Contents

Population, Health and Human Resources in India's Development

Editor

S.C. Gulati

ACADEMIC FOUNDATION
NEW DELHI

www.academicfoundation.com

First published in 2011
by

ACADEMIC FOUNDATION
4772-73 / 23 Bharat Ram Road, (23 Ansari Road),
Darya Ganj, New Delhi - 110 002 (India).
Phones : 23245001 / 02 / 03 / 04.
Fax : +91-11-23245005.
E-mail : books@academicfoundation.com
www. academicfoundation.com

in association with :

Institute of Economic Growth, Delhi
www.iegindia.org

Cataloging in Publication Data--DK
Courtesy: D.K. Agencies (P) Ltd. <docinfo@dkagencies.com>

Population, health and human resources in India's development / editor, S.C. Gulati.
p. cm.
Contributed articles.
ISBN 13: 9788171887859
ISBN 10: 8171887856

1. India--Population policy. 2. Medical policy--India. 3. Maternal health services--India. 4. India--Population–Economic aspects. 5. India--Population--Social aspects. I. Gulati, S. C., 1945-

DDC 304.60954 22

Typeset by Italics India, New Delhi.
Printed and bound in India.

Section VII: Population Growth Prospects and its Developmental Implications in India

List of Tables, Figures and Appendices

Tables

Figures

Appendices

About the Editor/Contributors

Editor:

S.C. Gulati is Professor in Population Research Center, Institute of Economic Growth, Delhi. He has authored and co-authored several books including: *Fertility in India: An Econometric Analysis of a Metropolis; Women's Status and Reproductive Health Rights; Reproductive Health in Delhi Slums; Contraceptive Use in India; Socioeconomic Root Causes of Biodiversity Loss in Chilika Lake; Migration, Common Property Resources and Environmental Degradation; and India: The State of Population 2007*. He has published more than 70 articles in reputed national and international journals covering a wide range of population, health, development and environmental issues in India. He has coordinated several crucial research projects for World Resource Institute (WRI), World Wide Fund for Nature (WWF), United Nations Population Fund (UNFPA), World Bank, Planning Commission (GoI), National Commission for Women (NCW), etc. He has been associated in various capacities as coordinator, consultant, technical advisory committees and task force member set up by GoI, etc. He was principal coordinator for large scale primary data based reproductive and child health projects like National Family Health Surveys (NFHS) and District Level Health Surveys (DLHS). His main areas of interest have been population, health, development, and environment.

Contributors:

Dhananjay W. Bansod is an Assistant Professor at the Population Research Centre, Institute for Social and Economic Change, Bangalore. He holds a PhD degree from International Institute for Population Sciences, Mumbai and Masters from Amravati University, Maharashtra. His area of research includes ageing and public health.

R.B. Bhagat is Professor, Department of Migration and Urban Studies, International Institute for Population Sciences (IIPS), Mumbai. He has extensively published on technical demography and environmental issues in national and international journals. He is editor of *Population and Environment Bulletin*, Population and Environment Center, IIPS, Mumbai.

Sandip Chakraborty is working as an Assistant Professor in Department of Statistics, MBB College Agartala, Tripura. Areas of interests are sample survey, demography and operations research. Published number of articles in reputed journals.

Alok Ranjan Chaurasia is Consultant, United Nation Children's Fund and Honorary Director, Shyam Institute, Madhya Pradesh, and formally professor at the Institute of Economic Growth, Delhi. He has authored several books, research articles on technical demography, health, family welfare, development, etc., in reputed national and international journals.

N.P. Das, former Director of PRC, Baroda, is currently with FIRD Pvt. Ltd., Lucknow as Director (Technical). In a career spanning four decades, he has executed important research projects on population, health and related issues funded by international and national organisations. He has a large number of publications, including books to his credit.

Puspita Datta is a research scholar at IIPS, Mumbai. She has submitted her thesis entitled "Impact of Fertility Decline on Child Schooling in India." Currently, she is working as a Senior Research Officer in District Level Health Surveys, IIPS, Mumbai.

Laxmi Kant Dwivedi is PhD Scholar at the IIPS, Mumbai. He has research interests in linkages between socioeconomic inequalities and utilisation of health care and nutritional status of women.

Tim Dyson is Professor of Population Studies at the London School of Economics. Much of his research has dealt with the past, present and future demography of India. He is a past President of the British Society for Population Studies, and was elected a Fellow of the British Academy in 2000.

Sujata Ganguly is PhD Scholar at the IIPS, Mumbai. She has research interests in mother and child health, especially obstetric care, and has published several articles in reputed journals.

Pradeep Guin was a Consultant at the Planning Commission, Government of India. He obtained his Masters in Statistics from the University of Delhi, and is currently a PhD student in Public Policy at the University of Maryland, Baltimore County.

Indrani Gupta, PhD from University of Maryland, USA, is Professor and Head of the Health Policy Research Unit of the Institute of Economic Growth, Delhi. Her areas of interest are demand for health and health care, health insurance and financing, poverty and health, costing and cost-effectiveness, economics of HIV and AIDS, and international agreements and their impact on public health.

Kamla Gupta is Professor and Head of the Department of Migration and Urban Studies at IIPS, Mumbai. She is one of the coordinators of NFHS-3, a globally recognised population and health survey in India. She has authored more than 40 research papers published in various journals of national and international repute.

Avishek Hazra is pursuing PhD from IIPS, Mumbai. His area of interest is health care financing and insurance systems. Presently, he is working with Population Council, New Delhi.

Prabhat K. Jha is Deputy Collector, Siwan, Bihar. He has done his Post-graduation from Benaras Hindu University and completed MPS degree from IIPS, Mumbai.

William Joe is Doctoral Scholar at the Centre for Development Studies, Thiruvananthapuram, Kerala. For his PhD, he is working in the area of measurement of health inequality with specific focus on inequalities in child health in India. His major research interest includes human development, health and poverty.

Arin Kar is PhD Scholar at the IIPS, Mumbai. He has research interests in regional differentials in women's nutritional status by socioeconomic status of households and communities.

Krishanu Karmakar is currently a graduate student at the Andrew Young School of Public Policy of Georgia State University, specialising in health policy in developing countries.

Sumati Kulkarni is Consultant, Population and Health Studies; Visiting Professor for Health Economics, at Poona University; former Professor, Population and Economic Development; Head, Department of Development Studies, IIPS, Mumbai; and all-India Coordinator, NFHS-2.

Chandan Kumar is Research Scholar at Indian Institute of Technology (IIT), Roorkee.

Subrata Lahiri is Professor, Department of Public Health and Mortality Studies, IIPS, Mumbai. Recipient of several prestigious national and international awards, he has authored several books and research articles in prestigious journals. His areas of interest are mathematical demography and actuarial methods' techniques of mortality analysis, population ageing and fertility and sex preferences.

Uday S. Mishra is Associate Professor at the Centre for Development Studies, Thiruvananthapuram, Kerala. He has research interests in measurement of poverty and inequality and assessment of indicators related to human development, gender and population health.

Anit N. Mukherjee is an Associate Professor at the National Institute of Public Finance and Policy (NIPFP). He previously worked as researcher in the Independent Commission for AIDS in Asia.

K.S. Natarajan retired as Deputy Registrar General (Demography), Census, India. He was convener of the successive expert committees of Planning Commission on Population Projections. He had been consultant for Post Enumeration Survey in Nepal, with UNICEF for Government of Maldives and country manager for Multiple Indicator Survey (2000) in India, with UNFPA for Post Enumeration Survey in Nigeria.

K. Navaneetham is Professor at the Centre for Development Studies, Thiruvananthapuram, Kerala. He has published several articles in national and international journals covering a wide range of population, health and development issues in India. His main areas of interest are population, human development, health and development.

Neelanjana Pandey is a research scholar at IIPS, Mumbai. She has been working on the age structural changes and its development implications and equity and accessibility issues of public health services.

Balram Paswan is Professor at IIPS, Mumbai. He obtained Master and M.Phil in geography from JNU, New Delhi and PhD in demography from IIPS, Mumbai. His research area is fertility and family planning and reproductive and child health.

Faujdar Ram is Senior Professor and Director, IIPS, Mumbai. Areas of interests are mathematical demography, fertility analysis and mortality analysis. Published number of articles in reputed national and international journals and books. Member of programme advisory committee of several health research organisations and government bodies.

Urvi Shah is associated with the Population Research Centre, Baroda since the last 25 years. Her expertise in social science and qualitative research has enabled her to be involved in several research projects in the area of gender, health and population issues. She has a number of publications, including books to her credit.

K. Shanthi is Professor, Department of Econometrics, University of Madras, Chennai. She is an awardee of Fulbright Post Doctoral Fellowship, Shastri Indo-Canadian Visiting Lectureship and ICSSR Senior Research Fellowship. Her fields of specialisation are women's studies and development studies. She is country representative for Feminist Approaches to Bioethics (FAB), an international association of feminist bioethists.

Aruna Sharma is Joint Secretary, National Human Rights Commission. She has authored several reports on human rights and published several articles on quality of life being instrumental towards population control and stabilisation.

Suresh Sharma is Assistant Professor at Population Research Centre, Institute of Economic Growth, Delhi. He has authored three books and published several articles in the reputed journals. He has coordinated several large scale projects on health and family welfare. His specialisation is reproductive and child health.

Avantika Singh specialises in organisation theory and health management. Her work has been published in national and international conference proceedings and international journals such as *IIMB Management Review, Policy and Society* and *Public Management Review.*

Raghubansh Mani Singh is Junior Consultant in Population Research Centre, Institute of Economic Growth, Delhi. He has coordinated several large projects in health and family welfare sponsored by MoHFW, Planning Commission, World Bank, etc. He has published several articles in national and international journals.

M. Sivakami is an Associate Professor at the Centre for Human Resource Development, Institute for Social and Economic Change (ISEC), Bangalore. She has published several research papers in the area of population, gender and health.

K. Srinivasan, demographer of international repute, was former Director and presently Prof. Emeritus, IIPS, Mumbai; former Director, Population Center, Bangalore; former Executive Director, Population Foundation of India. He was Consultant to United Nations Economic Commission for Asia and Far East (ESCAP), United Nation Population Fund (UNFPA), Adjunct Professor, School of Public Health, University of North Carolina, USA and member of various policy advisory committees on population set up of GoI.

Mayur Trivedi is currently working as a Lecturer with the Public Health Foundation of India and is deputed at the Indian Institute of Public

Health, Gandhinagar, Gujarat. His research interests are health and human development, economics of HIV/AIDS, health financing and insurance, and cost analysis of health care programmes.

R.P. Tyagi is Assistant Professor at Population Research Centre of the Institute of Economic Growth, Delhi. He has been extensively working on population programme and policy issues. He has been the Managing Editor of the journal *Demography India* for over three decades.

K. Narayanan Unni is Deputy Director General, National Sample Survey Organisation. He has worked in various capacities in the Office of the Registrar General, India, and has extensive experience in dealing with population statistics.

Introduction and Overview

India being signatory to the Plan of Action (PoA) of Cairo's International Conference on Population and Development (ICPD) endorsed by 179 participating countries in the conference, had responded positively and had taken several initiatives since 1994. The Cairo's conference Plan of Action (PoA) centred on considerations like population policies should not have the sole concern of fertility reduction but of reproductive health, reproductive rights and gender equity. The concerns over education of girls, gender equity and empowerment of women; infant, child and maternal mortality reduction; and the provision of universal access to reproductive health services, including family planning and sexual health were raised during the Cairo conference. The major paradigm shifts from earlier target-oriented to target-free approach (TFA) in April 1996 and then to client centred and demand-driven Community Needs Assessment (CNA) approach, which was later renamed as Reproductive and Child Health (RCH) approach, in October 1997 were initiated to translate promises made at Cairo into policy and programme actions in India.

India's National Population Policy (NPP-2000) had enshrined short-run objective to address unmet needs of contraception, health care infrastructure and health personnel, and to provide integrated service delivery for basic reproductive and child health care. The medium-run objective to bring down the total fertility rate (TFR) level to replacement levels by 2010, through vigorous implementation of inter-sectoral operational strategies and the long-term objective was to achieve a stable population by 2045, at a level consistent with the requirements of sustainable economic growth, social development and environmental protection (NPP-2000: 2). The Preamble of the National Rural Health Mission (NRHM) document, released in April 2005, recognised the importance of health in the process of social and economic development towards improving the quality of life of our citizens, especially underserved groups of society. The Government of India (GoI) resolved to launch the NRHM to carry out necessary architectural corrections in the basic health care delivery system, including merger/integration of vertical structures, delegation and decentralisation of administrative and financial powers, empowering of Panchayati Raj Institutions (PRIs), preparation of operational guidelines for the implementation of the Mission, logistic arrangements, IEC, MIS, etc. The Mission intended to adopt a synergistic approach by adopting not only programme interventions in increasing outreach of health care but also interventions relating to determinants of health like nutrition, sanitation, hygiene and safe drinking water.

India's demographic transition, initiated during the 1920s, represents both huge past achievements as well as substantial challenges that lie ahead. Despite huge past achievements on demographic and socioeconomic front, we find India is still facing huge challenges like massive poverty, malnutrition, demographic dividend, declining employment elasticity of economic development, unemployment and lack of gainful employment opportunities for increasing working age population resulting from age-structural changes during the process of demographic transition. Presently, India's massive population base of around 1100 million growing still at around 1.8 per cent per annum along with spectre of burgeoning population because of inbuilt demographic momentum, higher wanted as well as unwanted fertility in major states of India, still much higher levels of unmet need for contraception and lack of quality health care services is haunting India's development planners. The demographic dividend, where proportionate working age population is increasing faster than the overall population, can prove to be a blessing if declining dependency ratios and window of opportunity can be exploited to increase labour productivity with proper human resource development interventions. Otherwise, the demographic dividend would prove to be a bane for the country. India is facing other upcoming huge challenges like potential increase in HIV/AIDS pandemic, much higher incidence of reproductive tract and sexually transmitted diseases (RTIs/STDs) among passive women in India, epidemiological transition with changing regional morbidity profiles from communicable to non-communicable diseases. Also upcoming problems like increase in aged population and provisioning of social security and geriatric health care, co-existence of communicable and non-communicable diseases in different parts of the country are huge challenges for the country. Further, diseases like HIV/AIDS, cancer and cardio-vascular diseases warrant constant medical attention and sustained medical treatment, the cost for which is beyond the wherewithal of the average households. Thus, objective evaluation of existing health care system for general as well as high cost diseases is necessitated towards provision of quality health care for improvement in the quality of life and human well-being in India.

India's massive population base along with substantial population growth prospects in conjunction with other concurrent and prospective socioeconomic and health challenges calls for an objective evaluation of the linkages between population and development parameters. India is facing with duality in terms of demographic and epidemiological transition in different regions and socioeconomic groups. There are regions and groups where we still have much higher levels of fertility, both wanted as well as unwanted, higher unmet need of contraception, much higher levels of poverty and malnutrition, lack of health and educational infrastructure, abysmally low level of utilisation of health care services, co-existence of communicable as well as non-communicable disease, etc. The dualistic nature of demographic and socioeconomic scenario necessitates a critical examination of the system and intricate linkages between population, health, human resources and development in India. A critical examination of the linkages would provide prioritisation of programme interventions to bring around desirable results on socioeconomic and demographic fronts in India's constrained resource regime. The process would help the marginal groups to jump out of the vicious circle of lower levels of living, high fertility, lower utilisation of health and education facilities, and higher incidence of morbidity implying lower productivity, income and living standards.

In recognition of the significant body of new social science research on the linkages between population, health and human resource and socioeconomic development in India, a two-day conference was organised by Institute of Economic Growth, Delhi as a part of its Golden Jubilee Celebrations to bring together many of the leading Indian and international researchers involved in research on these issues. The conference was organised with the goal of presenting and synthesising the current 'state of the art' in terms of knowledge and understanding of these issues in India. A Golden Jubilee Lecture by Prof. Tim Dyson, London School of Economics and more than 35 papers by eminent national and international scholars were presented over the two-day International conference. Most of the crucial issues concerning population, health and human resources in context with socioeconomic development in retrospect and prospect got deliberated in the conference. Based upon the original nature and potential policy relevance of many of the findings of papers presented at the conference, a decision was reached at its conclusion that the papers warranted extensive dissemination efforts. This book represents synthesis of some of the selected papers presented at the conference.

This book would provide an insight into intricate linkages between population health, and socioeconomic and human resource development processes in historical and future perspective in India. The linkages between population growth parameters like fertility and mortality at national level and additionally migration at sub-national levels have theoretically and empirically been argued to be associated with the socioeconomic and cultural developmental processes in the past as well contemporary situations. A critical examination of the linkages and objective evaluation of the existing population and health policies and deficiencies in India's socioeconomic developmental programmes would provide basis for paradigm shifts and prioritisation of policy interventions in population, health and developmental strategies to bring about desired outcomes in terms of population control and stabilisation, sustainable development and utilisation of environmental resources towards improvements in the quality of life and human well-being. Quality of life and human well-being are multidimensional concept comprising of not only usual basket of material goods but also physical and mental health, social harmony, freedom of choice, participatory and inclusive development, etc. India's multifaceted challenges comprise quickening the process of population stabilisation, improvements in the quality of life and human well-being. We require concerted efforts to improve the health care system, enhance educational and gainful employment opportunities, alleviation of poverty and nutritional deficiencies, sustainable environment and natural resources like land, water and forest, and productive and optimal use of constrained natural and man-made resources. The selected papers have been divided into seven broad themes in the book.

First theme, "Demographic Transition in India" focusing on the demographic transition and its consequences for urbanisation and development process in India. Tim Dyson in his Golden Jubilee Lecture on the subject provided detailed account of mortality transition process initiated during the early 1920s and thereby fertility transition process initiated during the late 1960s. The study as chapter 1 in the book clearly reveals that India's demographic transition has contributed in a major way towards India's urbanisation and development process. Expressing caution over the applicability of drastic Chinese population policy in India's democratic structure towards accelerating population stabilisation process, he still emphasised that the role of family planning along with socioeconomic developmental process need not be relegated to the back-burner, which in turn would have substantial developmental implications over the coming future because of the interaction effects between population and developmental parameters.

Second theme, "Population and Health Policies in India" looks into the evolution and effectiveness of the population and health policies and paradigm shifts therein in the past. K. Srinivasan's study (chapter 2) focuses on role of governance towards effectiveness and utilisation of public health programmes at the state level. A critical evaluation of the policy interventions in NRHM like increased budget allocation for health sector and introduction of ASHA (the Accredited Social Health Activist) at the village level without proper governance may not yield the intended results like improvement in outreach of reproductive and child health services and its impact on infant, child and maternal mortality. The effective governance and optimal utilisation of effective governance at state level would be an important factor in mediating the impact of enhanced public sector allocations on health, nutrition and survival status of women and children. Aruna Sharma's study (chapter 3) in this book highlighted crucial challenges in population and health. The study emphasised that not only controlling population but also innovative interventions towards making population healthier, educated and productive and intersectoral convergence of resources is necessitated to achieve the desired goal of improvement of quality of life and human well-being. Avantika Singh (chapter 4) provides a detailed account of evolution of health policy in India during 1947-2007. The evolution was studied more from organisational perspective and contended that though remarkable achievements in terms of output indicators like life expectancy might have been achieved but still India faces a number of challenges like inadequate allocation of resources in public health system, low accessibility and utilisation of health services by marginal groups, and multifarious demands on the public health system compared to global standards. R.P. Tyagi (chapter 5) highlights challenges for the National Rural Health Mission (NRHM), which is an umbrella flagship comprehensive health programme of Government of India. The programme comprises curative, preventive and promotive health aspect towards improvement in the quality of life in general but especially for the underserved and marginal groups in India. The challenges are stagnant but higher infant and child mortality rates, higher levels of maternal mortality ratio and still higher levels of fertility contended that simultaneous concerted efforts on supply and demand side factors impacting the population parameters to achieve the desired health and demographic goals in India.

Third theme, "Fertility, Mortality and Contraception in India" focuses on the crucial determinants and interactions of the crucial population growth and socioeconomic developmental parameters in India. Sandip Chakraborty *(et al.)*'s study (chapter 6) focuses on fertility trends and differentials and childbearing behaviour among different social categories in India based on NFHS-2 data. The study contends that though fertility is declining among all social class and caste categories, the caste differentials are not only persisting but the gap is widening between different social and caste categories. Alok Ranjan Chaurasia (chapter 7) in this section highlights mortality transition phenomenon during 1970-2005 based on life tables of the Sample Registration System. The study reveals that rise in life expectancy in India has been slow by global standards. The improvement in life expectancy has been slow in urban areas compared to rural. Further, the improvement in survival probability in the first five years of life has decelerated over time, especially amongst females. Hastening the pace of mortality transition in India requires multi-dimensional and more pragmatic approach with focused attention on non-medical determinants of mortality apart from attention on health care delivery system. S.C. Gulati *(et al.)*'s study (chapter 8) is based on NFHS-2 data highlighting relative significance of socioeconomic, demographic and programme factors, influencing met and unmet need of contraception for spacing and limiting births in India. The study recommends that concerted efforts towards improvement in standards of living, interpersonal communications, counselling about family planning at health facilities, sensitisation of women about children's education, etc., would bring around pronounced effects of usage of contraception for spacing as well as limiting births. Puspita Datta (chapter 9) highlights social returns like improvement on educational attainment in the society as whole, and families in particular, from fertility declines in India. This study highlights that sibling's sex composition and birth order significantly affect school attendance of children. Earlier born children, especially girl children benefit more in terms of schooling when family size declines.

Fourth theme, "Maternal and Child Health in India" focuses on inequalities/differentials in health care utilisation by regions, social, economic and cultural groups, gender, etc. The sections also focuses on socioeconomic and cultural factors impacting utilisation of health care from private *versus* public sectors and also examines gender differentials in nutritional status in different regions of India. William Joe *(et al.)*'s study (chapter 10) based on NFHS-3 and NSSO's 60th round data highlights that despite several policy interventions for ensuring quality health care to the poorest households and vulnerable sections of the Indian society, we find that health care utilisation/deprivation by sex and income categories are quite substantial. The study highlights that rural population endures high degree of deprivation, more so, the girl child bears more of the deprivation. Economically better states like Gujarat and Maharashtra depict higher degree of malnourishment compared to Kerala and Tamil Nadu. Anit N. Mukherjee and Krishanu Karmakar (chapter 11) highlight demand side factors like income, perception about the gravity of illness, gender discrimination and level of education along with supply side factors like deficiencies in infrastructure depict significant effect on the health care utilisation. The study highlights that gender discrimination is less in rural compared to urban areas. Sujata Ganguly (chapter 12) reveals that utilisation of obstetric care is higher among women with wanted pregnancies compared to women with unwanted pregnancies. Similar patterns exist for utilisation of childcare like immunisation for wanted births compared to unwanted ones. Still, discrimination against girl child in terms of breastfeeding practices and treatment seeking behaviour gets reflected by the study. Chandan Kumar and R.B. Bhagat's study, (chapter 13) based on NSSO's 60th round data, highlights impact of various socioeconomic and demographic factors on health care utilisation for different aspect of health care during the life cycle like induced abortions, antenatal, delivery and postnatal care, children's immunisation, diarrhoea and pneumonia treatment and RTI/STD, etc. The study reveals that utilisation of private health care facilities is higher among richer compared to poorer women, Hindus compared to Muslim women, lower among SC/ST women compared to other castes, etc. The study clearly recommends a balanced approach in public-private partnerships in health care system in the light of inequalities of utilisation by socioeconomic and caste hierarchy and economic affordability. M. Sivakami's study (chapter 14) based on district level household survey data in 2002-2004 highlights regional differentials in utilisation of different aspects of maternal health care in Karnataka. The study reveals SC/ST women in Karnataka continue to be at disadvantage in securing institutional delivery in all regions. Further, regions like Gulbarga and Belgaum deserve focused attention and programmed efforts to enhance utilisation of maternal health care to further reduce maternal mortality in Karnataka. Suresh Sharma's paper (chapter 15) highlights differentials in child health care and mortality differentials by women's background characteristics. Malnutrition continues to affect newborns and young children and cause around 50 per cent of under-five deaths. About 55 million, or one-third of the world's underweight children under age five, live in India with the worst affected states being Madhya Pradesh, Jharkhand, Bihar, Gujarat, Orissa, Chhattisgarh, Uttar Pradesh and Meghalaya. Improvement in children's health and survival in India requires region/state specific and intersectoral approach in India.

Fifth theme, "Nutritional Status and HIV/AIDS in India" focuses on gender, regional and rural-urban differentials in nutritional status in India. Kamla Gupta's study (chapter 16) is based on NFHS-2 and NFHS-3 data which reveals that India is undergoing health transition and highlights gender differentials in levels of obesity by socioeconomic and cultural categorisation in different regions of India. The study reveals that proportional women being overweight or obese are much higher in cities and urban areas because of dietary habits and sedentary lifestyle. With increasing urbanisation, the problem of obesity or overweight may also get enhanced unless focused attention on sensitisation of men and women on these aspects is not taken care of. Laxmi Kant Dwivedi and Arin Kar's study (chapter 17), based on NFHS-2 data reveals that neighbourhood or community's standard of living effect on nutritional status or BMI levels of women from lower standards of living households turns out to be significant while controlling for other socio-demographic factors like education, caste, religion, age, parity and usage of contraception because of diffusion of knowledge through social learning. Indrani Gupta (*et al.*) (chapter 18) highlight key factors like quality of economic growth, nature of governance, and extent and inadequacy of interventions affecting the course of HIV/AIDS pandemic in district of Bellary of Karnataka. The paper concludes that economic growth inconsistent with human development can render even good set of interventions to be ineffective.

Sixth theme, "Ageing and Health Insurance in India" focuses on the process of ageing in terms of age structural changes implicit in the demographic transition process. Thus, increasing ratio of elderly population along with increasing feminisation and rural-urban distribution and provisioning of social security for elderly is the subject matter under discussion in this section of the book. K. Shanthi's study (chapter 19) based on NSSO's 52nd round data highlights that women in general suffer on account of providing care to elderly in the household during their young age at the cost of their career and thereby become dependent without any savings and suffer more because of chronic ailments and higher longevity during old ages compared to men. Thus, feminisation of ageing and poverty go hand in hand and thus, pangs of elderly women is not merely a women's issue but a social issue and warrants immediate public attention. Avishek Hazra and Subrata Lahiri's study (chapter 20) based on World Health Survey (2003) and NFHS-3 (2005-06) and exit interviews of beneficiaries of Employee State Insurance Scheme (ESIS) health services in West Bengal reveals that insurance coverage is very low among lower income quintiles groups and they spend a larger share of their meagre incomes to meet the health care costs. Predominantly the mandatory health insurance schemes like ESIS and CGHS (Central Government Health Scheme) and reimbursement of health costs by employers provide the health insurance coverage with privately purchased health insurance is only nominal so far. Predominantly, perception about free of cost treatment becomes more important compared with quality of services because of inaffordability due to economic reasons. Neelanjana Pandey and F. Ram's study (chapter 21) elicited ageing index for India and five zones characterising level of ageing and extent of oldness using data from 14 states of India encompassing almost 93 per cent of India's population. The demographic dividend indeed depends upon the stages of demographic transition. Thus, sharp declines in fertility results into sharp ageing process or larger demographic bonus. India's experience during liberalisation period, especially during 1999-2004, clearly reveals that source of growth of per capita national domestic product was primarily because of productivity per worker compared with the demographic bonus. If the appropriate vocational training and employment avenues are created to absorb the skilled manpower, India can surely take advantage of demographic dividend to boost economic growth and social development, otherwise it would lead to higher levels of unemployment and social unrest. Dhananjay W. Bansod and B. Paswan's study (chapter 22) based on primary data collected from 600 elderly in Maharashtra elicits functional and mental health indices along with living standard indices. The study clearly highlights that higher proportion of economically independent elderly living in joint families with higher standard of living (SLI) perceive their health condition to be good than their counterparts. Further, the study highlights that males are more independent and functionally healthier than women. The main cause of mental depression or weak mental health of elderly persons is financial dependence on the children.

Seventh theme, "Population Growth Prospects and its Developmental Implications in India" focuses on population projections and age structural shifts and their impact on demand for infrastructural and services in socioeconomic sectors like health, education and employment. Issues like young population of India and demographic dividend can be asset or liability, needs careful consideration. The massive population growth and age-structural shifts like dwindling school age population, increasing working-age and elderly population need to be critically examined with the current and prospective growth requirements in infrastructure and services for health, education, employment, etc. K.S. Natarajan's paper (chapter 23) critically examines the crucial fertility, mortality and migration assumptions in national and sub-national population projections and contends that India's population is poised to increase to 1.5 billion in 2051 and stabilise thereafter. Demographic transition started around 1921, with falling mortality and increasing life expectancy. While mortality is still falling, fertility started falling around 1975 and the fertility transition process is likely to be completed in all the states of India by 2030. IMR is likely to decline to 23 in 2051. Consequences of decline in fertility would be that child population

(5-14) would decline from 243 million in 2001 to 120 million in 2051 and the working-age population would increase from 620 million to 1046 million during the same period. Similarly, aged population would increase from 45 million to 205 million during 2001-2051. The study highlights implications for development in infrastructure for schooling and higher education and vocational training, employment generation and geriatric health care and provisioning of social security towards improvement of quality of life. K. Narayanan Unni's study (chapter 24) focused on age structural shifts, especially demographic dividend, and critically evaluates the references in the popular media and in academic circles whether the 'young' population of India is an 'asset' or liability. The study highlights that India's population is expected to overtake that of China in about 30 years, would increase to 1.5 billion in 2051 and fertility transition process would be completed in all the states of India by 2030. The study cautions that even to retain the current level of labour force participation, employment has to be provided to an additional 150-160 million people by 2026, which does not account for additional women who may join the labour force. Based on cross-country comparisons about the youthfulness of population, the study contends that employment opportunities offered by the developed countries because of the ageing process in their population would not help much towards changing employment or unemployment scenario in India. N.P. Das and Urvi Shah's study (chapter 25) focuses on current state level scenario about demographic and health parameters and some socioeconomic indicators and contends that unless adequate resource allocation from the Centre to states, especially those which are experiencing poor economic and social development, and without necessary political will and effective governance, the improvements in quality of life in terms of maternal and child health (MCH), malnutrition and poverty alleviation, etc., would be difficult to realise. Sumati Kulkarni's study (chapter 26) highlights implications of India's future population growth and age structural changes for educational and employment scenario. The study contends that translation of perspectives enshrined in the Vision 2020 document like GDP growth rate of 8.5 to 9.0 per cent resulting into quadrupling the per capita income and almost eliminate poverty and 100 per cent school enrolment of children aged 10-14 years, and creation of 200 million additional employment opportunities, etc., would largely depend on how far the success is achieved in four large north Indian states *viz.*, UP, Bihar, Rajasthan and Madhya Pradesh, which are going to contribute substantially to India's population and have relatively poor performance in terms of all socioeconomic development indicators. The study also cautions that not only increase in expenditure on education, like doubling of investment in education from current level of 3 to 4 per cent of GDP, would be sufficient rather appropriate changes in the educational system to suit the changing times and changing demographic scenario need to be looked into towards realisation of the Vision document's goals.

Twenty-six papers constituting 26 chapters in this book have been selected from the International Conference "Population, Health and Human Resources in India's Development" being held as one of the conferences during the Golden Jubilee Year of the Institute of Economic Growth during 24-25th March 2008. This book provides a fresh perspective on the linkages between populations, health and development parameters in India. We sincerely hope that this book will be of interest to policy formulators, development planners and other professionals concerned with population and development. It will be a valuable resource for researchers and students in the field of population-health-development nexus.

Section I

Demographic Transition in India

1

India's Demographic Transition and its Consequences for Development

TIM DYSON

Introduction

Population issues were a key concern of the Institute of Economic Growth (IEG) from its very beginning. Indeed, IEG was established with a focus on three specific academic fields—one of which was demography. Moreover, over the past 50 years the contribution of scholars based at the Institute to our understanding of population trends and processes has been great. The present lecture, for example, draws on the work of Pravin Visaria and Mari Bhat, both of whom did so much to increase our knowledge of India's population, and both of whom I was extremely fortunate to know well. However, the contribution to our understanding of population issues has also come from many other social scientists working at IEG. And the continuing central role of demographic concerns in the life of the Institute is reflected in the title of the international conference that is currently underway here, namely "Population, Health and Human Resources in India's Development".[1]

With this as background, the phenomenon that I want to address today is the demographic transition. My central contention will be that this transition is arguably the single most important feature for understanding India's development. The demographic transition represents both huge past achievements of the country, as well as substantial challenges that lie ahead. It provides an important overarching framework for the study of much of the India's socioeconomic development. The demographic transition has largely been responsible for the process of urbanisation—a fact that deserves much

1. The prominence of demography at IEG from the start no doubt partly reflected the interest in the field of V.K.R.V. Rao—the Institute's founder and first Director. In addition to demography, the other two initial fields of focus were economics and sociology (Institute of Economic Growth, 2008). In view of some of the points made below, it is important to stress that the contribution of scholars at IEG to our understanding of population matters has come from demographers—the name of Ashish Bose in particular springs to mind—but also from social scientists working in other disciplines (e.g., anthropology, economics and sociology).

greater recognition. And in bringing urbanisation about, the transition has had a huge effect in facilitating the process of economic growth (as well as being affected by it). Furthermore, the demographic transition allows us to make some comparatively firm statements about where the country is going.

India's demographic transition, therefore, is an immensely important subject. For the demographers present, there will be much in what follows that is well known. For the non-demographers, however, it seems appropriate to highlight just a few of the major ways in which the transition has contributed to India's development. I will begin by addressing mortality and fertility—in that order—and I then turn to the process of urbanisation. There follows a brief discussion of some of the implications of India's demographic transition for the country's future; this discussion draws on the results of a collaborative international study that benefited greatly from the advice and assistance of scholars based at IEG.[2] To spice things up for everyone—demographers and non-demographers alike—I finish the talk with some conclusions and issues for discussion. In particular, if we consider the next 50 years, then there is still considerable uncertainty regarding how much India's population will grow. Therefore, it is important to maintain a strong emphasis on the provision of high quality family planning services to all of the country's people.

Demographic India's Transition

Table 1.1 provides summary statistics relating to India's demographic transition. The principal source of the life expectation and total fertility rate estimates shown is Bhat (1989). To provide a better impression of what such dry statistical averages actually entail, Figure 1.1 plots annual registered crude death and birth rates during the first eight decades of the twentieth century for an area of central India that had comparatively good civil registration data.[3] Taken together, the table and the figure suggest that the country's demographic transition really began, rather hesitatingly, with a reduction in the average death rate during the 1920s and 1930s. These decades saw a decline in the frequency and scale of major famines and epidemics, which previously had made people's lives so incredibly precarious. As a result, there was a modest increase in life expectancy. And, with a prevailing crude birth

2. The study involved a team of researchers. The resulting book was co-edited by Robert Cassen, Leela Visaria and myself, and it was dedicated to the memory of Pravin Visaria (see Dyson *et al.*, 2004). Scholars closely associated with IEG who assisted the work in various ways included Kanchan Chopra, the Institute's current Director, Bina Agarwal, Ashish Bose, S.C. Gulati and the late P.N. Mari Bhat.

3. The area, formerly known as Berar, comprises the four districts in eastern Maharashtra of Akola, Amravati, Buldhana and Yavatmal. For the rates in Figure 1.1 see Dyson (1989a) and (1989b).

Table 1.1

Summary Demographic Estimates for India, 1901-2001

Period/ Year	Population (millions)	Increment Per Decade (millions)	Average Annual Growth Rate (per cent)	Crude Death Rate (Per 1000)	Crude Birth Rate (Per 1000)	Life Expectancy at Birth (years)		Total Fertility Rate Per Woman	Per cent Urban
						Male	Female		
(i)	(ii)	(iii)	(iv)	(v)	(vi)	(vii)	(viii)	(ix)	(x)
1901	238	-	-	-	-	-	-	-	10.8
1951	361	25	0.83	37.2	45.6	27.4	27.8	5.86	17.3
1961	439	78	1.96	25.9	45.5	36.8	36.6	6.11	18.0
1971	548	109	2.22	21.3	43.5	44.0	43.0	6.50	19.9
1981	683	135	2.20	16.0	38.0	50.0	49.0	5.40	23.3
1991	846	163	2.14	13.6	35.0	55.5	56.0	4.60	25.7
2001	1029	183	1.93	9.3	28.2	60.8	62.3	3.50	27.8

Note: Except for columns (ii) and (x), all the figures shown pertain to periods. For the first period (i.e., 1901-1951) the figures given are averages for the five intercensal decades.

Source: Most of the estimates are derived from Census data. For more detail on the sources, see Dyson (2004a: 20-21).

rate of about 45 per thousand, these small gains in mortality were sufficient to raise the average annual rate of population growth to over one per cent per year during the 1920s, the 1930s and the 1940s. This meant that by 1947, India's population had increased to around 336 million.

The late 1940s and the early 1950s then saw very rapid mortality gains—something that has often been missed by demographers. Indeed, it is possible that between 1946 and 1952 life expectation increased at a rate approaching two years per year.[4] Table 1.1 shows that there have been further sizeable increases in life expectation in each intercensal decade that has followed. Today average life expectancy is probably somewhere in the vicinity of 64 years; indeed, it may even be a little higher.

The social, economic, political, epidemiological and other developments that have underpinned the sustained mortality improvement of recent decades are many and complex. However, the increased control of many infectious and parasitic diseases (e.g., smallpox, malaria, cholera), the spread of immunisation coverage (especially with the Expanded Programme of Immunisation introduced around 1978), general progress in improving sanitation and water supplies, increased levels of education in the population, and a very considerable expansion of health facilities, have all been significant parts of the explanation for the sustained improvement in mortality. Also important, as the work of Caldwell *et al.* (1983) underlines, has been an increasing secularisation in attitudes towards sickness and disease.

For the country as a whole, it appears that female life expectation has generally tended to slightly exceed that of males. The work of Mari Bhat (1989) suggests that in the twentieth century, it was only during the period 1951-1981 that average male life expectancy was marginally higher than that of females. It is notable too that during 1961-2001, the momentum of mortality improvement—as measured by the average increment in life expectancy per decade—has apparently been somewhat greater for females. The average male increment has been smaller, and it has also diminished in size from decade to decade (see Table 1.1). Today, female life expectancy probably exceeds that of males by one or two years.

Of course, in general one would anticipate a still larger female mortality advantage. However, that for all-India female life expectancy exceeds that of males is worth noting. It is unclear why females are currently doing comparatively well. Perhaps, as Leela Visaria (2004a) has speculated, as non-communicable diseases have become more prominent in the overall health

4. This was also a period of rapid mortality decline in other parts of the world. In this context, the world war had ended, international trade increased and health measures that might otherwise have been introduced were implemented at last.

and mortality profile—they now account for a clear majority of all deaths—so the modest innate mortality advantage that females have has had greater opportunity to show through. Also, male mortality at later adult ages (e.g., over 30 years) is proving especially resistant to decline—a little-studied fact, that may well partly reflect the operation of behavioural factors such as greater alcohol and tobacco consumption. Of course, fertility decline is another factor that probably helps to explain the slightly faster mortality improvement experienced by Indian females in recent times. The fact that women are now having fewer births—especially at very young and later reproductive ages—has almost certainly worked to improve their health status, relative to what it would otherwise have been. That said, few analysts doubt that the current maternal mortality rate is high by international standards (e.g., see Bhat *et al.*, 1995; IIPS and ORC Macro, 2000). Although it is difficult to estimate, it is probably somewhere in the range of 300-500 maternal deaths per 100,000 live births.

In India, as elsewhere, there was a considerable delay between the occurrence of a sustained fall in the death rate and the start of a major—and compensatory—decline in the birth rate. Figure 1.1 shows this delay very clearly. During the 1960s, women were still having about six live births each. Moreover, both the figure and the table suggest that the level of fertility rose a little in the late 1950s and early 1960s. This rise was probably partly due to reduction in widowhood consequent upon the advent of sustained mortality decline. However, it may also have reflected various other modernisation effects—like increases in coital frequency (perhaps reflecting declines in traditional restrictions on sexual intercourse) and disruption to traditional patterns of breastfeeding.[5]

Table 1.1 shows that a fall in the country's birth rate is only really detectable in the 1970s. The average age of women at marriage has risen from about 15 years in 1951 to over 20 years for women marrying today—a trend that has certainly contributed to the fall in fertility at young ages (i.e., 15-19). That said, the main proximate cause of the decline in fertility, of course, has been a major rise in the use of contraception—especially female sterilisation. The proportion of married women aged 15-49 who are currently using modern methods of contraception is put at about 49 per cent by NFHS-3 and about three-quarters of these women are protected by sterilisation (see IIPS, 2008). It is this fact which explains why the total fertility rate at the

5. The extent of restrictions on sexual intercourse in the past is surprisingly little remarked upon in much of the literature. However, discussing south India, Caldwell, Reddy and Caldwell are an exception. They suggest, among other things, that the length of the traditional period of postnatal sexual abstinence was at least two years (see Caldwell *et al.*, 1988: 49).

beginning of the present century (i.e., during 2001-2006) was probably around 2.9 births per woman, with an associated crude birth rate of perhaps 25 per thousand population.

Figure 1.1

Registered Crude Death and Crude Birth Rates, Four Districts of Central India, 1901-1980

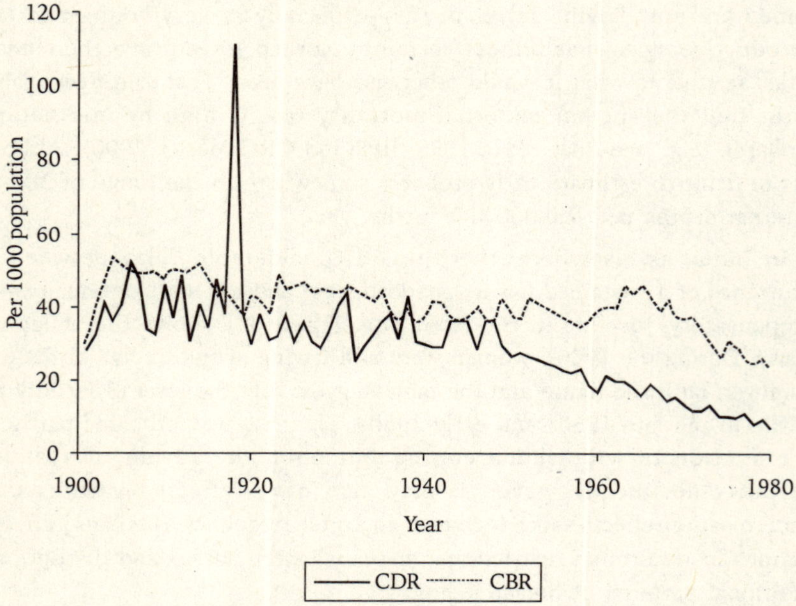

Nevertheless, it is important to stress that ultimately the fall in fertility from high to low levels almost certainly represents an unconscious adjustment by people to the preceding, sustained and huge fall in the death rate. In other words, the remote cause of fertility decline in India, as elsewhere, has been mortality decline. The figure hints strongly at what is happening in this respect. The country has been, and still is, going through a period of disequilibrium. This is the transition from a former state in which both the crude death rate and the crude birth rate were high, highly variable and roughly equal—to another state—still several decades away—in which both the death rate and the birth rate are low, fairly stable and roughly equal. This, of course, is the demographic transition. India's crude death rate during 1991-2001 was probably around 9 per thousand (see Table 1.1). It will probably never fall much lower than 7 per thousand. And, with population ageing, at some time in the not-too-distant future, the death rate will begin to increase a little. However, it will take several decades before the crude birth rate has fallen to roughly the same level as the crude death rate.

Conventional, essentially cross-sectional, regression-based demographic analyses—that usually contain little, if any, reference to history—cannot shed much light on such high-level causal processes whereby mortality decline causes fertility decline. However, when judged against criteria that are supportive of causal inference, mortality decline as the remote cause of fertility decline fares very well compared to the alternatives (see Ní Bhrolcháin and Dyson, 2007). For example, with reference to Figure 1.1, what we see occurring are events in which: (i) there is time order, the cause (i.e., the decline in the death rate) essentially precedes the effect (i.e., the decline in the birth rate); (ii) both the cause and the effect stretch over broadly similar durations; (iii) the effect is in the direction that would be expected, namely downwards; and (iv) the scale of the effect is proportional to the scale of the cause.

Again, many factors—including general ideational change in the area of family and sexual matters, and rising levels of education—have played important conditioning and often facilitatory roles in this process of adjustment. And India's family welfare programme has also helped to promote the idea of birth control, and service the rising demand for modern methods of contraception. Also, there is much cross-sectional survey evidence that more educated women are more likely to contracept (and marry later). That said, the fact that fertility decline is an adjustment process, that almost certainly will eventually occur across the whole of society, is reflected in the fact that a majority of recent fertility decline has happened among women with little or no education (see Bhat, 2002; McNay *et al.*, 2003). Poor, uneducated women (and their husbands) can also reduce their fertility, given the chance—although it generally takes them somewhat longer to do so. Family planning services, however, help to provide these people with the chance. In doing so, these services help to shorten the delay between the fall in the death rate and the fall in the birth rate i.e., the period during which the country's population is essentially in a state of disequilibrium.

Despite the fall in the birth rate, Table 1.1 shows that India's rate of population growth remained in the vicinity of 2 per cent per year in each intercensal decade following 1951. Thus, comparing 1951-1961 and 1991-2001, the birth rate has fallen appreciably, but the death rate has fallen by almost as much. Consequently, the population almost tripled in size during 1951-2001. The 2001 census enumerated slightly more than one billion people. If we make some allowance for census under-enumeration and subsequent population growth, then the country's population today is probably around 1,175 million. However, because the birth rate is almost certainly falling appreciably faster than the death rate, the 2011 census will probably register a significant decrease in the country's intercensal rate of demographic growth for the first time. It seems likely that the average intercensal population growth rate during 2001-2011 will be in the vicinity of 1.6 per cent per year (Dyson, 2004b).

Inevitably, for a country of such great scale and diversity, the preceding picture of the demographic transition is a massive oversimplification. Perhaps the most important reservation to be added is that the major southern states—Andhra Pradesh, Karnataka, Kerala, Maharashtra and Tamil Nadu—have been, and remain, nearly two decades ahead in their experience of the demographic transition—compared to the major populous northern states—in particular, Bihar, Madhya Pradesh (MP), Rajasthan and Uttar Pradesh (UP). For example, simple random sampling (SRS) data suggest that during 1996-2001 life expectancy in these five southern states averaged about 66.3 years, compared to 59.6 in the four northern states. Similarly, during the same period total fertility in these southern states averaged about 2.2 births per woman, compared to an average of 4.3 births for Bihar, MP, Rajasthan and UP combined. Without doubt, it is especially in the densely settled and landlocked northern states of Bihar and UP that death rates and reproductive behaviour have been slowest to change.

Urbanisation

Of course, urbanisation—i.e., the rise in the proportion of the population living in urban areas—has been another key development which, almost certainly, has facilitated the reductions in mortality and fertility that are integral components of the demographic transition. Among other things, urban areas offer economies of scale in terms of providing both health and family planning amenities. It is much harder to raise a large number of children if you live in a town. Also, modern forms of water supply, sewage and access to education, are usually somewhat better in the urban sector. There is no doubt that life expectation in the country's urban sector today is several years higher than in rural areas. And the level of total fertility per woman in the urban sector is probably about one birth below that holding in rural areas.[6]

It goes without saying that much of contemporary India's tremendous dynamism is located in the urban sector. This is true in terms of services, trade and production. But it is also true in relation to politics, culture, arts,

6. Of course, none of this is to deny the existence of considerable variation within the urban sector, perhaps particularly in relation to levels of mortality and health.

civil society and education, for example. If the word 'development' means anything, it refers to what goes on in the towns. And it is the movement of societies from being predominantly rural to being predominantly urban—i.e., the process of urbanisation—that underpins progress and development in our modern world. Therefore, the issue arises as to how urbanisation comes about.

Here, again, it is important to appreciate the crucial role played by the demographic transition. In particular, it is the sustained mortality decline of the demographic transition that effectively causes the process of urbanisation.

For example, in India between 1871 and 1941 census data show a very slow rise in the level of urbanisation—from 8.7 to 13.9 per cent. In this period of 70 years, the country's urban population increased by only about 3.7 million people during each decade. The main reason why the level of urbanisation was so low—and urbanisation and urban growth were both so restricted—was the key fact that mortality from most infectious diseases varied directly with population density. At this time, before India's demographic transition really got underway, the death rate in the urban sector was extremely high. Indeed, death rates in urban areas were almost certainly much higher than those prevailing in rural areas. And crucially, the death rates in urban areas were almost certainly very much higher than the birth rates. Therefore, the very existence of the towns depended upon a continual net inflow of people coming from rural areas. Nowhere was this more true than in Mumbai, where during the first decade of the twentieth century the average infant mortality rate was about 500 per thousand (Dyson, 1997: 123-31). Clearly, mortality was also extremely high in childhood and at other ages, so Mumbai's population could not have sustained itself without very considerable rural to urban migration.[7]

Efforts to address this lamentable situation met with some success, and they underpinned the growth of Mumbai's population from under 1 million in 1901 to 3.2 million in 1951, by which time the city's registered infant mortality rate was about 100. However, even as late as 1941 it remained the case that all of the country's major urban areas (e.g., Kolkata, Chennai and Mumbai) had appreciably higher death rates than prevailed in their rural hinterlands (see Dyson, 1997).

The huge and sustained fall in mortality that occurred during the second half of the twentieth century further transformed the situation as regards urban growth and urbanisation. India's urban sector has benefited much more from mortality decline than has the rural sector. Thus, SRS estimates suggest

7. This was probably true of all urban areas to varying degrees; Mumbai was an extreme case.

that by 1970-1975 life expectation in urban India was a massive 10.9 years higher than in the rural areas; and even by 1992-1996 the gap was still put as high as 6.9 years (Registrar General of India, 1999: 16). To reiterate, today the gap probably still amounts to several years.[8]

Anyhow, the massive improvement in urban mortality removed the restriction—essentially a ceiling—on the level of urbanisation. The census statistics in Table 1.1 imply that between 1951 and 2001, India's urban population grew from 62 to 285 million i.e., at an average of 44.6 million people during each decade. And the 2001 census put the level of urbanisation at 27.8 per cent. That said, this figure of 27.8 per cent would be much higher by some other criteria. For example, census data for 1991 showed that there were 13,376 villages with populations of 5000 people or more. Pravin Visaria (2000) pointed out that these villages contained about 113 million people; and were they to have been treated as 'urban' in 1991 then the country's level of urbanisation would have been raised from 25.7 to about 39 per cent. Relatedly, some states, such as Tamil Nadu have recently felt the need to reclassify many 'rural' areas as 'urban'.

Of course, and again, the proximate causes of urban growth and urbanisation are well-known. For example, reclassification can occur because units like villages cross certain thresholds to become designated as urban; and urban areas that are already established can expand their geographical area and thereby their population size. Essentially, however, the population of the urban sector as a whole grows either because of rural to urban migration or because of urban natural increase. In recent decades, the majority of urban population growth has resulted from urban natural increase, rather than from net rural to urban migration—although, of course, rural to urban migration has contributed as well.

The process of urbanisation occurs because the urban sector grows faster than the rural sector. It does so because during the demographic transition it has two main sources of growth—i.e., urban natural increase and rural to urban migration—rather than just one (i.e., natural increase, as holds in the rural sector). The volume of urban growth from either source reflects the overall population growth rate—which itself reflects mortality decline (e.g., see Preston, 1979; Visaria, 1997, 2000). The process of urbanisation in contemporary India would be impossible without mortality decline, especially in the urban sector. Thus, the mortality decline of the demographic transition can be regarded as the remote process which ultimately brings urbanisation about.

8. Recent sector-specific estimates of life expectation are unavailable. However, the Sample Registration System puts the infant mortality rates in urban and rural areas at 39 and 62 per thousand respectively in 2006 (see Registrar General of India, 2007).

So, and largely for demographic reasons, urbanisation in India is on a firmly upward path. And urban population growth is occurring at the relatively fast pace that it is because the country is still at an intermediate stage in the demographic transition. Relatedly, state-level differences in rates of urban population growth chiefly reflect state-level differences in rates of population growth.[9] The influence of economic differences on urban population growth is weaker and secondary. During 1991-2001, urban growth rates in states like Maharashtra and Gujarat—where levels of per capita income are relatively high—were fairly similar to those in poorer states like MP and UP.

The Future

As noted, the demographic transition provides an excellent framework for studying many aspects of development. Moreover, in broad terms it foretells what will happen. Thus, during the next few decades India's population will continue to grow, although at a slowing rate; it will continue to urbanise; and it will start to age (though gradually at first). Therefore, looking ahead, this section summarises selected conclusions from the study of India's future that was mentioned at the start. The study took projected demographic change at the state level as its point of departure. National figures were obtained through aggregation.[10]

The study's central demographic projection implies that India's population will increase by about 400 million between 2001 and 2026. The total population in 2026 will be about 1,420 million.[11] The central projection for the year 2051 is 1,579 million (Dyson, 2004b). According to this projection, all demographic growth in the period to 2026 will occur at ages above 15 years. There will be little change in the number of children aged less than 15 in 2026, and possibly a modest decline. By mid-century, the country's population will have surpassed that of China—it may do this around the year 2030—and it may well be approaching 1.6 billion. More than half of the demographic growth during 2001-2026 will occur in the main northern states i.e., Bihar, MP, Rajasthan and UP. The populations of these four states will increase by around 45-55 per cent over this period, but those of most of the other states will grow by only about 20-30 per cent.

9. Simple scatter-plots for 1991-2001 suggest this to be true, and it is even more apparent if Tamil Nadu—where there was considerable reclassification—is omitted.

10. On this study, see footnote 2 and associated text. I believe that social scientists have a responsibility to address the future, although it is inevitable that in doing so, they will often get things wrong.

11. The true figure in 2026 may be larger, because the projection does not allow for census under-enumeration. The most recent projection of the United Nations puts the population at 1,447 million in 2025 (see United Nations, 2008).

Turning to fertility and mortality, it seems reasonable to consider that by 2026 the total fertility rate for the country as a whole will be approximately two births per woman. It also seems plausible to suggest that women will continue to move towards a family building pattern in which they marry young, have two births in quick succession, and then get sterilised while still at a relatively young age. The average life expectation for both sexes combined in 2026 may well be about 69 years (perhaps with a 3-year advantage in favour of females). There is considerable scope for future mortality gains—e.g., through higher levels of immunisation, and better control and treatment of diarrhoeal and respiratory infections.

Importantly, however, India may well face an increasing 'double burden' of disease (see Visaria, 2004a). This means that various degenerative ailments (e.g., cancers, diabetes, hypertension) will grow in relative importance, but major infectious diseases (e.g., tuberculosis, malaria) will remain as serious health problems. Here there is a major issue—namely the capacity of aggregate indices of mortality to improve, without there being a commensurate advance in population health. Another way of putting this is to say that future mortality decline may occur on a rather fragile basis. In this context, it is worth noting some recent findings from NFHS-3. These indicate that nutritional deficiencies remain widespread. Between NFHS-2 in 1998-99 and NFHS-3 in 2005-06 there was apparently little change in the proportion of children who were underweight (the respective figures being 47 and 46 per cent), while the indicated prevalence of childhood anaemia actually rose (from 74 to 79 per cent). The NFHS-3 findings also imply that there has been an increase in anaemia among adult women—from about 52 to around 56 per cent (see IIPS, 2008).

Of course, we should not read too much into these particular figures. The point, however, is that the poor nutritional state of the population in general is changing slowly, if at all. In certain respects—e.g., relating to the intake of pulses and coarse cereals—the situation so far as food consumption is concerned may actually have deteriorated in recent decades (see Hanchate and Dyson, 2004). Just because per capita incomes are rising does not mean that the quality of people's food intake will improve. People do not always do what is good for themselves. And any small gains that may have occurred with respect to nutritional status may well have happened because of changes—e.g., rises in immunisation coverage—that have little to do with food consumption, let alone rises in average incomes.

So far as the urban sector is concerned, it seems likely that various states will set about reclassifying rural areas as urban in much the same way as Tamil Nadu has done. Clearly, this makes projections for the urban sector particularly hazardous. Nevertheless, provided there is no change in how areas are categorised, it is then plausible to project that the level of urbanisation will be about 36 per cent in 2026. The two especially dynamic urban regional systems—the first stretching throughout much of western Gujarat and Maharashtra, the second centred around Delhi—will continue to dominate the country's urban structure. There could be somewhere between 60 and 70 'million plus' cities in 2026. Of course, the size of a city depends upon where the boundary is drawn. Nevertheless, India's largest urban agglomerations (Delhi and Mumbai) could both have populations approaching 25 million by that year. It is clear that much future urban growth will happen in strands alongside major transport routes. And, as Pravin Visaria noted, commuting—an important, if rather neglected phenomenon—will continue to expand (Visaria, 1997).

India's future demographic evolution will also have significant implications for the economy, education and the environment. Economic growth may be enhanced by the 'demographic bonus' deriving from the projected diminishing age dependency ratio in the study's central projection in the period to about the year 2031. Benefits will arise if there are consequential increases in savings and investment. But such increases cannot be taken for granted. As Mari Bhat argued, there is nothing automatic about such potentially positive relationships (Bhat, 2001). It is virtually certain that the country's working age population is going to grow faster than the total population, and it may be roughly 50 per cent bigger in 2026 compared to 2001. McNay *et al.* (2004), among others, maintain that economic growth during the 1990s was not very employment-friendly. In terms of job generation, they contend, the situation appears to have deteriorated, and this is reflected in increased unemployment. The quality of the available employment also seems to have fallen—as the share of unorganised and casual work in total employment has risen. Without rapid economic growth and gains in the employment intensity of output, these authors argue that there could be a significant rise in unemployment.

Similarly, the expected reduction in school-age numbers will only bring a reward if there is a major increase in school quality. Kingdon *et al.* (2004) show that there were encouraging gains in literacy and school attendance in the 1990s. Gender gaps in education also fell. This progress was associated with demand-side increases in educational aspirations and supply-side improvements in terms of both the quantity and the quality of education. Nevertheless, significant regional variation remains. For example, in Kerala and Tamil Nadu the school-age population has already begun to decline. But in Bihar and UP the study's central projection indicates that it will rise in the period to 2026. All states are likely to see educational improvements, but significant education gaps are likely to remain. Similarly, gender gaps may well narrow in the future, but they seem certain to persist (Kingdon *et al.*, 2004).

So far as broader environmental issues are concerned, future demographic growth has obvious implications for food production. For example, average cereal yields must rise significantly. And in achieving this end there is little choice other than to increase chemical fertiliser applications substantially (Hanchate and Dyson, 2004). Future population growth will also have a major impact upon the country's demand for water—which is a resource that will have to be used much more efficiently, for example in agriculture (Vira *et al.*, 2004). Population growth will also have significant implications for the use of common pool resources like fodder and forest products (Vira and Vira, 2004). And, with continuing rapid urban growth in many states, issues relating to urban environmental quality are likely to become more and more important (Vira, 2004).

The addition of several hundred million more people by 2051 is likely to have major administrative ramifications, and quite possibly political implications as well. It seems plausible to suggest that, over the long run, further population growth will help to produce an increasingly differentiated administrative hierarchy and contribute to the increasing decentralisation of governance. The next few decades will surely see the creation of many more districts, and an increasing number of states. At the state-level, for example, it is significant that Uttarakhand, Chhattisgarh and Jharkhand were all carved out of extremely populous units. States with very large populations pose particular challenges in terms of administration. They are also more likely to contain ethnic minorities of sufficient size to justify—or bring about—the creation of new political units, hopefully in ways that do not involve conflict (Dyson, 2001: 354). The increasing disparity between the number of people in different states, and their number of elected representatives in Parliament, is another potential source of change.

Finally in this section, as Robert Cassen has remarked, a great challenge for India's future rests in limiting divergence. Of course—as with much else here—this basic point is well recognised. However, the experience of recent decades suggests strongly that the poor states are mostly growing slowly economically and fast demographically; and, conversely, the country's better-off states are mostly growing fast economically and slow demographically. In both cases, processes of cumulative causality apply. That is, faster demographic change would bring about faster economic change, and vice versa. Essentially it is the first of these possibilities that underpins the discussion below.

Discussion

I have tried to draw attention to the central place of the demographic transition in India's development. Both mortality and fertility decline are momentous developments in themselves. Indeed, it seems reasonable to claim that the increase in life expectation experienced since 1947 constitutes the biggest single improvement in the conditions of life in modern India. It is extremely difficult to think of a more significant change. Furthermore, the reduction in total fertility from around six births per woman to less than three is a hugely important development—one that will have immense ramifications for gender relations over the long run. The speed at which the position of women in society has changed in many Asian countries has taken social scientists by surprise. The spread of contraception and low fertility—coupled with other developments like the growth of education—have led to much less importance being placed upon the roles of marriage and childbearing in women's lives. Women have become more and more independent of men. Of course, this will happen—indeed it is beginning to happen—in India as well. For understandable reasons, social scientists have spent much time studying the poor position of women in society. But it will be important not to neglect improving shifts in gender relations.

The paths that the death rate and the birth rate have followed in India have led to a five-fold rise in population since 1901, i.e., from about 238 million to almost 1.2 billion. If the population does stop growing sometime around the middle of the present century, then the country's demographic transition will have stretched over a period of roughly 150 years. And if the population eventually flattens out at around 1.6 billion (as in the central projection), then the associated 'growth-multiple'—i.e., the ratio of the population at the end of the process to that at the start—will be somewhere between six and seven.

The demographic transition is a great framework for considering the future. But the level of detail that can be safely projected obviously diminishes the further one looks ahead. Nevertheless, it is certain that there will be considerable further population growth. It is certain that the regional composition of the country's population will continue to change. It is highly likely that there will be appreciable further mortality and fertility decline. However, whereas the crude death rate will not fall by much during the next few decades, the crude birth rate will fall by much more. It is certain, therefore, that the country's rate of population growth will decline in the coming decades. Furthermore, it is certain that the population will become increasingly old as a result of fertility decline. And it is certain that the population will become increasingly urban—this is an incredibly important part of the transition. The details of what will happen will depart from any specific projection. But the broad trends are definite. I know of no other social science that can make firmer statements about important future trends than can demography. Moreover, as has been discussed, these trends will have major practical implications—for example, in the areas of education, employment, food production, administration, politics and the environment (e.g., water, waste disposal).

The near-term future is largely determined. Demography allows us to forecast, for example, that the results of the 2011 census will reveal a population that is close to 1.2 billion and that the associated population growth rate during the 2001-2011 intercensal decade will be around 1.6 per cent per year.[12] Also, the country's level of urbanisation in 2011 will have risen to about 31 per cent (assuming no significant change in definition). In turn, this will imply an urban population of roughly 370 million. The associated urban growth rate for the 2001-2011 decade will be around 2.7 per cent per year.

However, looking to the longer run one has to be much more tentative. For one thing, surprises may occur. Also, as noted, the range of uncertainty becomes much greater the further one looks ahead. It is important not to be complacent. In particular, it is important not to forget the role of family planning and the path of future fertility. For example, while urbanisation is both inevitable and a good thing, rapid urban population growth is not. And, as Preston (1979) among others has noted, it is family planning that holds out the best hope of reducing urban population growth. This is because it influences both of the main proximate causes of this growth.

More generally, there is danger in placing too much confidence in the figures from individual population projections—like the study central projection referred to above. It is all too easy to assume that everything is settled, and that a figure of about 1.6 billion for India around the middle of this century is pretty much determined. Adopting such an attitude may be rather convenient for politicians—since it avoids an issue, and they tend to be preoccupied with the short run.

However, the same state-level central projections which imply a population in 2051 of 1,579 million also suggest that the figure could be as low as 1,458 million, or as high as 1,731 million. Of course, the different outcomes depend upon the future level and trend of fertility—especially, but not only in the major northern states. In the study's central projections, the 'floor' for state-level fertility was set at 1.8 births per woman. This is actually

12. For reasons alluded to in footnote 11, the true population in 2011 will be somewhat larger.

quite a low level. The 'floors' for the low and high projections were set at 1.5 and 2.1 births respectively. It should be clear that modest difference in future fertility can lead to very large differences in the eventual size of the population.

Thus, in the study's high scenario the country's population of 1,731 million in 2051 is still projected to be growing at 0.48 per cent per year in the middle of this century. Were this to happen, then it is very likely that the total population would eventually stabilise at a figure well beyond 1.8 billion. It is worth noting too that the United Nations has tended to raise its projected population totals for India in recent years. Thus, the 'medium' (i.e. middle) projection for 2050 made just a few years ago was 1,572 million (United Nations, 2001). But the UN's most recent medium projection puts the population in that year at 1,658 million—when it is projected to still be growing at 0.32 per cent per year. Moreover, the UN's latest 'high' projection puts the population in 2050 at 1,964 million, with an annual growth rate of 0.85 per cent (United Nations, 2008).[13] A recent study involving the Population Foundation of India (PFI) and the Population Reference Bureau (PRB) rightly raises the question as to whether India will be the one and only country ever to contain two billion people (Nanda and Haub, 2007). Such a concern cannot be taken lightly.

Many people, including me, would probably agree with a recent statement by Montek Singh Ahluwalia (2008) that China's population policy was too drastic (much too drastic). And, in any case, such a drastic policy would have been impossible in a democratic society, one where there is attention to due process, such as applies in India. It is inevitable that in such an open society policies evolve more slowly, and, therefore, fertility change is slower as a result. That said, many people would also agree with him that a faster rate of fertility decline in the past, one involving significantly less demographic growth, would, other things equal, have produced a contemporary population that is better off.[14] This might apply especially to those people who

13. The growth rate figures refer to the period 2045-2050.

14. "I do think that the one child policy [in China] perhaps was too drastic. On the other hand, had we [in India] been able to bring population growth under control—to get it closer to two children faster—we would have been better off. But you know, the difference would have been, instead of stabilising may be at 1.6 billion, we would have stabilised at 1.4 billion. The difference is not a difference that would alter India being one of the largest populations in the world" (Ahluwalia, 2008). However, if India had experienced China's fertility decline then its population would probably have been smaller by roughly 200 million in 2001, and it is possible that it would never have exceeded one billion people (see Dyson, 2004: 76 and 106-7). To reiterate, such a policy would have been impossible (and undesirable). Nevertheless it is important to have a good appreciation of the large differences in eventual population size that are implied by various fertility decline trajectories. As the 'high' projections cited in the previous paragraph show, this latter point is still relevant and important today.

experience the worst of the 'double burden' of disease i.e., many living in rural areas and the urban slums.

Anyone who neglects the role of India's family planning programme today are closing their eyes to an important instrument of past—and future—change. Clearly, it is far from immaterial whether the country ends up with an eventual population of 1.5 or 2.0 billion. And both of these outcomes are possible. The occurrence of rapid economic growth at present should not distract from this fact. Continuing attention to the provision of high quality family planning and reproductive health care services will benefit the poor—and especially women; there is a massive amount of good demographic evidence to this effect (e.g., see Merrick, 2001). Faster, rather than slower, fertility decline will make it easier to bring education of better quality to all people. It will reduce urban population increase, and growth of the labour force—making it easier to provide better living conditions in the urban sector and better employment prospects. It will reduce pressure on environmental resources, and it may also enhance economic growth. Since the large northern states are where fertility is highest, women are most disadvantaged, and services are still weak, it is in there, but not only there, that improved services are required.

References

Ahluwalia, M.S. (2008). "PM Programme", *BBC Radio 4*. Monday, 25 February.

Bhat, M. (1989). "Mortality and Fertility in India, 1881-1961: A Reassessment", in T. Dyson (ed.), *India's Historical Demography*. London: Curzon Press. pp.73-118.

———. (1998). "Demographic Estimates for Post-Independence India: A New Integration", *Demography India* 27(1): 23-57.

———. (2001). *A Demographic Bonus for India? On the First Consequence of Population Ageing*. Address to the Population Research Centre at the University of Groningen, Netherlands. November.

———. (2002). "Returning a Favour: Reciprocity between Female Education and Fertility in India", *World Development* 30(10): 1791-1803.

———., Navaneetham, K. and Rajan I. (1995). "Maternal Mortality in India: Estimates from a Regression Model", *Studies in Family Planning* 26(4): 217-32.

Caldwell, J.C., P.H. Reddy and P. Caldwell (1983). "The Social Component of Mortality Decline: An Investigation in South India Employing Alternative Methodologies", *Population Studies* 37(2): 185-205.

———. (1988). *The Causes of Demographic Change, Experimental Research in South India*. Madison: University of Wisconsin Press.

Dyson, T. (1989a). "The Historical Demography of Berar, 1881-1980", in T. Dyson (ed.), *India's Historical Demography: Studies in Famine, Disease and Society*. London: Curzon Press. pp.150-96.

———. (1989b). "The Population History of Berar since 1881 and its Potential Wider Significance", *The Indian Economic and Social History Review* 26(2): 167-201.

———. (1997). "Infant and Child Mortality in the Indian Subcontinent, 1881-1947", in A. Bideau, B. Desjardins and H.P. Brignoli (eds.) *Infant and Child Mortality in the Past*. Oxford: Clarendon Press. pp.109-34.

———. (2001). "The Preliminary Demography of the 2001 Census of India", *Population and Development Review* 27(2): 341-56.

———. (2004a). "India's Population—the Past", in T. Dyson, R. Cassen and L. Visaria (eds.), *Twenty-First Century India—Population, Economy, Human Development, and the Environment*. New Delhi: Oxford University Press. pp.15-31.

———. (2004b). "India's Population—The Future", in T. Dyson, R. Cassen and L. Visaria (eds.), *Twenty-First Century India—Population, Economy, Human Development, and the Environment*. New Delhi: Oxford University Press. pp.74-107.

Dyson, T., R. Cassen and L. Visaria (eds.) (2004). *Twenty-first Century India—Population, Economy, Human Development and the Environment*. New Delhi: Oxford University Press.

Hanchate, A. and T. Dyson (2004). "Prospects for Food Demand and Supply", in T. Dyson, R. Cassen and L. Visaria (eds.), *Twenty-First Century India—Population, Economy, Human Development, and the Environment*. New Delhi: Oxford University Press. pp.228-53.

IIPS (2008). "NFHS-3 National Factsheet". Available at: <<<*www.nfhsindia.org/factsheet. html*>>>. Accessed February 2008.

IIPS and ORC Macro (2000). *National Family Health Survey (NFHS-2), 1998-99:India*. Mumbai: International Institute for Population Sciences.

Institute of Economic Growth (2008). Available at: <<<*www.iegindia.org/phr.htm*>>>. Accessed February 2008.

Kingdon, G., R. Cassen, K. McNay and L. Visaria (2004). "Education and Literacy", in T. Dyson, R. Cassen and L. Visaria (eds.), *Twenty-First Century India—Population, Economy, Human Development, and the Environment*. New Delhi: Oxford University Press. pp.130-57.

McNay, K., P. Arokiasamy and R. Cassen (2003). "Why are Uneducated Women in India using Contraception? A Multilevel Analysis", *Population Studies* 57(1): 21-40.

McNay, K., J. Unni and R. Cassen (2004). "Employment", in T. Dyson, R. Cassen and L. Visaria (eds.), *Twenty-First Century India—Population, Economy, Human Development, and the Environment*. New Delhi: Oxford University Press. pp.158-77.

Merrick, T. (2001). "Population and Poverty in Households: A Review of Reviews", in N. Birdsall, A. Kelley and S. Sinding (eds.), *Population Matters*. Oxford: Oxford University Press. pp.201-12.

Nanda, A.R. and C. Haub (2007). *The Future Population of India—A Long-range Demographic View*. Washington DC: Population Reference Bureau.

Ní Bhrolcháin, M. and T. Dyson (2007). "On Causation in Demography", *Population and Development Review* 33(1): 1-36.

Preston, S. (1979). "Urban Growth in Developing Countries", *Population and Development Review* 5(2): 195-215.

Registrar General, India (1999). *Compendium of India's Fertility and Mortality Indicators, 1971-1997*. New Delhi: Office of the Registrar General.

———. (2007). *Sample Registration Bulletin* 42(1). New Delhi: Office of the Registrar General.

United Nations (2001). *World Population Prospects—The 2000 Revision*. United Nations: New York.

———. (2007). *World Population Prospects—The 2006 Revision*. United Nations: New York. Available at: <<<*http://www.un.org/esa/population/unpop.htm*>>>. Accessed February 2008.

Vira, B. (2004). "Common Pool Resources: Current Status and Future Prospects", in T. Dyson, R. Cassen and L. Visaria (eds.), *Twenty-First Century India—Population, Economy, Human Development, and the Environment*. New Delhi: Oxford University Press. pp.328-43.

Vira, B. and S. Vira (2004). "India's Urban Environment: Current Knowledge and Future Possibilities", in T. Dyson, R. Cassen and L. Visaria (eds.), *Twenty-First Century India—Population, Economy, Human Development, and the Environment*. New Delhi: Oxford University Press. pp.292-311.

Vira, B., R. Iyer and R. Cassen (2004). "Water", in T. Dyson, R. Cassen and L. Visaria (eds.), *Twenty-First Century India—Population, Economy, Human Development, and the Environment*. New Delhi: Oxford University Press. pp.312-27.

Visaria, L. (2004a). "Mortality Trends and the Health Transition", in T. Dyson, R. Cassen and L. Visaria (eds.), *Twenty-First Century India—Population, Economy, Human Development, and the Environment*. New Delhi: Oxford University Press. pp.32-56.

———. (2004b). "The Continuing Fertility Transition", in T. Dyson, R. Cassen and L. Visaria (eds.), *Twenty-First Century India—Population, Economy, Human Development, and the Environment*. New Delhi: Oxford University Press. pp.57-73.

Visaria, P. (1997). "Urbanization in India: An Overview", in G. Jones and P. Visaria (eds.) *Urbanization in Large Developing Countries*. Oxford: Clarendon Press. pp.266-88.

———. (2000). "Urbanization in India", unpublished manuscript. Delhi: Institute of Economic Growth.

Section II

Population and Health Policies in India

2

Need for a Review of Public Health Policies and Systems in India

K. SRINIVASAN

Background: Health Policy Evolution

The present system of delivery of health and medical care services within the public governance, i.e., the Central government, the state and local governments owe their origins to the recommendations and implementation thereof contained in the Health Survey and Development Committee (also called the Bhore Committee), constituted by the Government of India in 1943 under the chairmanship of Sir Joseph Bhore. The report of the committee submitted in 1946 identified India's major health problems as various infectious diseases, such as smallpox, cholera, leprosy, tuberculosis, malaria, filariasis, various other vector-borne diseases, high maternal mortality, infant and child mortality and gross malnutrition. It recommended various measures to improve the public health, environmental sanitation, nutrition and prevention of specific communicable diseases through national level programmes for mainly smallpox, cholera, tuberculosis, malaria and leprosy. It also recommended the organisational structure most appropriate for implementing these programmes. The main core of the recommendation was the setting up of a population-based system of maternity sub-centres (one for 20,000 population), primary health centres (one for 100,000 population), *taluka* level hospitals and district level hospitals and a state level public health department to supervise and monitor the activities at lower levels. Similar to the rural health structures, population-based urban health centres were also started. Based on public health principles developed from the experiences in the developed countries particularly in Great Britain, the public health care was stratified as primary health care (at the sub-centre and primary health centres), secondary care at the *taluka* level hospitals and tertiary or specialised care at the district level hospitals with increasing level of specialisation, at successive higher levels. This is a significant recommendation at that time for the setting up of a public health system in such a large country as India and it worked very well and rather effectively in the first few decades until the late sixties.

Over the years, the principles underlying the public health system were maintained, the main one being that it should be population-based and it should be three-tiered, but the populations served by these centres were reduced over time on the recommendations of a number of subsequent committees set up by the Government of India, notable among which are the Mudaliar Committee (1961), Srivastava Committee (1970), the Mukherjee Committee (1974) and the two National Health Policies of the Government of India formulated in 1983 and 2002. In all these committee recommendations, especially after the eighties, it was tacitly assumed that while the preventive health services should be made uniformly available to all the sections of the population, with regard to curative services the relatively better off sections of the population would be in a position to avail of such services from the private hospitals and private medical institutions on payment basis.

However, simultaneously with the setting up of the population-based public health system in the country, many specific disease control programmes were launched at the national level, from the fifties, significant among which are the National Smallpox Eradication Programme (NSEP), National Cholera Control Programme (NCCP), National Malaria Eradication Programme (NMEP), National Tuberculosis Control Programme (NTCP), National Guinea Worm Control Programme, National Leprosy Control Programme, National Blindness Control Programme, etc. The planning and specific resources needed additionally for these national programmes over and above the routine staff and facilities available with the Primary Health Centres set up under the state governments, were provided for from the budgets made available for these programmes from the Central government. The implementation of these programmes was done by the state governments but they were monitored and guided carefully and professionally, by subject experts from the then Ministry of Health, New Delhi. While the Central government in the Ministry of Health provided additional funds and technical know-how for most of these programmes and made a success of most of them, the state governments shared the credit for the disease control and/or eradication of some diseases as in the case of plague and smallpox.

Having adopted the socialistic pattern of society since Independence, the emphasis of the public health system was on meeting the basic health care needs of the poorer sections of the population on a free or a heavily subsidised basis. Over the years for the regular primary health care system, the only additions to the programmes that were made were the introduction of the community liaison workers, called by various names in different times as voluntary health worker, community health worker, village level health worker and the latest designation made popular in recent years is the *anganwadi* workers (AGWs) under the Integrated Child Development Scheme (ICDS) of the Government of India implemented by the Ministry of Women and Child Welfare since the seventies and the latest being the Accredited Social Health Activists (ASHA) under the National Rural Health Mission since 2005. AGWs and ASHAs have women selected from the communities at the rate of 1 per 1000 population or 1 per village, they receive short training in public health including nutrition and public health programmes and they are informed of the areas in which their cooperation, participation and assistance from the communities are expected. They are paid a token honorarium in addition to financial assistance on service basis such as the incentives given to ASHAs for accompanying a pregnant woman from her village to a medical institution for delivery. However, as we will see from the next section, these programmes have not so far paid any dividends in terms of significant declines in child mortality, child nutrition, maternal mortality, maternal health or better utilisation of the health and medical care facilities made available by the governments to people at large. After almost 50 years of such an expansion and diversification of health care services in the country, it is time to assess how far the public health services including the curative services are reaching the people, how the expansion of private health services have changed the extent of use of public services and the nature of modifications needed in the public health system in India. There is an increasing body of evidences, coming up in recent years, derived from analysis of data from the National Sample Survey and other sources that the public health services are being increasingly used by the relatively better off sections of the society, leaving the poor and deprived to the medical and health services from the private sector.

Current Policies: An Analysis

There are at present three policies directly relevant to population and health in India: the National Population Policy (NPP, 2000), the National Health Policy (NHP, 2002) and the recently launched National Rural Health Mission (NRHM, 2005). The last one though not declared, as a policy, is really a policy document in the statement of vision and objectives, setting up of goals, formulation of strategies and programmes and launched by no less a person than the Prime Minister of the country in May 2005. In recent years, this programme has become the cornerstone of the public health system in India. A comparative summary of the objectives and goals of these three current policies are given in Appendix A-2.1 and A-2.2 respectively.

NPP, 2000 and NHP, 2002 typify the impact or goal-obsessed approach to policy rather than the inputs-processes-outcome-oriented approach to policy. Knowing fully well that certain goals are impossible to be realised, they are still stated in the policy documents under the assumption that stating the goal is, in itself, half of the achievement of the goal. The three objectives, immediate, medium and long term and 14 quantitative goals, called the national socio-demographic goals, set to be achieved by the year 2010 in NPP, 2000 are given in the first column of Appendix A-2.1 and A-2.2, respectively.

Most of the health goals stated by the planners in the past were known to be impossible of realisation even at the time of policy formulation but the policy makers went ahead and put them in the document. As an illustration, let me take up the feasibility of the goals set with regard to infant mortality (specified in NPP, 2000 and NHP, 2002). Both NPP, 2000 and NHP 2002 have stated their goals for infant mortality rate as 30 per 1000 live births to be achieved by 2010. Recent trends in IMR indicate that the level has declined only by 14 points in 11 years (80 in 1990 to 66 in 2001) or at 1.3 points per year and during the subsequent five-year period, 2001 to 2006, the decline has been slightly more rapid, with the IMR declining by 9 points from 66 to 57 or by 1.8 points per year. Even if the IMR trend line observed during 2001 and 2006 is extrapolated into the future, the expected IMR by 2010 will be around 50. When the NPP, 2000 was being planned, an analysis was not made of the expected future declines in IMR on the basis of past trends, the gap between the desired and expected, and the additional resources necessary to be invested to fill in this gap. These additional inputs should be not only in the Ministry of Health and Family Welfare but also in much other development-related departments, such as Department of Women and Child Welfare, Ministry of Food and Agriculture, Human Resource Development etc. If the declining has to be accelerated what are the implications for additional resources, strategic changes and effective management of the programmes not only in the health sector but in other sectors? This requires inter-ministerial coordination, planning and implementation. I am afraid this has not been done.

Similarly, the NHP has stated that mortality rates due to TB, malaria, other vector and water-borne diseases should be reduced by 50 per cent by 2010 and achieve a zero level of growth in HIV/AIDS. Are these goals feasible or just stated desires by the planners? Even in the context of increased investments on health by the government as a per cent of GDP or as a per cent of total government expenditure these far-flung goals do not appear to be feasible.

Not only the paucity of public health funds at the state level but also how to make optimum use of the additional funds made available for health in the central in an effective manner are the major problems faced by the country. In most of the states, the state funded primary health care and secondary care system is in total disarray and states really look forward to the Central government for bailing them out of their tight financial situations. More than 80 per cent of the state health budgets in most of the states are used in the payment of the salaries of the health and medical personnel and there is very little funds available for programme services. Given this extremely difficult fiscal position of the state governments, the Central government will have to play a key role in the coming years in public health system. Though health is a state subject, the stagnation in the levels of child mortality, morbidity, the high prevalence of malnutrition among women and children and high cost of treatment of diseases in the private sector and the paucity of resources in most of the states for health programmes, makes it incumbent on the Central government to plan, direct and monitor many of their health programmes in the coming years. Taking into account the gap in health care facilities, it was planned, under the recent policy to increase health sector expenditure to 6 per cent of GDP, with 2 per cent of GDP being contributed as public health investment, by the year 2010. The Central government is committed to improving the health conditions of the population, especially the poorer sections of the society. The budget allocation for health for the year 2008-09 is Rs. 16,534 crores, an increase of 15 per cent over the previous years' budget but is still around 1 per cent of the GDP. The state governments are also expected commitment to the health sector. In the first phase, by 2005, it was planned to increase the commitment of their resources to 7 per cent of the Budget; and, in the second phase, by 2010, to increase it to 8 per cent of the Budget. This is not happening. With the stepping up of the public health investment, the Central government's contribution to the states is expected to rise to 25 per cent from the existing 15 per cent by 2010. The provisioning of higher public health investments will also be contingent upon the increase in the absorptive capacity of the public health administration so as to utilise the funds gainfully.

National Rural Health Mission

The National Rural Health Mission, 2005 (NRHM) recently launched by the Honourable Prime Minister is a departure from the earlier policy and plan documents in two aspects. First, it takes the programme in a "Mission Mode" probably encouraged by the success of the earlier missions such as the Technology Mission. Secondly, more importantly it is not obsessed by the desired goals of impact but rather it focuses on inputs, strategies and programmes to be done and leaves the ultimate impact as an outcome of what is done. This is a more realistic approach for the improvement of the health of the people. The 'preamble' of the 'Mission Document' states that "Recognising the importance of Health in the process of economic and social development and improving the quality of life of our citizens, the Government of India has resolved to launch the National Rural Health Mission to carry out necessary architectural correction in the basic health care delivery system. The Mission adopts a synergistic approach by relating health to determinants of good health *viz.*, segments of nutrition, sanitation, hygiene and safe drinking water. It also aims at mainstreaming the Indian systems of medicine to facilitate health care. The Plan of Action includes increasing public expenditure on health, reducing regional imbalance in health infrastructure, pooling resources, integration of organisational structures, optimisation of health manpower, decentralisation and district management of health programs, community participation and ownership of assets, induction of management and financial personnel into district health system, and operational zing community health centers into functional hospitals meeting Indian Public Health Standards in each Block of the Country. The Goal of the Mission is to improve the availability of and access to quality health care by people, especially for those residing in rural areas, the poor, women and children."

Experience has probably taught the planners that it is difficult to set targets on outcome parameters such as fertility rate, infant mortality rate, maternal mortality rate, prevalence rate of different diseases etc. What the programme personnel can and should do is to carry out certain functions in an effective and efficient manner in the direction of reduction of the above rates and the actual outcome will be a function of not only the inputs in the health programme but also in many other sectors, not necessarily under the control of any Ministry, nor even of the government at any level, state or the Centre. One can estimate through statistical regressions as to what can be expected in the various rates and ratios by a given input in any sector but such an estimate is bound to have a large error because not all the factors that affect each of the above parameter are fully known nor can be quantified. The NHRM places a high priority on care of pregnant mothers and promoting institutional deliveries. "Janani Suraksha Yojana" is an important component of NHRM. The Mission document provides for the selection, training and liaising with a community level female worker designated as "ASHA", acronym for Accredited Social Health Activist, one per 1000 population both in the rural and urban areas to function as the liaison between the official health system and the community. She is the equivalent of the AGW (the *anganwadi* worker) at the village level working solely for the health programmes. The *anganwadi* workers are under the Department of Women and Child Welfare and at present are contributing enormously to health programmes aimed at women and children. Since they have to shoulder many other responsibilities as well it is appropriate and necessary that the public health system develops its own community level liaison person. The "core" and "supplementary" strategies laid out in the Mission Document are focused on the appropriate training and enhancing the capacity of the panchayati raj institutions to own, control and manage public health services, establish a new link person in the community called ASHA (Accredited Social Health Activist) at one per 1000 population or a village; train her, and provide incentives to *panchayats* and ASHAs for their assistance and support in maternal and child care services. There will be about 1 million ASHAs in the country and their involvement is supposed to improve the health conditions of the population series of programmes, for training of trainers and training of ASHAs is underway with all national health institutions involved in such training.

Core strategies of NRHM are:

- Train and enhance capacity of Panchayati Raj Institutions (PRIs) to own, control and manage public health services.
- Promote access to improved health care at household level through the female health activist (ASHA).
- Health plan for each village through Village Health Committee of the *panchayat*.
- Strengthening sub-centres through an untied fund to enable local planning and action and more Multi Purpose Workers (MPWs).
- Strengthening existing primary health centres (PHCs) and community health centres (CHCs), and provision of 30-50 bedded CHC per lakh population for improved curative care to a normative standard (Indian Public Health Standards defining personnel, equipment and management standards).
- Preparation and implementation of an inter-sectoral District Health Plan prepared by the District Health Mission, including drinking water, sanitation and hygiene and nutrition.
- Integrating vertical Health and Family Welfare programmes at national, state, block and district levels.
- Technical support to national, state and district health missions, for Public Health Management.
- Strengthening capacities for data collection, assessment and review for evidence-based planning, monitoring and supervision.

- Formulation of transparent policies for deployment and career development of human resources for health.
- Developing capacities for preventive health care at all levels for promoting healthy lifestyles, reduction in consumption of tobacco and alcohol etc.
- Promoting non-profit sector particularly in under served areas.

In essence, the main principle underlying the NRHM is decentralisation of resources and responsibilities of the public health care system to lower levels, right down to *panchayats*, with great hopes placed in the person of ASHA on getting community support for the health programme. It is assumed that the public health services are well established and that only people are not coming forward to use them. This is far from truth as we will empirically prove from NFHS-3 data.

It is however, true that with regard to inputs into the programme the emphasis of the NHRM is somewhat different from the NPP and NHP, though one may question the validity of the assumptions behind the launch of ASHA scheme on such a massive scale. Unlike the latter two documents that talk about percentage of GDP or per cent of total government budget to be spent of public health, the NHRM talks about actual money to be spent at about Rs. 6,500 crores during 2005-06 and if needed, to be raised by 20 to 30 per cent every year. Similarly under inputs it talks of committees to be formed at each level, village, district and the state and the national levels, the activities including training and monitoring programmes to be initiated.

It is refreshing to note that the NRHM is more pragmatic in its approach and emphasising more on inputs and strategies. The policy envisages a key role for the Central government in designing national programmes with the active participation of the state governments. Also, the Policy ensures the provisioning of financial resources, in addition to technical support, monitoring and evaluation at the national level by the Centre. However, to optimise the utilisation of the public health infrastructure at the primary level, a gradual convergence of all health programmes under a single field administration is envisaged. Vertical programmes for control of major diseases like TB, malaria, HIV/AIDS, as also the Reproductiive and Child Health (RCH) and Universal Immunisation Programmes, would need to be continued till moderate levels of prevalence are reached. The NRHM envisages that while the programme implementation is effected through autonomous bodies at state and district levels, the interventions of State Health Departments may be limited to the overall monitoring of the achievement of programme targets and other technical aspects. The setting up of an independent Health Trust of India that will be financing the NRHM will give greater flexibility to the whole scheme. The relative distancing of the programme implementation from the State Health Departments will give the district team greater operational flexibility. Also, the presence of state government officials, social activists, private health professionals and MLAs/ MPs on the management boards of the autonomous bodies is expected to facilitate well-informed decision-making.

Programme Impact: Current Situation

Table 2.1(b) presents data available at the state level on some of the key indicators on maternal and child health available from the recently conducted National Family Health Survey-3 (NFHS-3) conducted by the International Institute for Population Sciences, Mumbai in collaboration with Macro International. NFHS-3 is the third in the series of such surveys, the first one conducted during 1991-92 and the second one during 1998-99. Like the previous two surveys, it is a large scale sample survey of a representative sample of households from each of the 29 states of the country at the national level and covered a wide range of topics on population, health, nutrition including anthropometric measurements on children below 5 years of age and adult men and women aged 15-54 and 15-49, respectively, domestic violence, prevalence of HIV/AIDS by analysis of blood samples etc. The field work for the survey was conducted during December 2005 to August 2006 and covered a sample of 109,041 households in which a sample of 124,385 women in the age group 15-49 and 74,369 men in the age group 15-54 were interviewed and/or examined. Table 2.1(a) presents data on 14 selected variables on maternal and child health including extent of registration of births that occurred in the households and utilisation of health services during the 5-year period prior to the interview date. They attempt to picture the present health situation in the states and the country as a whole in a summary form. The variables selected are: the extent of registration of births as an index of effective governance of the governments, eight indexes of extent of public contacts with the peripheral health system of the government either with the individual health worker or with the state health care institutions *viz.:* 1) the per cent of pregnant women who received a minimum of three antenatal care services from a health worker during the last pregnancy that occurred during 2000-2005; 2) per cent who received all the recommended antenatal care services; 3) per cent of births that took place in a medical institution; 4) per cent of births that were assisted by a trained health worker irrespective of whether it took place in an institution or at home; 5) per cent of children with diarrhoea who received treatment in a health facility; 6) children between 6 months and 6 years of age who received any service from an *anganwadi* worker (AGW); 7) per cent of households that did not generally use a government health facility during any sickness during the past one year; and 8) per cent of women without any contact with the peripheral health system during the past one year. We have also used five outcome variables *viz.:* 1) under 5 mortality rate; 2) children under age 5 who are malnourished (weight for age less than 2SD of the recommended mean); 3) per cent of children aged 6 months to 5 years who are anaemic (Hb less than 11 gms per dl); 4) per cent of women 15-49 years of age severely malnourished (BMI less than 18.5); and 5) per cent of men 15-49 age who have serious misconceptions about the spread of TB. A detailed description of the 14 variables is given in the note accompanying Table 2.1(a). On the whole, the table presents a depressing picture on the health situation in the country, more serious in some states than in others. The following are some of the specific findings that can be discerned from the table. A zero order correlation matrix of these variables is given in Table 2.1(b).

Registration of Births and an Index of Effective Governance (IEG)

The Birth and Death Registration Act was passed by the Indian Parliament in 1969 making it compulsory for a birth to be registered within 14 days and a death within 7 days. The responsibility for the implementation of this Act rests with the state governments. Even after 45 years of the passage of the act, it is rather distressing to note from Table 2.1(b) that among the births that occurred between 2000 and 2005, only 41 per cent of the births were registered, 35 per cent in the rural areas and 59 in the urban areas. Among the states the variation is very large, ranging from 95 per cent in Goa to a low of 6 per cent in Bihar, 7 per cent in Uttar Pradesh and 9 per cent in Jharkhand. Since the official responsibility for the registration of births and deaths is vested with the peripheral state government officials as the village *munsif/patel*, the auxiliary nurse midwife (ANM) or male multi purpose worker, or the *panchayat* secretary or the thane official depending upon the department of the state government with which the responsibility for the registration of vital events is vested, and since the vital events occur all over the place at all times, the extent of registration of births can be considered as a good proxy of the effectiveness of governance of the state government. It can be considered as a simple but good index of effectiveness of state governance (IEG). Viewed in this context, the IEG is highest, more than 80 per cent in Goa, Gujarat, Maharashtra, Himachal Pradesh, Kerala, Mizoram, Sikkim and Tamil Nadu and the lowest less than 20 per cent in Rajasthan, Uttar Pradesh, Bihar and Jharkhand. None of the states in north (except Himachal Pradesh), central and east India have good IEG, above 80 per cent registration.

Table 2.1 (a)

Zero Order Correlation Coefficients

Variable	*Statistics*	*X1*	*X2*	*X3*	*X4*	*X5*	*X6*	*X7*	*X8*	*X9*	*X10*	*X11*	*X12*	*X13*	*X14*
BRGN	Pearson Correlation	1													
	Sig. (2-tailed)														
U5MOR	Pearson Correlation	-0.701	1												
	Sig. (2-tailed)	0.000													
3ANCS	Pearson Correlation	0.721	-0.805	1											
	Sig. (2-tailed)	0.000	0.000												
ALLANC	Pearson Correlation	0.590	-0.749	0.822	1										
	Sig. (2-tailed)	0.001	0.000	0.000											
DELHEF	Pearson Correlation	0.653	-0.830	0.904	0.885	1									
	Sig. (2-tailed)	0.000	0.000	0.000	0.000										
DELAST	Pearson Correlation	0.679	-0.817	0.933	0.879	0.972	1								
	Sig. (2-tailed)	0.000	0.000	0.000	0.000	0.000									
DIACAE	Pearson Correlation	0.274	-0.267	0.453	0.378	0.369	0.380	1							
	Sig. (2-tailed)	0.150	0.161	0.014	0.043	0.049	0.042								
ICDS	Pearson Correlation	0.363	0.095	0.132	-0.006	-0.021	0.017	-0.109	1						
	Sig. (2-tailed)	0.053	0.623	0.495	0.973	0.914	0.931	0.573							
MALCH	Pearson Correlation	-0.472	0.711	-0.568	-0.444	-0.560	-0.575	0.193	0.187	1					
	Sig. (2-tailed)	0.010	0.000	0.001	0.016	0.002	0.001	0.316	0.331						
ANECH	Pearson Correlation	-0.463	0.697	-0.509	-0.486	-0.587	-0.539	0.161	-0.035	0.734	1				
	Sig. (2-tailed)	0.013	0.000	0.006	0.009	0.001	0.003	0.413	0.859	0.000					

contd..

...contd...

Variable	*Statistics*	*X1*	*X2*	*X3*	*X4*	*X5*	*X6*	*X7*	*X8*	*X9*	*X10*	*X11*	*X12*	*X13*	*X14*
THINWO	Pearson Correlation	-0.262	0.540	-0.306	-0.211	-0.304	-0.271	0.251	0.207	0.766	0.660	1			
	Sig. (2-tailed)	0.169	0.003	0.106	0.271	0.109	0.155	0.190	0.282	0.000	0.000				
TBNOTION	Pearson Correlation	-0.499	0.454	-0.532	-0.438	-0.532	-0.573	-0.120	-0.260	0.405	0.430	0.111	1		
	Sig. (2-tailed)	0.006	0.013	0.003	0.017	0.003	0.001	0.535	0.174	0.029	0.022	0.565			
NOUSEGF	Pearson Correlation	-0.189	0.126	-0.044	0.122	-0.004	0.062	0.460	-0.207	0.406	0.469	0.459	0.066	1	
	Sig. (2-tailed)	0.327	0.516	0.820	0.530	0.985	0.748	0.012	0.281	0.029	0.012	0.012	0.734		
ANYCOHW	Pearson Correlation	0.149	0.141	0.012	0.244	0.088	0.094	0.251	0.313	0.447	0.325	0.605	-0.069	0.395	1
	Sig. (2-tailed)	0.441	0.465	0.951	0.203	0.650	0.628	0.188	0.099	0.015	0.091	0.001	0.722	0.034	

Note: Sample size=29

Values (symbol < or = to) 0.01 depict significance at 0.01 level (2-tailed), and Values > 0.01 and (put symbol here for < or = to) 0.05 depict significance at the 0.05 level (2 tailed)

Table 2.1 (b)

Selected Indicators on Reproductive and Child Health during 2000-2005 from NFHS-3

Region/State	X1	X2	X3	X4	X5	X6	X7	X8	X9	X10	X11	X12	X13	X14
	BRGN	U5MOR	3ANCS	ALLANC	DELHEF	DELAST	DIACAE	ICDS	MALCH	ANECH	ANECH	THIWO	NOUSEGF	ANYCHOW
North														
Delhi	62.40	46.70	75.10	29.00	58.90	64.10	75.00	12.40	26.10	57.00	14.80	69.00	70.70	2.90
Haryana	71.70	52.30	59.20	14.70	35.70	48.90	81.70	27.60	39.60	72.30	31.30	39.40	72.30	11.20
Himachal Pradesh	89.00	41.50	62.60	17.40	43.00	47.80	68.90	37.50	36.50	54.70	29.90	55.10	17.30	9.10
Jammu & Kashmir	35.80	51.20	73.50	17.50	50.20	56.50	67.00	18.80	25.60	58.60	24.60	49.30	37.10	4.10
Punjab	76.80	52.00	74.80	19.60	51.30	68.20	75.20	14.10	24.90	66.40	18.90	38.90	80.80	11.90
Rajasthan	16.40	85.40	41.20	8.60	29.60	41.00	56.70	21.10	39.90	69.70	36.70	78.40	29.80	11.70
Uttarakhand	38.40	56.80	44.90	16.10	32.60	38.50	61.70	31.60	38.00	61.40	30.00	50.40	55.60	18.70
Central														
Chhattisgarh	73.00	90.30	54.20	11.30	14.30	41.60	61.60	65.20	47.10	71.20	43.40	45.00	63.70	19.40
Madhya Pradesh	29.70	94.20	40.70	7.20	26.20	32.70	58.10	49.80	60.00	74.10	41.70	75.90	62.60	16.90
Uttar Pradesh	7.10	96.40	26.60	4.10	20.60	27.20	58.30	22.30	42.40	73.90	36.00	60.40	84.70	19.80
East														
Bihar	5.80	84.80	17.00	5.80	19.90	29.30	53.90	9.90	55.90	78.00	45.10	58.50	93.30	19.20
Jharkhand	9.10	93.00	35.90	7.50	18.30	27.80	44.10	41.70	56.50	70.30	43.00	64.40	77.70	14.70
Orissa	57.00	90.60	61.80	18.40	35.60	44.00	58.90	65.80	40.70	65.00	41.40	24.80	24.00	22.60
West Bengal	75.80	59.60	62.00	12.30	42.00	47.60	67.40	42.30	38.70	61.00	39.10	57.20	71.20	23.30

contd...

contd...

Region/State	X1	X2	X3	X4	X5	X6	X7	X8	X9	X10	X11	X12	X13	X14
Northeast														
Arunachal Pradesh	32.40	87.70	35.50	6.50	28.50	30.20	35.50	15.80	32.50	56.90	16.40	56.50	17.50	9.60
Assam	43.00	85.00	39.30	9.60	22.40	31.00	31.40	29.80	36.40	69.60	36.50	44.90	34.80	8.90
Manipur	30.40	41.90	68.60	10.50	45.90	59.00	37.80	30.10	22.10	41.10	14.80	37.20	21.00	4.60
Meghalaya	43.30	70.50	54.00	8.10	29.00	31.10	72.20	48.10	48.80	64.40	14.60	53.50	35.20	7.60
Mizoram	93.30	52.90	59.30	8.70	59.80	65.40	27.40	55.80	19.90	44.20	14.40	30.40	9.40	6.20
Nagaland	36.90	64.70	32.70	1.90	11.60	24.70	17.60	39.30	25.20	#NULL!	17.40	47.30	47.90	4.50
Sikkim	85.70	40.10	70.10	27.20	47.20	53.70	33.40	41.60	19.70	59.20	11.20	73.70	8.20	13.20
Tripura	74.40	59.20	60.00	10.60	46.90	48.80	64.50	26.60	39.60	62.90	36.90	40.30	20.10	14.40
West														
Goa	94.70	20.30	94.90	55.70	92.30	94.00	72.10	35.40	25.00	38.20	27.90	25.30	70.40	14.50
Gujarat	85.60	60.90	67.50	25.60	52.70	63.00	56.80	43.90	44.60	69.70	36.30	49.20	72.50	27.30
Maharashtra	80.00	74.3	52	15	38.7	46.6	59.8	32.9	42.5	69.5	35.6	51.5	65.6	17.3
South														
Andhra Pradesh	40.30	63.20	85.40	28.20	64.40	74.90	65.30	30.50	32.50	70.80	33.50	38.90	74.30	9.00
Karnataka	58.30	54.70	79.50	29.60	64.70	69.70	65.60	35.50	37.60	70.40	35.50	52.80	64.00	19.90
Kerala	88.60	16.30	93.60	63.60	99.30	99.40	63.30	30.80	22.90	44.50	18.00	26.80	50.00	22.60
Tamil Nadu	85.80	35.50	95.90	34.00	87.80	90.60	63.30	42.50	29.80	64.20	28.40	28.20	47.00	15.20
India	**41.1**	**74.3**	**52**	**15**	**38.7**	**46.6**	**59.8**	**32.9**	**42.5**	**69.5**	**35.6**	**51.5**	**65.6**	**17.3**

Notes on Variables used in Table 2.1(b):

Variables	**Definitions**
X1**BRGNl**	Percentage of *de jure* total births of children under 5 years of age reported registered.
X2**U5MOR**	Under 5 mortality rates for the five-year period preceding the survey 2005-06.
X33**ANCS**	Among women with a live birth within five years preceding the survey percentage who had three or more ANC visits for the last live birth.
X4**ALLANC**	Among women with a live birth within five years preceding the survey percentage who had all recommended types of ANC care.
X5**DELHEF**	Percentage of births delivered in a health facility.
X6**DELAST**	Percentage of deliveries assisted by a health personnel.
X7**DIACAE**	Among children under age 5 who had diarrhoea during preceding two weeks percentage taken to an official health provider.
X8**ICDS**	Percentage of children under age 6 living in AGW covered centre who received any services within 12 months preceding the survey.
X9**MALCH**	Percentage of children under age 5 malnourished based on weight for age less than 2 SD from recommended median.
X10**ANECH**	Percentage of children age 6-59 months having anaemia (Hb less than 11 g/dl).
X11**THINWO**	Percentage of women aged 15-49 with thin body mass (BMI less than 18.5).
X12**TBNOTION**	Among men aged 15-49 who have heard of TB percentage who have misconceptions about transmission of the disease.
X13**NOUSEGF**	Percentage of households that do not generally use government health facilities.
X14**ANYCOHW**	Percentage of women,15-49, with any contact with a health worker.

Source: International Institute for Population Science (IIPS) and Macro International, 2007. National Family Health Survey (NFHS-3), 2005-06.

Outcome Indicators

If we look at the outcome indicators with regard to under 5 mortality, the level for the country as a whole during 2000-2005 was 74.3 children per 10000 births dying before the age of 5 and this ranged from a high of over 90 in Chhattisgarh (90.3), Madhya Pradesh (94.2), Uttar Pradesh (96.4), Jharkhand (93) and Orissa (90.6) to a low of below 40 in Goa (20.3), Kerala (16.3) and Tamil Nadu (35.5). Again the states in the central and east India depict a comparatively very dismal picture. The zero order correlation between the IEG and the effective governance by the state government, mentioned above and the child mortality level works out to—0.785 highly significant at .001 levels implying a very close association between state governance and child mortality. The states with good governance as indicated by a high proportion of births registered tend to have a low level of child mortality. The correlation matrix as given in Table 2.1(a), reveals a very high and significant correlation coefficient of extent of birth registration with most of the output and outcome variables in reproductive and child health.

Table 2.1(b) reveals that the prevailing conditions with regard to the nutritional status of women and children in India are the most depressing. The percentage of children under age 5 classified as malnourished in 2000-2005 in terms of weight for age (less than 2 SD units from the median levels of 2006 WHO International Reference Population) is as high as 42.5 per cent ranging from a very high of over 50 per cent (over half of the children) in the states of Madhya Pradesh (60 per cent), Bihar (56 per cent) and Jharkhand (57 per cent). The malnutrition is relatively better off (less than 25 per cent) in the states of Mizoram (20), Sikkim (20) and Kerala (23). Even in the state of Punjab which is considered as the most prosperous state in agriculture, 25 per cent of the children below the age of 5 are underweight. This is rather a serious situation needing an urgent investigation and corrective action.

Similarly the prevalence of anaemia among children (haemoglobin levels less than 11 gms. per decilitre of blood) in the age range of 6 to 59 months is a staggering 70 per cent in the country as a whole ranging from 78 per cent in Bihar to a low of 44.5 per cent in Kerala. There is greater homogeneity among the sates in the prevalence of anaemia than in the case of underweight or overall malnourishment among children. Again the correlation between the index of state governance and the two nutrition indicators of children are –0.472 and –0.463, both statistically significant at 10 per cent level.

With regard to the nutritional status of women in the age range 15-49, the body mass index (BMI) defined as the ratio of weight in kgms to the square of height in metres, is considered a sensitive index of adult malnutrition. BMI less than 18.5 units is considered to be an indicator of underweight by international standards. Table 2.1(b) reveals that 36 per cent of women in the country in the age group 15-49 are underweight ranging from a high of (over 40 per cent) in Bihar (45), Madhya Pradesh (42 per cent), Chhattisgarh (43 per cent), Orissa (41 per cent) and Jharkhand (43 per cent). It is below 20 per cent in many northeastern states (except for Assam and Tripura) and Kerala. There appears to be no significant association between extent of birth registration as an indicator of IEG and this indicator of woman's malnutrition, as was observed in the case of child malnutrition.

Process and Output Indicators

For any public health programme to succeed, frequent contacts by the peripheral health workers, ANM, AGW or ASHA, lady health visitor (LHV) and the medical officer of the PHC are essential to identify diseases at the early stages of onset, to provide appropriate care and treatment and to suggest necessary preventive measures. There are three indicators used in this regard; per cent of households that have stated that they do not generally use any government health facility when they are sick for various reasons (X13); per cent of women who did not have any contact with any peripheral health workers during the past 12 months (X14); per cent of children below 6 years of age who did not receive any services from the ICDS programme from the concerned *anganwadi* workers (AGW) during the past 12 months (X8). The percentage of households that do not generally use any government health facility is shockingly high at 66 per cent for the country as a whole ranging from a high of 93 per cent in Bihar and 85 per cent in Uttar Pradesh to a low of 9 per cent in Mizoram and 8 per cent in Sikkim. Even in the southern states that have well-developed private medical services even in the rural areas, more than half the households reported using the government health facility. Where there is a high level of non-use of government facility, the major reasons stated are "poor quality of care" and "long waiting times". Similarly the percentage of women aged 15-49 who had any contact at all within the past 12 months with the local health worker, auxiliary nurse midwife, lady health visitor, *anganwadi* worker or community health worker was only 17.3 per cent in the country as a whole and was as low as 2.9 per cent in Delhi. The maximum contact was found in Gujarat (27.3), Kerala (22.6) and Orissa (22.6). Similarly with regard to the extent of use of *anganwadi* centres for children below 6 years of age (X8), set up exclusively for the welfare of children below the age of 6 years, NFHS-3 reveals that the percentage of children in the age range 0-71 months, living in a AWC area, who received any services from the *anganwadi* centre was only 33 per cent in the country as whole ranging from a high of 65 per cent in Orissa and Chhattisgarh to a low of 10 per cent in Bihar and 12 per cent in Delhi.

Compared to other RCH services by the health department, the ICDS programme seems to have greater inroads and acceptance in the community. The correlation of these three variables with the percentage of birth registration taken as a proxy for effective governance is not significant. Under these circumstances one can question the presumption of the government that increasing the budgets for health would automatically improve the health conditions of the population under the existing public health system especially in the state of north, central and eastern regions of the country. Some fundamental structural changes seem to be called for in these states. As a result of such a poor health system with limited contacts and services for women and children, it is no wonder that the quality and extent of maternal and child health services availed of by pregnant mothers are quite low. These are obvious from looking at variables X3 to X6 in Tables 2.1(a) and (b). For example, the percentage of births that occurred during 2000-2005 and assisted by a skilled health personnel (whether delivered at home or in an institution—X6) was just 47 ranging from a high of 99 in Kerala to a low of 24 in Nagaland and 27 in Jharkhand and Uttar Pradesh. These output variables, X3 to X6 are highly correlated with the extent of registration of births, considered as proxy of effective state governance with the correlation coefficients at 0.721, 0.590, 0.653 and 0.679 respectively and all significant at 1 per cent level.

A multivariate analysis of taking child mortality (under 5 mortality—X2) with four selected predictors, *viz.*, the extent of birth registration (X1), per cent of pregnant women who received all prescribed antenatal care (X4), per cent of births delivered in a health facility (X5) and proportion of thin women with low body mass among women (X11) revealed that these four predictors were able to explain 81.3 per cent of the interstate variance (R=0.904) in child mortality and the regression equation using the standardised variables is

$$X2 + -0.24*X1 - 0.14*X4 - 0.460*X5 + 0.31*X11$$

The regression coefficients of the first three predictors (X1, X4 and X5) turning out to be highly significant. It is significant to note that a simple variable as the proportion of births registered retains its statistical significance even after controlling for the other three, which are expected to directly influence child mortality.

Discussions and Recommendations

Mainly as a result of the public health system coupled with improvements in personal hygiene, water supply and sanitation for larger sections of the population, a number of infectious diseases have been controlled and a few eradicated contributing to an increase in the expectation of life at birth from 32 years in 1951 to 66.5 years in 2005 and a reduction in the infant mortality rates by more than 60 per cent from 148 infant deaths per 1000 live births to 57 in the same period. However, during the same period many other large developing countries, China, Indonesia and Brazil have achieved better result in the reduction of mortality, especially infant and child mortality. Not only the mortality decline is slower in India compared to these countries but also the morbidity rates in our population have dramatically increased over the years partly as a result of the increase in the longevity of the population but mostly due to large-scale malnutrition as a consequence of poverty. With the continuation of many of the earlier communicable diseases, such as tuberculosis, malaria, water-borne diseases and number of newer communicable diseases such as HIV/AIDS and the burden of chronic diseases added on to the population heavily malnourished, no wonder the morbidity rates are high.

In recent years there are a number of research studies focusing on the extent to which the public health system in the country is meeting or responding to the changing health care needs of the population, especially the needs of the poorer and the vulnerable sections of the society for whom they were primarily intended. The findings are very depressing. The surveys by the National Sample Survey Organisation in their 52nd round conducted during July 1995-June 1996 revealed a sharply increased level of morbidity in the population, both acute and chronic illnesses (55 per cent in the rural areas and 54 per cent in the urban areas reporting some illness within the past 15 days of the 1995-96 survey), a significant proportion among them (16 per cent in the rural areas and 9 per cent in the urban areas) not taking any treatment at all because of financial reasons and a large proportion of those seeking medical treatment (81 per cent in the rural areas and 80 per cent in the urban areas) taking it from private sources (private medical practitioners and nursing homes) paying very high fees and almost driven to bankruptcy because of such payments to private doctors and nursing homes. Analysis of data available from the National Family Health Survey–2 conducted during 1998-99, revealed that the utilisation of public health services by the poorer sections of the society vary from state to state and in the states of Bihar and Uttar Pradesh, only less than 10 per cent of the poor used such facilities. The poor preferred to go to a private doctor, pay fees beyond their means and get indebted rather than go to a government medical centre. The data collected from the recently concluded National Family Health Survey–3 and presented above confirm the findings. The percentage of households that do not generally use any government health facility is shockingly high at 66 per cent for the country as a whole ranging from a high of 93 per cent in Bihar and 85 per cent in Uttar Pradesh to a low of 9 per cent in Mizoram and 8 per cent in Sikkim. Even in the southern states that have well-developed private medical services even in the rural areas, more than half of the households reported using the government health facility. Where there is a high level of non-use of government facility, the major reasons stated are "poor quality of care" and "long waiting times". Similarly, the percentage of women aged 15-49 who had any contact at all within the past 12 months with the local health worker, auxiliary nurse midwife, lady health visitor, anganwadi worker or community health worker was only 17.3 per cent in the country as a whole and was as low as 2.9 per cent in the capital of Delhi. The maximum contact was found in Gujarat (27.3), Kerala (22.6) and Orissa (22.6). Similarly with regard to the extent of use of *anganwadi* centres for children below 6 years of age, set up exclusively for the welfare of children below the age of 6 years, NFHS-3 reveals that the percentage of children in the age range 0-71 months, living in a AWC area, who received any services from the *anganwadi* centre was only 33 per cent in the country as whole ranging from a high of 65 per cent in Orissa and Chhattisgarh to a low of 10 per cent in Bihar and 12 per cent in Delhi. Compared to other RCH services by the health department, the ICDS programme seems to have greater inroads and acceptance in the community but far below the expectations. On the whole, the existing public health system has stopped delivering the goods and services expected of them.

The present government is committed for the improvement of the health and nutrition levels of the population, especially those below the poverty line. The budget for health for the year 2008-09, recently announced by the Finance Minister is Rs. 16,534 crores and marks an increase of 15 per cent in the budget of 2007-08. Based on the findings and arguments given in this paper, given the very inefficient and almost non-functioning (in some states) public health system in the country, one can question the presumption of the government that increasing the budgets for health would automatically improve the health conditions of the population especially in the states of north, central and eastern regions of the country. Some fundamental structural changes seem to be called for in these states. As a result of such a poor health system with limited contacts and services for women and children, it is no wonder that the quality and extent of maternal and child health services availed of by pregnant mothers are quite low. The extremely high prevalence of anaemia among women and children and malnourishment (underweight for age) among women and children are very high, over 40 per cent. Of course these conditions vary significantly from state to state but the general impression that emerges from these data is that the public health system including the network of PHCs, CHCs and district hospitals do not serve the needs of the poor for which they are intended to serve. Instead they are being increasingly exploited by the better off sections of the society both in the rural and the urban areas.

Since the quality of governance seems to be an important factor in mediating the impact of any investments in the public health sector on the health, nutrition and survival status of women and children, this is found to be low in many states (taking the extent of registration of births as an index), providing additional financial inputs to the health sector may not improve the situation. We found a very high degree of association between the percentage of births registered and child mortality, child nutrition and growth and use of ICDS services. In spite of increased investment in the health programmes during the past decade, the morbidity and mortality conditions in the country as a whole have not improved and in many areas it has worsened. In this context there is an urgent need for setting up a high level committee at national level (similar to the Bhore Committee of the forties) and redefine the role of state governments in the areas of health and medical care, the areas where there should be public-private partnerships and the specific roles of the primary health centres. The principles of democratic decentralisation whereby more powers, resources and responsibilities for primary health care are given to the *panchayats* may not be the best route for improving the health and nutrition of the population of the country.

References

Government of India (1946). *Report of the Health Survey and Development Committee.* Delhi: Manager of Publications. Vol.1.

———. (1961). *Health Survey and Planning Committee Report.* New Delhi: Ministry of Health.

National Sample Survey Organisation (1998). *Morbidity and Treatment of Aliments*, NSS Fifty–Second Round, July 1995-June 1996. GoI.

International Institute for Population Sciences (IIPS) (1994). *National Family Health Survey (NFHS 1)*, 1992-93. Mumbai: IIPS.

———. (2000). *National Family Health Survey (NFHS 2)*, 1998-99: India. Mumbai: IIPS.

International Institute for Population Sciences (IIPS) and Macro International (2007). *National Family Health Survey (NFHS 3)*, 2005-06, Vol. 1. India, Mumbai: IIPS.

Srinivasan, K. and S.K. Mohanty (2004). "Health Care Utilization by Source and Levels of Deprivation in Major States of India: Findings from NFHS-2," *Demography India* 3(2): 107-126.

Appendix A-2.1

Stated Objectives of the Recent Population and Health Policies

NPP 2000	*NHP 2002*	*NRHM 2005*
1. To address the unmet needs for contraception, health care infrastructure and health personnel and to integrate service delivery for basic reproductive and child health care.	1. To achieve an acceptable standard of good health among the general population of the country.	1. To provide effective health care to rural population throughout the country with special focus on 18 backward states.
2. To bring the TFR to replacement levels of 2.1 by 2010.	2. To increase the aggregate public health investment through a substantially increased contribution by the Central govt.	2. To raise public spending on health from 0.9% to 2-3% of GDP in five years.
3. To achieve a stable population by 2045.	3. To ensure the increased access to tried and tested systems of traditional medicine.	3. To undertake architectural correction of the health system to enable it effectively to handle increased allocations.
		4. To revitalise local health traditions and mainstream AYUSH into public health system.
		5. Aim at effective integration of health concerns with determinants of health like sanitation and hygiene, nutrition and safe drinking water.
		6. To address the interstate and inter-district disparities including unmet needs for public health infrastructure.

Appendix A-2.2

Stated Goals to be Achieved in Recent Population and Health Policies

NPP 2000 (To be Achieved by 2010)	*NHP 2002*	*NRHM 2005 (To be Achieved by 2012)*
1. Address the unmet needs for basic RCH services, supplies and infrastructures.	**1.** Eradicate polio and yaws by 2005.	**1.** Reduce IMR to 30 per 1000 live births.
2. Make school education upto 14 free and compulsory and reduce dropouts at primary and secondary levels.	**2.** Eliminate leprosy by 2005.	**2.** Reduce MMR to 100 per 100,000 live births.
3. Reduce IMR to 30 per 1000 live births.	**3.** Eliminate kala azar by 2010	**3.** Universal access to public health services such as women's health, child health, water, sanitation & hygiene, immunisation and nutrition.
4. Reduce MMR to 100 per 100,000 live births.	**4.** Eliminate lymphatic filariasis by 2015.	**4.** Prevention and control of communicable & non-communicable diseases, including locally endemic diseases.
5. Achieve universal immunisation of children against all vaccine preventable diseases.	**5.** Achieve zero level growth of HIV/AIDS by 2007.	**5.** Access to integrate comprehensive primary health care.
6. Promote delayed marriage for girls, not earlier than age 18 and preferably after age 20.	**6.** Reduce mortality by 50% on account of TB, malaria and other vector and water-borne diseases by 2010.	**6.** Population stabilisation, gender and demographic balance.
7. Achieve 80% institutional deliveries and 100% deliveries by trained persons.	**7.** Reduce prevalence of blindness to 0.5% by 2010.	**7.** Revitalise local health traditions and mainstream AYUSH.
8. Achieve universal access to information/ counselling	**8.** Reduce IMR to 30 per 1000 and MMR to 100 per 100,000 live births by 2010.	**8.** Promotion of healthy lifestyle.
9. Achieve 100% registration of births, deaths, marriage and pregnancy.	**9.** Increase utilisation of public health facilities from current level of <20% to >75% by 2010.	

contd...

...contd...

NPP 2000 (To be Achieved by 2010)	*NHP 2002*	*NRHM 2005 (To be Achieved by 2012)*
10. Contain the spread of AIDS and promote greater integration between the management of RTI, STI and NACO.	**10.** Establish an integrated system of surveillance, National Health Accounts and Health Statistics by 2005.	
11. Prevent and control communicable diseases.	**11.** Increase health expenditure by govt. as a % of GDP from the existing 0.9% to 2.0% by 2010.	
12. Integrate Indian system of medicine in the provision of RCH services and in reaching out to households.	**12.** Increase share of central grant to constitute at least 25% of total health spending by 2010.	
13. Promote vigorously the small family norm to achieve replacement levels of TFR.	**13.** Increasing state sector health spending from 5.5% to 7.0% of the budget by 2005 and further increase to 8.0% by 2010.	
14. Bring about convergence in implementation of related social sector programmes so that family welfare becomes a people centred programme.		

3

Challenges in Population and Health in India

Is One Billion an Asset or a Liability?

ARUNA SHARMA

Introduction

Challenges in population and health are not just in terms of controlling the population growth but more so in improving the quality of life. The challenges are therefore, whether the young population of India is an asset or a liability. The interventions for healthy, educated and productive population are to be in terms of assuring good nutrition, health care and specific targeted and time bound benchmarks for the 'left out' vulnerable and disadvantaged groups. The issue of population ought to be discussed in terms of direct interventions and conducive environment.

Population stabilisation in terms of encouraging use of contraceptives, increase of extent of unmet needs, basket of reproductive health choices available to women and men and terminal methods needs to be supplemented by focus on awareness building against child marriage, preference for male child, women's empowerment, efforts of state to improve child survival and also that on the reach, coverage and quality of services available to the vulnerable and marginalised groups. Challenges in population and health is therefore, not just advisory or advocatory but is to shift the debate on what works and what does not to achieve the desired objective of stabilisation of population on the one hand and on the other hand to have efforts for ensuring skilled, healthy and productive population contributing to the GDP. The efforts are therefore, to accelerate the interventions, which would give positive results and discourage the issues that have marginal or negative impact; it is to translate rhetoric to reality by bridging the gaps in the access and performance parameters.

There is no denial of the fact that the continuous rise in population in India is competing on the available financial, physical and opportunity resources. The issue turns more serious as 28 per cent of this population is categorised as poor i.e., who will perform poor in the parameters of health and nutrition. The challenge is, therefore, to work out a mechanism of not only checking the growth in population but also taking parallel steps to prevent the identified vulnerable and disadvantaged groups from perpetuating in poverty because of large family size. The failure is much argued as earmarking only 2 per cent of GDP to the health sector but the challenge of population and health is more to evaluate whether the available resources are used to the optimum to get qualitative and sustainable outcomes. The major hindrance and barrier is in terms of poor management of delivery of services and cultural dimensions. The poor get left out in having access to the interventions of health care and population stabilisation. Thus, the issue is not that of constraint in financial or manpower resource availability but is more of poor management of the mechanisms to improve the access. The responsibility becomes therefore more of the Government, civil society and implementing agency to strengthen the mechanism to achieve the dual objective of good health care and resultant population stabilisation by improving the delivery system by adopting effective management and resource convergence model to identified goals.

India is a country of 1020 million (2001 Census) and by the year 2030, at the current birth rate, India would have 1700 million people and acquire the distinction of being the most populous state in the world. India is also visualised as becoming a competitor to most developed countries by 2020 in terms of growth (GDP) potential and participation in the world's wealth. India's year-to-year growth rate could well hit double figures at some point in 2008 and the country may even grow faster than China but good economic performance is not by just having a consistent high growth rate but focused public policies to build capacity of the vulnerable. The increase in the number of vulnerable would be of 16 million in coming decade. Today, GDP grew by 9.2 per cent and average annual pace is more than 8 per cent compared with around 6 per cent in the 1980s and 1990s and measly 3.5 per cent during the three decades before 1980. The government's Eleventh Five Year Plan 2007-2012 has an ambitious target of 9 per cent average annual growth. However, much of this growth rate will be drained by rapid population growth imposing pressures on infrastructure due to intensive agriculture, environment, physical infrastructure and services, competing livelihood opportunities and thus, add to the number of vulnerable groups. The lopsided growth of having competence of world class to that of more than one-fourth of the population struggling for the basic survival with dignity is the challenge. Thus, addressing the population issue is critical for India's progress.

Health is the basic need of a human being and access to health care is a basic human right. Article 21 of the Constitution states that no person shall be deprived of his life and the right to life includes right to health.[1] Further, it has been emphasised that failure on the part of government hospitals i.e., public health care system to provide timely medical treatment to patients in need of such treatment amounts to violation of the right to life.[2] This when read with Article 47 stating the duty of the State to raise the level of nutrition and the standard of living, enjoins the state to improve the standard of public health by making it one of its primary duties. Improving standard of health services entails ensuring accessibility to such services at affordable prices so that it falls within the reach of all. India had adopted a three-tier hospital and health services structure. It is worthy to note that as far back as during the Sixth Five Year Plan; the national norms for a three-tier health care infrastructure consisting of the Sub-Centre (SHC), Primary Health Centre (PHC) and the Community Health Centre (CHC) were evolved. However, despite such efforts and more, the Human Development Report and NFHS-3 portrays a grim picture. It highlights the high rate of IMR and MMR with an increasing percentage of death rates among children due to lack of neo-natal care, low percentage of immunisation and thereby announcing the failure of the mandate enlisted in the Constitution.

As India races toward achieving superpowerdom, its children are still far behind in terms of health care, education and other facilities. Children are faced with lack of educational opportunities, malnourishment, infant mortality and early marriages. NFHS-3 (2005-06) has highlighted that all India average for malnourished children is 47 per cent. Every second child under 5 years is malnourished. Even in the prosperous states like Gujarat and Kerala, unfortunately there is rise in the number of malnourished children by 2 per cent in the last decade i.e., from 1991 to 2001. States like Madhya Pradesh have shown an increase of 6 per cent from 54 to 60 in the same time period. Thus, the impact of interventions in terms of supplementary diet is not reaching the desired groups. The outcome in terms of better performance in the indicator of nutrition is not reflecting. NHFS-3 further lists that three-fourth of all infants between 6-35 months of age are anaemic as for most of these children malnutrition must have started in the womb itself. This is also an indicator that the intervention of distribution of iron-folic tablets is not having the desired impact.

What is Needed is Micro Level Monitoring

The targeted beneficiary throws away much of the iron-folic tablets as it causes stomach irritation. With no sanitary toilets in villages and urban slums

1. State of Punjab, Mahinder Singh Chawala, AIR 1997 SC 1225.
2. Paschim Bengal Khet Mazdoor Society *vs.* State of West Bengal, AIR 1996 SC 2426, paragraphs 9, 15, 16 and Parmanand Katara *vs.* Union of India, AIR 1989 SC 2039 (1990).

in sufficient numbers, this adds to their problem and thus, they prefer not to have the iron-folic tablets. This, therefore, negates the very objective of intervention. Fifty-four (54) per cent of pregnant women are found anaemic. Comparison with NFHS-2 conducted five years ago shows that the proportion of wasted children has increased while underweight children are only marginally less.

Another indicator is high infant mortality rate where India is bettered by Pakistan, China, Brazil and even Nigeria. The all India average is 58 infant deaths for every 1000 live births and states like Uttar Pradesh (73), Rajasthan (65), a tiny state Arunachal Pradesh has as high as 61 and Gujarat has 50. The Millennium Development Goal (MDG) is committed for 2015 to reduce the IMR and child mortality by two-thirds which in absolute terms means to reduce IMR to 27 and under 5 mortality rate (U5MR) to 32. Here the NFHS-3 giving status for 2005 lists IMR to 58, does this mean that in coming seven years it will be a mere rhetoric to the commitment to MDG? The disturbing factor is the reduction in performance of the major intervention of immunisation. The children fully immunised are as low as 60 per cent in 6 states and in other 8 states less than half of the children born are fully immunised. This results ultimately in terms of huge economic burden in having malnutrition, sick and ill-equipped youth. The success till date is only to those who do manage to approach the agency imparting the services but the main challenge is to reach those who do not even access these agencies or manpower or the schemes available and targeted for them.

One Billion Population in India: An Asset or a Liability

The growth of population in last 50 years has jumped from 36.11 to 102.70 crores. The exponential growth rate in a decade is 1.93 per cent (1991-2001). India can definitely laud on increase in life expectancy and check in fertility but the wide base will continue to aggravate the challenge. Seventy-five (75) per cent of the projected increase in population over the next 30 years is likely to be on account of the 'population momentum'. And, to that extent, efforts to lower population growth rates are not likely to make a substantial difference as they can affect, at best reduce, as much as possible the numbers accounted for by the 25 per cent projected increase in population. Positive trends have reflected even in states like Uttar Pradesh, Bihar, Madhya Pradesh and Rajasthan, the TFR has been declining though not as fast. This is primarily because these states have lagged behind in the provisioning of comprehensive health care and basic education. Replacement level, or close to replacement level fertility, has been reached in several states including Sikkim, Kerala, Tamil Nadu, Karnataka, Goa, Andhra Pradesh,

Himachal Pradesh, Delhi and Punjab. This is more so in urban than in rural areas. Some of the laudable progress is listed below: The demographic chart is a pyramid with wide base thus, the efforts take 30-40 years to have the impact, thus the challenge is to translate this liability into a mission to educate more and more couples and improving the management of availability.

The challenge in population and health is not just limited to strengthen the interventions, which had positive impact, but to accelerate the pace of these interventions. The challenge is therefore, to identify the interventions that can accelerate the process of population stabilisation by striking the right balance of protection of the rights of individual to have choice and have the desired results. The success of the southern states within India in reducing fertility point to the importance of simultaneous actions along multiple fronts—quality health care services, education, women's empowerment, child survival and reducing human poverty. Indeed the lesson is "take care of people, and population will take care of itself". There is a strong correlation between lowering fertility rates on the one hand and empowering women, providing universal comprehensive primary health care (including reproductive health services), improving child survival and reducing poverty on the other.

The challenges are therefore,

- To capture the gap of number of children wanted and what they give birth to i.e., gap between 1.9 and 2.7.
- To capture the gap in contraceptive use which will enhance performance by 30-44 per cent from existing 61 per cent.
- To capture unmet need of adolescent awareness which is 13 per cent.
- To capture failure of access to public health services for preventive care by the disadvantaged and vulnerable groups.
- To capture failure of access to public health services for curative care by the disadvantaged and vulnerable groups which is 56 per cent.
- To capture optimal, nay 100 per cent usage of the financial, physical and social resources already earmarked for the health sector.
- To capture the gap between 'having access' and 'gaining access'.
- To build in mechanism for resource convergence among different schemes, agencies and funds of government targeted for similar objectives.

Figure 3.1

The Real Challenge is Bridging the Gaps

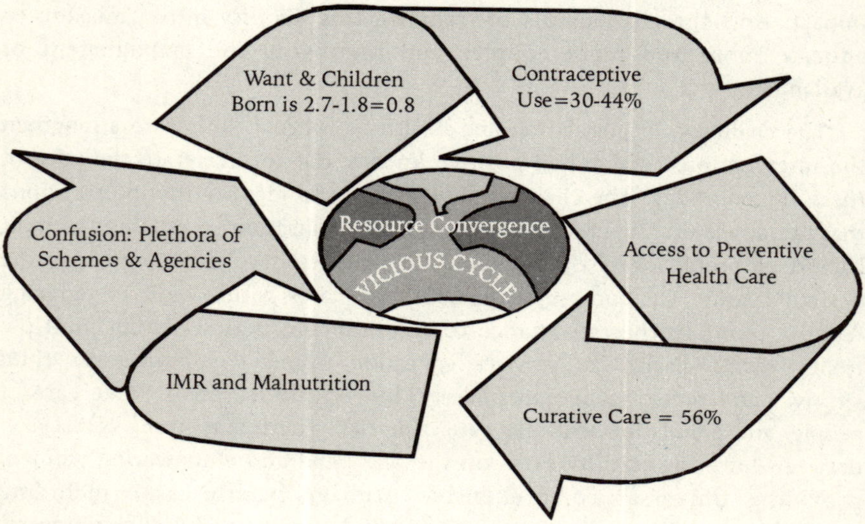

Bridging the Gap of Number of Children Wanted and that Given Birth will Improve Total Fertility Rate by 0.8

NFHS-3 has listed fertility level of 2.7 children but has also expressed concern that the decrease between NFHS-1 and NFHS-2 is 0.5 children whereas between NFHS-2 and NFHS-3 is just by 0.2 children. This reflects that the efforts to encourage small family norms have shown a decline. However, disaggregated figures reflect that the fertility rates among women in vulnerable and disadvantaged groups is 3.1 among ST; 2.9 among the SC and 2.8 is among the backward classes as compared to only 2.4 among others. Thus, the disadvantaged and vulnerable groups will be more prone to be in poverty trap and also miss out opportunities of high growth rate of GDP. Concentrated efforts are, therefore, required among these groups to ensure proper health care and access to contraceptives. The most interesting finding is "if all women were to have only the number of children they wanted, the total fertility rate would be 1.9 instead of 2.7. This is where the challenge is i.e., to ensure access to contraceptives, preventive and terminal methods to have children they wanted, however, with caution of selective female foeticide. The interventions should be to provide so that women get what they want.

Bridging Gap between Contraceptive Uses will Improve by 30-44 Per cent

It is encouraging that two-third of the women and men consider the ideal family size to be two children or less, however, strong preference for son still continues. The harm is more because of unplanned pregnancies, 11 per cent of which are unwanted. Contraceptive use among women is still 56 per cent. This is a gap which needs to be addressed for better management of health delivery system itself will bring an improvement of 30-44 per cent. Exposure to family planning messages is also as low as 61 per cent and reflects strongly the need to accelerate the awareness building efforts. The argument of incentive and disincentive makes it immaterial as the "want" for more children is not the reason for the continued high birth rate but the culprit is more of non-access to contraceptive methods and preference for male child. Thus, the focus is to be more on better delivery mechanism of awareness, monitoring the health delivery systems and contraceptive methods and terminal methods after two children.

Increasing Reach to Adolescents will Capture 13 Per cent

The experts advocating the two-child norm as necessary condition for achieving population stabilisation[3] considers human rights perspective will never accept a high mortality regime to achieve population stabilisation. The issue is not that of end but also of means. The NFHS-3 has clearly reflected that the families do 'want' only two children, thus the challenge is to enable them to have access to the contraceptive and terminal methods regime. The efforts are also to build up awareness against the preference for male child. The percentage of currently married women, who either want to space their next birth or stop child bearing, but are not using contraception is 13 per cent. Thus, this unmet need of 13 per cent is to be targeted through adolescent awareness, prevention of child marriage and resultant early child bearing.

Access to Preventive and Curative Health Care will Improve IMR by 27 Points

It has been an accepted norm that poverty is widely recognised as an impediment to good health. It plays a central role in an individual's health status, influencing his or her access to health care, housing condition, access to safe water and sanitation, sufficient food and nutrition, as well as control

---

3. "The Rationale for the Two-Child Norm", *Indian Journal of Population Education* 37: 65-85, (June 2007).

over his or her reproductive process.[4] The underlying adverse impacts of serious illnesses on households are costly, and potentially irreversible. Crisis coping mechanisms lead to "catastrophic health expenditure",[5] pushing these households into a poverty trap from which they rarely recover. In India, National Health Policy and the other related programmes of sanitation, food security in terms of public distribution system or supplementary nutrition, free housing, access to safe drinking water and above all the public health services are directed to the poor. Unfortunately the various studies have categorically listed and pointed that the poor are not using these free of cost preventive and curative health services available in the public health system. Health is clearly not the mere absence of disease. Good health, according to the Constitution of WHO, confers on a person or groups, freedom from illness and the ability to realise one's potential. Health is, therefore, best understood as the indispensable basis for defining a person's sense of well-being. If we take the issue of preventive health care, the NFHS-2 and 3 show disturbing trends. Child malnutrition[6] rates nearly one-half of children aged 0-35 months were underweight in 1998-99, the statistics show the figure as 45.9 per cent of children under three years of age underweight, 38.4 per cent stunted, and 19.1 per cent wasted. These indicators become all the more serious where all these services have been provided free of cost in the public health care system including those under Integrated Child and Development Scheme (ICDS) executed and monitored by Women and Child Welfare Ministry. It is thus imperative to note that the issue does not seem to be that of resource crunch as sufficient vaccines and schemes to cater to the services are available. If we talk of curative health services then even after 60 years of Independence, untrained doctors (quacks) are still in private sector with maximum percentage catering 68 per cent of the health care. The National Rural Health Mission (NRHM) has begun with great promise, now it remains to be seen whether the overall availability and quality of health care services for the poor and marginalised improves. Percentage of GDP of Government on public health is substantially low. It may be noted that the total health-related expenditure in India is roughly 5 per cent of the overall GDP. Of this, 1 per cent is the government's share and the rest is private spending. This again reflects denial by the poor of the available public health services. However, what is more disturbing that the benefit of 1 per cent that is spent

---

4. Basch, 1999.

5. Catastrophic health expenditure: Health expenditure exceeding 40 per cent of effective income remaining after fulfilling subsistence needs.

6. A child is considered underweight when his or her weight for age is more than two standard deviations below the NCHS reference weight.

is not reaching the target group. Thus, the challenge is not just of increase in the Government expenditure on health but also that of utilising the financial, physical and social resources that are already available in sufficient quantity.

Resource Convergence: As Schemes, Programmes, Finacial Resources and Delivery System in Place but Working in Watertight Compartments

Rural public health care and conditions in urban slums is choked nationwide for a number of reasons. To name two, provisioning of services is very top heavy and many major programmes continue to be conceived and run uncoordinatedly. The individual schemes work in watertight compartments with each of them having their own vertical structure, programmes, and extension staff and implementing agencies. If we analyse properly, the objectives are supplementary and complementary to each other. Infrastructure, accessibility in terms of proximity and affordability in terms of providing free services. The terms availability, accessibility and affordability needs to be understood to demonstrate low utilisation of public health services. Thus, the need is to distinguish between 'having access'[7] and 'gaining access'.[8] This points out that even where adequate services exist, issues relating to affordability, physical inaccessibility and acceptability can limit the extent to which patients can make use of them. Social or cultural obstacles can also restrict utilisation of basic services.

If we analyse the issue from adolescent to pre-birth to care till 18 years of age we cover the entire cycle. There are specific schemes targeted for the awareness building, hygiene, medical check ups, access to contraceptives, legal provisions against child marriage and survey reports showing the positive impact have endorsed the policies. However, the constant high growth of GDP to 9 per cent has on the one hand triggered the increase in opportunities but on the other hand has created conflict by increase in aspirations for those who do not have access to basic opportunities in terms of education, health care and job opportunities. For success in the stabilisation of population, the need is to focus on the awareness building among adolescents by converging the schemes under donor programmes, women and child development (WCD) department schemes, schemes under education sector and RCH. The exposure to health care, attack on anaemia and nutrients calls for converging schemes of WCD and food and health extension under RCH and NRHM. The legal awareness and social change in terms of resolution of not resorting to child

7. 'Having Access': when there is adequate supply of services and systems in place to facilitate utilisation.

8. 'Gaining Access': This relates to entry to, or actual utilisation of services.

marriage needs constant vigilance and awareness spread by opinion makers. The counselling to married couples and sexual and reproductive health (SRH) and HIV/AIDS convergence combined to awareness against female foeticide and spacing methods will go a long way. For women, the first contact point is often family planning or antenatal clinics and segregation of approach is again opportunity lost as women are often the one discriminated in access to health care and women also constitute a high percentage of non-planned pregnancies and abortions. In India, the National Rural Health Mission (NRHM) in its District Action Plan (DAP), and the Reproductive and Child Health (RCH II) activities and programmes have flagged the need for convergence in the field of institutional framework, manpower and proposed activities, which are generic as well as focused. It has also flagged the issue of inter-sectoral coordination. Thus, the challenges in population and health is first of all to catch up with the backlog of unmet needs in terms of 11 per cent of unplanned and unwanted pregnancies, catching up the gap of 44 per cent in the use of contraceptives, 61 per cent of gap of family planning messages not just reaching the target population and 13 per cent of the unmet need of terminal methods for stopping child bearing. Thus, sheer improvement in management without resorting to incentives or for that matter disincentives will show phenomenal progress in moving towards population stabilisation. This further assisted by assured health care, control over the IMR and MMR will accelerate the process. The need is to converge the village level functionaries like the ASHA, ANM, AGW and non-formal education employees to spread awareness and micro level monitoring. It is unfortunate that even at cutting edge the monitoring in village is more in terms of statistics of those who have availed the services than those who have missed the opportunity. The need is to monitor the individual. The target population of reproductive group is already listed and for a village as a unit with 3-4 village level workers spread between health, women and child, welfare of SC/ST/OBC departments need to converge their efforts and focus on the unmet needs. The performance level will indicate a straight jump of 25-30 per cent.

References

3i-Network (2007). *India Infrastructure Report: Rural Infrastructure*. Oxford Publication.

GoI (2006). *The Constitution of India, Ministry of Law and Justice and Company Affairs*. Government of India, New Delhi.

World Bank (2001). *India, Raising the Sights: Better Health Systems for India's Poor*. November.

———. (2006). *World Development Report*. New York: Oxford University Press.

Survey Reports:

Census (2001). "Sample Registration System (SRS): The SRS is the main source of data on Crude Birth Rate (CBR), Total Fertility Rate (TFR), Infant Mortality Rate (IMR), etc. at state level", These data are used for assessing the levels and studying the trends.

ICMR Surveys: Studies done by ICMR also provide information on many population-related issues.

Multi-indicator Surveys: Multi-indicator surveys done through UNICEF also provide information on various indicators.

National Family Health Survey (NFHS). Three rounds of National Family Health Survey (NFHS-1, NFHS-2 and NFHS-3) provide data on levels and change of various parameters at state level combined as well as by background characteristics such as literacy level, socio-economic groups etc.

RCH Rapid Household Surveys: At the district level data on population-related parameters are available through RCH/Rapid Household Surveys. These data are of immense use for identifying districts requiring special attention.

Books

Basch, P. (1999). "Health on the Edge", *Textbook of International Health*, (Ed. 2nd). London: Oxford University Press.

Berg, R. (2000). *Initiating Public/Private Partnerships to Finance Reproductive Health: The Role of Market Segmentation Analysis*. POLICY. May.

Berman, A.P. (1997). *Rethinking Healthcare Systems: Private Healthcare Provision in India*. Harvard School of Public Health. July.

Bhide, S. and A. Mehta, (2003). *Chronic Poverty in Rural India, An Analysis Using Panel Data: Issues and Findings*. Manchester, England: Chronic Poverty Research Centre.

Bird, K., D. Hulme, K. Moore and A. Shepherd (2002). "Chronic Poverty and Remote Rural Areas", CPRC *Working Paper* No. 13. Chronic Poverty Research Center: Birmingham, England.

BRAC (2004). *Annual Report*. BRAC Health Program. BRAC: Dhaka.

Dreze, Jean and Amartya Sen (1995). *India: Economic Development and Social Opportunity*. New Delhi: OUP.

Ellis, P.R. (1993). *Public and Private Interactions in the Health Sector in Developing Countries*. Health Financing and Sustainability (HFS) Project. February.

Gopalan, Sarala and Mira Shiva (2000). *National Profile on Women's Health and Development*. New Delhi: Voluntary Health Association of India (VHAI).

Gruskin, S. and D. Tarantola (2001). "Health and Human Rights", in Detels, McEwan, Beaglehole and Tanaka (eds.), *The Oxford Textbook of Public Health*. Oxford University Press.

Mahbub ul Huq Human Development Center (2005). *Human Development in South Asia*. Oxford Publication.

Qadeer, I. (1995). "Primary Health Care: A Paradise Lost", *IASSI Quarterly* 14(1&2): 1-20.

"Community Health Insurance in India." Friends of Women's World Banking, India. April 2005.

Articles

Dyna, Arhin Tenkorang (2000). "Mobilizing Resources for Health: The Case for User Fees Revisited", Unpublished paper for the Commission on Macroeconomics and Health, WHO, Geneva.

Jutting, J. (1999). "Public-Private-Partnership and Social Protection in Developing Countries: The Case of the Health Sector." Center for Development Research, University of Bonn. December.

Jutting, J. (1999). "Health Insurance for the Rural Poor?", Center for Development Research, University of Bonn. December.

Ahuja, R. (2004). "Health Insurance for the Poor in India", Indian Council for Research on International Economic Relations. March.

Schieber, G. and A. Maeda (1999). "Healthcare Financing and Delivery in Developing Counties", *Health Affairs*. May/June.

Garg, C. (1998). "Equity of Health Sector Financing and Delivery in India", Harvard School of Public Health. June.

Gullliford *et al.* (2001). "Access to Health Care: Report of a Scoping Exercise for the National Coordinating Center for NHS Service Delivery and Organization R&D", National Coordinating Center for NHS Service Delivery and Organization, London.

Hulme, D., A. Shepherd and K. Moore (2001). "Chronic Poverty: Meanings and Analytic Frameworks". Manchester, England: Draft. Chronic Poverty Research Center.

WHO (2005a). *World Health Organization: Global Atlas of Infectious Disease*. Retrieved on October 2005 from *http://globalatlas.who.int/*

———. (2005b). "Health Profile of Bangladesh", Retrieved on October 2005 from *http://www.whoban.org/country_health_profile.html*

World Bank (2001a). *Voices of the Poor: Dying for Change*. Washington D.C.: World Bank.

———. (2001b). *World Development Report 2000-2001: Attacking Poverty*. Washington D.C.: World Bank.

Zaman, S. *et al.* (2004). "Health Domain of the Ultra Poor: An Exploration", *Working paper* series No. 5, BRAC-AKFC Partnership for CFPR-TUP.

4

Evolution of Health Policy in India

An Analysis from an Organisation Theory Perspective

AVANTIKA SINGH

Introduction

In the 60 years since India achieved its Independence in 1947, the health status of the population has improved remarkably on numerous counts such as life expectancy (64.6 years during 2001-2006 as compared to 36.7 years in 1951) and infant mortality rate (58 infant deaths per 1000 live births during 2005 as compared to 146 in 1951)(MoHFW, 2002). However, a reputed public health scholar, N.H. Antia (2001), has attributed this improvement in health indicators to improvement in education, nutrition, living conditions and livelihoods, and not to the public health system of India, which he believes is curative and elitist. The country still faces a number of challenges, such as inadequate resources in the public health system,[1] low access to and utilisation of health services, particularly by marginalised groups and the multifarious demands on the public health system due to the demographic and epidemiological transition.[2] India has a federal polity, with explicit division of powers between the Union and the states. As mandated by the Constitution of India, the prime responsibility for provision of health care lies with the state governments[3] (Ministry of Law and Justice, 2007).

1. India spends about 5.2 per cent of its GDP on health care, of which 83 per cent is in the private sector.

2. Improvement in life expectancy, and reduction in total fertility rate and infant mortality rate have set off a gradual transition from high fertility and high mortality to low fertility and low mortality. Disease patterns and health-related behaviour are also changing. While diseases such as smallpox and guinea worm have been eradicated, poliomyelitis, tuberculosis (TB), malaria, leprosy and water-borne diseases continue to thrive. HIV/AIDS and non-communicable diseases such as cancer and coronary heart disease have become major health concerns.

3. Public health and sanitation, hospitals and dispensaries are defined and enlisted in List-II (State List) of the Seventh Schedule of the Constitution of India. Population control and family planning, medical education and medical profession are defined and enlisted under the List-III of the Seventh Schedule of the Constitution of India, which forms the Concurrent List. While only the State Legislatures can legislate on the subjects in the State list, both the Parliament and the State Legislatures can legislate on those in the Concurrent list, and the legislations made by the Parliament supersede those made by the State Legislatures.

Despite the state governments together spending 85 per cent of the total public health expenditure, and the Union government spending 15 per cent of it (MoHFW, 2005), policy-making in the health sector in India has implicitly been a function of the Union government. Consequently, identical policies and programmes are implemented across all states in India, through identically structured administrative machinery.

This chapter seeks to review various perspectives of public policy analysis, and draw relevant concepts to explicate the evolution of health policy in India during the post-Independence period (1947-2007). This chapter is based on a review of literature on health policy implementation in India and analysis of documents such as policy statements, implementation strategies, guidelines, performance reports, project implementation plans, etc. *Post facto* analysis through document research is a popular and accepted method in policy analysis (Allison, 1999; Sabatier and Jenkins-Smith, 1993; Yin, 2001). In Section 2, we present a review of the various perspectives of public policy analysis followed by a review of health policy in India in Section 3. We discuss our results in Section 4, followed by conclusions in Section 5.

Policy Analysis

The main approaches to policy analysis including policy implementation are discussed in this section.

Rationality and its Critics

Initial approaches to policy analysis were based on the assumption of rationality.[4] Through his behavioural theories of rational choice, Simon (1955; 1959; 1978; 1979) argued that individual decision-making is based on bounded rationality, limited information processing capability and satisfaction. Lindblom also described the incrementalism and messiness of the policy process as "muddling through" (Lindblom, 1959).

The rational model is also known as the policy cycle or the stagist model of policy analysis, because it describes policy-making as comprised of several sequential steps[5] (Parsons, 1995). One of the significant critiques of the stagist model is Hogwood and Gunn's (1984) model, according to which, several activities may be carried out simultaneously rather than sequentially in the

4. The concept of rationality implies that individuals have complete information about the problem, alternatives and consequences, that they have unlimited information processing capability and that each individual acts on the basis of maximising self-interest, benefit, output or value, which adds up to the social good.

5. These include identification of the problem, defining and ranking goals, generation of alternative courses of action and the consequences of each, evaluation of each alternative against consequences and selection of the alternative that maximises benefit, pay-off or value.

policy process. Baumgartner and Jones (1993) described the policy process as comprising of phases of instability and activity interspersed with relatively stable phases, akin to punctuated equilibrium in biological evolution. Cohen *et al.* (1972) described organisations as anarchies and "loose collection of ideas" rather than rational "coherent structures". All problems, solutions and choice opportunities are put into the organisational "garbage can" as they are generated. These are exogenous and flow in and out of the garbage can, independently of each other. Solutions and problems are coupled with each other—in a manner determined by the timing of their arrival or their simultaneity—to form policies.

State-Centric and Society-Centric Models of Policy Analysis

According to the state-centric approach, the object of analysis is the nature, role and intent of the state in policy-making[6] (Allison, 1999; 1971). The society-centric approaches or pluralistic approaches, on the other hand, regard policy-making as the negotiated outcome of contestations among multiple actors in society (Grindle and Thomas, 1991). The political economy addresses questions of who gets what, when and how (Lasswell, 1936).

Policy Networks

The term policy network connotes a cluster of actors or pressure groups, each of which has an interest or stake in a policy issue and the potential to influence the policy process (Peterson, 2003; Finer, 1958; Kavanagh *et al.*, 2006). These actors engage in game-like interactions for the exchange of resources and this process of exchange is regulated by the dominant coalition (Rhodes, 1981). Policy-making models can be classified into a continuum ranging from policy communities to issue networks[7] (Marsh and Rhodes, 1992; Heclo and Wildavsky, 1974). Roughly, policy communities may be

---

6. Allison analysed the Cuban missile crisis of 1962 (when the USSR placed its missiles in Cuba and then withdrew them) on the basis of three models of policy analysis, namely, the rational actor model, the organisational behaviour model and the governmental politics model. The rational actor model treats the government as a unitary actor, which makes a rational, calculated move in its best interests. According to the organisational behaviour model, the government is composed of several organisations linked with each other, and policy-making is the outcome of organisational routines, processes and culture. Thus, policy change is an incremental process. The governmental politics model recognises that government comprises of individuals who engage in "pulling and hauling" to push their agendas and interests, and policy-making is the resultant of bargaining games.

7. Policy communities are closed; tightly knit groups involved in policy-making and include governmental actors and 'insider' groups. Policy communities are the equivalent of "iron triangles" used to describe closely knit policy-making communities in the US during the 1960s, and the "village life" in British government. Issue networks are open, loosely joined groups involved in policy-making and comprise a wide range of interdependent organisations and groups, which share resources and information.

equated with the state-centric models and issue networks with society-centric models. In contrast to other scholars who argue that social environmental pressures and public opinion influence policy change, Sabatier (1988) and Haas (1992) hold the view that the policy-making process is dominated by elite opinion.

Agenda-Setting

Agenda-setting models describe, from a pluralist perspective, how 'problems' are identified, how issues are defined and how they become 'agendas' for policy[8] (Schattschneider, 1995; Cobb and Elder, 1995). Kingdon's (1995) policy streams framework builds upon the garbage can model and agenda-setting models. Kingdon describes the agenda-setting process as composed of three streams, namely, the problem stream, the policy stream and the political stream.[9] Policy entrepreneurs are people who are on the lookout for policy opportunities. When the three streams merge, a window of opportunity opens, and the policy entrepreneur pushes the policy idea to the policy agenda. Grindle and Thomas (1991) have used the term "policy elites", Kingdon (1995) has used the term "policy entrepreneurs" and Sabatier (1988) has used the term "policy brokers" to describe individuals or groups that are instrumental in setting agendas and pushing through policies.

Institutional Analysis

Institutions are the rules of the game in the society—the formal and informal constraints[10] which shape human behaviour and give stability and certainty to human interaction. Institutional analysis comprises mapping the institutional actors, studying the interactions, mechanisms of coordination, information exchange and resource dependencies between them. Institutions have been studied by economists (Alchian, 1950; Coase, 1937; North, 1990; Ostrom, 1991; Williamson, 1985), political theorists (March and Olsen, 1984) and sociologists and organisation theorists (DiMaggio and Powell, 1983; Meyer and Rowan, 1977; Powell and DiMaggio, 1991; Scott, 1987; 2001).

---

8. A trigger prompts the emergence of an issue, which then gets onto the political agenda and expands, first from a specifically concerned group to a well-informed and interested public and opinion leaders, and finally to the general public through the media.

9. Indicators, events and feedback prompt policy makers to focus their attention on certain problems whilst others are ignored (problem stream). The policy stream is a "primeval soup" where ideas float around. The national mood, organised political forces, government and consensus building mechanisms form the political stream.

10. Formal constraints are those which are codified in the form of rules, law, regulation, constitution etc., whereas informal constraints operate through norms, shared values, culture, trust, reciprocity and informal networks.

Alchian (1950) suggests that inefficient institutions are weeded out by efficient ones over time, and Williamson (1985) suggests that competition eliminates inefficient institutions. However, North (1990) argues that institutions are designed by those who have the bargaining power in order that their self-interests are maximised. Highlighting the significance of historical processes, North (1990) demonstrates that institutional change is path-dependent in the sense that once institutional change starts along a particular path, it continues along it even though the path may be inefficient. In their thesis of political institutions, March and Olsen (1984) explicate interdependence between relatively autonomous actors, complexity of processes at individual level, inefficiency of history and logics other than choice and allocate outcomes in influencing political behaviour. Preferences are neither stable nor exogenous (Axelrod and Cohen, 2000) and develop through a process of education, socialisation and experience. Political behaviour is the outcome of fulfilment of duties and obligations, such that political actors select actions that appear consistent and appropriate. Within a political structure, order is maintained through historical experience that builds up over generations, timing of events, internal institutional processes and normative processes among other factors.

From a sociological perspective, organisations adapt their structure in response to the expectations of constituencies and constraints and influences exercised by the institutional environment (Selznick, 1987). For instance, in the adoption of reforms, while early adopters may have acted on a rational basis, late adopters do so in order to gain legitimacy for a practice that has come to be regarded as 'appropriate' (Tolbert and Zucker, 1983). March and Olsen (1989) have described this as the "logic of appropriateness". Organisations embrace symbols, such as culture, normative beliefs or "rational myths" (Meyer and Rowan, 1977) because doing so can enhance their legitimacy and provide them access to an enlarged base of resources. "Institutional isomorphism"—the evolution of organisations in an industry in such a manner that their processes and behaviour attain homogeneity—occurs due to mimetic (cultural), coercive (legal) and normative (moral) factors[11] (DiMaggio and Powell, 1983). Scott (1987) has identified the ways in which institutional environments shape organisational structure. A summary of models of policy analysis is presented in Annexure Table A-4.1.

11. Under the influence of cultural factors, organisations imitate the best practices of other organisations, more so in uncertain environments. Under the influence of external pressures from government, regulatory bodies or influential organisations—in the form of rules, laws, sanctions or contractual obligations—an organisation may behave such that its actions are seen to be legitimate by constituencies in the external environment. Moral factors or normative forces include pressure to achieve professional standards and adopt techniques considered by the professional community to be effective.

Evolution of Health Policy in India

In this section, the evolution of health policy in India is traced over the period 1947-2007. Health policy evolution has been divided into the following phases for the purpose of analysis:

Phase I: 1947-1977

Phase II: The Alma-Ata Declaration 1978 and National Health Policy 1983

Phase III: Health Reforms (1991 onwards)

First phase of health reforms: 1991-2001

National Health Policy 2002

National Rural Health Mission 2005-2012

The major recommendations of various committees appointed to examine the health situation and suggest a way-forward, and the main objectives of various policies for health development are summarised in Annexure Table A-4.2.

Health Policy: 1947-1977

Policy development in the health sector in India during the post-Independence period was triggered by the Bhore Committee Report of 1946, which recommended adoption of the primary health care approach for improving the health status of the population of the country (Banerji, 2001; Goel, 1981; Sapru, 1997). Notwithstanding the Bhore Committee recommendations, India continued with the urban-based, elite-oriented and curative care-oriented health system inherited from the British (Banerji, 2001; Sapru, 1997; Qadeer, 2001; Banerji, 1983). While the first two Five Year Plans (FYPs) (1951-1956 and 1956-1961, respectively) focused on creating infrastructure, and improving water and sanitation, and maternal and child health services, the Third (1961-1966) and Fourth (1969-1974) FYPs shifted their focus to development of hospitals, specialist services and vertical disease programmes. Thus, the political commitment to implement the Bhore Committee recommendations was extremely short-lived (Banerji, 2001). From 1950 onwards, the obsession of the health ministry with the Family Planning programme, had a detrimental effect on the provision of other health services (Banerji, 2001), especially maternal and child health care. The coercive approach of the programme became one of the reasons for the downfall of the then-government in 1977 (Qadeer, 2001). The medical education system in India was elitist and the medical service exclusionary.[12]

---

12. The Indian Medical Council Act 1956 prohibits a person other than MBBS qualification to practice medicine, and the practitioners of Indian Systems of Medicine such as *Ayurveda*, Homoeopathy, *Siddha* and *Unani* are not even included in the 'formal public health system'. Despite the Bhore Committee's recommendations of preparing a cadre of social physicians, no steps have been taken in that direction.

The outcomes of the policies implemented from the Independence and till the 1970s were manifested in the fourfold problems of overpopulation, incidence of communicable diseases, malnutrition and inadequate health care infrastructure (Sapru, 1997).

The Alma-Ata Declaration and National Health Policy 1983

A paradigm shift came with the WHO-UNICEF conference at Alma-Ata, Kazakhstan in 1978 which, culminated in the adoption of 'Health for All by 2000 AD' through the 'primary health care' approach (WHO, 1978). Unfortunately, however, with the promotion of vertical programmes on universal immunisation, oral rehydration, child survival and safe motherhood and social marketing of contraceptives during the 1980s by WHO and UNICEF, the spirit of primary health care was undermined by the very agencies that had championed its cause at Alma-Ata in 1978 (Banerji, 2001).

The Government of India (GoI) articulated its commitment to the Alma-Ata Declaration through formulating the National Health Policy 1983 (NHP, 1983). In India, the primary health care approach came to be implemented by way of independent disease-specific programmes—which had more 'curative' content—rather than through the strategies envisaged at Alma-Ata (Qadeer, 2001). Qadeer (2001: 131) argues that the adoption of the Alma-Ata goals by India was in fact a "political move" by the then government to regain its legitimacy and "democratic image", which it had lost by way of the "excesses" committed during the Emergency.

Phase III: Health Reforms

3.3.1. First Phase of Health Reforms: 1991-2001

The need for reforms in the health sector was first recognised by the Eighth FYP (1992-1997), and reiterated in subsequent Plan documents as well as the National Commission on Macroeconomics in Health (MoHW, 2005b). During the early 1990s, reforms were initiated through structural adjustment to improve the macroeconomic situation of the country. The *World Development Report 1993* (World Bank, 1993) had a profound influence on health policy and budgetary allocations in India during the early 1990s. The slashing of public expenditure on social services including health, sanitation and drinking water by 20 per cent (Tulasidhar, 1993) resonated in the form of resurgence of several communicable diseases (Antia, 2001). While the allocation for preventive health care interventions was reduced, that for curative care increased (Antia, 2001). Despite evidence from other countries indicating that introduction of user charges leads to a decline in utilisation of curative health care (Bodart *et al.*, 2001; Gao *et al.*, 2001; DFID, 2006), user charges were introduced in the health system in India. The Ministry of Finance (MoF), GoI, has observed, "since the continuation of a universally free public health care system is unsustainable, strategies be evolved for levy and collection of user charges from above the poverty line" (MoF, 2003: 10, 152).

The outcomes of structural adjustment have been well-documented in an edited volume by Qadeer *et al.* (2001). The World Bank's (1993) approach recommending government to deal with basic, essential health care and the private sector to deliver secondary and tertiary health care services met with sharp criticism. Banerji (1994: 155) contested the "vivisection" of the "organic entity" of the health system. An unregulated private health sector, it was observed, would only serve to fulfil 'private' interests with public money siphoned off in the form of tax concessions and incentives, and subsidies directed at those who had paying capacity. Thankappan (2001) reports that the proliferation of the private health sector has actually escalated costs in the much-celebrated Kerala model of low-cost health care. The resurgence of the plague in Surat in 1994 has been attributed to the cuts in public expenditure due to SAP (Shah, 2001).

During the early and mid-90s, the World Bank became more active in funding vertical, disease-oriented, techno-managerial health programmes across various states of India[13] (World Bank, 2001; 2004). The Bank's inclination towards health could have come about because of its policy of strengthening social safety nets in countries where economic reforms are likely to exacerbate inequities. Banerji (1994) has been extremely critical of vertical programmes such as RCH or pulse polio, which have not succeeded despite the quantum of financial and human resources that have been pumped into them. Antia (2001) articulates that while poverty remains the cause for the low performance of health indicators, the 'solutions' adopted to address this problem include vertical programmes. Moreover, these programmes are further fragmented by contracting out the delivery of curative components to the private sector.

With the onset of reforms, the policy approach has shifted from egalitarianism to utilitarianism, i.e., from 'provision of health services to all' to 'maximising output/results with the least inputs' (Hearst and Blas, 2001;

13. World Bank assisted projects were initiated, such as India Population Project in three states, Cataract Blindness Control Project in seven states and Reproductive and Child Health Programme in all states of India. State Health Systems Development Projects (SHSDP) are under various phases of implementation in several states of India, the objectives of which are to develop policy and institutions so as to enhance the efficiency of the health system, and to improve quality, effectiveness and coverage of health care services at the secondary level, strengthen infrastructure and capacity, and improve the access of disadvantaged populations to health care.

Mills and Gilson, 1988). The nature and content of health reforms have been sharply criticised by public health scholars in India, mostly on grounds that they are far removed from peoples' participation (Antia, 2001), are "unscientific and insensitive to democratic processes" (Qadeer *et al.*, 2001: 30), ignore the social aspects of the costs of health care (Qadeer, 2001; Sen, 2001), "lack a systemic view as well as the welfare perspective" (Baru, 2001: 232), and lack a multi-dimensional approach to health care (Banerji, 2001). The form, content and outcomes of reforms have also been a cause of concern among multilateral agencies such as UNICEF as well as national governments. By the late 1990s, the Bank adopted a more humane approach by introducing mechanisms to cushion the vulnerable from the adverse impacts of adjustment. This was also partly due to the World Bank's desire to regain its eroding legitimacy, particularly with respect to human development (Baru, 2001). Though public expenditure on health care was augmented in the late 1990s (Dev and Mooij, 2002), it remained below the level of 1991 (Sen, 2001). The terms of discourse have now shifted from 'withdrawal of the state' to 'partnership' between government, private and voluntary sectors, and the revised agenda of health reforms is to develop a health system that is publicly funded and services are delivered through a network of private providers and non-governmental organisations (NGOs) (Berman, 1998; Peters *et al.*, 2002; Preker, 2003; Kettl, 2000).

National Health Policy 2002

The National Health Policy (NHP 2002) announced in 2002 marks a departure from "Health for All" and moves towards "equitable and affordable health care for the general population". Conceding that the Alma-Ata goals were "unrealistic", NHP 2002 recognises the limitations to administrative and financial capacity of the government to provide basic health care to all its citizens. NHP 2002 takes cognisance of the pluralistic nature of society, and calls for provision of health care by state, market and voluntary sectors, instead of the state being the sole provider of health care services. Thus, NHP 2002 heralds the shift from government to governance—the shift from hierarchical forms to network forms of governing (Minogue *et al.*, 1998; Kooiman, 2003; Gaudin, 1998).

NHP 2002 has also stated explicit, timebound targets for various health indicators as summarised in Appendix Table A-4.2. However, as of 2007, performance has fallen short of these targets[14] (CBHI, 2006; MoHFW, 2005;

14. 18.2 lakh cases of malaria were reported during 2005, 4.72 lakh people were at risk of lymphatic filariasis in 2005, more than 0.3 lakh cases of kala azar were reported during 2005, 116 deaths occurred due to acute poliomyelitis in 2006, and the prevalence rate of leprosy was 1.34 cases per 10000 populations during 2004-05. IMR was 58 in 2005 and MMR 408 in 1997.

2006) and public health expenditure has not exceeded one per cent of GDP (MoHFW, 2005). The utilisation of public health facilities is still low with the for-profit private sector accounting for 50 per cent of inpatient care and 60-70 per cent of outpatient care (Planning Commission, 2006).

NHP 2002 has suggested the need to divorce regulation and policy formulation from policy implementation (production and delivery of services) in order to attain greater "efficiency in programme implementation". Thus, MoHFW is to carry on with policy formulation, the state health departments are expected to play a monitoring role, and autonomous bodies (formed by agencification[15] (Pollitt and Talbot, 2004) or corporatisation of the state) at state and district levels are to implement health programmes (MoHFW, 2002). Vertical disease control programmes financed by the World Bank, for the control of TB, vector-borne diseases, leprosy, blindness and HIV/AIDS, and delivery of RCH services, are already implemented through agencies[16] at state level and district level. In some states, *viz.*, Punjab and Karnataka, health facilities at secondary and tertiary level are now governed by corporations, named Punjab Health Systems Corporation and Karnataka Health Systems Corporation, respectively. Gill (1996) reported that this was done in order to meet conditions for a World Bank loan. However, by articulating its support for agencies, NHP 2002 has legitimised the creation of 'agencies' for implementing Bank-supported programmes. NHP 2002 also seeks the gradual convergence of vertical, disease-specific health programmes under a single field administration. This is being accomplished through the National Rural Health Mission (NRHM) which is being implemented through the agency mode. The rationale for agencification seems to have emerged from the reinventing government movement (in the West) which reconceptualises the role of the state as shifting from "rowing" to "steering" (Osborne and Gaebler, 1992). However, agencification has its share of critics too. Gill (2002) proposes that a ministerial organisational structure is more appropriate for activities which are low on commercial focus and difficult to measure. In similar vein, Mintzberg (1996) argues that the agency model is more suited for apolitical, straightforward services such as driving licences, and not health care. Pressman and Wildavsky (1973) illustrated much before the current wave of agencification that separation of policy formulation from policy implementation was the major cause of implementation failure. Back

15. An 'agency' is an alternative form of organisation, and agencification is the process of carving out independent agencies from the government. Agencification involves transfer of activities hitherto done by the government to agencies.

16. In the public health system of India, agencies are autonomous bodies registered as not-for-profit organisations under the relevant legal framework, namely the Societies Registration Act 1860 or the Rajasthan Societies Act 1958.

home, Banerji (1994) laments that the dichotomy between policy formulation and policy implementation in the health sector, or in other words, between bureaucrats and medical professionals, has resulted in 'policy failure' as well as 'implementation failure'.

In a vein similar to the *World Development Report 1993* prescriptions (World Bank, 1993), NHP 2002 calls on the government to direct its attention to primary health care and allocate 55 per cent of the budget to primary health care. However, the suggestion that government fund provision of curative health care by the private sector may not directly translate into better health outcomes for the poor (Berman, 1998). Venkat Raman and Björkman (2007) report that the private sector is more interested in working with the government in sectors such as tertiary care and medical education and only in areas where there are high gains and low risks. Lamenting on the shift in the terms of the discourse, Banerji (2003: 44) has commented, "Preoccupying oneself with such refined discourses amounts to nothing less than a cruel joke on the helplessness of hundreds of the millions of the world's poor who do not get even two square meals all round the year, what to speak of such critically needed health promoting requirements such as access to adequate levels of potable drinking water, sanitation, housing and clothing". The paradox is that public health expenditure is dismal, and the government is under donor pressure to encourage further growth of the private sector by offering subsidies. Thus, resources which would otherwise have been spent for the poor are now being expropriated in the name of 'cost sharing' and 'cost recovery'.

Due to its public goods nature, preventive health care necessitates collective action (Weimer and Vining, 2004). However, in India, public expenditure on health can be cut while justifying, without qualms, the need to control the fiscal deficit. In contrast, in the West, health has high "political visibility" and gets a great deal of public attention and media coverage (Drèze and Sen, 1995: 42-43). Banerji (2003) and Drèze and Sen (1995) have suggested that health be recognised as a fundamental human right.

National Rural Health Mission 2005-2012

The National Rural Health Mission (NRHM) 2005-2012 focuses on provision of "equitable affordable, accountable and effective primary health care to rural population" with special focus on 18 states (out of 28), where performance of health indicators is low and/or infrastructure is weak. NRHM is to be implemented through coordination between MoHFW, Planning Commission, and Union Ministries of Panchayati Raj[17], Rural Development and Human Resource Development. During 2005-06, the Department of

17. The system of democratic local self-government is known as the Panchayati Raj in India.

Health and the Department of Family Welfare in MoHFW have been merged into a single department. The numerous vertical programmes have been amalgamated into autonomous agencies, known as the State Health Mission (SHM) at the state level and the District Health Mission (DHM) at the district level. Through a basket financing approach, earmarked funds from various sources are now funnelled through SHMs and DHMs. The management of DHMs has been professionalised. Though it is too early to comment on the effectiveness of this approach, DHM (headed by the District Collector, who is a civil servant) creates an implementation structure for NRHM, which is parallel to the existing district health administration (headed by the Chief Medical & Health Officer, who is a medical administrator).

Results and Discussion

Most analyses of health policy in India have been done from a political economy perspective. In this chapter, we attempt to employ alternative approaches to policy analysis. To begin with, we assume that the government as a 'rational' actor, has chosen such health goals and courses of action that the benefits, payoffs or values are maximised (Allison, 1999; 1971). In the context of a welfare state, maximisation would be understood as the maximisation of health benefits for all the citizens. However, given the experiences of implementation of health policy over a period of 60 years, one cannot argue with conviction that the government has acted as a rational actor. Therefore, we might tentatively accept that policy decisions by government could have been based on a 'satisfying' approach (Simon, 1955; 1959; 1978; 1979).

We find that the garbage can model (Cohen *et al.*, 1972) can more aptly explain the development of health policy in post-Independence India. Notwithstanding the fact that India had a well-developed private health sector at Independence[18] (Planning Commission, 2006; Aljunid, 1995; Baru, 1998; World Bank, 2001), policy makers in India seemed convinced that health care was the responsibility of the state, and thus, adopted the European model of the welfare state. In 1978, with the signing of the Alma-Ata Declaration, GoI re-affirmed its commitment to the primary health care approach. Policy makers picked up the 'prevailing health problems' and the 'primary health

18. Though India has a huge private sector in health, reliable estimates of the exact number, type, distribution and capacity of private providers (PPs) are not available (Planning Commission, 2006). Studies indicate that 73 per cent of the doctors were in the private sector at the time of India's Independence (Baru, 1998); more than half of the hospitals and 49 per cent of the dispensaries are privately owned (Aljunid, 1995); 93 per cent of all hospitals, 64 per cent of beds, 85 per cent of doctors, 80 per cent of outpatients and 57 per cent of inpatients are in the private sector (World Bank, 2001); and the for-profit private sector accounts for 50 per cent of inpatient care and 60-70 per cent of outpatient care (Planning Commission, 2006).

care' approach from the garbage can, coupled them, and announced the National Health Policy 1983. During the turbulent 1990s when economic reforms were initiated, the policy response to the problems of the health system (most of which were the same as in 1983) came in the form of public financing and private provision, public-private partnerships, and greater stress on efficient utilisation of resources. Thus, while problems have largely remained the same, different 'solutions' have been taken out of the garbage can at different times to address these 'problems'. The pairing of solutions with problems is determined by the timing of their arrival. Agenda-setting models and the role of policy entrepreneurs can be useful in explaining how problems and solutions move up the garbage can and are paired to form policies. For instance, three significant issues, namely, regulation of the health sector, reorientation of the medical profession towards rural health, and preparing a cadre of social physicians, have been floating around for long, but have not expanded into agendas for policy-making. This could be because of the lack of a policy entrepreneur, lack of sufficient media interest or public interest, and the lack of any trigger (Sabatier, 1988).

Given the sparse information on the actual nature of the policy-making process—the conflicts and the negotiations—available in the public domain, one may not be able to ascertain the "muddling through" or the messiness of the policy process, or to analyse health policy-making from pluralist perspectives, policy networks or policy streams models. Given the low political visibility of health in India (Drèze and Sen, 1995), and the relatively less public attention and media coverage accorded to it, we put forth the proposition that health policy-making is largely confined to elites (Sabatier, 1988) or policy communities (Marsh and Rhodes, 1992) comprising few tightly woven actors, such as government officials, medical professionals, few scholars and a couple of NGOs (Kavanagh *et al.*, 2006).

We now employ institutional analysis perspectives to analyse the development of health policy in India. Despite the Government of India articulating and rearticulating its commitment to the primary health care approach in all its policy pronouncements, the country has not been able to achieve a health system based on primary health care. From an institutional perspective, this can be understood from North's (1990) thesis that inefficient institutions persist because they fulfil the self-interests of those with the power to make or change rules. Therefore, we can put forth the proposition that it is against the interests of elites (policy makers, administrators and medical professionals) to develop a health system based on primary health care in India. Moreover, institutional change in the health system has been path dependent and has continued to move along the trajectory of a curative, urban-biased, elitist health care model. In line with March and Olsen's (1984) thesis, we make the proposition that health policy is the outcome of education, socialisation and experience of actors. Further that policy decisions are based not on a rational process of value maximisation alone, but are often inspired by the logic of appropriateness (March and Olsen, 1989) or the outcome of organisational processes, routines and culture (Allison, 1999).

Policy-making in the health sector in India has largely been driven by international "policy fevers" (Pollitt *et al.*, 2001) such as that of the welfare state during the 1940s and 1950s, primary health care at Alma-Ata in 1978, and structural adjustment, good governance, health reforms, efficiency and public-private partnerships from the 1990s onwards. From an institutional perspective, it can be explained that reforms are adopted not out of any rational justification, but just to seek conformity with what everyone else is doing (Tolbert and Zucker, 1983), the search for legitimacy (DiMaggio and Powell, 1983; Meyer and Rowan, 1977), or the influence of the institutional environment in shaping organisations (Scott, 1987). Thus, we make the proposition that the adoption of health reforms is not in pursuit of greater effectiveness or efficiency of health systems, but to seek conformity and legitimacy with the actions of other governments, or imposed by authority. Secondly, through mimetic, coercive and normative behaviour, the adoption of reforms is moving national as well as State governments towards institutional isomorphism (DiMaggio and Powell, 1983).

Conclusion

In this study, analytical models based on 'rationality' were not found appropriate for analysing the evolution of health policy in India. Due to lack of information available in the public domain on the actual process of policy formulation, analytical perspectives such as the pluralist perspective, agenda-setting and policy streams could not be applied to explain the evolution of health policy. Policy evolution in the health sector in India over the 60-year period between 1947 and 2007 can be better understood when explained by models such as the garbage can model (Cohen, 1972) and institutional analytical perspectives. The definition of 'problems' and 'solutions' has been motivated by international policy fashions, and is dependent on the timing of events.

Institutional analysis perspectives can also help explain several policy events in the public health system of India. Despite the fact that policy makers have recognised the importance of primary health care and recommended adoption of the same through policy pronouncements, institutional change in the public health system has been path dependent and has continued to move along the trajectory of a curative, urban-biased, elitist health care model. The adoption of health reforms in various states of India can be said to have been triggered by the changes in the overall policy environment (external events), the availability of soft loans (from the World Bank) to overcome the fiscal crisis in the states (inducements), and the pressing need to create the image of a progressive state interested in reforming the public health system to improve the health status of the citizens (legitimisation). The diffusion of a novel organisational pattern—institutional reforms in this case—across similar organisations may be the consequence of a deliberate choice, motivated by the logic of appropriateness, pressure for conformity or just because it seems to enhance the legitimacy of the organisation (March and Olsen, 1984; DiMaggio and Powell, 1983; Scott, 1987; Tolber and Zucker, 1983).

More information on the policy formulation process—who were the actors and what were their positions, which key issues were debated, which issues were pushed to the political agenda, what were the contestations about goals and resources and what were the resultants—could facilitate more rigorous analysis of policy. The movement of problems and solutions up the garbage can may be explained by one of the agenda-setting models through further research. The role of policy entrepreneurs, who opportunistically combine problems with solutions, and push them to the political agenda may also be examined through further research.

References

Allison, G.T. (1971). *Essence of Decision*. New York: Longman.

———. (1999). *Zelikow, P. Essence of Decision*. 2nd ed. New York: Longman, New Longman.

Alchian, A.A. (1950). "Uncertainty, Evolution and Economic Theory", *Journal of Political Economy* 58: 211-221.

Aljunid, S. (1995). "The Role of Private Medical Practitioners and Their Interactions with Public Health Services in Asian Countries", *Health Policy and Planning* 10: 333-349.

Antia, N.H. (2001). "Health for all through a Decentralized People's Movement", *Health for the Millions* 27: 10-11.

Axelrod, R., M.D. Cohen (2000). *Harnessing Complexity: Organizational Implications of a Scientific Frontier*. New York: The Free Press.

Banerji, D. (1983). "National Health Policy and its Implementation", *Economic and Political Weekly* 18: 105-108.

———. (1994). "A Simplistic Approach to Health Policy Analysis: The World Bank Team on the Indian Health Sector", *International Journal of Health Services* 24: 151-159.

———. (2001). "Landmarks in the Development of Health Services in India", in I. Qadeer, K. Sen, K.R. Nayar (eds.), *Public Health and the Poverty of Reforms: The South Asian Predicament*. New Delhi: Sage. p.39-50.

The support from Sir Ratan Tata Trust, Mumbai, India, for carrying out this research is gratefully acknowledged.

———. (2003). *Some Health Homilies from the Rich to the Poor, Health for the Millions.* Dec.-Jan.:44-45.

Baru, R.V. (1998). *Private Health Care in India: Social Characteristics and Trends.* New Delhi: Sage.

———. (2001). "Health Sector Reforms and Structural Adjustment: A State-level Analysis", in I. Qadeer, K. Sen, K.R. Nayar (eds.), *Public Health and the Poverty of Reforms: The South Asian Predicament.* New Delhi: Sage. p.211-234.

Baumgartner, F. and B.D. Jones (1993). *Agenda and Instability in American Politics.* Chicago: University of Chicago Press.

Berman, P.A. (1998). "Rethinking Health Care Systems: Private Health Care Provision in India", *World Development* 26: 1463-1479.

Bodart, C., G. Servais, Y.L. Mohamed, B. Schmidt-Ehry (2001). "The Influence of Health Sector Reform and External Assistance in Burkina Faso", *Health Policy and Planning* 16: 74-86.

CBHI (2006). "National Health Profile 2006". *http://www.cbhidghs.nic.in/cbhi%20book_content.pdf*

Coase, R.H. (1937). "The Nature of the Firm", *Economica* 4: 386-405.

Cobb, R.W. and C.D. Elder (1995). *Participation in American Politics.* 1972. Cited in Parsons W.

Cohen, M.D., J.G. March and J.P. Olsen (1972). "A Garbage can Model of Organizational Choice", *Administrative Science Quarterly* 17: 1-25.

Dev, S.M. and J. Mooij (2002). "Social Sector Expenditures in the 1990s: Analysis of Central and State Budgets", *Economic and Political Weekly* 37: 853-866.

DFID (2006). "Eliminating World Poverty: Making Governance Work for the Poor. A White Paper on International Development", *http://www.dfid.gov.uk/wp2006/default.asp.*

DiMaggio, P.J. and W.W. Powell (1983). "The Iron Cage Revisited: Institutional Isomorphism and Collective Rationality in Organizational Fields", *American Sociological Review* 48: 147-160.

Drèze, J. and A. Sen (1995). *India: Economic Development and Social Opportunity.* Delhi: Oxford University Press.

Finer, S.E. (1958). "The Anonymous Empire", *Political Studies* 6: 16.

Gao, J., S. Tang, R. Tolhurst and K. Rao (2001). "Changing Access to Health Services in Urban China: Implications for Equity", *Health Policy and Planning* 16: 302-312.

Gaudin, J.P. (1998). "Modern Governance, Yesterday and Today: Some Clarifications to be Gained from French Government Policies", *International Social Science Journal* 50: 155. pp. 47-56.

Gill, D. (2002). "Signposting the Zoo: From Agencification to a More Principled Choice of Government Organisational Forms", *OECD Journal on Budgeting* 2: 27-80.

Gill, S.S. (1996). "Punjab: Privatising Health Care", *Economic and Political Weekly* 31: 18-19.

Goel, S.L. (1981). *Health Care Administration: Policy Making and Planning.* New Delhi: Sterling.

Grindle, M.S. and J.W. Thomas (1991). *Public Choices and Policy Change.* Maryland: John Hopkins University Press.

Haas, P.M. (1992). "Epistemic Communities and International Policy Coordination", *International Organization* 46: 1-35.

Hearst, N., E. Blas (2001). "Learning from Experience: Research on Health Sector Reform in the Developing World", *Health Policy and Planning* 16: (Suppl)2: 1-3.

Heclo, H., A. Wildavsky (1974). *The Private Government of Public Money.* London: Macmillan.

Hogwood, B.W. and L.A. Gunn (1984). *Policy Analysis for the Real World.* New York: Oxford University Press.

Kavanagh, D., D. Richards, A. Geddes, M. Smith (2006). *British Politics. 5th ed.* Oxford: Oxford University Press.

Kingdon, J.W. (1995). *Agendas, Alternatives and Public Policies.* New York: Longman.

Kettl, D.F. (2000). "The Transformation of Governance: Globalization, Devolution and the Role of Government", *Public Administration Review* 60: 488-497.

Kooiman, J. (2003). *Governing as Governance.* London: Sage.

Lasswell, H. (1936). *Politics: Who gets What, When, How.* New York: Whittlesey House.

Lindblom, C.E. (1959). "The Science of 'muddling through'", *Public Administration Review* 19: 79-88.

March, J.G. and J.P. Olsen (1984). "The New Institutionalism: Organizational Factors in Political Life", *American Political Science Review* 78: 734-749.

———. (1989). *Rediscovering Institutions: The Organizational Basis of Politics*. New York: Free Press.

Marsh, D. and RAW Rhodes (eds.) (1992). *Policy Networks in British Government*. Oxford: Clarendon Press.

Meyer, J.W. and B. Rowan (1977). "Institutionalized Organizations: Formal Structure as Myth and Ceremony", *American Journal of Sociology* 83: 340-363.

Mills, A. and L. Gilson (1988). "Health Economics for Developing Countries: A Survival Kit", HEFP *Working Paper* 01/88, London: London School of Hygiene and Tropical Medicine.

Ministry of Law and Justice (2007). "Seventh Schedule", Constitution of India, *http://lawmin.nic.in/coi/SEVENTH-SCHEDULE.pdf*

Minogue, M., C. Polidano and D. Hulme (eds.) (1998). *Beyond The New Public Management: Changing Ideas and Practices in Governance*. Cheltenham: Edward Elgar.

Mintzberg, H. (1996). "Managing Government, Governing Management", *Harvard Business Review* May-June: 75-83.

MoF (2003). Social sectors. [Chapter 10]. *Economic Survey 2002-2003, http://indiabudget.nic.in/es2002-03/social.htm*

MoHFW (1983). *National Health Policy. http://mohfw.nic.in/kk/95/ii/95ii0101.htm#nhp9*

———. (2002). *National Health Policy 2002*. New Delhi.

———. (2005). *National Rural Health Mission (2005-2012) Mission Document*. New Delhi.

———. (2005a). "State-wise Infant Mortality Rate by Sex and Residence in India (2005)". *http://www.indiastat.com/india/ShowDataSec.asp?secid=409099&ptid=17794*

———. (2005b). *National Commission on Macroeconomics in Health*. New Delhi.

———. (2006). *Annual Report 2005-06*. New Delhi.

North, D.C. (1990). *Institutions, Institutional Change and Economic Performance*. Cambridge: Cambridge University Press.

Osborne, D. and T. Gaebler (1992). *Reinventing Government: How the Entrepreneurial Spirit is Transforming the Public Sector*. Reading: Addison-Wesley.

Ostrom, E. (1991). "Rational Choice Theory and Institutional Analysis: Toward Complementarity", *American Political Science Review* 85: 237-243.

Parsons, W. (1995). "Public Policy: An Introduction to the Theory and Practice of Policy Analysis", Cheltenham: Edward Elgar.

Peters, D.H., A.S. Yazbeck, R.R. Sharma, G.N.V. Ramana, L.H. Pritchett and A. Wagstaff (2002). *Better Health Systems for India's Poor: Findings, Analysis and Options*. New Delhi: Hindustan Publishing Corporation.

Peterson, J. (2003). *Policy Networks. No. 90. Political Science Series*. Vienna: Institute for Advanced Studies.

Planning Commission (2006). "Report on the Working Group on Clinical Establishments, Professional Services Regulation and Accreditation of Health Care Infrastructure for the 11th Five-Year Plan". New Delhi.

Preker, A.S. (2003). "Global Development Challenges and Health Care Reform", *World Hospitals and Health Services* 37: 2-11.

Pressman, J.L. and A. Wildavsky (1973). *Implementation*. Berkeley: University of California Press.

Pollitt, Christopher, Karen Bathgate, Janice Caulfield, Amanda Smullen and Colin Talbot (2001). "Agency Fever? Analysis of an International Policy Fashion", *Journal of Comparative Policy Analysis: Research and Practice*. 3(3): 271-290.

Pollitt, C. and C. Talbot (2004). *Unbundled Government: A Critical Analysis of the Global Trend to Agencies, Quangos and Contractualisation*. London: Routledge.

Powell, W.W. and P.J. DiMaggio (eds.) (1991). *The New Institutionalism in Organizational Analysis*. Chicago: University of Chicago Press.

Qadeer, I. (2001). "Impact of Structural Adjustment Programs on Concepts in Public Health", in I. Qadeer, K. Sen, K.R. Nayar (eds.) *Public Health and the Poverty of Reforms: The South Asian Predicament*. New Delhi: Sage. pp.117-136.

Qadeer, I., K. Sen, K.R. Nayar (2001). "Introduction", in I. Qadeer, K. Sen, K.R. Nayar (eds.) (2001). *Public Health and the Poverty of Reforms: The South Asian Predicament*. New Delhi: Sage. pp.27-36.

Rhodes, RAW (1981). *Control and Power in Central-Local Relations*. Aldershot: Gower.

Sabatier, P.A. (1988). "An Advocacy Coalition Framework of Policy Change and the Role of Policy-Oriented Learning Therein", *Policy Sciences* 21: 129-168.

Sabatier, P.A. and Jenkins-Smith, H.C. (1993). "The Advocacy Coalition Framework: Assessment, Revisions and Implications for Scholars and Practitioners", in Sabatier, P.A., H.C. Jenkins-Smith (eds.) *Policy Change and Learning: An Advocacy Coalition Approach*. Boulder: Westview Press.

Sapru, R.K. (1997). "Health Care Policy and Administration in India", *Indian Journal of Public Administration* 43: 731-748.

Schattschneider, E.E. (1995). *The Semisovereign People. 1960*. Cited in Parsons W.

Scott, W.R. (1987). "The Adolescence of Institutional Theory", *Administrative Science Quarterly* 32: 493-511.

Selznick, P. (1987). *Leadership in Administration*. New York: Harper and Row. 1957. Cited in Scott WR.

———. (2001). *Institutions and Organizations. 2nd ed.* Thousand Oaks: Sage.

Sen, K. (2001). "Health Reforms and Developing Countries: A Critique", in I. Qadeer, K. Sen, K.R. Nayar (eds.) *Public Health and the Poverty of Reforms: The South Asian Predicament*. New Delhi: Sage. pp.137-153.

Shah, G. (2001). "The Plague, The Poor and Health Services", in I. Qadeer, K. Sen, K.R. Nayar (eds.) *Public Health and The Poverty of Reforms: The South Asian Predicament*. New Delhi: Sage. pp.459-475.

Simon, H.A. (1955). "A Behavioural Model of Rational Choice", *Quarterly Journal of Economics* 69: 99-118.

———. (1959). "Theories of Decision-making in Economics and Behavioral Science", *American Economic Review* 49: 253-283.

———. (1978). "Rationality as Process and as Product of Thought", *American Economic Review* 68: 1-16.

———. (1979). "Rational Decision Making in Business Organizations", *American Economic Review* 69: 493-513.

Thankappan, K.R. (2001). "Some Health Implications of Globalization in Kerala, India", *Bulletin of the World Health Organization* 79: 892-893.

Tolbert, P.S., L.G. Zucker (1983). "Institutional Sources of Change in the Formal Structure of Organizations: The Diffusion of Civil Service Reform, 1880-1935", *Administrative Science Quarterly* 28: 22-39.

Tulasidhar, V.B. (1993). "Expenditure Compression and Health Sector Outlays", *Economic and Political Weekly* 28: 2473-2477.

Venkat Raman, A. and J.W. Björkman (2007). "Public/Private Partnership in Health Care Services in India", Research study funded by the Indo-Dutch Programme on Alternatives in Development.

Weimer, D.L. and A.R. Vining (2004). *Policy Analysis: Concepts and Practice*. New Jersey: Prentice Hall.

WHO (1978). "Declaration of Alma-Ata. International Conference on Primary Health Care, Alma-Ata, USSR", September 6-12, 1978, *http://www.who.int/hpr/NPH/docs/declaration_almaata.pdf*

Williamson, O.E. (1985). *The Economic Institutions of Capitalism*. New York: The Free Press.

World Bank (1993). *World Development Report 1993: Investing in Health*. New York.

———. (2001). "State Health Systems Development Project (02)", *http://web.worldbank.org/external/projectsmain?pagePK=64283627&piPK=73230&theSitePK=40941&menuPK=228424&Projectid=P035825*

———. (2001). *India: Raising the Sights: Better Health Systems for India's Poor*. Washington DC.

———. (2004). "Rajasthan Health Systems Development Project", *http://web.worldbank.org/external/projects/main?pagePK=64312881&piPK=64302848&theSitePK=40941&Projectid=P050655*

Yin, R.K. (2001). "Studying the Implementation of Public Programs", in William, W., (ed.) *Studying Implementation: Methodological and Administrative Issues*. Chatham: Chatham House; 1982. Cited in Schofield.

Appendix Table A-4.1

Summary of Models of Policy Analysis

Basis of Classification	*Different Types/Continuum*		
Rationality in Decision-Making	Comprehensive rationality (Programme Planning and Budgeting System; Quantitative techniques; Rational actor model)[1]	Bounded rationality[2] Institutional analysis[4]	Ambiguity (Garbage can model)[3]
Policy-Making as a Stagist Process	Stagist approach (Rational actor model[1]	Semi-stagist[5]	Non-stagist - Agenda-setting models[6, 7] - Institutional analysis[4]
Centre of Policy Making	State-centric (Rational actor model, organisational behaviour model, governmental politics model,[1] policy communities[9]	Society-centric + elitist[10]	Society-centric + diffused Marxist Pluralist[8]; Issue networks[11] Institutional analysis[4]
Networks	Policy communities State-centric[9]	'Elitist' policy communities (Advocacy coalitions)[10]	Issue networks[9] (society-centric) Institutional analysis[4]
Power	Diffused or equally distributed-Institutional analysis[4]		Contestation for power (governmental politics[1]; Marxist; agenda setting[6]; issue networks[9] - Institutional analysis[4]
Continuity in the Policy Process	Incrementalism (muddling through,[13] garbage can model[3] organisational behaviour model[1]		Punctuated equilibrium[12]
Policy Streams	Combination of society-centric,	Agenda-setting, garbage can[14]	
Institutional Analysis	New institutional economics (economics perspective)[15]	New institutionalism (politics perspective)[16]	Organisation theory (sociological perspective)[17]

contd...

...contd...

Note:

1. Allison, 1999; 1971.
2. Simon, 1955; 1959; 1978; 1979.
3. Cohen, 1972.
4. Alchian, 1950; Coase, 1937; North, 1990; Ostrom, 1991; Willianson, 1985; March and Olsen, 1984; DiMaggio and Powell, 1983; Meyer and Rowan, 1977; Powell and DiMaggio, 1991; Scott, 1987; Axelrod and Cohen, 2000; Selznic, 1987; Tolbert and Zucker, 1983; March and Olsen, 1989.
5. Hogwood, 1984.
6. Schattschneider, 1995.
7. Cobb and Elder, 1995.
8. Grindle and Thomas, 1991.
9. Marsh and Rhodes, 1992.
10. Sabatier, 1988.
11. Rhodes, 1981.
12. Baumgartner and Jones, 1993.
13. Lindblom, 1959.
14. Kingdon, 1995.
15. Alchian, 1950; Coase, 1937; North, 1990; Ostrom, 1991; Willianson, 1985.
16. March and Olsen, 1984.
17. DiMaggio and Powell, 1983; Meyer and Rowan, 1977; Powell and DiMaggio, 1991; Scott, 1987; Axelrod and Cohen, 2000; Selznic, 1987; Tolbert and Zucker, 1983; March and Olsen, 1989.

Appendix Table A-4.2

Evolution of Health Policy in India: Recommendations of Various Committees and Policy Objectives over the Period 1947-2007

S.No.	*Policy*	*Committee Recommendations/Policy Objectives*
Phase I: 1947-1977		
1.1.	Bhore Committee Report (1946)	No individual should be deprived of medical care because of the inability to pay for it. Prompt availability of preventive and medical care, particularly in rural areas. Active cooperation of the people in the development of health programmes. Training in preventive and social medicine to prepare social physicians. The ministry of health to take up the responsibility for health development.
1.2.	Mudaliar Committee (1962)	Strengthening referral linkages by provision of specialist care at district hospitals. Regionalisation of health services, i.e., setting up of regional health care institutions between the state and the districts. Improvement in the quality of services provided by Primary Health Centres (PHCs). Constitution of an All India Health Service.
1.3.	Mukerjee Committee (1966)	Recruitment of additional staff for effective implementation of health programmes.
1.4.	Jungwala Committee (1967)	Known as the Committee on "Integration of Health Services". Recommended integration of organisations and personnel in the health sector.
1.5.	Shrivastava Group (1975)	Known as the "Group on Medical Education and Support Manpower". Creation of a nationwide network of health services. Selection of semi-professional health workers from the community who could be trained to provide simple medication and preventive health care. Health workers to serve as linkages between the PHC and the community. Strengthening of referral linkages. Need for the government to constitute a Medical and Health Education Commission for coordinating and maintaining standards in medical and health education.
Phase II: The Alma-Ata Declaration 1978 and National Health Policy 1983		
2.1.	The Alma-Ata Declaration 1978	Primary health care is universal health care acceptable and affordable to all at the cost the community and society can afford. It encompasses preventive, promotive and rehabilitative aspects of health. It

contd...

...contd...

S.No.	*Policy*	*Committee Recommendations/Policy Objectives*
Phase II: The Alma Ata Declaration 1978 and National Health Policy 1983 (...*contd*...)		
		stresses an integrated and comprehensive approach to development of health services including health education, nutrition, maternal and child health, immunisation, family welfare, prevention and control of endemic diseases, treatment of common ailments and injuries, and supply of essential drugs.[1]
2.2.	National Health Policy 1983 (NHP 1983)	The objectives of NHP 1983 were as follows: To create a wide network of PHCs with a strong element of participation of people and auxiliary health workers. Large-scale transfer of knowledge, simple skills and technologies to community volunteers. Self-reliance and community participation in health care. Involvement of private sector and non-governmental organisations (NGOs) in health services delivery. Strong referral system; efforts towards physical and social rehabilitation for the disabled and the mentally sick.[2]
Phase III: Health Reforms		
3.1.	Health Reforms (1991-2001)	Cuts in public expenditure for macroeconomic management. Introduction of user charges in public health institutions. Government to focus on with a package of basic, cost-effective essential health care interventions and the private sector to deliver secondary and tertiary health care services. Government to encourage the proliferation of private sector through concessions and subsidies. Where economic reforms are likely to exacerbate inequities, strengthening social safety nets by making access provisions for the vulnerable groups, for e.g., waiving off user fee for poor patients. Focus on controlling specific diseases through vertical, disease-oriented, techno-managerial health programmes. Four-fold agenda for health reforms in India:[3] Government to assume responsibility for the health needs of the entire population, especially vulnerable groups. Government to develop appropriate health financing systems to sail through the health transition occurring in the country. Government to channelise the energy of the private health sector. Emphasis on quality, efficiency, and accountability in the public as well as private health sectors.
3.2.	National Health Policy 2002 (NHP 2002)	The main objective of NHP 2002 is to achieve "an acceptable standard of good health" through: Ensuring equitable access to health by strengthening infrastructure. Encouraging the private sector to deliver services, particularly to those who can afford to pay for health care.

contd...

...contd...

S.No.	Policy	Committee Recommendations/Policy Objectives
Phase III: Health Reforms (*...contd...*)		
		Top priority by government to preventive and first-line curative initiatives. Rational use of allopathic drugs, and improved access to Indian Systems of Medicine.[4] NHP 2002 strives to achieve time-bound goals such as eradication of Polio and elimination of leprosy by 2005, kala azar by 2010 and lymphatic filariasis by 2015, zero growth level of HIV/AIDS by 2007, reducing infant mortality rate to 30 infant deaths per 1000 live births and maternal mortality ratio to 100 maternal deaths per 100,000 live births. It also aims to increase utilisation of public health facilities from the current level of less than 20% to more than 75%, public health expenditure from 0.9% to 2.0% of GDP, total health expenditure to rise from 5.2% to 6% of GDP, and public health expenditure by states from 5.5% to 8% of their budgets, all by 2010. NHP 2002 underscores the need for a social health insurance scheme, funded by the government, with service delivery through the private sector, for increasing the coverage of curative services. It also highlights the need for inter-sectoral coordination between government, private sector, Panchayati Raj Institutions[19] (PRIs) and civil society.
3.3.	National Rural Health Mission 2005-2012 (NRHM)	With an annual budgetary outlay of Rs.6700 crores, the goals of NRHM are to reduce IMR and MMR, provide universal access to public health, and achieve population stabilisation (reduction of IMR to 30 per 1000 live births, MMR to 100 per lakh live births and total fertility rate to 2.1) over the seven-year period from 2005 to 2012. NRHM also aims to increase utilisation of First Referral Units (FRUs) from less than 20% to 75%. Like NHP 2002, NRHM envisages increasing public health expenditure to 2-3% of GDP from the existing 0.9%. NRHM is to be implemented through the following strategies: Integration of vertical disease programmes and basket financing[20] to correct the 'vertical' segregated approach and improve resource utilisation. Sector-wide approach and integrated district planning by integrating sanitation and hygiene, nutrition and safe drinking water with health. State budgets for these sectors are also to be integrated. People's participation in health care to enhance accountability. Interventions include selection of a

contd...

19. These are democratically institutions of local self-government in India.

20. Basket financing is a mechanism where all donor funds, local and Central governments subsidies and local revenues are gathered at one place at the district level and managed using common procedures, with a view to improve technical efficiency.[5]

...contd...

S.No.	*Policy*	*Committee Recommendations/Policy Objectives*
Phase III: Health Reforms (*...contd...*)		
		female health volunteer known as ASHA[21] (Accredited Social Health Activist) in each village, and preparation of village health plan with the involvement of the Health and Sanitation Committee[22] of the *panchayat*. Strengthening rural health care infrastructure at Community Health Centres (CHCs), Primary Health Centres (PHCs) and Sub Centres.[23] Mainstreaming AYUSH[24] (*Ayurvedic, Unani, Siddha* and Homoeopathy) practitioners. Promoting the private and voluntary sectors in service delivery. Enhancing measurability and accountability of services through Indian Public Health Standards (IPHS). NRHM also proposes to address issues such as regulation of the health sector, reorientation of medical education towards rural health, participation of the private sector and NGOs, and health financing including health insurance.

Note: 1. WHO, 1978.
2. MoHFW, 1983.
3. Peters; Yazbeck; Sharma; Ramana; Pritchett; Wagstaff, 2002.
4. MoHFW, 2002.
5. Bodart; Tang; Tolhurst and Rao, 2001.

21. ASHA would be a female health volunteer on honorary basis, selected by and accountable to the *panchayat*. She would serve as a bridge/interface between the village community and the public health system. She would receive performance-based compensation for promoting immunisation, referral and escort services for Reproductive and Child Health (RCH), construction of household toilets and other health care activities. Alongwith *Anganwadi* Worker (AWW), Auxiliary Nurse Midwife (ANM), functionaries of other departments, Self-Help Group (SHG) members and under the guidance of Village Health Committee (VHC) of the *panchayat* (the first level institution of PRIs whose representatives are democratically elected through adult franchise), ASHA would facilitate the preparation and implementation of the village health plan. She would be provided with a drug kit containing generic AYUSH and allopathic medicines. She would be provided an induction training of 23 days, followed by on-the-job training for a year.
22. This committee would consist of PRI representatives, ANM/MPW (Multi Purpose Worker), *Anganwadi* Worker, school teacher, ASHA and community health volunteers.
23. Each Sub Centre would be provided with an untied fund of Rs.10,000 (approx. US$250) per annum. The fund would be deposited in a bank account, operated jointly by ANM and *sarpanch* (Head of a *panchayat*, elected through adult franchise), in consultation with VHC. Other activities would include supply of essential drugs (Both AYUSH and allopathic) to the Sub Centres, recruitment of MPWs or ANMs where required, creation of new Sub Centres, upgrading of Sub Centres and construction of building where there is a rented premises.
24. NRHM seeks to augment the public health system by mainstreaming AYUSH infrastructure, manpower and drugs. AYUSH medicines would be included in the drug kit provided to ASHA, and be made available at rural (allopathic) health facilities such as Sub Centres, PHCs and CHCs. AYUSH practitioners and pharmacists would be made available at CHCs and PHCs.

5

Challenges for the NRHM

Study of Recent Demographic and Health Profile in NRHM States

R.P. TYAGI

Introduction

Health care is one of the seven thrust areas of the National Common Minimum Programme (NCMP) of the Government of India, where the importance of health has been realised in the process of socioeconomic development and improving the quality of life of the individual citizen. Under this programme, it is proposed to increase the public expenditure on health from the present level of 0.9 per cent of the GDP to 2-3 per cent of the GDP over the next five years. For accelerated achievements of the public health goals in the prevailing socioeconomic milieu, the National Health Policy (NHP) 2002 lays emphasis on providing increased accessibility to the decentralised public health system, enhancing public health investment and convergence of public health programmes.

For realisation of the goals of Health Policy (2002) and the National Population Policy (2000), the National Rural Health Mission (NRHM) was launched on April 12, 2005 for a period of 7 years (2005-2012). The NRHM is not a policy document, but a Mission launched to carry out 'architectural correction' in the basic health care delivery system. It adopts a 'synergetic' approach by relating health to determinants of good health. *Inter alia,* it seeks to provide access to women and children to safe water, sanitation and hygiene, immunisation and nutrition. It also aims at mainstreaming the Indian System of Medicine to facilitate health care. The second phase of Reproductive and Child Health (RCH) programme, initiated on 1st April 2005, is also included in NRHM. RCH-II programme intends to reduce the maternal, infant and child mortality and morbidity. It also intends to improve the performance of family welfare programme, reduce unwanted pregnancies, with the ultimate objective of population stabilisation.

Salient Features of National Rural Health Mission (NRHM)

The NRHM seeks to improve access to health care to rural population, especially the weaker sections, the women and children by providing affordable, equitable and accountable primary health care. The NRHM has given special focus to 18 states with relatively weaker population and health indicators and poor infrastructure. There are four north Indian states: Bihar, Madhya Pradesh, Rajasthan and Uttar Pradesh. The three smaller states bifurcated from these states are Jharkhand, Chhattisgarh and Uttarakhand. The seven sisters in northeastern India also form part of these special focus states, *viz.*, Arunachal Pradesh, Manipur, Meghalaya, Mizoram, Nagaland, Sikkim and Tripura. Besides, the states of Assam, Orissa, Jammu & Kashmir, and Himachal Pradesh are the other states included.

The main goals of the NRHM are to:

- Reduce infant mortality rate (IMR) to 30 per 1000 live births by 2012.
- Reduce maternal mortality ratio (MMR) to 100 per 100,000 live births by 2012.
- Reduce total fertility rate (TFR) to 2.1 by 2012.

Besides, it has laid down the targets of percentage reduction in mortality due to diseases like malaria, kala azar, filaria and dengue. It has also fixed targets for increasing cataract operations, reduction in the prevalence of leprosy, and maintaining high cure rate for tuberculosis. It has also been targeted that the utilisation of the first referral unit (FRU) be increased from 20 per cent to 75 per cent by 2010. It has also been targeted by the NHP 2002 to increase Central grant to constitute at least 25 per cent of the total health spending by 2010.

The NRHM also intends to promote the goals of the National Population Policy (NPP) 2000, which besides the goals of IMR, MMR and TFR already stated above has also set the following additional goals by 2010.

- Achieve universal immunisation of children against all vaccine preventable diseases.
- Achieve 80 per cent institutional deliveries and 100 per cent deliveries by trained persons.
- Promote delayed marriages for girls not earlier than age 18 and preferably after 20 years of age.
- Address the unmet need for basic reproductive services, supplies and infrastructure.

- Make school education up to age 14 free and compulsory, and reduce dropouts at primary and secondary levels to below 20 per cent for boys and girls.
- Integrate the Indian system of medicine (ISM) in the provision of reproductive and child health services and in reaching out to households.

Strategies

The strategies that the Mission has adopted are: (a) improve physical infrastructure for delivery of health care like buildings and equipment; (b) provide health and medical service according to the Indian Public Health Standards (IPHS); (c) augment manpower; (d) improve management; (e) provide flexibility in deploying funds to the states; (f) decentralisation of services; and (g) community participation.

More specifically, the strategies of the NRHM are the following:

- Capacity building of the Panchayati Raj institution (PRI) to own control and manage public health services.
- Improved access to health care at the household level through accredited social health activist (ASHA).
- Strengthening sub-centre through an untied fund to enable local planning and additional multi-purpose workers (MPWs).
- Strengthening primary health centres (PHCs) for quality preventive, promotive, curative, supervisory and outreach services.
- Strengthening the community health centres (CHCs) for the first referral care.
- Preparation and implementation of the district health plans by the district health mission on the basis of field responses through village health plans, including water supply, sanitation, hygiene and nutrition.
- Integration of Health and Family Welfare Programmes at national, state, district and block level.
- Technical support to national, state and district health missions for public health management.
- Strengthening capacities for data collection, assessment and review for evidence based planning, monitoring and supervision.
- Formulation of transparent policies for deployment and career development of human resource for health.

- Developing capacities for preventive health at all levels for promoting healthy lifestyles, reduction in consumption of tobacco and alcohol etc.
- Promoting non-profit sector, particularly in under-served areas.

The Present Study

It is as yet too early to assess the impact of the Mission on demographic and health indicators. However, on the basis the recent data released by the National Family Health Survey-3 (2005-06), the data from the earlier two rounds of National Family Health Surveys (NFHS), the Sample Registration System data and Official data released by the Ministry of Health and Family Welfare, the present study intends to examine the challenges before the NRHM in 18 states, which have been given special attention in NRHM because of weak public health indicators. The trend would be studied by comparison with the earlier two rounds of NFHS. The study will also examine the core strategies of the NRHM in the light of current health and demographic profile and the objectives of the NRHM.

Progress of NRHM as Reflected in Official Statistics

For observing the progress of NRHM as reflected by official figures, we will take only a selected few indicators, like selection, training and placement of ASHAs; strengthening of sub-centres, PHCs and CHCs; strengthening of FRUs, institutional deliveries, and the number of health *melas* observed.

Selection, Training and Placement of ASHA

Selection of ASHA

According to the timetable of NRHM, of the total number of ASHAs to be selected over the Mission period, 50 per cent fully trained ASHAs had to be placed for every 1000 population by 2007 and 100 per cent by 2008. The position as on 31st December 2007 shows that except in Himachal Pradesh, where not a single ASHA was selected, in all the other 17 high focus states and tribal areas in non-high focus states, a total of 87.7 per cent of the ASHAs were selected from those which were targeted to be selected. The percentage varied from a low of 20 per cent in Tripura and 56 per cent in Jharkhand to 100 per cent in Chhattisgarh and Manipur. In Uttar Pradesh and Jammu & Kashmir, it has exceeded a little over 100 per cent. Thus, except in Tripura and Jharkhand, the progress in the selection has been fairly good.

Training of ASHA

About training of ASHAs, they were to be trained in five modules. Of the total number of ASHAs selected, only 83.2 per cent were trained in the first module. The training calendar was not finalised in Meghalaya and Himachal Pradesh, where ASHAs have not been selected. So training even in the first module could not be imparted there. Even in Sikkim, the training could not be imparted in the first module, although the training calendar was finalised. In rest of the states, among the high focus, other than northeastern states, training in first module was imparted to all the selected ASHAs in Chhattisgarh, a little above 99 per cent in Uttarakhand, 97 per cent in Jammu & Kashmir, and 94 per cent in Rajasthan. On the other hand, in Orissa, only 27 per cent and in Jharkhand 54 per cent of the ASHAs were trained even in the first module. In five states, namely Jharkhand, Bihar, Uttar Pradesh, Orissa and Jammu & Kashmir, training was only confined to the first module. In Rajasthan and Uttarakhand, it was extended up to the second module. Only in Madhya Pradesh and Chhattisgarh, it went up to the fourth module.

In the northeastern states, of the total selected, only 47 per cent could be trained even in the first module. It varied from a low of 28 per cent in Manipur, 49 per cent in Tripura, 55 per cent in Assam to cent per cent in Mizoram and Nagaland. But the training never exceeded beyond the first module. From the analysis, it appears that the progress in training is lagging behind the desired level against the target of 50 per cent fully trained ASHAs by 2007.

ASHAs in Position with Drug Kits

In 11 out of 18 states, the selected and trained ASHAs are not in position with their drug kits by 31st December 2007. Only in Madhya Pradesh, 41 per cent are in position, in Rajasthan 62 per cent are in position, and in Orissa 20 per cent are in position. In rest of the three states, Chhattisgarh, Assam and Nagaland, all the selected ASHAs are in position with drug kits. Thus, the progress of placement of ASHAs with drug kits is painfully slow.

Strengthening of Sub-Centres, PHCs and CHCs

Strengthening of Sub-Centres

It was envisaged, while phasing and time lining of the NRHM activities that 30 per cent of the sub-health centres will be functional with 2 ANMs by 2007, 60 per cent by 2009 and 100 per cent by 2010. Against this target, in the high focus 10 states, other than the northeastern states, of a total of 68,207 sub-centres, which were functional with at least one ANM, 8,300 (12.2

per cent) were provided with additional ANM by 31st December 2007, which was much below the target of 30 per cent set at the launch of the NRHM. Even this figure of 12.2 per cent has been reached because in Jharkhand all the sub-centres have been provided with additional ANM. In other states—Bihar, Uttarakhand, Himachal Pradesh and Jammu & Kashmir, not a single sub-centre has been provided with additional ANM, while in Chhattisgarh, it is less than one per cent, in Uttar Pradesh, Madhya Pradesh and Orissa, it is less than 10 per cent and in Rajasthan, it is around 20 per cent.

In the northeastern states, the corresponding percentage was 36.1 per cent. In this respect, the position was below 10 per cent in Meghalaya and Tripura. In Sikkim and Arunachal Pradesh, it was nearly 18 per cent. Only in the state of Manipur, it was above 100 per cent, while in Mizoram, it was a little above 49 per cent. From a review of progress, it is clear that the progress is much slower than the targeted level.

Strengthening of PHCs

It was targeted that 30 per cent of the 30,000 PHCs will be strengthened with 3 staff nurses to provide service guarantee as per Indian Public Health Standards (IPHS) by 2007, 60 per cent by 2009, and 100 per cent by 2010. Against this target, it was observed that among the 10 high focus states, other than the northeastern states, by the end of 2007, only in 4.2 per cent of the total number of PHCs functioning on 24x7 basis, three staff nurses were positioned. Only in three states, namely, Madhya Pradesh (10.3 per cent), Uttarakhand (100 per cent) and Jammu & Kashmir (34.9 per cent), three staff nurses were provided. In rest of the 7 states, not a single PHC got the three staff nurses. This shows a very poor progress in strengthening of the PHCs.

In the northeastern states, out of a total of 678 PHCs, in 243 (35.8%), 3 staff nurses were positioned. Among the different states, in Meghalaya, in 6 out of 8 PHCs, in Tripura and Assam, a little over 54 per cent of the PHCs where 3 staff nurses were positioned. In Arunachal Pradesh, Nagaland and Sikkim, not a single PHC had positioned 3 staff nurses. This also shows not a very satisfactory position with regard to positioning of the 3 staff nurses to strengthen the service delivery at the PHCs.

Strengthening of CHCs

It was targeted that 30 per cent of the 6,500 CHCs will be strengthened with 7 specialists and 9 staff nurses by 2007, 50 per cent by 2009, and 100 per cent by 2010. For assessing the progress in strengthening the community health centres (CHCs), we would study the progress on two indicators: (i)

CHCs where facility survey has been completed; and (ii) CHCs where physical upgradation work has been taken up.

Completion of Facility Survey

Regarding the first, it was observed that of the total number of 1377 CHCs in high focus northern states selected for upgradation according to the IPHS, in 1187 (86.2 per cent) facility survey has been completed. Among different states, in Jharkhand more CHCs were surveyed than originally selected. In Madhya Pradesh, Bihar and Jammu & Kashmir, all the CHCs selected were surveyed. In other states also, quite a higher percentage of selected CHCs were surveyed for facilities, except Uttarakhand, where 26 out of 46 (53.1 per cent) were surveyed for facilities.

In northeastern states, the facility survey had been completed in more than 90 per cent of the CHCs selected in most of the states. In the states of Manipur and Tripura, more CHCs were surveyed than originally selected. Only in Nagaland in 18 out of 21 (85.7 per cent) CHCs selected, the facility survey could be completed. Thus, on this indicator the position appears to be satisfactory in both the northern states as well as the northeastern states.

Physical Upgradation Work Taken Up

In the northern states, out of 986 CHCs, which were identified for upgradation work, in 519 (52.6 per cent), the upgradation work could be started and only in 78 (15 per cent of those where work started), it could be completed. Among the different states, in Bihar and Jharkhand, the work could not be started. In other states, where the pace of start was low were Orissa (5 out of 30 identified), Uttar Pradesh (50 out of 169 identified) and in Chhattisgarh (25 out of 64 identified). In other states, pace of starting was somewhat satisfactory.

In the northeastern states, the physical upgradation work in CHCs could be started in 186 out of 191 identified for it. In Assam, Arunachal Pradesh, Manipur and Mizoram, the work could be started in all the CHCs identified. In Assam against the 93 identified, the work was started in 102. In the remaining other states, it could be started in majority of the CHCs identified. In the northeastern region as a whole, the work could be completed in about 49 per cent of the CHCs. The pace of completion was relatively slow in Assam, Mizoram, Sikkim and Tripura. In Arunachal Pradesh and Manipur, it was complete in nearly all the CHCs. In Nagaland and Meghalaya, it was complete in 41 and 50 per cent of the CHCs respectively. The pace of completion did not appear to be satisfactory, looking to the urgency of providing quality services to the people in the region.

Strengthening of Sub-Divisional Hospitals and District Hospitals

Strengthening of Sub-Divisional Hospitals (SDHs)

It was planned that 30 per cent of the 1800 SDHs be strengthened to provide quality health services by 2007 and 100 per cent by 2010. Against this target of 540 SDHs, to be strengthened by 2007, only 277 (51.3 per cent) sub-hospitals were strengthened by the end of December 2007. Quite a shortfall in the target! In the states of Jharkhand, Bihar and Chhattisgarh, there was not a single SDH by the end of 2007. Out of the 263 which existed in northern states by end of 2007, 44 (16.7 per cent) were working by the end of 2005, 71 (27 per cent) were added during 2005-06, 85 (32.3 per cent) during 2006-07 and 63 (24 per cent) during the most recent year 2007-08. So, in this region the progress in upgradation of SDHs has been slow, but uniform.

In northeastern states, out of 8 states, namely four, Manipur, Nagaland, Sikkim and Meghalaya did not have any sub-hospital. Only Arunachal Pradesh has 9 sub-divisional hospitals, Assam and Tripura has 2 each, while Mizoram has 1. Among these 14, 10 SDHs were already working as on 31st March 2005. During the next four years, only 4 have been added. Thus, the progress is painfully slow.

Challenges for the NRHM

In this section, we will examine the challenges for the NRHM. As already stated, the NRHM intends to achieve the goals set by NPP 2000 and NHP 2002 in a mission mode by strengthening the existing delivery of basic health care by synergetic approach by relating to determinants of good health. In the light of these objectives, we will examine the current demographic, health and socioeconomic indicators to assess how far the NRHM will be able to make significant effect on the key demographic and health indicators by a particular time period. More specifically, we will concentrate on infant mortality rate, maternal mortality rate, total fertility rate, teenage fertility, contraceptive prevalence rate, unmet need for family planning, the maternal care indicators, the nutritional level, and the age at marriage. This will not cover all the indicators, which will be affected by the NRHM effort, but will provide an idea of the challenges that the NRHM would have to face in achieving the goals set by the Mission.

Infant Mortality Rate

Infant mortality rate (IMR) the most sensitive index is affected by a large number of factors covered by the NRHM like prenatal care, natal care and postnatal care, breastfeeding, prelacteal feeds etc. Besides, it is affected by some of the demographic factors like age of the mother, birth interval, age at marriage, which are also covered in the goals of NPP 2000. For convenience of analysis and clarity of the argument, we will concentrate on the four bigger states of Bihar, UP, Rajasthan and Madhya Pradesh and the three bifurcated states, that is Jharkhand, Chhattisgarh and Uttarakhand.

The success of NRHM will be reflected in reduction in the level of IMR. On perusal of Table 5.3, we find that against the national level IMR of 58 (SRS), the level in Madhya Pradesh is as high as 76, in Uttar Pradesh 72, Rajasthan 67 and Bihar 61. The target is to attain a level of 30 by 2012.

Teenage Fertility

Against such high levels of IMR, when we examine the current situation of the factors, which determine IMR like teenage pregnancy, which is due to low age at marriage, we find that against the all-India level of 16 per cent of women aged 15-19 who have begun child bearing, the figure for Jharkhand is 27.5, and for Bihar 25 per cent (Table 5.13). Examining another index of teenage fertility, that is, the percentage of fertility in the age group (15-19) to total fertility rate, we find that it is as high as 16.29 per cent in Chhattisgarh and 15.61 per cent in Rajasthan, against the all-India level of 13.83.

Age at Marriage

The high teenage fertility is due to low age at marriage. The mean age at effective marriage as per SRS data in 2005 was 19 years in Bihar, 19.2 in Jharkhand, against 20.2 for all India. The percentage of women aged 18-29, who were first married by exact age 18 were 63.7 per cent in Bihar, 60.2 per cent in Jharkhand, against the all-India figure of 45.6 per cent. Such a high percentage of females were married below the legal age of 18 years. The goal of the National Population Policy (NPP) is to promote delayed marriages for girls not earlier than 18 and preferably after attaining 20 years.

Health and Nutritional Status of Females

The NFHS-3 has given two indicators of health and nutritional status of females. One is the anaemic status of women aged 15-49 by haemoglobin (Hb) level and another is the body mass index (BMI). Examining the anaemia level (haemogloin level <12 gms/dl), we find that 69.5 per cent of females in Jharkhand had Hb level below 12 gms/dl. In Bihar, it was 67.4 per cent and in Orissa, it was 61.2 per cent (Table 5.10). However, in UP it was 49.9 per cent. Moderate and severe level of anaemia (Hb <10 gms/dl) was the highest in Rajasthan (17.9%). Examining the BMI level, we observe that 45 per cent of women aged 15-49 in Bihar had less than BMI of 18.5, which is considered to be total thin. Respective percentages were 43.4 in Chhattisgarh, and 43 in Jharkhand. Nearly one-fifth (19.2%) of females in Bihar were severely thin (BMI of less than 17). Such is the nutritional status in these NRHM states.

Breastfeeding and Infant and Young Child Feeding Practices

Breastfeeding affects all the three key indicators, IMR, MMR and TFR, which we are discussing. Early initiation of breastfeeding within one hour of birth helps the child to get first breast milk (colostrums), which is highly nutritious and helps the child to fight many diseases. Instead of colostrums, introducing prelacteal feeds like honey, *ghutti*, glucose water etc., are potentially harmful. These practices may increase the level of IMR. Higher levels of such practices reflect the prevailing traditional attitude of the people. Examining these in the few selected NRHM states we find from the NFHS-3 data that in Bihar, only 3.7 per cent among the last-born children, born in the last five years started breastfeeding within one hour of birth. Such percentage was 7.3 in Uttar Pradesh (Table 5.9), 10.7 in Jharkhand and 14.1 per cent in Rajasthan. In Orissa and Himachal Pradesh, it was as high as 54.8 and 45.4 per cent respectively. About the per cent that received prelacteal foods, it was observed that in Bihar, 91 per cent received prelacteal feeds, in UP 86 per cent, in Rajasthan 71 per cent and in MP, it was received by 58 per cent. Surprisingly in Chhattisgarh, only 23.3 per cent received prelacteal feeds and 25 per cent of children were breastfed within one hour of birth. We take this as an index of tradition. Traditional parents do not start brestfeeding immediately and give prelacteal feeds.

Maternal Mortality Ratio (MMR)

Like IMR, the MMR has been another key indicator, which reflects on the progress of health and quality of life. But the estimates of MMR are fragmentary. Even the big surveys like NFHS-3 failed to give the estimates even at the national level because of the small size of sample. Recently, the sample registration system (SRS) has provided estimates of MMR for the period 1997-2003 through retrospective household reports and the special survey of deaths using RHIME (representative, re-sampled, routine household interview of mortality with medical valuation). These three surveys give MMR estimates at three points of time, 1997-98, 1999-2001 and 2001-2003 for five states, namely Assam, Bihar/Jharkhand, MP/Chhattisgarh, Orissa, Rajasthan and UP/Uttarakhand, which are given in Table 5.4. These are also the NRHM states.

A perusal of Table 5.4 reveals that at the national level, the MMR has declined from 398 deaths per 100,000 births in 1997-98 to 301 in 2001-2003. The highest level of MMR in 2001-2003 has been in UP (517), followed by Assam (490), Rajasthan (445). The lowest has been in Orissa (358).

Antenatal Care

The high level of MMR reflects on besides the general health conditions of the pregnant females, the state of antenatal care and the care during delivery. The NRHM envisages improving the antenatal care by ANC check-ups. A minimum of three ANC is required. For improving the natal care, institutional deliveries or deliveries with the assistance of trained medical practitioners are being promoted under the NRHM. From the available NFHS-3 data, let us examine the position of these indicators in selected NRHM states to know the challenges for the NRHM. Among the women who had live births during the preceding five years, only 17 per cent of females in Bihar had three or more ANC visits during their last pregnancy (Table 5.7). This percentage was also quite low in Uttar Pradesh (26.6 per cent) and Jharkhand (35.9 per cent) against the all-India level of 52 per cent. Another component of antenatal care is that the mothers receive any iron and folic acid (IFA) tablets or syrup for at least 90 days. On this component the position of Bihar, UP and Rajasthan is very poor. In UP, only 8.8 per cent received the IFA tablets, while in Bihar 9.7 per cent, for MP 12.4 and for Rajasthan 13.1 per cent against the all India level of 23.1 per cent. In the face of very high level of anaemia among females in these states, as discussed earlier, such a low level of taking of IFA tablets by the pregnant women is a big challenge for the NRHM. One needs to go deeper into underlying causes for this.

Natal Care

Two components have been particularly stressed in the NRHM, one the institutional deliveries, and the deliveries attended by trained personnel. Perusal of the NFHS data in Table 5.7 reveals that the percentage of births that were delivered in a health facility were as low as 14.3 in Chhattisgarh, 18.3 in Jharkhand, 19.9 in Bihar and 20.6 in UP. So, below one-fifth of the births during the last five years of the survey had taken place in a health facility against the national level of 38.7 per cent. About the other indicator of natal care, that is the percentage of deliveries assisted by a health personnel, we find that it is the lowest in Uttar Pradesh (27.2%), followed by Jharkhand (27.8%) and Bihar (29.3%). Thus, we observe a very low level of institutional deliveries and deliveries by skilled personnel. This is one of the biggest reasons of high maternal mortality.

High Level of TFR

As can be observed from Tables 5.5 and 5.6, the level of TFR is very high comparative to all-India in the states of Bihar, Jharkhand, Uttar Pradesh and Madhya Pradesh. According to NFHS-3 (2005-06), the TFR in Uttar Pradesh is the highest (2.95), followed by Bihar (2.87) and Madhya Pradesh (2.58). According to another set of data (SRS), we observe that for 2005, the TFR is 4.2 for Uttar Pradesh, 3.9 for Bihar, 3.7 for Rajasthan and 3.5 for Madhya Pradesh against the national level of 2.9. Here we are not going to discuss which data is more accurate, but will highlight that the TFR in these states is much higher than the other states.

The level of TFR is high generally where the initiation of child bearing is early, the childbirth is in quick succession, that is the birth interval is small and the level of contraceptive use is low. There are teenage pregnancies and childbirths as well as childbirths at higher ages like 35 years and above. We have already examined the teenage fertility and age at marriage while discussing the infant mortality rate and found the incidence to high. About the level of contraceptive use, we find the use of any modern contraceptive method to be lowest in Bihar at 28.9 per cent (NFHS-3), followed by 29.3 per cent in Uttar Pradesh and Jharkhand (31.1 per cent) against the all India level of 48.5 per cent. These factors explain the high level of TFR in these states.

Conclusion

The NRHM has been launched to provide comprehensive health to include curative, preventive and promotive health by increasing infrastructure by increasing allocation of resources. From the perusal of the performance of the NRHM on the basis of available official data, the performance has not been inspiring. But allocation of more funds and creation of infrastructure only strengthens the supply side of the programme. For achievement of the desired goals, besides supply side, the demand side factors need to be looked. These are embedded in the socio-cultural and economic change. With the present state of very poor socioeconomic indicators in the NRHM states, there is big challenge to achieve the goals set for the demographic and health indicators.

Table 5.1

Progress in Upgradation of Sub-Divisional Hospitals in High Focus Northern States during 2005 to 2008

High Focus Northern States	*SDHs Working by End of March 2005*	*Upgraded during 2005-06*	*Upgraded during 2006-07*	*Upgraded during 2007-08*	*Total*
1. Jharkhand	0	0	0	0	0
2. Madhya Pradesh	6	6	8	16	36
3. Rajasthan	0	0	28	12	40
4. Bihar	0	0	0	0	0
5. Uttarakhand	4	3	0	0	7
6. Chhattisgarh	0	0	0	0	0
7. Uttar Pradesh	20	25	30	35	110
8. Orissa	0	18	0	0	18
9. Himachal Pradesh	0	5	5	0	10
10. Jammu & Kashmir	14	14	14	0	42
Total	44	71	85	63	263

Source: Status Report on National Rural Health Mission available on website: *www.mohfw.nic.in/national_rural_health_mission*

Table 5.2

Progress in Upgradation of Sub-Divisional Hospitals in High Focus Northeastern States during 2005 to 2008

High Focus Northeastern States	*SDHs Working by End of March 2005*	*Upgraded during 2005-06*	*Upgraded during 2006-07*	*Upgraded during 2007-08*	*Total*
1. Assam	2	0	0	0	2
2. Arunachal Pradesh	7	1	1	0	9
3. Manipur	0	0	0	0	0
4. Mizoram	1	0	0	0	1
5. Nagaland	0	0	0	0	0
6. Sikkim	0	0	0	0	0
7. Meghalaya	0	0	0	0	0
8. Tripura	0	1	1	0	2
Total	10	2	2	0	14

Source: Same as in Table 5.1.

Table 5.3

Trend in Infant Mortality Rate in NRHM States

States	NFHS			SRS		
	1992-93	1998-99	2005-06	1992-1994	1998-2000	2004-2006
India	78.5	67.6	57.0	76	70	58
Northern States						
Bihar	89.2	72.9	64.9	70	64	61
Madhya Pradesh	85.2	86.1	70.0	103	92	76
Rajasthan	72.6	80.4	65.3	85	72	67
Uttar Pradesh	99.9	86.7	66.2	93	84	72
Northeastern States						
Arunachal Pradesh	40.0	63.1	60.7	63	44	38
Assam	88.7	69.5	66.1	78	76	67
Manipur	42.4	37.0	29.7	22	24	13
Meghalaya	64.2	89.0	44.6	49	55	52
Mizoram	14.6	37.0	34.1	NA	21	21
Nagaland	17.2	42.1	38.3	6	NA	18
Sikkim	NA	43.9	33.7	37	50	32
Tripura	75.8	NA	51.5	43	44	33
Other States						
Himachal Pradesh	55.8	34.4	36.1	63	62	50
Jammu & Kashmir	45.4	65.0	44.7	NA	48	50
Orissa	112.1	81.0	64.7	109	97	75

Source: India: National Family Health Survey (NFHS-3) 2005-06, Vol. I, Sept. 07, Table 7.4; India: National Family Health Survey (NFHS-2), 1998-99, Table 6.6; India: National Family Health Survey (NFHS-1), 1992-93, Table 8.8; Registrar General, India. *Sample Registration Bulletins* (various issues).

Table 5.4

Maternal Mortality Ratio (Number of Maternal Deaths Per 1000 Live Births) in India and NRHM States

India and NRHM States	Maternal Mortality Ratio (MMR)		
	1997-98*	1999-2001**	2001-2003***
India	398	327	301
Assam	568	398	490
Bihar/Jharkhand	531	400	371
Madhya Pradesh/Chhattisgarh	441	407	379
Orissa	346	424	358
Rajasthan	508	501	445
Uttar Pradesh/Uttarakhand	606	539	517
Sub-total@	520	461	438

Note: *1997-98 Retrospective MMR Surveys.
**1999-2001 SRS Retrospective Household Reports.
***2001-2003 Special Survey of Deaths using RHIME.
@ Sub-total refers to Empowered Action Group (EAG) states and Assam.

Source: India, Registrar General (2006). *Maternal Mortality in India: 1997-2003—Trends, Causes and Risk Factors*. October.

Table 5.5

Trend in Total Fertility Rate and Crude Birth Rate (CBR) in NRHM States

India and NRHM States	*Total Fertility Rate (TFR)*			
	NFHS-1	*NFHS-2*	*NFHS-3*	*NFHS-3 CBR*
India	2.70	2.27	2.06	18.8
Bihar	NA	2.61	2.87	23.5
Jharkhand	NA	2.95	2.32	21.0
Madhya Pradesh	NA	2.68	2.58	22.1
Chhattisgarh	NA	2.12	1.78	17.1
Rajasthan	2.77	2.98	2.21	19.8
Uttar Pradesh	NA	2.91	2.95	23.5
Uttarakhand	NA	2.14	2.21	18.5
Himachal Pradesh	2.03	1.74	1.57	14.6
Jammu & Kashmir	NA	1.66	1.63	15.0
Orissa	2.53	2.19	1.89	17.7
Northeastern States				
Arunachal Pradesh	NA	1.77	2.51	26.3
Assam	2.53	1.50	1.43	13.6
Manipur	NA	2.36	2.35	21.6
Meghalaya	NA	2.75	2.28	21.1
Mizoram	NA	2.37	2.50	23.3
Nagaland	NA	2.66	2.68	23.8
Sikkim	NA	NA	1.29	13.5
Tripura	NA	1.36	1.66	17.8

Source: National Family Health Survey (NFHS), 2005-06. *India*, Vol. I, September 2007, Table 4.3.

Table 5.6

Total Fertility Rate as per Sample Registration System (SRS) in Selected Four States

India/States	*Total Fertility Rate (TFR)*			
	1990	*1995*	*2000*	*2005*
India	3.8	3.5	3.2	2.9
Bihar	4.8	4.5	4.5	3.9
Madhya Pradesh	4.8	4.2	4.0	3.5
Rajasthan	4.5	4.4	4.1	3.7
Uttar Pradesh	5.2	5.0	4.7	4.2

Source: Registrar General, India. *Sample Registration Bulletins* (various issues).

Table 5.7

Selected Reproductive and Child Health (RCH) Indicators for NRHM States, 2005-06

(Percentage)

India/States	RCH Indicators							
	Contraceptive Use (Any Method)	*3 or More ANC Visits*	*IFA for at least 90 days*	*Institutional Deliveries*	*Deliveries by Skilled Persons*	*All Basic Vaccinations**	*ICDS Coverage for Children#*	*Mothers Received Health and Nutrition Education during Pregnancy from AWC*
India	56.3	52.0	23.1	38.7	46.6	43.5	32.9	20.5
Bihar	34.1	17.0	9.7	19.9	29.3	32.8	9.9	0.6
Jharkhand	35.7	35.9	14.2	18.3	27.8	34.2	41.7	34.7
Madhya Pradesh	55.9	40.7	12.4	26.2	32.7	40.3	49.8	31.0
Chhattisgarh	53.2	54.2	20.7	14.3	41.6	48.7	65.2	64.1
Rajasthan	47.2	41.2	13.1	29.6	41.0	26.5	21.1	17.0
Uttar Pradesh	43.6	26.6	8.8	20.6	27.2	23.0	22.3	9.6
Uttarakhand	59.3	44.9	26.4	32.6	38.5	60.0	31.6	18.9
Himachal Pradesh	72.6	62.6	37.9	43.0	47.8	74.2	37.5	33.6
Jammu & Kashmir	52.6	73.5	27.6	50.2	56.5	66.7	18.8	6.3
Orissa	50.7	61.8	33.8	35.6	44.0	51.8	65.8	44.6
Northeastern States								
Assam	56.5	39.3	16.2	22.4	31.0	31.4	29.8	12.7
Arunachal Pradesh	43.2	35.5	11.2	28.5	30.2	28.4	15.8	9.0
Manipur	48.7	68.6	13.1	45.9	59.0	46.8	30.1	3.7
Meghalaya	24.3	54.0	16.7	29.0	31.1	32.9	48.1	36.1
Mizoram	59.9	59.3	24.7	59.8	65.4	46.5	55.8	54.5
Nagaland	29.7	32.7	3.5	11.6	65.4	21.0	39.3	5.4
Sikkim	57.6	70.1	38.7	47.2	53.7	69.6	41.6	24.6
Tripura	65.7	60.0	18.0	46.9	48.8	49.7	26.6	6.8

Note: * BCG, measles and three doses each of DPT and polio vaccine.

Percentage of children aged 0-71 months who received any services from ICDS.

Source: National Family Health Survey (NFHS-3), 2005-06. *India*, Vol. I, Table 5.7; Table 8.10; Table 8.22; Table 9.24; Table 9.26; Table 9.5.

Table 5.8

Nutrition among Children Less than 5 Years of Age in NRHM States, 2005-06

India/NRHM States	*Indicators of Nutritional Status of Children*				
	Height-for-Age (Stunting) Per cent Below-2 SD	*Weight-for-Height (Wasting) Per cent Below-2 SD*	*Weight-for-Age (Underweight) Per cent Below-2 SD*	*Anaemia Status Moderate (7.7-9.9 g/dl)*	*Anaemia Status Severe (<7 g/dl)*
India	48.0	19.8	42.5	40.2	2.9
Bihar	55.6	27.1	55.9	46.8	1.6
Jharkhand	49.8	32.3	56.5	39.1	1.9
Madhya Pradesh	50.0	35.0	60.0	43.6	3.4
Chhattisgarh	52.9	19.5	47.1	45.2	2.0
Rajasthan	43.7	20.4	39.9	40.2	6.7
Uttar Pradesh	56.8	14.8	42.4	45.0	3.6
Uttarakhand	44.4	18.8	38.0	30.6	2.3
Himachal Pradesh	38.6	19.3	36.5	26.8	2.2
Jammu & Kashmir	35.0	14.8	25.6	30.4	2.4
Orissa	45.0	19.5	40.7	34.5	1.6
Northeastern States					
Assam	46.5	13.7	36.4	38.7	2.2
Arunachal Pradesh	43.3	15.3	32.5	29.1	0.8
Manipur	35.6	9.0	22.1	15.2	0.3
Meghalaya	55.1	30.7	48.8	31.7	1.0
Mizoram	39.8	9.0	19.9	20.0	0.6
Nagaland	38.8	13.3	25.2	NA	NA
Sikkim	38.3	9.7	19.7	29.5	0.8
Tripura	35.7	24.6	39.6	34.6	0.7

Source: National Family Health Survey (NFHS-3), 2005-06. *India,* Vol.I, Table 10.2; Table 10.13.

Table 5.9

Breastfeeding and Infant and Child Feeding Practices in NRHM States, 2005-06

India/NRHM States	Breastfeeding			Infant and Young Child Feeding (IYCF) Practices	
	Within One Hour of Birth	Exclusive Breastfeeding	Per cent who Received Prelacteal Feed#	Breastfed Children (6-23 Months) Fed 3+Food Groups and Minimum Number of Times	Non-breastfed Children (6-23 Months) with 3 IYCF Practices@
India	24.5	2.0	57.2	43.7	11.9
Bihar	3.7	0.7	90.6	54.8	11.9
Jharkhand	10.7	2.9	66.3	44.3	5.1
Madhya Pradesh	15.9	0.6	58.1	45.7	18.3
Chhattisgarh	25.0	5.8	23.3	53.2	NA
Rajasthan	14.1	1.4	71.6	38.7	6.6
Uttar Pradesh	7.3	2.4	86.0	35.2	8.2
Uttarakhand	33.5	0.7	44.9	40.4	16.8
Himachal Pradesh	45.4	1.1	21.7	49.0	33.5
Jammu & Kashmir	31.6	0.6	36.6	40.4	18.9
Orissa	54.8	2.3	42.1	56.3	19.9
Northeastern States					
Assam	50.9	3.5	32.7	41.1	NA
Arunachal Pradesh	58.6	3.0	16.7	63.9	NA
Manipur	57.8	3.4	37.5	66.1	15.0
Meghalaya	57.8	0.7	31.2	43.9	6.6
Mizoram	66.4	2.0	23.3	56.1	21.3
Nagaland	54.2	0.6	53.8	63.9	21.1
Sikkim	42.9	0.7	12.3	66.2	NA
Tripura	34.6	1.7	36.4	46.2	NA

Note: # Children given something other than breast milk during the first three days.

@ Non-breastfed children ages 6-23 months are considered to be fed with three IYCF practices if they receive milk or milk products and are fed at least the minimum number of times per day with at least a minimum number of food groups.

Source: National Family Health Survey (NFHS-3), 2005-06. *India*, Vol. I, Table 10.5; Table 10.10.

Table 5.10

Nutritional Status and Anaemia in Women of NRHM States, 2005-06

India/NRHM States	*Per cent Women Age 15-49 with Body Mass Index (BMI) in kg/m sq*			*Anaemia Status of Women Age 15-49 by Haemoglobin Level*	
	<17.0 (Severely Thin)	*<18.5 (Total Thin)*	*> = 30.0 (Obese)*	*Any Anaemia (<12.0 g/dl)*	*Moderate and Severe (< 10.0 gm/dl)*
India	15.8	35.6	2.8	55.3	16.8
Bihar	19.2	45.1	0.6	67.4	16.9
Jharkhand	18.0	43.0	0.9	69.5	19.9
Madhya Pradesh	18.9	41.7	1.4	56.0	15.1
Chhattisgarh	19.0	43.4	1.3	57.5	17.6
Rajasthan	15.2	36.7	1.8	53.1	17.9
Uttar Pradesh	14.9	36.0	1.7	49.9	14.8
Uttarakhand	11.7	30.0	2.7	55.2	14.8
Himachal Pradesh	13.2	29.9	2.1	43.3	11.7
Jammu & Kashmir	9.1	24.6	3.3	52.1	14.7
Orissa	18.3	41.4	1.1	61.2	16.4
Northeastern States					
Assam	15.2	36.5	0.9	69.5	24.6
Arunachal Pradesh	5.4	16.4	1.1	50.6	14.1
Manipur	3.1	14.8	1.9	35.7	5.6
Meghalaya	4.8	14.6	0.8	47.2	14.4
Mizoram	4.1	14.4	1.2	38.6	9.5
Nagaland	4.4	17.4	0.7	NA	NA
Sikkim	3.2	11.2	3.0	60.0	17.9
Tripura	16.1	36.9	0.7	65.1	16.1

Note: BMI is defined as weight in kilograms divided by height in metres squared (kg/m sq). g/dl: grams per decilitres.

Source: National Family Health Survey (NFHS-3), 2005-06. *India,* Vol. I, Table 10.23.1.

Table 5.11

State Domestic Product (SDP) at Current Prices, its Growth Rate, Per Capita SDP, its Growth Rate for NRHM States, 2005-06

	State Domestic Product (At Current Prices)		*Per Capita SDP*	
India/NRHM States	*Total*	*Growth Rate*	*Total*	*Growth Rate*
India	2,871,731	13.8	25,716	12.1
Bihar	71,006	7.3	7,875	5.5
Jharkhand	55,513	10.7	19,066	9.0
Madhya Pradesh	1,03,132	9.6	15,647	7.7
Chhattisgarh	45,743	13.5	20,151	11.5
Rajasthan	1,10,665	8.3	17,863	6.3
Uttar Pradesh	2,41,196	13.2	13,262	11.1
Uttarakhand	22,520	13.1	24,585	11.3
Orissa	67,090	7.3	17,299	6.1
Himachal Pradesh	22,390	10.5	33,805	8.6
Jammu & Kashmir	NA	NA	NA	NA
Northeastern States				
Assam	52,500	12.4	18,598	10.5
Arunachal Pradesh	2,767	6.8	23,788	5.5
Manipur	5,120	12.8	20,326	10.6
Meghalaya	5,757	8.2	23,420	6.9
Mizoram	NA	NA	NA	NA
Nagaland	NA	NA	NA	NA
Sikkim	1,527	12.6	17,863	6.3
Tripura	8,375	9.5	24,706	8.2

Source: Economic Survey, 2007-08, Appendix Table 1.7; 1.8.

Table 5.12

Socioeconomic Profile of Selected NRHM States, 2004-05

Socioeconomic Indicators	*States*								
	Bihar	*Himachal Pradesh*	*Madhya Pradesh*	*Orissa*	*Rajasthan*	*Uttar Pradesh*	*Chhattisgarh*	*Jharkhand*	*All India*
% Pop. Below Poverty Line	41.4	10.0	38.3	46.4	22.1	32.8	40.9	40.3	27.5
Av. MPCE–R	417	798	439.06	398.89	590.83	532.68	425.1	425.3	559
Av. MPCE–U	696	1390	903.68	757.31	964.02	857.05	989.97	985.43	1052
% Inadequate Food	2.7	0	1.6	5.3	0	1.5	2.2	0.6	1.9
Lorenz ratio-R	0.208	0.295	0.269	0.302	0.248	0.287	0.305	0.231	0.297
Lorenz ratio-U	0.339	0.318	0.397	0.355	0.369	0.370	0.439	0.354	0.373
GER (6-14) yrs.	65.2	108.7	114.1	108.5	102.7	87.0	112.6	75.8	93.5
GER (14-16) yrs.	22.5	134.9	45.7	53.7	43.7	48.9	43.9	26.5	51.7
GER (16-18) yrs.	9.8	127.7	25.3	32.9	21.6	22.9	30.4	2.5	27.8
% HH having electricity (2005-06)	27.7	98.4	71.4	45.6	66.1	42.8	71.4	40.2	67.9
% HH having access to toilet (2005-06)	25.2	45.6	27	19.3	30.8	33.1	18.7	22.6	44.5
% HH having safe drinking water (2001)	86.6	88.6	68.4	64.2	68.2	87.8	70.5	42.6	77.9

Note: MPCE: Monthly per capita expenditure; GER: Gross enrolment ratio; HH: Households; Av.: Average; R: Rural; U: Urban.

Source: GoI. *Economic Survey*, 2007-08. Table 2.3 (p.28).

Table 5.13

Mean Age at Effective Marriage (Females), Percentage of Women (18-29) who were Married by Exact Age of 18 and Teenage Pregnancy and Motherhood in Selected NRHM States, 2005-06

India/NRHM States	Age at Marriage		Teenage Pregnancy and Motherhood	
	Mean Age at Effective Marriage (Females) 2005#	% Women (18-29) who were Married by Exact Age 18*	Percentage of Women Age 15-19, who had begun Childbearing$	Percentage of Fertility in the Age Group (15-19) to Total Fertility Rate (TFR)@
India	20.2	45.6	16.0	13.83 (2.06)
Bihar	19.0	63.7	25.0	11.32 (2.87)
Jharkhand	19.2	60.2	27.5	15.51 (2.32)
Madhya Pradesh	20.5	52.6	13.6	10.27 (2.58)
Chhattisgarh	19.9	50.5	14.6	16.29 (1.78)
Rajasthan	19.9	58.4	16.0	15.61 (2.21)
Uttar Pradesh	19.8	52.2	14.3	10.00 (2.95)
Uttarakhand	Na	26.0	6.2	5.42 (2.21)
Orissa	20.5	37.5	14.4	4.55 (1.89)

Source: # Sample Registration System (as contained in *Family Welfare Statistics – 2006*, Table A.28, col.10).

* NFHS-3, Table 6.4.

$ NFHS-3, Table 4.12.

@ Calculated from NFHS-3, Table 4.3. Figures in parenthesis are the TFR.

Section III

Fertility, Mortality and Contraception in India

6

Fertility Trends, Differentials and Determinants among Social Categories in India

SANDIP CHAKRABORTY, PRABHAT K. JHA,
BALRAM PASWAN AND FAUJDAR RAM

Introduction

India is a country of immense religious, ethnic and cultural diversity evolving over the last five millennia. But the boundaries between different communities had not always been clear in past, prompting scholars to characterise Indians belonging to fuzzy communities (Das, 1994; Kaviraj, 1993). These social categories are very important socioeconomic and political reality in contemporary India. A new and modern dimension of demography was added during the colonial rule (Davis, 1951) and entered into the political consciousness led by the interest of the colonial government in the demographic size and distribution of religion and socio-cultural groups (Jones, 1981). Consolidation of caste identities, their complex and sometimes overlapping socio-cultural and politico-economic interplay present various permutations and combinations, fusion and fission of various castes which form very strong, relatively stable but dynamic caste groups that cooperating, competing and bargaining for higher status, opportunities and other rights and privileges provided by the governmental and other agencies (Srinivas, 1966; Kothari, 1970; Beteille, 1971; Singh, 1988). These are the logical outcomes in the evolution and spread of modern secular, scientific and utilitarian worldview, modernisation of economy and democratisation of polity (Chandra and Mukherjee, 1989). The Constitution of independent India is a blue-print of the transformation of traditional Indian society, culture, economy and polity into a modern set up by democratic means. Thus, the issue of caste group in contemporary socioeconomic and political arena became a focal point in recent intellectual debates, which got great impetus by the various executive and legislative measures taken after Independence and a series of new interpretations and directives given by the judiciary.

Caste has not been a fixed category historically, rather fluid, fuzzy and dynamic in Indian society. The forces shaping caste status lay in the way castes had perceived and defined themselves in relation to other castes (Gupta, 2004). However, Scheduled Castes (SCs), Scheduled Tribes (STs) and Other Backward Classes (OBCs) are already recognised in the Constitution as there are various special provisions enshrined in favour of these social groups by considering their historical deprivation and alienation from the mainstream. Caste is the most important identity of Indian people together with religion. Since, the very first census of 1872, the colonial government incorporated caste and religious categories in the enumeration of the Indian population. Along with caste, the census also incorporated the categories of tribe and race, but the distinction between them was often obscure (Bhagat, 2006). In independent India, enumeration of caste has ceased except for SCs and STs which were accepted as new official social categories under the provision of Article 341 of the Indian Constitution. However, in the absence of recent data, the 1931 census information on castes continues to be the only source on the size and proportion of OBCs in the country. Scheduled Castes and Scheduled Tribes are defined in Census 2001 as:

- List of the castes and tribes belonging to this group as declared by the President of India.
- Scheduled Caste could belong to only Hindu, Sikh and Buddhist religions.
- Scheduled Tribe could belong to any religion.

There are remarkable caste differentials on almost all important demographic indicators (Holsinger and Kasarda, 1976; Srinivasan *et al.*, 1977; Davis, 1951; Nag, 1989). Such caste differentials are persisting even today. For instance, 2001 census shows that the fertility performance of SC and ST was higher than other caste categories. The mean number of children ever born per ever married women in the age group of 45-49 years for SC and ST were 4.19 and 4.11 respectively while, the corresponding figures for all the communities put together was 3.88 (RGI, 2004). National Family Health Survey (1998-99) shows remarkable differences in fertility among the caste/ tribe categories, as SC having TFR 3.15 while, ST 3.06, OBC 2.83 and Others 2.66. So we need to find the trends and changes over the period and the underlying factors affecting it. While, we do not have sufficient data particularly, caste-wise and more specifically for OBC.

Objectives

- To comprehend the fertility trends and child bearing behaviour among different caste/tribe groups in India.
- To understand the differentials in fertility among the various social categories by their socioeconomic and demographic characteristics.

- To identify different socioeconomic and demographic factors affecting the levels of fertility among these social categories.

Data and Methodology

The data for the present study are obtained from the District Level Household Survey-II, 2002-2004, under Reproductive and Child Health programme. The data was collected from 620,107 households in India. From these households, 507,622 eligible women and 330,820 husbands of eligible women were interviewed. In DLHS-RCH-II, besides the information related with maternal and child health there are also some background information collected such as age of the women, children along with children's year of birth, month of birth, sex, whether child is alive or not, etc. From this data all the information of children are compiled to construct birth data (around 13.5 lakhs) with some basic information of their mothers.

Calculation of Period Parity Progression Ratio (PPPR)

Fertility trends and childbearing behaviour among the social categories like SC, ST, OBC and others are analysed by the method of period parity progression ratios (PPPR). Henry (1953) introduced the concept of parity progression as a measure of fertility. Feeney and Jingyuan Yu (1987) have estimated PPPR-based measures of fertility for China as a whole and for the rural and urban area for the period 1955-1981. It is the proportion of women who move from a given parity to the next during their lifetime. These are useful to study the family building process dynamics and can be linked to the total fertility rate. Generally cohorts of women or cohorts of births are used to measure fertility. However, in such analysis truncation caused by the survey makes it difficult to study recent changes. The PPPR methodology overcomes this problem by computing progression for synthetic cohorts.

The method used to calculate period parity progression ratio is similar to the one suggested by Feeney and Jingyuan Yu (1987). This method incorporates two basic information for a particular woman: (1) the calendar year of birth of her i^{th} order child and (2) the calendar year of birth of her $(i\text{-}1)^{th}$ order child. Suppose a group of women have their k^{th} birth in calendar year 't'. Let the proportion who have the next, that is $(k+1)^{th}$, birth in the same year be denoted by $q_E(t)$. Of the remaining women, proportion who have the $(k+1)^{th}$ birth in year $(t+1)$ be denoted by $q_0(t+1)$. Of the remaining women, proportion who have the $(k+1)^{th}$ birth in year $(t+2)$ be denoted by $q_1(t+2)$, and so on. Thus, $q_E(t)$, $q_0(t+1)$, $q_1(t+2)$,............, gives a series of duration specific period parity progression ratios for the cohort who had the kth birth in year t. If duration specific period parity progression ratios can be computed for various birth cohorts, a matrix $\{q_i(u)\}$ where i stands for duration (i= E,0,1,2,........) and u for calendar year, can be obtained. From these, synthetic parity progression ratio, called period parity progression ratio from k^{th} to $(k+1)^{th}$ parity for various calendar years can be computed. The period parity progression ratio from k^{th} to $(k+1)^{th}$ parity for calendar year t is computed as:

$$1 - \{(1-q_E(t))\ (1-q_0(t))\ (1-q_1(t))\ (1-q_2(t))\ldots\} \quad (1)$$

Since the chances of having a succeeding birth after a long time, say 10 years, has elapsed or remote, values of $q_i(t)$ became very small and nearly 0 for i>10. As a result, the number of terms in the product is not large.

Now the question is how to calculate the rates q_E and q_x for progression from first birth to second birth. Suppose t is the calendar year for which the parity progression ratio from parity l to $l+1$ is to be computed.

Then, $$q_E = \frac{No.\ of\ women\ who\ had\ both\ 1^{th}\ and\ l+1^{th}\ birth\ in\ year\ t}{No.\ of\ women\ who\ had\ 1^{th}\ birth\ in\ year\ t}$$

$$q_x = \frac{No.\ of\ women\ who\ had\ l^{th}\ birth\ in\ year\ (t-x-l)\ and\ l+1^{th}\ birth\ in\ year\ t}{No.\ of\ women\ who\ had\ l^{th}\ birth\ in\ year\ (t-x-l)\ but\ did\ not\ have\ the\ l+l^{th}\ birth\ until\ the\ beginning\ of\ year\ t}$$

For the purpose of consistency in computing parity progression ratios from woman's own birth to first birth (parity 0 to 1), the product chain in equation (2) is truncated at the duration of 30 years. That is, any first births beyond the age of 30 are ignored and thus, the PPPR relates to the probability of having the first birth before the age of 31. Further, since no births are expected below the age of 15 years, q_E, q_0,..........q_{14} would be zero for the progression to the first parity. Equation (1) is then modified to,

$$PPPR\ (0\ to\ 1) = 1 - (1-q_{15})\ (1-q_{16})\ (1-q_{17})\ (1-q_{18})\ldots(1-q_{30}) \quad (2)$$

Calculation of Total Fertility Rate (TFR) based on Calculated Period Parity Progression Ratios

Let p_0 be the proportion of all women in a hypothetical birth cohort who experience a first birth, assuming no significant premarital fertility. Then the total fertility rate (TFR) can be expressed as

$$TFR = p_0 + p_0 p_1 + p_0 p_1 p_2 + \ldots\ldots \quad (3)$$

Each of terms in the right hand side of (3) has its own significance. The term p_0 represents the proportions of all women in the cohort who ever have a first birth, the term $p_0 p_1$ is the proportion of all women who ever have a second birth and so on. Thus, TFR calculated in this way is a sum of multiplicative components representing the contribution of each birth order.

To fulfill the second objective cross-tabulation has been done by taking children ever born (more than four) to the women of 40-44 age group with different socioeconomic and demographic characteristics among the different social categories.

Multiple regression analysis is used to find out several socioeconomic correlates of fertility among these social groups. In the regression analysis, children ever born in the women 40-44 age group is taken as a dependent variable. Here, only Hindu women are considered because Scheduled Castes mostly belong to only Hindu, Sikh and Buddhist religions. Though, Schedule Tribe and Other Backward Classes could belong to any religion.

Findings

Fertility Trends among Caste/Tribe in India

The PPPRs have been computed for periods of one year during 1987 to 2002 for progressions up to sixth parity. The findings in Table 6.1 show that the trend in the PPPR to the first parity, i.e., from the birth of woman to her first birth, for women belonging to all the caste/tribe categories it is smoothly increasing over the period 1987 to 2002 among all the social categories. Barring few inconsistencies in SC and ST for first to second parity, though declining, consistently for all the higher parities among all the caste/tribe categories, for this period, there is clear decline in PPPRs. For parity 0-1 and 1-2 the values are very high suggesting that most of the women in their fertile period go for child bearing, that is common. But, as they move for higher parity over the period of time differences in value of PPPRs among SC-ST and OBC-Others decreases, particularly, 1990 onwards it is remarkable. Even, among OBC and others it becomes remarkable. After the period of 1995-1998 for parity three and higher parities among all the caste/tribe categories this decline is relatively sharp. Clearly, the PPPRs indicate that SC-ST fertility from the very beginning was substantially higher than OBC, and more so with Others, for 2-3 parity the pace of decline is sharper from 1995 onwards.

By converting all these progressions in TFRs, these findings can be more simplified. As Table 6.2 suggests that there is clear difference in TFRs among SC-ST, OBC and Others from even 1987-1990. Though, there is not much difference in TFRs between SC (3.78) and ST (3.73), but it is lesser in OBCs (3.62) and much lesser in Others (3.29). More or less, these differences continue though, slowly narrowing down. This finding is comparable with NFHS II (1998-99) based TFR by social categories. According to Table 6.2 TFRs of different social categories for the period 1999-2002 was as 3.15 for SC, 3.14 for ST, 2.91 for OBC and 2.46 for Others, which are very close to the figures shown by NFHS II (1998-99).

Table 6.1

Period Parity Progression Ratios by Social Categories in India, DLHS-RCH, 2002-2004

Period	Woman's Birth to 1st Birth	Parity Progression Ratio				
		1 to 2	2 to 3	3 to 4	4 to 5	5 to 6
			SC			
1987-1990	0.9745	0.9018	0.8407	0.7540	0.6746	0.6699
1991-1994	0.9754	0.9113	0.8370	0.7239	0.6722	0.6487
1995-1998	0.9804	0.9049	0.8108	0.6854	0.6431	0.6423
1999-2002	0.9827	0.8678	0.7128	0.5996	0.5587	0.5539
			ST			
1987-1990	0.9528	0.8981	0.8420	0.7603	0.6957	0.6937
1991-1994	0.9688	0.9012	0.8353	0.7243	0.6552	0.6609
1995-1998	0.9815	0.9052	0.8090	0.7015	0.6661	0.6350
1999-2002	0.9879	0.8634	0.7140	0.5984	0.5603	0.5429
			OBC			
1987-1990	0.9673	0.9032	0.8009	0.7123	0.6765	0.6957
1991-1994	0.9749	0.902	0.7837	0.6795	0.6491	0.6624
1995-1998	0.9785	0.8955	0.732	0.6467	0.6378	0.6299
1999-2002	0.9848	0.8534	0.6261	0.5534	0.5565	0.5392
			Others			
1987-1990	0.9630	0.8917	0.7371	0.6484	0.6253	0.6292
1991-1994	0.9747	0.8832	0.6981	0.5819	0.5722	0.5922
1995-1998	0.9792	0.8570	0.6206	0.5433	0.5424	0.5546
1999-2002	0.9877	0.7917	0.4989	0.4387	0.4584	0.4650

Table 6.2

Total Fertility Rates (TFR) by Social Categories in India, DLHS-RCH, 2002-2004

Category	Period			
	1987-1990	1991-1994	1995-1998	1999-2002
SC	3.78	3.75	3.60	3.15
ST	3.73	3.68	3.64	3.14
OBC	3.62	3.52	3.34	2.91
Others	3.29	3.11	2.86	2.46

Fertility trends among caste/tribe categories can also be seen in Table 6.3 by the percentage contributions by birth order in TFR to understand the family building process and differences among them. This table suggests the secular trend of increasing percentage contribution from 1st and 2nd birth order among all the caste/tribe categories. But, among others this trend is sharper; during 1987-1990 it was 55.5 per cent that increased to 72.3 per cent in 1999-2002. Contributions from 3rd and higher birth order are consistently declining but it is sharper among OBCs and Others.

Table 6.3

Percentage of Multiplicative Birth Order Component to the Total Fertility Rate by Social Categories in India, DLHS-RCH, 2002-2004

	1st and 2nd Birth Order				*3rd and Greater Birth Order*			
	SC	*ST*	*OBC*	*Others*	*SC*	*ST*	*OBC*	*Others*
1987-1990	49.1	48.6	51.0	55.5	50.9	51.4	49.0	44.5
1991-1994	49.8	50.1	52.7	59.1	50.2	49.9	47.3	40.9
1995-1998	51.9	51.4	55.5	63.6	48.1	48.6	44.5	36.4
1999-2002	58.8	58.8	63.1	72.3	41.2	41.2	36.9	27.7

Fertility Differentials by Social Categories in India

There are several arguments that can be advanced relating to caste groups and fertility. An argument of a "particularised group belief and socio-political identity" suggests that group identity inherently influences fertility, irrespective of any socioeconomic or demographic factors. On the other hand, it can be also argued that fertility differentials are the outcome of differences in the socioeconomic characteristics of the members of different caste groups. It can be further argued that caste group differentials in fertility could be result of discrimination in access to health care and family planning services among various caste groups. However, caste is not a homogeneous group, they present very complex and distorted feature. A single caste is not spread all over India but the caste categorisation is. Dyson and Moore (1983) opined that regional factors outweigh any other socio-cultural factors as social groups of castes show more similarities with each other within the regional demographic regimes than they do with at all India level.

By dichotomising children ever born(CEB) in 'less than four' and 'more than four', we cross tabulated RCH-2 data and taken 'more than four CEB' in the age group of women 40-44 years as dependent variable. As Table 6.4 suggests, there is a sharp contrast in fertility by place of residence among all the social categories. This difference (rural-urban within the caste group) is highest among ST (19 per cent) and lowest among SC (14 per cent) while this difference among OBC and Others is almost equal. In urban area it is 33.1 per cent among SC and 16.2 per cent in others. Strikingly, here fertility among ST and OBC is closer than the SC-ST what we generally found.

Table 6.4

Percentage of Women having 'Children Ever Born' More than Four by Different Background Characteristics among Different Social Categories in India, DLHS-RCH, 2002-2004

		SC	*ST*	*OBC*	*Others*
Place of residence	Rural	47.2	44.4	40.5	33.4
	Urban	33.1	25.5	23.2	16.2
Standard of living index	Low	52.2	47.3	51.4	47.1
	Medium	37.0	34.5	30.6	29.1
	High	27.0	18.8	17.8	12.9
Level of education of the couple	Both are illiterate	51.7	48.1	51.5	49.7
	Any of them is up to primary	42.1	41.7	37.6	41.8
	Any of them is up to middle	40.7	42.9	34.7	32.2
	Any of them is up to secondary	36.2	28.6	27.5	22.9
	Any one of them is above secondary	26.5	19.8	15.6	10.2
Child loss	No child loss	24.1	27.2	19.0	14.8
	One child loss	55.4	50.9	50.8	44.8
	Child loss 2+	88.1	85.4	88.2	84.1
Electronic media	No	50.6	47.0	49.6	44.6
	Yes	36.4	33.2	25.7	19.1
Contraception type	No use or traditional	52.6	48.0	45.5	32.0
	Limiting	36.7	36.5	27.5	21.1
	Spacing or other modern method	48.3	44.2	40.7	22.9
Region	North	47.3	47.9	41.4	22.0
	East	45.7	46.2	51.6	31.6
	West	29.6	30.4	23.6	15.7
	South	24.9	27.2	14.1	13.5
	Central	67.9	57.6	59.3	42.6
	North-East	28.2	39.2	17.7	29.6
Age at consummation of marriage	<18	49.3	47.1	44.1	38.1
	18 and above	31.0	33.0	21.9	14.1

Fertility differences are less among these categories for low standard of living (SLI) households. But, as the SLI increases differences widened, for medium SLI, SC it is highest (37 per cent) and for medium SLI Others, it is lowest (29.1 per cent). SC-ST and OBC-Others are closer with each other. Even for high SLI fertility among SC is higher (27.0 per cent) in comparison with ST (18.8 per cent), OBC (17.8 per cent) and Others (12.9 per cent).

'Level of education of couples' (in spite of taking female education we consider couples' education because it shows statistically more significant result) is categorised in five classes. When both the partners are illiterate there are not much fertility differences as it moves around 50 per cent in all the social categories. In the case of primary or middle standard of education though, the trend is declining but, not remarkable among the same caste categories. While secondary (SC-36.2 per cent, ST-OBC-28 per cent, Others-22.9 per cent) and above secondary education (SC-26.5 per cent, ST-19.8 per cent, OBC-15.6 per cent, Others-10.2) accelerate the decline and also show differences within the same category and between the categories. The important finding of the study shows that child loss plays important role in fertility differences. If there is more than two child loss, almost 85 per cent respondents go for more than four children among all the social categories and in the case of one child loss around 50 per cent go for the same, in almost all categories. Further, the household having electronic media, 36 per cent SC go for more than four children while 19.1 per cent Others go for same. If, there is no electronic media then there is not much difference in fertility. Use of contraceptive type also plays important role in fertility differences. Even in case of no use or traditional method there is difference in fertility, as 52.6 per cent SC go for more than four children while only 32.0 per cent Others go for that. In limiting method also 36.7 per cent SC and 21 per cent Others go for that. In case of spacing method fertility level is very high among SC (48.3 per cent) in comparison with Others (22.9 per cent). Within the all caste categories limiting method shows low level of fertility but in the case of SC even in this method fertility is very high in comparison with other categories. Region also plays important role in fertility differences, as in western, southern and north-eastern region in general there is low fertility level but it is highest in central region and more or less similar in northern and eastern region, which is also high. Barring central region (42.6 per cent) and eastern region (31.6 per cent), Others are always on low fertility. Within the northern region there is not much difference among SC, ST and OBCs but Others have substantially low level of fertility. In the eastern region, OBC was having highest level of fertility but in northern, western, southern and north-eastern region ST was having highest fertility. Age at consummation of marriage also plays a remarkable effect on fertility. If it is below 18 years then cases of having more than four children is around 45-50 per cent among SC, ST and OBCs and 30 per cent in Others.

Socioeconomic and Demographic Correlates of Fertility among the Social Categories

Fertility itself is likely to be influenced by a number of socioeconomic variables such as education, economic status of the household, occupation, religion and caste/tribe status. According to Bongaarts and Potter (1983), socioeconomic factors must be the principal causes of fertility trends and differentials. In demographic literature, rising levels of education, especially of women, is widely regarded as the major factor in fertility decline (Zachariah, 1984; Cochrane, 1988 and Unisa and Bhagat, 2000). In the case of Indian fertility transition too, the paramount role of female education has been argued forcefully in recent years by Dreze and Murthi (2001). But in a recent paper, Bhat (2002) has argued that fertility is declining in India primarily because of its decline among illiterate women, and they are doing so because of the diffusion of a new reproductive idea of having only a few children but investing more on their future. The occurrence of this trade-off is probably aided by easier access to contraception, and increased exposure to mass media (Bhat, 2002).

It is also important to note that fertility decline is not necessarily preconditioned, but there can be very important inducement factor among the uneducated by the government efforts in the areas of family planning and ideational changes brought about by the mass media (Bhat, 2002). In fertility study, it is generally believed that socioeconomic factors affect fertility via some proximate determinants. Davis (1951) observed that in pre-independent India, a major factor influencing caste group fertility differentials was the extent of widow remarriage differences. Though, Bhat (2004) believes that the difference in widow remarriages among communities has disappeared now because of decline in mortality levels. Thus, it is no longer a factor affecting fertility differentials. Other proximate determinants of fertility like polygyny and its role in increasing fertility is rejected by Bongaarts *et al.* (1984), Bhat (2004). Furthermore, there is little difference in median age at first marriage of women (SC-15.2, ST-15.9 and Others-16.6 years among the women in the age group of 20-49 by current age-NFHS I) and there is no plausible reason to believe differences in proportion currently married among these social categories. It is also found that post-partum abstinence (SC 3.7, ST 3.5, Others 3.4 median number of months) and the average duration of post-partum non-susceptibility (SC 11.0, ST 12.3, Others 9.5 median number of months) along with post-partum amenorrhoea (SC 10.7, ST 12.0, Others 8.5 median number of months) doesn't vary much among these social categories (NFHS I). Thus, it is evident that much of the proximate determinants related to cultural practices are no longer significant in causing caste group differentials in fertility. In such a situation, family planning can be considered the most significant proximate determinant influencing caste group fertility differentials. There is strong relationship between economic status and place of residence. Mostly, poor people belong to rural and tribal areas. Proportion of households being rich was highest among general caste category followed by OBCs, SCs and STs in urban areas (Prasad and Chopra, 2006). As well as, the literacy rate was very low among SC (32 per cent) and ST (25 per cent). Ever married women belonging to higher income groups within each caste category were older than those of the poor income groups (Prasad and Chopra, 2006).

To comprehend determinants of fertility differentials we have done multiple regression analysis in which children ever born in the women 40-

44 age group is taken as a dependent variable. Here, only Hindu women are considered because Scheduled Caste could belong to only Hindu, Sikh and Buddhist religions. While we have considered, type of residence (urban/rural), age at consummation of marriage (less/greater than 18 years), child loss (no/one/two), household having electronic media (yes/no), standard of living (low/medium/high), region (north/east/west/south/central/north-east) and lastly the combination of five levels of education of couple (illiterate, primary, middle, secondary and above secondary) and three types of contraceptive practices (no use or traditional/limiting/spacing), as independent variables, in which the first category was taken as reference category.

This multiple regression analysis suggests that barring SC-ST, among all the categories, place of residence positively and significantly affects fertility differentials. It means as proportion rural increase CEB also increase. Likewise, if age at consummation of marriage (below 18 years) declines, CEB significantly increases. In comparison with no child loss, even a single child loss increase CEB among all these social categories. Household having electronic media is not significant among SC-STs but is significant among all other categories and its presence shows negative effect on CEB. Similarly, standard of living index is negatively affecting CEB but, even for medium SLI among SC-STs it is statistically insignificant and among STs even high SLI is insignificant. In comparison with northern, eastern, western, southern and north-eastern regions of India are negatively and significantly affecting CEB invariably among all these categories. Though, barring ST Central region is always at higher level of fertility then any other regions including northern. We can see the effect of combination of education of couple and contraceptive practices on CEB in Table 6.5. This table suggests that in comparison with illiterate couple not using any or using traditional contraceptive methods, limiting method in all educational categories of all the caste/tribe categories is negatively and significantly affecting CEB. Spacing method with up to middle level of education is positively affecting CEB and more so significantly among OBC-Others. No use or traditional method of contraception even from the primary level of education is negatively affecting the fertility of all the social categories. This suggests the important role of even minimal education in fertility decline.

Conclusion

There is still a wide gap of the level of fertility among caste/tribe categories, particularly this difference is widened from SC, ST, OBC to Others though within each category it is declining. After the period of 1995-1998 for parity three and higher parities among all the caste/tribe categories, this

Table 6.5

Regression Analysis Results of Children Ever Born (CEB) by Level of Education and Types of Contraception, India, DLHS-RCH, 2002-2004[Y]

	Hindu	*SC*	*ST*	*OBC*	*Others*
Illiterate no use or traditional[@]					
Illiterate					
Limiting	-0.177*	-0.240*	-0.286*	-0.113*	0.031*
Spacing	0.565*	0.259	0.529	0.812*	0.546*
Primary					
No use or traditional	-0.475*	-0.273	-0.596*	-0.631*	-0.325*
Limiting	-0.206*	-0.233*	-0.215	-0.247*	0.083*
Spacing	0.124	0.067*	0.277	0.129	0.302*
Middle					
No use or traditional	-0.388*	-0.415*	-0.570*	-0.445*	-0.122*
Limiting	-0.231*	-0.302*	-0.251	-0.241*	-0.032*
Spacing	0.222*	0.240	0.434	0.197*	0.241*
Secondary					
No use or traditional	-0.418*	-0.011	-0.773*	-0.415*	-0.399*
Limiting	-0.171*	-0.179*	-0.246	-0.175*	-0.031*
Spacing	-0.235*	-0.112	-0.460	-0.223*	-0.100*
Above Secondary					
No use or traditional	-0.874*	-0.902*	-0.817*	-0.760*	-0.773*
Limiting	-0.364*	-0.432*	-0.178	-0.336*	-0.245*
Spacing	-0.815*	-0.669*	-0.876*	-0.746*	-0.694*
Social Categories					
Scheduled Caste					
Scheduled Tribe	-0.164*				
Other Backward Caste	-0.138*				
Others	-0.418*				
Dependent variable: Total children ever born					

Note: @ reference category

* $p<0.05$

North: Jammu and Kashmir, Haryana, Punjab, Himachal Pradesh, Rajasthan, Delhi, Chandigarh, Uttarakhand

East: West Bengal, Bihar, Orissa, Jharkhand

West: Maharashtra, Gujarat, Goa, Daman&Diu, Dadra and Nagar Haveli

South: Kerala, Karnataka, Tamil Nadu, Andhra Pradesh, Pondicherry, Andaman, Lakshadweep

Central: Uttar Pradesh, Madhya Pradesh, Chhattisgarh

North-east: Sikkim, Tripura, Assam, Mizoram, Meghalaya, Manipur, Arunachal Pradesh, Nagaland

[Y] Some more socioeconomic characteristics of women have also been taken into account as the predictor variables in the Regression analysis. The entire table is not shown here.

decline is very sharp. Three-fourth of the total births are coming from mainly up to 2nd birth order among others though, half of the total births are contributed by up to 2nd order birth in SC, ST and OBCs, that accelerated from 1995 onwards. So, we can say that small family norms are taking place particularly after the mid-90s. There is sharp contrast in fertility by place of residence among all the caste/tribe categories. This difference (rural-urban within the caste group) is highest among ST (19 per cent) and lowest among SC (14 per cent). In comparison with no child loss, even a single child loss increases CEB among all these social categories. This suggests the potential impact of health care system, particularly maternal and child health, on fertility reduction. Similarly, standard of living index is negatively affecting CEB but, even for medium SLI among SC-ST it is insignificant and among ST even for high SLI it is insignificant. It suggests that economic standard of living is not sufficient to explain the fertility behaviour among the downtrodden of our society. Regional effect on CEB substantiate the logic of diffusion effect, and also suggests that informal channels of information are still more efficient in the penetration of new ideas and techniques of family control than the formal channels of any other media. Spacing method with up to middle level of education is positively affecting CEB and more so significantly among OBC-Others. This suggests the incapability of taking proper care without getting higher than middle level of education. The important role of even minimal education can help in fertility decline. From secondary onwards, level of education is negatively and significantly affecting CEB among all these categories. Household having radio/TV is not significant among SC-ST but, is significant among all other categories and its presence shows negative effect on CEB. It suggests that media can be effective only after a minimum level of education or awareness.

References

Beteille, A. (1971). *Caste, Class and Power*. California: California University Press.

Bhagat, R.B. (2006). "Census and Caste Enumeration: British Legacy and Contemporary Practice", *Genus* LXII(2): 1-17.

Bhat, Mari P.N. (2002). "Returning a Favour: Reciprocity Between Female Education and Fertility in India", *World Development* 30(10): 1791-1803.

———. (2004). "Religion in Demographic Transition: The Case of Indian Muslims", in *Demographic Change, Health Inequality and Human Development in India*. ed. by S. Irudaya Rajan and K.S. James. Hyderabad: Centre for Economic and Social Studies.

Bongaarts, J. and Potter, R.J. (1983). *Fertility, Biology and Behaviour: An Analysis of the Proximate Determinants*. New York: Academic Press.

Bongaarts, J., O. Frank and R. Lesthaeghe (1984). "The Proximate Determinants of Fertility in Sub-Saharan Africa", *Population and Development Review* 10(3): 511-537.

Chandra, B. and M. Mukherjee (1989). *India's Struggle for Independence*. India: Penguin Book.

Cochrane, S.H. (1988). *Effects of Education, Health and Social Security on Fertility in Developing Countries.* Washington, DC: World Bank.

Das, A.N. (1994). *India Invented: A Nation in the Making.* New Delhi: Manohar Publications.

Davis, K. (1951). *The Population of India and Pakistan.* Princeton: Princeton University Press.

Dreze, J. and M. Murthi (2001). "Fertility, Education and Development: Evidence from India", *Population and Development Review* 27(1): 33-63.

Dyson, T. and M. Moore (1983). "On Kinship Structure, Female Autonomy and Demographic Behaviour in India", *Population and Development Review* 9: 35-60.

Feeney, G. and Y. Jingyuan (1987). "Period Parity Progression Measures of Fertility in China", *Population Studies* 41: 77-102.

Feeney, G. and Y. Jianhua (1994). "Below Replacement Fertility in China? A Close Look at Recent Evidence", *Population Studies* 48: 381-394.

Gupta, D. (2004). "Introduction—The Certitude of Caste: When Identity Trumps Hierarchy", *Contributions to Indian Sociology* 38(1&2): 5-15.

Henry, L. (1980). "Fertility of Marriages: A New Method of Measurement", *Population Studies Translation Series* No. 3. New York: United Nations.

Holsinger, D.P. and J.D. Kasarda (1976). "Education and Human Fertility: Sociological Perspectives", in *Population and Development* Review (ed.) by G. Ridker. Baltimore: The Jhons Hopkins University Press.

IIPS and ORC Macro (2001). National Family Health Survey-2, India, 1998-99. Mumbai: International Institute for Population Sciences.

IIPS and GOI (2006). District Level Household Survey, 2002-2004. Mumbai: International Institute for Population Sciences.

Jones, K.W. (1981). "Religious Identity and Indian Census", in *Census in British India: New Perspectives* ed. by N.G. Barrier, New Delhi: Manohar Publishers.

Kaviraj, S. (1993). "The Imaginary Institution of India", in *Subaltern Studies VII* ed. by P. Chaterjee and G.Pandey. New Delhi: Oxford University Press.

Kothari, R. (1970). *Caste in Indian Politics.* Hyderabad: Orient Longman.

Nag, M. (1989). "Alternative Routes of Fertility and Mortality Decline: A Study of Kerala and Punjab", in *Population Transition in India* (ed.) by S.N. Singh *et al.* New Delhi: B.R. Publishing Corporation.

Prasad, C.V.S. and P.K. Chopra (2006). "Economic Differentials of Fertility and Pradhan, J. Among Scheduled Caste and Schedule Tribe Population in India", Paper Presented at International Conference on *Emerging Population Issues in the Asia Pacific Region: Challenges for the 21st Century.* Mumbai: IIPS.

Registrar General India (2004). *Provisional Population Total: Census of India, 2001.* New Delhi: Controller of Publication.

Singh, Yogendra (1988). *Modernisation of Indian Tradition.* New Delhi: Rawat Publication.

Srinivas, M.N. (1966). *Social Change in Modern India.* California: University of California Press.

Srinivasan, K., P. Reddy, and K. Raju (1977). "Changes Over a Generation in Fertility Levels and Values in Karnataka", *Occasional Paper* No. 2, Bangalore Population Research Centre.

Unisa, S. and R.B. Bhagat (2000). "Social Dimension of Fertility in India: Insights from a Regional Study", *International Journal of Anthropology* 15(1-2): 361-74.

Zachariah, K.C. (1984). *Determinants of Fertility Decline in India.* Washington: World Bank.

Appendix Table A-6.1a

Percentage of Multiplicative Birth Order Component to the Total Fertility Rate among SC in India

Period	Birth Order					
	1	2	3	4	5	6
1987	25.5	22.9	19.7	15.2	10.0	6.8
1988	25.9	23.2	19.5	14.7	9.9	6.8
1989	27.4	24.1	19.3	14.0	9.5	5.8
1990	24.5	22.9	19.8	15.2	10.3	7.3
1991	26.4	24.0	20.2	14.3	9.4	5.7
1992	24.7	22.9	19.6	15.0	10.6	7.2
1993	27.2	24.4	19.8	14.0	9.0	5.6
1994	25.9	23.6	19.9	14.3	9.7	6.6
1995	27.4	24.5	20.1	13.7	8.7	5.6
1996	26.2	24.0	19.9	14.4	9.4	6.2
1997	28.3	25.3	20.0	13.3	8.1	5.0
1998	27.1	24.7	19.9	13.4	9.0	5.9
1999	28.8	25.9	19.8	13.0	7.8	4.7
2000	29.5	26.4	19.8	12.5	7.4	4.4
2001	30.4	27.2	19.8	12.1	6.7	3.8
2002	37.4	29.5	17.9	8.9	4.4	2.0

Appendix Table A-6.1b

Percentage of Multiplicative Birth Order Component to the Total Fertility Rate among ST in India

Period	Birth Order					
	1	2	3	4	5	6
1987	25.0	22.7	19.5	14.5	10.5	7.8
1988	26.0	22.7	19.2	15.0	10.1	7.0
1989	27.0	24.1	19.2	14.1	9.4	6.2
1990	24.4	22.4	19.4	15.3	10.9	7.5
1991	27.9	24.4	19.9	13.9	8.4	5.5
1992	24.7	22.8	19.6	15.1	10.4	7.4
1993	27.6	24.5	19.9	13.6	8.9	5.6
1994	25.4	23.3	20.0	14.9	10.0	6.4
1995	27.9	24.7	19.7	13.6	8.8	5.4
1996	26.1	23.9	20.0	14.3	9.6	6.1
1997	27.1	24.6	19.4	13.6	9.4	5.9
1998	26.8	24.4	19.8	13.9	9.1	6.0
1999	29.1	26.1	19.9	12.8	7.6	4.4
2000	29.7	26.5	19.9	12.6	7.2	4.1
2001	32.2	27.6	19.4	11.3	6.2	3.4
2002	35.5	28.7	18.4	9.9	5.2	2.4

Appendix Table A-6.1c

Percentage of Multiplicative Birth Order Component to the Total Fertility Rate among OBC in India

	Birth Order					
Period	*1*	*2*	*3*	*4*	*5*	*6*
1987	25.7	23.6	19.6	14.0	9.8	7.3
1988	27.3	24.3	19.2	13.8	9.2	6.2
1989	28.6	25.2	18.9	13.1	8.5	5.7
1990	25.6	23.7	19.7	14.2	9.9	6.9
1991	28.0	25.2	19.9	13.3	8.4	5.3
1992	26.4	24.3	19.7	13.9	9.2	6.6
1993	28.9	25.6	19.4	12.7	8.2	5.1
1994	27.6	25.0	19.3	13.3	8.7	6.0
1995	29.6	26.3	19.4	12.5	7.6	4.6
1996	28.6	25.6	19.3	12.7	8.3	5.5
1997	30.2	26.8	19.0	12.0	7.5	4.4
1998	28.8	26.1	19.0	12.4	8.3	5.4
1999	31.1	27.6	19.0	11.5	6.8	4.0
2000	32.0	28.2	18.7	11.0	6.4	3.8
2001	33.9	29.3	18.2	10.1	5.5	3.0
2002	39.6	30.9	16.4	7.6	3.8	1.7

Appendix Table A-6.1d

Percentage of Multiplicative Birth Order Component to the Total Fertility Rate among Others in India

	Birth Order					
Period	*1*	*2*	*3*	*4*	*5*	*6*
1987	28.0	25.5	19.5	13.4	8.4	5.1
1988	29.3	25.8	19.3	12.5	7.8	5.4
1989	31.4	27.2	18.6	11.6	7.1	4.1
1990	28.7	26.2	19.6	12.4	8.0	5.1
1991	31.2	27.5	19.6	11.5	6.5	3.7
1992	29.6	26.9	19.6	12.0	7.3	4.7
1993	32.6	28.2	19.2	10.7	5.9	3.3
1994	32.3	28.2	19.0	10.8	6.1	3.6
1995	34.1	29.1	18.4	10.0	5.4	3.0
1996	33.3	28.9	18.4	10.4	5.8	3.1
1997	35.4	29.8	17.8	9.3	4.9	2.8
1998	34.2	29.4	18.2	9.8	5.4	3.0
1999	36.7	30.8	17.4	8.8	4.2	2.1
2000	37.9	31.3	16.8	8.0	4.0	2.0
2001	40.1	32.4	16.0	7.0	3.1	1.5
2002	47.2	32.8	13.1	4.4	1.8	0.7

Appendix Table A-6.2

Regression Analysis Results of Children Ever Born (CEB) by Level of Education and Types of Contraception, India, DLHS-RCH, 2002-2004

	Hindu 40-44	*SC 40-44*	*ST 40-44*	*OBC 40-44*	*Others 40-44*
(Constant)	4.409*	4.475*	4.451*	4.254*	3.863*
Place of residence					
Urban @					
Rural	0.142*	0.051	0.170	0.114	0.195
Age at consummation					
<18@					
> 18	0.429*	-0.415*	-0.366*	-0.375*	-0.478*
Experience of child loss					
0@					
1	1.093*	1.103*	0.953*	1.061*	1.128*
2+	2.779*	2.853*	2.787*	2.748*	2.697*
Education*Contraception					
Illiterate no use or traditional@					
Illiterate and limiting	-0.177*	-0.240*	-0.286*	-0.113*	0.031
Illiterate and spacing	0.565*	0.259	0.529*	0.812*	0.546*
Primary and no or traditional	-0.475*	-0.273*	-0.596*	-0.631*	-0.325*
Primary and limiting	-0.206*	-0.233*	-0.215	-0.247*	0.083
Primary and spacing	0.124*	0.067	0.277	0.129	0.302
Middle and no use or traditional	-0.388*	-0.415*	-0.570*	-0.445*	-0.122
Middle and limiting	-0.231*	-0.302*	-0.251*	-0.241*	-0.032
Middle and spacing	0.222*	0.240	0.434	0.197*	0.241*
Secondary and no use or traditional	-0.418*	-0.011	-0.773*	-0.415*	-0.399*
Secondary and limiting	-0.171*	-0.179*	-0.246	-0.175*	-0.031
Secondary and spacing	-0.235*	-0.112	-0.460	-0.223*	-0.100
Above secondary and no use or traditional	-0.874*	-0.902*	-0.817*	-0.760*	-0.773*
Above secondary and limiting	-0.364*	-0.432*	-0.178	-0.336*	-0.245*
Above secondary and spacing	-0.815*	-0.669*	-0.876*	-0.746*	-0.694*
Household have electronic media					
No@					
Yes	-0.049*	-0.040	0.058	-0.059*	-0.106*
Standard of living					
Low@					
Medium	-0.110*	-0.111	-0.104	-0.099*	-0.110*
High	-0.266*	-0.235*	-0.238	-0.246*	-0.245*
Region					
North@					
East	-0.347*	-0.472*	-0.641*	-0.065*	-0.474*
West	-0.509*	-0.502*	-0.678*	-0.621*	-0.427*
South	-0.973*	-0.943*	-0.977*	-1.021*	-0.895*
Central	0.285*	0.339*	-0.085	0.284*	0.357*
Northeast	-0.412*	-0.589*	-0.660*	-0.451*	-0.307*
Social Categories					
SC@					
ST	-0.164*				
OBC	-0.138*				
Other	-0.418*				

Note: @: reference category.

*: $p<0.05$.

7

Mortality Transition in India

ALOK RANJAN CHAURASIA

Introduction

This chapter attempts an analysis of transition in mortality in India during the 35 years between 1970 through 2005. The primary objective of the chapter is to highlight salient features of changes in age patterns of mortality in India and in its constituent states in the recent past. Transition in mortality reflects improvements in the health and nutritional status of the population and hence improvements in the quality of life. Mortality transition, therefore, is regarded as a necessary requirement for improvements in the standards of living (United Nations, 1973). Mortality levels and trends also reflect the transition in health of the people. In recent years, poor state of health in India has been highlighted in a number of studies (Peters *et al.*, 2002) and the Government of India has launched the National Rural Health Mission to induce architectural corrections in the public health care delivery system in the country (Government of India, 2007).

Analysis of mortality transition is also expected to contribute to the evolution of the health policy and in analysing its impact of the policy in terms of the quality of life. Ideally, there should be congruence between mortality transition and evolution of the health policy as implementation of the health policy has a direct reflection on mortality transition through improvements in the health status of the population. On the other hand, evolution of health policy should essentially be a response to the health status of the population which has a reflection in the prevailing levels of mortality. It is well known that with the improvement in the health status of the population, the disease profile changes, there is a shift in the patterns of causes of death and there is a transition in the age pattern of mortality. The evolution of the health policy, therefore, should be a response to mortality transition.

The expectation of life at birth is the most widely used indicator of the level of mortality of a population. It is also the most widely used indicator for analysing trends and differentials in mortality (Pollard, 1982). The expectation of life at birth is essentially a synthetic measure of the level of mortality as it gives the number of years; a newborn is expected to survive, on an average, to prevailing age-specific death rates. The relationship between mortality transition and improvements in expectation of life at birth is essentially reciprocal but the exact connection is more complicated. Since analysis of mortality transition requires examination of the changes in the age-specific mortality rates, such an analysis results in numerous comparative indexes. As such, a single index of mortality is generally preferred, although there is no single summary measure of mortality that can replace the age-specific mortality rates. Indexes of mortality proposed in this regard are generally of two types: aggregative index such as directly standardised mortality rates that reflect absolute difference between corresponding age-specific mortality rates; and average of relative indexes which reflect proportional difference between those rates (Schoen, 1970). Spiegelman and Marks (1966) and Kittagawa (1964) have examined a number of suggested mortality indexes and discussed there advantages and drawbacks. Kittagawa (1966) has found that use of different indexes of mortality may provide different picture of mortality transition over time. In case of aggregative indexes, there are also problems of choosing appropriate standard population for weighing the age-specific mortality rates and various factors involved in the selection of the standard are of appreciable significance (Speigelman and Marks, 1966). On the other hand, there is no widely accepted average of relative index that is intuitively simple, easy to calculate, expressive of underlying mortality function and independent of the choice of a 'standard' population. It therefore, seems reasonable to focus attention on differences in the pattern of death rates over the whole spectrum of ages (Schoen, 1970).

In this chapter, we follow the life table approach of analysing mortality transition. This approach focuses on how changes in age-specific mortality rates contribute to the expectation of life at birth. Two ways have been suggested in this regard. The first is to analyse how the difference between two mortality schedules translates into the difference between the resulting expectation of life at birth (Pollard, 1982; United Nations, 1982). The second, on the other hand, focuses on how the rate of progress in mortality translates into the rate of progress in life expectancy (Keyfitz, 1977). The first approach has been applied by the author to analyse mortality transition in urban India (Chaurasia, 2006). In this chapter, we apply the approach pioneered by Keyfitz.

The chapter is organised as follows. The next section of the chapter describes the data source used for the analysis; third section discusses levels and trends in the expectation of life at birth; fourth section estimates and analyses trends and differentials in the probability of survival up to age 70 and contribution of the change in the survival probability in different age groups; fifth section measures entropy in the life tables and analyses trends and differentials in entropy. Finally, the last section of the chapter discusses the implications of mortality transition in the context of health policy.

Data Source

The present analysis is based on the life tables prepared on the basis of the age-specific death rates available through the Sample Registration System. The Sample Registration System is a large-scale demographic survey that provides annual estimates of key demographic indicators at national and sub-national levels. Initiated in 1964-65, the system is now operational in all the states and union territories. In the year 2004, the urban sample covered under the system consisted of 3164 sampling units covering a population of 1.798 million. The sample is replaced at every 10 years based on the latest sample frame in a staggered manner. However, in the year 2004, replacement of the sample was carried out in one go. Information on demographic events is collected under the system through a dual record procedure which consists of continuous enumeration by resident part time enumerators and independent survey every six months. Data obtained from these two independent sources are matched and unmatched and partially matched events are re-verified.

The annual rates estimated on the basis of the sample registration system have, however, been found to be associated with random fluctuations of unknown origin. To eliminate these random fluctuations, death rate in different age groups are averaged for a period of five years and these average death rates are used for the construction of life tables. One problem in using the life tables so prepared is that they are based on different methodologies of converting the observed age-specific death rate to the life table function ${}_nq_x$. The life tables for the periods 1971-1975, 1976-1980 and 1981-1985 are based on Greville's method (Greville, 1948) whereas life tables for the period 1986-1990 onwards are prepared by using the MortPak-Lite software package developed by the United Nations (United Nations, 1988). The methodology of MortPak-Lite software package uses a different approach of converting the observed age-specific death rates to the life table function ${}_nq_x$.

Expectation of Life at Birth in India

According to the Sample Registration System, the expectation of life at birth in India was 49.7 years during the period 1970-1975 which increased to 63.2 years during the period 2001-2005. This means that the average life of an Indian increased by about 13.5 years in the 30 years between 1970-1975 and 2001-2005 at an average annual rate of about 0.45 years per year. The increase in the average life of a male was, however, slower than that of a female. During the 30 years under reference, the male expectation of life at birth, in India, increased by around 11.8 years from 50.5 years during 1970-1975 to 62.3 years during 2001-2005 at an average annual rate of increase of less than 0.40 years per year. By contrast, the female expectation of life at birth increased by almost 15 years at an average annual rate of almost 0.50 years per year during this period.

The increase in the expectation of life at birth has been more rapid in rural as compared to the urban areas. In the rural areas, the expectation of life at birth increased by around 13.8 years between 1970-1975 and 2001-2005 whereas this increase was only around 9.6 years in the urban areas. Moreover, increase in the female expectation of life at birth has been more rapid than the increase in the male expectation of life at birth in both rural and urban areas of the country. In the urban areas of the country, the male expectation of life at birth increased by only about 8 years between 1970-1975 and 2001-2005 at an average annual rate of increase of just 0.27 years per year.

It is possible to characterise the increase in the expectation of life at birth in India by comparing the actual increase in male and female expectation of life at birth with the global model mortality improvement schedules developed by the United Nations (United Nations, 2004). The Population Division of the United Nations has developed five model mortality improvement schedules on the basis of the empirical evidence about the increase in the expectation of life at birth during the period 1950 to 2005 with the expectation of life at birth ranging between 50 to 85 years. These model mortality improvement schedules represent the average experience of improvement in mortality in the world during this period and are grouped according to the 90th percentile (very fast increase), the 75th percentile (fast increase), the arithmetic mean (medium increase), the 25th percentile (slow increase) and the lowest 10th percentile (very slow increase). The model mortality improvement schedules so obtained have then been extended to cover the levels of expectation of life at birth ranging from 40 years to 92.5 years by fitting the Lee-Carter mortality model (United Nations, 2004a). They have been expressed as average annual increments in the expectation of life at birth for a given level of expectation of life at birth. A comparison of actual increase in the expectation of life at birth in India as evident from the life tables based on the Sample Registration System with the expected increase according to the five model mortality improvement schedules developed by the United Nations provides the basis for characterising the improvement in the expectation of life at birth in the country and the pace of mortality transition.

Figure 7.2 compares the actual increase in the expectation of life at birth in India with the expected increase in the expectation of life at birth in the five model mortality improvement schedules. It may be seen from the figure that there has been a considerable slowdown in mortality improvement in both males and females in India after 1991-1995. Prior to 1991-1995, the male expectation of life at birth in India followed the medium trajectory of model mortality improvement schedules but after 1991-1995, there has been considerable slowdown in mortality improvement so that by the period 2001-2005, the male expectation of life in the country could increase to only 62.3 years which corresponds to the slow trajectory of model mortality improvement schedule of the United Nations. A similar trend may also be observed in case of female expectation of life at birth. Prior to 1981-1985, the increase in female expectation of life at birth in the country followed the very fast trajectory of model mortality improvement schedule. Between 1981-1985 and 1991-1995, increase in the female expectation of life at birth followed the medium trajectory but, after 1991-1995, there was a considerable slowdown in mortality improvement so that, during the period 2001-2005, female expectation of life at birth in India was very close to the slow trajectory of model mortality improvement schedule.

The pattern of increase in the expectation of life at birth in the rural and urban areas of the country has been different. The trend in the male expectation of life at birth in the rural areas has been very similar to the trend in the combined population. By contrast, the trend in the female expectation of life at birth followed very fast to fast trajectory till the period 1991-1995 but slowed down thereafter so that the female expectation of life at birth during the period 2001-2005 was in conformity with the medium trajectory of model mortality improvement. In the urban areas, on the other hand, improvement in mortality has been slower than that in rural areas with the increase in the male expectation of life at birth in the urban India being even slower than the very slow trajectory of model mortality improvement schedule of the United Nations till 1986-1990. It was only after 1986-1990, that the pace of improvement in the male expectation of life at birth in the urban areas accelerated marginally, although, the increase in the male expectation of life at birth in urban India has always been slower than the slow trajectory of model mortality improvement schedules.

Figure 7.1

Expectation of Life at Birth in India

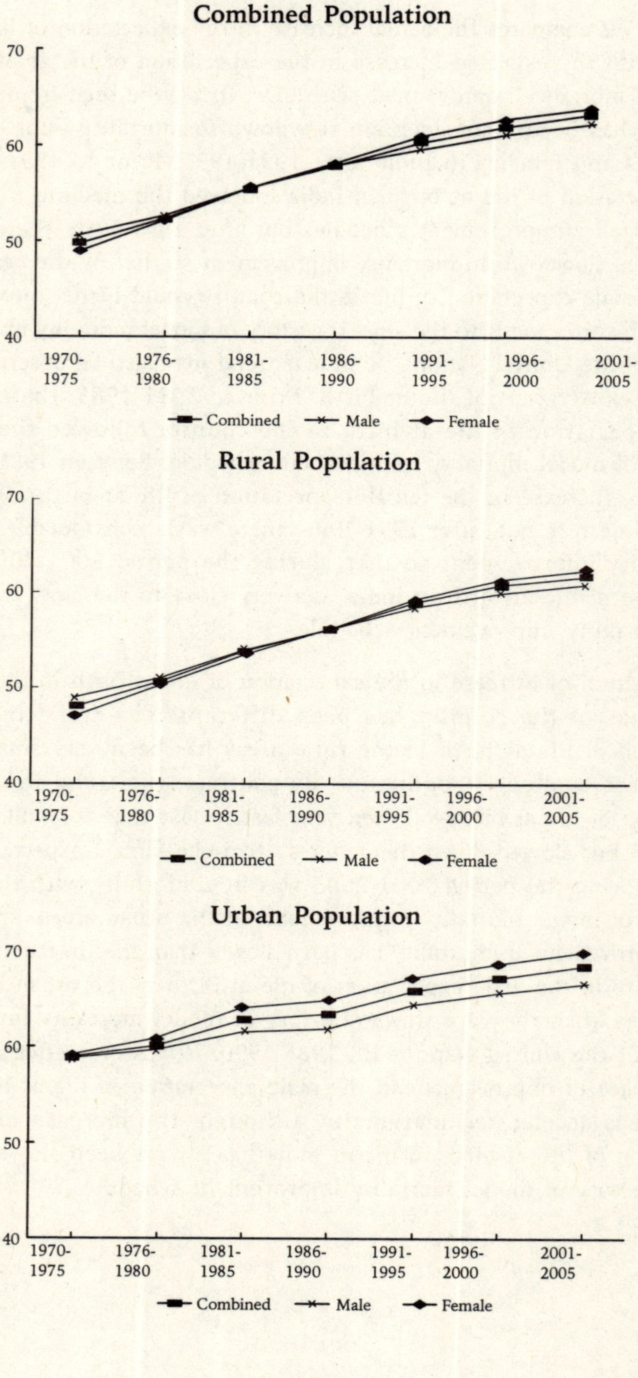

Figure 7.2

Trends in the Expectation of Life at Birth in India, 1970-2005

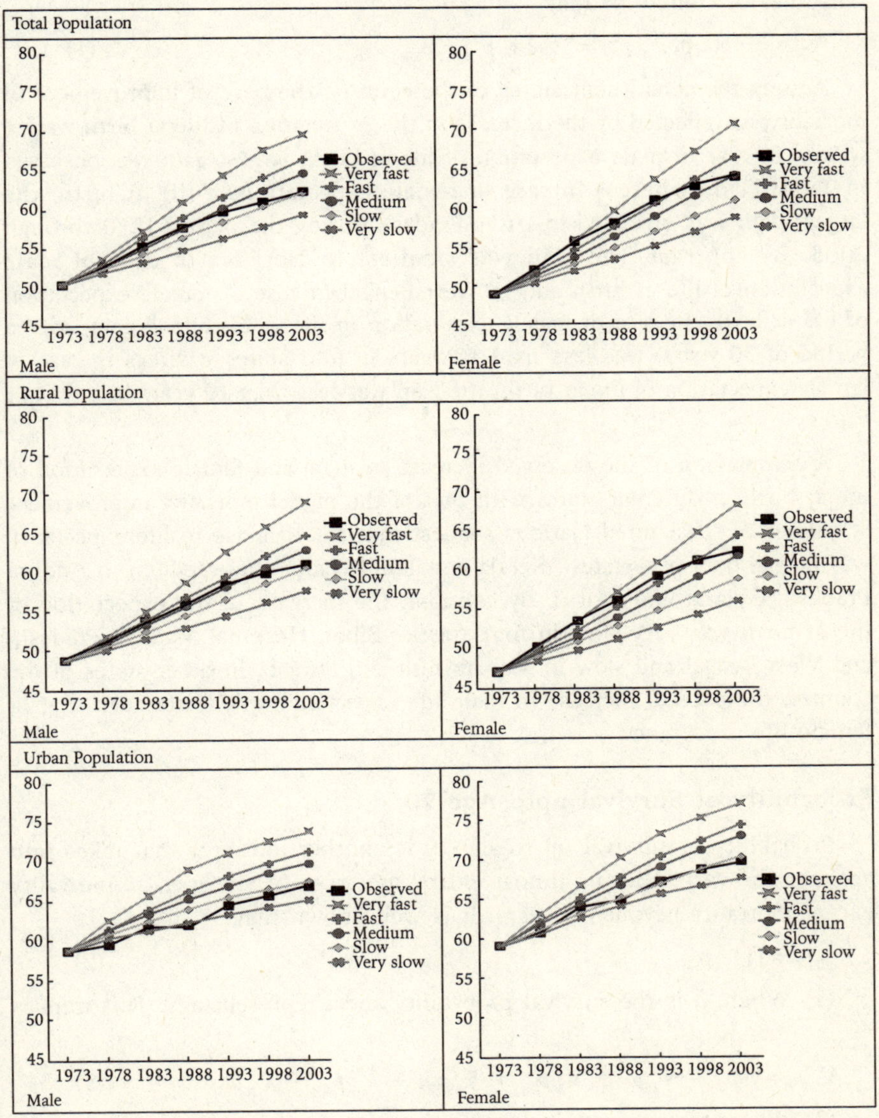

The increase in the female expectation of life at birth in the urban India, on the other hand, has also been very slow during the period 1970-1975 through 1976-1980 but it accelerated quite substantially during 1976-1980 through 1981-1985 but decelerated during 1981-1985 through 1986-1990.

After 1986-1990, the increase in the female expectation of life at birth in India has followed the slow trajectory of model mortality improvement schedules of United Nations.

$$\nabla_{70}p_0 = ln({}_{70}p_0^2 / {}_{70}p_0^1) = \sum_{i=1}^{70} ln({}_1p_{i-1}^2 / {}_1p_{i-1}^1 \quad (1)$$

Among the constituent states of the country, the pace of improvement in mortality, as reflected by the increase in the expectation of life at birth, varied widely. In case of male expectation of life at birth, largest gain was observed in Tamil Nadu whereas in case of female expectation of life at birth, the largest gain was observed in Uttar Pradesh during the period 1970 through 2005. By contrast, the gain was smallest in Haryana in case of male expectation of life at birth and in West Bengal in case of female expectation of life at birth. In case of male's expectation of life at birth, the gain, over a period of 30 years, was less than 10 years in four states whereas in case of female expectation of life at birth, the gain was less than 10 years in only two states.

A comparison of the observed increase in male and female expectation of life at birth in different states with that of the model mortality improvement schedules of the United Nations suggest that the increase in life expectancy was fast in only two states—Kerala and Tamil Nadu—and medium in Andhra Pradesh, Gujarat and Orissa. By contrast, the increase in the expectation of life at birth was very slow in four states—Bihar, Haryana, Madhya Pradesh, and West Bengal and slow in Maharashtra and Punjab. In other states of the country, the pace of increase in male life expectancy was faster than that of female life expectancy.

Probability of Survival upto Age 70

Probability of survival up to age 70 is another indicator that takes into account the variability in almost entire spectrum of age-specific mortality except mortality beyond 70 years. It is well known that

$${}_{70}p_0 = \prod_{i=1}^{70} {}_1p_{i-1} \quad (2)$$

(1) Where p is the survival probability and i represent age. This implies that

$$\nabla_{70}p_0 = \nabla_5p_0 + \nabla_{15}p_5 + \nabla_{30}p_{15} + \nabla_{45}p_{30} + \nabla_{60}p_{45} + \nabla_{70}p_{60} \quad (3)$$

(2) Where the superscript denotes the time. Equation (2) shows that the change in the probability of survival up to age 70 is the algebraic sum of the change in the probability of survival at different ages of the age interval 0-70 years.

(3) Clearly this suggests that the change in the probability of survival up to age 70 can be decomposed into changes in survival probability in different ages.

Information available through the Sample Registration System suggests that the probability of survival up to age 70 in India was around 32 per cent during the period 1970-1975 which increased to around 53 per cent during the period 2001-2005. This means that out of every 1000 live born, around 322 are expected to have survived to the 70 years of age when subjected to the age-specific mortality rates that prevailed in the country during the period 1970-1975 whereas the expected number to have survived to 70 years of age was around 529 when subjected to age-specific mortality rates prevailed in the country during the period 2001-2005. In other words, the probability of survival up to 70 years of age in India improved by about 62 per cent during the 30 years period between 1970-1975 and 2001-2005 at an average annual rate of 1.65 per cent per year.

The improvement in the probability of survival up to 70 years of age during the period under reference has been faster in rural (1.70 per cent per year on average) as compared to urban areas (1.17 per cent per year). Similarly, the rate of improvement has been faster in females as compared to males in the combined population as well as in rural and urban populations separately. Among the different population groups, the slowest improvement in the probability of survival up to 70 years of age has been observed in urban males (1.1 per cent per year on average) whereas the fastest improvement has been observed in case of rural females (1.90 per cent per year). As the result of this differential rate of increase in the survival probability, the female-male gap in the probability of survival up to 70 years of age has widened over time in the country.

The rate of change in probability of survival up to age 70 can be decomposed into the rate of change in the probability of survival in different age groups according to equation (3). This decomposition exercise suggests that most of the improvement in the probability of survival up to age 70 in India has been the result of improvement in survival probability (58 per cent) while improvement in survival probability in the age group 0-5 years accounted for about 25 per cent of the improvement in the probability of survival up to age 70. This pattern has been found to be more or less similar in the rural and urban populations as well as among males and females.

Figure 7.3

Average Annual Rate of Improvement in the Probability of Survival in India, 1970-2005

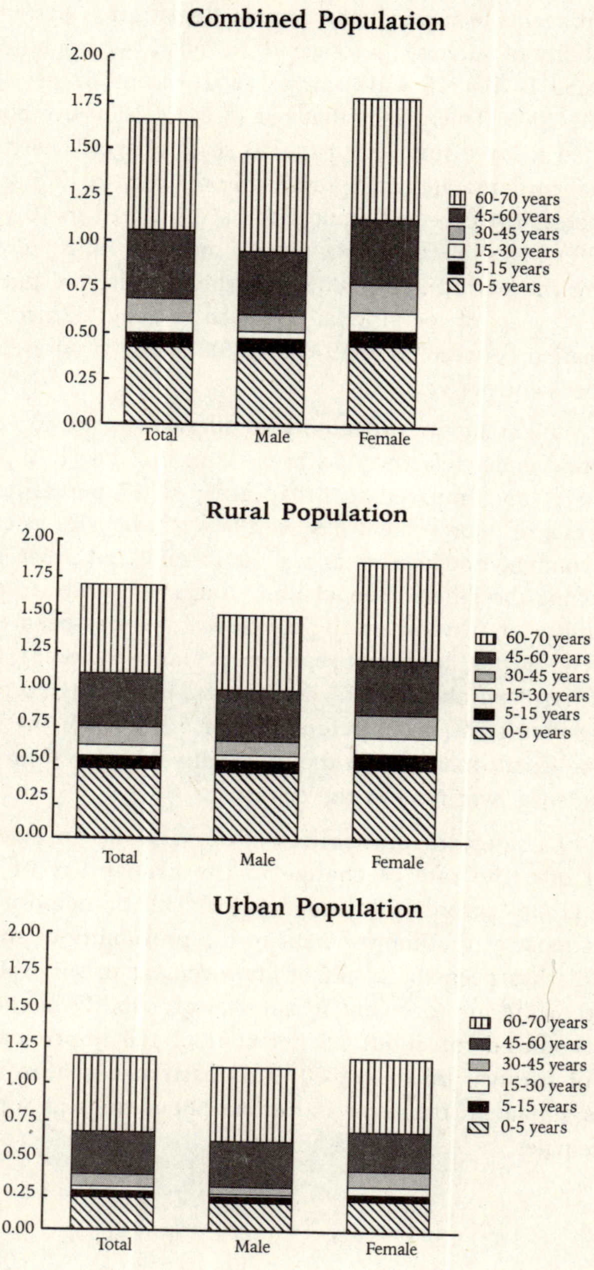

Figure 7.4

Average Annual Rate of Improvement in Probability of Survival up to 70 in Different Quinquennials in India, 1970-2005

Combined Population

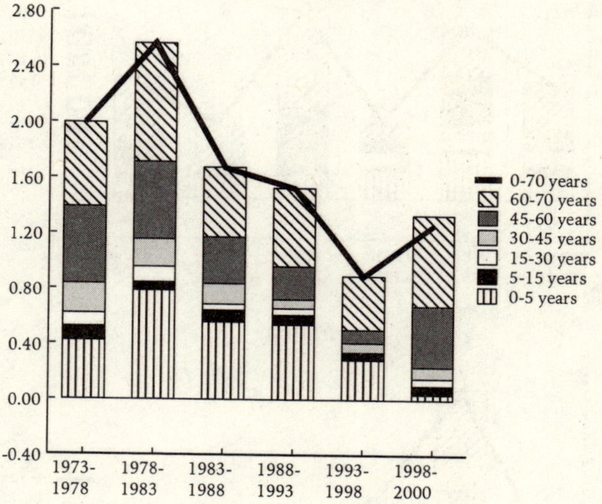

Rural Population

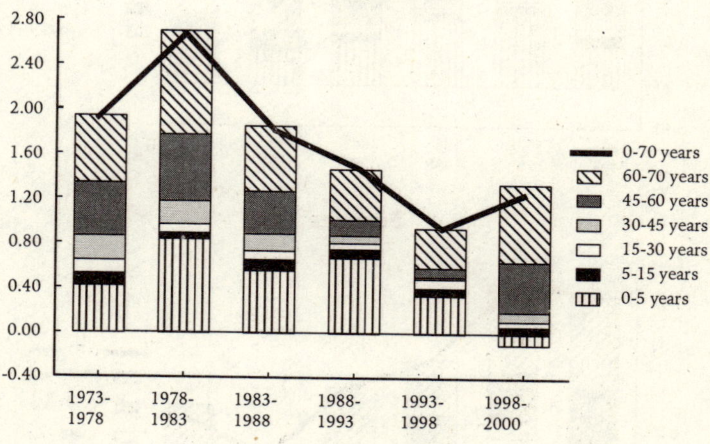

Urban Population

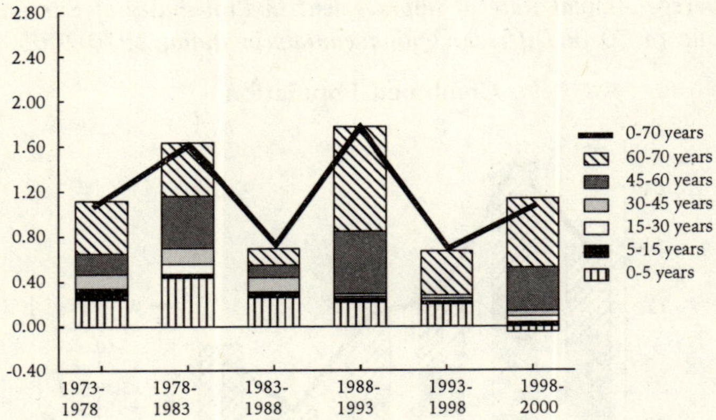

Males

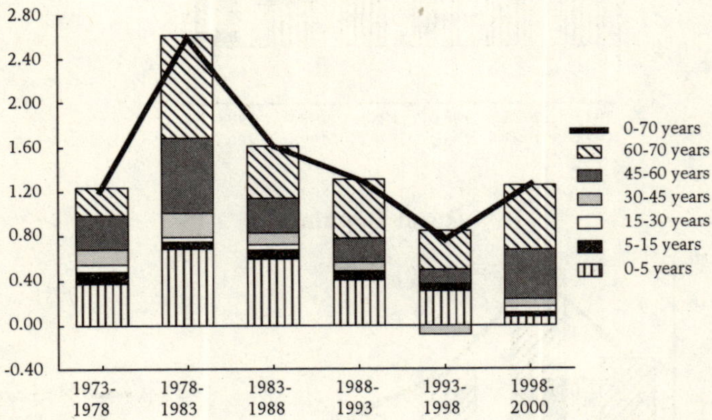

Females

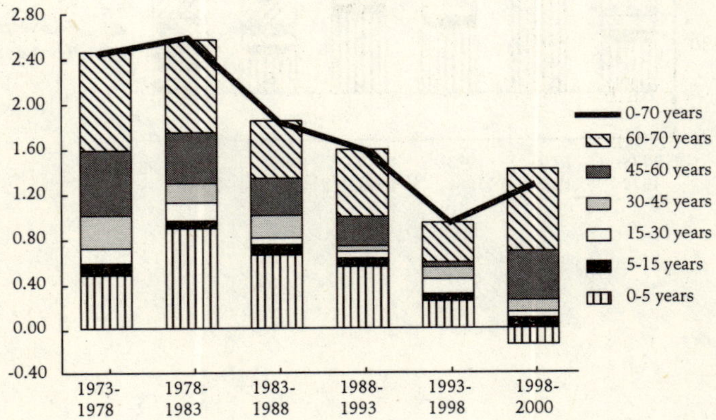

Improvement in the probability of survival up to age 70 has, however, not been uniform in different quinquennials of the period 1970-1975 through 2001-2005. Largest gain in the probability of survival up to age 70 was recorded during the period 1976-1980 through 1981-1985 while the gain was the least during the period 1991-1995 through 1996-2000. During the period 1976-1980 through 1996-2000, there has been a deceleration in the improvement in survival probability up to age 70 years. It was only after 1996-2000 that the improvements in the survival probability up to age 70 accelerated again. Moreover, the improvements in the survival probability up to age 70 have always been larger in females as compared to males whereas the deceleration in the improvement has been faster in males as compared to females.

Another discerning feature of the trend in the probability of the survival in different age groups is that the improvement in the probability of survival in the first five years of life decelerated sharply since 1976-1980 and during the period 1996-2000 to 2001-2005, the probability of survival in this age group actually decreased instead of increasing. As a result, the improvement in the probability of survival up to age 70 during the period 1996-2000 through 2001-2005 had largely been the result of the improvement in the probability of survival in the age group 45-70 years. The decrease in the probability of survival in the first five years of life in India during the period 1996-2000 to 2001-2005 has been the result of the increase in female mortality during the first five years of life as the male probability of survival in the first five years of life continued to improve during this period in both rural as well as urban areas of the country.

Among the constituent states, the probability of survival up to 70 years of age varies widely. As expected, highest probability of survival up to 70 years has been recorded in Kerala while the probability of survival up to 70 years of age has been estimated to be the lowest in Madhya Pradesh. There are only two states in India—Kerala and Punjab—where more than 60 per cent of the birth cohort was expected to survive up to 70 years when subjected to mortality levels prevailing during the period 2001-2005. By contrast, in Assam, Madhya Pradesh, Orissa and Uttar Pradesh, this proportion is still less than 50 per cent. Moreover, except Bihar, the probability of survival up to 70 years of age has been found to be higher in females as compared to males. Bihar is the only state in the country where female probability of survival up to 70 years of age is still lower than the male survival probability.

The rate of improvement in the probability of survival up to 70 years of age also varies from state to state. In general, it is observed that lower is the probability of survival up to 70 years of age during the period 1970-1975, the higher is the rate of improvement during the period 1970-1975 through 2001-2005. The exceptions to this pattern are Madhya Pradesh, Haryana, Punjab and Andhra Pradesh. In Madhya Pradesh, Haryana and Punjab, the rate of improvement in the probability of survival up to 70 years of age has been found to be exceptionally slow despite low levels of survival probability during the period 1970-1975. By contrast, the rate of improvement has been the fastest in Andhra Pradesh.

Survival Probability and Life Expectancy

How has improvements in survival probability influenced the expectation of life at birth? The dynamic relationship between the probability of survival and life expectancy can be approximated by the quantity H developed by Keyfitz (1977) and referred as entropy in the life table by Demetrius (1979). Entropy (H) can also be interpreted as a measure of heterogeneity of a population with respect to mortality at different ages (Vaupel, 1986). It is well known that with the decline in mortality, more and more deaths gets concentrated in the old ages and so the survival curve turns more and more rectangular. The change in the shape of the survival curve as the result of transition in mortality can be captured through entropy. In this way, it measures the impact of changes in the age-specific mortality rates on the expectation of life at birth (Demetrius, 1979; Goldman and Lord, 1986; Keyfitz, 1977). In its most simple conceptualisation, entropy (H) gives the proportional change in the expectation of life at birth as the result of a reduction of 1 per cent in the force of mortality at all ages. The value of H depends directly upon the concavity of the survivorship curve. If everyone dies at the same age, $H=0$; if the force of mortality is the same at all ages, $H=1$. When the force of mortality declines linearly with age, the value of H lies halfway between those described above, i.e., $H=1/2$. A high degree of life table entropy implies that the distribution of deaths by age is widely dispersed over the entire age range. In situations of a low degree of entropy, the dispersion of the distribution of deaths by age is small which means that deaths are concentrated in a very narrow age range (Glei and Horiuchi, 2007; Nusselder and Makenbach, 1996; Wilmoth and Horiuchi, 1999). An important result from formal demography is that the decline in mortality in the presence of high degree of life table entropy is associated with a very rapid increase in the expectation of life at birth. The reason is that a high proportion of deaths averted would have occurred among infants and young children.

Since the mortality risk in the adolescence and in the young adulthood are relative low, mortality decline in the youngest ages yields a much higher return in terms of the expectation of life at birth than the mortality decline in older ages. In situations of low entropy, deaths are concentrated at the older ages and so return in life expectancy as the result of an equivalent proportional reduction in mortality is considerably less (Wilmoth, 2001). Empirical evidence suggests that the historic rise in the expectation of life at birth was accompanied by a large reduction in entropy. For example, increase in life expectancy from 55 years in 1940 to 74 years in 1981 in the United States was associated with a decrease in entropy 0.37 to 0.16 (Goldman and Lord, 1986). In Sweden, entropy decreased from 0.772 to 0.157 as male life expectancy increased from 33.7 years in 1800 to 72.7 years in 1980 (Vaupel, 1986).

In India, life table entropy decreased from 0.352 during 1970-1975 to 0.188 during 2001-2005. This means that during 1970-1975, a one per cent reduction in the force of mortality in all ages would have resulted in an increase in the expectation of life at birth by about 0.35 per cent. By contrast, during the period 2001-2005, a one per cent decrease in the force of mortality would have resulted in an increase of only about 0.19 per cent in the expectation of life at birth. The decline in entropy reflects the concentration of deaths at older ages. If the rate of decline in entropy is low than the pace of concentration of deaths at older ages is also slow.

The average annual rate of decline in entropy in India is shown in Table 7.6 for different quinquennials of the period 1970-2005. The rate of decline in entropy in the country was highest during the period 1976-1980 through 1981-1985. Since then, the rate of decline in entropy has decelerated rapidly. This implies that the rate of concentration of deaths at older ages is increasingly slowing down in the country. As a result, the increase in the expectation of life at birth has also slowed down. This proportion was about 0.33 per cent in males and 0.37 per cent among females, which means, marginally faster increase in female as compared to males. Similarly, in the rural areas of the country, a reduction of 1 per cent in the force of mortality at all ages would have resulted in an increase of about 0.38 per cent in the expectation of life at birth during 1970-1975, compared to only 0.20 per cent during 2001-2005 corresponding to the increase in the urban areas of the country. It may also be seen from Table 7.6 that in most of the quinquennials of the period 1970-2005, the rate of decline in entropy in females has been faster than males. Similarly, the rate of decline in entropy has been faster in rural than in urban areas till the period 1996-2000. However, the trend has changed after 1996-2000. Between 1996-2000 and 2001-2005, the rate of decline in entropy has been faster in males as compared to females and in urban areas as compared to rural areas. This means that the shift in the concentration of deaths to older ages has slowed down in females and in rural areas in recent years, compared to the shift in males and in urban areas respectively.

Figure 7.5

Levels and Trends in Life Table Entropy in India, 1970-2005

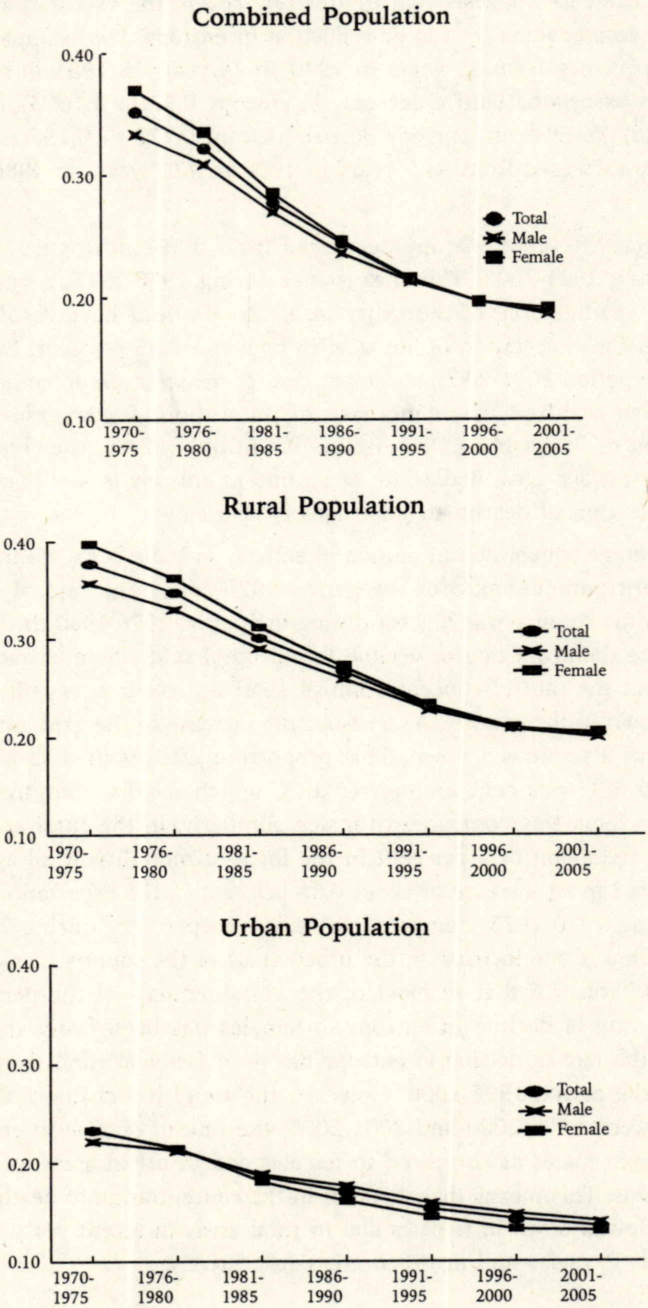

Among constituent states of the country, life table entropy varies widely. In Assam, Bihar, Madhya Pradesh, Orissa, Rajasthan and Uttar Pradesh, life table entropy was estimated to be more than 0.20 during the period 2001-2005 with largest entropy estimated in Madhya Pradesh. A value of entropy higher than 0.20, indicates that the distribution of deaths by age still has a high degree of dispersion. Deaths, in these states, are distributed over a broad age range. By contrast, Kerala is the only state in the country where the life table entropy has been estimated to be less than 0.10 during the period 2001-2005 which shows that the dispersion in the distribution of deaths by age in Kerala is small and nearly all deaths in Kerala are concentrated in older age groups. At the same time, the rate of decrease in life table entropy in Madhya Pradesh has been the second slowest in the country whereas it has been the fastest in Kerala during the period under reference. The rate of improvement in the probability of survival up to age 70 is also very slow in Madhya Pradesh despite the fact that mortality levels in these states are amongst the highest in the country.

Conclusions

Main conclusions of the analysis presented in the foregoing pages can be summarised as follows:

- The expectation of life at birth in India was around 62 years during the period 2001-2005. This shows that India has to go a long way as far as transition in mortality is concerned.
- By international standards, the rise in the expectation of life at birth in India has been slow. Moreover, there are indications that transition in mortality has slowed in the country despite the fact that expectation of life at birth.
- The probability of survival has improved in the country but most of the improvement in the survival probability has been confined to age 40 years and above. The rate of improvement in the probability of survival in the first five years of life has decelerated over time. Among the females, the probability of survival in the first five years of age has decreased, instead of increasing, in recent years.
- The transition in the concavity of the survival curve has shown down over the years. This shows that the shift in the concentration of deaths at older ages has slowed down.
- There are significant inter-state variations not only in the levels but also in the rate of change in different measures of mortality.

The analysis obviously presents a relatively bleak picture of mortality transition in the country. Unfortunately, mortality transition has been equated with the evolution and expansion of the health care delivery system, especially in the rural areas. The gross neglect of urban areas in the evolution of health policy is well reflected in terms of slow to very slow rise in life expectancy in urban areas despite the fact that the current levels of the expectation of life at birth in the urban areas remains low by international standards.

Another area of concern is the deceleration in the probability of survival in the first five years of life after 1991-1995. Interestingly, major efforts were initiated after 1995 to bring down the infant and child mortality in the country in the form of the reproductive and child health programme. The trends in the probability of survival in the first five years of life, however, suggests that there has been little impact of the reproductive and child health on the survival probability in the first five years of life.

The analysis presented here clearly highlights the limitations of the current approach of mortality reduction in India. One limitation of the current approach is that it is limited to the expansion and strengthening of the health care delivery system, especially, the public health care delivery system. Very little attention has so far been given to the non-medical determinants of mortality and how to address them. Even in much talked about National Rural Health Mission, launched in 2005, also focuses on the architectural corrections in the health care delivery system through increased public spending, decentralisation of the public health care delivery system and involvement of the community in managing and controlling health care at the grass roots level. A pragmatic, multi-dimensional approach towards mortality transition is still lacking in India.

References

Chaurasia, Alok Ranjan (2006). "Mortality Transition in Urban India: 1971-2002". Delhi: Institute of Economic Growth. *Discussion Paper No.* 113/2006.

Demetrius, L. (1979). "Relations between Demographic Parameters", *Demography* 16: 329-338.

Glei, D.A., Horiuchi S. (2007). "The Narrowing Sex Differential in Life Expectancy in High-income Populations: Effects of Differences in the Age Pattern of Mortality", *Population Studies* 61(2): 141-159.

Goldman, N., Lord G. (1986). "A New Look at the Entropy of the Life Table", *Demography* 23(2): 275-282.

Government of India (2007). *National Rural Health Mission*. New Delhi: Ministry of Health and Family Welfare.

Greville, TNE (1948). "Mortality Tables Analysed by Cause of Death", *Record of the American Institute of Actuaries* 37(76): 283-294.

Keyfitz, N. (1977). *Applied Mathematical Demography*. New York: John Wiley.

Kittagawa, E.M. (1964). "Standard Comparison in Population Research", *Demography* 1: 296-315.

Kittagawa, E.M. (1966). "Theoretical Considerations in the Selection of Mortality Index and Some Empirical Comparisons", *Human Biology* 38: 293-305.

Nusselder, W.J. and J.P. Makenbach (1996). "Rectangularisation of the Survival Curve in the Netherlands, 1950-1992", *The Gerentologist* 36(6): 773-782.

Peters, D.H., A.S. Yazbeck, R.R. Sharma, GNV Ramana, L.H. Pritchett and A. Wagstaff (2002). *Better Health Systems for India's Poor. Findings, Analysis and Options*. Washington DC: The World Bank.

Pollard, J.H. (1982). "The Expectation of Life and Its Relationship to Mortality", *Journal of the American Institute of Actuaries* 109(2): 225-240.

Schoen, R. (1970). "The Geometric Mean of the Age-Specific Death Rates as a Summary Index of Mortality", *Demography* 7(3): 317-324.

Spiegelman, M. (1955). *Introduction to Demography*. Chicago: The Society of Actuaries.

Spiegelman, M. and H.H. Marks (1966). "Empirical Testing of Standards for the Age Adjustment of Death Rates by the Direct Method", *Human Biology* 38: 280-292.

United Nations (1973). *The Determinants and Consequences of Population Trends*. New York: United Nations.

United Nations (1982). *Levels and Trends of Mortality Since 1950*. New York: United Nations.

United Nations (1988). *Mortpak-Lite. The United Nations Software Package for Mortality Measurement*. New York: United Nations.

United Nations (2004). *World Population Projections: The 2004 Revision, Volume III: Analytical Report*. New York: United Nations.

United Nations (2004a). *World Population Prospects: The 2002 Revision. Vol III, Analytical Report*. New York: United Nations.

Vaupel, J.W. (1986). "How Changes in Age-Specific Mortality Affects Life Expectancy", *Population Studies* 40: 147-157.

Wilmoth, J.R. (2001). "How Long can We Live? A Review Essay", *Population and Development Review* 27(4): 791-800.

Wilmoth, J.R., Horiuchi S. (1999). "Rectangularisation Revisited: Variability of Age at Death within Human Populations", *Demography* 36(4): 475-495.

Table 7.1

Expectation of Life at Birth in India, 1970-2005

Period	*Expectation of Life at Birth*			*Absolute Increase*		
	Total	*Male*	*Female*	*Total*	*Male*	*Female*
Combined Population						
1970-1975	49.7	50.5	49			
1976-1980	52.3	52.5	52.1	2.6	2	3.1
1981-1985	55.4	55.4	55.7	3.1	2.9	3.6
1986-1990	57.7	57.7	58.1	2.3	2.3	2.4
1991-1995	60.3	59.7	60.9	2.6	2	2.8
1996-2000	61.9	61	62.7	1.6	1.3	1.8
2001-2005	63.2	62.3	63.9	1.3	1.3	1.2
Increase				13.5	11.8	14.9
Type of increase					Slow	Medium
Rural Population						
1970-1975	48.0	48.9	47.1			
1976-1980	50.6	51	50.3	2.6	2.1	3.2
1981-1985	53.7	54	53.6	3.1	3	3.3
1986-1990	56.1	56.1	56.2	2.4	2.1	2.6
1991-1995	58.9	58.5	59.3	2.8	2.4	3.1
1996-2000	60.7	59.9	61.3	1.8	1.4	2
2001-2005	61.8	61	62.4	1.1	1.1	1.1
Increase				13.8	12.1	15.3
Type of increase					Slow	Medium
Urban Population						
1970-1975	58.9	58.8	59.2			
1976-1980	60.1	59.6	60.8	1.2	0.8	1.6
1981-1985	62.8	61.6	64.1	2.7	2	3.3
1986-1990	63.4	62	64.9	0.6	0.4	0.8
1991-1995	65.9	64.5	67.3	2.5	2.5	2.4
1996-2000	67.3	65.7	68.8	1.4	1.2	1.5
2001-2005	68.5	66.9	69.8	1.2	1.2	1
Increase				9.6	8.1	10.6
Type of increase					Very slow	Very slow

Source: Government of India, 2008.

Table 7.2

Increase in the Expectation of Life at Birth in Indian States

State	Expectation of Life at Birth (Male)			Type of Increase	Expectation of Life at Birth (Female)			Type of Increase
	1970-1975	2001-2005	Increase		1970-1975	2001-2005	Increase	
Andhra Pradesh	48.4	62.7	14.3	Medium	49.3	65.2	15.9	Medium
Assam	46.2	58.3	12.1	Slow	44.8	59.0	14.2	Medium
Bihar	54.2	62.0	7.8	Very slow	51.5	60.1	8.6	Very slow
Gujarat	48.8	62.8	14.0	Medium	48.8	65.0	16.2	Medium
Haryana	59.0	65.6	6.6	Very slow	55.6	66.0	10.4	Very slow
Himachal Pradesh	54.8	66.3	11.5	Slow	50.9	67.1	16.2	Fast
Karnataka	55.4	63.4	8.0	Very slow	55.1	66.9	11.8	Slow
Kerala	60.8	71.3	10.5	Fast	63.3	76.3	13.0	Fast
Madhya Pradesh	47.6	57.8	10.2	Very slow	46.3	57.5	11.2	Very slow
Maharashtra	53.3	65.8	12.5	Slow	54.5	68.1	13.6	Slow
Orissa	46.0	59.2	13.2	Medium	45.3	59.2	13.9	Medium
Punjab	59.0	68.1	9.1	Slow	56.8	70.1	13.3	Slow
Rajasthan	49.2	61.2	12.0	Slow	47.5	62.2	14.7	Medium
Tamil Nadu	49.6	64.8	15.2	Fast	49.6	67.1	17.5	Fast
Uttar Pradesh	45.4	60.1	14.7	Medium	40.5	59.3	18.8	Fast
West Bengal	56.8	63.9	7.1	Very slow	58.0	65.5	7.5	Very slow

Source: Government of India, 2008.

Table 7.3

Probability of Survival up to Age 70 in India, 1970-2005

Period	Survival Probability			Rate of Improvement		
	Total	Male	Female	Total	Male	Female
Total Population						
1970-1975	0.322	0.315	0.334			
1976-1980	0.356	0.335	0.378	2.008	1.231	2.475
1981-1985	0.405	0.382	0.430	2.579	2.626	2.578
1986-1990	0.440	0.414	0.471	1.658	1.609	1.821
1991-1995	0.475	0.442	0.510	1.531	1.309	1.591
1996-2000	0.497	0.460	0.535	0.906	0.798	0.957
2001-2005	0.529	0.490	0.570	1.248	1.264	1.267
Rural Population						
1970-1975	0.305	0.299	0.312			
1976-1980	0.337	0.318	0.357	1.995	1.232	2.695
1981-1985	0.385	0.366	0.406	2.663	2.812	2.572
1986-1990	0.423	0.400	0.449	1.883	1.777	2.013
1991-1995	0.456	0.426	0.488	1.502	1.260	1.666
1996-2000	0.478	0.440	0.514	0.942	0.647	1.038
2001-2005	0.509	0.469	0.548	1.257	1.277	1.281
Urban Population						
1970-1975	0.424	0.399	0.457			
1976-1980	0.448	0.417	0.485	1.101	0.883	1.189
1981-1985	0.487	0.450	0.530	1.669	1.523	1.775
1986-1990	0.504	0.458	0.555	0.686	0.352	0.922
1991-1995	0.551	0.507	0.601	1.783	2.033	1.593
1996-2000	0.569	0.526	0.617	0.643	0.736	0.525
2001-2005	0.601	0.555	0.649	1.094	1.073	1.011

Source: Author's Calculations.

Table 7.4

Decomposition of the Rate of Improvement in Probability of Survival up to 70 Years of Age into Rate of Improvement in Probability of Survival in Different Age Groups

Period	*Age Group*					
	0-5	*5-15*	*15-30*	*30-45*	*45-60*	*60-70*
Total						
1970-1975/1976-1980	0.419	0.105	0.099	0.210	0.560	0.601
1976-1980/1981-1985	0.785	0.061	0.109	0.199	0.561	0.852
1981-1985/1986-1990	0.557	0.087	0.042	0.150	0.333	0.508
1986-1990/1991-1995	0.539	0.071	0.048	0.065	0.240	0.568
1991-1995/1996-2000	0.286	0.058	0.068	0.011	0.081	0.387
1996-2000/2001-2005	-0.038	0.063	0.053	0.083	0.444	0.655
Male						
1970-1975/1976-1980	0.376	0.104	0.067	0.132	0.306	0.259
1976-1980/1981-1985	0.685	0.060	0.042	0.221	0.685	0.937
1981-1985/1986-1990	0.595	0.082	0.048	0.103	0.317	0.478
1986-1990/1991-1995	0.408	0.065	0.011	0.084	0.209	0.540
1991-1995/1996-2000	0.307	0.056	0.006	-0.080	0.127	0.351
1996-2000/2001-2005	0.075	0.038	0.054	0.066	0.442	0.589
Female						
1970-1975/1976-1980	0.470	0.104	0.138	0.292	0.584	0.882
1976-1980/1981-1985	0.890	0.064	0.168	0.172	0.453	0.831
1981-1985/1986-1990	0.649	0.094	0.064	0.197	0.333	0.508
1986-1990/1991-1995	0.543	0.076	0.059	0.053	0.260	0.601
1991-1995/1996-2000	0.241	0.060	0.135	0.102	0.042	0.361
1996-2000/2001-2005	-0.149	0.091	0.054	0.101	0.435	0.735

Source: Author's calculations.

Table 7.5

Inter-State Variations in the Probability of Survival up to Age 70, 2001-2005

State	Trend			Differentials					
	2001-2005	1970-1975	Rate of Increase (Per cent)	Male	Female	M-F	Rural	Urban	R-U
Andhra Pradesh	0.532	0.290	2.027	0.478	0.589	-0.111	0.513	0.594	-0.081
Assam	0.434	0.208	2.445	0.404	0.469	-0.065	0.417	0.563	-0.146
Bihar	0.512	na	na	0.514	0.507	0.007	0.502	0.590	-0.088
Gujarat	0.550	0.327	1.737	0.501	0.602	-0.101	0.532	0.585	-0.053
Haryana	0.585	0.480	0.654	0.535	0.642	-0.107	0.580	0.604	-0.024
Himachal Pradesh	0.601	na	na	0.565	0.639	-0.074	0.598	0.650	-0.052
Karnataka	0.560	0.383	1.261	0.500	0.625	-0.125	0.535	0.621	-0.086
Kerala	0.687	0.499	1.066	0.606	0.773	-0.167	0.686	0.692	-0.006
Madhya Pradesh	0.461	0.312	1.306	0.428	0.496	-0.068	0.445	0.535	-0.090
Maharashtra	0.586	0.372	1.513	0.542	0.633	-0.091	0.564	0.628	-0.064
Orissa	0.470	0.237	2.282	0.448	0.493	-0.045	0.460	0.563	-0.103
Punjab	0.613	0.501	0.669	0.577	0.651	-0.074	0.605	0.630	-0.025
Rajasthan	0.542	0.315	1.810	0.504	0.594	-0.090	0.531	0.602	-0.071
Tamil Nadu	0.561	0.292	2.183	0.525	0.600	-0.075	0.531	0.625	-0.094
Uttar Pradesh	0.486	0.265	2.019	0.467	0.503	-0.036	0.473	0.544	-0.071
West Bengal	0.556	na	na	0.522	0.596	-0.074	0.531	0.624	-0.093

Source: Author's calculations.

Table 7.6

Life Table Entropy in India, 1970-2005

State	Total			Rural			Urban		
	Total	*Male*	*Female*	*Total*	*Male*	*Female*	*Total*	*Male*	*Female*
Degree of Entropy									
1970-1975	0.352	0.333	0.370	0.377	0.357	0.397	0.233	0.222	0.233
1976-1980	0.322	0.309	0.335	0.347	0.330	0.362	0.214	0.212	0.215
1981-1985	0.277	0.270	0.285	0.301	0.290	0.312	0.186	0.189	0.181
1986-1990	0.244	0.236	0.246	0.266	0.258	0.273	0.170	0.177	0.161
1991-1995	0.214	0.213	0.215	0.230	0.227	0.234	0.153	0.159	0.145
1996-2000	0.197	0.197	0.196	0.210	0.209	0.211	0.142	0.148	0.133
2001-2005	0.188	0.186	0.191	0.204	0.200	0.206	0.136	0.140	0.131
Average Annual Rate of Decrease									
1970-1975/1976-1980	-1.782	-1.496	-1.987	-1.658	-1.573	-1.846	-1.701	-0.922	-1.608
1976-1980/1981-1985	-3.011	-2.698	-3.233	-2.844	-2.584	-2.973	-2.805	-2.297	-3.443
1981-1985/1986-1990	-2.537	-2.692	-2.943	-2.472	-2.338	-2.671	-1.799	-1.312	-2.342
1986-1990/1991-1995	-2.624	-2.051	-2.694	-2.908	-2.560	-3.083	-2.107	-2.145	-2.093
1991-1995/1996-2000	-1.655	-1.562	-1.850	-1.819	-1.652	-2.069	-1.492	-1.434	-1.728
1996-2000/2001-2005	-0.935	-1.149	-0.517	-0.580	-0.880	-0.480	-0.863	-1.111	-0.303
1970-1975/2001-2005	-2.091	-1.941	-2.204	-2.047	-1.931	-2.187	-1.795	-1.537	-1.919

Source: Author's calculations.

Table 7.7

Entropy in the Life Table of Indian States

State	1970-1975			2001-2005			Rate of Change		
	Total	*Male*	*Female*	*Total*	*Male*	*Female*	*Total*	*Male*	*Female*
Andhra Pradesh	0.351	0.352	0.350	0.174	0.185	0.163	-2.339	-2.144	-2.547
Assam	0.418	0.378	0.398	0.230	0.227	0.233	-1.991	-1.700	-1.785
Bihar	na	na	na	0.214	0.205	0.232	na	na	na
Gujarat	0.368	0.356	0.379	0.171	0.174	0.166	-2.555	-2.386	-2.752
Haryana	0.257	0.231	0.285	0.173	0.165	0.180	-1.319	-1.122	-1.532
Himachal Pradesh	na	na	na	0.147	0.152	0.142	na	na	na
Karnataka	0.279	0.271	0.288	0.161	0.169	0.151	-1.833	-1.574	-2.152
Kerala	0.186	0.194	0.177	0.074	0.098	0.054	-3.072	-2.276	-3.957
Madhya Pradesh	0.399	0.379	0.419	0.248	0.243	0.255	-1.585	-1.482	-1.655
Maharashtra	0.291	0.291	0.289	0.140	0.149	0.131	-2.439	-2.231	-2.637
Orissa	0.393	0.386	0.401	0.228	0.226	0.230	-1.815	-1.784	-1.853
Punjab	0.253	0.238	0.268	0.142	0.148	0.137	-1.925	-1.584	-2.237
Rajasthan	0.381	0.356	0.408	0.206	0.204	0.208	-2.050	-1.856	-2.246
Tamil Nadu	0.341	0.341	0.342	0.143	0.154	0.132	-2.897	-2.650	-3.173
Uttar Pradesh	0.469	0.421	0.522	0.223	0.213	0.235	-2.478	-2.271	-2.660
West Bengal	na	na	na	0.166	0.170	0.161	na	na	na

Source: Author's calculations.

8

Unmet and Met Need of Contraception in India

S.C. GULATI, ALOK RANJAN CHAURASIA
AND RAGHUBANSH MANI SINGH

Introduction

Hitherto, theoretical literature and empirical evidences have often highlighted the crucial role of contraception in fertility regulation in historical and contemporary situations. It has always been contraception together with other conducive and concomitant socioeconomic factors that have facilitated fertility control. The advent and usage of effective contraception has rendered fertility as a choice variable in most of the socioeconomic theoretical frameworks evolved during the 60s and 70s.

Realising the potential dangers of burgeoning population, India was the first country to launch an official national family planning programme in 1952 to promote the usage of contraception and responsible parenthood to control fertility and hasten the process of demographic transition to achieve population stabilisation in India. Interestingly, the official statistics reveal that the official efforts have succeeded in averting about 252 million births till 2004. Though fertility decline has set-in all over India, yet the slow pace of decline in some parts of India remains a serious concern to population and development planners.

Major paradigm shifts in India's population policies have occurred since Cairo's International Conference on Population and Development in 1994 (ICPD), in which India too participated and was one of the signatories amongst 179 participating countries. The method-mix target-oriented approach has given way to a client-centred demand-driven quality reproductive and child health services in 1996-97. This new approach got predominantly reflected in the National Population Policy 2000 in which 14 National Socio-Demographic Goals for the year 2010 got enshrined with tangential reference to fertility control in the form of vigorous promotion of small family norm to achieve replacement levels of fertility by 2010.

Recently the Preamble of the National Rural Health Mission launched in 2005 brought focus on provision of health care towards improvement in the quality of life, especially amongst underprivileged and underserved groups amongst Indian citizens. Possibly, the underlying presumption in most of such national and international strategic pronouncements over the quality of life or standards of living could be that improvement in the quality of life would motivate people to limit their family size and thus fertility regulation and population stabilisation processes would get accelerated. Nevertheless, the report submitted by the working group on population stabilisation constituted by the Planning Commission has aptly concluded that "there appears to be an urgent need for bringing back promotion of contraception as the main concern of Family Welfare programmes in the high fertility states of India and thus the couples' felt need for contraception should be fully met".

However, promotion of contraception as a fertility control strategy seems to have been consigned to the back burner in India in recent years despite the fact that almost all the empirical studies have demonstrated that contraception had always been the most significant catalytic factor and cost effective strategy for fertility control in almost all the circumstances. In fact, curtailment of unwanted fertility through contraception usage has always been stressed for achieving population stabilisation in developing countries (Robey *et al.*, 1996; Westoff and Bankole, 2000).

The prominent explanations extended for the lack of demand for contraception in developing countries are lack of knowledge about contraception, health concerns, high costs, limited supplies, fear of side effects of contraception methods, familial and societal objections to the usage of contraception, etc. In the Indian context it may be of interest to mention that apart from the fact that the current unwanted fertility being higher, the prospective decline in the wanted fertility because of improvements in quality of life would imply increased demand for contraception. It is obvious in the context of hastening the pace of population stabilisation processes in the country that a focused attention is given not only to the current substantial unmet need of contraception but also to the prospective increased demand for contraception resulting from the improvements in the quality of life.

The Demand for Contraception in India

The demand for contraception comprises of both met as well as unmet need for contraception for the purpose of spacing as well as limiting births. The unmet need for contraception describes the extent of discrepancy between women's stated fertility preferences and observed contraception usage behaviour. Similarly, met need for contraception depicts the extent of effective usage of contraception in concurrence with the desired fertility preferences. The sum of met and unmet need for contraception is equal to the total need or demand for contraception.

Over 100 million women in the developing countries alone have discerned to have unmet need for contraception as these women would either prefer to postpone or avoid pregnancy but don't use contraceptives. India alone depicts highest proportion of fecund married women of around 20 per cent numbering around 31 million with the unmet need for contraception (Packard Foundation, 1998). Unmet need of contraception has drawn lot of attention of public-health policy makers and reproductive-health programme planners all over the world since 1970; especially in the developing countries where about one-fourth of pregnancies are unintended i.e., either unwanted or mistimed (Haub and Herstad, 2002).

Several empirical studies have highlighted the influence of several socioeconomic, demographic and programme factors like age, religion, caste, place of residence, standard of living, female education, status of women, sex-composition of living children, exposure to mass media, spousal communication on family planning, etc., on the unmet and met need for contraception in India and abroad (Bongaarts and Bruce, 1995; Casterline and Sinding, 2000; Chaudhury, 2001).

Conceptual modifications on the measurement of unmet need for contraception in a society have brought forth lot of literature over the recent past.[1] It refers to proportion of women who are fecund, married or living in union, and thus presumed to be sexually active and exposed to the risk of pregnancy and who either do not want any more children or who wish to postpone the birth of their next child for at least two more years but are not using any method of contraception are presumed to have unmet need for contraception. Further, the women who are currently pregnant but state that their pregnancy is mistimed or never wanted to have the pregnancy but were not using contraception before the pregnancy also belong to the unmet need category of women. Still further, all women who are amenorrhoeic but their last child was unwanted or mistimed also depict the unmet need for contraception.

The unmet need for contraception has further been categorised into unmet need of contraception for spacing births and unmet need of contraception for limiting births. The unmet need for spacing comprises women who are pregnant but the pregnancy is mistimed, amenorrhoeic women whose last

1. A critical appraisal of the conceptual modifications has been provided in Westoff, 1992; Bhushan, 1997; and Casterline and Sinding, 2000.

birth was mistimed, and women who are neither pregnant nor amenorrhoeic and who are not using any method of family planning but want to wait at least for two more years for their next pregnancy. The unmet need for spacing group includes women who are sure whether they want another child or not but are unsure when to have the child. Unmet need for limiting refers to pregnant women whose pregnancy is unwanted, amenorrhoeic women whose last birth was unwanted and who are neither pregnant nor amenorrhoeic and are not using any method of family planning and who want no more children.

Second National Family Health Survey was conducted in 24 states and the National Capital Territory of Delhi of India during 1998-99 and elicited the extent of unmet and met need of contraception for spacing as well as limiting births. The information from over eighty-nine thousand currently married women aged 15-49 was collected through canvassing a detailed questionnaire. The survey provides information on fertility, mortality, family planning and important aspects of nutrition, health and health care. Information on no-use of contraception with reasons was also elicited. Thus, extent of unmet and met need for contraception for spacing as well as limiting births could be elicited from the survey data (IIPS, 1998).

The definitional aspects of unmet and met need for spacing as well as limiting births are provided in reports of the National Family Health Survey conducted in 1998-99. The unmet need of contraception for spacing births referred to all pregnant women whose pregnancy was mistimed, amenorrhoeic women whose last birth was mistimed, and women who are neither pregnant nor amenorrhoeic and who are not using any method of family planning and who say they want to wait for at least two more years for their next birth. Also included in unmet need for spacing are women who are unsure whether they want another child or not but are unsure when to have the child. Unmet need for limiting births refers to pregnant women whose pregnancy was unwanted, amenorrhoeic women whose last child was unwanted and women who are neither pregnant nor amenorrhoeic and who are not using any method of family planning and who want no more children. Met need for spacing refers to women who are using some method of family planning and say they want to have another child or are undecided whether to have another child. Met need for limiting refers to women who are using some method and who want no more children. Note that spacing and limiting refer to the reason for using contraception rather than to the particular method used (IIPS, 1998: 172).

From a policy perspective, increasing the demand for contraception and at the same time reducing the unmet demand is important for both achieving demographic goals and enhancing individual rights. From the demographic standpoint, increasing the demand and reducing unmet demand for contraception would contribute to lowering fertility. Unwanted fertility is likely to be nearly non-existent at the two extreme stages of transition—initially when fertility desires are mostly unrestricted and at the end of the transition when couples have nearly complete control over their fertility (Kulkarni and Choe, 1998). Reducing the unmet demand for contraception is also important for helping couples achieve their reproductive goals and enhancing well-being of women and children (Potts, 2006) and may help in reducing unintended pregnancies that lead to abortions and unwanted births—both of which are unacceptably high in many developing countries witnessing fertility transition (Becker, 1999). Interestingly, unwanted fertility or proportion of unwanted births was discerned to be low in countries with very low or very higher levels of fertility and highest in countries with intermediate levels of fertility (Bongaarts, 1990, 1997).

One particularly harmful consequence of unintended pregnancies is unsafe abortion. An estimated 18 million unsafe abortions take place each year in less developed regions, contributing to high rates of maternal death and injury in these regions (Murray and Lopez, 1998: 280). Additionally, unwanted births pose risks for children's health and well-being and contribute to rapid population growth in resource constrained countries.

Objectives of the Study

The study intends to analyse factors influencing different components of the total demand for contraception *viz.,* met as well as unmet need for spacing as well as limiting births, in India. For the purpose some selected socioeconomic, demographic and programme factors affecting met and unmet need for contraception in India have been brought under the purview of the present study. Identification of the key contributing factors and their relative significance in impacting the different components of the total need of contraception would be elicited using multinomial logit regression analysis.

Database of the Study

The second National Family Health Survey (NFHS-2) collected detailed information on fertility, mortality, family planning, and important aspects of nutrition, health and health care including maternal and child health. Primary data from 25 states and union territories of the country got collected from 88,562 households and 84,862 currently married women aged 13-49 years and cohabiting with their husbands. The households were selected using a systematic, multi-stage, stratified sample design. Information related to wide range of socioeconomic, demographic and cultural characteristics pertaining to selected households and eligible women facilitates multivariate analysis in the study.

Methodology

The study employs the cross tabular analysis and multinomial logit regression analysis to explore linkages between different components of demand for contraception and some selected socioeconomic, demographic and cultural background factors of the respondents. Thereby, the multinomial logit regression analysis highlights the effects and relative significance of the predictor variables on the response variable which has been categorised into five mutually exclusive and exhaustive categories—respondents not using any type of contraception, respondents having unmet need for spacing births, respondents having unmet need for limiting births and respondents whose need for contraception having been met in terms of both spacing and limiting births. Each respondent can fall into one and only one of these five categories of the response variable. The reference category for the multinomial logit regression analysis comprises of those respondents who were not using any family planning method and had no unmet need for contraception at the time of the survey.

The multinomial logit regression model specified in log-odds form would consist of four equations plus a constraint as follows:

$$\text{Log } (Pi/P_0) = \alpha_i + \Sigma \beta ik \; Xk; \; (i=1...4, \; k=1...M) \quad (1)$$

And the constraint as;

$$\Sigma Pi + P_0 = 1; \quad (i = 1.... 4) \quad (2)$$

Where Pi/P_0 is interpreted as the odds-ratio, α_i's and βik's are the multinomial logit regression coefficients and Xk's are the M predictor variables in the system.

The quantities P_1/P_0, P_2/P_0, P_3/P_0 and P_4/P_0 are interpreted as odds-ratios, which are not strictly the odds as in the binary logit regression model, as numerator and denominator of the odds in the multinomial logit regression do not necessarily sum to one. In fact, each of these odds has for its denominator the probability of the reference category (P_0) of the response variable, and P_1, P_2, P_3 and P_4 are the probabilities of the other categories of the response variable.

The multinomial logit model in the present study is fitted with the maximum likelihood method. We choose the values of the coefficients (α's and β's) to maximise the likelihood function. The estimated multinomial logit regression coefficients in turn can be used to estimate probabilities of respondents in the relevant categories under study as follows:

$$P_1=P_0\ e^{(\alpha_1+\beta_{11}X_1+\beta_{12}X_2+\dots\dots+\beta_{1k}X_k)} \quad (3)$$

$$P_2=P_0\ e^{(\alpha_2+\beta_{21}X_1+\beta_{22}X_2+\dots\dots+\beta_{2k}X_k)} \quad (4)$$

$$P_3=P_0\ e^{(\alpha_3+\beta_{31}X_1+\beta_{32}X_2+\dots\dots+\beta_{3k}X_k)} \quad (5)$$

$$P_4=P_0\ e^{(\alpha_4+\beta_{41}X_1+\beta_{42}X_2+\dots\dots+\beta_{4k}X_k)} \quad (6)$$

Where P_0 is the probability of no-use and no unmet need for the reference category:

$$P_0=1/\ (1+\Sigma\ e^{\alpha_i+\beta_{i1}X_1+\beta_{i2}X_2+\dots\dots+\beta_{ik}X_k};\ i=1\dots4) \quad (7)$$

The effects of the predictor variables on the response variable have been presented in the form of estimated probabilities based on parametric estimates in the present study.

The odds-ratios or logs of odds-ratios in the multinomial logit model needs cautious interpretation as logs of odds-ratios in the multinomial logit model may not necessarily ensure increase or decrease in the odds-ratios or probabilities. In the binary logit regression model the sum total of probabilities in numerator and denominator add upto one and hence log of the odds-ratios (Ωs) become monotonically increasing functions of probabilities (Pj's). In the multinomial logit regression analysis the sum total of probabilities in numerator and denominator do not add up to one and thus, the logs of odds-ratios and odds-ratios may not be monotonically increasing or decreasing functions of the probabilities.[2]

Unmet and Met Need of Contraception by Background Characteristics

Currently married women who are not using any method of contraception but who do not want any more children or want to wait two or more years before having another child are defined as having an unmet need for family planning. Current contraceptive users are supposed to have met the need for contraception. The total demand for contraception is the sum of met and unmet need. Table 8.1 depicts the extent of unmet need and met need for contraception for spacing as well as limiting births, total demand for contraception and proportion demand satisfied by selected background characteristics of the women.

Perusal of Table 8.1 reveals that around 16 per cent of currently married women in India have an unmet need for contraception comprising need for

2. Proper interpretations of odds-ratios or logs of odds-ratios in the multinomial logit regression analysis and other finer details are provided in author's earlier study using the multinomial logit regression technique (Gulati, 1996b). For further details on formulations, estimation procedures and proper or cautious interpretations of the odds-ratios in multinomial logit regressions one can look in literature, especially Retherford's statistical models for Causal Analysis (Retherford *et al.*, 1993).

spacing births of 8.2 per cent and for limiting births of 8 per cent. Thus, if all women who say they want to space or limit their births were to use family planning, the contraceptive prevalence rate would increase from 48.9 per cent to 65.1 per cent of currently married women, implying that around 25 per cent of total family planning need is yet to be met.

Comparison of NFHS-2 results with NFHS-1 indicates that the proportion of women with unmet need for family planning declined from around 19.5 per cent in NFHS-1, conducted during 1992-93 to 15.8 per cent in NFHS-2 during 1998-99. Thus, over a span or around six years between the two surveys there was a decline of around 3.7 per cent points in the unmet need for family planning. Also we find that the proportion of met need to total demand for family planning increased from 68 per cent to 75 per cent. It may be of interest to mention that drop in the unmet need for contraception need not be viewed as reflection on family planning programme as such changes may also occur due to changes in the fertility preferences over the period (Ashford, 2003).

Components of need or total demand for contraception comprising the unmet need for FP for spacing births (UNFS) and for limiting births (UNFL), met need or use of contraception for spacing births (MNFS) and for limiting births (MNFL) and per cent demand satisfied (MNPTD) by selected background characteristics of women are provided in Table 8.1.

Need for Family Planning by Women's Age

Perusal of Table 8.1 and Figure 8.1 reveals that the unmet need is highest (27.5) among women below age 20 and the unmet need in this youngest age group is almost entirely for spacing births (25.7) rather than for limiting births (1.8). Unmet need is also relatively high among women age 20-24 (24.6 per cent), with almost 75 per cent of the need being for spacing births. Among women age 25-29, 19.4 per cent have an unmet need, and more than half of this need is for limiting births. In higher age groups beyond 30 years we find that the unmet need is predominantly for limiting compared with spacing births.

Table 8.1

Need for Family Planning Services Percentage of Currently Married Women with Unmet Need, Met Need and Total Demand for Family Planning (FP) Services and Percentage of Total Demand Satisfied by Selected Background Characteristics, India, 1998-99

Background Characteristic	Unmet Need of FP for		Met Need of FP (Currently Using) for		Total Demand for FP	Per cent Demand Satisfied	Number of Currently-Married Women
	Spacing Births (UNSB)	Limiting Births (UNLB)	Spacing Births (MNSB)	Limiting Births (MNLB)	(TDFP)	(MNPTD)	
Age							
15-19	25.7	1.8	5.8	2.0	35.3	22.1	6888
20-24	18.6	6.0	8.7	16.6	49.9	50.7	15529
25-29	8.8	10.6	6.1	41.8	67.3	71.2	17486
30-34	3.5	11.0	2.8	60.0	77.3	81.2	15042
35-39	1.4	9.6	0.9	66.5	78.4	86.0	12779
40-44	0.5	6.6	0.3	65.3	72.7	90.2	9852
45-49	0.2	3.9	0.0	57	61.1	93.3	7286
Residence							
Urban	6.4	6.9	6	53.5	72.8	81.7	26308
Rural	9.0	8.4	3.1	41.1	61.6	71.8	58554
Education							
No education	7.7	9.3	1.7	41.0	59.7	71.5	41798
Primary edn.	8.1	7.4	3.0	50.3	68.8	77.5	14335
Secondary edn.	9.6	6.3	6.3	48.4	70.6	77.5	20618
Higher edn.	7.8	6.5	11.9	47.1	73.3	80.5	8111

contd...

...contd...

Background Characteristic	Unmet Need of FP for		Met Need of FP (Currently Using) for		Total Demand for FP	Per cent Demand Satisfied	Number of Currently-Married Women
	Spacing Births (UNSB)	Limiting Births (UNLB)	Spacing Births (MNSB)	Limiting Births (MNLB)	(TDFP)	(MNPTD)	
Religion							
Hindu	7.6	7.4	3.6	46.8	65.4	77.1	66136
Muslim	10.4	12.0	5.1	32.9	60.4	62.9	10121
Christian	12.8	8	5.9	38.2	64.9	68.0	4544
Other	7.2	6.5	5.8	51.4	70.9	80.7	4061
Caste							
SC/ST	9.5	8.3	3.3	39.3	60.4	70.5	24334
OBC	8.5	7.6	2.9	44.8	63.8	74.8	24477
Others	7.2	8	5.2	48.9	69.3	78.1	36051
Standard of Living							
Very low	9.5	9.5	2.2	35.7	56.9	66.6	22569
Low	8.4	7.9	3.6	45.4	65.3	75.0	44409
Medium	6.3	6.3	7	55.2	74.8	83.2	15738
High	4.9	5.3	9.1	55.5	74.8	86.4	2146
Occupation							
Not working	9.1	8.2	4.7	43.2	65.2	73.5	54828
Working without cash	7.9	8.4	2.1	41.9	60.3	73.0	11267
Working with cash	5.8	6.8	3	51.7	67.3	81.3	18767

contd...

...contd...

Background Characteristic	Unmet Need of FP for		Met Need of FP (Currently Using) for		Total Demand for FP	Per cent Demand Satisfied	Number of Currently-Married Women
	Spacing Births (UNSB)	Limiting Births (UNLB)	Spacing Births (MNSB)	Limiting Births (MNLB)	(TDFP)	(MNPTD)	
Number of Living Children							
0	13.4	0.4	3.9	0.7	18.4	25.0	9481
1	20.0	3.2	14.2	11.7	49.1	52.7	13587
2	7.9	7.7	3.4	54.7	73.7	78.8	20594
3	4.1	8.4	1.4	66	79.9	84.4	18138
4	2.9	10.1	0.8	65.2	79	83.5	11333
5+	2.6	17.3	0.4	49.9	70.2	71.7	11729
Exposure to FP by Media							
No	8.9	9.7	1.7	35.6	55.9	66.7	30666
Yes	7.8	7	5.3	50.2	70.3	78.9	54196
Exposure to FP by HF							
No	8.3	7.9	3.9	44.6	64.7	75.0	83450
Yes	4.5	8.6	11	65.2	89.3	85.3	1412
Total	8.2	8.0	4.0	44.9	65.1	75.2	84862
Number of women	6980 (8.2)	6747 (8.0)	3392 (4.0)	38135 (44.9)	55254 (65.1)	(100)	84862

Figure 8.1

Unmet, Met and Total Need for FP by Age of Women

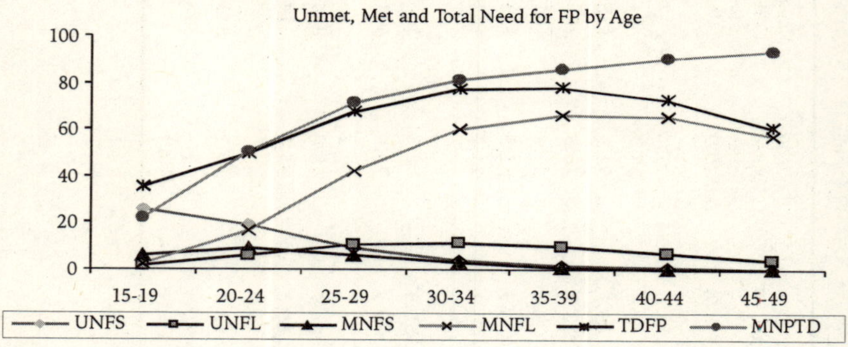

Coming to met need or contraceptive usage we find that except youngest age group of 15-19 years the usage of contraception for limiting births is higher compared with usage for spacing births. Further, beyond age 30 we find that in all the age groups the usage of contraception is for limiting births ranging between 60-67 per cent, and marginally for spacing births ranging between 0 to 3 per cent. Thus, predominant component of total demand for contraception comprises for limiting births rather than for spacing births, except in the younger age groups.

Interestingly, only 22 per cent of the total demand for family planning is being satisfied or met (MNPTD) amongst married women aged 15-19. This proportion rises sharply to 51 per cent for women aged 20-24 to 71 per cent for women aged 25-29 and gets much higher ranging between 81-93 per cent for women aged 30-49. It may be of interest to note that both met and unmet need for contraception among women is higher for limiting births compared with for spacing births excepting the youngest age group of 15-19 years.

Need for Family Planning by Rural-Urban Residence

Perusal of Table 8.1 and Figure 8.2 reveals that the unmet need for family planning for spacing as well as limiting births is higher in rural areas than in urban areas. The met need or usage of contraception for spacing as well as limiting births is higher in urban areas than in rural areas. Further, the total demand for family planning turns out to be much higher in urban areas (72.8) than in rural areas (61.6).

It is of interest to note that contraception usage in rural as well as urban areas is predominantly for limiting births than for spacing births. Also, we find that proportion of total demand for family planning being satisfied (MNPTD) also turns out to be higher in urban areas (81.7) than in rural areas (71.8).

Figure 8.2

Need for FP by Rural-Urban Residence of Women

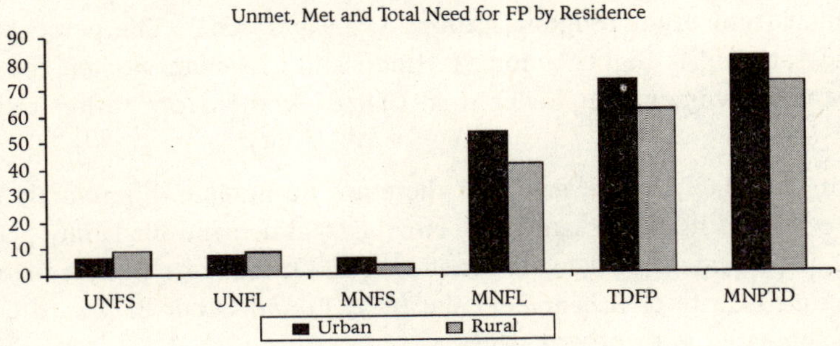

Need for Family Planning by Women's Education

Unmet need for family planning varies within a narrow range of 17 per cent for illiterate women to 13.7 per cent for women with higher education. Total demand for family planning depicts positive relationship with the education of women as it varies from 59.7 per cent amongst illiterate women to 73.3 per cent amongst women with education higher than secondary. Interestingly we find that proportionate usage of spacing methods depicts positive linkage with women's education varying from 1.7 per cent amongst illiterate women to almost 11.9 per cent amongst women with the higher education. Similarly extent of demand for family planning being satisfied varies systematically from 71.5 per cent amongst illiterate women to 80.5 per cent amongst women with the higher education.

Figure 8.3

Unmet, Met and Total Need for FP by Women's Education

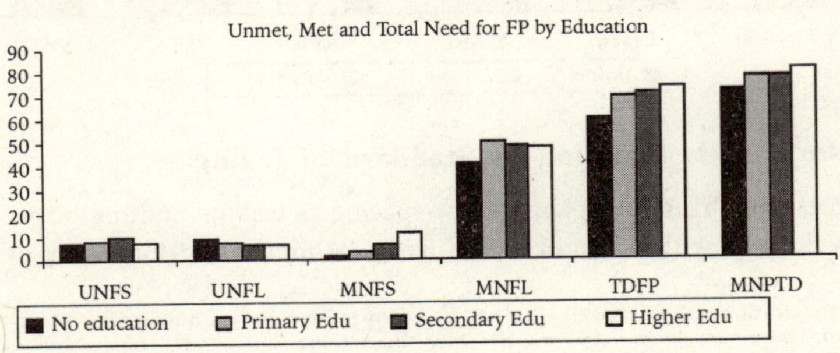

Need for Family Planning by Religion and Caste

Perusal of Table 8.1 reveals that Hindu and Christian women have a lower unmet need for family planning than Muslim women but a higher unmet need than women from other religious groups. Similarly, total demand for family planning is higher amongst Hindu and Christian women of the order of 65 per cent compared with Muslim women (60.4 per cent) but lower than that of women from other religious groups (70.9 per cent). The percentage of demand satisfied is higher amongst Hindu and Christian women compared with Muslim women, but lower than that of women from other religious groups (80.7).

Perusal of Table 8.1 reveals that there are no notable differentials in the extent of unmet need by caste/tribe, but the total demand for family planning as well as percentage of demand satisfied is lower amongst women belonging to Scheduled Caste or Scheduled Tribe (SC/ST) and Other Backward Classes (OBC) compared with other castes.

Figure 8.4 clearly reflects that unmet need for spacing methods (MNFS) is substantially higher amongst Muslim compared with Hindu women, whereas met need for limiting methods (MNFL) of family planning is much lower amongst Muslim compared with Hindu and Christian women.

Figure 8.4

Unmet, Met and Total Need for FP by Religion and Caste

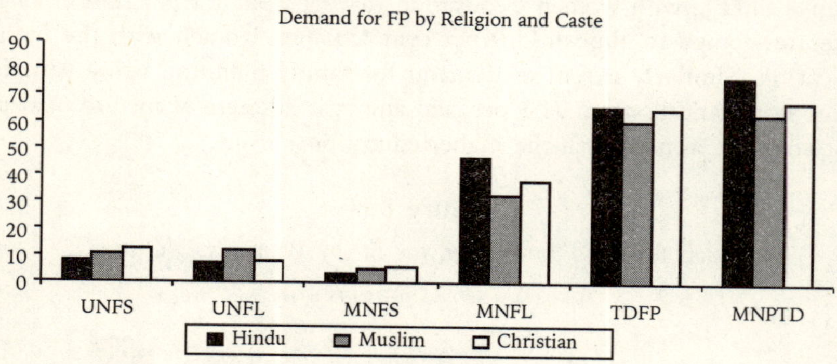

Need for Family Planning by Standard of Living

Unmet need for family planning for spacing as well as limiting births depict negative linkage with the standard of living.[3] Unmet need for family planning

3. Standard of living of households was based on possession of household inventories like radio, television, bicycle, two wheeler, four wheeler, etc. The weights assigned to possession of the individual household inventories as inverse of the percentage of households possessing the item and accordingly the weights assigned to individual items was such as radio or bicycle (2), refrigerators or two wheelers (7), four wheelers (41), etc. Thereby, the assigned weights were added up and the categorisation of the households subject to the total score for possession of the individual inventory items was like very low, low, medium and high pertaining to total score ranges of 0, 2-6.7-20, 21-61, respectively.

for spacing births vary from 9.5 per cent in very low category of standard of living to 4.9 per cent amongst women in high standard of living households. Similarly, we find that unmet need for limiting also varies from 9.5 per cent amongst women from very low standard of living households to 5.3 per cent women from high standard of living households. On the other hand, we find usage of contraception for spacing as well as for limiting births improves consistently amongst women from low to high standard of living households. Overall we find that total demand for family planning as well as per cent demand satisfied also depicts positive linkage with the standard of living.

Figure 8.5

Unmet, Met and Total Need for Family Planning by Standard of Living

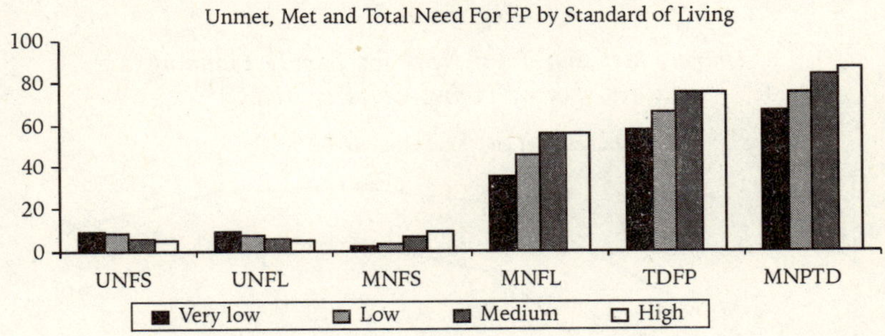

It may be of interest to mention that usage of contraception for spacing births is higher amongst women from higher standards of living households. Similarly, demand for family planning as well as proportion of demand being satisfied is also higher amongst women from higher standards of living households.

Need for Family Planning by Women's Work Status

Perusal of Table 8.1 reveals that unmet need for family planning for spacing as well as limiting births is lowest amongst women who are working for cash payments or for wages and salaries being paid in cash. Similarly, women working for cash also depict higher demand for family planning and per cent demand satisfied compared with women who are either not working or working without any remuneration in the form of cash. However, we don't find any consistent relationship of met need for family planning or usage of contraception with occupational categories from not working to working with cash in the table.

Need for Family Planning by Number of Living Children

Unmet need for family planning amongst women with no living child is primarily for spacing births (13.4 per cent). Amongst women with one living child we find that unmet need for spacing births is maximum (20 per cent) whereas for limiting births is marginal (3.2 per cent). The unmet need for family planning is primarily for spacing births amongst women with no or one living child. However, unmet need for family planning for limiting births keeps on increasing althrough with the number of living children. The proportion of unmet need that is for limiting births rises from 47 per cent among women with two living children to 91 per cent among women with six or more living children.

Figure 8.6

Unmet, Met and Total Need for Family Planning by Number of Living Children (NLC)

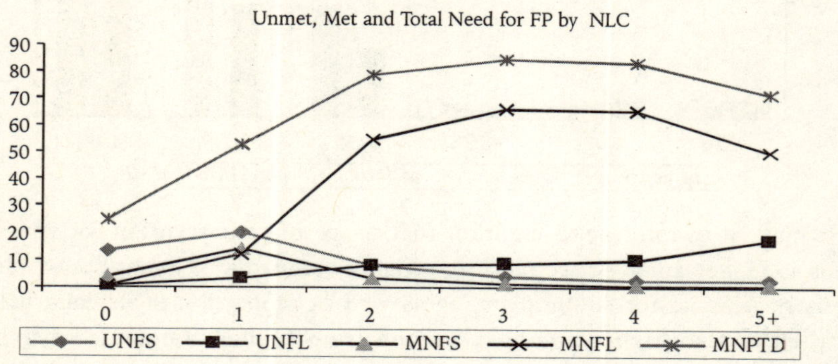

Met need or usage of contraception for spacing (3.9) as well as limiting (0.7) births is just marginal amongst married women with no living child. However, usage of contraception for spacing as well as limiting births jumps substantially amongst women after having one living child compared with women with no child. Thus, amongst women with one living children, the demand for family planning as well as proportion of demand satisfied jumps to almost 49.1 and 52.7 per cent, respectively.

Total demand for family planning jumps sharply amongst women with 2 or more living children. However, the demand for family planning is predominantly for limiting births than for spacing births. The proportion of demand satisfied also rises sharply to 80-85 per cent amongst women with 2 to 4 living children and then declines to 71.5 per cent amongst women with 5 or more children. These results indicate that family planning programmes strong emphasis on sterilisation, especially female sterilisation, results in failure to meet the spacing needs of young women who are still in the process of forming their families.

Need for Family Planning by Women's Exposure to Family Planning by Media or at Health Facility

Table 8.1 reveals that unmet need for family planning for spacing as well as limiting births is lower amongst women who had exposure to family planning messages over media, print and electronic, and also counselling or discussion on FP by health workers at public health facilities visited by women. Interestingly, usage of contraception especially for limiting births is substantially higher amongst women who were exposed to family planning by the media or the health facilities. Similarly, proportion of the demand satisfied also is quite high amongst women with exposure to FP by media.

Reasons for No-Use of Contraception

Reasons extended by the respondents for no-use of contraception can provide important clues whether the constraints for no-use are from supply side or demand side of contraception (Zappella, 1997). The supply side constraints like inaccessibility or effectiveness of contraceptive methods, or misapprehensions about available contraception methods suggest that programme interventions can improve the demand for contraception. On the other hand, demand side constraints like familial or societal opposition to family planning or lack of knowledge may suggest strengthening of IEC component towards improvement in the demand for family planning. Let us briefly look into the main reasons extended by women in NFHS-2 for non-use of contraception. Table 8.2 provides information on reasons for no-use amongst women who have unmet need of contraception for spacing and limiting births as well amongst women who have neither unmet need nor using contraception.

Perusal of Table 8.2 reveals the majority of the women with unmet need of contraception for spacing of births have extended fertility related reasons for non-use of contraception. Around 44 per cent of such women reports non-use because of desire for more children.

Out of 6980 women, who reported unmet need for spacing births, we find 16.4 per cent i.e., 1145 women, are not using contraception as they are pregnant, which clearly depicts that these pregnancies are mistimed. Around 7.7 per cent of these women extend fertility related reasons like not having sex or infrequent sex, or post-partum amenorrhoea, or infecundity because of menopausal conditions, hysterectomy, etc. Around 4.3 per cent of such women report opposition on usage of family planning, predominantly from their husbands (2.6 per cent). However, around 4.7 per cent of the women report family planning methods related problems like worries about side effects and health-risks. Thus, overall we find that majority of women with unmet need for spacing children extend reasons for no-use like additional desired children, familial opposition especially from husbands and worries about side effects and health-risks.

Amongst 6747 women with unmet need for limiting births we find around 9.2 per cent women i.e., 621 women, are not using contraception as they got pregnant and these pregnancies can be straightaway categorised as unwanted pregnancies. Other predominant reasons for non-usage of contraception amongst these women are fertility related (10.5 per cent), opposition to family planning (10.5 per cent) and contraceptive method specific reasons (15.5 per cent). However, even lack of knowledge about methods (1.7 per cent) and about source of contraception (3.9 per cent) also depict an important reason for non-usage amongst 5.6 per cent of these women. However, societal and spousal opposition to usage of contraception or sterilisation here, termed as high social cost from the social influence group (Nag, 1984), also turns out to be an important reason for non-usage of contraception amongst women with unmet need for limiting births or women who don't want to have any more child. Other predominant reasons for no-use of contraception amongst women with unmet need of contraception for limiting births are fear of side effects (6.4 per cent) and health-risks (5.3).

Coming to the category of women with no-use and no unmet need of contraception we find that predominant reasons extended for the non-use are desire for more children (35.8 per cent), pregnancies (16.0 per cent), menopausal/hysterectomy (8.2 per cent), post-partum/breastfeeding (5.1 per cent), husband's opposition to the usage (2.1 per cent) and fear of side effects (2.2 per cent).

All women with unmet need may not be potential users of contraception (Ashford, 2003). However, analysis of reasons for non-use in Table 8.2 reveals that the usage of family planning can be conveniently enhanced by around 19.2 per cent amongst these non-user category of women through assuaging method-specific reasons for non-use (numbering 2817), elimination of familial and societal opposition through IEC interventions (numbering 2283), increased knowledge and accessibility of contraception (numbering 1542) and taking care of mistimed pregnancies (1067) and unwanted pregnancies (numbering 599). It may be of interest to note that around 16.4 per cent i.e., 1067 out of a total of 6508 pregnancies are mistimed and another 9.2 per cent i.e., 599 out of 6508 are altogether unwanted. Thus, overall around 25.6 per cent of the total pregnancies amongst non-users of contraception category women can be categorised as unintended comprising mistimed and unwanted, which implies that extent of unfulfilled demand for contraception is still quite substantial. However, the proportions of unintended conceptions in developing countries are quite substantial due to several such reasons (Potts, 2006).

Table 8.2

Per cent Distribution of Non-Users Categories of Women by Reasons for No-Use of Contraception

Reasons	*Unmet Need for Spacing Births*	*Unmet Need for Limiting Births*	*No-Use & No-Unmet Need*	*Total Number of Women*
Wants More Children	44.1	—	35.8	13834
Pregnant	16.4	9.2	16.0	6508
Fertility Related Other Reasons	7.7	10.5	19.2	6901
Not having sex	0.6	1.3	1.1	448
Infrequent sex	0.5	1.4	0.8	365
Menopausal/Had hysterectomy	0.0	0.2	8.2	2436
Sub-fecund/Infecund	0.2	1.0	4.0	1257
Postpartum/Breastfeeding	6.4	6.6	5.1	2395
Opposition to Use	4.3	10.5	4.3	2283
Respondent opposed	0.3	1.1	0.6	281
Husband oppose	2.6	6.2	2.1	1206
Other people oppose	0.5	1.1	0.3	201
Against religion	0.9	2.1	1.3	595
Lack of Knowledge	4.6	5.6	2.8	1542
Knows no method	1.1	1.7	1.1	511
Knows no source	3.5	3.9	1.7	1031
Method Related Reasons	4.7	15.5	5.0	2817
Health concerns	1.2	5.3	2.0	1028
Worry about side effects	2.5	6.4	2.2	1243
Hard to get method	0.3	0.9	0.2	126
Costs too much	0.6	2.3	0.5	347
Inconvenient to use	0.1	0.6	0.1	73
Other Miscellaneous Reasons	6.9	13.5	7.3	3548
DK	11.6	35.3	9.7	5902
Total Number of Women	6980	6747	29608	43335

Thus, accounting for predominant reasons of non-use like unwanted pregnancies (1067 mistimed and 599 unwanted), societal and spousal opposition to contraception (2283), lack of knowledge about methods and supply sources (1542), method related reasons (2817) out of a total of 43335 users can easily lead to an increase in the usage of contraception by around 19.2 per cent amongst non-user category women.

Let us now shift toward highlighting relative significance and directions of effects of different factors in influencing the unmet and met needs of contraception for spacing and limiting births in the following sections.

Multinomial Logit Regression Results

Factors influencing unmet and met needs for contraception for spacing and limiting births are highlighted through the Multinomial Logit Regression analysis. For the purpose the categorisation of the response variable for underlying Multinomial Logit Model the response from all the 84862 currently married women staying with husbands, covered under all India National Family Health Survey-2 during 1998-99, got classified in five mutually exclusive categories comprising 6780 women with unmet need for contraception for spacing births, 6747 women with unmet need for limiting births, 3392 women with met need for spacing and 38135 women with met need for limiting births and the rest of the women numbering 29428, who reported neither unmet nor met need for contraception, and were not using any method of contraception got classified as the reference category of no-use.

The selected predictor variables are both quantitative as well as categorical. The quantitative predictor variables are women's age (AGE) and its squared term (AGESQ), number of living sons (NLS) and its squared term (NLSSQ), number of living daughters (NLD) and its squared term (NLDSQ). The categorical predictor variables in the model are women's education with illiterate or no education as reference category, women's religion with Hindus as reference category, women's rural-urban residence with rural as reference category, women's caste with others as reference category, with standard of living with low-standard as reference category, women's occupation with not-working out of home as reference category, exposure to family planning through media with no exposure as reference category, exposure to family planning through public health facility with no-exposure as reference category, discussion of family planning with friends, husbands, etc., with no discussion as reference category, with aspirations for children's education upto primary, secondary or higher education, etc., with no aspiration as reference category.

The parametric estimates of the Multinomial Logit Regression coefficients by the Maximum Likelihood procedure of all the predictor variables, quantitative as well as categorical, are presented in Table 8.3. The estimated coefficient (bi) depicts the additive effect of one-unit change in the predictor variable (Xi) on the log of odds (log Ω) of the response variables, which are categorised as women with unmet or met need of contraction for spacing or limiting births in relation to women in no-use and no unmet need of family planning category. Equivalently, the term (e^{bi}) depicts the multiplicative effect on the odds-ratio or the ratio at which the odds of the response variable would increase or decrease depending upon the positive or negative sign of the coefficient, respectively. If the sign of the estimated coefficient is positive then the multiplicative effect would be greater than one and thus the odds of the response variable would increase and thus, depicts positive effect on the probability of having demand or components of demand for contraception in the present analysis. The parametric estimates of the coefficients and levels of significance of underlying models for unmet and met need for contraception for spacing and limiting births are provided in Table 8.2. Let us examine the effects of different predictor variables on the four components of demand for contraception in India. It must always be kept under consideration that the effect of any predictor variable on the odds ratios or probabilities is net of accounting for other predictor variables under the purview of the model.

Effects of Age of Women

Perusal of Table 8.3 reveals that women's age depict significant and positive impact on all the components of demand for contraception *viz.*, unmet need for contraception for spacing births (UNSB), unmet need for contraception for limiting births (UNLB), met need for contraception for spacing births (MNSB) as well as met need for contraception for limiting births (MNLB). Thus, probability of usage of contraception as well as unmet need for contraception increases alongwith age of women. However, the effect is much more substantive on the met need or usage of contraception for limiting births compared with effects on other components of demand for contraception.

Further, we find that coefficients pertaining to non-linear term or squared of age also turns out to be significant but negative for all the four components of demand for contraception. This depicts that the unmet need for contraception for spacing births tends to increase with age upto some threshold level of age, beyond which it tends to level off and even decline. Similar interpretations can be extended for all other components of demand for contraception in India. Nevertheless, the impact of age of women on usage of contraception for limiting births (MNLB) turns out to maximum compared with effects on other components of demand for contraception.

Effects of Number and Sex Composition of Children

Number of living sons (NLS) as well as daughters (NLD) depict significant and positive impact on all the four components of demand for contraception i.e., for unmet need for contraception for spacing (UNFS) as well as for

Table 8.3

Multinomial Logit Regression Coefficients of the Model with Unmet Need for Spacing Births (UNSB), Unmet Need for Limiting Births (UNLB), Met Need for Spacing Births (MNSB) and Met Need for Limiting Births (MNLB), with No-Use and without Unmet Need for Contraception as Reference Category in the Response Variables

Predictor Variables	*UNSB Log(P1/P0)*		*UNLB Log(P2/P0)*		*MNSB Log(P3/P0)*		*MNLB Log(P4/P0)*	
	Coeff.	σ	*Coeff.*	σ	*Coeff.*	σ	*Coeff.*	σ
intercept	-1.044	0.00	-10.592	0.00	-8.265	0.00	-13.556	0.00
AGE	0.051	0.00	0.438	0.00	0.379	0.00	0.612	0.00
AGESQ	-0.004	0.00	-0.007	0.00	-0.008	0.00	-0.009	0.00
NLS	0.363	0.00	1.650	0.00	0.294	0.00	2.044	0.00
NLSSQ	-0.035	0.00	-0.196	0.00	-0.139	0.00	-0.334	0.00
NLD	0.424	0.00	1.077	0.00	0.187	0.00	0.913	0.00
NLDSQ	-0.037	0.00	-0.125	0.00	-0.043	0.00	-0.165	0.00
WEDNP	0.157	0.00	0.248	0.00	0.470	0.00	0.460	0.00
WEDNHS	0.331	0.00	0.425	0.00	0.906	0.00	0.570	0.00
WENHIGR	0.624	0.00	0.782	0.00	1.408	0.00	0.404	0.00
RELMUS	0.114	0.01	-0.277	0.00	0.276	0.00	-0.885	0.00
RELCHR	0.718	0.00	-0.324	0.00	0.314	0.00	-0.776	0.00
RELOTH	0.147	0.04	-0.173	0.02	0.240	0.00	-0.107	0.02
EXFPM	0.075	0.03	0.168	0.00	0.457	0.00	0.583	0.00
EXFPHF	0.115	0.45	0.787	0.00	1.706	0.00	1.638	0.00
ASDEDNM	0.011	0.93	0.046	0.68	-0.025	0.92	0.157	0.05
ASDEDNH	0.192	0.10	0.264	0.02	0.121	0.61	0.669	0.00
ASDEDND	0.242	0.04	0.334	0.00	0.183	0.44	0.727	0.00

contd...

...*contd*...

Predictor Variables	UNSB *Log(P1/P0)*		UNLB *Log(P2/P0)*		MNSB *Log(P3/P0)*		MNLB *Log(P4/P0)*	
	Coeff.	σ	*Coeff.*	σ	*Coeff.*	σ	*Coeff.*	σ
ASSEDNM	-0.301	0.04	-0.099	0.52	0.697	0.02	0.236	0.03
ASSEDNH	-0.242	0.08	-0.084	0.56	0.218	0.45	0.146	0.15
ASSEDND	-0.340	0.01	-0.090	0.53	0.114	0.69	0.225	0.03
LSSLow	0.039	0.23	0.043	0.22	0.296	0.00	0.213	0.00
LSSMed	0.076	0.15	0.076	0.17	0.514	0.00	0.353	0.00
LSSHigh	-0.099	0.40	-0.126	0.29	0.595	0.00	0.326	0.00
WWNoCash	-0.103	0.02	-0.175	0.00	-0.132	0.08	0.028	0.34
WWWCash	-0.171	0.00	-0.035	0.37	0.100	0.06	0.422	0.00
SC/ST	-0.003	0.93	-0.270	0.00	-0.169	0.00	-0.398	0.00
OBC	0.022	0.54	-0.148	0.00	-0.415	0.00	-0.194	0.00
FPWOthers	0.172	0.00	0.127	0.03	-0.171	0.01	0.158	0.00
FPDHus	0.074	0.04	0.557	0.00	0.993	0.00	-0.015	0.58
FPDFriends	-0.101	0.04	0.060	0.21	0.194	0.00	0.342	0.00
RES-Urban	-0.027	0.46	0.130	0.00	0.259	0.00	0.306	0.00
n	(n=6980)		(n=6747)		(n=3392)		(n=38135)	

Note: σ : Level of significance.

N=84862; Total number of currently married women.

n= 29608, women in reference category i.e., no-use and no unmet-need of FP category.

limiting births (UNFL), met need for contraception for spacing (MNFS) as well as limiting births (MNFL). Thus, the probability of having unmet need for contraception for spacing as well as limiting and also probability of usage of contraception for spacing as well as limiting increases alongwith increase in the number of living sons as well as daughters. Interestingly, we find that number of living sons as well number of living daughters depict significant and positive impact on met as well unmet need of contraception for spacing as well as limiting births.

It may be of interest to mention that number of sons depict much stronger impact on usage of contraception for limiting births (β=2.044) compared with the impact of daughters (β=0.913). Thus, the positive effect of number of living sons (e^{β} =7.723) are much more pronounced compared with the number of living daughters (e^{β} =2.491) on the usage of contraception for limiting births.[4] However, the phenomenon of son preference in Indian society clearly gets reflected in terms of usage of contraception for limiting births as the probability of usage of contraception for limiting births increases much faster alongwith number of living sons compared with number of living daughters.

Interestingly, we find that coefficients pertaining to non-linear terms i.e., squared of NLS as well as NLD also turn out to be significant but negative for all the four components of demand for contraception. Thus, significant but positive coefficient pertaining to linear term and significant but negative coefficient pertaining to squared term depicts that all the four components of demand for contraception increase with number of living sons as well as daughters upto some threshold levels of number of living sons as well as daughters, beyond which it tends to level off or even decline.

Impact of number of living sons as well as daughters on unmet need for contraception for spacing as well as limiting births is significant and positive. However, the effect of number of living daughters is higher than that of number of living sons on the unmet need for contraception for spacing births. Alternatively, the probability of having unmet need for contraception for spacing births is higher amongst women with more of female children compared with women having more of male children, which again reflects the phenomenon of son-preference in the Indian society. Alternatively, women with more of daughters depict higher probability of having unmet need for contraception for spacing births compared to women having more of sons and thus desire for additional children seems to be higher amongst women with

4. The multiplicative effects on odds-ratios of the response variables in the Multinomial Logit Regression analysis are provided in Appendix Table A-8.2.

more of female children compared to women having more of sons, which again manifests the son-preference phenomenon in the Indian society.

Effects of Women's Education

Education of women depicts significant and positive impact on all the four components of demand for contraception. Further, we find that as the level of education of women improves from primary to secondary to higher levels, the magnitude of impact improves consistently for unmet need for contraception for spacing as well as limiting births and also for met need or contraception usage for spacing births. However, the probability of use of contraception for limiting births is higher amongst educated women of all levels compared with illiterate women, but the consistent increase in the probability of contraceptive usage for limiting births alongwith education does not get reflected as was with other components of the demand for contraception. Possibly, the usage of contraception for limiting births is higher amongst all educated women compared with illiterate women, irrespective of the level of education of women.

Effects of Religion

It is of interest to mention that usage of contraception as well as unmet need for limiting births is significantly higher amongst Hindu women compared to Muslim, Christians and other religious community's women whereas usage of contraception for spacing births is significantly lower amongst Hindu women compared to others. Thus, demand for spacing methods seems to be significantly higher amongst Muslim, Christian and other religious group women compared to Hindu women. It may be of interest to mention that though religious differentials in usage of contraception for spacing and limiting births seems to have narrowed down between Hindu, Muslim and other religious community women after accounting for other socioeconomic and demographic predictors but still the differentials in the usage are significant.

A close examination of the magnitude of coefficients reveals that met need or usage of contraception for limiting births (-.885) turns out to be minimum amongst Muslim and Christian (-.776) women compared to Hindu women, which would get reflected in terms of probabilities of the usage in the next section also.

Thus, overall we find that demand for contraception for limiting births is significantly higher amongst Hindu women compared to all other religious groups' women. On the other hand, demand for contraception for spacing births is significantly higher amongst Muslim, Christian and other religious group women compared to Hindu women.

Effects of Exposure on Family Planning through Mass Media

Exposure of women to family planning through mass media, comprising of all electronic and print media like radio, TV, newspapers, posters, brochures, etc., depicts significant and positive impact on met as well as unmet need for contraception for spacing as well as limiting births or total demand for family planning. Thus, demand for family planning for spacing as well as limiting births seems to be significantly higher amongst women who get exposed to family planning messages through media compared to the reference category women, who are not exposed to FP through media. Thus, mass media seems to have significantly increased demand for family planning in India, of course even while accounting for all other predictor variables under the purview of the regression.

Effects of Exposure on Family Planning through Health Facilities

Exposure of women to family planning at health facilities visited by them depicts significant and positive impact on met need or usage of contraception for spacing as well as limiting births. However, the exposure also depicts significant impact on unmet need for limiting births but not on spacing births. Possibly, there seems to be more emphasis on counselling on family planning for limiting births compared to for spacing births at health facilities in India.

It is of interest to note that multiplicative impact on usage of contraception for spacing of births is much higher when women get exposed to family planning counselling at health facility ($e^{1.706}=5.508$) compared to exposure to FP by the mass media ($e^{.457}=1.579$). Similarly, impact on probability of contraception usage for limiting births while exposed to FP at health facility is much higher ($e^{1.638}=5.147$), almost five times more, compared with exposure of women by the mass media ($e^{.583}=1.792$), around 80 per cent more. The probability of increased use of contraception for spacing as well as limiting births is much higher amongst women who are counselled about family planning at health facility compared to women who get exposed to family planning messages by the mass media.

Effects of Aspirations for Children's Education

Aspirations for children's education depict significant impact on the met need or usage of contraception for limiting births. Further, the impact is much more on the usage for limiting births if women have aspirations for daughters' higher education. Possibly, women or couples who don't discriminate between son's and daughter's education depict higher probability of use of contraception for limiting births compared with other couples. However, the aspirations for children's education do not depict any significant impact on the unmet need for contraception for spacing as well as limiting births.

Effects of Standard of Living

Standard of living depicts significant but positive impact on met need or usage of contraception for spacing births (MNSB) as well as limiting births (MNLB). Thus, usage of contraception improves consistently alongwith increase in the standard of living of the households. Further, the unmet need for limiting births also declines consistently alongwith increase in the standard of living. Overall, the demand or total need for family planning improves alongwith improvements in the standard of living of the households.

Effects of Working Status of Women

Working women, especially for wages or cash, depict significantly higher usage of contraception for limiting births. Rather the usage of contraception for limiting births is higher by around 52 per cent amongst women working for wages ($e^{.422}=1.525$) compared to non-working women. Also, we find that unmet need for contraception for spacing as well limiting births is also significantly lower amongst women working for wages compared to non-working women. Possibly, economic empowerment of women helps in increasing the demand or usage of contraception for spacing as well as limiting births.

Effects of Caste

All currently married women were classified under caste categories as Scheduled Caste or Scheduled Tribe (SC/ST), Other Backward Class (OBC) and Others belonging to none of the two i.e., SC/ST or OBC. Perusal of the parametric estimates pertaining to caste reveals that women belonging to SC/ST and OBC depict significantly lower usage of contraception for spacing (MNSB) as well as limiting births (MNLB). Rather, the extent of usage of contraception for spacing births is lower amongst SC/ST women by 33 per cent ($e^{-.398}=.671$) and amongst OBC women by 18 per cent ($e^{-.194}=.824$) compared with women belonging to other castes. Similarly, we find that usage of contraception for spacing births in lower amongst SC/ST women by 26 per cent and amongst OBC women by 34 per cent. Thus, usage of contraception is significantly lower amongst SC/ST and OBC women compared to other caste women.

Effects of Discussion of Family Planning

The impact of discussion on family planning with husband, friends, relatives, etc., on demand for contraception seems to be positive and significant. The currently married women were classified under categories of discussion on family planning with partner/husband, with friends/neighbours, with other relatives like sister, mother, sister-in-law, mother-in-law, etc., and the women with no discussion on family planning with anybody were classified into the reference category. Perusal of the Table 8.2 reveals that discussion on family planning with husband depicts significant and positive impact on usage of contraception for spacing births and discussion on family planning with friends/neighbours on the usage of contraception for limiting births. Rather probability of usage of contraception for spacing births amongst women who had discussed FP with husband was higher by 2.7 times ($e^{.993}=2.699$) compared with women with no discussion on FP with anybody. Similarly, usage of contraception for limiting births (MNLB) was higher amongst women who had discussed FP with friends or neighbours were higher by around 41 per cent ($e^{..342}=1.408$) compared to the reference category women.

Effects of Rural-Urban Residence

The demand for contraception is significantly higher in urban areas compared to rural areas. Precisely, we find that usage of contraception in urban areas for spacing children is higher by around 30 per cent ($e^{.259}=1.296$) and for limiting births by around 36 per cent ($e^{.306}=1.357$). However, we find that unmet need for contraception for limiting births is higher in the urban areas compared to the rural areas. Thus, overall usage of contraception or met need of contraception for spacing as well as limiting births is significantly higher in urban compared to the rural areas.

Probabilities of Needs of Contraception by Background Characteristics

We now consider the probabilities of having unmet and met need of contraception for spacing and limiting births amongst women with different background characteristics. The responses on usage of contraception from currently married women were categorised into 5 mutually exclusive and exhaustive categories discussed earlier. The category of women with response of no-use and no unmet need of contraception was taken as reference for the response variable for the Multinomial Logit Regression analysis in the present study. The elicited parametric estimates of the regression coefficients have been utilised in the formulas described in the Methodology to highlight the probabilities of having met and unmet need for contraception for spacing and limiting births. The multiple classification analysis table for the adjusted values of probabilities (Pj, j=0,1,..,4) for different categories of women by background characteristics is furnished in Table 8.4.

Met Need of Contraception for Limiting Births (MNLB)

Perusal of column (4) in Table 8.4 reveals probability of usage of contraception for limiting births (P_4) for women with different background characteristics. The usage of contraception for limiting births increases alongwith women's age upto around 35 and thereby levels off or even declines and that is how we find that the probability of usage declines from .58 at age 35 to .39 at age 45. The curvilinear nature of relationship depicted by the estimated structural coefficients pertaining to age of women in earlier section get reflected in terms of patterns of probabilities of use of contraception which increases alongwith age but levels off and even declines amongst women towards later ages during their reproductive career.

The probabilities of usage of contraception for limiting births also increase alongwith increase in number of sons as well as daughters, but increases faster with having sons compared to daughters. It may be of interest to mention that patterns of probabilities of use of contraception for limiting births reflect that couples or women depict choice for having balanced sex composition of children. We find that that there is marginal difference in the probability of use of contraception for limiting births amongst women with two sons (.52) compared to women with one son and one daughter (.45). However, the son-preference in India get clearly reflected as probability of use of contraception for limiting births is much higher amongst women with only two sons (.52) compared to women with only two daughters (.20) and still higher amongst women with three living sons (.57) compared to women with 3 living daughters (.20).

The use of contraception for limiting births increases alongwith increase in education of women and exposure to family planning messages by mass media. Though the coefficient pertaining to exposure to FP at health facility is significantly higher and positive in MNLB equation (1.638) in Table 8.3, and the probability of usage for limiting births amongst such women also turns out to be much higher (.72) in Table 8.4 compared to the reference category i.e., no exposure at the health facility (.41) in Table 8.4.

Table 8.4

MCA Table of Adjusted Values of Probabilities (Pj) from the Model for Unmet and Met Need of FP for Spacing and Limiting Births and No-Use and No Unmet Need for FP

Predictor Variable	UNSB (P_1) (1)	UNLB (P_2) (2)	MNSB (P_3) (3)	MNLB (P_4) (4)	No-Use (P_0) (5)	Number of Women
Women's Age						
p age 15	0.40	0.04	0.03	0.04	0.49	
p age 25	0.10	0.14	0.04	0.37	0.35	
p age 35	0.01	0.13	0.01	0.58	0.27	
p age 45	0.00	0.08	0.00	0.39	0.53	
Sex Composition of Children						
p 0s 0d	0.03	0.02	0.03	0.08	0.84	9481
p 1s 0d	0.03	0.06	0.03	0.31	0.58	7346
p 0s 1d	0.03	0.04	0.03	0.15	0.74	6241
p 2s 0d	0.02	0.10	0.01	0.52	0.35	6369
p 0s 2d	0.04	0.08	0.03	0.20	0.65	3412
p 1s 1d	0.03	0.10	0.02	0.45	0.40	10813
p 2s 1d	0.02	0.15	0.01	0.63	0.20	8227
p 1s 2d	0.03	0.16	0.02	0.51	0.30	6139
p 3s 0d	0.02	0.15	0.01	0.57	0.26	2420
p 0s 3d	0.05	0.12	0.03	0.20	0.60	1352
Women's Education						
Edn-nil®	0.04	0.15	0.02	0.25	0.54	41798
Primary	0.03	0.13	0.02	0.48	0.34	14335
Secondary	0.03	0.16	0.03	0.38	0.40	20618
Higher	0.04	0.19	0.04	0.40	0.34	8111
Religion						
Hindu®	0.03	0.13	0.01	0.45	0.38	66136
Muslim	0.04	0.14	0.03	0.26	0.53	10121
Christian	0.07	0.12	0.03	0.28	0.50	4544
Other Rel. Comm.	0.03	0.11	0.02	0.43	0.40	4061
By Media-No®	0.03	0.14	0.01	0.34	0.48	30666
By Mass Media	0.03	0.12	0.02	0.47	0.37	54196
At Health F-No ®	0.03	0.13	0.02	0.41	0.41	83450
At Health Facility	0.01	0.10	0.03	0.72	0.14	1412
Aspirations for Children's Education						
Aspiration-No®	0.05	0.16	0.02	0.19	0.59	
Daughter's Edn. Mid.	0.04	0.15	0.02	0.28	0.52	11426
Dauther's Edn. Sec	0.04	0.15	0.01	0.38	0.42	33465
Dauther's Edn. Des	0.04	0.15	0.01	0.39	0.40	37356
Son's Edn. Mid.	0.03	0.12	0.03	0.30	0.51	2781
Son's Edn. Sec.	0.03	0.13	0.02	0.29	0.53	31242
Son's Edn. as Des	0.03	0.13	0.02	0.30	0.52	49392
Living Style Score						
lss0®	0.03	0.14	0.01	0.38	0.44	22569
lss1	0.03	0.13	0.02	0.42	0.40	44409
lss2	0.03	0.12	0.02	0.45	0.37	15738
lss3	0.02	0.11	0.02	0.46	0.39	2146

contd...

...contd...

Predictor Variable	*UNSB* (P_1) *(1)*	*UNLB* (P_2) *(2)*	*MNSB* (P_3) *(3)*	*MNLB* (P_4) *(4)*	*No-Use* (P_0) *(5)*	*Number of Women*
Women' Working Status						
Not Working®	0.03	0.14	0.02	0.39	0.42	54828
Working No-Wage	0.03	0.12	0.01	0.41	0.43	11267
Working With Wage	0.02	0.11	0.02	0.50	0.35	18767
Caste						
Others®	0.03	0.13	0.02	0.45	0.37	36051
SC/ST	0.03	0.12	0.02	0.37	0.45	24334
OBC	0.03	0.13	0.01	0.42	0.41	24477
Discussion on Family Planning						
With Nobody®	0.03	0.12	0.01	0.42	0.42	51419
With Relatives	0.03	0.12	0.01	0.45	0.39	5855
With Husband	0.03	0.19	0.03	0.37	0.38	17742
With Friends	0.02	0.11	0.01	0.50	0.36	9846
Residence						
Rural®	0.03	0.13	0.02	0.40	0.43	58554
Urban	0.03	0.13	0.02	0.46	0.37	26308

Note: 1. ® : Reference Category
2. Pj adjusted values are obtained using estimated coefficients from Table 8.2 in the formulae and putting other predictor variables on their mean values and for the requisite variable the exact value.

The usage of contraception for limiting births also increases amongst women who depict aspirations for higher education for children. The probability of the use also significantly increases amongst working women for wages. Also, we find that probability of the usage increases alongwith increase in the standard of living and is also higher in the urban compared to the rural areas.

Met Need of Contraception for Spacing Births (MNSB)

Probabilities of usage of contraception for spacing births (P_3) amongst women with different background characteristics are provided in column (3) in Table 8.4. Overall we find that the met need or usage of contraception for spacing births is comparatively much lower than for limiting births. However, the curvilinear relationship between the usage for spacing births also get depicted alongwith age, number of living sons and daughters. The probability of use for spacing births increases marginally uptil age 25 and thereby it levels off or even declines in higher age groups. Probabilities of usage of contraception for spacing births are substantially higher amongst women who are working with wages compared to others working without wages and amongst women in urban compared to rural areas.

Unmet Need of Contraception for Limiting Births (UNLB)

Probabilities of having unmet need of contraception for limiting births (P_2) amongst women with different characteristics are provided in column (2) in Table 8.4. The unmet need for limiting births increases with age but tapers off and even declines amongst women in higher age groups. Thus, curvilinear nature of relationships also gets depicted between the unmet need for limiting births and women's age. The probability of unmet need for limiting births is higher amongst women with only two sons compared to women with only two daughters. Interestingly, unmet need for contraception for limiting births increases alongwith education of women. Possibly, more educated women depict stronger intentions for limiting births compared to their counterparts i.e., less educated women. Also, we find unmet need for limiting births is higher amongst Hindu women compared to Muslim, Christian and other religious community's women. Again, we find that probability of unmet need for contraception for limiting births is higher amongst women who have discussed family planning with husbands. Also we find that women who have been counselled about family planning at health facilities also depict higher intentions or unmet need for limiting births.

Unmet Need of Contraception for Spacing Births (UNSB)

Probabilities of having unmet need of contraception for spacing births (P_1) are provided in column 1 of Table 8.4. Overall we find that the unmet need of contraception for spacing births was only 8.2 per cent. However, the unmet need for spacing births is quite high amongst women in younger age groups and almost declines to nil above age 35. Also we find that unmet need for spacing births is marginally low amongst women with more sons than daughters. It may be of interest to mention that probability of having unmet need for spacing births is relatively high amongst Muslim and Christian women compared to Hindu women. Also, we find that unmet need for spacing births is also high amongst women who don't reflect any aspiration for education.

No-Use and No-Unmet Need of Contraception

The extent of non-usage of contraception and also no-unmet need of contraception can be elicited from column 5 in Table 8.4. Rather, one can discern the extent of overall demand for contraception in India, which is complementary to probability of no-use and no-unmet need for spacing as well as limiting births. Thus, the probability of no-use and no-unmet need (P_0) seems to decline alongwith education of women implying that overall demand for contraception comprising unmet and met need for spacing and limiting births increases alongwith women's education. Thus, we find that overall demand for contraception also depicts curvilinear relationship with women's age. Also, we find that overall demand for contraception is higher amongst women with more of sons than daughters. We also find that overall demand for contraception is high amongst women exposed to family planning messages by mass media. Also, we find overall demand for contraception is higher amongst Hindu women compared to Muslim and Christian women. Again, we find that overall demand for contraception increases alongwith increase in standard of living. We also find that overall demand for contraception is higher amongst women working for wages. The demand for contraception is lower amongst SC/ST women compared with OBC and other caste women. Overall demand for contraception is also found to be higher amongst women who have discussed family planning compared to those who have not. Also, the demand for contraception is higher in urban compared to rural areas.

Summary and Concluding Remarks

The study has highlighted effects of selected socioeconomic and demographic predictor variables on the four components of demand for contraception *viz.*, met and unmet need of contraception for spacing and limiting births. The selected predictor variables under the purview of the study comprise women's age, number and sex composition of children, women's education, religion, exposure on family planning by mass media and at health facility visited by her, living standards, women's working status, caste, discussion on FP with others, and rural-urban residence. The Multinomial Logit Regression analysis has elicited relative significance and directions of effects of selected socioeconomic and demographic predictor variables on the four components of demand for contraception.

Total need or demand for family planning in India is 65 per cent as per NFHS-2 and only 75 per cent of the demand is satisfied implying that still 25 per cent of the need for FP remains unfulfilled. The unmet need for contraception for spacing and limiting births is around 16.2 per cent comprising half for spacing (8.2) and half for limiting births (8.0).

The unmet need of contraception for spacing births is predominantly amongst younger age group, married women in the age groups 15-24, and that for limiting births is predominantly amongst women in later reproductive age groups of 25-39. Similarly, the usage of contraception for spacing births is high amongst the younger age group women with no or one living child and for limiting births amongst women with two or more living children. Further, the usage of contraception for limiting births gets much higher amongst women with more of sons compared with daughters, implying deep-rooted son-preference phenomenon in the Indian society.

All women with unmet need of contraception may not be potential users of contraception. However, analysis of reasons for no-use amongst non-users category women, numbering 43335 out of the total of 84862, reveals that the usage of family planning can be conveniently enhanced by around 19.2 per cent amongst these non-users category of women through assuaging method-specific reasons for non-use like elimination of familial and societal opposition through IEC interventions, alleviation of fear of side effects and health risks through proper counselling through mass media and at health facilities, imparting correct information and easy accessibility of quality contraception services and methods, etc. Thus, the increase of 19.2 per cent amongst these non-users categories of women would imply an increase in met need of contraception by 9.9 per cent or increase in the usage of contraception from 48.9 per cent to 58.8 per cent in the present analysis.

However, 27 per cent of the total pregnancies amongst non-users of contraception category of women are unintended comprising mistimed and unwanted pregnancies, which implies lot of unfulfilled demand for contraception and thus potential users of contraception could be many more. The Multinomial Logit Regression analysis clearly reveals curvilinear nature of relationship between all the four components of demand for contraception *viz.*, unmet need of contraception for spacing births (UNSB), the unmet need for limiting births (UNLB), met need of contraception for spacing births (MNSB) and the met need for limiting births (MNLB); and the three predictor variable *viz.*, age of respondent, number of living sons and number of living daughters, clearly reflect that the effects on the response variables increase alongwith age, number of living sons and daughters, upto some level beyond which the effects taper off or even decline.

Usage of contraception for limiting births increases much faster amongst women having more of living sons compared to daughters. Rather, the usage increases much faster after having two sons, which clearly reflects that there is still a deep rooted son-preference in the Indian society.

Women's empowerment, especially economic empowerment characterised by working for wages, as well as overall improvements in the economic conditions characterised by improvements in the standards of living of the households also result into significant improvement in the demand for family planning in India. Women's education also depicts positive and significant effect on the usage of contraception for spacing as well as limiting births. Interestingly, impact of women's education on the usage of contraception for spacing births are much more pronounced compared with effects on the usage for limiting births.

Religious differentials in usage of contraception for limiting as well as spacing births narrow down after accounting for other socioeconomic factors in the multivariate analysis, but still the usage for limiting births remains significantly higher amongst Hindu compared to Muslim and Christian women. On the other hand, the usage for spacing births remains significantly high amongst Muslim and Christian women compared to Hindu women. This could be because of religious bias against limiting methods of contraception amongst Muslim and Christian women. Such religious biases can be alleviated through interventions from religious leaders or proper and effective IEC interventions through mass-media.

Exposure to family planning by media as well at health facilities depicts significant impact on the usage of contraception for spacing as well as limiting births. Interestingly, exposure to family planning or counselling on family planning at the health facilities depict much stronger impact on the demand for contraception compared to exposure through mass media. Thus, counselling on family planning at health facility can be much more effective in terms of increasing demand for contraception compared to exposure on mass media. Further, interpersonal communication in terms of discussion on family planning with friends, relatives and husbands by women also imparts significant effect on demand for contraception in India.

Aspirations for children's education amongst women also facilitate higher demand for contraception. Interestingly, probabilities of usage of contraception for limiting births improve significantly amongst women with aspiration for children's education, especially for daughters, to higher levels.

Higher standards of living depict significant and positive impact on the usage of contraception for spacing as well as limiting births. Thus, women from higher standards of living households also depict higher usage of contraception for spacing as well as limiting births. Rather, impact of standard of living depicts relatively higher impact on the usage of contraception for spacing births compared with limiting births.

Usage of contraception or met need of contraception for limiting as well as spacing births seems to be significantly lower amongst the SC/ST women as well as the OBC women compared to other caste women.

Interpersonal communications, especially discussion of women with their friend and relatives, depict significant and positive impact on the usage of contraception for limiting births. However, discussion on family planning with husbands depict positive impact on the usage of contraception for spacing births or in other words, only of the usage of spacing methods.

Usage of contraception for spacing as well as limiting births is significantly higher in urban compared with the rural areas possibly because of higher accessibility and awareness about the family planning methods.

Policy Imperatives

The study's primary recommendations are that policies and programmes should focus on promoting contraception usage amongst non-users categories of women by assuaging method specific misapprehensions through proper counselling on fears of side effects and health risks, imparting correct information on contraceptive methods through mass media and proper counselling at health facilities, increased supply and accessibility of quality contraceptive methods, etc., would increase usage of contraception and result into reduction in unintended pregnancies, which often lead to unsafe abortions and thus, detrimental to women's health.

Though all women in the non-use of contraception category may not be the potential users of contraception but assuaging some important reasons of non-use like religious and familial opposition to use contraception, alleviation of misapprehensions about side effects and health risks, awareness and accessibility of contraceptive methods, etc., can conveniently facilitate increased demand for contraception by 19.4 per cent amongst non-users category women implying usage of contraception could easily be increased from 48.9 to 57.5 per cent. Still we find that increased awareness and accessibility of quality contraception is necessitated and can conveniently enhance usage of contraception.

Unmet need of contraception for spacing of births is much higher amongst women in younger age groups and with no or one living child. Thus, spacing methods need to be advocated especially amongst younger and low parity women for spacing children which have implications for child and maternal morbidity and mortality too.

Unmet need of contraception for limiting births is higher amongst women beyond age 25 and after having at least two children. Thus, advocacy of limiting methods need to be focused amongst women in the middle age groups and predominantly amongst women with at least one or two children, with special focus on women with daughters only because of extremely low usage due to desire for having a son. Thus, alleviation of son-preference, which is deep rooted in the Indian society, can definitely lead to changes in fertility preferences and enhancement in the contraception usage for limiting births.

Women's empowerment through better education and gainful employment helps in increasing demand for contraception for spacing as well as limiting births and is an ideal goal by itself. Counselling about family planning at health facilities compared to exposure through mass media depicts relatively pronounced effects on usage of contraception for spacing as well as limiting births.

Religious differentials in usage of contraception for limiting as well as spacing births narrow down after accounting for other socioeconomic factors in the multivariate analysis, but still the usage for limiting births remain significantly higher amongst Hindu compared to Muslim and Christian women. On the other hand, the usage for spacing births remains significantly high amongst Muslim and Christian women compared to Hindu women. This could be because of religious bias against limiting methods of contraception amongst Muslim and Christian women. Such religious biases can be alleviated through interventions from religious leaders or proper and effective IEC interventions through mass media.

Concerted efforts towards improvements in standards of living, interpersonal communications, counselling about family planning at health facilities, sensitisation of women about children's education, will also bring about pronounced effects on usage of contraception for spacing as well as limiting births.

However, increased usage and demand for family planning and easy accessibility of wider range of quality contraception methods would be an important step towards improving health of women, fertility reduction, achievement of demographic goals and enhancing individual rights.

Contraception, which has been relegated to the back-burner as per recent population policy pronouncements, need to be prioritised and focused attention on supply as well as demand side factors influencing usage of contraception would facilitate fertility reduction, improvement in women's and children's health, hastening the process of demographic transition and population stabilisation in India.

References

Ashford, Lori (2003). "Unmet need for Family Planning: Recent Trends and Their Implications for Programs", Policy Brief; Population Reference Bureau Measure Communications, Washington DC.

Becker, Stan (1999). "Measuring Unmet Need: Wives, Husbands or Couples", *International Family Planning Perspectives* 25(4): 172-80.

Bhushan, Indu (1997). "Understanding Unmet Need", The John Hopkins School of Public Health: Center for Communication Programs; *Working Paper No*. 4. Baltimore.

Bongaarts, John (1990). "The Measurement of Wanted Fertility", *Population and Development Review* 16(3): 487-506.

———. (1997). "The Proximate Determinants of Unwanted Childbearing in the Developing World", Paper presented at the 1997 Annual Meeting of the Population Association of America, Washington, D.C., 27-29 March.

Bongaarts, J. and Bruce J. (1995). "The Causes of Unmet Need for Contraception and the Social Content of Services", *Studies in Family Planning* 26(2).

Carl, Haub and Brit Herstad (2002). "Family Planning Worldwide 2002 Data Sheet", Population Reference Bureau, Washington DC.

Casterline, John B. and Steven W. Sinding (2000). "Unmet Need for Family Planning in Developing Countries and Implications for Population Policy", *Population Council*. New York.

Choudhry, R.H. (2001). "Unmet Need for Contraception in South Asia: Levels, Trends, and Determinants", *Asia-Pacific Population Journal* 16(3).

Gulati, S.C. (1996a). "Contraceptive Method's Use and Choice in Kerala and Uttar Pradesh: Multinomial Logit Analysis of the National Family Health Survey in 1992-93 (NFHS-1) Data", in *Demography India* 25(1): 205-220, July.

———. (1996b). "Contraceptive Use in India, 1992-93", National Family Health Survey Subject Reports, No. 2, October 1996; International Institute for Population Sciences, Mumbai, India and East-West Center Program on Population, Honolulu, Hawaii, USA. (Jointly with B.M. Ramesh and Robert D. Retherford).

———. (2005). "Levels and Determinants of Contraceptive Use" Packard Foundation Project Reports, No 7, April 2005; Population Research Center, Institute of Economic Growth. (Jointly with P.N.Mari Bhat and A.J. Francis Zavier).

IIPS (International Institute for Population Sciences) (1998). National Family Health Survey, 1998-99 (NFHS-2).

Kulkarni, Sumati and Minja Kim Choe, "Wanted and Unwanted Fertility in Selected States of India", National Family Health Survey Subject Reports, No 6. February 1998; International Institute for Population Sciences, Mumbai, India and East-West Center Program on Population, Honolulu, Hawaii, USA.

Murray, Christopher and Lopez Alan (eds.) (1998). *Health Dimensions of Sex and Reproduction*. Vol. 3, Global Burden of Disease. Boston: Harvard University Press.

Nag, M. (1984). "Some Cultural Factors Affecting Costs of Fertility Regulation", *Population Bulletin of United Nations* (17).

Packard Foundation (1998). "The Unmet Need for Contraception in Developing Countries", Rand Policy Brief, RB-5024.

Potts, Malcolm (2006). "The Unmet Need for Family Planning", *Population Press*, Packard Foundation.

Retherford, Robert D. and Minja Kim Choe (1993). *Statistical Models for Causal Analysis*. New York: John Wiley & Sons Inc.

Robey, B., J. Ross and I. Bhushan (1996). "Meeting Unmet Need: New Strategies", *Population Reports*, Series J, No. 43. Baltimore, Johan Hopkins School of Public Health, Population Information Program.

Westoff, C.F. (1992). "Measuring the Unmet Need for Contraception: Comment on Bongaarts", *Population and Development Review* 18(3).

Westoff, C.F., Bankole A. (2000). "Trends in the Demand for Family Limitation in Developing Countries", *International Family Planning Perspectives* 26(2).

Zappella, M. (1997). "Beyond Access: Addressing the Unmet Need for Family Planning", *People and Development Challenges* 4(7).

Appendix A-8.1

Descriptive Statistics of the Selected Variables under Study

Variable	*Description of the Variable*	*Min.*	*Max.*	*Mean*	*Std. Deviation*
AGE	Current age—respondent	15	49	31.0	8.6
AGESQ	Age squared	225	2,401	1,037.5	559.3
NLS	Number of living son	0	10	1.4	1.2
NLSSQ	Nlssq	0	100	3.2	4.9
NLD	Number of living daughter	0	11	1.3	1.2
NLDSQ	Nldsq	0	121	3.1	5.3
WEDNP	Primary education	0	1	0.2	0.4
WEDNHS	Secondary education	0	1	0.2	0.4
WENHIGR	Higher education	0	1	0.1	0.3
RELMUS	Muslim	0	1	0.1	0.3
RELCHR	Christian	0	1	0.1	0.2
RELOTH	Other religion	0	1	0.0	0.2
EXFPM	Exposure about family planning by mass media	0	1	0.6	0.5
EXFPHF	Exposure about family planning at health facility	0	1	0.0	0.1
ASDEDNM	Aspirations for daughter's education upto middle level	0	1	0.1	0.3
ASDEDNH	Aspirations for daughter's education upto higher level	0	1	0.4	0.5
ASDEDND	Aspirations for daughter's education upto her desired level	0	1	0.4	0.5
ASSEDNM	Aspirations for son's education upto middle level	0	1	0.0	0.2
ASSEDNH	Aspirations for son's education upto higher level	0	1	0.4	0.5
ASSEDND	Aspirations for son's education upto his desired level	0	1	0.6	0.5
LSS1	Living style score low	0	1	0.5	0.5
LSS2	Living style score medium	0	1	0.8	0.4
LSS3	Living style score high	0	1	1.0	0.2
WWNoCash	Working without wage	0	1	0.1	0.3
WWWCash	Working with wage	0	1	0.2	0.4
SC/ST	Caste SC/ST	0	1	0.3	0.5
OBC	Caste OBC	0	1	0.3	0.5
FPDWOthers	Family planning discussed with others	0	1	0.1	0.3
FPDWHus	Family planning discussed with husband	0	1	0.2	0.4
FPDWFriends	Family planning discussed with friends	0	1	0.1	0.3
RES-Urban	Urban residence	0	1	0.3	0.5

Appendix A-8.2

Multiplicative Effects of Predictor Variables (e^{β}) on the Odds Ratios (Ω's) in the Multinomial Logit Model

Abbreviated	*Exp (β)*			
Variable	*UNSB*	*UNLB*	*MNSB*	*MNLB*
AGE	1.053	1.549	1.461	1.845
AGESQ	0.996	0.993	0.992	0.991
NLS	1.438	5.205	1.342	7.723
NLSSQ	0.965	0.822	0.87	0.716
NLD	1.528	2.935	1.206	2.491
NLDSQ	0.964	0.883	0.958	0.848
WEDNP	1.17	1.281	1.6	1.584
WEDNHS	1.392	1.53	2.474	1.769
WENHIGR	1.866	2.185	4.086	1.498
RELMUS	1.12	0.758	1.317	0.413
RELCHR	2.051	0.723	1.369	0.46
RELOTH	1.159	0.841	1.272	0.899
EXFPM	1.077	1.183	1.579	1.792
EXFPHF	1.122	2.197	5.508	5.147
ASDEDNM	1.011	1.047	0.976	1.17
ASDEDNH	1.212	1.303	1.128	1.95
ASDEDND	1.274	1.397	1.201	2.068
ASSEDNM	0.74	0.906	2.009	0.79
ASSEDNH	0.785	0.92	1.244	0.864
ASSEDND	0.712	0.914	1.121	0.799
LSS1 (Low)	1.04	1.044	1.345	1.238
LSS2 (Med)	1.079	1.079	1.673	1.423
LSS3 (High)	0.905	0.881	1.813	1.385
WWWNoCash	0.902	0.839	0.876	1.029
WWWCash	0.843	0.966	1.105	1.525
SC/ST	0.997	0.764	0.844	0.671
OBC	1.022	0.862	0.661	0.824
FPDWOthers	1.188	1.135	0.843	1.172
FPDWHusband	1.077	1.746	2.699	0.985
FPDWFriends	0.904	1.062	1.214	1.408
RES-Urban	0.974	1.139	1.296	1.357

9

Social Returns from Family Planning and Fertility Decline in India

PUSPITA DATTA

Introduction

It has been widely established that child schooling has far reaching influence on shaping a child's subsequent living, in particular and social and economic development of the society, in general. It is a well known fact that there has been a decline in the fertility over the years. Almost half of the married couples in developing nations now use some form of modern contraception. Consequently, desired family sizes reported by both women and men in various survey responses are found to be remarkably decreasing in most of the developing countries including India. It is unlikely that these two virtually simultaneous changes in educational opportunities and fertility have no causal links. A growing interest has been noticed in recent years, to investigate the relationship between fertility decline in terms of family size and child schooling (Knodel *et al.*, 1990; Montgomery and Lloyd, 1999), which is mainly associated with the child's quantity-quality trade-off.

Family size is an important determinant of children's education. Even after adjustment for many other powerful correlates of educational attainment, a strong inverse association remains between family size and child's education (Knodel, 1992; Knodel and Wongsith, 1991). The relationship of fertility in terms of family size with child schooling, is seen to vary over time and among countries according to several factors; the stage of economic development, role played by the state, the phase of demographic transition and the nature of the family system. The relationship between child's schooling and family size may also vary within different subgroups of the population (Diamond *et al.*, 1999). This decision varies according to various social, economic and demographic characteristics of the parents (Ilahi, 2001). Some of the main factors that have an influence on child schooling are wealth of the family, educational level of the parents, rural-urban residence, sex of the child and their birth order.

There are significant gender differences in child schooling in the Indian states (Pal, 2003). Birth order is also said to affect educational attainment especially for girl child (Sudha, 1997). The first-born daughters appear to be the greatest beneficiary of the changing emphasis on quality over quantity from the decline in the family size and changing reproductive outcomes as she is released from the burden of attending to younger siblings (Bhat, 2002). The economic implications of findings from some psychology and sociology literatures suggest that in the presence of capital constraints, families may not be able to afford to send their earlier born children to school, but may be able to send their later born children due to the income earned by their older siblings. In fact, male first-born children are less likely to attend school than their later born siblings and more likely to work as child labourers. Household income is expected to have a negative effect on children's market work and home production and a positive effect on children's schooling. (Emerson and Souza, 2002; DeGraff *et al.*, 1992).

The first section of this chapter enlightens a theoretical framework for how family size is associated with child schooling and also some empirical evidences to show the family size-child schooling relationship and gender and birth order effect on child schooling. The next section discusses the methods and data used in this study and its next part presents the results and discussion of the analysis, with some concluding remarks.

Association between Family Size and Child Schooling

In India, considerable increase in educational level can be noticed during the last few decades. The literacy rate has increased almost 30 per cent during the period of 1971 to 2001. It is a documented fact that there has also been a substantial decline in fertility during the same period. According to SRS data, TFR has declined from 5.2 in 1971 to 3.1 in 2001. It is unlikely that these two virtually simultaneous changes in educational opportunities and fertility have no causal links. At macro level, a reduction in the total number of children at any point of time may be reflected after 5-6 years on the number of children of school entrance age (Jones, 1975). This also implies that there will be an increase in the quality of education as teacher-pupil ratio will increase and this in turn helps individuals to obtain a better job in future and thereby replace the unskilled workforce of the nation with skilled manpower in future. Addressing the issue of long term implications of low fertility in Kerala, Rajan and Zachariah (1998) stated that the pressure on schools and colleges now is not a matter of concern and presently there are ample opportunities for the educational system to concentrate on the quality of education rather than on quantity. When the volume of total consumers or in other words, number of children becomes less in number, there may be an increase in the savings level at the national as well as household level (Coale and Hoover, 1958). Providing education to the children involve an increase in consumption by creating new expenses relating to schooling and this decreases the benefit derived from children by removing them from family productive system or earning system at household level (Axinn, 1993; Caldwell, 1980). Accordingly, the parents take the decisions regarding child schooling which explains the relationship between family size and child schooling at family level.

Theoretical Reasons for Relating Family Size and Child Schooling

The relationship between family size and child schooling is generally explained through the quantity-quality trade-off theory. A key element of the quantity-quality model is an interaction between quantity and quality in the budget constraint that leads to rising marginal costs of quality with respect to family size; this generates a trade-off between quality and quantity (Becker and Lewis, 1973; Rosenzweig and Evenson, 1977; Becker, 1981; Hanushek, 1992; Kaplan, 1994). Economic theories of fertility are generally built on the premise that fertility and children's schooling are jointly determined outcomes of a common set of exogenous determinants.

When considering that the choices of quality and quantity of children, in a household, are thus determined simultaneously by the parents, that is, it is assumed that the total investment in human capital for each child as well as the level of fertility of the parents, are endogenous variables. In this case, one can observe the presence of a bias due to the occurrence of endogenous decisions, that are made conjointly and that are influenced by common determinants. This statistical bias is called simultaneity bias. The estimates of the impact of family size on human capital investment in children can be compromised given the existence of this bias. In models where fertility and education are determined in the same time, the direction of the simultaneity bias depends on how the size of the family relates to the costs of education, and of schooling in relation to family size. In general, the bias will be less in low-income countries, in rural areas, where levels of education are low. In a developing country like India, parents may not have full control on their fertility behaviour, especially in the presence of elder members in the family. In addition, there is uncertainty about the survival of the children (Bhat, 2002). Couples generally cannot plan their family size well in advance with a calculation of net lifetime return of schooling especially if the parents are illiterate. Probably, in these situations, the decision about family size is not substantially affected by decisions regarding educational investment in children, which makes the simultaneity bias weak or even non-existent. In other words, in this case, the fertility can be considered a "less" endogenous variable. On the other hand, the simultaneity bias should be stronger among more educated women, in urban regions and, of course, in times of low fertility (Verona, 2006). Thus, it can be said that in Indian rural set-up and among the illiterate parents, the effect of fertility on child schooling is causal and unidirectional in nature and free from the simultaneous bias.

Empirical Evidences Relating Family Size with Child Schooling, Gender Effect and Birth Order Effect

Literatures addressing the issues of children's schooling decisions at household levels mostly combined child labour with child schooling and more emphasis were laid on child labour. Child schooling was identified as the opportunity costs of child labour (Deb and Rosati, 2004; Jeong, 2005; Ray, 2000; Kulkarni *et al.*, 2004; Emerson and Souza, 2002). Studies based on primary surveys in Thailand and Vietnam exhibit that, even after adjustment for the many other powerful correlates of educational attainment, a strong inverse association operates between family size and the percentage of children who enter lower and upper secondary (Knodel and Wongsith, 1991; Knodel, 1992; Sudha, 1997; Anh *et al.*, 1998).

In order to identify the effect of fertility transition on child's education in Brazil, a study by Marteleto (2005) considered the cohorts of children born in pre- and post-transitional period. The findings based on a nationally representative data show that the fertility decline advantaged the younger cohort by increasing the proportion of smaller families, although the negative effect of family size on children's education did not decline. In India, Bhat (2002) using NCAER data has shown that there exist a trade-off among illiterate parents, and he argued that first-born daughters have the most to gain from this development as in smaller families they are less likely to forgo schooling to take care of younger siblings. Children with many or closely spaced siblings are often thought to be disadvantaged with respect to their schooling in comparison with other children (Eloundou-Enyegue, 1999; DeGraff *et al.*, 1992).

In this light of discussion, the present chapter first attempts to examine the impact of family size on child schooling in India and then, to find out whether there exist any family level discrimination. This chapter made an effort to observe how family size influences child schooling with respect to child's sex and birth order composition using NFHS-2 and NFHS-3 datasets.

Data and Methods of Analysis

The study used the secondary dataset from the National Family and Health Survey-2 (1998-99) and National Family and Health Survey-3 (2005-2006). In the household schedule of NFHS dataset, for each member of the household aged 6 and above questions were asked about years of schooling, whether the member is still going to school or not and reasons for continuing/discontinuing school. Information is also available for women's educational aspirations for both boys and girls. In the study, fertility will be expressed through the component family size and to express child schooling two variables will be used—whether enrolled in school that is, ever been to school or not and school attendance that is, whether the member is still in school or not.

In NFHS datasets, the schooling information is given in the household file for all the members of the household, whereas detailed information about women's fertility behaviour and contraceptive behaviour, and birth history of each child is provided in the individual file. After matching the mother from the women's individual file of the member of household aged 6-14 years, the required dataset has been created, where along with children aged 6-14 years all the information of their mother's fertility behaviour can be found. The final working data files consists of total 83105 and 87764 children of age 6-14 years of illiterate parents in the rural areas of India in NFHS-2 and NFHS-3 respectively. Literate parents, even if any one of the parents is literate, are excluded from the analysis because of the explicit fact that, when parents are literate they obviously want educated children as well. It is mentioned earlier, that in rural areas and among illiterates the simultaneity bias will be almost negligible. Thus, the results will be free from the bias and moreover, it is also important from the policy point of view.

Results and Discussion

The profile of the children (6-14 years) of illiterate parents in rural India according to socioeconomic and demographic characteristics is described through Table 9.1. The percentage of children in the age 6-14 varies between 9 to 13 per cent in various ages. The sex ratio (F/M) of the child population in the above mentioned age group is around 923 for both NFHS-2 and NFHS-3. In both NFHS-2 and NFHS-3 around 27 per cent of those children are of the first order birth, while around 31 per cent of them belong to birth order of four or more in NFHS-2, the percentage belonging to the same group in NFHS-3 is almost 29 per cent. More than half of the children (almost 56 per cent) are born to the non-working mother ageing between 25-34 years in both the datasets. More than two-third of these children are from those mothers who are using any contraceptives in NFHS-2 while the share of children aged 6-14 years is three-fourth of those mothers who used any contraception. In NFHS-2, around 63 per cent of these children belonged to the parents having four or more surviving children while 37 per cent are from those parents whose desired family size were two. On the other hand, according to NFHS-3, around 57 per cent of children aged 6-14 belongs to the parents with four or more living children which is less compare to NFHS-2 and 48 per cent are from those parents whose desired family size were two which is much higher compared to NFHS-2. This may occur as the demand for desired family size is decreasing and people are having smaller family compared to earlier preferences. These children are mostly from the general caste Hindu families with medium standard of living.

Table 9.1

Percentage Distribution of Children Aged 6-14 Years of Illiterate Parents by Selected Background Characteristics in Rural India for NFHS-2 (1998-99) and NFHS-3 (2005-06)

Background Characteristics	*Percentage of Children*	
Characteristics of the Child	*NFHS-2*	*NFHS-3*
Age of the Child		
6	12.7	12.1
7	11.3	11.6
8	12.7	12.5
9	10.2	10.1
10	12.7	12.6
11	9.4	9.6
12	12.0	11.8
13	9.2	10.7
14	9.7	8.9
Sex of the Child		
Male	52.1	51.9
Female	47.9	48.1
Order of Birth		
1	26.7	27.1
2	24.0	25.4
3	18.6	18.6
4+	30.7	28.9

contd...

...contd...

Background Characteristics	*Percentage of Children*	
Characteristics of the Child	*NFHS-2*	*NFHS-3*
Characteristics of the Parents		
Age of the Mother		
<25 years	4.1	3.2
25-34	56.2	54.3
35 and above	39.8	42.5
Mother's Working Status		
Not working	56.4	55.9
Working	43.6	44.1
Contraceptive Use		
Yes	67.0	76.7
No	33.0	23.3
Number of Surviving Children		
1	1.8	2.3
2	13.5	17.4
3	21.7	22.8
4+	63.0	57.4
Desired Family Size		
1	2.2	3.3
2	36.9	47.9
3	27.0	26.6
4+	33.8	21.3
Socioeconomic Characteristics		
Religion		
Hindu	79.1	78.5
Muslim	15.7	16.5
Other religions	5.2	5.1
Caste		
General	38.9	28.2
Scheduled caste	19.3	20.4
Scheduled tribe	9.3	9.2
Other backward castes	32.5	42.2
Standard of Living		
Low	36.0	31.0
Medium	47.3	35.2
High	16.7	32.2
Total Number of Children	83105	87764

From bivariate analysis (Table 9.2) it was evident that proportion of children ever enrolled in school has declined slightly from 86 per cent in NFHS-2 to 84 per cent in NFHS-3, but among those enrolled children the proportion who continued schooling or attending school increased in NFHS-3 to 94 per cent while it was only 78 per cent in NFHS-2. As the main focus of this chapter is on how family size and contraceptive use are related with child schooling, so the stress is given on the discussion of these two variables. The children enrolled in school are more among the users of any contraceptives compared to non-user of any contraceptives in both the datasets. It can be noticed that as number of surviving children increases the percentage of school enrolment as well as school attendance both decreases, though the percentages are higher for NFHS-3.

Table 9.2

Percentage of Children (6-14 years) of Illiterate Parents in Rural India according to Ever been to School and School Attendance NFHS-2 (1998-99) and NFHS-3 (2005-06)

Background Characteristics	*Ever been to School*		*School Attendance*	
Characteristics of the Child	*NFHS-2*	*NFHS-3*	*NFHS-2*	*NFHS-3*
Age of the Child				
6	78.2	56.7	69.4	95.4
7	85.6	77.1	82.7	98.3
8	86.3	83.1	83.6	98.5
9	89	89.7	86.5	98.3
10	86.6	89.6	82.4	97.3
11	88.5	93.0	83.1	96.0
12	84.5	90.6	75.7	92.0
13	87.4	90.4	74.3	88.3
14	84.8	91.3	66.6	83.4
Sex of the Child				
Male	89.4	86.0	82.6	94.7
Female	81.4	82.1	73.7	93.9
Order of Birth				
1	89.4	87.7	82.6	95.5
2	87.9	87.5	81.3	94.7
3	85.4	84.5	78.3	94.1
4+	80.4	77.5	72.3	92.7

contd...

...contd...

Background Characteristics	*Ever been to School*		*School Attendance*	
Characteristics of the Child	*NFHS-2*	*NFHS-3*	*NFHS-2*	*NFHS-3*
Characteristics of the Parents				
Age of the Mother				
<25 years	82.4	67.4	74.5	97.6
25-34	86.2	83.9	79.8	95.6
35 and above	84.9	85.6	76.6	92.4
Mother's Working Status				
Not working	88.6	84.1	83	95.4
Working	82.4	84.1	74	92.9
Contraceptive Use				
No	74.7	71.9	67.2	92.4
Yes	90.8	87.8	83.8	94.8
Number of Surviving Children				
1	94.1	89.1	89	97.9
2	95.3	92.2	90.7	97.5
3	92.7	89.4	86.7	95.8
4+	80.8	79.4	72.5	92.3
Desired Family Size				
1	95.6	85.9	90.8	97.9
2	93.5	95.3	87.4	95.7
3	86.9	85.9	79.3	93.3
4+	75.2	81.6	66.9	91.2
Socioeconomic Characteristics				
Religion				
Hindu	86.1	85.8	78.8	94.7
Muslim	80.3	74.8	72.6	91.6
Other religions	93.4	88.6	88.5	94.8
Caste				
General	90.1	87.8	83.8	95.4
Scheduled caste	82.1	83.4	74.1	92.7
Scheduled tribe	74.8	76.0	66.3	92.0
Other backward classes	85.5	83.5	78.1	94.7
Mass Media Exposure				
No exposure	76.1	74.5	67.8	91.4
Any exposure	93.9	89.0	87.7	95.5
Standard of Living				
Low	73.5	72.3	64.4	90.9
Medium	90.1	86.0	82.9	93.5
High	98.5	93.7	95.4	97.6
Total	85.5	84.1	78.3	94.3

Though it came out that the parents using any contraceptives are more inclined to send their children to school. The parents those who are deliberately trying to control their family size by using contraception have a higher tendency to send their children to school, which is clear from the difference of the percentages in Table 9.3 of children attending school. Though this percentage declines with the increase in the number of surviving children, there is a considerable difference in percentage of children attending school among 'never user' and 'ever user'. The difference between the percentage of school attendance among the 'never user' and 'ever users' of contraceptive increases from 10 per cent to 15 per cent as the number of surviving children increases from one to four and above in NFHS-2, while the differences are small in NFHS-3. It can be observed that in NFHS-3, if the number of surviving children is one or two, the differences of school attendance among the children of 'ever user' of contraceptive and 'never users' became very minor whereas this difference is more in NFHS-2. This result clearly indicates that though the situation of child schooling is improving, still there is a quantity-quality trade-off. The trade-off is prominent among the female children compared to their male counterparts in NFHS-2, while the trade-off became weak in NFHS-3.

Table 9.3

Percentage of Children Aged 6-14 Years of Illiterate Parents Attending School by Mother's Contraceptive Use and Family Size in Rural India (NFHS-2)

Use of Contraceptives	*Number of Surviving Children*	*% of Children Attending School*					
		Total		*Male*		*Female*	
		NFHS-2	*NFHS-3*	*NFHS-2*	*NFHS-3*	*NFHS-2*	*NFHS-3*
Never used	1	83.1	97.6	84.4	98.0	81.9	97.1
	2	78.1	95.3	81.2	95.6	74.7	95.1
	3	73.2	93.5	78.0	93.4	68.8	93.5
	4+	62.7	91.3	69.0	91.5	57.0	91.0
Ever used	1	93.0	98.2	94.0	98.7	91.4	97.3
	2	92.2	97.7	92.7	97.8	91.3	97.7
	3	87.7	96.1	89.0	96.0	86.1	96.2
	4+	77.8	92.7	82.2	93.2	73.6	92.2

There exists male-female difference in school enrolment and attendance. The illiterate parents intend to send their sons to school more compared to their daughters. The results of Z-test revealed that the difference is significant at one per cent level of significance. To observe whether there are any sex-specific birth order effect of schooling among the children the sample is divided into two categories i.e., first order birth and higher order birth, for each sex. Higher birth order children are less enrolled in school and they are attending school less compared to the first order born children irrespective of their sex. Table 9.4 shows that significant birth order difference exists irrespective of the sex of the children. It may happen due to the fact that the higher order sons or daughters are privileged, as when they are getting admission to school the number of children born to their parents are less and as they are not supposed to share their part of resources they got from their parents. But after that, whether the child will continue schooling or dropout from school that becomes dependent on the number of siblings, so that the difference of school attendance between first order boy or girl to their higher order boy or girls is small, though it is statistically significant.

Table 9.4

Results of Z-Test for Significance Differences in School Enrolment and School Attendance of Children according to Sex and Birth Order, NFHS-3

	Percentage of Children Ever been to School	*Significance*	*Percentage of Children Attending School*	*Significance*
Sex of the Child				
Male	86.0	ψ	94.7	ψ
Female	82.1		93.9	
Birth Order Composition of Child (Male)				
First order male	89.2	ψ	95.9	ψ
Higher order male	84.8		94.2	
Birth Order Composition of Child (Female)				
First order female	86.2	ψ	95.1	ψ
Higher order female	80.6		93.4	

Note: ψ = Difference is significant at 1 per cent level of significance.

Though previously the influences of different socioeconomic and demographic factors were analysed, it is necessary to control the effect of other factors through multivariate analysis to know the significance of each factor. Binary multivariate logistic analyses have been carried out for this purpose, considering school attendance as the dependent variable. Controlling for other socioeconomic factors family size has a significant negative impact on child's school attendance. Irrespective of its effect of

Table 9.5

Logistic Regressions of School Attendance of Children Aged 6-14 Years of Illiterate Parents in Rural India, NFHS-3 (2005-06)

Background Characteristics	*Exp(B)*		
	All Son	*All Daughter*	*All Children*
Characteristics of the Child			
Age of the child	2.81**	2.00**	2.37**
Age of child square	0.94	0.95**	0.95**
Birth order of child (reference=first order)			
Higher birth order	0.96	1.13	0.71**
Sex of the Child (reference=male)			
Female			1.06
Characteristics of the parents			
Age of the mother	1.01	1.00	1.00
Mother's Working Status (reference=not working)			
Working	1.04	0.82	0.92
Contraceptive use (reference=not using/never used)	1.23	1.27	1.26*
Number of surviving children	0.91*	0.94	0.92**
Mass media (reference=no exposure)	1.31*	1.47**	1.38**
Socioeconomic Characteristics of the Household & Community			
Landholding (reference=own no land)	1.27	1.13	1.19
Religion (reference=Hindu)			
Muslim and others	0.63*	0.90	0.74*
Caste (reference=general)			
Scheduled caste	0.94	1.18	1.07
Scheduled tribe	0.83	1.07	0.93
OBC	0.83	0.86	0.84
States (reference=low fertility states)			
Moderate fertility states	1.34	1.37	1.34*
High fertility states	1.51**	1.65**	1.59**
Constant	0.34	1.19	0.78
-2 Log likelihood	3208.38	3266.39	6492.04
Cox & Snell R Square	0.060	0.062	0.062
Total number of cases	8486	8085	16571

Note: *p<0.01, **p<0.001

school attendance through family size, contraceptive use is found to be a significant factor controlling for all other independent variables. Though the effect of sex and birth order were negatively significant for all children it was not significant for the daughters. The binary logistic analysis (in Table

9.6) was carried out for each sex and birth order to understand the impact of family size on child schooling. It was found that except for first order male children there is no significant influence of family size on child schooling. To understand clearly the effect of family size according to birth order, when further analysis carried out considering the higher family size taking the households with illiterate parents and more than 3 children in rural areas, it is found that the effect of family size is significantly negative for the first order or earlier born children. From Table 9.6 it can be said that in the case of earlier born male children the chance of attending school became significantly negative as the family size or number of surviving siblings increases. In probability terms, if the family size increases the probability of school attendance decreases by 11 per cent for all children and it is more for the female children, though the results are not statistically significant. As family size increases, male children are more benefited compared to female children in terms of the school attendance though for female children the results are not statistically significant.

From Table 9.2, it is also clear that all the children of ages 6-14 years of illiterate parents in rural India are not enrolled in school. Only around 84-86 per cent of them are enrolled in school, though, among them 94 per cent continue schooling in 2005-06 (NFHS-3), still in absolute number there are children who are not enrolled and even if they are getting enrolled they are withheld from school. Thus, the result depicts that still there exists school dropout though it declined in 2005-06 (NFHS-3) from 1998-99 (NFHS-2). Therefore, this result calls for a further explanation of the reasons for not enrolled in school and discontinuing school.

To observe the reasons for discontinuance in schooling according to sex, Tables 9.7 and 9.8 have been given. It can be observed that apart from 'not interested in studies', 'cost of schooling' is the main reason for the children irrespective of their sex in NFHS-3. Around 17 per cent female children between ages 6-14 in NFHS-3 are not continuing school as they are required for household work and sibling care. Looking at the reasons for discontinuing schooling according to children's sex, it is found that while the daughters of illiterate parents aged 6-14 years are withheld from school as they have to be engaged in household work and sibling care, for the sons that motive is economic, i.e., sons are withheld from school as they are required for work in the family business or required to work outside home and earning.

Table 9.6

Logistic Regressions of School Attendance of Children Aged 6-14 Years of Illiterate Parents in Rural India, NFHS-3 (2005-06)

Background Characteristics	*Exp(B)*			
	First Order Son	*Higher Order Son*	*First Order Daughter*	*Higher Order Daughter*
Characteristics of the Child				
Age of the child	4.45**	2.50**	1.36	2.25**
Age of child square	0.92**	0.94**	0.97	0.95**
Characteristics of the Parents				
Age of the mother	1.06	1.00	0.99	1.00
Mother's working status (reference=not working)				
Working	1.15	1.02	0.77	0.82
Contraceptive use (reference=not using/never used)	1.31	1.21	1.14	1.32
Number of surviving children	0.78*	0.93	0.88	0.96
Mass media (reference=no exposure)	1.14	1.33	1.82*	1.38*
Socioeconomic Characteristics of the Household & Community				
Landholding (reference=own no land)	1.62	1.19	1.13	1.13
Religion (reference=Hindu)				
Muslim and others	0.69	0.62*	1.14	0.85
Caste (reference=general)				
Scheduled caste	0.73	1.00	0.96	1.23
Scheduled tribe	0.94	0.82	1.03	1.07
Other backward classes	0.52	0.93	0.60	0.94
States (reference=low fertility states)				
Moderate fertility states	1.21	1.39	1.35	1.37
High fertility states	1.74	1.49	2.28	1.51*
Constant	0.01	0.73	13.17	0.69
-2 Log likelihood	618.544	2571.840	704.985	2550.9
Cox & Snell R Square	0.0671	0.062	0.081	0.0597
Total Number of Cases	1562	6924	1599	6486

Note: *p<0.01, **p<0.001

Table 9.7

Reasons for Discontinue Schooling for the Children Aged 6-14 of Illiterate Parents in Rural India, NFHS-3 (2005-06)

Reasons	*Frequency*	*Per cent*
No proper school facility/No transport/School far away	127	4.7
Education not considered necessary	91	3.3
Required for household work and sibling care	341	12.5
Required for family business/earning outside	271	9.9
Cost too much	490	18.0
Not interested in studies	847	31.0
Repeated failure	104	3.8
Got married	7	0.3
No facility for girls/Not safe for girls/No female teacher	71	2.6
Other reasons	379	13.9
Total	2728	100

Table 9.8

Reasons for Discontinue Schooling by Sex of the Children Aged 6-14 Years of Illiterate Parents in Rural India, NFHS-3 (2005-06)

Reasons	*Sex of Child*	
	Male	*Female*
No proper school facility/No transport/School far away	2.2	7.1
Education not considered necessary	2.8	3.8
Required for household work and sibling care	7.7	17.1
Required for family business/earning outside	13.0	6.9
Cost too much	16.2	19.7
Not interested in studies	39.2	23.2
Repeated failure	3.5	4.1
Got married	0.0	0.5
No facility for girls/Not safe for girls/No female teacher	0.5	4.6
Other reasons	14.9	12.9
Total	1344	1385

Conclusion and Policy Implication

The above discussion of results specify that family size plays an important role in child schooling. It is a well-established fact that parent's education has a significant impact on child's school attendance (Pal, 2003). To control the effect of parental education and other diffusion effect of education, the present study considers only the rural illiterate parents and the results show that smaller the family size, more is the child school attendance. Significant sex and birth order differentials are also found to exist. This calls for a better gender discrimination free society, so that all the girl children receive education along with the boys.

As cost of schooling is found to be the most prime reason for not sending a child to school, the planners and policy-makers need to give special attention to reduce the cost (both direct and indirect cost) related to schooling. Direct cost of schooling can be reduced through providing free education, and establishing schools in every village so that it can also reduce the transportation cost. If the child is required to earn for the better livelihood of their family, then there involves indirect cost of schooling for that household when they are sent to schooling. As not interested in studies is found as a main reason for school dropout, action should be to find out the reasons behind what may influence people to discourage them to not send their child to school and should take necessary steps.

With the fertility transition, as people are using contraceptives and desire smaller family, the next consequences of the fertility decline can be seen in the form of more schooling among children. In other way, the returns of fertility decline in terms of smaller family size will result in providing more schooling and, therefore, increase the overall educational level of a society. So far in the fertility research the fact is established that education has a strong negative effect on fertility, i.e., as educational level increases the people desire smaller family. Thus, it can be said that not only schooling can influence the people to achieve their desired smaller family in the context of fertility decline, on the other hand the smaller family during fertility transition can be helpful for fulfilling the target of achieving 'education for all'. While schooling influences to have smaller family size, small family provides more education to children.

References

Anh, T.S., J. Knodel, D. Lam and J. Friedman (1998). "Family Size and Children's Education in Vietnam", *Demography* 35(1): 57-70.

Arokiasamy, P., Kirsty McNay and Robert H. Cassen (2004). "Female Education and Fertility Decline, Recent Developments in the Relationship", *Economic and Political Weekly*, October 9: 4491-4495. available at *http://www.utas.edu.au/ecofin/Library/discussion_papers/papers_00/2000-05.pdf*

Axinn, W.G. (1993). "The Effects of Children's Schooling on Fertility Limitation", *Population Studies* 47(3): 481-493.

Becker, G.S. (1981). *A Treatise on the Family.* Cambridge: Harvard University Press.

Becker, G., and H. Lewis (1973). "On the Interaction between the Quantity and Quality of Children", *Journal of Political Economy* 81(2): s279-s288.

Bhat, P.N. Mari (2002). "Demographic Transition, Family Size and Child Schooling". *Working Paper Series No. 86.* National Council of Applied Economics Research, New Delhi.

———. (2002). "Returning Favour: Reciprocity between Female Education and Fertility in India", *World Development* 30(10): 1791-1803.

Caldwell, J.C. (1980). "Mass Education as a Determinant of the Timing of Fertility Decline", *Population and Development Review* 6(2): 225-255.

Coale, A.J. and E.M. Hoover (1958). *Population Growth and Economic Development in Low-Income Countries.* Princeton NJ: Princeton University Press.

Deb, Partha and Furio Rosati (2004). "Estimating the Effect of Fertility Decisions on Child Labor and Schooling", *Understanding Children's Work,* a joint research project of the ILO, World Bank and UNICEF. *http://www.ucw-project.org/resources/pdf/fertility_child_labor.pdf*

DeGraff, Deborah S., Rechard E.Bilsborrow and Alejandro N. Herrin (1992). "The Implications of High Fertility for Children's Time Use in the Philippnes", in Cynthia B. Lloyd (ed.) *Fertility and Family Size and Structure-Consequences for Families and Children.* The Population Council, New York.

Diamond, I., M. Newby and S. Varle (1999). "Female Education and Fertility: Examining the Links" in C.H. Bledsoe, J.B. Casterline, J.A. Johnson-Kuhn and J.G. Haaga (eds.) *Critical Perspectives on Schooling and Fertility in the Developing World.* Washington DC: National Academy Press.

Eloundou-Enyegue, Parfait M. (1999). "Fertility and Education: What Do We Now Know?", in C.H. Bledsoe, J.B. Casterline, J.A. Johnson-Kuhn and J.G. Haaga (eds.) *Critical Perspectives on Schooling and Fertility in the Developing World.* Washington DC: National Academy Press.

Emerson Patrick, M. and Andre Portela Souza (2002). "Birth Order, Child Labour and School Attendance in Brazil". *Working Paper No. 0212.* Department of Economics, Vanderbilt University.

Hanushek, E. (1992). "The Trade-off between Child Quantity and Quality", *Journal of Political Economy* 100(1): 84-117.

Ilahi, Nadeem (2001). "Children's Work and Schooling: Does Gender Matter? Evidence from the Peru LSMS", *Policy Research Working Paper Series*, No. 2745, The World Bank.

Jeong, Juhyun (2005). "The Determinants of Child Labour and Schooling in Honduras, Nicaragua, and Panama". Department of Economics, Stanford University, Stanford, USA. *http://www-econ.stanford.edu/academics/Honors_Theses/Theses_2005/Jeong.pdf*

Jones, Gavin (1975). *Growth and Educational Planning in Developing Nations*. A Population Council Book. New York: Irvington Publishers Inc.

Kaplan, H. (1994). "Evolutionary and Wealth Flows Theories of Fertility", *Population and Development Review* 20(4): 753-791.

Knodel, J. and M. Wongsith (1991). "Family Size and Children's Education in Thailand: Evidence from a National Sample", *Demography* 28(1): 119-131.

Knodel, J., N. Hvanon and W. Sittitrai (1990). "Family Size and Education of Children in the Context of Rapid Fertility Decline", *Population and Development Review* 16(1): 31-62.

Knodel, John (1992). "Fertility Decline and Children's Education in Thailand: Some Macro and Micro Effects" in Cynthia B. Lloyd (ed.) *Fertility and Family Size, and Structure-Consequences for Families and Children*. The Population Council, New York.

Kulkarni, Sumati, Acharya Rajib and Y. Vaidehi (2004). "Child Labour, Schooling and Fertility: What Does NFHS-II Indicate?", *Demography India* 33(2): 265-294.

Marteleto, Leticia (2005). "Family Size, Demographic Change, and Educational Attainment: The Case of Brazil", *Population Studies Center Research Report 05-584* Survey Research Center, University of Michigan.

McNay, K., P. Arokiasamy and R.H. Cassen (2003). "Why are Uneducated Women in India Using Contraception?: A Multilevel Analysis", *Population Studies* 57(1): 21-40.

Montgomery, Mark R. and C.B. Lloyd (1999). "Excess Fertility, Unintended Births and Children's Schooling" in C.H. Bledsoe, J.B. Casterline, J.A. Johnson-Kuhn and J.G. Haaga (eds.). *Critical Perspectives on Schooling and Fertility in the Developing World*. Washington DC: National Academy Press.

Montgomery, Mark R., Mary Arends-Kuenning and Cem Mete (1999). "The Quantity-Quality Transition in Asia", *Policy Research Division Working Paper* 123, Population Council, New York.

Pal, Sarmistha (2003). "How much of the Gender Difference in Child School Enrolment can be Explained? Evidence from Rural India". Available at *http://129.3.20.41/eps/hew/papers/0309/0309004.pdf*

Rajan, S. Irudaya and K.C. Zachariah (1998). "Long Term Implications of Low Fertility in Kerala, India", *Asia Pacific Population Journal* 13(3): 41-66.

Ray, Ranjan (2000). "The Determinants of Child Labour and Child Schooling in Ghana", *Discussion Paper*, University of Tasmania.

Rosenzweig, M.R. and K.I. Wolpin (1980). "Testing the Quantity-Quality Fertility Model: The Use of Twins as a Natural Experiment", *Econometrica* XLVIII: 227-240.

Rosenzweig, M.R. and R. Evenson (1977). "Fertility, Schooling, and the Economic Contribution of Children in Rural India: An Econometric Analysis", *Econometrica* 45(5): 1066-1079.

Schultz, T. Paul (1988). "Education Investments and Returns", *Handbook of Development Economics*, Volume 1. Amsterdam: North Holland Press.

Sudha, S. (1997). "Family Size, Sex Composition and Children's Education: Ethnic Differentials over Development in Peninsular Malaysia", *Population Studies* 51(2): 139-151.

Verona, A.P.A. (2006). "The Relationship between Fertility and Children's Education in Brazil: A Natural Experiment using Twin Data", available at *http://paa2006.princeton.edu/download.aspx?submissionId=61540*

Section IV

Maternal and Child Health in India

10

Health Inequality in India
Evidence from NFHS-3

WILLIAM JOE, UDAYA S. MISHRA
AND K. NAVANEETHAM

Introduction

Of late, several of the Indian health policies and programmes including the National Rural Health Mission (NRHM) has identified the need for ensuring quality health services to the poorest households residing in the remotest rural regions of the Indian union. Likewise, key international agencies and a lot of non-governmental organisations in the health field have concomitantly stressed upon the actions to improve the health of the deprived. Undoubtedly, these policy initiatives and programmes strongly perceive that the health sufferings arising out of certain systematic deprivations are unfair and iniquitous. Notwithstanding the motivations behind such interventions, much is still left to be explored and scrutinised as regards the efficacy of the policy matrix *per se*. The prime concern arises out of the fact that most of these interventions are, and would be, mediated through distribution of health care facilities—either for direct treatment of health ailments or in the form of certain preventive measures—and therefore, to facilitate this intent a prior and proper knowledge of the distribution of health among the population holds immense significance as the distribution of the former, which is an instrumental matter, is ought to be based upon the latter, which is a more fundamental concern.

In spite of these inherent anxieties involved in designing health interventions, the issue of health deprivation and its measurement to facilitate policy and governance in India has, by and large, remained an untailored exercise. For instance, several of the policy vision documents and official reports assessing the health conditions of the Indian population have firmly placed its focus upon population averages or aggregates. Undeniably, such an approach for assessing health outcome discounts off the possibility wherein the advances toward the envisaged goals may be escorted by engorging gaps among different sections or groups of the population. Apparently, there exists a plethora of academic literature on health disparities in India that widely discusses the region-specific health profiles as well as the group-related scenarios through which health disparities predominantly gets exemplified. But in most of these exercises what gets discounted is the fact that while comparing any health outcome between population subgroups we are ought to observe a disparity positioned around the aggregate outcome, hence these disparities could not be directly termed as inequities unless they are derived subject to the application of different ethical or economic ideals. Moreover, for ensuring an equitable and efficient allocation of public health resources, across varied socioeconomic or geographic clusters, it is imperative to unravel the depth and varied dimensions of health outcomes through adopting measures especially sensitised for equity[1] concerns.

Our intention, here, acknowledges the wider opinion that measures based on averages are no longer considered to be a sufficient indicator; rather, inclusion of health distribution within the defined sets (such as subsets of income or access) has become a fundamental requirement (Gakidou *et al.*, 2003). Measurement based on certain disciplinary principles invariably offers deeper insights regarding the disadvantages suffered by different socioeconomic groups in terms of their health status and helps to provide a true account of health deprivation. In addition, if the measures employed are sensitised for group-related distributional details, it can prove to be more effective in exposing the real troubles of the vulnerable segments. This emphasis on inter-group rather than inter-personal inequality is also motivated by the fact that between-group disparities are politically more salient and often personal destinies and identities are so intimately bound into group affiliations that the resulting patterns of social stratification which emerge are quite entirely lost to social analysis when a thorough-going individualistic approach to inequality assessment is adopted (Majumdar and Subramanian, 2001). In other words, while measuring health inequality it is rather imperative to elevate the socioeconomic dimensions as it forms an integral part of the measurement exercise and perhaps should not be pushed back to the explanation exercises alone (Wagstaff and Doorslaer, 2000), and more so, because an approach that emphasises upon important social determinants of health inequalities can invariably offer better policy inferences (Macinko and Starfield, 2002).

1. Equity, as defined by the International Society for Equity in Health (ISEH), is: "the absence of potentially remediable, systematic differences in one or more aspects of health across socially, economically, demographically, or geographically defined population groups or subgroups".

In the wake of the problem identified above, this chapter is an attempt to contextualise and approach the problem of health disparities in India through the domain of distribution-sensitised and principle-based measurement of health inequity and, thereby, intends to capture its major facets. For the present analysis, we focus upon the health problems of children. Undoubtedly, healthy children assume significance for human and economic development of a country but what is more important is to regard it as their right to survival, protection, participation and development as ratified by the Government of India in 1989 through the Convention on the Rights of the Child (CRC), drafted by the United Nations Commission on Human Rights. Unfortunately, most of the preventable deaths among young children in India, which are caused due to the untoward combination of undernourishment and infectious diseases, are inimical to all these rights. Although the subject of child health and welfare have been a prime agenda for the Central and the various state governments, certainly their intent cannot proceed very far without a prior assessment of its magnitude and varied dimensions. In this regard, fuller information on group-specific child health deprivation and distributive-sensitive summary indices can help lay bare the multiple facets of deprivation in child health and pave the way for successful action.

However, before we set out to define our measurement exercise, it is a matter of analytical interest to briefly discuss the three specific socio-economic dimensions considered for the present analysis, namely income, location and gender. Our choice of these particular dimensions has been motivated by the fact that these dimensions—as discussed in the health literature—have significant bearing upon health outcomes; a fact that is also evident from the larger and consistent variations observed in terms of health profiles of these population groups in India (see NFHS-India Reports, Rajan and James, 2004; Dasgupta *et al.*, 1996). By disclosing the special problems of such disadvantaged groups by employing distributive-sensitive measures one can facilitate better interventions. The rest of the chapter is organised as follows. Section 2 briefly discusses the measurement techniques employed to gauge the disparities in child health. Section 3 briefly discusses the data sources and the variables identified for the analysis. Section 4 presents the empirical findings obtained for the income-related dimension of health inequality and Section 5 attempts to comprehend the results theoretically. In Section 6, the group-related disadvantages are computed and discussed. Section 7 provides the composite index of nutritional deprivation in India which is adjusted for the group-specific incidence by using a 'group-analogue' of Gini coefficient of interpersonal inequality. Section 8 concludes with some policy recommendations.

Methods

As we have argued above, the assessment of health status can be enhanced by resorting to certain distributional-sensitised measures along with the identified dimensions. In order to examine income-related inequality we adopt the standard technique of employing concentration curves and concentration indices. The concentration curve (CC) and concentration index (CI) have certain attractive properties as compared to certain other measures of health disparities (Wagstaff *et al.*, 1991; Kakwani *et al.*, 1997) and are employed here as a means for quantifying the degree of income-related inequality in certain specific health variables. The CC plots the cumulative proportions of the population (beginning with the most disadvantaged in terms of income and ending with the least disadvantaged) on the X-axis against the cumulative proportions of ill-health on Y-axis. For interpretative purposes, if the burden of ill-health (for example child mortality) is equally distributed across socioeconomic groups, the concentration curve will coincide with the diagonal. If poor health is concentrated in the lower socioeconomic groups, the health CC lies above the diagonal and the further the CC is from the diagonal, the greater would be the degree of inequality. The CI is defined as twice the area between the CC and the diagonal. The CI provides a measure of the extent of inequalities in health that are systematically associated with socioeconomic status. The CI can be computed very simply by making use of the convenient covariance result (Kakwani, 1980; Jenkins, 1988; Lerman and Yitzhaki, 1989) as follows.

$CI = 2\ cov(y_i, R_i)/\mu,$

Where y is the health variable whose inequality is being measured, μ is its mean, R_i is the ith individual's fractional rank in the socioeconomic distribution and $cov(y_i, R_i,.)$ is the covariance. The CI ranges between +1 and -1 and takes negative values when the CC lies above the line of equality, indicating disproportionate concentration of the ill-health outcome among the poor.

Further, we employ a distinct approach developed by Jayraj and Subramanian (2002) for measuring group inequities in the form of relative deprivations. This measure derives the deviation from an ideal situation which says that the population subgroup share should be equal to the share in vulnerability. To derive the relative deprivation, we begin with a measure that provides the incidence of health deprivation in the population and term it as the Ill-health Incidence Rate (IIR). For a given population it is defined as the headcount ratio of the number of individuals with ill-health to the total population. Further, we make use of N_i which is the population share of group i in the total population and IIR_i which is the ill-health incidence rate of group i. Here i denotes the number of population subgroups (ranging from i=1,2,...,k). Utilising this group-specific information, the RDI for the ith group is computed in the following manner,

$$RDI_i = \left(\frac{N_i}{1-N_i}\right)\left(\frac{IIR_i}{IIR} - 1\right)$$

if $N_i \geq IIR$,

and $RDI_i = \dfrac{IIR_i - IIR}{1 - IIR}$ if $N_i \leq IIR$.

RDI finds an easy and interesting interpretation in the sense that a group is said to be relatively disadvantaged whenever RDI_i is positive and is recognised relatively advantaged whenever RDI_i is negative. A ranking of i number of groups in ascending order of the obtained values of RDI_i will place the least disadvantaged (most advantaged) group at the top of the index and the most disadvantaged (least advantaged) at the bottom of the index.

It is not sufficient to comprehend the group-specific disadvantages alone rather than making an attempt at providing a fuller account by sensitising the health outcomes with group-related distributional details. To accomplish this task, we adopt the approach of Majumdar and Subramanian (2001) to provide an 'inequality adjusted' measure of child undernourishment levels in India and thereby develop a composite index of child nutritional failure based upon group-differentiation. Methodologically[2], this process involves adjusting the mean level of deprivation by a factor incorporating the extent of between group disparity in the distribution of deprivation, as described by the group analogue of Gini coefficient. This particular measure portrays the aspects of child nutritional failures which the summary measures often seem to smooth over. Such an exercise is warranted as it helps in recognising the exact extent of child undernourishment accounting for group-related distributional profile and thus lends better insights for policy-making. Since we are dealing with a nutritional failure ratio, we begin the measurement process by making use of the three standard indices of physical growth that describe the nutritional status of children, *viz.*, stunting, wasting and underweight. The conceptual and definitional issues related with these variables are presented in the next section on data and variables. As regards the method, first of all, we obtain the child undernourishment rates or child nutritional failure ratio along the dimensions of all the three identified variables of stunting (S), wasting (W) and underweight (U). The composite NFR is then obtained as a simple

2. Also see Hicks (1997).

average of its constituent failure ratios. Since our inclination is to construct an adjusted version of the NFR—name it NFR*—we proceed as follows. The relevant populations are classified in the sets of S_S, S_W, S_U in order to assess group-specific health failures along the dimensions mentioned above. This sub-groups classification could depend upon the relevance of any particular grouping either from the policy perspective or along the concerns of data availability and accuracy. Here the technique is demonstrated to adjust nutritional failure for the indicator pertaining to prevalence of wasting, however, other nutritional outcome indicators could also be calculated in an analogous fashion. Let $W_1, \ldots, W_{\#SW}$, be the group-specific prevalence of wasting, arranged in non-increasing order, namely $W_1 \geq W_2 \geq \ldots \geq W_{\#SW}$. Of course, for every group i belonging to S_W, the wasting incidence of the ith group should be considered. Then, since W is decomposable, it could be expressed as:

$W = \sum_{i=1}^{SW} t_i^W W_i$ where for every i in S_W: t_i^W is the share of the ith group in total population. To adjust the value of W, we estimate W* using the following technique proposed by Majumdar and Subramanian (2001),

$$W^* = \frac{1}{(\#S_w - 1)} \sum_{i=1}^{S_W} [(\#S_w - 1 - i)t_i^W + T_i^W] W_i,$$

where, T_i^W is the cumulative proportion of the population who belong to groups whose deprivation levels do not exceed the deprivation level of the ith group. Note that W*/W is a measure of the extent to which 'average' nutritional failure because of wasting is inflated owing to the presence of inter-group disparities in the distribution of the wasting. Analogous considerations would apply to the estimation and interpretation of the other ill-health indicators of child health. The overall adjusted index of nutritional failure ratio, NFR*, is now obtained as a simple average of its component-wise adjusted failure ratios.

Data and Variables Used

Notwithstanding the measurement techniques, availability of health information, disaggreagated to the level of groups, becomes crucial in evaluating health inequities. Prior to the advent of National Family Health Surveys (NFHS), health information was restricted to aggregate measures and, therefore, examining inequities was deemed to be a task only next to impossible. The genesis of NFHS, its wide coverage and the nature of information collected through it has presented an exclusive opportunity to employ robust measures to comprehend health disparities across the Indian union. In order to portray the status of health deprivation in India and its spatial and group-related dispersal, we have relied and mined the unit level information available in the third and the latest round of NFHS, jointly conducted by International Institute for Population Sciences and ORC Macro in 2005-06. To retain the sensitivity of health outcome indicators the domain of child health has emerged as a major criterion as it allows for better interventions right from the preliminary stages of life. Therefore, in our analysis we engage ourselves with the analysis of health outcome variables related to child health across states as well as among different socioeconomic groups. As the key indicators of child health, this article employs the information available on under-5 mortalities, child immunisation, child under nutrition as well as prevalence of diarrhoea among the child population. For measuring the inequities in child under nutrition, we use the NFHS-3 information provided on the basis of the new international reference population released by World Health Organization (WHO) in April 2006 (WHO Multicenter Growth Reference Study Group, 2006) and accepted by the Government of India. All these variables are specifically defined in Table 10.1. To focus on issues of association and causation we have obtained information on two other economic variables. One, being the state-wise net state domestic product 2004-05 at factor cost, which is obtained through the statistics published by Central Statistics Organisation (CSO) and the other, pertaining to public spending on health as a share of total health spending, is taken from Rao *et al.* (2005). In addition, it was also required to compute the income inequality levels across the different Indian states. For this purpose, the consumption expenditure of the households have been taken as a proxy for income and we have computed the Gini coefficient of inequality for all the states of India in terms of per capita monthly consumption expenditure, using the unit level records of National Sample Survey's (NSS) 61st round on Consumer Expenditure Survey.

Interstate Differences in Health Inequalities

In this section we examine the income-related inequalities in health across the different Indian states. For this purpose we have computed the concentration index (CI) for the selected indicators of child health across all the Indian states and have reported the same in Table 10.2. The CI values for a range of child health indicators for the country as a whole are negative confirming on the prevalence of income-related health inequalities that manifest primarily among the poor. On comparison of these inequalities across varied indicators of child health, inequalities are observed to be more pronounced in case of under-5 mortalities, undernutrition and in the receipt of all basic vaccinations. The under-5 mortality concentration curves (CC) for all-India as well as its three other major states (Maharashtra, Gujarat and Madhya Pradesh) with higher inequality levels are shown in Figure 9.1. What is immediately discernible from these CCs is that they all lie above the diagonal and thus indicate a greater concentration of health eventualities among the poorer groups. While the CI value for under-5 mortality at the national level is computed to be –0.1582, it presents a reasonably wider range across various states with the minimum of -0.0388 in West Bengal and –0.4107 in Uttarakhand. Among other major states, Maharashtra, Madhya Pradesh, Gujarat, Tamil Nadu and Punjab experience greater income-related inequalities in under-5 mortality as against the states of Uttar Pradesh, Rajasthan and Bihar with relatively low inequalities. Apart from the differences in the magnitude of these inequalities across the board, the negative values indicate adversities among the poor. Another highlight worth mentioning here relates to the inequality levels being higher with better levels of the event as against the worse situation. Undoubtedly from a policy

Table 10.1

Definitions of Maternal and Child Health Indicators used in the Analysis

Under-5 mortality rate(U5MR)	The number of deaths to children under 5 years of age per 1,000 liver births. Figures are based on births in the 5 years preceding the survey.
Stunting (H/A)	Children whose height-for-age is below minus two standard deviations (-2 SD) from the median of the reference population are considered short for their age, or stunted.
Wasting (W/H)	Children whose weight-for-height measures are below minus two standard deviations (-2 SD) from the median of the reference population are too thin for their height, or wasted.
Underweight (W/A)	Children whose weight-for-age measures are below minus two standard deviations (-2 SD) from the median of the reference population are underweight for their age.
Prevalence of anemia (ANE)	Children between 6-59 months are classified as anaemic if the haemoglobin concentration is found to be less than 11.0 g/dl.
Not fully immunised (NFI)	A child (12-23 months) is considered not to be fully immunised if the child has not received either of the vaccinations, namely; BCG, a measles vaccination, three DPT vaccinations, and three polio vaccinations.
Diarrhoea (DIA)	Whether any of the children under five years of age had had diarrhoea during the two-weeks preceding the survey.

perspective, focused attention needs to be laid towards improving the mortality situation in these backward states and perhaps inequality aversion measures need to be promoted in states like Maharashtra and Gujarat with lesser under-5 mortality rates of 47 and 61 per thousand live births where more and more concentration of this misfortune among the poor could be avoided.

Table 10.2

Concentration Index (CI) for Inequalities in Child Health Indicators

States	*CIU5MR*	*CIANE*	*CIDIA*	*CIH/A*	*CIW/A*	*CIW/H*	*CINFI*
Andhra Pradesh	-0.0704	-0.0367	0.1054	-0.1311	-0.1650	-0.0974	-0.0963
Arunachal Pradesh	-0.1401	-0.0587	-0.0536	-0.1167	-0.1816	-0.2139	-0.1296
Assam	-0.0541	-0.0581	-0.0246	-0.1302	-0.1373	-0.0295	-0.1079
Bihar	-0.0882	-0.0389	0.0375	-0.0861	-0.0962	-0.0660	-0.1340
Chhattisgarh	-0.0764	-0.0389	0.1536	-0.0669	-0.1133	-0.0997	-0.1443
Delhi	-0.1835	-0.0666	-0.0959	-0.1313	-0.1410	0.0498	-0.2079
Goa	-0.1282	-0.1126	-0.0293	-0.2867	-0.3063	-0.1857	-0.2893
Gujarat	-0.2198	-0.0658	-0.0459	-0.1127	-0.1432	-0.0859	-0.1542
Haryana	-0.1304	-0.0524	-0.0195	-0.1408	-0.1260	-0.1028	-0.3341
Himachal Pradesh	-0.2186	-0.0406	0.0261	-0.1305	-0.1323	-0.0820	-0.1589
Jammu & Kashmir	-0.1656	-0.0169	0.0398	-0.1690	-0.2258	-0.0549	-0.2341
Jharkhand	-0.0546	-0.0624	-0.0904	-0.0803	-0.0876	-0.0734	-0.1131
Karnataka	-0.1325	-0.0339	0.0463	-0.1284	-0.1648	-0.0898	-0.1823
Kerala	-0.1274	-0.0314	-0.0295	-0.1628	-0.2026	-0.0634	-0.2719
Madhya Pradesh	-0.2081	-0.0406	0.0661	-0.0683	-0.0835	-0.0679	-0.1810
Maharashtra	-0.2481	-0.0444	0.0247	-0.1427	-0.1796	-0.1227	-0.1795
Manipur	-0.3458	-0.0097	-0.0201	-0.1409	-0.1805	-0.1552	-0.1975
Meghalaya	-0.1152	-0.0525	0.2120	-0.0325	-0.0811	-0.0515	-0.0957
Mizoram	-0.1942	-0.1363	-0.0728	-0.1606	-0.2400	-0.1593	-0.2130
Nagaland	-0.1646	NA	0.0624	-0.1328	-0.1645	-0.0752	-0.1113
Orissa	-0.0844	-0.0827	-0.0851	-0.1865	-0.1811	-0.1224	-0.1328
Punjab	-0.1688	-0.0331	0.0514	-0.2082	-0.2597	-0.2469	-0.2505
Rajasthan	-0.0801	-0.0198	0.1164	-0.1043	-0.1337	-0.0585	-0.0898
Sikkim	-0.0581	-0.0171	-0.0850	-0.0848	0.0200	0.0405	-0.0725
Tamil Nadu	-0.1749	-0.0346	-0.0368	-0.1463	-0.1936	-0.1287	-0.0523
Tripura	-0.2251	-0.0381	-0.1677	-0.1113	-0.1421	-0.1120	-0.2306
Uttar Pradesh	-0.0960	-0.0271	0.0247	-0.0885	-0.1181	-0.0803	-0.0754
Uttarakhand	-0.4107	-0.0710	-0.1090	-0.1924	-0.1997	-0.1592	-0.2302
West Bengal	-0.0388	-0.0919	-0.0310	-0.1716	-0.1660	-0.1190	-0.1231
All India	-0.1582	-0.0518	-0.0010	-0.1249	-0.1600	-0.1211	-0.1595

Note: Computed by authors using NFHS-3 (2005-06) unit level records.

Figure 10.1

Under-5 Mortality Concentration Curves

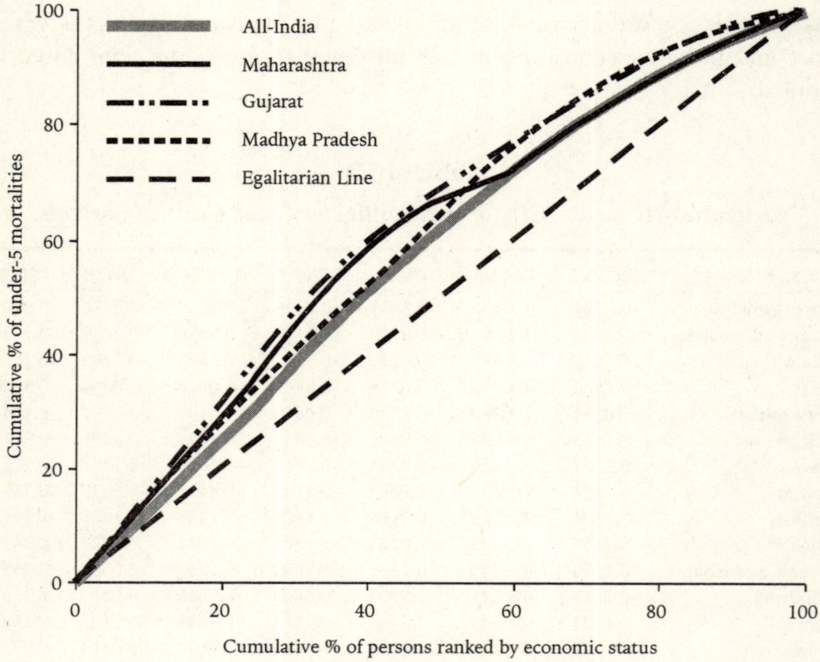

Other than under-5 mortality, similar inequality is assessed for a set of child health indicators, which include nutritional make-up, anaemia, child-immunisation and experience of diarrhoea. As regard nutritional make-up, the three dimensions namely stunting (low height-for-age), underweight (low weight-for-age) and wasting (low height-for-weight) manifest inequalities at the all-India level ranging between -0.1211 and –0.1600. The all-India level inequality in weight-for-age based nutritional assessment being the largest depicts a similar pattern across states as well. Compared with stunting and wasting, the inequality in nutrition according to underweight criterion has a wider range between –0.0835 in Madhya Pradesh and –0.3063 in Goa. Moderate range of inequality across states for the alternative nutritional measures could also be conditioned by the level of overall prevalence of the same. This is obvious from the fact that prevalence of undernutrition according to underweight criterion is by far the largest when contrasted with the same evaluated on alternative criterion like stunting or wasting. Further, weight-for-age in its own construct has a propensity for larger variation during childhood. As regard stunting, the all-India concentration index value is –0.1249 with a variation range of –0.0325 in Meghalaya and –0.2867 in Goa.

Not only the range of variation in this inequality measure is relatively lower compared to the same according to underweight criterion, but also the high inequality magnitudes are lesser in this case. According to the third criterion wasting, the inequality at the national level is –0.1211 which is the least among all the nutrition-based inequalities. The largest inequality according to this criterion is observed in Punjab and the least is in Assam. Apart from wide ranging variation in inequality in three domains of child-nutrition outcomes, there is some degree of agreement in magnitude of inequality across three domains like the inequality being manifested largely in underweight followed by stunting and wasting.

For the indicator of anaemia the all-India CI value of -0.0518 is observably lower and could be due to the widespread prevalence of anaemia across the population but still the poorer groups are found to remain at a higher disadvantage compared to the richer groups. The inequities in child-anaemia does not vary significantly across the major states, however, the states of West Bengal and Orissa still emerge to be more inequitable. Considerable variations were found in the CI values for prevalence of diarrhoea across Indian states, but it was found to be very low (-0.0010) at the all-India level. Our contention is that the mixed pattern of CI observed for diarrhoea reflects a greater tendency in some states than other for the poor to identify and report unjustifiably low levels of diarrhoea. To give a quick illustration of this observation we can compare the CI values of educationally backward (particularly in terms of maternal education) states of Uttar Pradesh, Rajasthan, Orissa and Bihar where the CI for diarrhoea registers a positive value meaning its concentration is more among richer households whereas in literate and better organised (in terms of health awareness) states such as Kerala, Tamil Nadu and West Bengal, the CI registers a negative value. Such results, therefore, warrants caution while drawing any broad conclusion regarding the phenomenon or its causation. In addition to these indicators, we have also tried to probe whether income-related inequities are present in the attainment of basic vaccinations, which is provided through the public health machinery. What is found is that there are evidently higher income-related inequities inherent in the distribution of non-immunised child. Though the rates for complete immunisation among children are generally lower across the Indian states but in states like Haryana, Punjab and Kerala with better coverage, the children belonging to the poorer sections of the population are at a greater disadvantage, as the concentration of these incomplete immunisations is higher among them. Undoubtedly, apart from income, inequality in such outcomes could be due to interplay of several factors including education and health awareness and as such, it would be an important and challenging task to probe inequalities obtained due to reasons other than the elementary issue of privation.

Until now what we have gathered from the information presented above is that inequalities in child health in India do get manifested along the lines of household income. However, the said observation does not necessarily imply such inequalities to be coincident with the state's income profile or the prevailing levels of income inequality in the state. For instance, high-income states like Maharashtra and Gujarat demonstrate coexistence of higher levels of income inequality along with higher levels of inequality in under-5 mortalities whereas low-income states such as Uttar Pradesh and Bihar which have lower income inequalities were among the states with lower inequalities in under-5 mortalities. Based on such observations, one could perhaps quickly presume that inequalities in health are directly related with income and income inequality; however, it may turn out to be an inference in haste. This is substantiated when we find some evidence among middle and low income states such as Tamil Nadu and Madhya Pradesh which have higher income inequalities coupled with higher health inequalities (in terms of under-5 mortalities) and a state like Kerala with similar income and income inequality levels but depicting lower levels of health inequality (also in terms of under-5 mortalities). Hitherto, it could be agreed that there is enough ambiguity in the said association as far as major states are concerned but once we consider all the 29 states of the Indian union, we may find the relationship between income, income inequality and health getting even more blurred.

Hence, this calls for an exposition of the theoretical underpinnings of income-related health inequality. But prior to doing so, let us explore the correlations between the concentration indices of the five important child health indicators to comprehend whether the states that exhibit a high degree of inequality in one indicator are the same states that exhibit similar levels of inequality in the other indicators? Table 10.3 (a) and (b) presents the correlation matrices for the concentration indices obtained for Pearson correlations and Spearman's rho (rank correlation). Unsurprisingly, there are high and significant correlations between the concentration indices for these indicators. The concentration indices for the three indicators of child malnutrition *viz.*, stunting, wasting and underweight are strongly correlated with each other. In fact the inequalities in under-5 mortalities are significantly correlated, not only with the indicators of malnourishment but also, with the inequities in incomplete immunisation. In other words, with the exception of CI for stunting, states with high level of inequality in under-5 mortality consistently have high levels of inequality on the other indicators. Following this, it would be worthwhile to comprehend the reasons behind these interstate differences in the levels of health inequalities and we can focus upon inequalities in under-5 mortalities for illustration. Because of significant correlations between these different indicators of child health, comprehending the determinants of inequities in under-5 mortalities can go a long way to explain the inequalities in the other indicators of child health as well.

Table 10.3

Pearson and Spearman's Correlations of Concentration Indices

(a) Pearson Correlations (Two Tailed Significance)					
	CIU5MR	*CIH/A*	*CIW/A*	*CIW/H*	*CINFI*
CIU5MR	1.000	0.233 (0.215)	0.317* (0.088)	0.326* (0.079)	0.413** (0.023)
CIH/A	0.233 (0.215)	1.000	0.848*** (0.000)	0.524*** (0.003)	0.551*** (0.002)
CIW/A	0.317* (0.088)	0.848*** (0.000)	1.000	0.692*** (0.000)	0.518*** (0.003)
CIW/H	0.326* (0.079)	0.524*** (0.003)	0.692*** (0.000)	1.000	0.314* (0.091)
CINFI	0.413** (0.023)	0.551*** (0.002)	0.518*** (0.003)	0.314* (0.091)	1.000
(b) Spearman's Rho (Two Tailed Significance)					
	CIU5MR	*CIH/A*	*CIW/A*	*CIW/H*	*CINFI*
CIU5MR	1.000	0.266 (0.155)	0.345* (0.062)	0.376** (0.040)	0.514*** (0.004)
CIH/A	0.266 (0.155)	1.000	0.875*** (0.000)	0.530*** (0.003)	0.499*** (0.005)
CIW/A	0.345* (0.062)	0.875*** (0.000)	1.000	0.651*** (0.000)	0.471*** (0.009)
CIW/H	0.376** (0.040)	0.530*** (0.003)	0.651*** (0.000)	1.000	0.327* (0.078)
CINFI	0.514*** (0.004)	0.499*** (0.005)	0.471*** (0.009)	0.327* (0.078)	1.000

Note: N = 30; Two tailed significance - ***at one per cent, ** at five per cent and * at ten per cent.

Income, Income Inequalities and Health

Although we drift a little from the central theme of the chapter but perhaps it is equally important to briefly touch upon the relationship between the obtained income and income-related health inequities. Prior to interpreting this association, it would be useful to shed some light on some of the explanations forwarded in the literature to comprehend inequalities in health. One of them is the psychosocial explication, which comes from the work of Emile Durkheim and has been used at two different levels to comprehend health inequalities. At a micro level, it is argued that income inequality results in 'individual processes of social comparison' that enforce social hierarchies causing chronic stress leading to poorer health outcomes for those at the bottom and at macro level, it erodes social bonds that allow people to work together, decreases social resources, and results in less trust and civic participation, greater crime, and other unhealthy conditions (Macinko *et al.*, 2003). The other important explication is termed as the neo-material explanation, which advocates that high degrees of income inequalities leaves the poor with fewer economic resources and thus increases their vulnerability against illness. Recent research has witnessed considerable engagement with this task and has found that the burden of ill-health is borne disproportionately by different groups wherein people of lower socioeconomic status consistently appear to have much worse health outcomes (Smith, 2004; Macinko *et al.*, 2003). Besides, several empirical studies have acknowledged the existence of income-related inequalities in health propounded as the absolute income hypothesis (Kakwani *et al.*, 1997, van Doorslaer *et al.*, 1997, Humphries and van Doorslaer; 2000). However, studies remain largely inconclusive in finding evidence of the relative income hypothesis which states that in developed regions income inequality has a larger impact on individual health than absolute income[3] (Wilkinson, 1996).

Undoubtedly, all the above explanations have their own merit and relevance and a corresponding empirical enquiry would prove to be an ideal complement. However, especially after providing a preliminary account of income-related child health inequality in India, it is of interest here to examine the determinants of the observed patterns and since we have build the present issue of health inequality around the income domain we pursue an explanation closer to the neo-material explanation. To be precise, in economic literature, health is largely conceived as a product resulting from a production process with inputs like consumption behaviour, income, education, environmental conditions and medical care and it is accepted that individuals with better endowments of these inputs have better health (Grossman, 1972). Therefore, the distribution of these inputs, particularly income, within societies should also play a decisive role in determining the population health. To understand health inequality through this channel, we engage with the simplified version of the theoretical model developed by

3. Wagstaff and van Doorslaer (2000) conducted a literature review of individual level studies on the impact of income inequality on health. In their review of six major studies, they found that the literature reveals strong support for the absolute income hypothesis and little or no support for the relative income hypothesis. Also see Macinko *et al.* (2003).

Grossman (1972) and Wagstaff (1986) presented in Wagstaff (2002). In this model, the relationship between health and medical care is assumed to be concave, meaning that medical care is subject to diminishing returns in the production of health. According to the model, richer individuals are likely to end up with higher levels of health and wherein increases in income inequality results in higher levels of health inequality. Further, it is inferred that if medical care is subsidised through public spending it helps to lower the levels of health inequality. It also suggests increases in health inequality if rising incomes are accompanied by technological improvements in the health care.

In order to quickly verify these theoretical predictions, Wagstaff (2002) undertakes a modest empirical analysis and finds that neither income inequality nor public share of health spending proves to be a significant determinant of health inequities but interestingly, observes that average income of the population turns out significant in determining the same. These empirical insights raise a question that why, to some extent, these empirical findings differ from the theoretical insights offered by the model regarding the relationship between income inequality and health? Does it imply that the supposedly strict concave relationship between health and medical care is a weaker one? To answer this, instead of a strictly concave relationship we work with a convex-concave relation between income and health which is shown in Figure 10.2. Here, income is represented along the X-axis and health is depicted along the Y-axis. The proposed framework elucidates the expected relationship between health and medical care expenditure—particularly in a developing country—by capturing the indivisible nature of health expenditure and hence is able to comprehend health inequality in a striking manner. What motivates us to engage with such a relation is the fact that in a developing country whenever an individual decides to seek medical care, the first task would be to arrange for an array of health care related expenses, such as travelling cost and so on. Also, in the initial phases of the treatment process, often, the individual is advised to undergo a few diagnostic tests which help detect the ailment accurately, and importantly requires additional expenditure. It must be noticed that many such expenses are indivisible and unavoidable under conditions of feeble health systems, as present in many developing countries. Such specific difficulties in accessing quality medical care provide inadequate or lower returns to health at very low levels of income. This line of reasoning is captured by the initial convex region of the income-health function depicted in Figure 10.2.

Figure 10.2

Income-Health Relationship

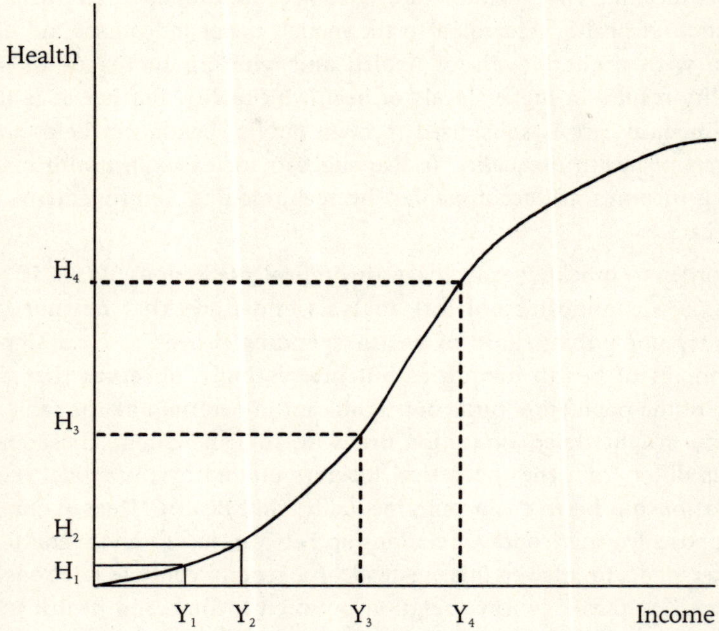

Under such a framework, even if the income inequality remains higher among a low-income society (incomes ranging between Y_1 and Y_2), i.e., if majority of the population have a relatively lower income of Y_1 and the rest have relatively greater income of Y_2 (implying absolute and relative income inequality given by $Y_2 - Y_1$, Y_2/Y_1 is high) the degree of health inequality (given by $H_2 - H_1$, H_2/H_1) would be relatively lower. This framework also allows us to discuss a threshold income level beyond which individuals are able to afford for quality health care and are able to bring about considerable improvements in their health status. This phase can very well begin at the point of inflexion (between Y_3 and Y_4) in the income-health function plotted in Figure 10.2. Now, if the average income of the society is somewhere around this inflexion-point, then it could pose serious consequences for health inequity in the society. For instance, consider the case of two subgroups of population, wherein the major subgroup has an average income of Y_3 and the other subgroup has an average income of Y_4, also we allow for a considerable degree of income inequality within the society (i.e., $Y_4 - Y_3$, Y_4/Y_3). But unlike the case of low-income societies, here we would find that given similar degrees of income inequality, the health inequality ($H_4 - H_3$, H_4/H_3) in the society with higher average income has worsened. Further, we can proceed towards the much flatter part of the concave region in the proposed function and argue that these inequalities may eventually diminish at very high levels of average income. In a dynamic sense, when we also account for the rapid technological advancements in the health field, it is inevitable that the marginal returns to health in the proposed function remain positive and in fact at no point of time gives way to a flatter slope. In other words, with increasing incomes and ongoing technological improvements, the returns to health diminishes but at a very slow pace and this can happen only at very high levels of income. Well, it remains an empirical question to determine that how high is this high level of income and how does it vary among different societies.

Another related discussion could be made here regarding the impact of public health spending upon health inequality as it can be combined in the income space to provide greater health benefits. Though it is necessary that such facilities should be distributed more evenly across the population but the true picture remains desolate as the health facilities provided through public health spending often tend to concentrate in particular regions such as urban areas or in certain other target location thereby often failing miserably in guaranteeing universal access and the opportunity to benefit from it. Such unevenness in the distribution of health facilities may have a dampening impact on health and could instigate further inequities. Given the brief theoretical reasoning now we can proceed towards some empirical formulations and corroborate the predictions. However, before concluding this section let us quickly summarise the major predictions of the proposed theoretical framework. In a nutshell, the modification of the income-health function allows one to infer that for a given level of income inequality, if overall income levels are lower (higher) in the society then health inequalities are also lower (higher). Another inference which could be drawn here is that the levels of income inequality also have significant bearing upon health inequality, but the impact is more observable if the income inequities are coupled with higher levels income. And more importantly, under conditions of lower income and high-income inequality, the health inequality levels would get enhanced whereas if the income levels are higher and income inequality is low then it has a moderating impinge on the health inequality levels.

Approximating Wagstaff (2002), now we proceed and present a simple regression exercise to corroborate the predictions of the two different frameworks on income-health relationship. This exercise could also be viewed as an attempt to comprehend the differences in health inequality across the different states of India in terms of income inequality, per capita income and share of public health spending. We have selected the negative of the under-5 mortality concentration index as an indicator to represent child health inequality. For explanatory variables, the Gini measure of inequality in per capita monthly consumption expenditure is taken as a proxy for income inequality, per capita NSDP at factor cost is utilised to represent the state per capita income and public spending on health as a share of total health spending to represent the role of subsidies in health care. These results, presented in Table 10.4. Model 1 shows that in the Indian context, income inequality is positively but insignificantly related with the levels of health inequality. The R-squared value suggests that hardly two per cent of the variations in health inequality are actually explained by the differences in income inequalities. This finding is similar to what Wagstaff (2002) had arrived in his study on comprehending the differences in health inequality across developing countries. Given the inability of the income inequality alone to capture the variations in health inequality, therefore, we add other important variables to comprehend the causation. Specifically, in Model 2 we control for income inequality and public health spending levels and thereby attempt to elicit the role of per capita income in determining health inequalities. The results hint that increases in average income also increases the levels of health inequality as presented by the positive and significant coefficient of NSDP per capita. This relationship has been predicted by the theoretical framework discussed earlier. However, it is also observed that the coefficient obtained for the variable of public health spending as a share of per cent total health spending though possesses a negative sign suggesting its favourable effect for reducing health inequalities but turns out to be statistically insignificant. One of the reasons could be that specifying public health spending as a per cent total may not be the appropriate way to capture the true value of the variable because statistically, it is possible that even at very low levels of public health spending we may obtain a statistically higher share because of the possibility that the private health spending component may be even lower. Nonetheless, the overall results obtained here, especially in relation to income inequality and average income, are partly in agreement with the strictly concave relationship between health and income but does not lend any concrete support to the relative income hypothesis. In other words, it may also be opined that the outlined theory of concave relationship between income and health is incomprehensive in capturing the conditions presented in developing countries. Therefore, let us now turn towards the alternate framework while discussing the convex-concave relationship between health and income and test its predictions. What is necessary here is to conceive of a variable, which should be sensitive to both, average income levels as well as income inequality levels.

Table 10.4

Regression Results for Concentration Indices of Under-5 Mortality

Variable	*Model 1*	*Model 2*	*Model 3*
	Parameter (t-statistics)	*Parameter (t-statistics)*	*Parameter (t-statistics)*
Constant	0.076 (0.992)	0.080 (0.920)	0.048 (1.482)
Gini coefficient	0.183 (0.767)	-0.160 (-.0546)	
NSDP per capita		9.49E-06** (2.429)	
Public spending on health as per cent total		-0.00012 (-0.124)	
Avg. of Gini and normalised NSDP per capita			0.211*** (2.894)
F statistic for model	0.588	2.438*	8.378***
R-squared	0.024	0.249	0.267
Adjusted R-squared	-0.017	0.147	0.235
N	26	26	25

Note: *** significant at 10 per cent, ** at 5 per cent, and * at 1 per cent.

For this purpose we develop a simple composite index of income and income inequality in two small steps as follows. Firstly, we normalise the NSDP per capita across the states in such a way that the state with the highest income obtains a value of one and the lowest-income state is assigned a value of zero. In the second step we obtain the composite index for each state, by taking a simple average of the Gini coefficient for the state and the normalised NSDP per capita values for the respective states obtained through the previous step. This new index represents the relative levels of both the important variables of income and income inequality. Model 3 uses this particular index as a variable to comprehend health inequality in the Indian context and finds that this new composite index measure given by the average of Gini and the normalised NSDP per capita turns out to be statistically a significant factor explaining the variations in health inequality and possesses an explanatory power of 27 per cent, greater than the previous two models. This result also supports the theoretical prediction that if higher levels of average incomes are accompanied by higher income inequities then it increases health inequality. Further, effects on health inequality gets cushioned if either the distribution of income is more equitable or if the average income levels are lower. Although we have strayed a bit from the central task, nonetheless, we would consider this exercise as a preliminary attempt at gauging the proposed health-income relationship and a more comprehensive examination can help to draw further insights because income alone is insufficient in describing the larger variations observed in health inequity.

Relative Disadvantages in Child Health

Having discussed the income-related health inequality, both theoretically and empirically, we revert back to the prime concern of the chapter but we may notice that the previous section had one very important conclusion to offer. It suggested that not all the variations in the health status of the population could be interpreted and explicated in terms of the income domain and there exist certain other dimensions along which such differences manifest themselves wherein these dimensions either act independently or foster through the income domain. To uncover this, in this section we engage ourselves to gauge the health disadvantages suffered across two other important dimensions. One of these dimensions is related with the larger issue of gender-based inequities which has the potential to act independently of the income domain to induce health differences.

However, the other dimension of spatial location (rural-urban areas) of the individual does remotely shapes itself into income domain wherein an individual residing in a disadvantaged location (rural area) bears a greater burden of ill-health eventualities. In order to obtain the picture of related disadvantages, we resort to the binary classifications of the child population by gender (as 'male child' and 'female child') and by sector of origin or spatial location (as 'rural' and 'urban') and compute the index of relative disadvantage discussed in Section 2 for the largely conceived disadvantaged subgroup (namely, female and rural) in each pair of population groups. Thus, obtained picture of group-related disparities in the distribution of child health across the major Indian states is reported in Table 10.5. At first, we discuss here the relative disadvantages observed for being a rural child in terms of the selected indicators of basic immunisation and nutritional status and thereafter proceed to comprehend the same across the gender dichotomy.

The NFHS-3 report suggests that around 58 per cent of the total urban children in India receive all the basic vaccinations, however, this proportion falls to around 39 per cent in case of rural children. This picture becomes all the more clearer from the information presented in column (ii) where one may observe that the picture of disparity that obtains between the rural and the urban areas in the distribution of the burden of incomplete immunisation is rather startling. The bottom row of column (ii) shows that for all-India, the RDI value is hugely positive (25 per cent) meaning that rural children constitute the relatively disadvantaged group while urban children constitute the relatively advantaged group. Less developed states like Madhya Pradesh,

Chhattisgarh, Jharkhand and Rajasthan depict higher degree of relative disadvantages for rural children, ranging from 24 per cent to 51 per cent. What is more staggering is to observe that these rural agonies for child immunisation is not confined only to the backward states but is also present among relatively advanced states like Kerala, Haryana and Maharashtra. In fact, a rural child in Kerala and Haryana suffers with relative disadvantages to the magnitude of 54 per cent and 49 per cent respectively compared to their urban counterpart. Basic immunisation is central in sustaining through the initial upheavals of life and therefore, such relative disparities are unjustified. The most disturbing fact here relates to reigning location disadvantage irrespective of the developmental status of the state. In this regard, the present findings are expected to be suggestive of the intricacies posed due to the spatial dichotomy and therefore, demand prompt attention to dismantle such blockade. Definitely, the NRHM is a leap forward in this direction and such informational inputs could be expected to go a long way in enhancing its efficacy, design and performance.

Table 10.5

Estimated Index of Relative Disadvantage for Selected Indicators: India and Major States (NFHS-3, 2005-06)

	RDI for being Rural				*RDI for being a Girl Child*			
States	*NFI*	*W/A*	*H/A*	*DIA*	*NFI*	*W/A*	*H/A*	*DIA*
Column (i)	*(ii)*	*(iii)*	*(iv)*	*(v)*	*(vi)*	*(vii)*	*(viii)*	*(ix)*
Andhra Pradesh	0.097	0.169	0.166	-0.319	0.160	0.029	-0.003	-0.089
Assam	-0.032	0.398	0.318	0.047	-0.062	0.068	-0.016	-0.133
Bihar	0.190	0.163	0.159	-0.125	0.189	0.040	0.036	-0.027
Chhattisgarh	0.505	0.517	0.391	-0.420	-0.042	-0.004	-0.037	-0.069
Gujarat	0.168	0.158	0.114	-0.004	0.082	-0.043	-0.002	-0.052
Haryana	0.491	0.129	0.198	0.201	-0.051	-0.014	-0.029	-0.062
Jharkhand	0.251	0.472	0.445	0.240	0.066	-0.030	-0.042	-0.066
Karnataka	0.102	0.223	0.222	-0.037	-0.010	-0.025	-0.020	-0.130
Kerala	0.543	0.589	0.102	-0.100	-0.061	-0.048	-0.046	-0.136
Madhya Pradesh	0.476	0.176	0.126	-0.275	0.108	0.012	0.008	-0.111
Maharashtra	0.225	0.223	0.097	0.098	0.050	0.001	-0.030	0.012
Orissa	0.020	0.358	0.290	0.123	-0.062	0.029	0.036	-0.066
Punjab	0.107	0.168	0.036	0.053	0.153	0.042	-0.004	-0.019
Rajasthan	0.243	0.314	0.288	-0.470	-0.008	-0.017	-0.016	-0.013
Tamil Nadu	-0.164	0.126	0.017	0.223	-0.008	-0.051	-0.045	-0.145
Uttar Pradesh	0.130	0.220	0.129	0.020	0.101	0.027	0.015	-0.087
Uttarakhand	0.181	0.636	0.717	0.013	0.031	0.003	-0.042	-0.113
West Bengal	0.169	0.602	0.542	0.214	-0.068	0.039	-0.009	0.038
All India	0.251	0.230	0.171	0.000	0.048	0.011	0.000	-0.061

Note: Computed by authors using NFHS-3 (2005-06) unit level records.

In an attempt to discern the nutritional disadvantages endured by the rural children we have estimated the RDI values separately for two important indicators of stunting and underweight. Our decision to perform the analysis in terms of stunting and underweight is guided by the argument that stunting reflects cumulative growth failure in the children, and therefore, is useful to measure long term effect of undernourishment while underweight helps to capture short-term fluctuations in nutritional status, i.e., if the child has inadequate food intake or has suffered from some ailments in the immediate past it would get reflected through this indicator. The RDI index-values for these indicators for all the major Indian states as well as for all-India are reported along column (iii) and (iv). As depicted in the last row of these columns, we find that for all-India the degree of disparities is computed to be 23 per cent in terms of underweight and 17 per cent in terms of stunting and thus insinuates that the rural children are at a higher disadvantage compared to their urban counterpart. In absolute terms, as per NFHS-3, around 51 per cent of the rural children are found to be stunted compared to 40 per cent of the urban children and similarly 46 per cent of the rural children are underweight compared to 33 per cent of the urban children. Rural children in almost all the low-income states are facing higher relative disadvantages. Although, the problem of child undernourishment is relatively lesser among the middle and high-income states but still the degree of relative disadvantages engendered due to location disparities are by no means insignificant. The final variable of diarrhoea prevalence across the rural-urban divide does not prove to be of immense importance as evident from column (v) of Table 10.5. There was no specific disadvantage or advantage for rural children as far as the prevalence of diarrhoea was concerned and which we opt not to discuss here as it may also require us to address other issues such as reporting behaviour across rural and urban regions.

Proceeding towards the second dimension of analysis of relative disadvantages across gender lines, it is essential to acknowledge the fact that the disparities along these divide may not be directly and easily remedied through direct policy prescriptions as it requires larger institutional and behavioural changes to rectify the problem. And precisely because of such prevailing outlook towards gender issue, we may also expect the different Indian states to depict those patterns differently. Unlike the case of an overall rural disadvantage, what would be more interesting to observe is whether, we arrive at different conclusions for the same state, wherein the girl child is found to be at disadvantage in terms of absolute and unbiased measures but turns out to be advantaged in terms of indicators subject to reporting behaviour. From column (vi) in Table 10.5 we can find that at all-India level, being a female child may pose a relative disadvantage of 5 per cent. Though it turns out to be relatively lower for the country as a whole but has significant variations across different states. An elementary scrutiny of the table would suggest us that the disadvantages posed to girl child are excessive in the north Indian states of Uttar Pradesh, Punjab, Madhya Pradesh, Jharkhand and Bihar. With the exception of Andhra Pradesh, all other southern Indian states suggest the absence of disadvantages for girl child. In terms of nutritional status, we find that the obtained value of RDI (see column vii and viii) at all-India level does not suggest any specific degree of disadvantage for the girl child. However, a closer look at the index-values across the states elicits that unlike the high-income states, the low-income states like Bihar, Uttar Pradesh, Orissa and Madhya Pradesh show smaller disadvantages for the female child in terms of her nutritional outcome measured through the indicators of stunting and underweight. Certainly, this argument of gender disparity gains strength if we look at the performance of these states across certain other indicators. Our index-values suggest that these low-income states have consistency in terms of presenting disadvantageous position to the female child. But if we glance through the RDI values for the disadvantages for female child in terms of diarrhoea, we come across altogether a reversal of findings wherein the female child appears to be at a slight advantage. This finding makes us all the more suspicious as regards the reported estimates on diarrhoea prevalence, particularly in these states and validates our concern discussed above.

Group Disparities and Inequality Adjusted Nutritional Outcomes

After verifying the presence of income as well as spatial and gender-related disparities in child health, the current exercise would remain incomplete unless we present an account of health deprivation which is sensitised to these group-related distributional details. It is to this task that we motivate ourselves and firstly attempt to provide fuller information on group-specific disparities across the major Indian states. Such an exercise offers valuable insights for effective designing of child health programmes and can also be helpful in arriving at optimal budgetary interventions. Following the methodology for deriving an inequality adjusted index of deprivation as spelt out in Section 2, we here encompass the three specific dimensions of nutritional failure namely stunting, wasting and underweight to provide an overall measure of inequality-adjusted nutritional failure among the child population of India and its different states. We believe that there is sufficient evidence to justify our choice of incorporating these nutritional indicators in our analysis. As a matter of fact, researchers have observed that a person born undernourished is also more likely to face undernourishment in subsequent years. Moreover, there is substantial evidence that undernutrition that starts at foetal level and hence results in low birth weight for babies and in the absence of favourable factors this nutritional disadvantage continues and gets cumulated in later years. If interventions in the form of food supplements during pregnancy and proper pre- and post-partum care are not provided, it largely leads to a cycle where underweight babies become underweight mother themselves and again give birth to underweight babies. Malnourishment in early stages of life leaves the individual susceptible to severe illness, including diarrhoea, pneumonia, jaundice, various physical disabilities, blindness and memory loss. Not only that, infectious diseases and ailments obtained due to unhygienic living conditions may actually contribute to malnourishment and reflects a reverse causality wherein children who are infected with either of these ailments depict poor nutritional status. The problems get further accumulated for a country like India with a large rural and poverty-laden population wherein strict physical labour is the sole mean of earnings and therefore, widespread prevalence of undernourishment in the earliest stages of life can affect the physical productivity in adolescence as well as in the prime years. Thus, several layers of social and economic disadvantages get wrapped up within the summary statistic of undernutrition, hence focusing on threats to child nutrition becomes one of the important and direct ways of assessing child health deprivations and the disparities therein.

Stunting

Firstly, as reported in Table 10.6, we provide a detailed profile of nutritional deficiencies measured in terms of stunting from which various population groups across the major states of India suffer. Cross classified by gender, sector of origin and wealth profile, stunting figures of eight mutually exclusive and completely exhaustive sub-groups, namely, rural poor female (RPF), rural poor male (RPM), rural non-poor female (RNPF), rural non-poor male (RNPM), urban poor female (UPF), urban poor male (UPM), urban non-poor female (UNPF), urban non-poor male (UNPM).

What is immediately discernible from the figures presented in Table 10.6 is that the magnitude of stunting across India is unacceptably high and there are large and systematic differences between population groups in terms of stunting in all major states of India. The data reveals that Kerala, Punjab and Tamil Nadu possess relatively lower levels of stunting while in Uttar Pradesh, Bihar, Chhattisgarh and Gujarat more than half of the child population is stunted. But what this method has allowed is to reveal a more detailed profile of stunting outcomes in India and its states, by focusing on the inequality in its distribution across space, income groups and gender.

Evidently, the problem of stunting is severe among poor girl child irrespective of the sector of origin. For all India, around 60 per cent of the poor rural female children are stunted and with the exception of Kerala and Tamil Nadu, all other states have appalling levels (more than half) of stunting among children belonging to this population group. Yet another disquieting observation emerges in the form of stunting differentials observed along the lines of wealth profile. This divide between poor and the non-poor subgroups presents an unequivocal testimony of the plight of the children irrespective of their gender and spatial location.

Table 10.6

Group-Specific Stunting (Height-for-Age) Indices: India and Major States (NFHS-3, 2005-06)

States	*RPF*	*RPM*	*RNPF*	*RNPM*	*UPF*	*UPM*	*UNPF*	*UNPM*	*ALL*
Andhra Pradesh	0.616	0.617	0.429	0.437	0.795	0.519	0.332	0.356	0.427
Assam	0.544	0.597	0.437	0.432	0.544	0.278	0.355	0.333	0.465
Bihar	0.650	0.622	0.556	0.511	0.589	0.533	0.441	0.498	0.556
Chhattisgarh	0.569	0.591	0.528	0.578	0.643	0.534	0.359	0.385	0.529
Gujarat	0.697	0.610	0.519	0.532	1.000	1.000	0.452	0.466	0.517
Haryana	0.530	0.665	0.460	0.474	0.000	0.000	0.358	0.402	0.457
Jharkhand	0.519	0.581	0.494	0.496	0.427	0.817	0.322	0.343	0.498
Karnataka	0.500	0.609	0.458	0.464	0.555	0.819	0.348	0.347	0.437
Kerala	0.200	0.800	0.229	0.273	0.000	0.000	0.241	0.210	0.245
Madhya Pradesh	0.547	0.549	0.496	0.463	0.568	0.667	0.419	0.428	0.500
Maharashtra	0.605	0.653	0.480	0.443	0.962	0.858	0.360	0.462	0.463
Orissa	0.613	0.584	0.360	0.314	0.579	0.760	0.331	0.292	0.450
Punjab	0.580	0.500	0.334	0.391	1.000	0.500	0.399	0.319	0.367
Rajasthan	0.507	0.528	0.442	0.434	1.000	0.606	0.292	0.373	0.437
Tamil Nadu	0.327	0.426	0.281	0.332	0.569	0.454	0.296	0.300	0.309
Uttar Pradesh	0.673	0.671	0.540	0.531	0.630	0.428	0.516	0.487	0.568
Uttarakhand	0.675	0.592	0.471	0.500	0.500	0.500	0.240	0.302	0.444
West Bengal	0.578	0.593	0.395	0.410	0.347	0.475	0.296	0.286	0.446
All India	0.594	0.603	0.468	0.463	0.626	0.587	0.379	0.396	0.480

Note: Computed by authors using NFHS-3 (2005-06) unit level records.

What we have encountered in this discussion so far is that the characters of these health disparities are not only interstate in nature but they reside as well within the same political territories. Indisputably, the impairments of being female, poor or rural pose its own disadvantages for health but deplorably the syndicate of these three adversities has developed itself into a perilous snare. To expose this kind of desolate picture of inequities in subgroup stunting outcomes we present in Table 10.7, both the simple headcount ratio of the stunted population and the between-group disparity 'adjusted' estimates of stunting. As mentioned earlier, the intent behind such an exercise is to penalise the inter-group disparities and thereby lay bare the real health scenario in the society.

Table 10.7

Stunting and the Effect of Adjustment for Inter-Group Inequalities: India and Major States (NFHS-3, 2005-06)

States	Incidence of Stunting (S)	Rank (in ascending order) according to S	Inequality Adjusted Incidence of Stunting* (S)*	Rank (in ascending order) according to S*	Factor (in per cent) by which Incidence of Stunting is Adjusted due to Inter-group Inequalities (S*/S)	Rank (in ascending order) according to S*/S
Andhra Pradesh	0.427	4	0.35	2	82	3
Assam	0.465	11	0.501	12	108	8
Bihar	0.556	17	0.438	3	79	2
Chhattisgarh	0.529	16	0.584	17	110	10
Gujarat	0.517	15	0.484	8	94	4
Haryana	0.457	10	0.513	15	112	13
Jharkhand	0.498	14	0.296	1	59	1
Karnataka	0.437	5	0.529	16	121	15
Kerala	0.245	1	0.471	6	192	18
Madhya Pradesh	0.500	13	0.497	11	99	5
Maharashtra	0.463	12	0.511	14	110	9
Orissa	0.450	9	0.48	7	107	7
Punjab	0.367	3	0.497	10	135	16
Rajasthan	0.437	6	0.503	13	115	14
Tamil Nadu	0.309	2	0.439	4	142	17
Uttar Pradesh	0.568	18	0.628	18	111	12
Uttarakhand	0.444	8	0.444	5	100	6
West Bengal	0.446	7	0.493	9	111	11
All India	0.480		0.488		102	

Note: Computed by authors using NFHS-3 (2005-06) unit level records.

The results indicate that, with the exception of the states of Andhra Pradesh, Bihar, Gujarat, Jharkhand, Madhya Pradesh and Uttarakhand, in all other major states there is an increase in the 'adjusted' index *vis-à-vis* the unadjusted one, owing to the existence of inter-group disparity in the distribution of stunting. Thus, after adjustment the average stunting in India gets inflated to 49 per cent. In states of Kerala, Tamil Nadu, Punjab and Karnataka, the stunting levels gets significantly inflated once we 'adjust' the average measure. After the adjustments in the average level of deprivation to reflect inter-group disparities in the distribution of stunting we witness that the ranking of the states have altered. As Table 10.7 indicates, the actual ranking changes are not only significant but to some extent rank reversals are also observed. For instance, Bihar and Jharkhand emerge to possess one of the lowest incidences of adjusted-stunting outcomes. Certain other states like, Gujarat, Andhra Pradesh, Madhya Pradesh, Orissa and Uttarakhand gain in their rankings after inequality adjustment. Rest of the states has registered a drop in their rankings and among these, larger drop is observed for Karnataka, Rajasthan, Punjab and Kerala.

The ratio of S*/S which is a measure of the extent to which deprivation is worsened by inter-group inequality is more pronounced among these states. In terms of average stunting, as captured by the index S, the relatively middle and high-income states possess smaller values of stunted population in comparison to the low-income states of India. However, in terms of inter-group disparity in the distribution of stunting as captured by the ratio S*/S, these higher-income states turn out to be the worst performer. Though it indicates that the group-related disadvantages tend to increase as income goes up but before that one must also consider the fact that inequalities tend to be silent when the burden of deprivation is, more or less, ubiquitous. Given the economic prospects of India, these low-income states, as hoped, would sooner or later join the path of prosperity but in this process they need to devise policies and programmes that must be considerate enough to address this austerity.

Wasting

The indicator of wasting or low weight-for-height provides an important means to measure the overall stature of the child population and has been incorporated as the second component of our composite NFR. The population groupings identified in this section are parallel in construction to the one discussed in the previous section on stunting. Table 10.8 reports the extent to which the chances of wasting among child population vary across the identified sub-groups within the population. In an unadjusted aggregate sense, Punjab has the lowest levels (nine per cent) of wasting whereas states like Madhya Pradesh have wasting incidence of 35 per cent which comes to around four times that of Punjab. Apart from Madhya Pradesh, other backward states like Jharkhand and Bihar also present greater burden of wasting among its child population. Certainly such stark realities await proficient policy interventions pertaining to child welfare. Further, the incidence of wasting is higher among the poorer groups of the population irrespective of their sector of origin and gender. For instance, at all-India level it is observed, that the gap between the rural poor and the urban non-poor is to the extent of 8 to 9 per cent. In particular, states like Madhya Pradesh, Bihar, Jharkhand, Haryana and Gujarat show greater accretion of wasting among the poorer section. Moreover, after controlling for location and income dimensions, it is also observed that the female child show a slight advantage over the male child in terms of low weight-for-height, however, the margins are too narrow to derive any firm conclusion.

Table 10.8

Group Specific Wasting (Weight-for-Height) Indices: India and Major States (NFHS-3, 2005-06)

States	RPF	RPM	RNPF	RNPM	UPF	UPM	UNPF	UNPM	ALL
Andhra Pradesh	0.077	0.107	0.147	0.129	0.247	0.030	0.093	0.113	0.122
Assam	0.168	0.130	0.133	0.127	0.179	0.139	0.154	0.124	0.137
Bihar	0.282	0.321	0.245	0.274	0.307	0.378	0.224	0.259	0.271
Chhattisgarh	0.233	0.260	0.175	0.144	0.179	0.270	0.152	0.210	0.195
Gujarat	0.227	0.237	0.191	0.200	0.500	0.333	0.159	0.159	0.187
Haryana	0.383	0.335	0.167	0.202	0.000	0.000	0.160	0.190	0.191
Jharkhand	0.373	0.359	0.276	0.333	0.045	0.366	0.253	0.257	0.323
Karnataka	0.203	0.268	0.175	0.174	0.220	0.271	0.163	0.163	0.176
Kerala	0.000	0.000	0.178	0.191	0.000	0.000	0.105	0.105	0.159
Madhya Pradesh	0.341	0.427	0.334	0.353	0.519	0.417	0.311	0.294	0.350
Maharashtra	0.185	0.173	0.181	0.184	0.000	0.284	0.111	0.159	0.165
Orissa	0.221	0.265	0.170	0.166	0.194	0.141	0.115	0.140	0.195
Punjab	0.170	0.096	0.088	0.088	0.000	0.250	0.061	0.104	0.092
Rajasthan	0.254	0.249	0.175	0.183	0.000	0.000	0.195	0.231	0.204
Tamil Nadu	0.250	0.246	0.196	0.249	0.144	0.454	0.182	0.213	0.222
Uttar Pradesh	0.146	0.180	0.157	0.142	0.208	0.241	0.120	0.130	0.148
Uttarakhand	0.267	0.246	0.194	0.219	0.500	0.250	0.106	0.111	0.188
West Bengal	0.196	0.205	0.134	0.180	0.347	0.173	0.143	0.128	0.169
All India	0.237	0.262	0.185	0.193	0.255	0.289	0.155	0.169	0.198

Note: Computed by authors using NFHS-3 (2005-06) unit level records.

A comparison of average wasting rates and inequality 'adjusted' ones captured respectively through the indices of W and W* is attempted in Table 10.9. After this adjustment, the all India average wasting incidence of 0.198 gets inflated by 106 per cent and becomes 0.209, though it is a small increase for all-India but owing to the incorporation of inequalities in the distribution of wasting phenomenon across groups, the incidence of wasting gets adjusted accordingly in several states, though in different degrees as observed from the ratio W*/W. On one hand, states of Gujarat, Uttarakhand, Punjab and Haryana indicate of the higher inequities present in the distribution of wasting across the different groups whereas on the other hand, Kerala, Jharkhand, Rajasthan, Orissa and Bihar demonstrate lower levels of inter-group disparity. With or without adjustment, Punjab leads the rest of the country in terms of averting stunting outcomes whereas Madhya Pradesh, Bihar and Jharkhand remain the laggards.

Table 10.9

Wasting and the Effect of Adjustment for Inter-group Inequalities: India and Major States (NFHS-3, 2005-06)

States	*Incidence of Wasting (W)*	*Rank (in ascending order) according to W*	*Inequality Adjusted Incidence of Wasting* (W)**	*Rank (in ascending order) according to W**	*Factor (in per cent) by which Incidence of Wasting is Adjusted due to Inter-group Inequalities (W*/W)*	*Rank(in ascending order) according to W*/W*
Andhra Pradesh	0.122	2	0.13	2	107	11
Assam	0.137	3	0.132	3	96	5
Bihar	0.271	16	0.266	16	98	6
Chhattisgarh	0.195	12	0.202	11	104	9
Gujarat	0.187	9	0.243	15	130	18
Haryana	0.191	11	0.218	12	114	15
Jharkhand	0.323	17	0.303	17	94	2
Karnataka	0.176	8	0.191	9	109	13
Kerala	0.159	5	0.144	4	91	1
Madhya Pradesh	0.350	18	0.352	18	101	7
Maharashtra	0.165	6	0.17	6	103	8
Orissa	0.195	12	0.187	8	96	4
Punjab	0.092	1	0.116	1	126	16
Rajasthan	0.204	14	0.195	10	96	3
Tamil Nadu	0.222	15	0.237	13	107	12
Uttar Pradesh	0.148	4	0.157	5	106	10
Uttarakhand	0.188	10	0.242	14	129	17
West Bengal	0.169	7	0.185	7	109	14
All India	0.198		0.209		106	

Note: Computed by authors using NFHS-3 (2005-06) unit level records.

Underweight

In this sub-section, we consider the magnitude of underweight, as measured by the simple headcount index and incorporate it as our third component to arrive at the composite index of NFR. Here as well, the overall child population has been divided into the same number of subgroups as was done in the previous two sub-sections on stunting and wasting. Thus, obtained information on the group-specific incidence of underweight children is presented in Table 10.10. Across the major states, Kerala, Punjab and Tamil Nadu depict lower levels of the underweight problem. Similar to the cases of stunting and wasting, it is immediately discernible from Table 10.10 that, irrespective of gender, the headcount indices of underweight are systematically of a significantly higher magnitude for the poorer children than for the non-poor. In fact, this pattern is true not only for the country as a whole but also for every major state of the Indian union. Indisputably, these results indicate that poverty turns out to be the prime factor in determining health status wherein health is heavily biased in favour of the non-deprived. In rural areas, the incidence of underweight among the non-poor is around 20 per cent less than that among the poor, whereas in urban areas the difference gets intensified to around 30 per cent. Another related observation here is that among the other two identified groups, child's nutritional status gets more influenced with locational disadvantages compared to the gender gap. To give a quick illustration, at all-India level the underweight outcome among rural non-poor (both girls and boys) is around 40 per cent whereas the same among their urban counterpart is around 30 per cent which is less than almost 10 percentage points. Given such systematic patterns, undoubtedly, the states burdened with the twin problems of privation and backwardness (such as Bihar, Madhya Pradesh and Jharkhand) is observed to possess greater levels of this misfortune.

In Table 10.11, data are presented on both the indices U and U*(the 'unadjusted' and 'adjusted' values respectively of the underweight headcount ratio), for each major state and for the country as a whole. At the all-India level, the 'adjusted' underweight headcount ratio climbs to a value of 45.8 per cent from its 'unadjusted' value of 42.5 per cent—making for an escalation by a factor of 108 per cent. A glance at the 'adjusted' underweight figure suggests that except Haryana, all other high-income states are plagued with highly inequitable distribution of underweight outcomes across income and locational subgroups. In particular, the states of Punjab, Tamil Nadu, Karnataka and Gujarat could be pointed out to have the highest inequities in the distribution of underweight wherein the 'adjusted' estimates of underweight prevalence gets inflated to the extent of around 10 per cent. At

Table 10.10

Group Specific Underweight (Weight-for-Age) Indices: India and Major States (NFHS-3, 2005-06)

States	*RPF*	*RPM*	*RNPF*	*RNPM*	*UPF*	*UPM*	*UNPF*	*UNPM*	*ALL*
Andhra Pradesh	0.384	0.511	0.373	0.304	0.547	0.438	0.244	0.284	0.325
Assam	0.512	0.364	0.361	0.349	0.456	0.278	0.266	0.239	0.364
Bihar	0.677	0.655	0.551	0.499	0.615	0.578	0.441	0.490	0.559
Chhattisgarh	0.565	0.554	0.448	0.457	0.410	0.534	0.305	0.307	0.471
Gujarat	0.636	0.560	0.433	0.486	0.500	1.000	0.351	0.417	0.446
Haryana	0.500	0.515	0.397	0.408	0.000	0.000	0.339	0.364	0.396
Jharkhand	0.615	0.656	0.569	0.550	0.522	0.817	0.362	0.389	0.565
Karnataka	0.527	0.549	0.380	0.392	0.555	0.910	0.285	0.301	0.376
Kerala	0.000	0.400	0.250	0.276	0.000	0.000	0.143	0.158	0.229
Madhya Pradesh	0.654	0.695	0.590	0.556	0.850	0.751	0.504	0.458	0.600
Maharashtra	0.506	0.547	0.409	0.370	0.038	0.574	0.285	0.320	0.370
Orissa	0.535	0.537	0.343	0.290	0.541	0.620	0.281	0.255	0.407
Punjab	0.420	0.398	0.260	0.261	0.000	0.750	0.250	0.183	0.249
Rajasthan	0.512	0.537	0.378	0.376	0.606	0.606	0.277	0.329	0.399
Tamil Nadu	0.289	0.459	0.295	0.336	0.713	0.546	0.242	0.254	0.298
Uttar Pradesh	0.517	0.533	0.419	0.382	0.524	0.477	0.362	0.324	0.424
Uttarakhand	0.675	0.515	0.406	0.405	0.500	0.250	0.240	0.241	0.380
West Bengal	0.507	0.492	0.375	0.346	0.370	0.317	0.264	0.229	0.387
All India	0.563	0.570	0.418	0.395	0.581	0.590	0.313	0.318	0.425

Note: Computed by authors using NFHS-3 (2005-06) unit level records.

the same time, it is discernible that the best performer in terms of the index U (namely Punjab) turns out to be the worst performer in terms of the index U*/U. The low-income states though depict higher levels of unadjusted underweight outcomes but do not show larger inequities in its distribution. This may be due to the fact that this particular problem of undernourishment is present in almost equal proportion among all the classified sub-groups hence a lower inequity is observed along these dimensions. However, if certain other population grouping criterion is adopted or the present grouping is further sub-divided to include other important determinants such as caste, maternal education, availability of child health facilities or any other proximate determinant, we might be able to obtain a more closer view of the inequity situation prevailing in these states. One indisputable truth that emerges even after adjusting for the group-related disparities in the prevalence of underweight among children is that there is a wide disparity between the states at the two extremes of income (high-income and low-income), irrespective of the fact that whether their performance is assessed in terms of U and U*. To gain insights into the acute sub-national welfare divisions which prevail in the country, one has only to compare the lot of the rural poor female child in Bihar with that of the urban non-poor male child in Kerala; for the former sub-population, the underweight incidence (at 67.7 per cent) exceeds that of the latter sub-population (at 15.8 per cent) by a factor of over 400 per cent.

Table 10.11

Underweight and the Effect of Adjustment for Inter-Group Inequalities: India and Major States (NFHS-3, 2005-06)

States	Incidence of Underweight (U)	Rank (in ascending order) according to U	Inequality Adjusted Incidence of Underweight* (U)*	Rank (in ascending order) according to U*	Factor (in per cent) by which Incidence of Underweight is Adjusted due to Inter-group Inequalities (U*/U)	Rank(in ascending order) according to U*/U
Andhra Pradesh	0.325	4	0.375	4	115	14
Assam	0.364	5	0.354	3	97	4
Bihar	0.559	16	0.532	16	95	2
Chhattisgarh	0.471	15	0.451	13	96	3
Gujarat	0.446	14	0.527	15	118	15
Haryana	0.396	10	0.376	5	95	1
Jharkhand	0.565	17	0.558	17	99	6
Karnataka	0.376	7	0.482	14	128	16
Kerala	0.229	1	0.232	1	101	9
Madhya Pradesh	0.600	18	0.602	18	100	8
Maharashtra	0.370	6	0.403	8	109	11
Orissa	0.407	12	0.44	11	108	10
Punjab	0.249	2	0.338	2	136	18
Rajasthan	0.399	11	0.444	12	111	13
Tamil Nadu	0.298	3	0.387	7	130	17
Uttar Pradesh	0.424	13	0.421	10	99	7
Uttarakhand	0.380	8	0.418	9	110	12
West Bengal	0.387	9	0.378	6	98	5
All India	0.425		0.458		108	

Note: Computed by authors using NFHS-3 (2005-06) unit level records.

A Consolidated Picture of Nutritional Failure and its Inequality-adjusted Version

Table 10.12 presents a consolidated picture of nutritional failure in India, and what happens to it when it is adjusted to reflect inter-group disparities in the distribution of such nutritional inadequacies. For the country as a whole and for each of its major states, data are presented for the magnitude of each of the components S, W and U of the Nutritional Failure Ratio (NFR), the NFR itself (given by NFR = [S+W+U]/3), the values of the adjusted components of the NFR (namely S*, W* and U*), and the value of the overall adjusted Nutritional Failure Ratio, NFR* (given by NFR* = [S*+W*+U*]/3). Also presented in the table is information on the ranking of the various states by both NFR and NFR* and the extent of inequality in group-specific deprivation levels (captured by the index NFR*/NFR). Table 10.12 indicates that at the all-India level, the nutritional failure ratio stands at the disturbingly high value of 37 per cent, and its 'adjusted' value—at 39 per cent—is computed to be more than 105 per cent in excess of the unadjusted value. Measured in terms of NFR*, the most deprived of the 18 states turns out to be Madhya Pradesh which, with an index-value of 60 per cent, has an undernutrition level that is almost three times that of the least deprived state, Kerala, which has a NFR* value of 22.4 per cent.

Employing the all-India figure of NFR* as a cut-off level, we could classify the states into 'high nutritionally deprivation' and 'low nutritionally deprivation' ones depending on whether their respective NFR* values exceed or fall short of the cut-off level. On this basis the 'high nutritionally deprived' states, in descending order of NFR*, are Madhya Pradesh, Gujarat, Jharkhand, Bihar, Karnataka, Maharashtra and Chhattisgarh: it is noteworthy that the relatively higher income states of Karnataka and Maharashtra do not fall in this categorisation if we consider the unadjusted NFR. The 'low nutritionally deprived' states, again in descending order of NFR*, are Rajasthan, Uttarakhand, Orissa, Uttar Pradesh, Haryana, West Bengal, Andhra Pradesh, Tamil Nadu, Punjab, Assam and Kerala: this once again acknowledges the pre-eminence of Kerala as a 'model' state (though it is worth noting that even this exemplar's NFR* figure of nearly 22.4 per cent is by no means a comforting small real number). Perhaps, this may also offer further insights into the longevity status enjoyed by its population which is the highest among the Indian states.

Let us next, in analogous fashion, consider the relative performance of the states in terms of: (a) the 'unadjusted' nutritional failure ratio (NFR), and (b) the disparity index NFR*/NFR, which we shall designate by m (to signify that it is an inequality-induced multiplier). Table 10.8 indicates that the 'high NFR' states, in descending order of NFR are, Madhya Pradesh, Bihar, Jharkhand, Chhattisgarh, Gujarat and Uttar Pradesh while the low NFR states (also in descending order of NFR) are Orissa, Haryana, Rajasthan, Uttarakhand, West Bengal, Maharashtra, Karnataka, Assam, Andhra Pradesh, Tamil Nadu, Punjab

Table 10.12

A Consolidated Picture of Nutritional Failure and its Inequality-Adjusted Version: India and Major States (NFHS-3, 2005-06)

States	*Incidence of Stunting (S)*	*Incidence of Wasting (W)*	*Incidence of Underweight (U)*	*Nutritional Failure Ratio (NFR) [= S+W+U)/3]*	*Rank (in ascending order) according to NFR*	*Adjusted Incidence of Stunting (S*)*	*Adjusted Incidence of Wasting (W*)*	*Adjusted Incidence of Underweight (U*)*	*Adjusted Nutritional Failure Ratio (NFR*) [= S*+W*+U*/3*	*Rank (in Ascending order) according to NFR**	*Factor by which NFR is Inflated due to Inter-group Inequalities (NFR*/NFR) (in per cent)*	*Rank (in ascending order) according to NFR*/NFR*
Andhra Pradesh	0.427	0.122	0.325	0.291	4	0.497	0.13	0.375	0.334	5	115	13
Assam	0.465	0.137	0.364	0.322	5	0.444	0.132	0.354	0.310	2	96	2
Bihar	0.556	0.271	0.559	0.462	17	0.513	0.266	0.532	0.437	15	95	1
Chhattisgarh	0.529	0.195	0.471	0.398	15	0.503	0.202	0.451	0.385	12	97	3
Gujarat	0.517	0.187	0.446	0.383	14	0.628	0.243	0.527	0.466	17	122	17
Haryana	0.457	0.191	0.396	0.348	11	0.438	0.218	0.376	0.344	7	99	6
Jharkhand	0.498	0.323	0.565	0.462	16	0.501	0.303	0.558	0.454	16	98	5
Karnataka	0.437	0.176	0.376	0.330	6	0.493	0.191	0.482	0.389	14	118	16
Kerala	0.245	0.159	0.229	0.211	1	0.296	0.144	0.232	0.224	1	106	9
Madhya Pradesh	0.5	0.350	0.600	0.483	18	0.48	0.352	0.602	0.478	18	99	7
Maharashtra	0.463	0.165	0.370	0.333	7	0.584	0.17	0.403	0.386	13	116	14
Orissa	0.45	0.195	0.407	0.351	12	0.497	0.187	0.44	0.375	9	107	10
Punjab	0.367	0.092	0.249	0.236	2	0.484	0.116	0.338	0.313	3	132	18
Rajasthan	0.437	0.204	0.399	0.347	10	0.511	0.195	0.444	0.383	11	111	11
Tamil Nadu	0.309	0.222	0.298	0.276	3	0.35	0.237	0.387	0.325	4	117	15
Uttar Pradesh	0.568	0.148	0.424	0.380	13	0.529	0.157	0.421	0.369	8	97	4
Uttarakhand	0.444	0.188	0.380	0.337	9	0.471	0.242	0.418	0.377	10	112	12
West Bengal	0.446	0.169	0.387	0.334	8	0.439	0.185	0.378	0.334	6	100	8
All India	0.48	0.198	0.425	0.368		0.488	0.209	0.458	0.385		105	

Note: Computed by authors using NFHS-3 (2005-06) unit level records.

and Kerala. The high disparity states (also in descending order of m) are Punjab, Gujarat, Karnataka, Tamil Nadu, Maharashtra, Andhra Pradesh, Uttarakhand, Rajasthan, Orissa and Kerala, while the 'low disparity states, (again in descending order of m) are West Bengal, Madhya Pradesh, Haryana, Jharkhand, Uttar Pradesh, Chhattisgarh, Assam and Bihar. Indeed, there is a strong inverse relationship between 'average nutritional deprivation' (as measured by NFR) and disparity in the distribution of sub-group deprivation levels (as measured by m). Gujarat emerges as the only state which not only exemplifies higher unadjusted incidence of nutritional disadvantages but also reveals higher levels of inter-group disparity.

After discussing these major highlights of the exercise it is important to consider the differences obtained in NFR* in comparison to the index NFR. It must be remembered that the difference between NFR* and NFR brings out the true account of deprivation which is adjusted for between-group disparities in health deprivation. It can also be interpreted as a composite 'equally distributed equivalent deprivation' indicator. From this perspective, it implies that the average nutritional failure rate in India which is 37 per cent if evenly distributed would increase the nutritional failure rate to 39 per cent. Though at all-India level the overall discrepancy appears to be of two per cent but such discrepancies are prominent among the states of Gujarat, Punjab and Karnataka. The adjustments of the nutritional outcome could be used in arriving at optimal budgetary allocations for such child welfare schemes as such an exercise renders useful in enhancing the efficiency in the allocation of scarce resources.

Policy Note and Conclusion

We shall begin this concluding section by reiterating the motivation behind the present engagement of ours. What lies beneath this empirical exercise is the sheer urgency to contemplate over the inadequacies of plain summary measures of health outcomes and to evoke policy concerns pertaining to social justice and equity. It is disconcerting to witness, especially from an ethical perspective, that certain identifiable groups in India bear the brunt of health disadvantages especially when they also are incompetent to prevail over their share of insecurities merely because of imperious social and economic misfortunes. Although, certain policy interventions are in place to deal with such adversities but, all the same, it is a little surprising to observe that they are seldom formulated on the basis of any distribution-sensitised measure which, undeniably, can go a long way to optimise resource allocation and enhance targeting efficiency of such interventions. The present analysis pursues this deliberation and endeavours to enhance the informational base for policy-making by incorporating into the summary measures, a more elaborated account of health inequality obtained due to factors such as income inadequacies, locational disadvantages and gender bias.

While analysing along the income component, it was observed that poorer section of the population were beleaguered with ill-health whether it be the quest for child survival or the anxieties pertaining to child nutrition. A simple theoretical model was resorted to comprehend its association and causation. The analysis revealed that the degree of health inequalities gets escalated when the rising average income levels of the population is accompanied by greater income inequalities. On the one hand, such an association does reflect that the product of economic growth in the form of rising average income and income inequalities present certain impediments in the path of equitable health by allowing the better-off population to secure greater benefits of the growth process. On the other hand, it is also evident that the summary measures of health also improve with the income profile of a region. The interplay of these two impacts may actually lead the policy makers to trade-off a little bit of health inequality for gaining higher health levels. However, a social planner needs to sail through such quandaries and should arrive at prudent mechanisms to utilise the resources and technology obtained through economic growth by devoting greater resources towards those sections of the population who have been excluded from the growth process. Invariably, such an exercise requires fuller information as regards the sources of inequality and the recognition of the vulnerable groups.

In second part of the chapter, an attempt was made to highlight such disadvantages among the vulnerable groups. Our findings suggest that the rural population endures high degrees of disadvantages and they are secluded in terms of health achievement. With the implementation of NRHM, it is expected that such discrepancies are narrowed down over a period of time but it is equally important here to monitor its performance on the equity front. In the third and final part of the chapter, such an attempt was presented for the prevalence of undernourishment among the child population of India and its different states. It is encouraging to observe that such an analysis succeeds in presenting the group-wise prevalence of health disadvantages and thus proves of high merit for guiding public policy on health. The present analysis brought out that a rural income-poor female child has the largest share of health sufferings. However, the poverty factor was also observed to cut across the other two dimensions of location and gender and had emerged as the major factor along which health disparities were getting manifested. Being a suggestive exercise, we have restricted ourselves to examine disparities along the three important identified groupings of income, location and gender but it would be of immense help for policy purposes if distribution-sensitive measures are obtained accounting for other important dimensions associated with child health such as child ailments or child mortalities across characteristics like maternal education, caste and availability of health facilities. Since our analysis was largely confined to examine the group-related disparities in child nutrition it would be useful to briefly discuss the policy contexts and the lessons therein. To eradicate the risk of undernutrition, it is warranted that interventions are made towards provisioning of basic services such as food supplementation, complete basic immunisation and better health care for children and their mother. However, the unacceptably higher malnourishment levels of India raise several concerns regarding the policies pertaining to child health interventions in India. In India, nutritional intervention is primarily covered through the Integrated Child Development Scheme (ICDS), which provides eight types of services to its beneficiaries—children and mothers. These are supplementary feeding, immunisation, health check-ups, referral, and nutrition and health education for mothers, micronutrient supplementation, and introduction to formal education to child aged between 3 to 6 years. While its haphazard implementation and performance has not offered much to celebrate, nonetheless, the ICDS villages have better nutritional status for their children in contrast to non-ICDS ones. Given the current state-of-affairs, the government—both Central and state—should work towards enhancing the effectiveness of the existing schemes or should engineer new mechanisms to resolve the problem. For instance, the state of Tamil Nadu has designed the Tamil Nadu Integrated Nutrition Project (TNIP), which targets the children below two years of age wherein, if they are found to be underweight for 90 consecutive days, they are directly provided with food supplementation. Besides, the programme also provides health care to children in terms of treatment of diarrhoea, deforming, immunisation as well as regular check-ups for child and mother. These services are extended to pregnant and lactating women as well. As identified by several studies, there are a slew of factors (including its economical design and political sensitivity) beneath this success story, but eventually, what really matters is to observe that Tamil Nadu has accomplished a great deal to reduce the severe magnitude of undernourishment and in a relative sense is observed to be faring well in terms of overall NFR and NFR*. The moral of this story is that political commitment and peoples' will can help realise enormous changes and can make a dent in the discoloured fabric of child health. This argument gains further strength if we observe the unparallel story of Kerala that secures a firm national lead in terms of superior health performance. Moreover, it makes a statement regarding the role of social mobilisation and awareness as the best weapons to combat health deprivation and there is no real necessity to await rapid economic growth and wealth accumulation. Both these states offer valuable lessons not only to several backward states of India but also to income-rich states such as Gujarat and Maharashtra who depict not only greater magnitude of the problem but are marked with stark inequities in its distribution.

References

Central Statistical Organisation (2007). *National Sample Survey-Consumer Expenditure Survey 61st Round*. CSO New Delhi.

Dasgupta, M., L. Chen and T.N. Krishnan (eds.) (1996). *Health, Poverty and Development in India*. New Delhi: Oxford University Press.

Gakidou, E.G., Christopher J.L. Murray, Julio Frenk (2003). "A Framework for Measuring Health Inequality", in C.J.L Murray and D.B. Evans (eds.), *Health system performance assessment: Debates, methods and empiricism*. Geneva: World Health Organization.

Grossman, M. (1972). "On the Concept of Health Capital and Demand for Health", *Journal of Political Economy* 80: 223-255.

Hicks, D.A. (1997). "The Inequality-adjusted Human Development Index: A Constructive Proposal", *World Development* Vol.7.

Humphries, K.H. and E. van Doorslaer (2000). "Income Related Health Inequalities in Canada", *Social Science and Medicine* 50: 663-671.

International Institute for Population Sciences (IIPS) and ORC Macro (2007). *National Family Health Survey* (NFHS-3), 2005-06. India, Mumbai: IIPS.

Jayraj, D & S Subramanian (2002). "Child Labour in Tamil Nadu in the 1980s: A Preliminary Account of its Nature, Extent and Distribution", *Economic & Political Weekly*, March 9.

Jenkins, S. (1988). "Calculating Income Distribution Indices from Microdata", *National Tax Journal* Vol.61.

Kakwani, N.C. (1980). *Income Inequality and Poverty; Methods of Estimation and Policy Applications*. New York: Oxford University Press.

Kakwani, N.C., A. Wagstaff and E. van Doorslaer (1997). "Socioeconomic Inequalities in Health: Measurement, Computation and Statistical Inference", *Journal of Economterics* 77(1): 87-104.

Lerman, R.I. and S. Yitzhaki (1989). "Improving the Accuracy of Estimates of Gini Coefficients", *Journal of Econometrics* 42(1).

Macinko, J.A. and B. Starfield (2002). "Annotated Bibliography on Equity in Health, 1980-2001", *International Journal for Equity in Health* 1: 1.

Macinko, J.A., L. Shi, B. Starfield, J.T. Wulu, Jr. (2003). "Income Inequality and Health: A Critical Review of the Literature", *Medical Care Research and Review* 60(4).

Majumdar, M. and S. Subramanian (2001). "Capability Failure and Group Disparities: Some Evidence from India for the 1980s", *Journal of Development Studies* 37(5).

Murray, C.J.L. *et al.* (1999). "Health Inequalities and Social Group Differences: What should We Measure?", *Bulletin of the World Health Organization* 77(7): 537-543.

Rajan, S.I. and K.S. James (2004). *Demographic Change, Health Inequality and Human Development in India.* Hyderabad: Centre for Economic and Social Studies.

Rao, K.S., S. Selvaraju, S. Nagpal, S. Sakthivel (2005). "Financing of Health in India, Background Paper on Financing and Delivery of Health Care Services in India", National Commission on Macroeconomics and Health, New Delhi.

Smith, J.P., (2004). "Unraveling the SES and Health Connection" *Population and Development Review.*

Starfield, B. (2001). "Improving Equity in Health: A Research Agenda", *International Journal of Health Services* 31(3): 545-66.

van, Doorslaer E. *et al.* (1997). "Income Related Inequalities in Health: Some International Comparisons", *Journal of Health Economics* 16: 93-112.

Wagstaff, A. (1986). "The Demand for Health Care: A Simplified Grossman Model", *Bulletin of Economic Research* 38(1): 93-95.

Wagstaff, A. and E. van Doorslaer (2000). "Equity in Health Care Finance and Delivery", in A.J.Culyer and J.P. Newhouse eds., *Handbook of Health Economics* (1B), Elsevier, Amsterdam, Chapter 34: 1803-1862.

Wagstaff, A., P. Paci and E. van Doorslaer (1991). "On the Measurement of Inequalities in Health", *Social Science and Medicene* 33(5): 545-557.

Wagstaff, A. (2002). "Inequalities in Health in Developing Countries: Swimming Against the Tide?", Policy research *Working Paper* no.2795, World Bank.

Wildman, J. (2003). "Modelling Health, Income and Income Inequality: The Impact of Income Inequality on Health and Health Inequality", *Journal of Health Economics* 22: 521-538.

Wilkinson, R.G. (1996). *Unhealthy Societies: The Afflictions of Inequality*. London: Routledge and Kegan Paul.

11

Human Development Constraint to Demand for Health Care in India

ANIT N. MUKHERJEE AND KRISHANU KARMAKAR

Introduction

The current health scenario in India is often described as 'dismal' or 'disturbing'[1]. Except a few states like Kerala, Goa and Tamil Nadu which have done relatively well, the situation in most parts of the country is a cause for worry. Levels of infant and neo-natal mortality, child malnutrition, female anaemia, non-institutional delivery etc., are higher in some states in India than countries of Sub-Saharan Africa. Going by present trends, India is in danger of missing the health targets set by the Millennium Development Goals (MDGs).

One major reason put forward for this low level of achievement of health in India is the systematic lack of investment by the government, which adversely affects the poor. Public expenditure on health stands at less than one per cent of GDP, with state governments sharing most of the burden. In the light of economic reforms in the decade of the 90s, the squeeze on public expenditure in health has been aggravated further especially at the state level.[2]

There have been a series of studies documenting the precarious situation *vis-à-vis* the provision of public health facilities in India. Most of them focus on access and quality issues, which deter people from utilising government health services. Recent papers have also investigated the links between non-utilisation and administrative factors such as absenteeism among the health staff in the rural areas, as well as the presence of alternative informal sources of medical care.[3] They also find instances of untrained and uninformed quacks being frequently consulted in the rural areas. Even in fee-paying urban private

---

1. See Bose (2007) for a discussion on child and maternal health in the light of the latest NFHS-3 data.
2. Mooij and Dev, 2002.
3. Banerjee and Duflo, 2006.

sector, one particular study reports a lack of knowledge among medical practitioners in Delhi for common symptoms of diseases such as tuberculosis.[4]

However, the demand for health care has received relatively little attention, particularly because of the non-availability of representative household-level datasets. The National Sample Survey (NSS) data is the most suitable for this kind of analysis. Over the last two decades, there have been only three rounds where health care data has been collected in detail—42nd, 52nd and 60th rounds conducted in 1986-87, 1995-96 and 2004-05 respectively. While the time gap of the surveys is useful in comparing changes in the utilisation rates of public and private facilities, expenditure by households and individuals etc., changes in questionnaire design and data collection methodology has rendered such comparative analysis difficult.

The latest (60th) round of the NSS included detailed questions on household characteristics, economic profile, expenditure on inpatient cases over the past year, details of diagnostic and other charges, lost income due to illness and caring for the sick, and utilisation of outpatient services due to illness with a recall period of 15 days. Our interest lies in those cases where individuals reported being ill just before the survey, but did not seek medical advice. This seems to be a plausible starting point for an analysis of the demand for health care.

We use the unit (household)-level data from the 60th round to understand the reasons behind why individuals do not seek treatment for reported ailments. Intuitively, there are both systemic as well as personal reasons—lack of access and quality of care from the supply side, financial constraints from the economic side as well as constraints of knowledge and perception about the nature and severity of the ailment at a personal level. The report of the 60th round does not delve deeply into the issue, certainly not at a disaggregated level. However, this aspect of demand constraint is important to understand the next steps in the debate—public *versus* private, burden of expenditure etc.

The chapter focuses on three key determinants of demand for health care which can be grouped under the generic title of human development—age profile, income group and literacy level. In all the three aspects, we would present our results from the unit level analysis disaggregated by sector (rural and urban) and gender (male and female). What comes out of the exercise is that in all the three determinants, location of the household and the gender

---

4. Das and Hammer, 2006.

of the ailing member plays a significant role in determining whether treatment is taken or not.

The following section describes the data in brief and the steps taken to remove inconsistencies in the NSSO dataset. In Section 3, we analyse the data on untreated morbidity for demographic characteristics such as age of household members and intra-household familial relationships; Section 4 reports the results classifying households in terms of literacy level of the household head. Section 5 stratifies the data according to expenditure quintiles, exploring the relationship between the proxy for income/wealth status on access to medical care. We end with some conclusions and proposals for future extension.

Data Description and Trends across Rounds

Our total sample consists of 383,312 individuals out of which 36462 (9.5 per cent) reported an ailment within 15 days before the survey was conducted. The design of the questionnaire is such that these individuals who reported an ailment could be divided into those who did seek medical advice and those who did not. As per the field instruction for filling up the survey, medical advice was recorded in those cases where the individual went to a health post either public or private. Medical advice in the private sector was stated to be only in case the individual went to registered medical practitioners in all streams—allopathic, homeopathic, *ayurveda* and *unani*, or else to the outpatient department of a private hospital or medical college.

The decision tree of the individual is given in Figure 11.1. If the answer to the first question was in the affirmative, then the respondent was asked about the type of service he or she availed (public or private), and then other supplementary questions. In case the answer to the first question was negative, then the respondent was given six pre-coded reasons, which are the same across all the three health rounds mentioned above. Finally, the respondent was asked whether they took any other measure such as consulting with friends and/or family members, medicine shop owner etc., and how much it cost.

For the whole sample, 85.2 per cent of those who reported ailing in the last 15 days said that they sought medical advice while the rest 14.8 per cent did not. In rural areas, 16.6 per cent of those reporting morbidity did not seek medical care, while it was 11.7 per cent for the urban areas. Clearly there is a large difference in their demand for medical services between the two sectors.

The reason for not seeking treatment for illness spells across all the three health rounds is given in Table 11.1. It is interesting to note that over the last

Figure 11.1

Questionnaire Tree (Question Sequence for those Individuals who were Ill within the 15 Days Previous to the Survey)

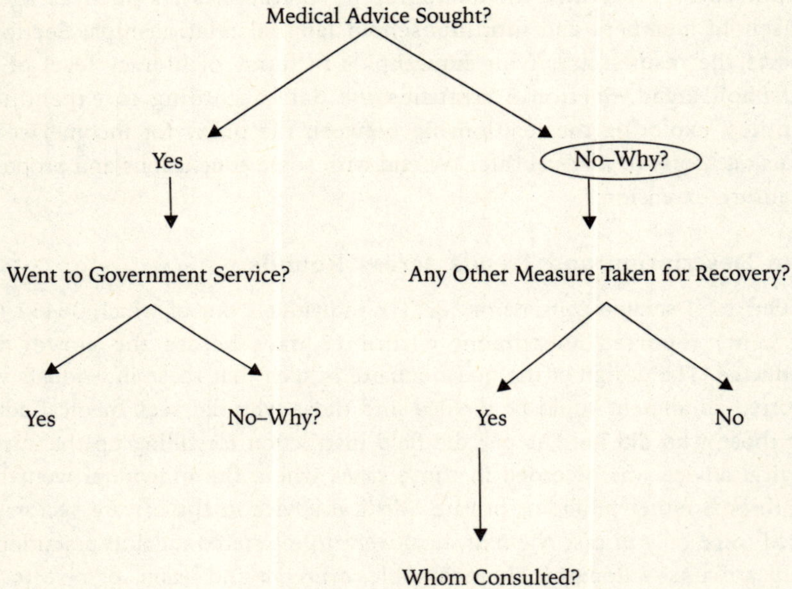

Table 11.1

Distribution of Untreated Ailments by Reason of No Treatment

Reason for Not Seeking Medical Treatment	*Rural*			*Urban*		
	42nd	*52nd*	*60th*	*42nd*	*52nd*	*60th*
No medical facility	3	9	12	0	1	1
Lack of faith	2	4	3	2	5	2
Long waiting	0	1	1	1	1	2
Financial problem	15	24	28	10	21	20
Ailment not serious	75	52	32	81	60	50
Others	5	10	24	6	12	25
Total	**100**	**100**	**100**	**100**	**100**	**100**

Note: Estimates for Others include the cases where the reason is not reported; For 42nd and 52nd rounds estimates refer to untreated persons.

Source: Table 4.9 of NSSO 52nd Round Report and Statement 16 of NSSO 60th Round Report.

two decades, the proportion of rural respondents citing lack of health infrastructure as a reason for not accessing medical care has gone up significantly from 3 to 12 per cent. There has been a very dramatic decline in the proportion of people stating illness not serious as the reason for not treating morbidities. This is true both for urban as well as for rural areas. What this signifies is that there is a better awareness of the medical condition, but demand for health care is constrained due to financial and 'other' reasons.

The last category is interesting in itself and merits more attention. It may reveal an increasing trend towards getting treatment informally, either from family members, or from the untrained and unregistered informal sector. Overall, more than one-third of the cases of illness is not considered serious enough to merit a visit to a medical professional. Therefore, apart from supply and economic constraints, increase in the demand for health care would depend on the individual's perception of their medical condition.

The gender and sector desegregations are presented in Table 11.2. The proportion of male and female reporting untreated morbidity is nearly equaled in rural, while there is a large difference in the urban areas. Rate of untreated morbidity in urban females is about 20 per cent higher than the reported untreated cases for males.

Table 11.2

Sector and Gender Distribution of Untreated Cases of Illness

Reason for Not Seeking Medical Treatment	*Rural*		*Urban*	
	Male	*Female*	*Male*	*Female*
No medical facility	6.00	5.52	0.41	0.79
Lack of faith	1.67	1.36	0.76	1.13
Long waiting	0.51	0.36	0.29	1.35
Financial problem	13.15	15.12	8.07	12.47
Ailment not serious	14.86	17.38	24.68	25.60
Others	11.84	12.24	11.54	12.91
Total	**48.02**	**51.98**	**45.75**	**54.25**

Source: NSSO 60th Round data.

Also noteworthy is the fact that among the reasons cited for not accessing health care, there is very little difference among males and females in the rural areas. However, for the urban sample, there is a 3 to 4 per cent gender gap for respondents citing financial reasons and self-assessment of their illness. This may point to the persistence of gender bias in utilisation of health care as already noted in studies using the 52nd round data.[5]

As we shall see subsequently, this gender disparity among the two sectors persists even if we stratify the data by demographic characteristics, income class or education levels. One important lesson from a policy perspective is that urbanisation may aggravate, rather than mitigate, the gender disparity in health seeking behaviour in future.

Demographic Characteristics

Demand for health care has been shown to have a non-linear relationship with demographic factors—principally age.[6] Newborn babies and children need greater care, hence the emphasis on neo-natal and child health in policy formulation. Lower infant mortality is positively correlated with better standards of health care and also as an indicator of the general level of development of a country or region. The example of Kerala has often been cited in the literature—high standard of health care has reduced infant mortality and malnutrition to levels seen in advanced countries. On the other hand, Uttar Pradesh has infant mortality and malnutrition rates comparable to the least developed nations of the world.[7]

The demand for health care reduces during the productive years of adolescence and middle age, and then rises again when a person gets old. In the years between 15 and 45, the perception of the gravity of the illness is also much lower. Individuals making rational decisions about their health status may sometimes discount the long-run cost and prefer not spending time and resources in accessing health care during the productive age. This can very often result in increasing the probability of developing serious ailment in old age due to untreated morbidity. What it also means is that in the case where public provision of health care is deficient, untreated morbidity may actually raise the economic dependence of the old on the younger generation. In the context of declining fertility rates, demographic composition that is now favourable for India may in the long run turn out to be a significant challenge for health policy, as is evident in ageing societies such as Japan, Western Europe, the United States and even China.

Our analysis of the 60th round data supports the points raised above. We disaggregate the data on untreated morbidity by age groups and by gender—the rationale for dividing the age-group in six categories is dictated by the

---

5. Sen, Iyer and George, EPW, 2002.

6. Musgrove, 2003.

7. Source data from NFHS-3; reported in Bose (2008).

non-linearity in demand for health services discussed above. Overall, we find that in both rural and urban areas, the proportion of untreated morbidity is greater for females than for males, and the difference is greater in the urban as compared to the rural areas. Out of the total number of instances of untreated morbidity, 13 per cent is in the first age-group (below 5 years) and a similar proportion in the second (between 6 and 15 years). The highest rate is found in the third group—the young adult and middle age population, tapers off in the fourth group (late working age) but rises significantly in the age group of 60-70 years (see Figure 11.2 below).

Figure 11.2

Cases of Untreated Morbidity by Age-Groups: Rural and Urban

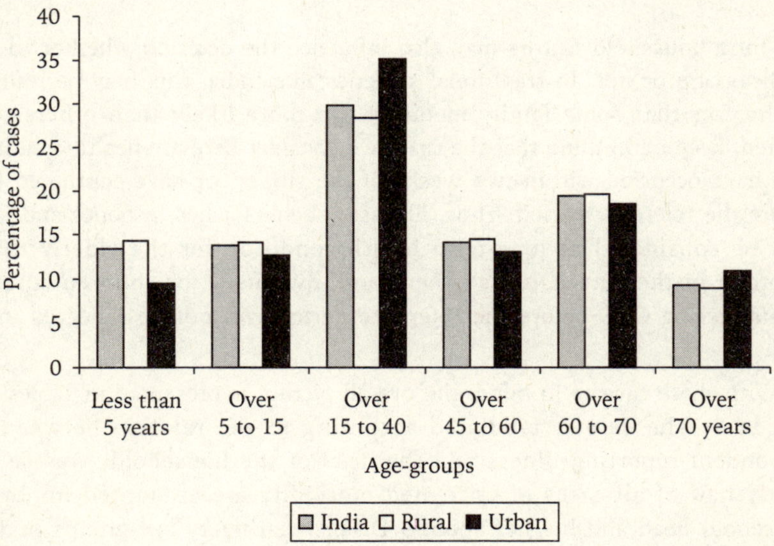

Table 11.3 gives a summary of the untreated morbidity scenario by age-groups and location. In the rural areas, the rates of untreated morbidities for children below 15 are lower for females as compared to males. The difference is not very significant for those above 60. In the urban areas, however, the gender inequality is higher—in the lower age-groups the difference is one per cent or less in favour of girls, while in all others, women are less likely to get treated in the case of temporary illnesses.

Table 11.3

Untreated Morbidity by Gender and Age-Groups (%)

Age Group	India			Rural			Urban		
	Male	Female	Total	Male	Female	Total	Male	Female	Total
Less than 5 years	7.03	6.40	13.42	7.56	6.80	14.36	4.81	4.72	9.53
Over 5 to 15	7.10	6.78	13.87	7.38	6.76	14.14	5.94	6.84	12.77
Over 15 to 40	12.60	17.12	29.72	11.77	16.65	28.42	16.05	19.10	35.15
Over 45 to 60	6.57	7.63	14.20	6.68	7.79	14.47	6.12	6.96	13.07
Over 60 to 70	9.32	10.07	19.39	9.62	9.99	19.61	8.10	10.38	18.48
Over 70 years	4.96	4.42	9.38	5.02	3.98	9.00	4.73	6.26	11.00
Total	**47.58**	**52.42**	**100.00**	**48.02**	**51.98**	**100.00**	**45.75**	**54.25**	**100.00**

Source: NSS 60th Round.

Intra-household factors may also influence the decision whether to seek medical care or not. In traditional societies like India, this may be reflected in the fact that some family members are more likely than others to be treated, keeping in mind that the cases we consider here are health conditions that have occurred within two weeks of the survey, or have continued from before the reference period. Thus, illnesses such as aches in bones and joints may be considered as long-term health condition for the elderly that is recorded in the data. On the other hand, dysentery for children cured by administering ORS before the reference period will not be reflected in the data.

With these caveats in mind, the overall picture is presented in Tables 11.4 and 11.5. The data is tabulated according to the relation between the respondent reporting illness and the head of the household. We see that nearly half of all cases of untreated morbidity are accounted for by the household head and his/her spouse. Disaggregating by age-groups in Table 11.4, we find that the chances of untreated morbidity are higher if the head of household is over 60 years of age. On the other hand, the major proportion of untreated morbidity for spouse is between ages 15 to 60, especially in the lower age bracket.

Unmarried children upto 15 years constitute over 80 per cent of total untreated morbidity for all unmarried children, reflecting, to a certain extent, the low age at marriage prevalent in India. The third largest proportion of untreated morbidity is for the elderly—father, mother or in-laws of the household head. Understandably, most of the untreated morbidity in this category is in the over-60 age group.

Disaggregating the data by gender, Table 11.5 provides some clues regarding the extent of gender differences in treatment of illness *vis-à-vis* the relation to the head of household. We find that elderly female members of the household (mothers or mothers-in-law of the head of household) have far higher rates of untreated morbidity as compared to elderly male members—the difference is nearly 6 per cent for the whole sample. As noted above, male head of household is the group who are most likely to ignore temporary illnesses.

It is difficult to assign reason for this finding from the data without an explicit model of household decision-making structure. Overall, it seems that elderly heads of households may not value their health condition given the fact that they are no longer the earning members of the family. The social dynamics may also be the reason why illnesses of elderly women are not given as much importance as that of men when the head of household is presumably their son. It is therefore, unclear whether preference for male children within the household is reflected in health outcomes for the elderly.

Table 11.4

Untreated Morbidity by Relation to Head and Age-Groups (%)

Relation to Head	*Age Group*						
	Less than 5 years	*Over 5 to 15*	*Over 15 to 40*	*Over 45 to 60*	*Over 60 to 70*	*Over 70 years*	*Total*
Self	-	-	8.90	7.34	10.41	4.13	30.78
Spouse of head	-	-	10.26	4.53	2.09	0.38	17.26
Married child	-	0.03	1.66	0.04	0.05	-	1.79
Spouse of married children	-	-	1.83	0.03	-	-	1.87
Unmarried child	10.26	11.90	5.36	0.04	-	0.01	27.57
Grand child	2.91	1.49	0.25	-	-	-	4.66
Father/mother/ father-in-law/mother-in-law	-	-	0.17	1.74	6.22	4.28	12.41
Brother/sister/brother-in-law/ sister-in-law/other relatives	0.26	0.45	1.27	0.47	0.62	0.57	3.64
Servants/employees/other Non-relatives	-	-	0.02	0.01	-	0.01	0.03
Total	13.42	13.87	29.72	14.20	19.39	9.38	100.00

Source: NSS 60th Round.

Table 11.5

Untreated Morbidity by Relation to Head and Gender (%)

Relation to Head	*Male*	*Female*	*Total*
Self	24.05	6.74	30.78
Spouse of head	0.11	17.15	17.26
Married child	1.44	0.34	1.79
Spouse of married children	0.04	1.82	1.87
Unmarried child	14.76	12.81	27.57
Grand child	2.64	2.02	4.66
Father/mother/father-in-law/mother-in-law	3.10	9.31	12.41
Brother/sister/brother-in-law/sister-in-law/other relatives	1.44	2.20	3.64
Servants/employees/other non-relatives	0.00	0.03	0.03
Total	47.58	52.42	100.00

Source: NSS 60th Round.

Education Level

The connection between education level and health status is well-established. In the case of Kerala for example, studies have pointed to the fact that there is almost universal school education, and also a much higher standard of health compared to other states in the country—especially in terms of maternal and child mortality. Paradoxically, the NSS report also indicates that the proportion reporting ailment is also the highest in India. This may be due to causal linkages between better education standards and greater health-seeking behaviour.

From another standpoint, number of years of education is one of the determinants of income level of an individual. We would, therefore expect to find that for persons who are either illiterate or with a few initial years of school education, financial factors as well as their self-assessed health condition are the primary reasons for not accessing organised medical service. If access to health centres is difficult, the opportunity cost of transport and man-days lost can also become critical. This will disproportionately affect persons with lower rather than higher education—and consequently income levels.

To describe the data on the demand for health care by varying levels of education, we first stratify the data using the level of schooling of the head of the household as a proxy for the general standard of education of the household. If the household head is over 60, there is a higher probability that he/she would be less educated than the next generation. In case of a representative household of middle-aged parents and young children, the level of education of the head of the household would be better correlated to the demand for health services for the entire family. For the purposes of our analysis, we do not separate out the two cases mentioned here, and report the results using the full sample of those who reported ill but did not seek medical advice.

Table 11.6 describes the data for the whole sample, while Table 11.7 presents the picture in the rural and urban areas separately. We divide the sample into four classes as far as the education of the household head is concerned—illiterate, upto primary, upto secondary, and higher secondary and above. As expected, the share of untreated morbidity for those cases where the head of household is illiterate is over 45 per cent, which drops progressively to below 7 per cent in the highest education level. Therefore, overall, there is a distinct inverse relationship as far as household head's education level and demand for health care is concerned.

The data in Table 11.6 also confirms the hypothesis that having lower level of education in a household increases the chances of financial difficulty in the access to health care. Financial reason is cited by 16.3 per cent of the household heads who are illiterates. On the contrary, the major reason for not accessing health care for other education groups is "ailment not considered serious". What is clear is that the cost of medical care restricts access for those with low education levels. Furthermore, health infrastructure is also more of a hindrance in accessing care for persons with lower education levels. The linkages between supply and demand sides, therefore, need to be looked at more carefully in multiple contexts of human development.

Table 11.6

Reasons for Not Accessing Treatment by Education Level of Household Head (% in sample)

Reason for Not Seeking Medical Treatment	*Education Level of the Head of the Family*				
	Illiterate	*Primary*	*Secondary*	*Higher Sec.*	*Total*
No medical facility	4.70	2.61	1.79	0.41	9.52
Lack of faith	1.31	0.96	0.49	0.05	2.81
Long waiting	0.19	0.26	0.49	0.08	1.02
Financial reasons	16.35	6.76	3.04	0.62	26.77
Ailment not serious	12.88	10.68	8.38	3.79	35.73
Others	10.22	6.38	5.64	1.92	24.16
Total	**45.65**	**27.65**	**19.83**	**6.87**	**100.00**

Note: Higher Sec: Higher Secondary.
Source: 60th Round NSS.

The overall picture masks significant differences between the rural and urban areas as far as education level is concerned, as seen from Table 11.7. For the rural areas, the broad conclusion of Table 11.6 still holds, except for the fact that the 'return to education' is higher. That is, the decline in the rate of untreated morbidity decreases faster across education levels in the rural area compared to the general picture. From a policy perspective, it points to the importance of adult education, which may have first-round impact on reducing untreated morbidity. In the long term, demand for health care would improve with improvement in the general level of education.

For the urban area, the picture is very different. The proportion of untreated morbidity is the highest for those instances where the head of household has at least secondary level education. It is nearly 6 per cent higher than those where the head of household is illiterate. This result is counter-intuitive, but may be explained by the fact that most of the households with low levels of education are likely to be daily-wage manual labourers, who cannot afford not to treat temporary ailments such as fever, injuries or respiratory problems. Given the greater availability of private health care facilities in the urban areas and higher wage rates, the proportion of the illiterate who reported not accessing health care for infrastructure or financial reason is much lower than the rural areas. In fact, 75 per cent of untreated morbidities are either due to the individual perception of their illness not being serious enough or 'other' reasons given by the respondent. As we shall show later, most of those who gave 'other' reasons have taken medical advice from their friends, family members or medical shop attendants. This implies that compared to rural areas, health care demand being met by informal sources such as medical shop attendant, friends and family etc., in urban areas may actually be higher.

Economic Group

The proportion of untreated morbidity will be expected to vary across various economic groups as well. However, the direction of causality is more difficult to hypothesise. Higher income groups may have a lesser degree of financial constraint, but that may not necessarily translate into higher demand for health care. The interplay between the various socioeconomic factors—two of which have already been examined above—may determine the proportion of reported illnesses that go untreated.

The NSS questionnaire enables us to stratify the sample by monthly expenditure level of the household. We divide the whole sample into five expenditure groups on the basis of increasing monthly household expenditure and tabulate the results for untreated morbidity for each quintile.

Table 11.7

Demand for Outpatient Care Classified by Education Level of Head of Household (% in Sub-Sample)

Reason for Not Seeking Medical Treatment	Education Level of the Head of the Family									
	Rural					Urban				
	Illiterate	Primary	Secondary	Higher Sec.	Total	Illiterate	Primary	Secondary	Higher Sec.	Total
No medical facility	5.70	3.21	2.18	0.42	11.52	0.53	0.12	0.18	0.35	1.19
Lack of faith	1.40	1.07	0.52	0.03	3.03	0.90	0.49	0.36	0.13	1.88
Long waiting	0.14	0.27	0.38	0.09	0.87	0.41	0.21	0.96	0.06	1.64
Financial reasons	17.75	7.04	2.83	0.64	28.26	10.50	5.59	3.93	0.52	20.54
Ailment not serious	13.35	10.78	6.40	1.70	32.24	10.93	10.26	16.6	12.49	50.28
Others	11.35	6.64	5.08	1.01	24.09	5.51	5.29	7.98	5.67	24.45
Total	**49.70**	**29.01**	**17.39**	**3.90**	**100.00**	**28.79**	**21.96**	**30.02**	**19.23**	**100.00**

Note: Higher Sec: Higher Secondary.
Source: 60th Round NSS.

As per the expenditure group classification, Table 11.8 provides the summary for the entire sample which reported ailing within the survey recall period of 15 days. We find that for rural and urban areas combined, there is little variation in the distribution of untreated cases across expenditure quintiles. However, two points emerge from the table: (i) in the poorer quintiles, financial reasons dominate, and (ii) in the higher quintiles, the perceived health condition is the major reason for not seeking care. Interestingly, access to health infrastructure as a constraint to seeking care in the fourth quintile is highest among all expenditure groups.

Table 11.8

Distribution of Cases of Untreated Illness according to Family Expenditure Category and Stated Reason for not Seeking Medical Advice (Percentage in Sub-Sample)

Expenditure Quintile	*Reason for Not Seeking Treatment*						
	No Medical Facility Nearby	*Lack of Faith*	*Long Wait at the Facility*	*Financial Reasons*	*Ailment Not Serious*	*Others*	*Total*
Very poor 20%	2.17	0.49	0.15	7.41	5.04	3.96	19.22
Poor 20%	1.77	0.81	0.07	7.25	6.51	4.41	20.81
Middle 20%	1.75	0.57	0.21	6.00	6.99	3.54	19.06
Richer 20%	2.47	0.47	0.20	4.01	8.20	5.75	21.10
Richest 20%	1.36	0.47	0.39	2.10	8.98	6.51	19.80
Total	**9.52**	**2.81**	**1.02**	**26.77**	**35.73**	**24.16**	**100.00**

Source: NSS 60th Round.

Table 11.9 presents the data disaggregated by rural and urban sectors. Within each expenditure quintile, we present the share of the reasons for not accessing health care as a proportion of total untreated morbidity. The contrasts are very clear: (i) the proportion of untreated morbidity due to financial reason within each expenditure quintile shows a secular decline from poorest to richest expenditure levels both for rural, but not for urban areas; (ii) Access to health care facility is not a constraint in urban areas, but is still reported in the rural sector across all expenditure quintiles; (iii) From the second quintile onward, more than half the share of untreated morbidity is due to self-assessment of the disease as well as 'other' reasons; (iv) Even for the richest quintiles in the rural areas, issues of access, quality and financial constraints cannot be disregarded; (v) Among the poorest urban quintile, the proportion of reported untreated morbidity due to financial reason is nearly eight per cent more than the poorest rural quintile.

Table 11.9a

Untreated Morbidity by Relation to Head and Age-Groups: Rural

Expenditure Quintile	*Reason for Not Seeking Medical Treatment*						
	No Medical Facility	*Lack of Faith*	*Long Waiting*	*Financial Reasons*	*Ailment Not Serious*	*Others*	*Total*
Very poor 20%	2.61	0.56	0.17	8.13	5.48	4.53	21.49
	(12.16)*	(2.61)	(0.81)	(37.84)	(25.51)	(21.07)	(100.00)
Poor 20%	2.18	0.97	0.08	8.26	6.74	4.89	23.12
	(9.42)	(4.20)	(0.35)	(35.74)	(29.15)	(21.14)	(100.00)
Middle 20%	2.15	0.58	0.15	6.26	7.43	3.87	20.44
	(10.50)	(2.86)	(0.74)	(30.61)	(36.37)	(18.92)	(100.00)
Richer 20%	3.07	0.51	0.12	3.76	7.23	5.70	20.39
	(15.04)	(2.51)	(0.60)	(18.45)	(35.46)	(27.94)	(100.00)
Richest 20%	1.51	0.40	0.34	1.85	5.35	5.11	14.56
	(10.38)	(2.74)	(2.35)	(12.71)	(36.74)	(35.08)	(100.00)
Total	**11.52**	**3.03**	**0.87**	**28.26**	**32.24**	**24.09**	**100.00**

Note: * The values within brackets are proportions within each expenditure quintiles.

Table 11.9b

Untreated Morbidity by Relation to Head and Gender (%): Urban

Expenditure Quintile	*Reason for Not Seeking Medical Treatment*						
	No Medical Facility	*Lack of Faith*	*Long Waiting*	*Financial Reasons*	*Ailment Not Serious*	*Others*	*Total*
Very poor 20%	0.30	0.21	0.07	4.39	3.20	1.57	9.74
	(3.06)*	(2.17)	(0.67)	(45.11)	(32.89)	(16.10)	(100.00)
Poor 20%	0.07	0.12	0.03	3.02	5.55	2.41	11.19
	(0.59)	(1.04)	(0.23)	(26.99)	(49.58)	(21.58)	(100.00)
Middle 20%	0.10	0.50	0.48	4.94	5.15	2.16	13.33
	(0.79)	(3.75)	(3.58)	(37.08)	(38.60)	(16.21)	(100.00)
Richer 20%	0.00	0.30	0.50	5.05	12.25	5.97	24.06
	(0.00)	(1.23)	(2.08)	(20.97)	(50.91)	(24.81)	(100.00)
Richest 20%	0.73	0.76	0.58	3.14	24.13	12.34	41.68
	(1.74)	(1.82)	(1.38)	(7.53)	(57.91)	(29.61)	(100.00)
Total	**1.19**	**1.88**	**1.64**	**20.54**	**50.28**	**24.45**	**100.00**

Note: * The values within brackets are proportions within each expenditure quintiles.

Supplementary questions were asked whether those reporting no treatment for ailments took any other measure, for example, consulting friends and family, medicine shop etc. In Table 11.10, we tabulate the data by expenditure group where the respondent gave the reason for no treatment as 'other'. For the highest expenditure quintile in the urban area, this reason itself constitutes half of the cases of untreated morbidity. The distribution is more even in the case of rural areas.

Table 11.10

Distribution of Cases of Untreated Morbidity due to "Other Reasons"

Expenditure Quintile	*Rural*	*Urban*	*Total*
Very poor 20%	18.80	6.41	16.37
Poor 20%	20.29	9.87	18.25
Middle 20%	16.06	8.84	14.64
Richer 20%	23.65	24.41	23.80
Richest 20%	21.20	50.47	26.93
Total	**100.00**	**100.00**	**100.00**

Source: NSS 60th Round.

To summarise, we find that economic condition of the households can partly explain the non-treatment of morbidity in terms of the reasons asked during the survey. A relaxation of the financial constraint, i.e., moving from lower to higher expenditure groups, is accompanied by a greater proportion of untreated morbidity being due to the individual's own health perception, as well as due to access to informal sources of health care. This contrast is greater for urban as compared to rural areas. In the latter, physical access to health facilities and the quality of treatment still remain important—something which needs urgent attention at the policy level.

Conclusion

Analysis of unit-level data from NSS 60th Round throws up interesting set of issues related to the demand for health care in India, and the challenge faced in formulating public policy towards the health sector. In this chapter, we investigated the health-seeking behaviour of the respondents of the survey and explored three avenues through which health and human development outcomes may be related—demographic characteristics, education level of the head of the household and expenditure groups. We find that the NSS data points to large differences in the demand for health care when we disaggregate according to gender and geographical location. The intra-family relationship as well as the level of education of the head of household exerts considerable influence on health-seeking behaviour. As expected, for lower expenditure groups, financial reasons play an important role in lack of demand for health care. Interestingly, the proportion of cases within the lowest quintile citing lack of resources is higher in urban than in rural areas.

References

Banerjee, A. and E. Duflo (2004). "Healthcare Delivery in Rural Rajasthan", *Economic and Political Weekly* 39(9): 944-949.

Bose, A. (2007). "India's Disturbing Health Card", *Economic and Political Weekly*: 10-13 September 15.

Das, J. and J. Hammer (2007). "Money for Nothing: The Dire Straits of Indian Medical Care", *Journal of Development Economics* 83(1): 1-36.

Mooij, J. and S. Mahendra Dev (2004). "Social Sector Priorities: An Analysis of Budgets and Expenditures in India in the 1990s", *Development Policy Review* 22(1): 97-120.

12

The Extent of Pregnancy Intentions and its Association with Maternal and Child Health Care in India

SUJATA GANGULY

Introduction

Information about women's intention to become pregnant (hereafter pregnancy intention) has been used for a variety of purposes, from estimating the number of unintended pregnancies to assessing the effects of pregnancy intention on behaviours during pregnancy, birth outcomes, health and development of children born as a result of unintended pregnancies (Joyce *et al.*, 2002). Over the last several decades, researchers and policy makers have devoted considerable attention to women's pregnancy intentions (Pulley *et al.*, 2002). A 1995 report by the Institute of Medicine (IOM) of the National Academy of Sciences (Brown and Eisenberg, 1995: 1) concluded:

"The consequences of unintended pregnancy are serious, imposing appreciable burdens on children, women, men and families. A woman with an unintended pregnancy is less likely to seek early prenatal care and is more likely to expose the foetus to harmful substances (such as tobacco and alcohol). The child of an unwanted conception especially (as distinct from a mistimed one) is at greater risk of being born at low birth weight, of dying in its first year of life, of being abused and of not receiving sufficient resources for healthy development (cited in Joyce *et al.*, 2002)."

Unintended pregnancy is correlated with income, race, marital status, education, cognitive ability and other parental characteristics, all of which are also related to prenatal behaviour, child health and child development (Joyce *et al.*, 2000). Despite the association of unintended pregnancies with adverse consequences, few researches have examined the meaning of unintended pregnancy and how that meaning is constructed in women's lives (Fischer *et al.*, 1999). The traditional measures of intendedness were based on a model in which a married couple either selects a family-size target at marriage and then pursues it, or revises it periodically, but at any given time agrees on what the target had been decided, i.e., one child, two children, three children etc.(Peterson and Mosher, 1999). Most analyses of pregnancy intention in the United States uses the classification devised by the National Survey of Family Growth (NSFG) which divides pregnancy into three categories—intended, mistimed and unwanted—on the basis of women's answers to a series of questions about their feelings at the time they became pregnant (Pulley *et al.*, 2002).

According to NSFG (1995), a pregnancy is unwanted when the woman had not ever wanted to have any other child. A pregnancy is classified as mistimed if the woman did not want it at the time it occurred. Intended pregnancies are those that were wanted at the time they occurred and those that were wanted earlier (cited in Pulley *et al.*, 2002). Developing a more complete understanding of pregnancy intentions should advance efforts to increase contraceptive use, to prevent unintended pregnancies and to improve health of women and their children (Santelli *et al.*, 2003). As a result of this, question remains: Are women's pregnancy-related behaviours and the health of their newborns directly linked to the planning status of their pregnancy or do the apparent effects of planning status actually reflect demographic and socioeconomic differences between women who had intended to conceive and those whose pregnancy were unplanned? (Kost *et al.*, 1998).

Women's behaviour during pregnancy, which can affect the health of their infants, may be influenced by their attitude towards the pregnancy (Kost *et al.*, 1998). The mother may be at greater risk of depression and of physical abuse herself and her relationship with her partner is at greater risk of dissolution. Both mother and father may suffer economic hardship and may fail to achieve their educational and career goals. Such consequences undoubtedly impede the formation and maintenance of strong families. Accurate measurement of pregnancy intendedness, including women's attitudes toward pregnancy and motivations to achieve or avoid a pregnancy, is important in understanding fertility-related behaviours, estimating unmet need for contraception and building stronger family planning programmes (Speizer *et al.*, 2004).

Review of Literature

Baydar (1995) found that out of 1,327 children younger than two whose mothers were participants in the National Longitudinal Survey of Youth, 61 per cent were wanted, 34 per cent were mistimed and 5 per cent were unwanted. Planning status is associated with the level of developmental resources the child receives at home: At ages one and older, mistimed and unwanted children score significantly lower on a scale measuring opportunity for skill development and on a scale measuring non-authoritarian parenting style than their wanted peers; by preschool age, they also have significantly less-positive relationships with their mothers. Measures of the direct effects of planning status on development also indicate that mistimed and unwanted children are at a disadvantage; those younger than two have higher mean scores for fearfulness than wanted infants and lower scores for positive affect; unintended preschoolers score lower on a measure of receptive vocabulary.

Dye *et al.* (1997) assessed the effect of unintended pregnancies on breastfeeding behaviours. All women delivering a live birth between January 1, 1995 and July 31, 1996 in the 15 county central New York regions were asked whether they had intended to become pregnant and their breastfeeding plans. Women with mistimed and unwanted pregnancies were significantly less likely to breastfeed than were women whose pregnancies were planned. Moreover for women whose pregnancies were not planned, breastfeeding is particularly important. First, breast milk may provide protection from morbidity for which unplanned infants are at risks. Second, the act of breast-feeding may stimulate mother-infant bonding and subsequently help the mother and infant overcome the difficulties associated with parenting among women with unplanned pregnancies.

Korenman *et al.* (2002) carried out logistic regression analyses using 1979-1992 data from the National Longitudinal Survey of Youth to assess the effects of unintendedness and parents' disagreement on outcomes related to infants' health and development. Analyses are conducted separately for married and unmarried women; for women of each marital status, one set of analyses includes extensive controls for socioeconomic background, and a second compares effects of intended and unintended pregnancies within the same family and found that despite the well-established literature on couples' pregnancy intentions and on the consequences of unintended pregnancy, the effects of parents' disagreement in fertility intentions have not been explored. Parental disagreement in pregnancy intention, as well as a father's pregnancy intention, may affect infant health. Infants whose conception was intended by their mother but not their father are at elevated risk of adverse health events. When a pregnancy was not intended by the mother, risks are higher than they are if both parents intended the pregnancy, but they differ little according to the father's intention. Thus, it may be useful to classify pregnancies as intended by both parents or not intended by at least one. In comparisons of siblings, unintended fertility (so defined) is associated with delayed prenatal care and reduced initiation of breastfeeding.

Remez (2003) found that pregnancy intention status has little or no effect on medical supervision at delivery, child vaccination or adequacy of growth, once the impact of socioeconomic and demographic characteristics is accounted for; intendedness does appear to independently affect the odds of obtaining adequate prenatal care, however. According to an analysis of Demographic and Health Survey data from five developing countries, only in Peru was unwantedness at conception consistently associated with deficits in all four health indicators.

Marston and Cleland (2003) investigated whether children later reported as having been unwanted or mistimed at conception will, when compared with children reported as wanted, show adverse effects when the following criteria are applied: receipt of antenatal care before the sixth month of gestation, supervised delivery, full vaccination of the child and child growth (stunting). The study uses data from recent Demographic and Health Survey enquiries in Bolivia, Egypt, Kenya, Peru and the Philippines. In Peru, children unwanted at conception were found to have significantly worse outcomes than other children but in the other countries, a systematic effect was found only for receipt of antenatal care. Weak measurement of the complex concept of wantedness may have contributed to these results. Birth order of the child, with which wantedness is inextricably linked, has more powerful and pervasive effects, with first-born and second-born children being much less likely to show adverse effects.

D'Angelo *et al.* (2004) sought to examine the components of pregnancy intention and to assess whether women with a mistimed pregnancy and those with an unwanted pregnancy should be examined separately—analytically and in practice—rather than together. Data from 15 states participating in the Pregnancy Risk Assessment Monitoring System (1998) were used to calculate the prevalence of intended, mistimed and unwanted conceptions, by selected variables. Associations between unintendedness and women's behaviours and experience before, during and after the pregnancy were assessed through unadjusted relative risks.

Johnson *et al.* (2004) concluded that over the past two decades in Jordan, contraceptive use has risen and total fertility has declined. However, the proportion of pregnancies resulting in live births that are reported as wanted when conceived has declined over time. There is therefore, a need to explore the risk factors for experiencing unintended pregnancy in Jordan. The multivariate analysis indicated that several factors significantly influence the likelihood that a woman would classify her most recent pregnancy as unwanted or mistimed. Risk factors that independently increase the likelihood of an unintended pregnancy included ever-use of modern contraception, use of the contraceptive pill and number of previous births. Factors associated with pregnancy reported as intended include obtaining contraceptive services from private medical providers and the ability to pay for health care with little difficulty. They analysed the risk factors associated with having a mistimed pregnancy, or a pregnancy that occurred at a time when the mother had wished for no more children, in the Hashemite kingdom of Jordon. Social, geographic and economic indicators have been assessed for their influence on the probability that a woman has.

According to Crissey (2006), prior research has documented a relationship between unintended pregnancy and negative consequences for infants and children. Using the 1988 National Maternal and Infant Health Survey and its 1991 Longitudinal Follow-Up, a composite measure of reported pregnancy intention and birth control use is constructed. This composite measure is compared to more conventional measures through analyses predicting the effects of pregnancy intention on child health, activity and development. Across the different constructions of the pregnancy intention measure, children from unintended pregnancies have poorer outcomes. They are more likely to have less than excellent health, undesirable activity levels and below median scores on a development assessment.

Vlassoff C. (1990) compares fertility and family planning intentions of rural Indian women in 1975 with actual outcomes in 1987. Ninety-four of 103 respondents who had fewer children than they wanted in 1975 and had stated definite intentions with respect to future fertility and contraceptive use were re-interviewed in 1987. These observations, taken from diary notes recorded in a study conducted from September 1975 through June 1976, reflected the high priority attributed to children by women in this Maharashtrian community. The study, which used questionnaires and participant observation, investigated the relationship between cultural factors, fertility and family planning among women of childbearing ages. In 1987, a follow-up survey was carried out in order to study change over the 12-year period. This report compares fertility and family planning intentions in 1975-76 with actual outcomes in 1987 for a selected cohort of women those aged 15-49 who had not exceeded their stated fertility goal in 1975. It was felt that, by 1987, most of these women would have had the opportunity to complete their families, or at least to have the number of children they said they wanted in 1975.

Life circumstances, support from family and friends, attitudes toward children and abortion, and general feelings of readiness for a pregnancy may be more correlated to wantedness than they are to intending or planning to become pregnant (Fischer *et al.*, 1999). Few researches have been published on the possible effects of intention status of pregnancies carried to terms (Marston and Cleland, 2003). Hence, there is a need to study the prevailing situation in India and analyse the underlying factors for the intentions of pregnancy planning.

Objectives of the Study

The broad objective of the study is to analyse the extent of pregnancy intentions and its association with maternal and child health care. The specific objectives are as follows:

- To study the pregnancy intentions according to demographic, social and economic conditions among the currently married women.
- To examine the association between pregnancy intention and the utilisation of maternal health care services by the currently married women.
- To determine the gender differences in association between pregnancy intentions and child health.

Data and Methodology

NFHS-2 (1998-99) data has been used for the study that provides information on fertility, mortality, family planning and important aspects of nutrition, health and health care. The NFHS-2 survey covered a nationally representative sample of more than 90,000 ever-married women aged 15-49 from 26 states that comprise more than 99 per cent of India's population. The survey used uniform questionnaires, sample designs and field procedures to facilitate comparability of the data and to achieve a high level of data quality. The NFHS-2 reports that in India, the wantedness of the pregnancies for the births in the three years preceding the survey are 78.4 per cent whereas the mistimed pregnancy is around 12 per cent and unwanted pregnancy is 9.4 per cent.

Unintended pregnancies can have serious health, social and economic consequences. Such pregnancies may be unwanted (a baby is not wanted at any time) or mistimed, yet wanted (a baby is wanted eventually). Intended pregnancies are those conceived when desired (Kaufmann *et al.*, 1997). Hence, in order to determine the pregnancy intention of currently married women, the variable considered is the time when women wanted pregnancy. The specific question asked regarding this variable is "At the time you were pregnant with (name), did you want to become pregnant then, did you want to wait until later or did you want no (more) children at all?" This question is asked for the last two children born in the last three years preceding the survey.

The bivariate analysis has been done for studying the percentage distribution of currently married women and percentage distribution of pregnancy intention among currently married women by background characteristics in each category. For this purpose many predictor variables have been used like age, type of place of residence, religion, ethnicity, age at first birth, women's and husband's education as well as occupation, total children ever born, birth order, birth interval, standard of living, exposure to mass media, number of household members and women's autonomy.

Some of the critical variables used in the analysis have been discussed briefly in the following sections:

Religion

Three categories of religion have been made i.e., Hindu, Muslim and Others. The last category includes Christian, Sikh, Buddhist/Neo Buddhist, Jain, Jew, Zoroastrian/Parsi and no religion.

Ethnicity

Scheduled Caste, Scheduled Tribe and Others are included in this category. Others include Other Backward Classes or those who belong to none of these aforesaid categories.

Birth Order

The live births of women are classified according to their order or rank e.g., first order birth, second order birth etc. Accordingly, birth order one, two, three and four and above have been formed.

Birth Interval

Birth interval has been taken from the birth history and it is defined as the length of time between two successive live births which indicates the space of childbearing. Birth interval of less than 12 months, 12-24, 24-36 and 36 and above months have been taken into consideration.

Standard of Living Index

The standard of living index has been formed by considering the house type, toilet facility, source of lighting, source of drinking water, separate room for cooking, ownership of house and agricultural land, ownership of irrigated land, livestock and durable goods. Scores have been given to different categories and accordingly low, medium and high categories have been created.

Women's Occupation

This variable include those women who are not engaged in any occupation, those engaged in primary sector namely, agricultural self-employed and agricultural employee, those engaged in professional jobs namely, professor, teaching, management, clerical, sales, services and skilled manual and lastly, those engaged in other kind of jobs that include domestic and household and unskilled manual work.

Exposure to Mass Media

This variable has been created by considering those women who have access to newspaper, television and radio. Accordingly, those women who have no access to either of these three media have been categorised as having no exposure to mass media, those women who have access to any one of these have partial exposure and those who have access to all have full exposure to mass media.

Women's Autonomy

For this variable, an index has been calculated. Women's autonomy have been considered on the basis of their decision-making power regarding health care, going to the market, visiting friends or relatives, power to keep aside money and decision regarding spending money. All these five aspects have been equally weighted and aggregate of all these five aspects give the output with values ranging from zero to five. Finally the values from zero to one have been categorised as low, between two and three as medium and four to five as high autonomy.

Further, bivariate analyses have been done to study the utilisation of maternal health care services among currently married women by pregnancy intention. The variables included are—"How many times did you receive antenatal check-up during this pregnancy?" This variable has been categorised as none, once, twice, thrice and above; "How many months pregnant were you when you first received an antenatal check-up?" This variable has been re-formed into first, second and third trimester; "When you were pregnant with (name), were you given an injection in the arm to prevent you and your baby from getting tetanus?" Three categories have been made as none, once, twice and above; "When you were pregnant with (name), were you given any iron folic tablets or syrup?" If yes: "Did you consume all the iron folic tablets or syrup you were given?". Another variable that has been considered is the place of delivery of the child which has been divided into three categories namely, home (own, parent's, others), public (government/municipal hospital, government dispensary, UHC/UHP/UFWC, CHC/rural hospital/ PHC, sub-centre, other public sector health facility), private (private medical sector/private hospital/clinic/maternity home, other private sector health facility). Apart from these three categories for the place of delivery, there is one more category for others which show negligible cases and so it has been dropped from the analysis.

The child health according to pregnancy intention has also been considered. Here, apart from analysing the prevailing situations according to different levels of fertility, gender-wise percentage distributions have been done. The variables included are:

Immunisation

It considers whether the child has received immunisation. For this variable, those children who are above one year of age has been included. The analysis consists of BCG, three doses of DPT, three doses of polio and measles. Accordingly, the new variable formed is the per cent of children having no immunisation, partial immunisation i.e., those who had either of the doses mentioned above and full immunisation i.e., those who had all the doses.

Birth Weight

This variable includes the per cent distribution of those children who were not weighed at birth, those who were weighed and were below or above 2.5kg.

Size of Child at Birth

The question asked was: "When (name) was born, was he/she: large, average, small or very small?"

Undernourishment

The three indices of nutritional status are expressed in standard deviation units (z-score) from the median for the international reference population. Children who are more than two standard deviations below the reference median on any of the indices are considered to be undernourished. Undernourished children on the weight-for-age index are referred to as 'underweight', on the height-for-age index as 'stunted' and on the weight-for-height index as 'too thin' or 'wasted'.

Anaemia

Haemoglobin levels are less than 7.0 grams/decilitre for children with severe anaemia, 7.0-9.9 g/dl for children with moderate anaemia and 10.0-10.9 g/dl for children with mild anaemia.

Vitamin A

The question addressed was: "Was a dose of Vitamin A liquid or capsule ever given to (name) to protect him/her from night blindness?"

Breastfeeding

The question was: "How long after birth did you first put (name) to the breast?". In accordance with this question, the variable has been categorised as immediately, within an hour, within 24 hours and beyond 24 hours.

Duration of Breastfeeding

It includes the question: "For how many months did you breastfeed (name)?". Hence, the categorisations are not breastfeeding and exclusive breastfeeding (for those who have breastfed their children for six months).

Morbidity and Treatment Seeking Behaviour

The questions that were asked: "When (name) was ill with a cough (at any time in the last two weeks), did he/she breathe faster than usual with short rapid breaths?"; "Has (name) been ill with a fever at any time in the last two weeks?" If yes: "Did you seek advice or treatment for the cough/fever?"; "Has (name) had diarrhoea in the last two weeks?" If yes: "Did you seek advice or treatment for the diarrhoea?"

In order to determine the factors influencing the pregnancy intention, multinomial logistic regression has been used. The dependent variable is pregnancy intention (wanted, mistimed and unwanted). For fulfilling the first objective, certain variables have been dropped like age at first birth, total children ever born, husband's education and occupation and number of household members. The first two variables have been dropped to avoid collinearity, husband's education and occupation have been dropped due to the fact that it hardly shows any variation with its complementary variable i.e., women's education and occupation. Further, birth order has been classified as low and high by taking into consideration the first and second birth order as low and third and fourth and higher birth order as high. The birth interval has been classified as less than 24 months and above 24 months.

For the second objective, binary logistic and for the third objective, multinomial logistic regression has been applied by controlling the other predictor variables like age, birth order, birth interval, place of residence, religion, ethnicity, education, exposure to mass media, standard of living and occupation. For binary logistic, the variables have been made dichotomous e.g., if the women have any ANC visit or not, if the women has any ANC visit in the first trimester or not, if the women have taken any tetanus toxoid injection or not, if the women have taken any iron folic tablets and the women who have done so then whether they have consumed all and lastly if the place of delivery is institutional (public and private) or non-institutional (home). The fourth objective has been fulfilled mainly by bivariate analysis.

Multinomial regression has been applied for immunisation. The other variables have not been considered as most of the children are not weighed or measured in India and hence, considering these variables for multivariate analysis may not be authentic.

Findings and Discussions

Births or pregnancies may be unwanted because they either pose a serious threat to health of mothers or children or they do not conform to certain social norms or they occur after specific family size desired by couples has been achieved (Kulkarni and Choe, 1997). The prevalence of unwanted births typically increases with age and parity because women who have already reached their desired family size do not want any more pregnancies (Kaufmann *et al.*, 1997). The research on pregnancy intention enables one to weigh the pros and cons of fertility transition. Various predictor variables can have significant impact on the pregnancy intention of the women. Age, type of place of residence, religion, ethnicity, age at first birth, women's education, husband's education, total children ever born, birth order, birth interval, standard of living, women's occupation, husband's occupation, exposure to mass media, number of household members and women's autonomy are the underlying variables that determine the pregnancy intention. Moreover, states of India differ not only in levels of development but also in socioeconomic and demographic background.

Pregnancy Intention by Background Characteristics in India

The pregnancy intention of the currently married women may vary widely according to the socioeconomic background. It is of utmost importance to consider the differences in pregnancy intention as per the age, place of residence, religion, education, occupation etc. As shown in Table 12.1, the percentage distribution of pregnancy intention among currently married women according to selected background characteristics in India, the wanted pregnancy is high irrespective of the control variables. However, lot of variation can be observed in case of mistimed and unwanted pregnancies. Unwanted pregnancy increases with age. This increase is quite steep in the age group 35 and above. The unwanted pregnancy increases from around 3 per cent in the age group 15-24 to 13.5 per cent in the age group 25-34 and lastly to 31.7 per cent in the age group 35 and above. Mistimed pregnancy shows an inverse relation with age. It is 12.9, 9.3 and 5.2 per cent, respectively. One striking observation that can be mentioned is that there is not much variation in pregnancy intention according to the place of residence. The unwanted pregnancy is around 9 per cent whereas the mistimed pregnancy is 12.2 and

Table 12.1

Percentage Distribution of Pregnancy Intention among Currently Married Women according to Selected Background Characteristics, India, NFHS-2 (1998-99)

Background Characteristics	Pregnancy Intention			
	Wanted	Mistimed	Unwanted	Total
Women's age (years)				
15-24	84.0	12.9	3.1	16679
25-34	77.2	9.3	13.5	13556
35+	63.0	5.2	31.7	2035
Place of residence				
Urban	78.8	12.2	9.0	7176
Rural	80.1	10.6	9.3	25094
Religion				
Hindu	80.9	10.4	8.7	25569
Muslim	74.3	13.0	12.8	5098
Others	79.2	13.5	7.3	1570
Ethnicity				
Scheduled Caste	78.5	10.7	10.7	6435
Scheduled Tribe	83.2	9.3	7.5	3070
Others	79.8	11.1	9.0	22385
Age at first birth (years)				
Less than 20	78.7	11.1	10.2	23985
More than 20	83.1	10.4	6.5	8285
Women's education				
No education	79.9	8.7	11.4	17474
Primary education	78.5	11.9	9.6	5077
Secondary education	79.5	15.0	5.5	7148
Higher education	82.8	12.7	4.6	2560
Husband's education				
No Education	79.4	9.0	11.5	9317
Primary education	78.9	10.3	10.8	5623
Secondary education	80.5	11.6	7.9	11494
Higher education	80.2	13.1	6.7	5736
Total children ever born				
Less than 2	86.9	11.6	1.5	16670
2-4	77.0	12.0	11.0	9784
4+	64.1	7.2	28.7	5816

contd...

...contd...

Background Characteristics	*Pregnancy Intention* Wanted	*Mistimed*	*Unwanted*	*Total*
Birth order				
1	90.9	8.5	0.7	9306
2	82.1	15.5	2.4	8344
3	78.0	12.6	9.4	5718
4+	67.3	8.2	24.6	8902
Birth interval (Months)				
Less than 12	69.7	19.9	10.4	628
12-24	69.7	19.2	11.1	5606
24-36	74.5	13.1	12.3	7441
36+	79.6	6.0	14.4	9227
Standard of living index				
Low	79.3	10.0	10.7	11658
Medium	79.7	11.1	9.2	15089
High	81.4	12.2	6.4	5127
Women's occupation				
Not working	79.6	11.6	8.9	22333
Primary sector	81.5	8.6	9.8	7032
Professional	75.7	14.0	10.3	1899
Others	81.4	6.6	12.0	967
Husband's occupation				
Not working	78.8	15.4	5.8	603
Primary sector	81.0	10.0	9.0	12507
Professional	79.1	11.7	9.2	15066
Others	79.1	10.0	11.0	3760
Exposure to mass media				
No	80.3	8.7	11.0	15221
Partial	78.8	12.9	8.3	13803
Full	81.6	13.1	5.3	3232
Number of household members				
Less than 4	87.4	10.4	2.2	5782
4-6	80.0	11.0	9.0	9284
6+	77.2	11.0	11.8	17205
Women's autonomy				
Low	80.4	10.5	9.1	5306
Medium	79.9	11.0	9.1	24613
High	77.2	10.9	11.9	2352
Total	**25754**	**3525**	**2992**	**32271**

10.6 per cent in the urban and rural areas respectively. Similarly, the mistimed pregnancy is around 10, 13 and 14 per cent among Hindu, Muslim and Others respectively. The unwanted pregnancy is around 13 per cent among the Muslims whereas it is around 8 per cent among the other two categories. Mistimed and unwanted pregnancies range between 9 to 11 per cent according to ethnicity.

If the age at first birth is below 20 years, then mistimed and unwanted pregnancies are around 11 and 10 per cent respectively whereas if the age at first birth is above 20 years, then the mistimed and unwanted pregnancies are around 10 and 7 per cent respectively. A negative relation can be seen between the level of women's education attainment and unwanted pregnancy. The women who have no education, has primary, secondary and higher education have unwanted pregnancy ranging from 11.4 per cent to 4.6 per cent. The mistimed pregnancy is 8.7, 11.9, 15 and 12.7 per cent respectively. Similar result can be seen in case of husband's education. An inverse relation exists between husband's education and unwanted pregnancy whereas the opposite pattern can be seen in case of mistimed pregnancy.

If the total children ever born are less than two, then the unwanted pregnancy is 1.5 per cent. As the total children ever born increases, the unwanted pregnancy also increases from 11 per cent to around 29 per cent (if the total number of children is between two to four children and above four children respectively). The mistimed pregnancy shows a declining trend with the increase in the total children ever born i.e., around 12 per cent in the first two categories and 7 per cent in the last category. With birth order first, second, third and fourth and above, the unwanted pregnancy increases drastically from 0.7, 2.4, 9.4 to 24.6 per cent respectively. However the mistimed pregnancy shows a wedge-like pattern i.e., 8.5, 15.5, 12.6 and 8.2 per cent respectively. As the birth interval increases, the unwanted pregnancy increases. However, the difference is not that much notable. The mistimed pregnancy decreases with increase in the birth interval from around 20 per cent to 6 per cent as the birth interval increases from less than 12 months to above 36 months.

The high standard of living index (SLI) shows lowest unwanted pregnancy (6.4 per cent). The low and medium SLI has around 11 and 9 per cent unwanted pregnancy. However, the mistimed pregnancy increases with increase in the SLI from around 10 per cent to 12 per cent. The unwanted pregnancy shows an upward trend with women's and husband's occupation. The unwanted pregnancy is around 11 per cent among women who have no exposure to mass media and it decreases to 8.3 and 5.3 per cent among women having partial and full exposure to mass media respectively. On the other hand, the mistimed pregnancy shows an increasing pattern from 8.7, 12.9 to 13.1 per cent from among women having no, partial and full exposure to mass media respectively. If the total number of household members is less than four, then the unwanted pregnancy is around two per cent. However, if the total number of household members is between 4-6 and 6 and above, then the unwanted pregnancy is around 9 and 12 per cent respectively. There is not much variation between mistimed pregnancy and total number of household members (11 per cent). Women's autonomy does not show much influence on pregnancy intention.

Factors Determining Pregnancy Intention in India

A look into the important determining factors that influence wanted, mistimed and unwanted pregnancies are essential from the programme point of view. Table 12.2 shows the determining factors for pregnancy intention in India. It can be observed that in case of wanted *versus* mistimed pregnancy, mistimed pregnancy is 30 per cent less likely among women in the age group 25-34 and 50 per cent less likely among women in the age group 35 and above as compared to the women in the age group 15-24. Women with birth interval of more than 24 months are 50 per cent less likely to have mistimed pregnancy than those who have birth interval less than 24 months. Muslims are 30 per cent more likely to have mistimed pregnancy than the Hindus and Scheduled Tribes are 20 per cent less likely than the Scheduled Castes to have mistimed pregnancy. Women with primary, secondary and higher education are 20, 60 and 70 per cent respectively more likely to have mistimed pregnancy than those women who are illiterate. Those with partial exposure to mass media are 30 per cent more likely to have mistimed pregnancy. Women in medium and high SLI are 10 and 20 per cent respectively less likely to have mistimed pregnancy than those women in the low SLI. Women engaged in the primary and other kinds of job are 20 and 30 per cent respectively less likely and women in the professional sector are 40 per cent more likely to have mistimed pregnancy than those women who are not working. States with TFR between 2.1 and 3.1 and above 3.1 are 20 per cent less likely to have mistimed pregnancy than states with TFR less than 2.1.

In case of wanted *versus* unwanted pregnancy, as age increases, the likelihood of unwanted pregnancy also increases as compared to those women in the age group 15-19. Women having their children in the higher birth order are 6.3 times more likely to have unwanted pregnancy than those women who have children in the lower birth order. Women in the rural areas are 20 per cent less likely than the women in the urban areas to have unwanted pregnancy. Muslims are 30 per cent more likely than Hindus and

Table 12.2

Multinomial Logistic Regression Showing the Association between Pregnancy Intention and Selected Background Characteristics among Currently Married Women, India, NFHS-2 (1998-99)

Background Characteristics	*Mistimed*	*Unwanted*	*Background Characteristics*	*Mistimed*	*Unwanted*
Women's age			**Women's autonomy**		
15-24®			Low®		
25-34	0.7***	1.8***	Medium	1.0	0.9
35+	0.5***	3.8***	High	1.0	1.1
Birth order			**Standard of living index**		
Low®			Low®		
High	1.0	6.3***	Medium	0.9**	1.0
			High	0.8***	0.8**
Birth interval (Months)					
<24®			**Women's occupation**		
>24	0.5***	0.9	Not working®		
			Primary sector	0.8***	0.9
Place of residence			Professional	1.4***	1.1
Urban®			Others	0.7**	1.0
Rural	1.0	0.8***			
			TFR		
Religion			<2.1®		
Hindu ®			2.1-3.1	0.8**	2.4***
Muslim	1.3***	1.3***	>3.1	0.8	3.2***
Others	1.2	1.1			
Ethnicity					
Scheduled Caste®					
Scheduled Tribe	0.8**	0.6***			
Others	0.9	0.9***			
Women's education					
No education®					
Primary education	1.2**	1.2***			
Secondary education	1.6***	1.1			
Higher education	1.7***	1.3**			
Exposure to mass media					
None®					
Partial	1.3***	1.2***			
Full	1.1	1.2			

Note: ®=Reference Category, Significance level: ***p<0.01; **p<0.05.

Scheduled Tribe and others are 30 and 60 per cent respectively less likely than Scheduled Castes to have unwanted pregnancy. Women with primary and higher education as compared to women who are illiterate are 20 and 30 per cent respectively and women with partial exposure to mass media than women with exposure to mass media are 20 per cent more likely to have unwanted pregnancy. Women in the high SLI are 20 per cent less likely to have unwanted pregnancy than the women in the low SLI. States with TFR between 2.1 and 3.1 are 2.4 times and those states having TFR above 3.1 are 3.2 times more likely to have unwanted pregnancy than those states having TFR less than 2.1.

Pregnancy Intentions and Utilisation of Maternal Health Care Services in India

The pregnancy intention can have its implication on the utilisation of the maternal and child health care services. However, pregnancy intention has little or no effect on medical supervision at delivery, child vaccination or adequacy of growth, once the impact of socioeconomic and demographic characteristics is accounted for; intendedness does appear to independently affect the odds of obtaining adequate prenatal care (Remez, 2003). Unintended pregnancies affect the well-being of women, children and families. In fact, some health experts believe that unintended pregnancies carried to term are more likely to involve complications. Women with unintended pregnancies may be subject to increased physical abuse by their partners during pregnancy (cited in IGWG and WHO, 2005). The planning status of births is a factor in maternal behaviour during pregnancy. In the specific behaviours examined, whether pregnancies were wanted exhibits significant net relationships with timing of prenatal care (Weller *et al.*, 1987).

The study focuses mainly on the maternal health care facilities availed by the women as there will be negative discrimination in the use of antenatal, intranatal and postnatal care in cases where pregnancies are unwelcome (Marston and Cleland, 2003). Women with unwanted pregnancy may initially attempt to deny their pregnancy to themselves and to conceal them from others, either from a desire that the pregnancy "go away" or because of fear of the consequences. Thus, these women may be less likely to obtain prenatal care, especially early in pregnancy (Weller *et al.*, 1987). It seems reasonable to assume that a woman who has planned a pregnancy will be more highly motivated to seek early prenatal care to ensure a highly successful outcome, more concerned about the well-being of the foetus and less reluctant to adopt what may be major changes in lifestyle to increase foetal well-being (cited in Weller *et al.*, 1987).

The percentage distribution of selected maternal health care (MHC) services according to pregnancy intention among currently married women in India (Table 12.3) shows that those women who have perceived their pregnancy as unwanted have higher percentage of not having any ANC visits (46.7 per cent) than those whose pregnancies are wanted (33.6 per cent) and mistimed (28.2 per cent). The percentage of women increases with increase in the number of ANC visit. However, the increase is drastic among women with wanted and mistimed pregnancies. Those women having three and more than three visits are lesser among women with unwanted pregnancy (29 per cent) than those with wanted (45.3 per cent) and mistimed (49.7 per cent) pregnancies. Fifty per cent women with wanted pregnancy have taken their first ANC in the first trimester whereas 48 per cent women with unwanted pregnancy have ANC visit in the same period. The women having their first ANC in the third trimester are around 12 per cent irrespective of their pregnancy intention. Specifically, women who choose to become pregnant are apt to be better prepared emotionally and financially for the demands of pregnancy and childbearing. Thus, they may be more likely to seek out prenatal care earlier and in general to have a more heightened concern for the impact of their behaviour on the health of the foetus than are women whose pregnancies are unwanted or unintended (Joyce and Grossman, 1990). Studies have found that women who report not wanting their pregnancy tend to initiate antenatal care (ANC) later than women who want their pregnancy (cited in Marston and Cleland, 2003).

About 35.5 per cent women with unwanted pregnancy have not taken tetanus toxoid injection whereas for wanted pregnancy it is only 23.6 per cent. This difference persists in case of those women who have taken two and above injections i.e., 54.8 per cent and 68.5 per cent for unwanted and wanted pregnancies respectively.

About 45 per cent women with unwanted pregnancy and 59 per cent with wanted pregnancy have taken iron folic tablets. Sixty-three per cent of those women who have perceived their pregnancy as mistimed have taken iron folic tablets. Among those who have taken iron folic tablets and have consumed all are 81 per cent for women with wanted pregnancy and 78 per cent for unwanted pregnancy. Similar is the pattern for mistimed pregnancy.

Around 77 per cent of the deliveries for unwanted pregnancy take place at homes whereas 65.7 per cent of wanted pregnancy is delivered at homes. The unwanted pregnancy delivered in public (12.8 per cent) and private (10.1 per cent) places are comparatively lower than the wanted pregnancy (16.1 and 18.2 per cent respectively).

Table 12.3

Percentage Distribution of Selected MHC Services according to Pregnancy Intention among Currently Married Women, India, NFHS-2 (1998-99)

	ANC Visit				
Pregnancy Intention	*None*	*1*	*2*	*3+*	*Total*
Wanted	33.6	7.8	13.4	45.3	25640
Mistimed	28.2	8.4	13.8	49.7	3517
Unwanted	46.7	11.5	12.7	29.1	2970
Total	34.2	8.2	13.4	44.2	32127
	Timing of First ANC				
Pregnancy Intention	*1st Trimester*	*2nd Trimester*	*3rd Trimester*	*Total*	
Wanted	49.8	38.6	11.6	17097	
Mistimed	53.7	37.0	9.3	2529	
Unwanted	48.0	40.7	11.3	1594	
Total	50.1	38.6	11.3	21220	
	Tetanus Toxoid Injection				
Pregnancy Intention	*0*	*1*	*2+*	*Total*	
Wanted	23.6	7.9	68.5	25626	
Mistimed	19.2	9.5	71.4	3496	
Unwanted	35.5	9.7	54.8	2972	
Total	24.2	8.3	67.5	32094	
	Given Iron Folic Tablets			*Consumed All Tablets****	
Pregnancy Intention	*Yes*	*Total*		*Yes*	*Total*
Wanted	58.7	25748		81.3	15102
Mistimed	63.0	3524		77.9	2216
Unwanted	45.2	2990		77.6	1346
Total	57.9	32262		80.6	18664
	Place of Delivery				
Pregnancy Intention	*Home*	*Public*	*Private*	*Total*	
Wanted	65.7	16.1	18.2	25689	
Mistimed	60.4	20.7	18.9	3516	
Unwanted	77.2	12.8	10.1	2983	
Total	66.1	16.3	17.5	32188	

Note: *** Women who started consuming Iron and Folic tablets

The Utilisation of Maternal Health Services Determined by Pregnancy Intention in India

Pregnancy intention is determined by various socioeconomic and demographic factors. However, if pregnancy intentions have an effect on the utilisation of maternal health care services is a major question. Table 12.4 shows that as compared to the women with wanted pregnancy, women with mistimed pregnancy is 20 per cent more likely and women with unwanted pregnancy is 10 per cent less likely to go for ANC visit. In accordance with the bivariate analysis, it can be observed that timing of first ANC do not give the result in the direction that women with unwanted pregnancy will prefer less to go for ANC in their first trimester than the women with wanted pregnancy. The multivariate analysis shows that women with mistimed and unwanted pregnancy are 20 and 40 per cent more likely to go for their first ANC in the first trimester than women with wanted pregnancy. Women with unwanted pregnancy are 10 per cent less likely to take tetanus toxoid injection and women with mistimed pregnancy is 20 per cent less likely to consume all iron folic tablets and 10 per cent more likely to go for institutional delivery than the women with wanted pregnancy.

Table 12.4

Odds Ratios Showing the Association between Selected MHC Services and Pregnancy Intention among Currently Married Women, India, NFHS-2 (1998-99)

Pregnancy Intention	*Exp (β)*	*Pregnancy Intention*	*Exp (β)*
ANC visit		**Intake of iron folic tablets**	
Wanted®		Wanted®	
Mistimed	1.2**	Mistimed	0.9
Unwanted	0.9	Unwanted	0.9
ANC visit in the 1st trimester		**Consumed all iron folic tablets**	
Wanted®		Wanted®	
Mistimed	1.2***	Mistimed	0.8***
Unwanted	1.4***	Unwanted	0.9
Intake of tt injection		**Place of delivery (Institutional)**	
Wanted®		Wanted®	
Mistimed	1.1	Mistimed	1.1**
Unwanted	0.9***	Unwanted	1.1

Note: Other variables controlled are age, birth order, birth interval, place of residence, religion, ethnicity, education, occupation, exposure to mass media, autonomy, standard of living and regions by different levels of fertility.

®=Reference Category; Significance Level: ***$p<0.01$ **$p<0.05$.

Pregnancy Intentions and Child Health Care in India

More than a decade has now passed since the International Conference on Population and Development (ICPD) in Cairo. At the time, the Programme of Action (POA), with its emphasis on improving reproductive health and promoting gender equity, marked a major shift in national population policies and donor strategies worldwide. Now, however, governments and organisations everywhere are asking a question that goes one step further: Does taking a gender-based approach to policy and programming as proposed in the POA have an effect on health, particularly reproductive health outcomes? (IGWG and WHO, 2005). Moreover, when mention is made about pregnancy intention, special focus should also be given to gender as pregnancy intention is also affected to some extent by the gender differences. The impending birth of any child takes place within a complex of social relations, the dynamics of which carry implications for the child itself, the family affected by the pregnancy, and the community and society within which the pregnancy and birth take place. When a pregnancy comes sooner than desired or comes at a time when the mother had wished for no more children, the complexities associated with the birth of that child are more likely to be perceived as complications (Johnson *et al.*, 2004).

According to Bustan (1994), being unwanted puts children at increased risk of a range of adverse health outcomes, including child abuse and delayed cognitive and social-emotional development. Women with unwanted pregnancy are less likely to seek early and adequate prenatal care and may, thus, be at increased risk of delivering infants with adverse pregnancy outcomes. In a Finnish study, women reporting infants unwanted at birth were more likely to have infants of lower birth weights and higher rates of infant mortality. Many of these adverse outcomes are more strongly associated with unwanted than with mistimed conceptions (Kaufmann *et al.*, 1997).

Mothers who have positive expectations about mothering and who act on these expectations by good adaptation to being a mother tend to have children with high levels of cognitive, social maturity (Marsiglio and Mott, 1988).

The child born out of unwanted pregnancy may be subjected to negligence. Hence, Table 12.5 shows the percentage distribution of selected factors determining child health according to pregnancy intention among currently married women in India. It can be observed that 13 per cent of the children born out of wanted and mistimed pregnancies are not immunised at all whereas children of unwanted pregnancy who are not immunised are around 23 per cent. Similarly, children who are fully immunised are 41, 42 and 28 per cent among wanted, mistimed and unwanted pregnancies respectively. About 85 per cent of unwanted births are not weighed during births whereas it is 73 and 67 per cent respectively among wanted and mistimed births. The size of child at birth does not show variation according to the pregnancy intention. The differences are not that notable.

Table 12.5

Percentage Distribution of Selected Factors Determining Child Health according to Pregnancy Intention among Currently Married Women, India, NFHS-2 (1998-99)

	Immunisation				
Pregnancy Intention	*None*	*Partial*	*Full*	*Total*	
Wanted	13.5	45.1	41.4	15892	
Mistimed	13.3	44.3	42.3	2075	
Unwanted	23.3	48.9	27.8	1864	
Total	14.4	45.4	40.2	19831	
	Birth Weight				
Pregnancy Intention	*Not weighed*	*<2.5 kg*	*>2.5 kg*	*Total*	
Wanted	73.1	10.9	15.9	24562	
Mistimed	67.2	14.1	18.7	3372	
Unwanted	85.3	6.3	8.3	2879	
Total	73.6	10.8	15.5	30813	
	Size of Child at Birth				
Pregnancy Intention	*Larger than Average*	*Average*	*Smaller than Average*	*Very Small*	*Total*
Wanted	14.2	61.9	19.2	4.7	25740
Mistimed	14.8	59.0	20.4	5.8	3523
Unwanted	11.2	61.2	20.8	6.8	2989
Total	14.0	61.6	19.5	5.0	32252
	Undernourishment				
Pregnancy Intention	*Ht/A*	*Wt/A*	*Wt/Ht*	*Total*	
Wanted	64.7	67.7	58.4	25754	
Mistimed	67.9	71.6	63.3	3525	
Unwanted	66.3	68.6	60.6	2992	
Total	65.2	68.2	59.1	32271	
	Anaemia				
Pregnancy Intention	*Severe*	*Moderate*	*Mild*	*Total*	
Wanted	4.7	42.2	23.0	18884	
Mistimed	4.7	42.1	24.0	2721	
Unwanted	6.1	44.7	24.4	2147	
Total	4.8	42.4	23.3	23752	

contd...

...contd...

Pregnancy Intention	Intake of Vitamin A Yes	Total
Wanted	23.4	22894
Mistimed	24.2	3225
Unwanted	16.5	2715
Total	22.8	28834

	Breastfeeding				
Pregnancy Intention	Immediately	Within an Hour	Within 24 hr	Beyond 24 hr	Total
Wanted	16.0	0.7	22.6	60.6	24779
Mistimed	16.9	0.9	28.1	54.2	3425
Unwanted	12.2	0.7	20.6	66.5	2894
Total	15.8	0.7	23.0	60.5	31098

	Duration of Breastfeeding		
Pregnancy Intention	Not Breast Fed	Exclusive Breastfeeding	Total
Wanted	3.7	26.0	25680
Mistimed	2.8	29.6	3517
Unwanted	3.1	25.2	2974
Total	3.5	26.3	32171

	Illness and its Treatment				
Pregnancy Intention	Cough with Fast Breathing	Fever	Treatment for Fever/Cough	Diarrhoea	Treatment for Diarrhoea
Wanted	17.4	28.1	68.1	18.2	71.2
Mistimed	19.7	31.3	68.4	21.3	69.9
Unwanted	21.1	33.8	66.2	22.6	71.5
Total	19.4	31.1	67.6	20.7	70.8

Likewise, nourishment of the children i.e., children who are stunted, underweight and wasted does not show any variation among wanted, mistimed and unwanted births. About 6 per cent unwanted births have severe anaemia whereas about 5 per cent wanted and mistimed births have severe anaemia. However, negligible difference exists among those having moderate and mild anaemia as per the pregnancy intention. 16.5 per cent unwanted births are given Vitamin A whereas among wanted and mistimed births, it is around 24 per cent. Sixteen per cent of wanted, 17 per cent of mistimed and 12 per cent of unwanted births are put to the breast immediately after the birth. However, duration of breastfeeding does not have many differences. The children suffering from cough with fast breathing, fever and diarrhoea are more among unwanted births than those born of mistimed and wanted pregnancies. Nevertheless, treatment-seeking behaviour hardly shows any difference.

The gender-wise analysis for the child health does have certain prominent observations (Tables 12.6 and 12.7). In case of immunisation, it is clear that unwanted births have more percentage of having no immunisation for both males and females alike. Moreover, the unwanted males are at a favourable condition than their counterparts. Females are at a disadvantage from the point of view of having none, partial or full immunisation. The percentages of unwanted male births that are not weighed are around 84 per cent whereas among females it is around 87 per cent. It can also be observed that those with more than 2.5kg weight are 10 and 7 per cent among males and females respectively. The percentage is comparatively higher among the wanted births. Size of child at birth also shows variation in case of wantedness and unwantedness of the child and among males and females. The positive results are in the favour of males than the females. The births with very small size do not show notable differences. The other categories show a difference of three to four percentages.

Table 12.6

Percentage Distribution of Selected Factors Determining Child Health (Male) according to Pregnancy Intention among Currently Married Women, India, NFHS-2 (1998-99)

	Immunisation				
Pregnancy Intention	*None*	*Partial*	*Full*	*Total*	
Wanted	12.6	44.4	43.0	8324	
Mistimed	14.2	41.6	44.2	987	
Unwanted	22.7	48.8	28.5	918	
Total	13.7	44.5	41.8	10229	
	Birth Weight				
Pregnancy Intention	*Not Weighed*	*<2.5 kg*	*>2.5 kg*	*Total*	
Wanted	72.8	10.5	16.6	12974	
Mistimed	66.5	13.9	19.6	1624	
Unwanted	83.6	6.9	9.6	1380	
Total	73.1	10.6	16.3	15978	
	Size of Child at Birth				
Pregnancy Intention	*Larger than Average*	*Average*	*Smaller than Average*	*Very Small*	*Total*
Wanted	15.2	62.3	17.9	4.6	13583
Mistimed	15.3	60.0	19.2	5.5	1703
Unwanted	12.7	62.5	18.4	6.4	1444
Total	15.0	62.1	18.1	4.8	16730

contd...

...contd...

Pregnancy Intention	*Undernourishment*			
	Ht/A	*Wt/A*	*Wt/Ht*	*Total*
Wanted	65.0	68.2	58.3	13589
Mistimed	67.1	70.8	62.9	1703
Unwanted	67.3	69.1	61.9	1445
Total	65.4	68.6	59.1	16737

Pregnancy Intention	*Anaemia*			
	Severe	*Moderate*	*Mild*	*Total*
Wanted	5.2	43.2	22.6	10023
Mistimed	4.2	45.8	21.9	1300
Unwanted	7.3	45.8	22.6	1050
Total	5.3	43.7	22.5	12373

Pregnancy Intention	*Intake of Vitamin A*	
	Yes	*Total*
Wanted	24.0	12096
Mistimed	24.3	1550
Unwanted	17.7	1318
Total	23.5	14964

Pregnancy Intention	*Breastfeeding*				
	Immediately	*Within an Hour*	*Within 24 hr*	*Beyond 24 hr*	*Total*
Wanted	16.3	0.7	22.9	60.1	13043
Mistimed	15.5	1.1	28.3	55.1	1647
Unwanted	12.2	0.9	22.1	64.8	1400
Total	15.9	0.7	23.4	60.0	16090

Pregnancy Intention	*Duration of Breastfeeding*		
	Not Breast Fed	*Exclusive Breastfeeding*	*Total*
Wanted	3.9	26.3	13560
Mistimed	3.2	31.2	1698
Unwanted	2.7	24.5	1439
Total	3.8	26.6	16697

Pregnancy Intention	*Illness and its Treatment*				
	Cough with Fast Breathing	*Fever*	*Treatment for Fever/Cough*	*Diarrhoea*	*Treatment for Diarrhoea*
Wanted	18.6	29.0	78.5	18.5	71.8
Mistimed	21.4	32.9	71.2	22.1	73.9
Unwanted	23.7	34.9	66.6	22.5	73.9
Total	19.3	29.9	70.2	19.2	72.2

Table 12.7

Percentage Distribution of Selected Factors Determining Child Health (Female) according to Pregnancy Intention among Currently Married Women, India, NFHS-2 (1998-99)

	Immunisation			
Pregnancy Intention	*None*	*Partial*	*Full*	*Total*
Wanted	14.5	45.9	39.6	7568
Mistimed	12.6	46.8	40.6	1088
Unwanted	23.9	49.0	27.1	946
Total	15.2	46.3	38.5	9602

	Birth Weight			
Pregnancy Intention	*Not Weighed*	*<2.5 kg*	*>2.5 kg*	*Total*
Wanted	73.5	11.3	15.2	11588
Mistimed	67.8	14.3	17.9	1750
Unwanted	87.0	5.7	7.2	1498
Total	74.2	11.1	14.7	14836

	Size of Child at Birth				
Pregnancy Intention	*Larger than Average*	*Average*	*Smaller than Average*	*Very Small*	*Total*
Wanted	13.0	61.6	20.6	4.8	12157
Mistimed	14.3	58.1	21.6	6.0	1821
Unwanted	9.8	60.0	23.0	7.2	1546
Total	12.8	61.0	20.9	5.2	15524

	Undernourishment			
Pregnancy Intention	*Ht/A*	*Wt/A*	*Wt/Ht*	*Total*
Wanted	64.4	67.2	58.5	12164
Mistimed	68.7	72.4	63.7	1822
Unwanted	65.5	68.1	59.3	1547
Total	65.0	67.9	59.2	15533

	Anaemia			
Pregnancy Intention	*Severe*	*Moderate*	*Mild*	*Total*
Wanted	4.2	41.1	23.5	8864
Mistimed	5.1	38.7	25.9	1421
Unwanted	4.9	43.7	26.2	1421
Total	4.4	41.1	24.0	11706

contd...

...contd...

Pregnancy Intention	Intake of Vitamin A	
	Yes	Total
Wanted	22.6	10800
Mistimed	24.1	1675
Unwanted	15.5	1398
Total	22.1	13873

Pregnancy Intention	Breastfeeding				
	Immediately	Within an Hour	Within 24 hr	Beyond 24 hr	Total
Wanted	15.7	0.7	22.3	61.2	11736
Mistimed	18.2	0.7	27.8	53.3	1778
Unwanted	12.2	0.5	19.2	68.1	1493
Total	15.7	0.7	22.7	61.0	15007

Pregnancy Intention	Duration of Breastfeeding		
	Not Breast Fed	Exclusive Breastfeeding	total
Wanted	3.4	25.8	12119
Mistimed	2.4	28.1	1819
Unwanted	3.4	25.8	1536
Total	3.3	26.1	15474

Pregnancy Intention	Illness and its Treatment				
	Cough with Fast Breathing	Fever	Treatment for Fever/Cough	Diarrhoea	Treatment for Diarrhoea
Wanted	16.0	27.1	65.0	17.8	70.5
Mistimed	18.1	19.9	65.5	20.6	65.9
Unwanted	18.7	32.7	65.7	22.8	69.2
Total	16.5	28.0	65.1	18.6	69.7

The differences between children who are stunted, underweight and wasted among those who are wanted and unwanted are below 5 per cent. Not much conclusion can be drawn between the pregnancy intention and the status of nourishment among the children. Another observation that is worth mentioning is that, though the unwanted births are prone to anaemia, the anaemic condition is mainly prevalent among males than the females. However, the difference is by a per cent or two. More number of unwanted males has not been given Vitamin A as compared to wanted males. Similar is the situation with females. However, the percentage of females is higher than the males. There is not much variation between wanted and unwanted pregnancies and between males and females, if breastfeeding is taken into consideration. Parallel to this is the situation with duration of breastfeeding.

The illnesses among the children do show some differences between wanted and unwanted pregnancies but the differences between male and female children is not that notable.

Influence of Pregnancy Intention on Child Immunisation

The pregnancy intentions have shown that it affects child immunisation. In accordance to it, Table 12.8 shows that the unwanted births are less likely to be immunised than the wanted births whether it is partial or full immunisation.

Table 12.8

Multinomial Logistic Regression Showing the Association between Immunisation and Pregnancy Intention among Currently Married Women, India, NFHS-2 (1998-99)

Pregnancy Intention	*Immunisation [exp(β)]*	
	Partial	*Full*
Total		
Wanted®		
Mistimed	1.0	0.9
Unwanted	0.8***	0.7***
Male		
Wanted®		
Mistimed	0.8	0.8
Unwanted	0.8***	0.6***
Female		
Wanted®		
Mistimed	1.1	1.0
Unwanted	0.8	0.8**

Note: Other variables controlled are age, birth order, birth interval, place of residence, religion, ethnicity, education, occupation, exposure to mass media, autonomy, standard of living and regions by different levels of fertility.

®=Reference Category; Significance Level ***$p<0.01$ **$p<0.05$.

Summary and Conclusions

It can be concluded that there are wide range of factors that play an important role in determining pregnancy intentions among women in India:

- Women's age is one of the important determining factors for mistimed and unwanted pregnancies. It can be observed that in case of wanted *versus* mistimed pregnancy, mistimed pregnancy is 30 per cent less likely among women in the age group 25-34 and 50 per cent less likely among women in the age group 35 and above as compared to the women in the age group 15-24. The unwanted pregnancy is 1.8 and 3.8 times more likely in the age group 25-34 and 35 and above respectively as compared to women in the age group 15-24.

- The unwanted pregnancy increases with increase in the birth order. It is 6.3 times more likely in the higher birth order than the lower birth order.
- Muslims are 30 per cent more likely to have both mistimed and unwanted pregnancies than the Hindus.
- Increase in women's educational attainment lead to increase in the likelihood to have more unwanted and mistimed pregnancies. The women with higher education are 70 and 30 per cent more likely to have mistimed and unwanted pregnancies respectively as compared to women with no education.
- Women's decision to avail maternal health care services is influenced by the perception of the women about her pregnancy.
- The women with unwanted pregnancy mostly do not go for any ANC or for full ANC as compared to women with wanted pregnancy.
- However, if the women avail ANC services irrespective of their pregnancy intention, then the timing of first pregnancy do not vary much though the women with unwanted pregnancy differ slightly.
- The utilisation of other maternal health care services and the place of delivery show that the women with unwanted pregnancy are less probable to have positive response.
- Female child are at a disadvantage than the male child.
- Moreover, if the female child is unwanted, then the condition is more deplorable.
- Whatever the factors may be i.e., birth weight, size of child at birth, anaemia, illness, immunisation etc., a clear distinction is observed as per the pregnancy intention.

Policy Implications

The unwanted pregnancy shall require a new national understanding about this problem and a new consensus that pregnancy should be undertaken only with clear intent. For this, the mass should be educated about the major social and public health burdens of unwanted pregnancies and to undertake a comprehensive set of activities at national, state and local levels to reduce the burden of unwanted pregnancies resulting either due to contraceptive failure or unmet need of modern contraceptive methods. There is an urgent need to impart comprehensive knowledge on contraindications and side effects of different contraceptive methods, which can improve use and continuation rates of modern methods of contraception and hence reduce incidences of unwanted pregnancies. This has long lasting implications for improving the overall reproductive health status of women in India. The above findings may lay out the following specific recommendations:

1. The mass should be educated about the repercussion, the unwanted pregnancy has on the health of the mother and the child.
2. All the efforts to educate the people should be started from the grass-root level by reaching out to even the most outreach people.
3. Efforts should be stimulated to fully understand the determinants and antecedents of unwanted pregnancies.
4. Policy should be oriented in such a way that apart from focusing on the reproductive health of the women and the child, due emphasise should also be given to the pregnancy intentions.

Limitations of the Study

There are certain situations where exact explanation for the queries cannot be given. There may be certain reasons behind it e.g., the question on pregnancy intention can suffer from number of limitations like—if a son is born after four daughters, then that son is not considered unwanted. On the contrary, the daughters may be considered unwanted. Hence, preferences for a particular sex composition can create bias. Another important factor is that of replacement as well as insurance effect i.e., to have more children for compensating child loss. The unwantedness of the child can become wanted after its birth e.g., 4 in 10 married white women who said that they wanted no more children and subsequently had a birth reported that birth as wanted and said their reaction to it had been positive. Only 7 per cent of those who said they wanted more children reported a subsequent birth as unwanted (Westoff, 1980). Moreover, the respondent may respond so as to present a favourable image to the interviewer. Hence, such situation can create response bias. Besides, there are cases where there are non-numeric responses when question on ideal number of children is asked. The influence of the family members can also be important in determining the pregnancy intention.

References

Baydar, N. (1995). "Consequences for Children of Their Birth Planning Status", *Family Planning Perspectives* 27: 228-234.

Brown, S.S. and L. Eisenberg (1995). "The Best Intentions: Unintended Pregnancy and the Well-Being of Children and Families", Committee on Unintended Pregnancy, Institute of Medicine ISBN. Website: *http://www.nap.edu/catalog/4903.html*

Bustan (1994). "Maternal Attitude Toward Pregnancy and the Risk of NeoNatal Deaths", *American Journal of Public Health* 84(3): 411-414.

Crissey, S.R. (2006). "Effect of Pregnancy Intention on Child Well-Being and Development: Combining Retrospective Reports of Attitude and Contraceptive use", *Population Research and Policy Review* 24 (6): 593-615.

D'Angelo, D.V., B.C. Gilbert, R.W. Rochat, J.S. Santelli and J.M. Herold (2004). "Differences between Mistimed and Unwanted Pregnancies among Women Who have Live Births", *Perspectives on Sexual and Reproductive Health* 36(5): 192-197.

Dye, T.D, M.A. Wojtowycz, R.H. Aubry, J. Quade and H. Kilburn (1997). "Unintended Pregnancy and Breastfeeding Behaviour", *American Journal of Public Health* 87(10): 1709-1711.

Fischer, C.R., J.B. Standford, P. Jameson and M. Jann De Witt (1999). "Exploring the Concepts of Intended, Planned and Wanted Pregnancy", *Journal of Family Practice* 48(2): 117-122.

IGWG and WHO (2005). *A Summary of the 'So What? Report*. Department of Women and Health Family and Community Health. Geneva, Switzerland: WHO.

International Institute for Population Sciences (2000). National Family Health Survey 1998-1999: India. Mumbai: IIPS and ORC Macro.

———. (2007). National Family Health Survey 2005-2006: India. Mumbai: IIPS and ORC Macro.

Johnson, Kiersten, Zoubi al Osama and Wulfe Martin (2004). *Mistimed and Unwanted Pregnancies in Jordon*. Maryland, USA: Department of Statistics, ORC Macro Calverton.

Joyce, T.J. and M. Grossman (1990). "Pregnancy Intentions and Early Initiations of Prenatal Care", *Demography* 27(1): 1-17.

Joyce, T.J., R. Kaestner, S. Korenman (2000). "The Effect of Pregnancy Intention on Child Development", *Demography* 37(1): 83-94.

———. (2002). "On the Validity of Retrospective Assessments of Pregnancy Intention", *Demography* 39(1): 199-213.

Kaufmann, R.B., L. Morris, A.M. Spitz (1997). "Comparison of Two Question Sequences for Assessing Pregnancy Intentions", *American Journal of Epidemiology* 145(9): 810-816.

Korenman, S., R. Kaestner, T. Joyce (2002). "Consequences for Infants of Parental Disagreement in Pregnancy Intention", *Perspectives on Sexual and Reproductive Health* 34(4): 198-205.

Kost, K., D.J. Landry and J.E. Darroch (1998). "The Effects of Pregnancy Planning Status on Birth Outcomes and Infant Care", *Family Planning Perspectives* 30(5): 223-230.

Kulkarni, S. and M.K. Choe (1997). "Unwanted Fertility in Selected States of India", Paper presented at the 1997 Annual Meeting of the Population Association of America, 27-29 March, Washington, D.C.

Marsiglio, W. and F.L. Mott (1988). "Does Wanting to Become Pregnant with a First Child Affect Subsequent Maternal Behaviours and Infant Birth Weight?", *Jounal of Marriage and the Family* 50(4): 1023-1036.

Marston, C. and J. Cleland (2003). "Do Unintended Pregnancies Carried to Term Lead to Adverse Outcomes for Mother and Child? An Assessment in Five Developing Countries", *Population Studies* 57(1): 77-93.

Peterson, L.S. and W.D. Mosher (1999). "Options for Measuring Unintended Pregnancy Inc Cycle 6 of the National Survey of Family Growth", *Family Planning Perspectives* 31(5): 252-253.

Pulley, L., V. Klerman, H. Tang and B.A. Baker (2002). "The Extent of Pregnancy Mistiming and its Association with Maternal Characteristics and Behaviours and Pregnancy Outcomes", *Perspectives on Sexual and Reproductive Health* 34(4): 206-211.

Remez, L. (2003). "Unintended Pregnancy Is Linked to Inadequate Prenatal Care, but Not to Unattended Delivery or Child Health", *International Family Planning Perspectives* 29(3): 146-147.

Santelli, J., R. Rochat, Hatfield-Timajchy, B.C. Gilbert, K. Curtis, R. Cabral, J.S. Hirsch, L. Schieve and Unintended Pregnancy Working Group (2003). "The Measurement and Meaning of Unintended Pregnancy", *Perspectives on Sexual and Reproductive Health* 35(2): 94-101.

Speizer, I.S., J.S. Santelli, A. Afable-Munsuz and C. Kendall (2004). "Measuring Factors Underlying Intendedness of Women's First and Later Pregnancies", *Perspectives on Sexual and Reproductive Health* 36(5): 198-205.

Vlassoff, C. (1990). "Fertility Intentions and Subsequent Behaviour: A Longitudinal Study in Rural India", *Studies in Family Planning* 21(4): 216-225.

Weller, R.H., I.W. Eberstein and M. Bailey (1987). "Pregnancy Wantedness and Maternal Behaviour during Pregnancy", *Demography* 24(3): 407-412.

Westoff, C.F. (1980). "Women's Reactions to Pregnancy", *Family Planning Perspectives* 12(3): 135-139.

13

Utilisation of Health Services and Scope for Public-Private Partnership in India

CHANDAN KUMAR AND R.B. BHAGAT

Introduction

In the present era of substantial demographic restructuring, as is evidenced in almost all over the world, with significant control on mortality factors, the burden on health care has increased. Many countries all over the world has made the solution of the increasing burden for providing health services to various kinds of health problems of their citizen by just expanding the services with the help of non-governmental organisations (NGOs). However, this is not a permanent solution, especially in developing democratic countries like India, where the prime duty of the Government is to provide better and eqi-accessible services to every strata of the population. Nonetheless, concerns about the ability of governments to finance health services adequately, the poor performance of public health service delivery systems, and the desire to expand the choices available to patients have led a number of countries in Asia to adopt a strategy of encouraging the expansion of the private sector (see William and Patricia, 1997). India is also not the exception; private sector in health care services in India is spreading its realm tremendously. Almost 75 per cent of health services in India are being currently provided by the private sector (NRHM, 2005-2012).

The major drawback of this unregulated spread of privatisation of health services in India is the poor who really needs better and cheap services are not able to afford highly-priced private health care services. In fact, if the Government mutes on this issue and think that the people prefer private services over public services as a matter of choice and thus the Government should only motivate private services to enter into the health sector, is a real problem for the country. The present study makes an attempt to realise this issue of public-private dichotomy in provision of health care services in India. We will see in later section of this chapter that how people, especially the women which are the focal point of country's reproductive and child health care services, switch over to private health services, once they get their first treatment in public health care services. We will also look into the matter of influencing factors, which determine the patient's decision to go for private health care sources as against the public sources.

In a country like India, where almost 70 per cent of total population lives in rural areas with a lack of adequate facilities, even private services too are not able to cater the people's health care needs. Private health care providers are concentrated where they can receive better infrastructural facilities and can get more benefits in monetary terms. And if the private services are available in rural areas, the quality differs again, when we compare the private health care providers in rural and urban areas. Of course, there is no doubt, that the private health services to some extent satisfy the needs of patients as against the public health care services. However, in some cases we find that the amount of failure in providing cure (treatment) is more in private services as against the public services, but still for the post-treatment complication, people[1] prefer to visit private services again and again.

Private health services don't bother about the concept like equality and equity; they only cater the services to those who can pay better health care services. So, the increasing gaps in health service utilisation from public *versus* private sources actually promote inequality in health care system in the country. The richer gets benefit from both sides, on the one hand, they get better quality health care services by paying affordable prices to private health services and on the other hand, they also get benefited from some of the subsidised services from government sources. And the poor neither get better quality health care services from public sources, nor do they get unaffordable private health care services.

Equality of utilisation is best understood as being a situation where patients with equal needs for health care receive equal treatment, both in terms of the volume and the quality of the services (Mooney, 1983). A potentially important factor influencing utilisation of health services is accessibility of the services. Equality of access represents a situation where people with equal needs have equal opportunity to use health services (Mooney *et al.*, 1991). It is a supply side phenomenon; equal access is achieved when patients with the same needs face the same costs of health care consumption both in terms of time and money.

1. The use of the term 'people' actually refers to 'women' in most places in this chapter, because the informations gathered on different demographic and health issues in RCH surveys are mainly based on the responses of the ever married women (age 15-49) in the household. And we think that the health care services all over the world in general, discern the needs of women and children's health mostly. So, to some extent, we can generalise the women's attitude towards utilisation of health services as the utilisation pattern of the general people.

Utilisation of health services differ by various demographic and socio-economic status of individual too, in addition to the availability, accessibility and quality of services in different places or regions. In various studies based on the European countries like Norway etc., the factors like the perceived symptoms of disease, health status and the time price have also been considered in determining utilisation of health services.

However, in the Indian context, out-of-pocket price is likely to have an important impact on health care utilisation. Bice *et al.* (1972, 1973), Mechanic (1969) and Montiero (1973) also conclude that socio-cultural differentials in utilisation are greatly diminished where capacity to pay for services is equalised. There appears to be considerable convergence of both research and opinion leading to the conclusion that ability to pay is the major determinant of the utilisation of health services once symptoms are perceived as serious, and that cultural and social psychological factors once thought to account for much of the observed variations among social classes and ethnic groups in their utilisation behaviour are largely irrelevant.

In later sections of this chapter, we will see how the economic status[2] of the individual affects the utilisation of health care services in different states of India. Finally, the selected states of India, for which the sample size was sufficient, have been ranked on the basis of extent of inequality in terms of the economic standard of the population in utilising public and private health care services.

Public-Private Dichotomy in Health Sector in India: A Background

Since the inception of the planning process, the Central and state governments have experienced a number of constraints in implementing health programmes effectively. In 1982, the National Health Policy (NHP) acknowledged these constraints and suggested an integrated and comprehensive approach for the future development of health care services. The NHP's emphasis on promoting private and voluntary health curative services has been an important step towards providing clear direction to the states. Planning to help state government develop their own strategies to utilise untapped resources and strengthen their ability to meet the growing health needs of their people has been carried out through the NHP process (Bhat, 1997).

---

2. Economic status of the people is considered in this chapter on the basis of the household standard of living and the monthly per capita expenditure, used for services received from DLHS-RCH-II survey and National Sample Survey respectively.

Bhat (1997) also sheds light on the growth of private sector over the years. He is of the opinion that it has been triggered by a number of factors, including a new national economic policy, the rapid influx of medical technology, growing deficits of public sector hospitals, and a rising middle class. Its growth has profound implications for the character of the current Indian health care system and its future course.

Recent studies indicate that private health care significantly affects both the cost and quality of health care services in India (Uplekar, 1989a, b; Duggal and Amin, 1989; Vishwanathan and Rohde, 1990; Yesudian, 1990). It is evident that the people of India, including the poor, make considerable use of the private health sector. But at what cost? This is a crucial dimension of the private health sector in India, unfortunately under-researched. NSS data reveals that the average cost of treatment in the private sector for rural in-patients was 2.1 times higher, and for urban inpatients 2.4 times higher, than in the public sector during 1995-96 (India Health Report, 2003). The NRHM document has also stated that curative services favour the rich, for every rupee spent on the poorest 20 per cent population, Rs. 3 are spent on the richest quintile (Singh, 2006).

Over the years, the access to health facilities in India has become too costly to afford. The recent findings (NSS, 2004), reveals that most of the people in north (especially Uttar Pradesh and Uttarakhand) and northeastern states (Nagaland, Mizoram, Assam etc.) are financing more than 80 per cent of their health treatment expenditure from other sources, like borrowings, contributions from friends and relatives, and by selling of ornaments etc. If such would be the case in future, it would really be a pathetic condition for the country as a whole.

Significantly, despite the problems resulting from the rapid growth of the private sector, there has been little effort to establish market or regulatory mechanisms to ensure its appropriate growth. This is unfortunate, since it is well known that leaving health care to market forces does not necessarily lead to an effective and efficient health care system (Bhat, 1997).

Therefore, the emphasis should be on partnership and not on privatisation, since there is some skepticism about PPPs and it is reframed by many as an agenda for privatisation. Prof. Peter Berman, leading economist, World Bank in his presentation during the National Planning Workshop, organised by NIHFW in November 2005, puts emphasis that the PPP "doesn't imply abdication of roles of Govt., but re-orientation and re-assuring provision of public health through private partnership. Health care in India is already privatised and the issue is not to talk about more privatisation but a reorientation of the role of the Govt." We should be pragmatic and not ideologists. Emphasis should be on the most effective way to improve the outcome. The question is of coverage, reaching people and improving quality of service, cost and outcome (Berman, 2005).

Hence, the challenge is to find out strategies that will facilitate a far more substantial participation by NGOs in the health sector, particularly in the backward states and remote areas, and to ensure systems that will keep such participation accountable and transparent.

According to a rough estimate, the number of voluntary organisations working in health care areas is more than 7000. Despite the lack of comprehensive documentation on the contribution of NGOs, there is no disputing the fact that NGOs have the potential to improve access to, and the quality and equity of services, either through direct provision or through advocacy and other action. This potential to contribute substantially to public health goals has not been realised due to several reasons. Their limited size and spatial distribution is a major cause. That they are missing where they are most needed hinders effective partnership with the public health system (India Health Report, 2003).

The present study draws motivation from the National Rural Health Mission Document (Component-H), 2005-2012, to deal with an explicable plan of action, i.e., to identify the areas of public-private partnership (PPP) in health sector, which are need based, thematic and geographically relevant. Therefore, we attempt to observe this issue with the theme of economic status of the people and accordingly the utilisation of health services from public and private sources. We will try to see in which state the inequality is high in utilisation of different RCH services and for the general health treatment (as inpatient) from public and private sources separately.

Data and Methods

The study utilises data from National Sample Survey (NSS, 60th Round: January-June, 2004), schedule 25.0: Morbidity and Health Care, conducted by the Government of India, National Sample Survey Organisation (NSSO). The survey covered the curative aspects of the general health care system in India and also the utilisation of health care services provided by the public and private sector, together with the expenditure incurred by the households for availing these services. It is based on the information collected during the six months in 2004 from 47,302 rural and 26,566 urban households covering all over the country. The enquiry on morbidity was conducted with a reference period of 15 days. All spells of ailment suffered by each member, both present as well as the deceased, of the sample household, during the 15 days preceding the date of enquiry, whether or not the patient was hospitalised for treatment, however, information was collected for every event of hospitalisation of a member, whether living or deceased at the time of survey, during the 365 days preceding the date of enquiry. The sample design adopted for the survey was essentially a two-stage stratified design, with census villages and urban blocks as the first stage units (FSUs) for the rural and urban areas respectively, and households as the second-stage units (SSUs). The survey period, January-June 2004, was split up into two sub-rounds of three months each. The rural and urban samples of FSUs of each sub-sample were allocated for the two sub-rounds.

The informations on the utilisation of health care services by household members as inpatient of hospital during the last 365 days before survey, separately for rural and urban areas have been extracted from the above mentioned source.

Moreover, informations on the utilisation of health services for different reproductive and child health care components have also been drawn from the DLHS-RCH–II, women file. The survey extends the informations on induced abortions, antenatal, natal and postnatal care, family planning services and the RTI/STI related components of the women in reproductive age-group. This also provides the informations on child health care.

Maps have been prepared to reveal marked state-wise variations in the utilisation of public and private health services in general, for different reproductive and child health care component and for the utilisation of health care services by residence and by economic standard of the people, using Geographical Information System (GIS) package (Arc Catalogue/Arc Map).

According to the recent survey (2004) of NSS, almost 97 per cent of rural inpatients and 96 per cent of urban inpatients of hospital received health treatment from the private sources during the period of one year before survey. So, it was a matter of great interest that such a clear bias towards the private health services must be taken into consideration with regard to the general socioeconomic and other related background characteristics of those people or inpatients. This is attempted by employing a logistic regression, separately for rural and urban areas. The dependent variable is the population, who received treatment as inpatient from private health services (Public health services=0/Private health services=1) during the last one year before survey. Independent variables are the age-group, sex composition, marital status, religion, social groups, education level, household size, monthly per capita expenditure group and nature of ailment.

Seven more separate regressions have been carried out considering the inclination towards private health sources in case of other reproductive and child health care services. These services are related to: induced abortion,

Figure 13.1

India (Rural): Treatment of Household Members (As Inpatients) by Public and Private Sources Exclusively, 2003-04

Figure 13.2

India (Urban): Treatment of Household Members (As Inpatients) by Public and Private Sources Exclusively, 2003-04

Figure 13.3

India: Utilisation of Private Health Services for Different RCH Care Components, 2002-2004

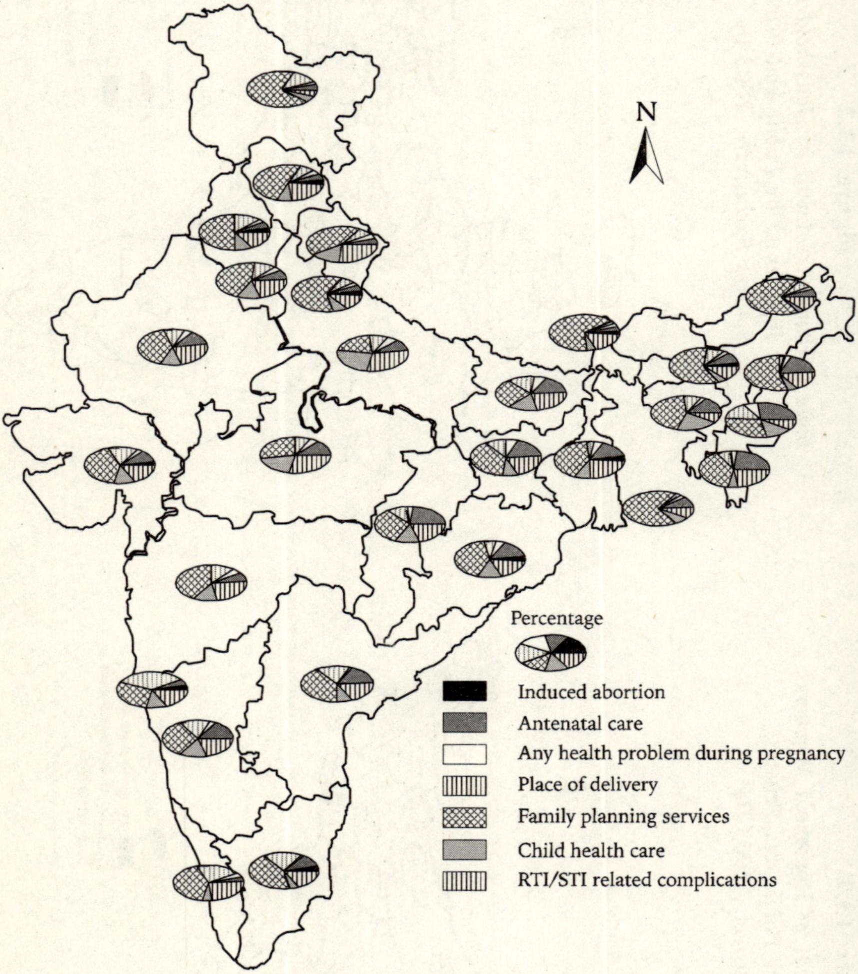

Figure 13.4

India: Utilisation of Public Health Services for Different RCH Care Components, 2002-2004

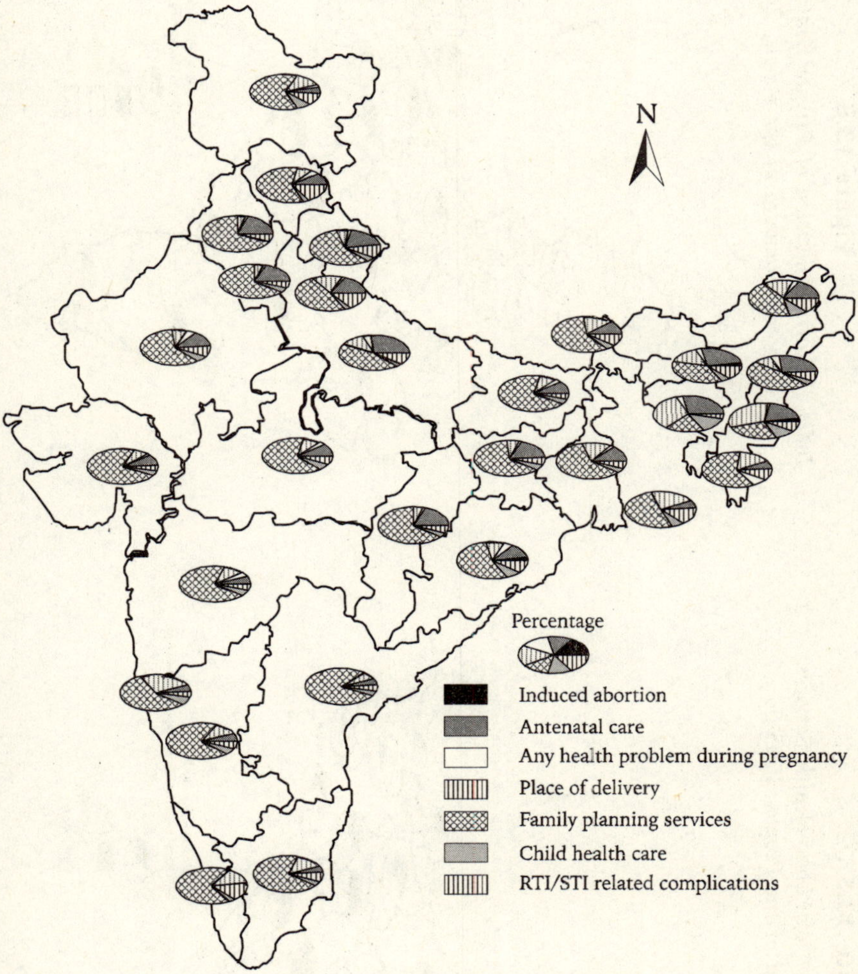

Figure 13.5

India (Rural): Utilisation of Public Health Services by Economic Standard of the People, 2003-04

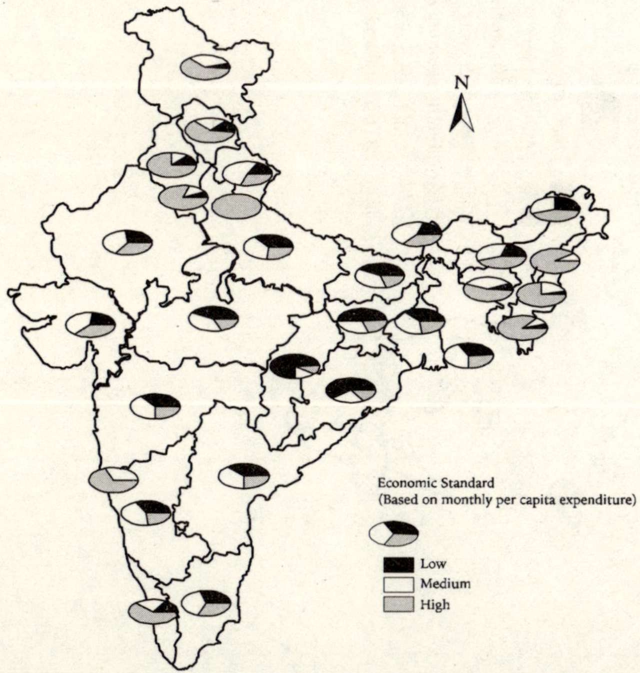

Figure 13.6

India (Rural): Utilisation of Private Health Services by Economic Standard of the People, 2003-04

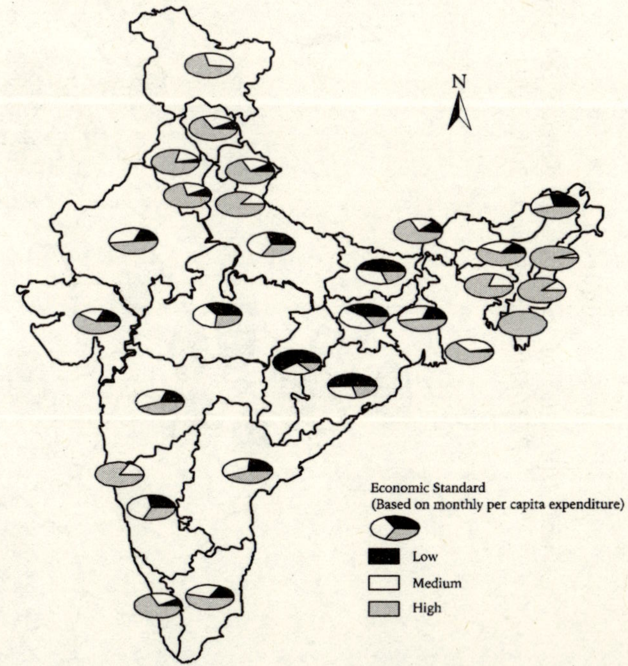

Figure 13.7

India (Urban): Utilisation of Private Health Services by Economic Standard of the People, 2003-04

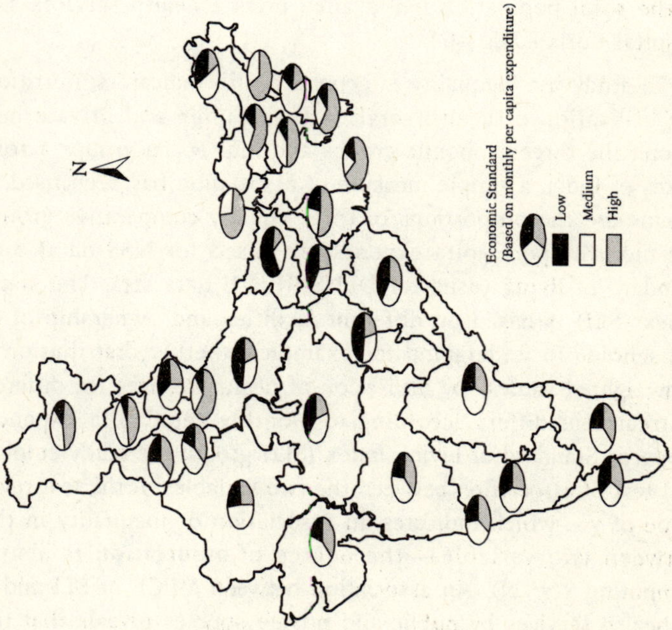

Figure 13.8

India (Urban): Utilisation of Public Health Services by Economic Standard of the People, 2003-04

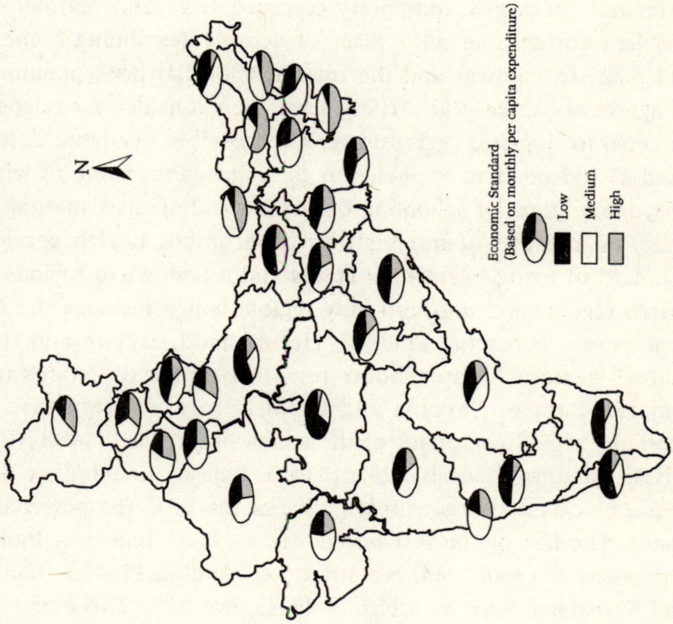

antenatal check-ups, temporary contraceptive use, treatment for any health problem during pregnancy, place of delivery (excluding home delivery), RTI/STI related treatment and the treatment of diarrhoea/pneumonia to children of age below three years. These have been considered as dependent variables in separate logistic regressions. The possible available determinants were used as independent variables in the regression. Some of which are the age of women, years of schooling of women and spouse, marital duration, caste, religion, reasons of not visiting government health services, household standard of living, residential status and a few macro regions of India. These macro regions are: northern hilly region, which includes the states of Jammu & Kashmir, Himachal Pradesh, Uttarakhand, Sikkim and the northeastern states; western high economy region includes the states of Maharashtra, Gujarat, Punjab, Haryana and Delhi; central-western-eastern (CWE) low economy region comprises of the states like Uttar Pradesh, Bihar, Jharkhand, Orissa, Madhya Pradesh, Chhattisgarh, Rajasthan and West Bengal. The later might be called as the representative of the EAG (Empowered Action Group) states. The last or the rest one is the southern region of India, which clearly represents the four southern states i.e., Andhra Pradesh, Tamil Nadu, Kerala and Karnataka. Such an arbitrary division of India into four regions pleads for the rationale considering the geographical as well as the developmental component. The northern hilly region has been found as the least potential region in terms of the utilisation of private health services, still 89 per cent of the rural population had availed private health services as inpatients of hospital during 2003-04.

To study the inequality in general health indicators, nutritional status and the utilisation of health services (i.e., public and private health services) among the three economic groups and four social groups across the selected states of India, a simple measure of association has been used. The economic groups are the proportions of three equally comparative groups in terms of the monthly per capita expenditure (used for NSS data) and in terms of standard of living (used for DLHS-RCH-II data set). The standard of living index (SLI) is based on different facilities and ownership of amenities in a household. To understand for example, whether distribution of population (unweighted values) by utilisation of health services for different health care or treatment differs according to Monthly Per Capita Expenditure (MPCE) group or Standard of Living Index (SLI) group, the study employ a chi-square (χ^2) test of association between the two variables. If the test reveals significant value of χ^2—which indicates an association or inequality in the distribution between two variables—the degree of association is also measured by computing $\sqrt{(\chi^2/N)}$. An association between MPCE or SLI and the utilisation of health services by public and private sources reveals that the populations of different economic groups are not equal in terms of use of two different health services. Then the states were ranked according to the value of $\sqrt{(\chi^2/N)}$. The lower rank indicates a strong association, which implies high inequality while a higher rank indicates weak association which implies low inequality. In case of states with the same values of $\sqrt{(\chi^2/N)}$, they are given tied ranks.

Utilisation of Health Services in India

There is dearth of adequate and reliable information related to the utilisation of health services for different aspects of health care and treatment. Therefore, it is always considered risky to conclude the result on the basis of a few subgroups of the population. However, the National Sample Survey, 2004 with its 250,862 sample size in rural areas and 132,638 samples in urban areas; out of that more than 40 per cent of household members in both rural as well as urban areas, had anyhow experienced any health problem during one year before survey and also got treatment as inpatients of hospitals. If we have no information at all for the out-patient cases during the period, still the samples for inpatient cases are sufficient to understand the general inclination towards the either services (i.e., public or private health services). Out of these 40 per cent population, 2 per cent received services exclusively from public health sources, 53 per cent exclusively from private sources and 45 per cent of the inpatients got treatment from both health care sources in rural areas. The figures for the same in urban areas are 3, 57 and 40 per cent respectively. If we look at the information in other way, we would see almost 97 per cent inpatients in rural and 96 per cent in urban areas got treatment at least once in private health services during the period of one year (2003-04).

Moreover, the second round of DLHS-RCH provides informations on the treatment seeking behaviour for almost all important components of reproductive and child health care services. For instance, a woman in reproductive age-group might experience ever the cases of induced abortions, antenatal, natal and postnatal health care services or any health problem during pregnancy, extended further to the use of contraceptives etc., and the treatment of their children in infancy. Considering the last three year period before survey, 2002-2004 (DLHS-RCH-II), we got information about almost 38,182 women with the result of their last pregnancy outcome. Out of these 94 per cent women had live births, 1 per cent experienced stillbirths, 2 per cent had spontaneous abortions and almost 3 per cent women had gone for induced abortion. About 66 per cent of these induced abortions were performed by private services and 67 per cent of these abortions (i.e., performed at private health services) experienced health problems within six weeks of abortion, compared to only 26 per cent such problematic cases in public health care services.

Table 13.1

India: Performed Induced Abortions and Health Problems Experienced After Abortion by Health Services, 1999-2001 to 2002-2004 (DLHS-RCH II)

	Induced Abortion Performed during 3 years before Survey		*Health Problem Experienced within 6 weeks of Abortion*	
	No. of Cases	*Per cent*	*No. of Cases*	*Per cent*
Govt. services	314	27.4	60	25.8
Private services	752	65.6	156	66.7
Others	80	7.0	17	7.5
Total	1146	100.0	233	100.0

However, still during the second term of the treatment for the emerged health problems due to induced abortion, 27 per cent women plied for private health services, who had earlier performed their abortions at public health centres. On the other hand, despite having the large number of unsuccessful cases of induced abortions in private health care centres, only 7 per cent of women went for public services for their treatment, who had earlier performed their abortions at private health centres, and 12 per cent of those cases received treatment or consultation from other sources (see Table 13.2).

Table 13.2

India: Health Treatment after having Health Problem due to Abortion by Health Services: 1999-2001 to 2002-2004 (DLHS-RCH II)

	Health Treatment or Consultation Received After Abortion	
	Per cent of Abortions, Earlier Performed by Govt. Health Services	*Per cent of Abortions, Earlier Performed by Private Health Services*
Govt. services	68.8	6.8
Private services	27.1	81.5
Others	4.1	11.7
Total	100.0	100.0

Since the Government of India draws special attention on the reproductive and child health care among all other public health services after the International Conference on Population and Development (ICPD), 1994, the services like antenatal check-ups and the distribution of other supplementary courses in terms of iron folic acid (IFA) tablets and/or tetanus injections etc., have substantially improved. However, still 49 per cent of women get antenatal check-ups from private sources, in comparison to only 45 per cent from public sources and 6 per cent from other sources. On the other hand, the maximum proportion of women (55 per cent) got the IFA tablets during pregnancy from public sources, compared to only 18 per cent from private sources and 28 per cent from other sources. Such distribution might be understood with this fact that the service was free of cost.

During the period 1999-2000 to 2002-2004 (three years), out of 507,622 women in reproductive age-group (15-44), 13 per cent women experienced any type of health problem during their pregnancy. Out of these 13 per cent women (66,747), more than 60 per cent women availed the treatment or consultation from private sources. Though there is no evidence of substantial variation in availed services for different types of health problems during pregnancy, but the distribution of proportions of women went for different health services for major health problems during pregnancy can be observed in Table 13.3.

Table 13.3

India: Health Services Received by Women for Health Problems during Last Pregnancy: 1999-2001 to 2002-2004

Health Problems during Pregnancy	*Services Received From*		
	Govt. Sources	*Private Services*	*Others*
Swelling of hands and feet	31.9	64.2	3.9
Paleness	34.1	61.9	4.0
Visual disturbances	36.3	54.1	9.5
Convulsions	37.0	54.0	9.0
Others	31.0	62.4	6.6
Total	32.9	61.2	6.0

In India, most of the mothers deliver their child at home. During the period 1999-2000 to 2002-2004, almost 59 per cent of women (22,956) delivered their child at home. However, out of rest 41 per cent institutional deliveries, 22 per cent women delivered their child at private health centres, compared to only 19 per cent in public health centres. As Table 13.4 shows, the chances of post-delivery complications is the most among home deliveries, followed by other institutional deliveries, deliveries at government or public health centres and the lowest complications have been reported for deliveries at private health care centres.

Out of 33 per cent of post-delivery complications emerged out after the deliveries performed at home, more than 60 per cent of women went for private health care services, compared to only 21 per cent for public services and 18 per cent for other services (see Table 13.5).

Table 13.4

India: Place of Delivery and Post-delivery Complication by Women for their Last Live or Still Births by Health Services during the 3 Years before Survey, 2002-2004

	Place of Delivery		*Post-Delivery Complication (During the first week after delivery)*	
	No. of Women	*Per cent*	*No. of Women*	*Per cent*
Govt. services	7471	19.1	2104	28.2
Private services	8407	21.5	2024	24.1
Home	22956	58.6	7634	33.3
Others	313	0.8	94	30.1
Total	39146	100.0	11856	30.3

Table 13.5

India: Post-delivery Treatment by Health Services during the 3 Years Period before Survey, 2002-2004

	Per cent of Deliveries Earlier Performed at		
	Govt. Services	*Private Services*	*Home*
Govt. services	46.4	13.0	20.5
Private services	45.4	79.4	61.1
Others	8.2	7.5	18.4
Total	100.0	100.0	100.0

The family planning movement in India started since early 70s and the most oldest and popularised means of family planning is the sterilisation. The temporary methods of family planning in the form of Intra Uterine Device (IUD), pills and condom etc., have been introduced later; some of these methods are still not much popularised. Due to the free services available for sterilisation including some other benefits, most of the cases of family planning get services from the public health care services. However, a clear distinction among sterilisation and other temporary contraceptive use by health services is shown in Table 13.6.

Table 13.7 shows the proportion of health treatment or consultation sought after having problem with contraceptive use by health services during the last 3 years before survey, 2002-2004. Almost 41 per cent and 49 per cent of women plied for private health services, who had earlier received contraceptives from public and other sources respectively.

Table 13.6

India: Modern Contraceptive Use and Resulted Health Problems by Health Services during the Last 3 Years before Survey, 2002-2004

Modern Contraceptive Methods	*Govt. Services*		*Private Services*		*Others*	
	*C.U.**	*H.P.***	*C.U.*	*H.P.*	*C.U.*	*H.P.*
Female sterilisation	80.4	17.3	18.0	14.2	1.6	21.8
Vasectomy	78.4	11.2	12.3	23.8	9.4	18.8
IUD/Copper-T/Loop	44.6	18.0	53.7	12.3	1.7	28.6
Oral pills	16.5	18.8	78.5	15.6	5.0	14.2
Condom/*Nirodh*	13.5	2.4	82.5	1.6	4.0	0.0
Total	58.9	16.8	38.6	10.5	2.5	14.8

Note: * Contraceptive use ** Health problem emerged after contraceptive use.

Table 13.7

India: Health Treatment or Consultation Received after having Problem with Contraceptive Use by Health Services during the Last 3 Years before Survey, 2002-2004

	Per cent of Women, who used Contraceptive Methods Earlier from		
	Govt. Sources	*Private Sources*	*Others*
Govt. services	47.1	4.6	9.2
Private services	40.5	80.3	44.8
Others	12.4	15.1	45.9
Total	100.0	100.0	100.0

Moreover, other sensitive health care treatment is also served distinctly by the private health services. As can be seen in Table 13.8, almost 60 per cent of women seem to get treatment or consultation for menstruation related problems and 61 per cent for RTI/STI related problems from private sources. Similarly, 58 per cent of women liked to go for private services in case of any abnormal vaginal discharge.

In case of child care too, one can clearly observe the bias towards the private health services, except the immunisation of the children. Almost 13 per cent children of age 0-71 months had diarrhoea during the last two weeks before survey and for the same reference period, about 16 per cent cases of pneumonia were reported. Out of these cases, 68 per cent of children with diarrhoea were treated in private health services and about 69 per cent treated for pneumonia (see Table 13.9).

Table 13.8

India: Treatment or Consultation for RTI/STI Related Problems by Health Services during the Last 3 Years before Survey, 2002-2004

	Treatment or Consultation (per cent of women) for Problems Related to		
	Menstruation	RTI/STI	Any Abnormal Vaginal Discharge
Govt. services	25.5	22.0	23.8
Private services	59.5	60.9	55.7
Others	15.0	17.1	20.4
Total	100.0	100.0	100.0

Table 13.9

India: Child Health Care by Health Services during the Last 3 Years before Survey, 2002-2004

	Per cent of Children, who were Treated for or Immunised		
	Diarrhoea	Pneumonia	Immunised
Govt. services	18.7	17.5	62.3
Private services	67.8	68.9	15.1
Others	13.5	13.6	22.6
Total	100.0	100.0	100.0

Determinants Influencing the Utilisation of Health Care Services

To understand the differentials in the utilisation of health services by different background characteristics of the population, a bivariate analysis was done. Among the inpatient cases, the use of private health services was recorded more among children of age below 5 years in rural areas and about 61 per cent among older age-group in urban areas. There was no clear distinction found between both the sex (i.e., male and female) and among the inpatients of different marital status regarding the use of private health services. Among different religion and social groups, both in rural and urban areas, the proportion of population using private health services make difference. In rural areas, the use of private health services was found more prevalent among Hindu and OBC caste, while in urban areas, the use seems more prominent among Scheduled Tribes. With the increase in the level of education, the use of private health services also increases, but it doesn't appear to put prominent impact upon the use of private services, because the higher proportion of illiterate people also look forword to use the private health services equally. Further, with the increase in household size and the increase in income level or the economic status, the use of private health services also increases. The use of private health services is likely to be more in sensitive diseases like gynaecological disorders or heart diseases, compared to other kind of ailment. In rural areas, the highest proportion (67 per cent) of population seeks private health services in case of gynaecological disorders; similarly 64 per cent in urban areas.

Further, by adjusting the influence of different socioeconomic and demographic determinants, the impact of income level of population seems more prominent and highly significant, when compared to the lowest quintile of MPCE; among all other quintiles, the probability of using private health services is more. The use of private health services among Muslims is about half of that among Hindus and almost five times more among Christians in comparison to Hindus. In comparison to Scheduled Tribes, which is also believed as the most deprived social group, the inpatients of all other social groups or castes the use of private health services was found more. So, the inequality in utilisation of health services appears more among different income groups as well as different social groups.

Similarly, regarding the use of private health services among all other reproductive and child health care services (here in the present chapter, seven health care services have been considered), the impact of different standard of living of the women appear significant and imply that the utilisation of private health services are more in high and middle SLI group in comparison to the women of low SLI group except in the services regarding induced abortion. The most important thing which comes out from the present study is that such bias towards the use of private health services is due to this opinion that the government health care services do not provide better quality of services and the clients are not entertained or examined properly. As we can clearly observe in Table 13.10, that the women who went to private health services for performing induced abortions reported six times more the poor quality of government services and they were of the opinion that in government health care services, the cases are not examined properly being inconvenient location of the government health services, when they were asked to give reasons for not visiting government health services.

Among four macro regions of India, in western higher economy region, the use of private health services was found more regarding all selected reproductive and child health services in comparison to the other three macro regions. This also suggests the influence of income level or the economic standard of the women plays more prominent role in the use of private health services.

Table 13.10 also shows some of the important findings, which are not here being described comprehensively.

Table 13.10

Results of Logistic Regression Models (Odds Ratios) for the Population, who Received Treatment as Inpatient from Private Health Services (during the Last 1 year before Survey, January-June, 2004) in India

Demographic and Socioeconomic Characteristics	*Exp β (Odds Ratio)*	
	Rural	*Urban*
Age composition		
Below 5		
5-15	0.925	0.973
15-35	0.646**	0.482***
35-60	0.567***	0.365***
60 and above	0.591**	0.538**
Sex composition		
Male		
Female	1.011	1.052
Marital status		
Never married		
Currently married	1.002	1.014
Others	1.200	1.262
Religion		
Hindu		
Muslim	0.582***	1.558***
Christian	5.908***	1.558**
Others	0.986	1.864**
Social groups		
ST		
SC	1.284*	2.345***
OBC	1.512**	1.953***
Others	1.564**	2.149***
Education level		
Illiterate		
Below primary	0.727**	0.978
Primary	0.796**	0.881
Middle	1.021	0.925
High school and above	1.070	1.095
Household size		
1 to 5		
5 to 10	1.119	1.243**
10 and above	2.150***	2.006***

contd...

...contd...

Demographic and Socioeconomic Characteristics	*Exp β (Odds Ratio)*	
	Rural	*Urban*
MPCE[<] (in quintile)		
Q1		
Q2	1.736***	1.148
Q3	1.977***	1.033
Q4	1.707***	1.238*
Q5	1.790***	2.308***
Nature of ailment		
Diarrhoea/dysentery		
Gastritis/gastric or peptic ulcer	1.109	3.009***
Heart disease	0.734**	1.981***
Gynaecological disorders	2.486***	3.027***
Fever (unknown origin)	0.909	3.988***
Accidents/injuries/burns/fractures/poisoning	1.098	1.663***
Other diagnosed ailments	1.381**	2.215***

Note: [<] Monthly per capita expenditure ® Reference category
* Significant at 10% level ** Significant at 5% level *** Significant at 1% level.

Ranking of States by Extent of Inequality in the Utilisation of Health Services

After getting this result that there is marked inequality among the people of different economic groups, it is essential to see which states are characterised by higher extent of inequality among different economic categories by using a complete summary measure of inequality. Statewise values of $\sqrt{(\chi^2/N)}$ given in Table 13.12 for the utilisation of different health services respectively, show whether there is significant association between economic or social groups and the given indicator. If the value is not significant, it implies that economic status does not have any effect on that indicator and the situation with respect to that indicator is more or less the same among the given groups. If the value is significant but low it means economic group has only a moderate effect on that indicator. If the value is statistically significant and high, it shows a strong correlation between given categories and that indicator implying that the specific category does affect the dimension represented by that particular indicator and that the value of that indicator is high in certain group and not in others. It is obvious that if there is notable inequality among economic groups regarding the dimensions reflected in these indicators, value of $\sqrt{(\chi^2/N)}$ is likely to be high and significant. Value which is not significant but low can be taken as an indication of low inequality among four groups with respect to that particular indicator. In this sense, state ranks given in all the above tables, represent the

Table 13.11

Results of Logistic Regression Models for the Utilisation of Private Health Services in case of Various Health Care Components

Independent Variables		*Reference Category*	*IA*[1]	*ANC*[2]	*PDT*[3]	*TCU*[4]	*RTI/STI*[5]	*Dia./Pnea.*[6]	*AHP*[7]
Age in completed years			1.112*	-	-	-	-	-	-
Women's years of schooling			1.111**	1.085***	1.110**	1.048**	1.047**	0.985*	1.053
Spouse's years of schooling			1.022	1.042***	0.977	1.059***	1.017	1.046	1.027**
Marital duration			0.869**		0.985	0.990	0.994		1.005*
Age at consummation of marriage		18 years and above							
	< 18 years		3.858**	-	-	1.147	-	-	-
Age of women		< 25 years							
	25 years & above		-	0.942	0.742	1.057	1.126	-	0.957
Social groups	(SC)	Others	0.394**	0.581***	1.277	0.951	0.697**	1.321	0.584***
	(ST)		0.683	0.828	1.263	0.656	1.478	0.955	0.664**
	(OBC)		0.844	1.101*	1.426	1.203*	1.092	0.971	1.093
Religion	(Muslim)	Hindu	0.291**	1.149*	3.593**	0.910	0.963	0.871	0.934
	(Christian)		0.473	1.526**	1.549	1.509	0.732	0.329**	1.007
	(Others)		1.609	0.833	2.693	1.352	0.750	0.400**	1.121
Daughter (surviving)	(2)	1	1.381	-	-	-	-	-	-
	(3 and more)		6.579*	-	-	-	-	-	-
Children (surviving)	(4 and more)	1-3	0.631	-	-	-	-	-	-
Reasons of abortion		unplanned pregnancy							
	complication in pregnancy		2.010*	-	-	-	-	-	-
	last child too young		0.743	-	-	-	-	-	-
Reasons of not visiting govt. services		not conveniently located							
	Time not suited		1.142	0.787**	0.822	0.870	0.632**	0.470**	0.899
	Poor quality of services		6.429***	1.659***	0.871	1.520***	1.294**	0.760	1.695***
	Not examine properly		3.710**	1.678***	1.757	1.369**	1.728**	0.868	1.774***

contd...

...contd...

Independent Variables	*Reference Category*	*IA*[1]	*ANC*[2]	*PDT*[3]	*TCU*[4]	*RTI/STI*[5]	*Dia./Pnea.*[6]	*AHP*[7]
Standard of living (Medium)	Low	0.350	1.165**	1.675*	1.112	0.975	1.061	0.952
(High)		0.292*	1.940***	1.246	1.537**	1.300	2.084**	1.493**
Residential status (Urban)	Rural	1.426	0.987	1.608	2.090***	1.187	1.310	1.066
Macro regions	Northern hilly region							
Western higher economy region		3.701	1.845***	1.268	0.747	2.543**	3.207**	1.894**
CWE[8] low economy region		2.499	1.182	1.781	0.876	1.304	1.228	1.917**
Southern region		3.927	2.318***	0.830	0.303***	1.264	1.656	1.796**

Note: [1]Induced Abortion [2]Antenatal Check-ups [3]Post-delivery treatment in private services of those women who delivered her child at home [4]Temporary Contraceptive Use [5]Problems related to RTI/STI [6]Treatment of diarrhoea/pneumonia to children of age below 3 years [7]Treatment for any health problem during pregnancy [8]Central-western-eastern; * $p < 0.1$ ** $p < 0.5$ *** $p < 0.01$.

Table 13.12

India: Ranking of Selected States by Extent of Inequality across Three Economic Groups based on SLI[1] and MPCE[2] Groups in Utilisation of Health Care Services

States	Utilisation of Public Health Services[3]		Utilisation of Private Health Services[4]		Utilisation of Health Services in Rural Areas[5]		Utilisation of Health Services in Urban Areas[6]	
	$\sqrt{(\chi^2/N)}$	Rank	$\sqrt{(\chi/N)}$	Rank	$\sqrt{(\chi^2/N)}$	Rank	$\sqrt{(\chi^2/N)}$	Rank
Uttar Pradesh	0.152	6	0.331	7	0.095	13	0.112	13
Bihar	0.108	12	0.253	15	0.012*	15	0.043*	16
West Bengal	0.242	1	0.284	12	0.236	1	0.322	2
Andhra Pradesh	0.103	13	0.326	8	0.193	4	0.207	8
Maharashtra	0.155	5	0.348	6	0.215	2	0.258	6
Rajasthan	0.112	11	0.315	9	0.134	8	0.102	14
Madhya Pradesh	0.145	7	0.400	2	0.121	10	0.282	3
Assam	0.198	2	0.259	14	0.096	12	0.271	5
Tamil Nadu	0.118	10	0.301	11	0.213	3	0.328	1
Orissa	0.196	3	0.303	10	0.074	14	0.151	11
Karnataka	0.102	14	0.386	4	0.105	11	0.199	9
Haryana	0.129	8	0.265	13	0.105	11	0.218	7
Gujarat	0.119	9	0.398	3	0.177	5	0.183	10
Jharkhand	0.159	4	0.377	5	0.122	9	0.057*	15
Chhattisgarh	0.155	5	0.477	1	0.172	6	0.124	12
Kerala	0.046*	15	0.172	16	0.141	7	0.273	4

Notes: [1] Standard of Living Index [2] Monthly Per Capita Expenditure

* not significant

[3] Extent of inequality across three SLI groups in utilisation of Public health services for different RCH health care components.

[4] Extent of inequality across three SLI groups in utilisation of Private health services for different RCH health care components.

[5] Extent of inequality across three MPCE groups in utilisation of public and private health services (for inpatient cases) in rural areas.

[6] Extent of inequality across three MPCE groups in utilisation of public and private health services (for inpatient cases) in urban areas.

relative position of states by inequality among three economic groups regarding each of the selected indicators of health status and utilisation of health services. The first rank shows the highest inequality while 14th or 15th rank shows the lowest inequality. For the same values tied ranks have been given.

The result shows that among the general heath indicators in rural areas, the highest inequality among the economic and social groups combinedly regarding the utilisation of public and private health services has been found in West Bengal, followed by Andhra Pradesh, Maharashtra, Tamil Nadu, Rajasthan, Gujarat and Chhattisgarh. In rural areas, very less inequality have been found in Madhya Pradesh and Assam. Similarly, in urban areas, the highest inequality has been recorded in Maharashtra and Kerala.

Among the four nutritional status indicators, on an average, the highest inequality has been recorded in Gujarat, followed by West Bengal and Orissa. Rajasthan, Madhya Pradesh and Tamil Nadu have recorded relatively better position in comparison to other states.

Likewise, in utilisation of health services for different health care or treatment indicators, on an average, the highest inequality among three SLI groups, has been recorded in Tamil Nadu, followed by Karnataka, Assam, Maharashtra and Chhattisgarh.

References

Berman, Peter (Presentation) in National Planning Workshop on Public Private Partnerships in the Health Sector in India (28.11.2005 to 30.11.2005), organised by National Institute of Health & family Welfare (NIHFW), New Delhi.

Bhat, R. (1997). "Regulation of the Private Health Sector in India", in William New Brander (Eds). *Private Health Sector Growth in Asia: Issues and Implications.*

Bice, Thomas W., David L.Rabin, Barbara H. Starfield, and Kerr L. White (1973). "Economic Class and Use of Physician Services", *Medical Care* 11: 287-296.

Bice, Thomas W., Robert Eichhorn, and Peter D. Fox (1972). "Socioeconomic Status and Use of Physician Services: A Reconsideration", *Medical Care* 10: 261-271.

DAINET NGO Directory (A Directory of Non Governmental Organizations in India) (1998). Published by Development Alternatives. New Delhi.

Duggal, R. and S. Amin (1989). Cost of Health Care. Bombay: FRCH.

Government of India (2005). National Rural Health Mission: Mission Document. Ministry of Health and Family Welfare.

India Health Report (2003). Published by Oxford University Press, New Delhi.

Jamison, Dean T. *et al.* (Ed.) (2006). *Priorities in Health.* Washington, D.C.: World Bank.

Mechanic, David (1969). "Illness and Cure", in John Kosa, Aaron Antonavsky, and Irving Kenneth Zola (eds.), *Poverty and Health.* Cambridge: Harvard University Press.

Montiero, Lois (1973). "Expense is No Object: Income and Physician Visits Reconsidered", *Journal of Health and Social Behaviour* 14: 99-115.

Mooney, G.H. (1983). "Equity in Health Care: Confronting the Confusion", *Effective Health Care* 1: 179.

Mooney, G., Hall J., Donaldsen C, Gerard K. (1991). "Utilization of as a Measure of Equity: Weighing Heat?", *Journal of Health Economics* 10: 475.

Newbrander, William (ed.) (1997). Private Health Sector Growth in Asia. Chichester: John Wiley & Sons.

Private Participation in Health Services (Ed). Published by the World Bank, Washington, D.C.

Singh, Amarjit (2006). "Private Public Partnership: A Solution to Maternal Mortality", *The Journal of Family Welfare* 52(79), Special Issue.

Uplekar, M. (1989a). "Implications of Prescribing Patterns in Private Doctors in the Treatment of Pulmonary Tuberculosis in Bombay, India", *Research Paper* No. 41. Takemi Program in International Health. Cambridge: Harward School of Public Health.

———. (1989b). "Private Doctors and Public Health: The Case of Leprosy in Bombay., India", *Research Paper* No. 40. Takemi Program in International Health. Cambridge: Harward School of Public Health.

Vishwanathan, H., Rohde, J. (1990). *Diarrhoea in Rural India: A Nation–wide Study of Mothers and Practitioners.* New Delhi: Vision Books.

William, N. and M. Patricia (1997). "The Future of Health Sector Reforms in Asia", in William Newbrander (ed.), *Private Health Sector Growth in Asia.* Chichester: John Wiley & Sons.

Yesudian, C. (1990). "Utilization Pattern of Health Services and its Implications for Urban Health Policy", Takemi Program in International Health. Cambridge: Harward School of Public Health.

14

Does Utilisation of Maternal Health Care Services Vary across Regions in Karnataka?

Evidence from the District Level Household Survey, 2002-2004

M. SIVAKAMI

Introduction

Complications related to pregnancy and childbirth are among the leading causes of mortality among women of reproductive age in many developing countries (United Nations, 1995). More than 5,00,000 maternal deaths occur worldwide every year due to pregnancy related complications, out of which 99 per cent occur in developing countries (WHO, 2000). India has the dubious distinction of having the highest estimated number of maternal deaths: an estimated 1,36,000 women die each year from causes related to pregnancy, childbirth and abortion (WHO, 2004). Many more suffer serious complications that can have a severe impact on their quality of life and of their families (ESCAP, 2007).

Existing literature suggests that there are strong linkages between maternal health care use and maternal health. Researchers and policy makers have highlighted the positive impact of antenatal care during pregnancy and hygienic professional institutional care on maternal mortality. The impact of maternal health care on factors other than maternal mortality, namely, family planning, child morbidity, child mortality, reproductive health etc., have also been highlighted. Not surprisingly, therefore, studies have also tried to highlight the determinants of maternal health care use. Important factors that might improve maternal health care use that have been highlighted are education, socioeconomic conditions, awareness and access to health care facilities.

However, regional analyses of both maternal health care use and its determinants are few and far between. At best, studies focus on state-level analysis pointing out for example that south Indian states fare better than north Indian states. This ignores intrastate differences that might be significant. Determinants of health care use might also vary significantly within states and state-level policies might fail to capture these differences. This chapter undertakes such an analysis in Karnataka, a state that fares well over all but has districts that fare as badly as many of the north Indian states.

Maternal Health: Contextualising the Study

According to the Ministry of Health and Family Welfare (MOHFW), Government of India, the major causes of death during pregnancy and child birth include bleeding during pregnancy and puerperum, abortion and anaemia (MOHFW, 1999). Radkar and Parasuraman (2007) in their recent article state that more than 80 per cent of maternal deaths in India are due to six medical causes, namely haemorrhage, eclampsia, obstructed labour, sepsis, complication due to unsafe abortion and anaemia.

Many of these deaths are avoidable by ensuring all pregnant women get adequate antenatal care during pregnancy and that deliveries take place under hygienic conditions with professional health assistance (Fauveau *et al.*, 1988; Fortney *et al.*, 1988). The impact of maternal health care on factors other than maternal mortality, namely, family planning, child morbidity, child mortality, reproductive health etc., are also significant (See Ahmed, 1988; Kapil, 1988; Bhatia, 1989; Ramachandran, 1992 for child mortality and low birth weight; Govindasamy and Ramesh, 1997 for infant mortality; Kogan *et al.*, 1998; Wiecha and Gann, 1994; Butz *et al.*, 1993 for childhood vaccinations; Gemperline *et al.*, 1989; Freed *et al.*, 1999; Ramchandran, 1989; Phillips *et al.*, 1998; Pandey *et al.*, 2004 for child care; Taylor and Singh, 1975; Arole and Arole, 1975; Mishra *et al.*, 1998 for family planning; Magadi *et al.*, 2000; Bhatia and Cleland, 1995; Becker *et al.*, 1993 for reproductive health). But about 50 per cent of Indian women do not receive the minimum three antenatal check-ups during their pregnancy and about 60 per cent of the deliveries take place at home (IIPS and ORC Macro, 2000).[1]

Given the link between maternal health care use and maternal health, it is not surprising that many studies, especially in developing countries, have attempted to identify factors that determine utilisation of maternal health

1. Ante natal care provides an opportunity to identify women who are anemic and encourages mothers to consume iron and folic acid tablets and educate them about the benefits of nutrition that help both the mother and the baby. Tetanus toxoid vaccinations, an important component of ante natal care, given to women during pregnancy, help reduce neonatal mortality (Bhatia, 1989). Ante natal care also helps identify women with high risk pregnancies to ensure safe delivery at a health institution. Ante natal care ensures that the health of the expectant mother, more specifically her nutritional status, is periodically supervised and avoidable complication of pregnancy prevented or treated. It also results in the administration of skilled care and attention by trained health personnel during child birth.

care services. Several studies have also found that education of the mother is an important factor that has a positive impact on utilisation of maternal health care services (Kanitkar and Sinha, 1989; Obermeyer and Potter, 1991; Elo, 1992; Obermeyer, 1993; Goldman and Pebley, 1995; Bhatia and Cleland, 1995; Govindasamy and Ramesh, 1997; Khan *et al.*, 1997; Addai, 1998; Addai, 2000; Navaneetham and Dharmalingam, 2002; Celik and Hotchkiss, 2000; Pandey *et al.*, 2004).

Some others argue that socioeconomic status *per se* has an important bearing on maternal health care use. For example, women who belong to traditionally oppressed castes such as Scheduled Castes and Scheduled Tribes (SCs/STs), who normally live in separate settlements or hamlets and are poor, receive poor maternal health care (Kavitha and Audinarayana, 1997 and Suganthan *et al.*, 2001). But this contention is not universally accepted. Sivakami and Kulkarni (2003) found no caste difference in terms of utilisation of maternal health care services in Tamil Nadu. Navaneetham and Dharmalingam (2002), using NFHS-1 data for all the southern states separately, also found that there is no caste difference in terms of utilisation of ANC care services across all states.

The evidence regarding economic status is also mixed. Numerous studies have highlighted that women from low income families or having a low standard of living are at a disadvantage. Sivakami and Kulkarni (2003) found a strong correlation between economic status and utilisation of ANC services based on their analysis of NFHS-1 data. Other studies have also reached similar conclusions (Umamani and Yogananda, 2006; Pandey, *et al.*, 2002; Bhatia and Cleland, 1995; Obermeyer, 1993; Obermeyer and Potter, 1991; Kanitkar and Sinha, 1989). However, Kavitha and Audinaryayana (1997) found no significant association between income and utilisation of MCH services.

A number of other variables also appear to be important. High parity or high order birth women seem to use maternal health care facilities less (Kwast and Liff, 1988 and Khandekar *et al.*, 1993). In other words, women who are pregnant for the first time tend to use maternal health care services more than women who are pregnant for a second time or more. However, Sivakami and Kulkarni (2003) found that rural women at third order birth are more likely to be visited at home by medical practitioners, a finding that goes contrary to received wisdom. This is possibly because of the selectivity of health workers in terms of their visits to rural areas for the purpose of motivating people to use family planning techniques.

Access to health care facilities in terms of distance also seems to be an important factor that influences utilisation of health care services (Rao and

Richard, 1984; Kumar *et al.*, 1997). Many studies have found that there are also marked rural-urban differences in access to antenatal care services and institutional delivery (Govindasamy and Ramesh, 1997; Obermeyer, 1993) despite the fact that there are networks of primary health centres with auxiliary nurses, midwives, training *anganwadi* workers, accredited social health activists from the community etc. Both these factors are important given the finding of a few studies that when access to health facilities improve, the effect of socioeconomic factors that influence the utilisation of health care facilities becomes less important (Rosenzweig and Schultz, 1982; Govindasamy and Ramesh, 1997).

Unfortunately, most studies have focused on a specific location (state or sub-state) or on a comparative analysis across states. This is not surprising given the fact that until recently there was a paucity of data at the regional level on maternal health care indicators. The District Level Household Survey (DLHS-RCH), however, fills this gap by providing information on maternal health care service use for districts in India. Taking advantage of this data, this chapter sets out to examine whether the level of utilisation of maternal health care varies by different regions in Karnataka. It then attempts to analyse the correlates of maternal health care service use across different regions in Karnataka.

Scenario of Karnataka

While Karnataka appears to be doing well in terms of women receiving antenatal care services, i.e., 90 per cent of women receive such service, there are huge regional variations within the state. There are studies that have highlighted regional variations in fertility levels, population growth and infant and child mortality, and the factors for such regional variations in Karnataka (Sekhar *et al.*, 2001; Government of Karnataka, 1999; Bhat and Zavier, 1999; Bhat, 1996). However, practically no study exists on regional variations in maternal health care indicators in Karnataka, especially using data from large scale surveys. Bhat and Zavier (1999) using NFHS-1 data highlight the regional disparities of a few maternal health care indicators in Karnataka; however, they do not examine the determinants of such disparities especially individual and household level factors (as the purpose of their paper was to highlight the regional variations of various demographic and health indicators). The present chapter hence aims to fill this gap in identifying the individual and household level factors that may not be the same across regions within a state.

Data and Methodology

Data for this study are drawn from Round II, otherwise known as the District Level Household Survey (DLHS), of the RCH programme conducted during 2002-2004. DLHS-RCH collected information from all the 593 districts of the country as per the 2001 Census.[2] DLHS-RCH collected information from currently married women of age 15-44 and their husbands. A total of 28,167 households were covered in Karnataka. From the interviewed households, 22,656 eligible women (usual residents or visitors who stayed in the sample households the night before the interview), who were currently married women and 13,903 husbands of eligible women were interviewed. Detailed information on antenatal, natal and postnatal for all the women whose pregnancy terminated in a live/still birth in the three years preceding the survey was obtained in the survey. Using these information, the following five indicators of maternal health care services were examined in the chapter.

Antenatal Check-up

Various information on antenatal care like whether antenatal care was received, where the antenatal care was sought (private or government), who provided the antenatal care (health professional or trained *dai*/untrained *dai*/ relatives and friends), duration of pregnancy at which the first antenatal check-up was sought and the number of antenatal care check-ups was collected. In this chapter, only one indicator for antenatal care is used: whether women received any antenatal care (yes or no)? This information is computed from two questions in the women's questionnaire: whether women went for an antenatal check-up? (q213) and whether any health worker visited home for an antenatal check-up? (q218). One (1) if women received antenatal care from some one or went for an antenatal check-up, zero (0) if not received.

Tetanus Toxoid (TT) Injection

Women were asked about whether they were given a tetanus toxoid injection to prevent them or their babies from getting tetanus (q228). They were also asked about the number of injections they had during their pregnancy (q229). As two doses of tetanus toxide, one month apart, is the recommended dose, women who received two doses of injection or more are considered as women who had a TT injection. The rest are treated as not having had a TT vaccination. One (1) if received two or more doses of TT injection, zero (0) if received one does or none.

---

2. The information was collected in two phases. Each phase covered half of the districts of all the states and union territories, the same being true of the 27 districts in Karnataka.

Iron and Folic Acid Tablet (IFA) Consumption

Women were asked about the number of iron and folic tablets they consumed during their entire pregnancy (q226). In this chapter, we treat a woman as having consumed iron and folic acid tablets if she has consumed at least 100 tablets, otherwise she is treated as not having consumed iron and folic acid tablets. One (1) if consumed 100 or more iron and folic acid tablets, zero (0) if consumed less than 100 (including none).

Place of Delivery

The place of delivery is an important factor in determining the risk of infant and maternal death. Women were asked about the place in which they delivered (q235). In this chapter, deliveries that took place in any public or private health facility are considered as institutional deliveries and deliveries that took place at home considered as home deliveries. One (1) if delivery took place either in public hospital, sub-centre, primary health centre, trust hospital, private hospital or clinic, zero (0) if delivery took place at home.

Assistance During Delivery

Assistance during delivery is very important especially for the deliveries that take place at home. Generally, assistance during delivery could be provided by health professionals and relatives and friends. If more than one type of attendant assisted the delivery, only the most qualified attendant was considered. Women whose delivery took place at home were asked who assisted or conducted the delivery (q237). One (1) if doctor, auxiliary nurse midwife (ANM), nurse, lady health visitor, trained birth attendant or *dai* assisted the delivery, zero (0) if untrained *dai*, relatives or friends assisted the delivery.

Explanatory Factors

The following are the explanatory factors that could potentially affect the above mentioned maternal health care indicators. These factors were based on the theoretical and empirical evidence obtained from national and international literature on use of maternal health care services. It is worth mentioning here that there are a few variables that have been highlighted as important in existing literature that were not collected in the DLHS-RCH survey and hence those variables were not included in the analysis which are discussed in the section 'limitations of the study'. The explanatory variables can be broadly divided into three categories, namely demographic characteristics, socioeconomic characteristics and other characteristics.

Demographic Characteristics

Age of the woman is considered as one of the important determinants of use of maternal health care services. Earlier studies have found that younger women use health care services more than older women as mentioned earlier (Addai, 2000, Pandey *et al.*, 2004). Age of the woman is categorised into three categories in this chapter: 15-19, 20-34 and 35-44 years. Other demographic variables that determine the use of maternal health care services are parity, order of birth and number of births (Pandey *et al.*, 2004; Sivakami and Kulkarni, 2003; Govindasamy and Ramesh, 1997; Bhatia and Cleland, 1995; Elo, 1992). Only one of the above three variables is normally included in the analysis as these variables are highly correlated. Total number of live births is being used in this chapter to capture this effect. Women are classified into four categories: women with no live birth and one live birth,[3] women with two live births, women with three live births and women with four or more live births. Studies have also found that women who experienced a still birth tend to use health care services more than other women due to known risk factors (Bhatia and Cleland, 1995). A dichotomous variable, women who have experienced still birth and women who have not experienced still birth is used to capture this effect separately.

Socioeconomic Characteristics

Education of women influences their likelihood to seek maternal health care services (Mosley and Chen, 1984; Cleland and Van Ginneken, 1988; Becker *et al.*, 1993; Addai, 1998; Addai, 2000). Hence, in this chapter, the education of the respondent is included. Women are classified into three categories: women who are illiterate, women who are literate to nine years of schooling and women who have 10 or more years of schooling. Place of residence has also been included in the analysis in order to capture the effect of accessibility and availability to health care facilities.

Earlier studies also show a strong association between caste and utilisation of maternal health care services (Kavitha and Audinarayana, 1997; Govindasamy and Ramesh, 1997). In order to capture this effect, two categories of caste are being included in the analysis. The SC/ST category comprises households where the head of the household has specified their caste as SC or ST. The other category includes households that do not belong to SC/ST. Religion is another social variable that could potentially affect use

3. DLHS-RCH 2002-2004 collected information on ANC from women who gave still births as well, hence there are a few women included who had no live birth.

of health care services. Three categories of religion are included in the analysis:[4] Hindu, Muslim and Christian.

The economic dimension also cannot be ignored. In DLHS-RCH, information on household income was not collected and therefore, cannot be included in the analysis. However, a composite measure, *viz.*, standard of living index (SLI) was available which was calculated based on the data on ownership of assets, consumer goods and housing condition.[5] Hence, the SLI is used as a proxy for income in the analysis. Three categories of SLI are included in this chapter: low, medium and high.

Other Characteristics

Women's tendency to seek antenatal care could also be influenced by pregnancy related morbidities. In particular, women who do not normally go for an antenatal check-up may do so in case of acute pregnancy related morbidities such as bleeding, visual disturbances etc. (Liskin, 1992). Further, women who experience pregnancy related morbidities, especially women with acute pregnancy related morbidities, are more likely to seek institutional care (Bhatia and Cleland, 1996; Mahler, 1987). DLHS-RCH, 2002-2004, collected information on various pregnancy related morbidities.[6] Using this information, the variable complication during pregnancy was created. It includes two categories: women who experienced at least one complication during pregnancy and women who experienced no pregnancy complication. This particular variable is also included as one of the explanatory variables for the first three dependent variables, i.e., any antenatal care, TT injection and IFA tablets.

Further, studies have also highlighted that women with complications during delivery are likely to seek institutional care and professional health

---

4. There are a few households that belonged to the Jain religion. These households were included along with Hindus in order to not omit them from the analysis.

5. The SLI was calculated based on the scores of the following items: Source of drinking water: 3 for Tap (own), 2 for Tap (shared), 1 for hand pump and well, and 0 for other; Type of house: 4 for pucca, 2 for semi pucca, and 0 for kachcha; Source of lighting: 2 for electricity, 1 for kerosene, and 0 for other; Fuel for cooking: 2 for LPG gas/ electricity, 1 for kerosene, and 0 for other; Toilet facility: 4 for own flush toilet, 2 for own pit toilet, 2 for shared toilet, and 0 for no toilet; Ownership for items: 4 each for care and tractor, 3 each for television, telephone and motorcycle/scooter, and 2 each for fan, radio/transistor, sewing machine and bicycle. The total score may vary from the lowest of 0 to maximum of 40. On the basis of the total score households were defined into three categories: Low (if total score was less than or equal to 9), Medium (if total score was greater than 9 but less than or equal to 19) and high (if total score was greater than 19).

6. Information on eight pregnancy related morbidities were obtained in DLHS-RCH, 2002-2004. They are: Swelling of hands and feet, paleness, visual disturbances, excessive bleeding, convulsions, weak or no moment of fetus, abnormal position of fetus and any other.

assistance (Bhatia and Cleland, 1996; Mahler, 1987). DLHS-RCH, 2002-2004, collected information on complication during delivery.[7] From this information, the variable complication during delivery was created with two categories: women who experienced at least one complication during delivery and women who experienced no delivery complication. Women's tendency to seek institutional care during delivery could also be influenced by whether women sought antenatal care or not during pregnancy. The antenatal care variable has two categories: no antenatal care received and antenatal care received either at home or at an institution.

These three variables, namely complication during pregnancy, complication during delivery and antenatal care are included along with other explanatory variables in analysing two dependent variables, namely place of delivery and assistance during delivery.

Regional Classification

It should be noted at the outset that the terms 'division' and 'region' are used interchangeably throughout this chapter. The analysis has been done separately for the different divisions/regions in Karnataka. There are various ways to classify districts depending on the focus of the study. For example, for agricultural purpose the districts are grouped into agro-ecological regions. Similarly, the department of revenue has a four-fold 'division' of Karnataka, purely for administrative convenience, divisions that do not overlap with the other systems of classifications. Likewise in this chapter, the classification of districts is based on 'health' divisions, i.e., the administrative classification by the Directorate of Health Services (DHS), Government of Karnataka (GoK), since the focus is on health care services. Further, in the traditional classification,[8] there appears to be a lack of sensitivity towards cultural differences within the regions. For example, in the northern Maidan region, districts within Hyderabad-Karnataka and Mumbai-Karnataka are grouped together although there are significant differences between them. Such a lack of cultural sensitivity appears to be minimum in a classification based on the health division even if the relative homogeneity is not the purpose of such a classification.

The districts of Karnataka are grouped into four health divisions; Gulbarga Division (Gulbarga, Koppal, Bidar, Raichur and Bellary districts), Belgaum

7. Information on six problems experienced during delivery were obtained in DLHS-RCH, 2002-2004. They are: premature labour, excessive bleeding, prolonged labour, obstructed labour, breech presentation and any other.

8. The traditional regional classification of Karnataka is threefold, namely Coastal and Malnad, Southern Maidan and Northern Maidan. Each of these regions covers a huge area. Implementing programs at that scale would miss sub-regional differences.

Division (Belgaum, Bagalkot, Bijapur, Dharwad, Gadag, Haveri and Uttara Kannada districts), Mysore Division (Mysore, Mandya, Mangalore, Chikmagalur, Chamarajanagar, Kodagu, Hassan and Udupi districts) and Bangalore Division (Bangalore Urban, Bangalore Rural, Chitradurga, Davanagere, Kolar, Shimoga and Tumkur districts).

Method of Analysis

Since in the present analysis the dependent variables are dichotomous in nature (whether a service was received or not), the technique of logit regression has been adopted to help assess the influence of certain variables on the probability of occurrence of an event, in this case, the probability of receiving specific maternal health care services. The logit of the probability of occurrence (p) is expressed as a function of explanatory variables in the following manner:

$$\text{logit (p)} = \log (p/(1\text{-}p) = \beta_0 + \Sigma\beta_i X_i ,$$

where X_i are explanatory variables and β_i are regression coefficients to be estimated. The predicted probability of occurrence given a set of values X_i is computed as

$$\frac{e^{\beta_0+\Sigma\beta_i X_i}}{1+e^{\beta_0+\Sigma\beta_i X_i}}$$

As mentioned earlier, the analysis has been done separately for each of the health divisions/regions in order to see if the effects of covariates on the utilisation of maternal health care services differ between the four health divisions/regions.

Results

Table 14.1 presents the distribution of individual and household characteristics of women who had a live birth or still birth in the three year period preceding the survey. Most births, in all the four health divisions in Karnataka, were to women aged 20-34 (over 75 per cent). About 30 per cent of women in Gulbarga division had four or more live births. In the case of Belgaum region it was 16 per cent, Bangalore region 10 per cent and Mysore region 7 per cent. About 6 per cent of women each in Gulbarga and Bangalore divisions and about 4 per cent each in Belgaum and Mysore divisions have had a still birth in the past.

Two-thirds of the women in Gulbaraga region (67 per cent) and about one-third of the women in Mysore (27 per cent) and Bangalore regions (29 per cent) in the sample were illiterate; in Belgaum region, this figure was 43 per cent. Nearly 50 per cent of the respondent's husbands were illiterate in Gulbarga region; it was approximately one-third in Belgaum (32 per cent) and Bangalore divisions (29 per cent) and one-fourth in Mysore region (25 per cent). A majority of the population live in rural areas in all the four regions. The sample was predominately Hindu (about 80 per cent). About one-fourth of the sample households in Mysore and Bangalore divisions were classified within the high standard of living index; it was 19 per cent in Belgaum division and 11 per cent in Gulbarga division.

Utilisation of Maternal Health Care Services

The utilisation of maternal health care services for all four divisions in Karnataka is presented in Table 14.2. Almost all women in Mysore and Bangalore regions received antenatal care (over 95 per cent). The corresponding figure for Belgaum division was 91 per cent. In Gulbarga region, one in every five women neither visited antenatal care centres nor were medically checked at home. Although most women (except in Gulbarga region) received antenatal check-ups, a considerable number of women in Karnataka did not receive the required two doses of TT injection during delivery. Most women in Mysore region received the required doses of TT injection (about 90 per cent). However, 37 per cent of women in Gulbarga region and 21 per cent in Belgaum region did not receive two doses of the TT injection. The corresponding figure for Bangalore region was 14 per cent.

As mentioned earlier, in order to tackle the issue of anaemia, pregnant women are advised to consume 100 iron and folic acid tablets during pregnancy. However, only very few women consumed the required iron and folic acid tablets (IFA) in all the four regions. Over 70 per cent of women each in Gulbarga and Belgaum regions did not consume the required amount of IFA tables. The corresponding figure for Mysore and Bangalore regions was 66 and 60 per cent respectively.

Table 14.1

Individual and Household Characteristics of Women in Karnataka, RCH 2002-2004$

Background Characteristics	*Gulbarga Division*	*Belgaum Division*	*Mysore Division*	*Bangalore Division*
Age group (in yrs)				
15-19	18.5	19.3	10.5	14.3
20-34	76.0	77.7	85.5	82.1
35-44	5.4	3.0	4.0	3.5
Number of live births&				
0	0.8	0.7	0.6	1.0
1	25.2	31.1	38.8	37.0
2	24.6	32.4	39.1	36.5
3	20.0	20.3	14.2	15.9
4 and more	29.5	15.5	7.3	9.6
Women ever had still birth#				
No	94.4	95.8	95.6	93.7
Yes	5.6	4.2	4.4	6.3
Education of the women				
Non-literate	67.0	42.6	27.1	29.3
0-9 years@	18.7	33.5	43.5	38.7
10 years and above	14.3	23.9	29.4	31.9
Education of the husband				
Non-Literate	47.5	32.0	25.2	28.6
0-9 years@	22.5	29.3	39.5	32.0
10 years and above	29.9	38.7	35.3	39.4
Place of residence				
Rural	75.6	66.3	69.3	61.6
Urban	24.4	33.7	30.7	38.4
Religion				
Hindu	79.9	82.6	82.4	80.4
Muslim	18.2	16.1	14.9	16.6
Christian	1.8	0.6	1.8	1.9
Others	0.1	0.8	0.9	1.0
Caste				
SCST	32.4	23.8	26.0	30.8
Non SCST	67.6	76.2	74.0	69.2
Standard of living index				
Low	58.4	43.3	40.3	35.9
Medium	30.2	37.8	36.7	38.8
High	11.4	18.9	23.0	25.3
N	1912	2078	1730	1819

Note: Missing cases are excluded for computing percentages.

$: Women who had live births/still births in the three years preceding the survey.

&: DLHS-RCH 2002-2004 collected information on ANC from women who gave still births as well, hence there are a few women included who had no live birth.

@: Literate women/men with no years of schooling but who are able to read and write are also included.

#: Information on still birth was available from two questions in the women's questionnaire: 1) Whether women experienced any still birth (w121) and 2) what was the outcome of the last pregnancy (w202). The still birth variable for the present analysis was computed based on question w121 as it provides information of women who ever experienced still birth in their life time. However, there were 21 cases considered missing cases where the last pregnancy resulted in still birth. These were included in the present analysis.

Table 14.2

Utilisation of Maternal Health Care in Karnataka, RCH 2002-2004[$]

Maternal Health Care Indicators (in Per cent)	*Gulbarga Division*	*Belgaum Division*	*Mysore Division*	*Bangalore Division*
Ante natal care received				
Not received	20.4	9.4	2.1	5.0
Received	79.6	90.6	97.9	95.0
TT injection during pregnancy				
Not taken or single dose	37.3	20.6	10.8	16.3
Two doses and more	62.7	79.4	89.2	83.7
IFA tablets consumed during pregnancy				
Not taken or less than 100	75.3	70.4	65.5	60.0
100 and more	24.7	29.6	34.5	40.0
Place of delivery				
Home	70.0	44.2	24.8	35.7
Health Institution	30.0	55.8	75.2	64.3
N	1912	2078	1730	1819
Assistance during delivery for home delivery				
Non health professional	72.1	63.1	62.7	62.4
Health Professional[#]	27.9	36.9	37.3	37.6
N	1338	919	431	651

Note: Missing cases are excluded for computing percentages.

$: see footnote to table 14.1.

TT: Tetanus Toxoid injection.

IFA tablets: Iron and Folic Acid tablets.

#: Health professionals include doctors, nurses, midwives, Auxiliary Nurse Midwives, Lady Health Visitors, and trained traditional birth attendants.

Table 14.3

Regional Differentials in Utilisation of Maternal Health Care Services after Controlling for Socioeconomic and Demographic Factors in Karnataka, RCH 2002-2004$

Divisions	*Antenatal Check Up*		*TT Injection*		*IFA Tablets*		*Institutional Delivery*		*Assistance during Delivery*	
	Odds Ratios	*Beta Coefficients*	*Odds Ratios*	*Beta Coefficients*	*Odds Ratios*	*Beta Coefficients*	*Odds Ratios*	*Betas Coefficients*	*Odds Ratios*	*Beta Coefficients*
Gulbarga (reference)	1.000	0.000	1.000	0.000	1.000	0.000	1.000	0.000	1.000	0.000
Belgaum	0.705***	-0.349	0.959***	-0.041	0.903**	-0.101	0.929	-0.072	1.063	0.061
Mysore	2.616***	0.961	1.756*	0.563	0.983	-0.016	2.270***	0.820	1.093	0.089
Bangalore	1.177*	0.163	1.094***	0.090	1.298***	0.261	1.157***	0.146	1.053	0.051
Constant	3.982		1.835		-0.807		0.776		-0.282	
-2 log likelihood	3706.111		7022.710		9027.689		7320.929		4003.485	
N	7539		7537		7539		7536		3339	

Note: Missing cases are excluded from the analysis

$: see footnote to table 14.1.

TT: Tetanus Toxoid injection.

IFA tablets: Iron and Folic Acid tablets. *** significant at 1 per cent level; ** significant at 5 per cent level; * significant at 10 per cent level.

Control variables included in the model are: Age of the women, number of live births, women ever had still birth, education of the women, education of the husband, place of residence, religion, caste, standard of living index and complication during pregnancy. In addition to these variables, complication during delivery and ante natal care check up were also included in the case of place of delivery and assistance during delivery.

Table 14.4

Determinants of Receiving Antenatal Check-up in Karnataka, RCH 2002-2004[$]

(1 if Received from Someone or Went for Check-up, 0 if not Received)

Background Characteristics	*Gulbarga Division*	*Belgaum Division*	*Mysore Division*	*Bangalore Division*
Age group (in yrs)				
Below 20 (reference)	1.000	1.000	1.000	1.000
20-34	1.193*	1.061	1.718**	1.072
35 and above	0.919	1.313	0.700	0.938
Number of live births[&]				
0-1 (reference)	1.000	1.000	1.000	1.000
2	1.170	1.177	0.950	1.411*
3	0.762**	0.673***	1.474	1.173
4 and more	0.673***	0.462***	0.424**	0.335***
Women ever had still birth[#]				
No (reference)	1.000	1.000	1.000	1.000
Yes	0.769**	0.877	0.902	0.988
Education of the women				
Non-literate (reference)	1.000	1.000	1.000	1.000
0-9 years[@]	1.227	1.015	0.817	1.228
10 + years	2.211***	1.789**	2.461*	1.976*
Education of the husband				
Non-Literate (reference)	1.000	1.000	1.000	1.000
0-9 years[@]	0.979	1.115	1.964	1.414
10 and more	1.189	1.094	0.754	0.917
Place of residence				
Rural (reference)	1.000	1.000	1.000	1.000
Urban	1.158	1.188	0.940	1.039
Religion				
Hindu (reference)	1.000	1.000	1.000	1.000
Muslim	0.590	0.317	0.194	0.197
Christian	4.018**	10.507	22.654	12.414
Caste				
SCST (reference)	1.000	1.000	1.000	1.000
Non SCST	0.952	1.240**	0.951	1.413***
Standard of living index				
Low (reference)	1.000	1.000	1.000	1.000
Medium	0.996	0.851	1.113	0.847
High	1.545*	1.533*	1.084	2.548*
Complication during pregnancy				
No (reference)	1.000	1.000	1.000	1.000
Yes	1.431***	1.678***	1.582	1.464*
Constant	3.281	4.159	5.398	4.858
-2 log likelihood	1665.893	1108.999	312.983	550.907
N	1912	2078	1730	1819

Note: Missing cases are excluded from the analysis.

$, &, @ and #: see footnote to table 14.1. *** significant at 1 per cent level; ** significant at 5 per cent level; * significant at 10 per cent level.

Table 14.5

Determinants of Receiving Tetanus Toxoid (TT) Injection during Pregnancy in Karnataka, RCH 2002-2004[$]

(1 if Received 2 or More Doses, 0 if not Received)

Background Characteristics	*Gulbarga Division*	*Belgaum Division*	*Mysore Division*	*Bangalore Division*
Age group (in yrs)				
Below 20 (reference)	1.000	1.000	1.000	1.000
20-34	1.123	0.976	0.996	0.946
35 and above	0.880	1.067	0.881	1.047
Number of live births[&]				
0-1 (reference)	1.000	1.000	1.000	1.000
2	1.084	1.068	1.053	1.397***
3	0.875	0.977	1.414*	1.071
4 and more	0.763***	0.772**	0.509***	0.591***
Women ever had still birth[#]				
No (reference)	1.000	1.000	1.000	1.000
Yes	0.966	1.024	0.880	0.978
Education of the women				
Non-literate (reference)	1.000	1.000	1.000	1.000
0-9 years@	1.187**	1.199**	1.089	1.096
10 + years	1.697***	1.353**	1.038	1.172
Education of the husband				
Non-literate (reference)	1.000	1.000	1.000	1.000
0-9 years@	0.898	1.051	0.949	1.191
10 and more	1.346***	1.026	1.006	1.143
Place of residence				
Rural (reference)	1.000	1.000	1.000	1.000
Urban	1.058	0.886*	0.888	0.970
Religion				
Hindu (reference)	1.000	1.000	1.000	1.000
Muslim	0.771	0.236	0.165	1.257
Christian	2.276**	19.257	29.808	0.891
Caste				
SCST (reference)	1.000	1.000	1.000	1.000
Non SCST	1.027	1.005	0.961	1.048
Standard of living index				
Low (reference)	1.000	1.000	1.000	1.000
Medium	1.141*	1.121	1.039	0.926
High	1.389**	1.091	1.284	1.258
Complication during pregnancy				
No (reference)	1.000	1.000	1.000	1.000
Yes	1.183**	0.934	0.757***	0.969
Constant	1.674	2.939	3.386	1.663
-2 log likelihood	2226.984	2025.861	1133.076	1524.305
N	1912	2078	1728	1819

Note: Missing cases are excluded from the analysis

$ & @ and #: see footnote to table 14.1. *** significant at 1 per cent level; ** significant at 5 per cent level; * significant at 10 per cent level.

Table 14.6

Determinants of Iron and Folic Acid (IFA) Tablets Consumed during Pregnancy in Karnataka, RCH 2002-2004$

(1 if Consumed 100 or More Tablets, 0 if not Received)

Background Characteristics	*Gulbarga Division*	*Belgaum Division*	*Mysore Division*	*Bangalore Division*
Age group (in yrs)				
Below 20 (reference)	1.000	1.000	1.000	1.000
20-34	1.137	1.370***	1.281**	0.809**
35 and above	1.303	1.164	0.942	1.422**
Number of live births&				
0-1 (reference)	1.000	1.000	1.000	1.000
2	0.883	0.908	1.020	1.199
3	0.820**	1.208	0.974	1.003
4 and more	0.682***	0.665***	0.799	0.624***
Women ever had still birth#				
No (reference)	1.000	1.000	1.000	1.000
Yes	0.992	1.177	0.847	1.066
Education of the women				
Non-literate (reference)	1.000	1.000	1.000	1.000
0-9 years@	1.138*	1.125*	1.003	1.144*
10 + years	1.275**	1.247**	1.212**	1.169*
Education of the husband				
Non-literate (reference)	1.000	1.000	1.000	1.000
0-9 years@	0.991	1.046	0.994	0.966
10 and more	1.237**	1.030	1.309***	1.173**
Place of residence				
Rural (reference)	1.000	1.000	1.000	1.000
Urban	1.211***	1.204***	0.884	0.963
Religion				
Hindu (reference)	1.000	1.000	1.000	1.000
Muslim	0.894	0.893	0.971	0.913
Christian	1.382	1.062	1.237	0.891
Caste				
SCST (reference)	1.000	1.000	1.000	1.000
Non SCST	1.076	1.085	1.041	1.122
Standard of living index				
Low (reference)	1.000	1.000	1.000	1.000
Medium	0.906	0.912	0.986	0.970
High	1.364**	1.066	1.057	1.054
Complication during pregnancy				
No (reference)	1.000	1.000	1.000	1.000
Yes	1.076	1.094	0.999	0.896
Constant	-0.702	-0.889	-1.025	-0.623
-2 log likelihood	1984.609	2410.687	2160.387	2367.894
N	1912	2078	1730	1819

Note: Missing cases are excluded from the analysis
$, &, @ and #: see footnote to table 14.1. *** significant at 1 per cent level; ** significant at 5 per cent level; * significant at 10 per cent level.

Table 14.7

Determinants of Institutional Delivery of Birth in Karnataka, RCH 2002-2004$

(1 if Delivered at Health Care Institution, 0 if Delivered at Home)

Background Characteristics	Gulbarga Division	Belgaum Division	Mysore Division	Bangalore Division
Age group (in yrs)				
Below 20 (reference)	1.000	1.000	1.000	1.000
20-34	1.019	1.195	0.853	0.885
35 and above	1.592**	1.009	2.143***	1.615**
Number of live births&				
0-1 (reference)	1.000	1.000	1.000	1.000
2	0.886	0.786	0.950	0.865
3	0.843	0.900	0.904	0.787**
4 and more	0.611***	0.622***	0.521***	0.633***
Women ever had still birth#				
No (reference)	1.000	1.000	1.000	1.000
Yes	1.481***	0.784*	1.112	0.940
Education of the women				
Non-literate (reference)	1.000	1.000	1.000	1.000
0-9 years@	0.876	0.866	1.120	0.942
10 + years	1.821***	1.738***	1.276**	1.652***
Education of the husband				
Non-literate	1.000	1.000	1.000	1.000
0-9 years@	0.877	1.040	1.061	0.885
10 and more	1.346***	1.303***	1.191	1.577***
Place of residence				
Rural (reference)	1.000	1.000	1.000	1.000
Urban	1.628***	1.849***	1.526***	1.592***
Religion				
Hindu (reference)	1.000	1.000	1.000	1.000
Muslim	1.112	0.650	0.652	0.950
Christian	0.924	1.479	2.719	1.573
Caste				
SCST (reference)	1.000	1.000	1.000	1.000
Non SCST	1.174**	1.253***	1.336***	1.088
Standard of living index				
Low (reference)	1.000	1.000	1.000	1.000
Medium	0.852	0.973	0.877	0.909
High	1.387**	1.457***	2.236***	1.489***
Complication during pregnancy				
No (reference)	1.000	1.000	1.000	1.000
Yes	1.156*	1.173**	0.877	1.085
Complication during delivery				
No (reference)	1.000	1.000	1.000	1.000
Yes	1.631***	1.627***	1.504***	1.432***

contd...

contd...

Background Characteristics	*Gulbarga Division*	*Belgaum Division*	*Mysore Division*	*Bangalore Division*
Ante natal care visit				
No (reference)	1.000	1.000	1.000	1.000
Yes			1.933***	1.473***
Constant	-0.053	0.313	1.742	1.086
-2 log likelihood	1736.811	2173.025	1517.769	1806.790
N	1912	2076	1729	1819

Note: Missing cases are excluded from the analysis
$, &, @ and #: see footnote to table 14.1. *** significant at 1 per cent level; ** significant at 5 per cent level; * significant at 10 per cent level.

Table 14.8

Determinants of Assistance during Delivery by Health Professional for Non-Institutional Delivery in Karnataka, RCH 2002-2004[$]

(1 if Assisted by Health Professional, 0 If Assisted by Untrained Birth Attendant or Friends and Relatives)

Background Characteristics	*Gulbarga Division*	*Belgaum Division*	*Mysore Division*	*Bangalore Division*
Age group (in yrs)				
Below 20 (reference)	1.000	1.000	1.000	1.000
20-34	1.081	1.318	0.980	1.021
35 and above	0.850	0.807	0.987	1.216
Number of live births[&]				
0-1 (reference)	1.000	1.000	1.000	1.000
2	0.970	0.895	1.051	0.966
3	0.998	1.087	0.907	0.782
4 and more	0.855	0.782	0.740	0.862
Women ever had still birth[#]				
No (reference)	1.000	1.000	1.000	1.000
Yes	0.956	0.886	1.002	0.765
Education of the women				
Non-literate (reference)	1.000	1.000	1.000	1.000
0-9 years[@]	0.830	0.911	0.985	0.968
10 + years	1.528**	1.532**	1.429	1.262
Education of the husband				
Non-literate (reference)	1.000	1.000	1.000	1.000
0-9 years[@]	1.107	1.070	0.909	0.883
10 and more	1.074	0.883	1.506*	1.120
Place of residence				
Rural (reference)	1.000	1.000	1.000	1.000
Urban	1.321***	0.952	1.909***	1.228
Religion				
Hindu (reference)	1.000	1.000	1.000	1.000
Muslim	0.862	0.251	6.055	1.065
Christian	1.530	16.135	0.028	0.644

contd...

contd...

Background Characteristics	*Gulbarga Division*	*Belgaum Division*	*Mysore Division*	*Bangalore Division*
Caste				
SCST (reference)	1.000	1.000	1.000	1.000
Non SCST	1.161**	1.107	1.302**	1.324***
Standard of living index				
Low (reference)	1.000	1.000	1.000	1.000
Medium	0.997	1.005	0.979	0.941
High	1.225	1.263	1.131	1.515
Complication during pregnancy				
No (reference)	1.000	1.000	1.000	1.000
Yes	0.944	0.924	1.078	0.881
Complication during delivery				
No (reference)	1.000	1.000	1.000	1.000
Yes	1.397***	1.126	1.146	1.039**
Ante natal care visit				
No (reference)	1.000	1.000	1.000	1.000
Yes	1.113	1.415***	2.685**	1.195
Constant	-0.152	0.562	-2.343	-0.750
-2 log likelihood	1490.770	1157.235	500.289	802.251
N	1338	919	431	651

Note: Missing cases are excluded from the analysis.

$, &, @ and #: see footnote to table 14.1.

*** significant at 1 per cent level; ** significant at 5 per cent level; * significant at 10 per cent level.

References

Addai, I. (1998). "Demographic and socio cultural factors influencing use of maternal health services in Ghana", *African Journal of Reproductive Health* 2: 73-80.

Addai, I. (2000). "Determinants of sue of maternal child health services in rural Ghana", *Journal of Bio Social Sciences* 32(1): 1-15.

Ahmed, F.U. (1988). "The impact of maternal health on child health", *In Touch* 12(89): 19-22.

Arole, G. and R. Arole (1975). "A comprehensive rural health project in Jamkhed (India)", in Newell K.W. (ed.), Health by the People, World Health Organisation, Geneva.

Basu, A.M. (1997). "Mother's education and childhood mortality: The status of women as a proximate determinant", in Visaria L., J. Simons and P. Berman (eds.), *Maternal Education and Child Survival*. Delhi: Vikas Publishing House Pvt. Ltd.

Becker, S., H.P. David, H.G. Ronald, G. Connie and E.B. Robert (1993). "The determinants of use of maternal and child health services in Metro Cebu, the Philippines", *Health Transition Review* 3(2): 77-89.

Bhat, Mari P.N. (1996). "Contours of fertility Decline in India: A district level study based on 1991 Census", in Srinivasan K. (ed.), *Policy and Reproductive Health*, Hindustan Publisher Corporation, New Delhi.

Bhat, Mari P.N. and F. Zavier (1999). "Findings of national family health survey: Regional analysis", *Economic and Political Weekly* 34(42 and 43): 3008-3032.

Bhatia, J.C. and J. Cleland (1995). "Determinants of maternal care in a region of South India", *Health Transition Review* 5(1): 127-142.

Bhatia, J.C. and J. Cleland (1996). "Obstetric morbidity in south India: Results from community survey", *Social Science and Medicine* 43(10): 1507-1516.

Bhatia, S. (1989). "Patterns and cause of neonatal and post neonatal mortality in rural Bangladesh", *Studies in Family Planning* 20(3): 136-146.

Butz, A.M., A. Funkhouser, L. Caleb and B.J. Rosenstein (1993). "Infant health care utilization predicted by pattern of prenatal care", *Pediatrics* 92(1): 50-54.

Caldwell, J.C., P.H. Reddy and P. Caldwell (1983). "The social component of mortality decline: An investigation in south India employing alternative methodologies", *Population Studies* 37(2): 185-205.

Celik, Y. and D.R. Hotchkiss (2002). "The socio economic determinants of maternal health care utilization in Turkey", *Social Science and Medicine* 50(12): 1797-1806.

Cleland, J. and J. Van Ginneken (1988). "Maternal education and child survival in developing countries: The search for pathways of influence", *Social Science and Medicine* 27(12): 1357-1368.

Dyson, T. and M. Moore (1983). "On kinship, female autonomy and demographic behavior in India", *Population and Development Review* 20(1): 115-136.

Elo, I.T. (1992). "Utilization of maternal health care services in Peru: The role of women's education", *Health Transition Review* 2(1): 49-69.

ESCAP (2007). "Population Headliners", *Economic and Social Commission for Asia and the Pacific*. July-August. No 319.

Fauveau, V., M. Koenig, Chakraborty and A. Chowdhury (1988). "Causes of maternal mortality in rural Bangladesh: 1976-1985", *Bulletin of the World Health Organization* 66: 643-51.

Fortney, J.A., I. Susanti, S. Gadalla, S. Saleh, P.J. Feldblum and Potts (1988). "Maternal mortality in Indonesian and Egypt", *British Journal of Gynecology and Obstetrics* 26(1): 21-32.

Freed, G.L., S.J. Clark, D.E. Pathman and R. Schectman (1999). "Influences on the receipt of well child visits in the first two years of life", *Pediatric (Journal of the Ambulatory Pediatric Association)* 103: 864-869.

Gemperline, P., J. Brockert and L.M. Osborn (1989). "Preventive health care utilization, prenatal and first 3 years in a Utah population", *Clinical Pediatrics* 28: 24-37.

Goldman, N. and A.R. Pebley (1994). "Childhood immunization and pregnancy related services in Guatemala", *Health Transition Review* 4(1): 29-44.

Govindaswamy, P. and B.M. Ramesh (1997). "Maternal education and utilization of maternal and child heath services in India", *NFHS Survey Subject Report No. 5*. International Institute for Population Sciences, Mumbai, India and Macro International Inc. Calverton, Maryland, USA.

International Institute for Population Sciences (IIPS) and ORC Macro (2000). *National Family Heath Survey (NFHS-2), 1998-99: India*, Mumbai, India: IIPS.

International Institute for Population Sciences (IIPS) (2007). "National family health survey-3 (NFHS-3), 2005-06, Facts sheets for India (provisional data)", *International Institute for Population Sciences*, Mumbai.

Kanitkar, Tara (1979). "Development of maternal and child health services in India", in Srinivasan K. *et al.* (eds.), *Demographic and Socio Economic Aspects of the Child in India*, Himalaya Publishing House, Bombay.

Kapil, U. (1988). "Strategies to reduce perinatal and neonatal mortality", *Indian Pediatrics* 26(3): 301-302.

Karve, I. (1965). *Kinship Organization in India*. Bombay: Asia Publishing House.

Kavitha, N. and N. Audinarayana (1997). "Utilization and determination of selected maternal and child health care in rural areas of Tamil Nadu", *Health and Population Perspectives and Issues* 20(3): 112-125.

Khan, A.G., N. Roy and S. Surender (1997). "Utilization of reproductive health services in rural Maharashtra", *The Journal of Family Welfare*.

Khandekar, J.S., M. Dwivedi and M. Bhattacharya (1993). "Childbirth practices among women in slum areas", *The Journal of Family Welfare*.

Kogan, M.D., G.R. Alexander, B.W. Jack and M.C. Allen (1998). "The association between adequacy of prenatal care utilization and subsequent pediatric care utilization in the United States", *Pediatrics*, 102.

Kumar, R., M.M. Singh and M. Kaur (1997). "Impact of health centre availability on utilization of maternity care and pregnancy outcome in a rural area of Haryana", *Journal of the Indian Medical Association* 95(8): 448-450.

Kwast, B.E. and J.M. Liff (1988). "Factors associated with maternal mortality in Addis Ababa, Ethiopia", *International Journal of Epidemiology* 17(1): 115-121.

Liskin, L.S. (1992). "Maternal Morbidity in developing countries: A review and comments", *International Journal of Gynecology and Obstetrics* 37(1): 77-87.

Magadi, M.A., N.J. Madise and R.N. Rodrigues (2000). "Frequency and timing of antenatal care in Kenya: Explaining variations between women of different communities", *Social Science and Medicine* 5(4): 551-561.

Mahler, H. (1987). "The safe motherhood initiative: A call to action", *Lancet* 1(8534): 668-670.

Mishra, U.S., T.K. Roy and S.I. Rajan (1998). "Antenatal care and contraceptive behaviour in India: Some evidence form NFHS", *The Journal of Family Welfare*.

MOHFW (1999). *Health Information of India 1997-98*. Ministry of Health and Family Welfare, Government of India. PP 255.

Mosley, W.H. and L.C. Chen (1984). "An analytical framework for the study of child survival in developing countries", in Mosley W.H. and L.C. Chen (eds.), *Child Survival: Strategies for Research, Population and Development Review* 10 supplement.

Navaneetham, K. and A. Dharmalingam (2002). "Utilization of maternal health care services in Southern India", *Social Science and Medicine* 55(10): 1849-1869.

Obermeyer, C.M. (1993). "Culture, maternal health care and women's status: A comparison of Morocco and Tunisia", *Studies in Family Planning* 24(3): 354-365.

Obermeyer, C.M. and J.E. Potter (1991). "Maternal health care utilization in Jordan: A study of patterns and determinants", *Studies in Family Planning* 22(3): 177-187.

Pandey, A., M. Pradeep and A. Ojha (2002). "An analysis of the child spacing effect of the utilization of maternal health care services in some selected states of India", in Pandey CM, Pradeep Mishra and Uttam Singh (eds) in *Biostatistical Aspects if Health and Epidemiology*, pp 91-100.

Pandey, A., N. Roy, A. Sahu and R. Acharya (2004). "Maternal health care services: Observations from Chhattisgarh, Jharkhand and Uttaranchal", *Economic and Political Weekly* 39(9): 713-720.

Phillips, J.F., S. Wayne, S. Bhatia, M. Rahman and J. Chakraborty (1998). "The demographic impact of the family planning health services project in Matlap, Bangaldesh", in Foreit, J.R. and T. Frejka (eds.), *Family Planning Operations Research*. New York: The Population Council.

Radkar, A. and S. Parasuraman (2007). "Maternal deaths in India: An exploration", *Economic and Political Weekly* 42(31): 3259-3263.

Ramachandran, L. (1989). "The effect of antenatal and natal services on pregnancy outcome and health of the mother and child", *Journal of Family Welfare* 35(5): 34-46.

Ramachandran, Prema (1992). "Need for organization of antenatal and intra-partum care in India", *Demography India* 21(2): 179-193.

Rao, P.S. and J. Richard (1984). "Socio economic and demographic correlated of medical care and health practices", *Journal of Biosocial Science* 16(3): 343-55.

Ray, S.K., B.B. Mukhopodhyay, R. Das, M.M. Ganguly, A. Maidal and S.C. Roy (1984). "Extent of utilization of maternal health care services of PHC by families of rural area", *Indian Journal of Public Health* 28(3): 122-127.

Rosenzweig, M. and T.P. Schultz (1982). "Child mortality and fertility in Colombia: individual and community effects", *Health Policy and Education* 2(4): 305-348.

Sekher, T.V., K.N.M. Raju and M.N. Sivakumar (2001). "Fertility transition in Karnataka: Levels, trends and implications", *Economic and Political Weekly* 36(51): 4742-4752.

Sivakami, M. and P.M. Kulkarni (2003). "Are socially and economically weaker sections deprived of maternal health care in Tamil Nadu, India?", *Journal of Health and Population in Developing Countries*, August 07: pp 1-15.

Sugathan, K.S., V. Mishra and R.D. Retherford (2001). "Promoting institutional deliveries in rural India: The role antenatal-care services", *National Family Health Survey Subject Reports. Number 20*. International Institute for Population Sciences, Mumbai, India and East West Center, Population and Health Studies, Honolulu, Hawaii, USA.

Taylor, C.E. and R.D. Singh (1975). "The Narangwal population study: Integrated health and family planning services", *Rural Health Research Centre*, Narangwal, Punjab, India, Mimeographed.

Umamani, K.S. and C. Yogananda (2006). "Choice of birth places-home vs hospital: Evidence from rural Karnataka", *Demography India* 35(1): 15-30.

United Nations (1995). *Report of the International Conference on Population and Development*, Cairo, 5-13 September 1994, New York: United Nations.

WHO (2000). "Pregnancy exposes women in poor states to 200 fold risk of death compared with rich ones says WHO", *Populi* 27(2).

WHO (2004). *Maternal mortality in 2000: Estimates developed by WHO, UNICEF, UNFPA*. Report. World Health Organization, Geneva.

Wiecha, J.M. and P. Gann (1994). "Does maternal prenatal care use predict infant immunization delay?", *Family Medicine* 26(2): 172-178.

15

Child Mortality and Health in India

SURESH SHARMA

Introduction

Childhood mortality is one of the important indicators of a country's general medical and public health conditions and consequently, the country's level of socioeconomic development. Its decline is therefore not only desirable but also indicative of an improvement in general living standards. The history of childhood as a modern concept is embedded in the narrative of the modern, welfare state. Childhood as a protected and prolonged period of life owes its recognition to popular struggles for welfare waged by the working classes in the context of the sweeping changes brought into their lives by the industrial revolution during the 18th and the 19th centuries.

In India, 2.1 million children die before their fifth birthday. Half of these children die even before they are 28 days old, according for one-fourth global infant deaths. Of the 9.7 million child deaths worldwide annually, one-third occur in India. The statistics are equally shocking among neonates—children new born to a maximum age of 28 days old. While around 4 million children die within the first 28 days of life across the planet every year, India records around one million of these cases. Among the reasons cited for the poor state of infant and child health in India are inadequate neonatal care, insufficient breastfeeding, malnutrition, low immunity and high incidence of communicable diseases. Breastfeeding a baby within an hour of birth is said to markedly increase its change of survival since breast milk contains vital nutrients and antibodies that enhance a baby's immunity. Benefits accrue to the mother too for breastfeeding helps her uterus contract post-delivery and burn calories and fat accumulated during pregnancy. It also releases beneficial hormones into the mother's baby. Of the 19 million infants in the developing world who have low birth (less than 2,500 gram), 8.3 million are in India. This means that approximately 43 per cent of all the world's infants who are born with a low birth weight are born in India.

The infant mortality rate (IMR)—probability of dying before one year of age expressed per 1000 live births—and under-five mortality rate (U5MR)—probability of dying between birth and age 5 expressed per 1000 live births—have been used as measures of children's well-being for many years. The Sixth and Seventh Five Year Plans had aimed at nationwide programmes to realise this goal. The twenty-point programme included, as a key component, rapid improvement in the conditions of women and children. In 1979, the Expanded Programme of Immunisation (EPI) was established to provide tetanus toxoid (TT) vaccine to pregnant women and BCG, DPT, polio and measles vaccine to children. The Universal Immunisation Programme (UIP) and Oral Rehydration Therapy (ORT) were both launched in 1985 and the Safe Motherhood Programme initiated during the Eighth Plan was a prominent component of the Family Welfare Programme. In the early 1990s, these programmes were integrated and further strengthened to shape the Child Survival and Safe Motherhood (CSSM) Programme. In 1994, the CSSM Programme was further expanded to the Reproductive and Child Health (RCH) services. These programmes had the desired effect of reducing child mortality and improving child health as evidenced from the child mortality statistics of 1978–2002. The National Population Policy (2000) and National Health Policy (2002) addressed the issues of child survival and maternal health, and increased the outreach and coverage of the comprehensive package of RCH services through the government as well as the voluntary non-government sector together in partnership.

The objective of this paper is to examine the determinants of childhood mortality and child health in India and the factors explaining the differential performance of the child immunisation and treatment of childhood diseases. It also looks into the levels of IMR and U5MR among socially and economically disadvantaged groups. The knowledge of these factors is important for policy formulation and implementation because it will enable policymakers to formulate appropriate policies for the reduction of childhood mortality by paying special attention to the disadvantaged sub-groups.

Data and Methods

The NFH surveys have emerged as an important source of reliable information on demographic, health and nutrition for India. Data from India provide a unique opportunity to examine how changes in under-five mortality are related to the changes in risk factors under varying economic and social conditions in some detail. Virtually, all of the analysis in this paper is based on two sets of national household surveys. First, unit record data from two rounds of the nationally-representative National Family Health Survey

(NFHS) are used to analyse the correlates of infant mortality and child malnutrition (underweight) (International Institutes for Population Science (IIPS), 1995). Second, record data from the two most recent quinquennial, 'thick' rounds of the National Sample Survey (NSS)—the 55th Round conducted in 1999-2000—are used for two groups of states. Since the NSS data do not contain information on infant mortality or child weights, the NFHS data remained as the only alternative to analyse these indicators. In addition, the sample registration system (SRS) under the Registrar General of India provides the estimates of births and deaths at state/national level. For two groups of states: poor states (i.e., those that have a monthly per capita consumption expenditure of Rs. 676 or less according to the NSS 1999-2000 Round) and non-poor states (those having a per capita consumption expenditure of more than Rs. 676). Defined in this manner, the poor states are Andhra Pradesh, Assam, Madhya Pradesh, Manipur, Orissa, Rajasthan, Sikkim, West Bengal, Uttar Pradesh and Tripura. Other (non-poor) states are Goa, Gujarat, Haryana, Himachal Pradesh, Jammu & Kashmir, Karnataka, Kerala, Maharashtra, Meghalaya, Mizoram, Nagaland, Punjab, Tamil Nadu, New Delhi and Arunachal Pradesh.

Results and Discussion

Status and Trends

The U5MR, including infant, neonatal and child mortality rates, started declining since the late 1970s and until 1993 the rate of decline was substantial. The decline was, however, slow during 1993–1998. The country's goal to achieve a U5MR of less than 100 per 1000 live births and reducing the IMR to less than 60 per 1000 live births by the year 2000 could not be achieved despite improved interventions and an increase in the overall resources. In the present scenario of IMR (2002), 25 per 1000 newborns died within the first week of birth; 40 per 1000 newborns died before reaching the age of 1 year and 85 per 1000 newborns died before reaching the age of 5 years. The major uncertainty seems to be whether the IMR is approaching a limiting value. This value does not have an ultimate cap that will hold forever. Perhaps the progress in reducing mortality in early infancy is possible with innovative interventions for newborn care. Nevertheless, the IMR and U5MR have become increasingly important indicators that need to be monitored.

Figure 15.1

Under-Five Mortality Rate by Residence and Sex

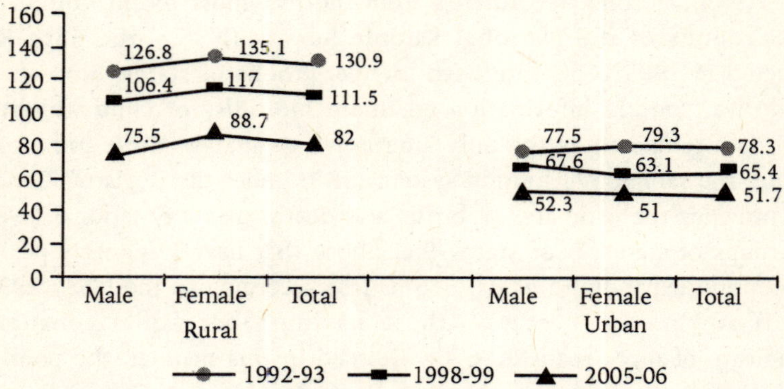

The U5MR is the probability (expressed as a rate 1000 live births) of a child born in a specified year dying before reaching the age of five if subject to current age specific mortality rates. U5MR at national level has declined during the last decade. It has come down from 109.3 per thousand (1992-93) to 74.4 per thousand during the period 2005-06. More declines are noticed for males compared with female children such as the U5MR has come down from during NFHS-1 to NFHS-3, for males it declined from 126.8 per thousand to 75.5 per thousand and females also declined from 135.1 per thousand to 88.7 per thousand in rural areas during the corresponding periods in Figure 15.1. In urban area, declines are slow, for males it declined from 77.5 per thousand to 52.3 per thousand and females also declined from 79.3 per thousand to 51.0 per thousand in rural areas during the corresponding periods. Perceptible decline in the rate has taken place in rural areas as compared to urban parts of the country. This implies that the government's programmes like universal immunisation are being successfully implemented in the rural areas.

Table 15.1 show differentials in infant and child mortality rates for the five year period preceding the survey by demographic characteristics, separately for rural, urban and total areas of India. Considering first the data for India as a whole, it is seen that the infant mortality rate is marginally higher for females (58) than males (56). However, in the neonatal period, like elsewhere, mortality in India is lower for females (37) than for males (41). As children get older, females are exposed to higher mortality than males. Females have 36 per cent higher mortality than males in the post-neonatal period, but a 61 per cent higher mortality than males at age 1-4 years. The infant mortality rate is lowest for mothers aged 20-29 years (50)

Table 15.1

Childhood Mortality Rates by Demographic Characteristics

Demographic Characteristics	*IMR (per 1000)*	*CMR (per 1000)*	*U5MR (per 1000)*
Child's Sex			
Male	56	14	70
Female	58	23	79
Mother's Age at Birth			
<20	77	20	95
20-29	50	16	65
30-39	56	26	81
40-49	72	(37)	107
Birth Order			
1	64	11	75
2-3	47	16	62
4-6	62	25	86
7 or more	80	39	116
Previous Birth Interval			
<2 years	86	32	115
2 years	50	20	69
3 years	30	15	44
4 years or more	37	9	45
Birth Size			
Very small	129	40	164
Small	62	14	75
Average or larger	49	18	66
Total	57	18	74
NFHS-1	86	35	119
NFHS-2	73	31	101

Note: () Based on 250-499 unweighted children surviving to the beginning of the age interval. Excludes first-order births. IMR = Infant mortality rate CMR = Child mortality rate (the probability of dying between first and fifth birthday). U5M rate = Under-five mortality rate (the probability of dying before the fifth birthday).

and is substantially higher for mothers aged less than 20 years (77) and 40-49 years (72). The birth order also shows a similar effect. The infant mortality rate is lowest for births of order 2 or 3 (47) and higher for first order births (64) and for births of later orders (62 or higher). Similar differentials by birth order are observed at age less than one month, but child mortality increases steadily with birth order. The interval between the previous birth and the current birth shows a strong negative effect on infant and child mortality rates. When a birth occurs less than two years after an earlier birth, the infant mortality rate is 86. If the interval is 24-35 months, the infant mortality rate is 50 and if the interval is 36-47 months, it is only 30. But when the interval is four years or more, the infant mortality rate is somewhat higher (37). Child mortality, however, is negatively related to the previous birth interval throughout, with mortality being lowest for intervals of four years or more. In India, the weight of babies is not measured at birth in most cases. Taking the reported size of the baby at birth as a proxy for birth weight, one finds that birth weight has a substantial effect on infant and child mortality rates. The infant mortality rate is 49 for an average or large size baby, but it is 62 for a smaller than average baby and 129 for a very small baby. The risk of mortality is particularly high for small babies during the neonatal period. Similar demographic differentials are observed in infant and child mortality in rural and urban areas, with the exception of sex differentials. Infant and under-five mortality rates are higher for females in rural areas and are higher for males in urban areas.

Disparity across Social Groups

In India, social groups, such as scheduled castes (SCs), scheduled tribes (STs) and other backward classes (OBCs), have been historically under-privileged, and tend to have poorer socioeconomic indicators than the general population. The NFHS-2 data indicate that these groups have higher infant mortality rates than the general population, although there are differences among these groups as well (Table 15.2). Of the three groups, STs have the highest infant mortality, followed by SCs. Although SC/STs in the poor states have the highest absolute IMRs of any group in the country, the relative position of SC/STs *vis-à-vis* the non-SC/ST/OBC groups is worse in the non-poor states relative to the poor states. For instance, in the poor states, STs have an IMR that is 54 per cent greater than that of forward castes, but this differential is only about 37 per cent in the non-poor states.

Rural infrastructure can have powerful influences on health outcomes. For instance, rural roads enable easier access to health centres and referral district hospitals, thereby reducing the risk of an infant dying because of neonatal and post-neonatal infections. Access to safe drinking water and sanitation are important environmental hygiene interventions that significantly reduce the exposure of an infant to water- and vector-borne diseases and increase the probability of his or her survival. Likewise, access to electricity can also improve infant survival probabilities by improving hygiene, cooking and health practices in the household as well as the health practices of local health providers. The NFHS-2 data show significant association between infant mortality and access to infrastructure (Table 15.2).

Table 15.2

Infant Mortality Rate by Various Individual, Household, Child and Community Characteristics and by Poor and Non-Poor States, 1994-1998

Characteristics	*Poor States*	*Other States*	*All States*
Household has			
No electricity	85	66	82
Electricity	64	45	55
Electricity Supply in Village is			
Irregular	81	57	75
Regular	78	49	65
Household has			
No piped water	80	54	75
Piped water	59	45	51
Household has			
Some toilet access	49	34	42
No toilet access	84	60	78
% of Villages in District having *Pucca* Road			
50% or fewer	81	53	77
50-90%	78	52	71
>90%	59	45	51
Social Group of Household	84	58	77
Scheduled caste	88	65	81
Scheduled tribe	80	47	70
Other backward classes	83	53	74
SC, ST or OBC	65	42	57
Forward caste (all groups)	76	49	67

Source: NFHS-2, 1998-99.

The infant mortality rate is nearly 50 per cent greater among households without access to electricity as compared to households with electricity, although this difference is somewhat smaller in the poor states than in the non-poor states. It is not just the availability of electricity but also the regularity in its supply is associated with health outcomes. The regularity of electricity supply in a village is associated with significantly lower levels of infant mortality, although this relationship too is more predominant in the better-off states than in the poor ones. On the other hand, the presence of piped water and rural roads has a much stronger association with infant mortality reduction in the poor states than in the rich states (Table 15.2). This suggests that the health 'appropriateness' of infrastructure differs across poor and non-poor states; in the former, drinking water and rural roads matter more than electricity. Access to sanitation is another infrastructural intervention that is observed to have strong association with health outcomes. Households with no toilet access have an infant mortality rate that is nearly double that of households with toilet access. This pattern does not differ much across poor and non-poor states.

Child Immunisation

Among all the indicators, immunisation is one, which lacks authentic information. The available figures vary according to different sources. While the Government of India statistics quote a higher level of measles coverage as compared to other survey figures such as NFHS, the NFHS indicates coverage of 50.7 per cent of children aged 12 to 23 months for measles during 1998-99 and the same survey indicates a still lower coverage of 41.7 per cent for children (Table 15.3). However, there has been a considerable improvement when compared to NFHS-I during 1992-93. The male-female differences in the measles immunisation has declined considerably (male 51.6 per cent, female 49.8 per cent). The urban areas have much higher coverage (69.2 per cent) than the rural areas (45.3 per cent).

Figure 15.2

Per cent of Children 12-23 Months Old Fully Immunised and Children Under-Three taken to Health Facility while Suffering from Illness, EAG States, NFHS-3

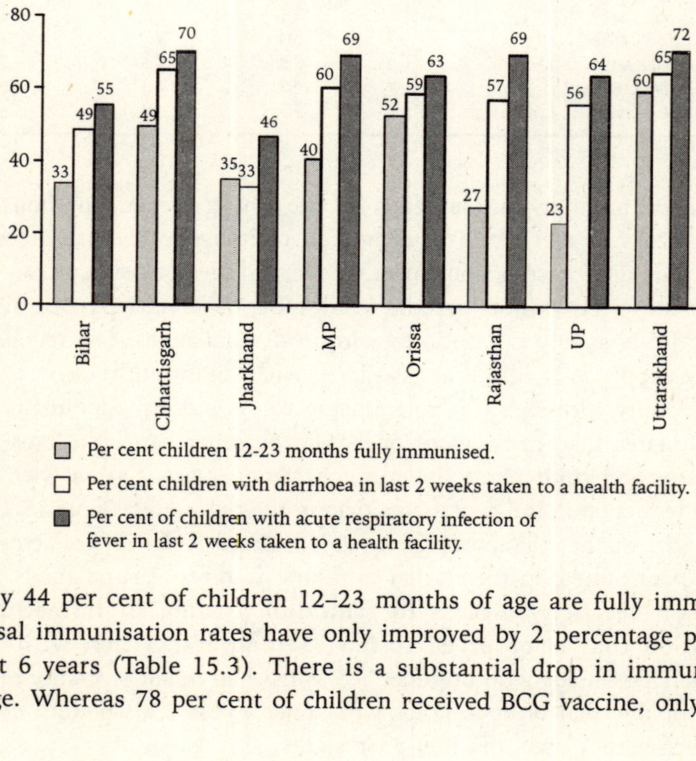

Only 44 per cent of children 12–23 months of age are fully immunised. Universal immunisation rates have only improved by 2 percentage points in the last 6 years (Table 15.3). There is a substantial drop in immunisation coverage. Whereas 78 per cent of children received BCG vaccine, only 59 per cent of children were given measles immunisation. Health-seeking behaviour for childhood illnesses are far from satisfactory. Only half of the children who suffered from diarrhoea are taken to a health facility for treatment. Only two out of three children suffering from acute respiratory infection or fever are taken to a health facility for treatment (Figure 15.3). Though there has been significant improvement in full immunisation coverage in some of the states such as Bihar, Jharkhand, Chhattisgarh and Uttarakhand, still most of the Empowered Action Group (EAG) states have lower coverage than the national average. Table 15.3 reveals that only 44 per cent of children of 12-23 months were fully immunised in 2005-06, up from 42 per cent in 1998-99 and 36 per cent in 1992-93.

Table 15.3

Trend in Access to and Reach of Basic Health Services (Per cent)

	NFHS-3 (2005-06)	*NFHS-2 (1998-99)*	*NFHS-1 (1992-93)*
Child Immunisation Vitamin A Supplementation			
Children aged 12-23 months fully immunised (BCG, measles, and three doses each of polio/DPT)	44	42	36
Children aged 12-23 months who have received BCG	78	72	62
Children aged 12-23 months who have received three doses of polio vaccine	78	63	64
Children aged 12-23 months who have received three doses of polio DPT vaccine	55	55	52
Children aged 12-23 months who have received measles vaccine	59	51	42
Treatment of Childhood Disease (Children under five years)*			
Children with symptoms of ARI treatment sought from a health facility	69	64	66
Children with symptoms of fever treatment sought from a health facility	15	29	20
Treatment of Childhood Disease (Children under three years)*			
Children with diarrhoea in the last two weeks who received ORS	26	27	18
Children with diarrhoea in the last two weeks taken to a health facility	60	63	61
Child Feeding Practices*			
Children under three years breastfed within one hour of birth maternity care (for births in the last three years)	23	16	10
Mothers who had at least three antenatal care visits for their last birth	51	44	44
Birth assisted by a doctor/nurse/LHW/ANM/ other health personnel*	48	42	33
Institutional births*	41	34	26

Note: * Based on the last two births in the three years before the survey.

Source: NFHS-3.

Treatment was sought from a health facility or provider for 69 per cent of children with symptoms of ARI. Fifteen per cent of children under age five years had a fever during the two weeks before the survey. Children's access to certain critical components of treatment of childhood diseases has declined over the past seven years (Table 15.3). For instance, the proportion of children with diarrhoea who received ORS in the two weeks preceding the survey had risen from 18 per cent in 1992-93 to 27 per cent in 1998-99; but since then it has fallen to 26 per cent in 2005-06. The critical public health messages are simply not reaching the families with children. For example, in 2005-06, only 23 per cent if infants aged 0-5 months were being exclusively breastfed in 2005-06, up from 16 per cent in 1998-99, an increase of 7 percentage points over seven years, despite the importance of exclusive breastfeeding in the initial months of a child's life. There are huge gaps in women's access and reach of maternal health services. Improvements in women's access to safe delivery, for instance, have been minimal. Between 1998-99 and 2005-06, the proportion of births assisted by a doctor, nurse, LHW, ANM or other health personnel went up marginally from 42 to 48 per cent and institutional births went up from 34 per cent to 41 per cent over the same period.

Has the Decline in Childhood Mortality Rates Slowed in India?

Several indicators of childhood mortality are used to measure levels and trends, including the neonatal and post-neonatal mortality rates, the infant mortality rate, the child mortality rate and the U5MR. Over the 15-year period before the 1992–93 National Family Health Survey (NFHS), all measures of childhood mortality declined in India at rates slightly greater than the average for other low-income countries, excluding China.[1] Figure 15.4 summarises the decline of several childhood mortality indicators measured in the NFHS. Another source of infant mortality data is the Indian Sample Registration System (SRS), whose annual estimates are consistent with those of the NFHS.[2] The SRS was started in a few states in 1965, with coverage extended to all states in 1970, and tracks births through the use of continuous enumeration and biannual surveys. Infant mortality rates and child deaths are published annually, but not child mortality rates. The continuous registration and survey results are matched and verified in the field to minimise duplication and omission. At the national level, the results are generally believed to be quite accurate. Improvements in the accuracy of the data are likely to have occurred in some states over time, which may

1. *Demographer*, World Bank, Washington DC, USA.
2. Senior Public Health Specialist, Health, Nutrition and Population, South Asia Department, The World Bank, Washington DC, USA.

underestimate the pace of decline; but this is not likely to affect the estimation of national trends.

Figure 15.3

Trends in Childhood Mortality Indicators

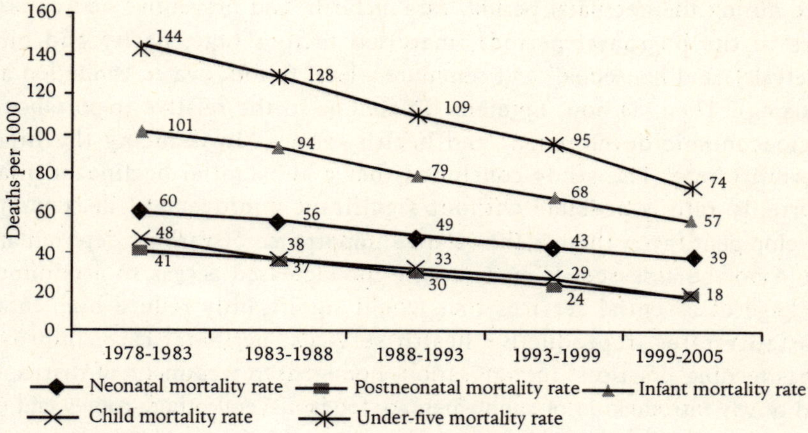

A 1980 survey into omissions of vital events found that death rates were underestimated by about 3 per cent nationally; by 1985, this had improved to 2.5 per cent. We have compared SRS estimates of the annual infant mortality rate for the most recent 5-year period (1993–1997) with retrospective data going back to 1981. Throughout this interval, the rate of decline in the infant mortality rate tended to stagnate for brief periods, and was often followed by a subsequent rapid decline. During the most recent 5-year period, however, the marked reduction in the rate of decline has been sustained, and the observed estimates are now significantly above the 1981–1993 trend line. Based on the longer-term trend, the predicted value for the 1997 infant mortality rate was 63.5 per 1000 live births, whereas the observed rate was 71 per 1000 live births. In terms of numbers, this means that about 200,000 more infants died in 1997 than would have been the case had the longer-term trend continued. As infant and child mortality rates fall, further gains become more difficult to achieve. However, childhood mortality rates in India are still at elevated levels, and the observed reduction in the decline is not readily explainable. The failure to reduce infant mortality during this period means that India will not achieve its year 2000 health goals.

Why is the Decline in Child Mortality Rates Slowing?

Child mortality trends, differentials and determinants in India have been the subject of many studies. One of the studies attempted to account for the pace of decline in the infant mortality rate over the period 1968–1978 and provided a framework for analysing factors that contributed to it (Jain, 1988). These included proximate factors (such as non-medical factors and medical care during the antenatal period, care at birth, and preventive and curative care in the postnatal period); maternal factors (age, parity and birth intervals); and household- and community-level factors (water, sanitation and housing). Then, as now, opinions differed as to the relative importance of socioeconomic development and health services in reducing the infant mortality rate. The study concluded that a substantial decline in infant mortality rate is possible without significant improvement in economic development, even though the relative importance of various determinants could not be assessed. It made a case for increased access to a minimum package of essential services that would significantly reduce high infant mortality rates: reproductive health services; perinatal care; improved breastfeeding practices; immunisation; home-based treatment of diarrhoea; and timely introduction of supplementary foods. Several other studies laid out intervention strategies and directions based on similar analyses and assumptions.

Causes of Child Mortality

It is estimated that under-nutrition and anaemia are contributory factors in over 50 per cent of under-five deaths in the country. Malnutrition is an area to be tackled as studies have revealed a synergy between malnutrition and mortality. Major causes of infant mortality continue to be pre-mature birth and low birth weight, poor intrapartum and newborn care, diarrhoeal diseases, acute respiratory infections and other infections.

Neonatal Mortality

Neonatal mortality accounts for more than two-third of infant mortality rate in India. Over the last decade, postneonatal mortality has declined much faster than neonatal mortality. This is mainly due to increased programme interventions focused on postneonatal such as immunisation, management of diarrhoea and acute respiratory infections (ARI) etc. Policies and programmes should emphasise on interventions to perinatal and neonatal mortality. Antenatal care, safe delivery and quality of newborn care are key requirements for reduction of all types of mortality.

Gender Disparity

There are gender differences in IMR and under-five mortality rates. Though there is no biological reason for a higher mortality rate in females in the age group 0-4 years, it is the social causes that adversely affect the mortality rate of girls, and this needs to be tackled. Girls have a higher mortality rate than boys during the postneonatal period to five years. The risk of mortality is higher among girls than boys as their malnutrition levels are higher.

Urban-Rural Bias

Bridging the gap between urban and rural child mortality rates and immunisation coverage is another challenge to be tackled with. There is a large urban-rural disparity in the infant, U5MR and immunisation coverage for measles. One of the reasons is the lack of accessibility to services either by remoteness of the location and higher proportion of disadvantaged groups. Providing adequate services to specific vulnerable groups and those in the remote areas is the key to bring down the gap.

Conclusion

Infant and U5MR are often used as indicators of national health development. In India over the last 35 years, the rate of deaths to infants under one year of age has more than halved from 129 per 1000 live births in 1971 to 57 in 2006. Under-five child mortality has declined by one-third from 109 per 1000 live births in 1991-92 to 74 in 2005-06. Despite this progress, current child mortality rates in India are high compared to other countries of similar socioeconomic conditions. The National Rural Health Mission aims to reduce the infant mortality rate to 30 per 1000 live births by 2012. This will require a further halving of infant mortality in a relatively short period of time. Though ambitious, this goal can be achieved with intensive efforts to scale up evidence-based child survival interventions backed by strong leadership, effective programme management, and increased human and financial resources.

The improvement in childhood mortality is the result of a combination of factors. Amongst these are the expansion of health care facilities and services, disease-specific health interventions, changes in diets and health behaviour, and the success of developmental programmes such as the Water and Sanitation Programme. The significant improvement in Indian women's educational attainment must also have played an important role in reducing mortality.

Policy Implications—Lesson Learned

To understand what other policy interventions might be needed to help India attain its infant mortality MDG, one needs an understanding of the proximate—or intermediate—causes of infant mortality in India. An answer to this question can be found in the data on timing of deaths, obtained from analysis of unit record data from the National Family Health Survey.

The lesson learned for child survival in India is the need for state-specific strategies and the adoption of multisectoral approaches to achieve greater impact and accelerate progress towards the health goals. Policy options for child survival include:

1. Enhancing capacity to use information to support child-health programmes.
2. Establishing strong and unified leadership at national and sub-national levels.
3. Strengthening health systems for sustainable gains in child survival.
4. Adequate and targeted resources to rapidly scale-up child survival interventions while assuring quality of care.
5. Generating awareness and commitment beyond the public health community to mobilise support for child survival interventions.

Regions or states with high U5MRs and slow decline need to strengthen the health systems, prioritise essential elements of child health and nutrition services (high impact interventions) and develop and expand community participation for the prevention and treatment of childhood illnesses.

The multisectoral approach would include female education and nutrition, increasing the use of health services during pregnancy and delivery, eliminating the gender gap in child health services and improving nutrition throughout the lifecycle.

References

Anker, R. and J. Knowles (1977). "An empirical analysis of mortality differentials in Kenya at the macro and micro levels", *Population and Employment Working Paper* No. 60. Geneva: International Labour Organization.

Claeson, M., E.R. Bos, T. Mawji and I. Pathmanathan (2000). "Reducing child mortality in India in the new millennium", *Bull World Health Organ* 78(10): 1192-1199.

Das Gupta, M. (1990). "Death clustering, mothers education and the determinants of child mortality in rural Punjab, India", *Population Studies* 44(3): 489-505.

International Institute for Population Sciences (IIPS) and ORC Macro (1995). *National Family Health Survey (NFHS-1), India, 1992-93.*

———. (2001). *National Family Health Survey (NFHS-2), India, 1998-99.*

———. (2001). *National Family Health Survey (NFHS-3), India, 2005-06.*

Jain, A. (1988). "Determinants of regional variations in infant mortality in rural India", in A. Jain and L. Visaria (eds.), *Infant Mortality in India: Differentials and Determinants.* Sage Publications. pp. 127-167.

Ministry of Health and Family Welfare (MoHFW) (2005). *Annual Report 2004-2005.* New Delhi: MoHFW.

———. (2006). *National Rural Health Mission (2005-2012), Mission Document.* New Delhi: MoHFW.

Mishra, Vinod, T.K. Roy and Robert D. Retherford (2004). "Sex differentials in childhood feeding, health care and nutritional status in India", *Population and Development Review* 30(2): 269-295.

National Sample Survey Organisation (NSSO) (1998). "A note on the consumption of tobacco in India: NSS 50th round (1993-94)", *Sarvekshana* 21(3): 51-61.

Office of the Registrar General (2006a). *Sample Registration System, Statistical report 2004.* New Delhi: Office of the Registrar General, India.

———. (2006b). *SRS Bulletin* 40(1). New Delhi: Office of the Registrar General, India.

———. (1998). *Compendium of India's Fertility and Mortality Indicators, 1971-1997.* New Delhi: Office of Registrar General.

Pandey, A., B.N. Bhattacharya, D. Sahu and Rehena Sultana (2005). "Componets of under-five mortality trends, current stagnation and future forcasting levels", NCMH *Background papers* "Burden of Disease in India".

Pandey, A. *et al.* (1998). "Infant and child mortality in India". International Institute for Population Sciences Mumbai, India and East-West Center Program on Population Honolulu, HI, USA (*National Family Health Survey Subject Reports No. 11*).

Sharma, Suresh (2005). "Child health and nutritional status of children: The role of sex differentials", *Working Paper* series no.e/262/2005. Delhi, India: Institute of Economic Growth.

———. (2007). "Immunization coverage in India", *Working Paper* series no.e/2683/2007. Delhi, India: Institute of Economic Growth.

Victora, C. and A. Wagstaff *et al.* (2003). "Applying an equity lens to child health amd mortality: More of the same is not enough", *Lancet* 362: 233-41.

Wagstaff A. and M Claeson (2004). *The Millennium Development Goals for Health: Rising to the Challenges.* Washington DC: World Bank.

World Bank (2003). *Attaining the Millennium Development Goals in India: How Likely and What will it Take?.* Washington DC.

Section V

Nutritional Status and HIV/AIDS in India

16

Gender Differentials in Nutritional Status by States and Socioeconomic and Cultural Groups in India

KAMLA GUPTA

Introduction

Proper nutrition is the basic ingredient of good health outcomes. Consequently good nutrition and health since long have been considered as prerequisites for human development. Many developing countries, particularly southern Asiatic countries and Sub-Saharan African countries are known for their high levels of under-nutrition and sincere efforts are made by country governments for improving the nutritional status of their people through planned development. However, of late in many developing countries problems of overweight and obesity have also assumed significant proportions. In many of the developing countries this "double burden" of malnutrition wherein both under- and overnutrition occur simultaneously among different population groups has become a major health burden and the most important risk factor for illness and death. According to WHO (2002), underweight and obesity are both among the top ten leading risk factors for the global burden of disease. Worldwide, an estimated 852 million people were undernourished in 2000-2002. Of these, 815 million or 96 per cent were found in developing countries only. Around the same time, more than one billion people worldwide were estimated obese and some 300 million of these were estimated to be clinically obese. For quite sometime the problem of overweight and obesity was confined mainly to developed countries but now it prevails globally and not limited to upper-income developing countries only. Countries with very different cultures and dietary customs are now faced with the overweight and obesity problem. There is accumulating evidence that when economic conditions improve, obesity and diet related non-communicable diseases may escalate in countries even with high level of undernutrition.

Obesity[1] and related ill health are becoming serious problems in parts of the developing countries also, most notably in Asia. Concerns about the environmental effects of large-scale industrialised livestock production, an important problem in many high-income countries, are gradually becoming important around large cities in many developing countries (Pinstrup-Andersen and Pandya-Lorch, 2001). The etiology of obesity is multifactorial. Problems of overweight and obesity are caused by a chronic imbalance between energy intake and actual energy needs of the body.

Of late, fast economic development in India has attracted worldwide attention. There is sharp increase in per capita income, particularly in urban areas. With fast economic development and increasing income levels, the nutritional and health status of the Indian population is expected to improve significantly. Since 1975, the National Nutrition Monitoring Bureau (NNMB) has been providing data on dietary intake and nutritional status for 10 states (Kerala, Karnataka, Andhra Pradesh, Tamil Nadu, Maharashtra, Orissa, Gujarat, Madhya Pradesh, West Bengal and Uttar Pradesh) of India. A one-time district level nutrition survey was carried out in the mid 1990s in order to obtain data on the dietary intake and nutritional status of individuals in other states. These data show that over the last three decades there has been a progressive decline in undernutrition and some increase in overnutrition in both rural and urban areas. Though India is typically known for high prevalence of undernutrition, significant proportion of overweight and obese people now coexist with those who are undernourished (Popkin, 2002).

For the first time the National Family Health Survey 1998-99 (NFHS-2) measured the height and weight of all ever-married women in ages 15-49 in all the states of India and provided national and state level estimates of nutritional status of ever-married women in ages 15-49. The survey results showed that along with high level of undernutrition among Indian women, for several socio-cultural groups and in several more developed states, overweight and obesity problem was quite visible. Overall in India, 3 per cent of ever-married women were found obese and 8 per cent overweight. The problem of overweight (18 per cent) and obesity (7 per cent) was found more widespread in urban than in rural areas (5 per cent and 2 per cent

1. Quatelet in 1869 was the first person to observe that among adults of normal built but different heights, weight was roughly proportional to height squared. The Quatelet Index (weight in kg./height in metres^2) was later renamed 'the body mass index (BMI)' by Keys *et al.* (1972). Despite its inherent limitations like being independent of the age of the respondent and not providing information on a person's percentage of body fat, BMI has been widely used as a measure to determine the nutritional status of the population. A BMI ranging from 18.5 to 24.99 indicates a proper normal nutritional condition and a BMI less than 18.5 represents underweight. It is generally agreed that a BMI of greater than 35 is indicative of clinical obesity, BMI of 30.0-34.99 indicative of obesity while a BMI of 25.0-29.9 is suggestive of overweight in an individual.

respectively). Delhi showed the highest prevalence of obesity and overweight among women followed by Punjab and Gujarat. The survey clearly showed that in several states of India (11 states), the proportion of overweight or obese women was higher than the national average. Similarly problem of overweight and obesity was also found high in several groups of women. Several earlier studies also show that prevalence of overweight and obesity is found higher among women compared to men (Shetty and James, 1994; Gopalan, 1998; Misra *et al.*, 2001; Zargar *et al.*, 2000; Gopinath *et al.*, 1994). Older women are found to be relatively more overweight and obese than younger women (Agrawal, 2002). In a recent study (Agrawal and Mishra, 2004) among women in northern India, it was seen that urban residence significantly increases the risk of obesity.

The 2005-06 National Family Health Survey (NFHS-3) has also collected information about the nutritional status of all women in the ages 15-49 and all men in the ages 15-54. The height and weight was measured from a representative sample of 124,385 women in ages 15-49 and 74,369 men in ages 15-54 in all the 29 states of India. In this chapter, we examine the prevalence of overweight and obesity problem by several background characteristics of the male and female population and by state. We also look into the overweight and obesity prevalence in some large cities of India by slum and non-slum areas.

Trend in Overweight and Obese between NFHS-2 and NFHS-3

Between NFHS-2 and NFHS-3 the problem of overweight and obesity has increased among ever-married women in India and that of undernutrition has decreased. According to NFHS-2, nearly 36 per cent of ever-married women were underweight and 11 per cent were overweight. The proportion of underweight has declined to 33 per cent in NFHS-3 and that of overweight women has increased to 15 per cent.

Prevalence of Overweight and Obesity in India according to Background Characteristics

Table 16.1 presents the prevalence of overweight (BMI 25.0-29.9) and obesity (BMI > 30.0) among all women aged 15-49 and men aged 15-54 in India according to age, marital status, residence, education, religion, caste, and by wealth quintiles. NFHS-3 shows that among all women in ages 15-49, 13 per cent of women were overweight or obese (10 per cent overweight and 3 per cent obese). In the same age-group, the percentage of overweight and obese men is somewhat lower (9 per cent overweight and 1 per cent obese). The proportion of overweight or obese men does not change much even for

Table 16.1

Nutritional Status of Women and Men Percentage of Women and Men Aged 15-49 with Specific Body Mass Index (BMI) Levels (Overweight or Obese), by Background Characteristics, India, 2005-06

Background Characteristic	Body Mass Index (BMI) in kg/m² — Women[1]				Men			
	≥ 25.0 (Overweight or Obese)	25.0-29.9 (Over-Weight)	≥ 30.0 (Obese)	Number of Women	≥ 25.0 (Overweight or Obese)	25.0-29.9 (Over-Weight)	≥ 30.0 (obese)	Number of Men
Age								
15-19	2.4	2.1	0.2	22,147	1.7	1.4	0.2	12,251
20-29	8.2	6.8	1.4	36,413	6.5	5.8	0.7	21,396
30-39	17.4	13.5	3.9	31,321	13.0	11.2	1.8	18,015
40-49	23.7	17.4	6.4	21,900	15.2	12.9	2.3	14,079
Marital status								
Never married	4.5	3.8	0.7	24,053	4.2	3.7	0.5	23,578
Currently married	14.9	11.5	3.4	82,145	12.2	10.5	1.7	41,274
Widowed	14.4	11.1	3.2	3,865	5.8	5.1	0.7	499
Divorced/separated/deserted	14.4	10.7	3.7	1,718	5.2	4.7	0.4	391
Residence								
Urban	23.5	17.4	6.1	36,366	15.9	13.5	2.4	23,304
Rural	7.4	6.2	1.3	75,416	5.6	5.0	0.6	42,438
Education								
No education	7.3	5.9	1.4	44,926	3.6	3.3	0.3	11,828
<5 years complete	10.7	8.6	2.1	9,120	5.3	4.7	0.6	6,720
5-7 years complete	14.2	10.7	3.5	17,032	6.5	5.5	1.0	10,949
8-9 years complete	14.0	10.9	3.1	15,781	7.2	6.2	1.0	13,695
10-11 years complete	18.1	13.3	4.8	11,718	12.5	10.5	1.9	9,741
12 or more years complete	23.8	18.4	5.4	13,198	18.8	16.3	2.5	12,794

contd...

contd...

Background Characteristic	≥ 25.0 (Overweight or Obese)	25.0-29.9 (Over-Weight)	≥ 30.0 (Obese)	Number of Women	≥ 25.0 (Overweight or Obese)	25.0-29.9 (Over-Weight)	≥ 30.0 (obese)	Number of Men
Religion								
Hindu	11.8	9.3	2.6	90,593	8.9	7.7	1.2	54,099
Muslim	14.1	10.7	3.5	14,510	8.4	7.4	1.1	7,926
Christian	18.2	14.7	3.6	2,788	13.6	11.9	1.7	1,505
Sikh	31.6	21.5	10.1	2,080	25.5	20.9	4.7	1,224
Buddhist/Neo-Buddhist	10.1	8.6	1.5	939	9.0	8.5	0.6	572
Jain	26.6	20.4	6.2	348	28.2	24.6	3.5	187
Other	3.9	3.0	0.9	421	2.3	2.3	0.1	216
Wealth index								
Lowest	1.8	1.6	0.2	18,995	1.4	1.3	0.1	10,531
Second	3.9	3.4	0.5	21,106	2.2	1.9	0.2	12,077
Middle	7.4	6.5	0.9	22,867	5.0	4.6	0.4	13,666
Fourth	15.4	12.5	2.9	23,756	10.2	9.1	1.0	14,544
Highest	30.5	22.0	8.4	25,058	23.6	19.6	4.0	14,923
Total age 15-49	12.6	9.8	2.8	111,781	9.3	8.0	1.3	65,742

Note: Total includes women with missing information on education and religion, who are not shown separately.

1 Excludes pregnant women and women with a birth in the preceding 2 months.

15-54 age groups. Table also makes it clear that overweight and obesity have become substantial problems among several groups of women and men in India.

The problem of overweight and obesity among women was more than three times higher in urban (24 per cent) than in rural areas (7 per cent). It was true in case of men also (proportion of overweight or obese among males was 6 per cent in rural areas but 16 per cent in urban areas. The overweight and obesity increased with increasing age for both men and women. The proportion of overweight and obese was more than three times as high among women with an education level 12 or more years as among women with no education level. Distribution of the women and men by wealth quintiles also shows significant differences in the prevalence of overweight and obesity. Higher the wealth status of men and women, higher is the prevalence of overweight and obesity.

Among all the groups, Sikh women (32 per cent) showed the highest level of overweight and obese followed by women belonging to wealthiest households (31 per cent). In general, the differentials in the prevalence of overweight and obesity by background characteristics men were similar to women. Among all groups of men, Jains followed by Sikhs showed the highest level of overweight and obesity (26-28 per cent). Almost one-fourth men in the wealthiest households were overweight or obese. But interesting thing is that in each group, overweight and obesity is more widespread among women than among men. The prevalence estimates of overweight and obese between males and females also shows some interesting results. The highest difference in the prevalence of overweight and obesity among different groups is found among widowed, divorced, separated and deserted women and men (more than 9 percentage points), followed by difference between older women and men (9 percentage points) and in urban areas (8 percentage points). Another interesting thing is that among Jains, proportion of overweight and obese male is higher than females. The nutritional status of Indian women shows that Indian women are suffering from a dual burden of malnutrition more than Indian males as one out of two women is either thin or too thin or overweight or obese (49 per cent) whereas this proportion is 44 per cent among males.

State Level Differentials in the Overweight and Obese Male and Female

Across states of India, the proportion of overweight or obese women ranged from 30 per cent in Punjab to 5 per cent in Bihar (Table 16.2). In Delhi and Kerala also, more than one-fourth of all women were overweight or obese. Tamil Nadu and Goa are the other two states where one in every five

Table 16.2

Nutritional Status of Adults Percentage of Women and Men Aged 15-49 with Body Mass Index (BMI) ≥ 25.0 kg/m² (Overweight or Obese), India and States 2005-06

	Residence		Education				Wealth index					
	Urban	Rural	No Education	<5 years Complete	5-9 years Complete	10 or more Years Complete	Lowest	Second	Middle	Fourth	Highest	Total
					Women							
Andhra Pradesh	25.9	10.2	10.2	14.2	20.6	22.0	3.9	6.5	7.5	19.5	37.4	15.6
Arunachal Pradesh	11.4	7.8	6.5	9.0	8.0	16.7	2.1	2.0	7.4	14.1	19.0	8.8
Assam	19.6	5.1	2.2	4.6	8.4	17.7	1.0	2.2	4.5	13.2	25.9	7.8
Bihar	12.6	3.0	2.4	2.6	7.2	11.1	0.9	1.4	3.4	7.5	18.2	4.6
Chhattisgarh	16.9	2.1	2.9	5.8	5.4	16.5	0.9	1.6	5.2	8.7	27.9	5.6
Delhi	27.3	16.7	23.8	(4.5)	21	30.5	*	12.1	9.1	13.7	31.0	26.4
Goa	24.4	14.9	16.7	14.0	17.7	23.8	1.8	2.3	4.1	13.2	29.0	20.2
Gujarat	25.9	9.6	11.8	16.0	17.3	22.6	1.6	3.6	6.2	15.0	29.5	16.7
Haryana	28.3	12.5	13.6	12.8	17.3	22.8	2.7	6.2	8.9	12.3	31.5	17.4
Himachal Pradesh	29.4	11.6	11.0	14.0	13.5	14.6	(7.1)	6.1	6.1	10.7	22.6	13.5
Jammu & Kashmir	30.5	11.2	15.0	17.4	14.4	22.1	5.0	4.9	8.0	15.8	32.2	16.7
Jharkhand	15.5	1.5	2.0	5.3	5.7	17.0	0.8	2.8	1.7	7.6	23.9	5.4
Karnataka	25.9	8.4	10.5	11.4	16.2	21.7	2.8	4.7	9.4	17.0	36.7	15.3
Kerala	32.9	25.5	26.7	29.1	30.8	25.8	(3.7)	14.3	16.5	23.9	36.1	28.1
Madhya Pradesh	18.6	3.1	4.4	7.5	7.6	18.5	1.1	2.9	5.7	11.5	25.9	7.6
Maharashtra	22.3	6.9	9.5	13.3	15.0	18.3	2.1	3.7	7.4	13.9	26.3	14.5
Manipur	19.8	10.1	12.9	10.8	10.0	17.6	2.2	5.2	7.6	16.5	25.4	13.3
Meghalaya	8.0	4.3	3.6	6.4	3.9	8.8	2.8	2.2	3.3	6.0	10.7	5.3

contd...

contd...

	Urban	Rural	No Education	<5 years Complete	5-9 years Complete	10 or more Years Complete	Lowest	Second	Middle	Fourth	Highest	Total
Mizoram	14.6	5.3	1.1	7.2	10.5	14.5	0.0	1.2	3.3	8.6	16.4	10.6
Nagaland	12.1	4.1	5.2	5.4	5.9	9.2	0.0	2.0	4.6	8.0	13.4	6.4
Orissa	17.7	4.2	2.1	6.0	8.9	13.8	1.0	3.4	5.0	10.5	27.0	6.6
Punjab	36.3	26.2	27.8	22.9	30.4	31.7	(13.8)	11.5	17.6	23.3	39.2	29.9
Rajasthan	17.7	5.2	7.1	9.4	9.2	17.1	2.7	4.8	4.6	9.3	21.1	8.9
Sikkim	19.9	14.2	16.0	14.6	15.1	15.6	*	11.4	10.3	13.6	20.7	15.4
Tamil Nadu	29.5	13	12.6	16.2	21.9	27.3	4.9	8.8	11.8	25.3	45.4	20.9
Tripura	17.2	5.0	2.4	6.0	6.6	17.1	0.7	2.2	4.4	12.1	31.5	7.1
Uttar Pradesh	19.1	5.9	6.7	7.3	9.5	16.0	2.3	3.5	7.1	12.6	25.4	9.2
Uttaranchal	23.7	8.6	7.9	16.9	9.4	20.0	5.9	1.6	4.3	7.7	25.8	12.8
West Bengal	24.8	5.3	5.4	8.4	10.9	29.1	1.4	3.6	8.0	16.7	37.2	11.4
Men												
Andhra Pradesh	20.9	9.6	6.2	11.7	13.4	19.0	2.0	4.3	6.8	16.8	33.7	13.6
Arunachal Pradesh	7.3	7.1	3.5	4.0	6.0	13.8	1.7	2.7	6.6	4.4	20.6	7.1
Assam	10.9	3.4	1.1	1.9	2.7	12.1	0.7	0.0	1.5	8.4	22.6	5.0
Bihar	7.9	5.8	3.2	0.8	2.2	13.5	1.9	1.6	3.0	9.2	21.8	6.3
Chhattisgarh	13.7	2.0	2.6	2.6	2.0	12.7	0.9	3.5	2.9	5.2	20.8	4.9
Delhi	17.9	5.9	14.2	*	9.8	21.8	*	(15.1)	3.0	8.1	21.2	16.8
Goa	17.9	12.5	8.5	5.7	14.2	19.0	(3.6)	3.9	5.5	9.5	23.5	15.4
Gujarat	16.5	7.2	6.0	5.6	8.3	19.1	3.7	2.0	2.9	10.6	20.0	11.3
Haryana	19.9	6.4	4.0	8.0	9.5	14.5	(3.6)	0.8	6.4	5.3	23.5	10.8
Himachal Pradesh	17.2	9.6	(12.2)	-3.5	5.5	13.4	*	2.1	4.4	8.3	18.5	10.6

contd...

contd...

	Urban	Rural	No Education	<5 years Complete	5-9 years Complete	10 or more Years Complete	Lowest	Second	Middle	Fourth	Highest	Total
Jammu & Kashmir	13.1	3.2	4.0	7.2	4.6	8.9	0.0	0.8	2.7	4.1	15.3	6.2
Jharkhand	10.6	2.4	1.0	3.5	2.5	11.0	1.3	3.4	2.4	5.2	19.2	4.9
Karnataka	18.4	5.8	5.2	6.1	9.1	16.9	2.4	2.8	5.0	11.6	29.9	10.9
Kerala	21.7	15.7	*	7.9	16.1	21.0	*	(5.4)	8.4	12.1	26.8	17.8
Madhya Pradesh	9.2	2.1	1.7	4.0	1.6	10.6	1.8	1.2	2.2	5.2	15.2	4.3
Maharashtra	16.9	6.5	6.5	8.5	8.3	16.9	1.3	2.5	6.9	11.0	21.9	11.9
Manipur	14.8	6.4	4.0	5.6	4.6	14.0	0.0	1.6	4.2	10.4	24.7	9.2
Meghalaya	5.0	6.3	4.4	8.3	3.1	10.0	(8.3)	6.3	1.7	6.5	10.0	5.9
Mizoram	15.6	6.5	0.0	12.2	10	15.9	*	0.0	1.0	7.9	20.0	11.4
Nagaland	10.8	3.4	2.6	2.1	4.5	10.5	0.9	2.0	3.2	7.2	13.5	5.7
Orissa	14.3	4.0	0.4	2.7	4.3	15.3	1.0	2.2	4.8	5.4	31.4	6.0
Punjab	25.6	19.5	15.3	15.6	17.5	29.9	*	3.1	10	13.1	32.9	22.2
Rajasthan	13.2	2.9	2.8	4.1	4.2	13.3	1.2	0.9	3.7	5.5	16.8	6.2
Sikkim	17.3	10.4	14.1	7.1	8.9	18.6	*	(4.3)	7.4	8.9	19.0	11.9
Tamil Nadu	18.8	10.1	7.9	11.1	11.4	20.1	2.9	5.1	9.0	16.2	31.9	14.5
Tripura	15.6	18.8	25.7	20.1	20.7	7.2	22.9	23.0	21.8	5.9	-3.4	18.3
Uttar Pradesh	15.0	4.2	2.6	3.7	5.0	13.8	1.2	2.2	4.5	9.3	23.0	7.3
Uttaranchal	12.2	5.6	7.1	(3.2)	4.0	12.0	0	0.8	1.8	3.2	17.2	7.9
West Bengal	12.3	2.0	0.8	2.1	4.5	12.9	0.3	0.9	3.6	6.8	20.0	5.5

Note: Total includes women/men with missing information on education, who are not shown separately.

( ) Based on 25-49 unweighted cases.

* Percentage not shown; based on fewer than 25 unweighted cases.

women is overweight or obese. As far men, the proportion of overweight and obese across states of India ranged from 4 per cent in Madhya Pradesh and Chhattisgarh to 22 per cent in Punjab. Statewise figures also show that in general, proportion of overweight and obese among women was higher than among men. In a number of states, the proportion of women with overweight and obesity in urban areas was very high. In urban areas of Punjab, Jammu & Kashmir and Kerala, 40 per cent or more women were found overweight and obese. In Himachal Pradesh, Haryana, Tamil Nadu, Goa, Gujarat, Karnataka, Andhra Pradesh and Uttarakhand also, between 30-40 per cent women in urban areas were found overweight and obese. In Punjab and Kerala, even in rural areas atleast 30 per cent women were found overweight and obese. Thus, the problem of overweight and obesity among ever-married women is quite widespread, particularly in urban areas and in better-off states.

For men also, the overweight and obesity problem was more prominent in urban than in rural areas. The proportion of overweight or obese men was nearly three times higher (22 per cent) in urban areas than in rural areas (7 per cent) for all India. In all the states also, the proportion of overweight or obese men was much higher in urban areas than in rural areas; and in several states the urban-rural ratio in overweight or obese males was very high. For example in Chhattisgarh and West Bengal for every overweight and obese male in rural areas, there are 7 overweight or obese males in urban areas.

A strong negative relationship was found between overweight and obesity and the education level of the women and men in almost every state of India. In most of the states the proportion of overweight and obese women was several times higher among women with atleast 10 years of education than among women with no education level. For example, in some of the poorer states like Assam, Bihar, Chhattisgarh, Jharkhand, Orissa, West Bengal etc., where overall overweight and obesity levels among women are low, quite a substantial proportion of women (25-37) with higher level of education are overweight and obese. In Delhi, Tamil Nadu, Jammu & Kashmir and Punjab, 40-46 per cent women with education level 10 years or more are overweight or obese.

The differences in the proportion of overweight or obese males by education level are even more pronounced. In India, almost one in five males with education level 10 years or more is overweight or obese. In no other state of India except Punjab, Delhi, Sikkim and Himachal Pradesh, the proportion of overweight or obese among men with no education level is above 10 per cent. However, in 18-20 states of India, the proportion of overweight and obese among men with atleast 10 years of education is 20 per cent or more. In Punjab, Kerala, Tamil Nadu and Andhra Pradesh, one-third or more males with education level 10 years or more (31-40 per cent) are overweight or obese.

Overweight and Obesity in Cities

Thus, we see that a disproportionately large number of overweight or obese women and men in India are concentrated in urban areas, more prominently in large metros and belong to more educated group. The proportion of overweight or obese men and women in Mumbai, Kolkata and Chennai is much higher than the urban areas of their respective states (Table 16.3). In Chennai, almost 2 out of 5 women are overweight or obese. Even in slum areas of Chennai, one in three women is overweight or obese. In Hyderabad also, one in three women is overweight or obese. We tried to study the prevalence of overweight and obesity among women and men by food habits.

Table 16.3

Nutritional Status of Adults in Selected Cities Percentage of Women and Men Aged 15-49 with Specific Body Mass Index (BMI) Levels for Slum/Non-Slum Areas, Selected Cities, India, 2005-06

City/Residence	*Women* ≥ 25.0 (Overweight or Obese)	*Women* ≥ 30.0 (Obese)	*Men* ≥ 25.0 (Overweight or Obese)	*Men* ≥ 30.0 (Obese)
Delhi	27.3	8.2	17.9	2.8
Slum	20.3	6.4	10.5	1.4
Non-slum	28.9	8.6	20.0	3.2
Meerut	29.6	9.6	18.7	3.7
Slum	24.6	6.9	16.0	2.3
Non-slum	33.5	11.8	21.0	4.8
Kolkata	29.8	6.9	18.0	3.0
Slum	25.0	5.3	15.3	1.6
Non-slum	32.3	7.8	19.6	3.8
Indore	22.3	6.1	13.7	1.6
Slum	19.4	4.8	8.8	0.8
Non-slum	23.1	6.4	15.0	1.8
Mumbai	27.4	8.1	18.2	2.9
Slum	25.1	7.7	16.4	2.4
Non-slum	30.4	8.7	21.0	3.7
Nagpur	19.3	4.7	13.3	2.4
Slum	13.5	2.9	9.5	1.5
Non-slum	22.8	5.8	15.5	3.0
Hyderabad	33.4	10.6	24.5	4.4
Slum	31.4	9.6	21.9	4.0
Non-slum	33.9	10.8	25.1	4.5
Chennai	39.2	12.1	23.4	4.3
Slum	33.5	11.5	17.8	2.3
Non-slum	40.6	12.2	24.8	4.7

Prevalence of Overweight and Obesity according to Food Habits

Diet has been considered as an important risk factor of obesity. Large-scale epidemiological studies on diet and obesity have been performed in many countries. With respect to the frequency of meals, it has been reported that the prevalence of obesity rises as the frequency of meals decreases (Bellisle *et al.*, 1997). However, this issue does not yet seem to have been settled because some other studies have come to the opposite conclusion. The large-scale surveys performed in various parts of Europe and the United States have demonstrated that the body weight increases as the total dietary calorie intake increases (Williamson, 1996). In large-scale surveys like National Health and Nutrition Examination Surveys (NHANES) performed in the United States and other surveys performed in Germany, Scotland and Denmark, the BMI was higher in the high-fat diet group than in low-fat diet group (Lissner and Heitmann, 1995). A distinct feature of Indian diet is the high intake of dairy products and added sugar (Popkin *et al.*, 2001). Also, there seems to be an inexorable shift to the higher fat Western diet, reflected in a large proportion of the population consuming over 30 per cent of energy from fat. Unfortunately vegetable *ghee* in India appears to have very high trans fatty acid levels. According to Dr. Walter Willett, Chairman, Department of Nutrition, Harvard University, a major source of edible oil in India, "Dalda," a vegetable *ghee*, has trans fatty acid levels of about 50 per cent.

In NFHS-2, data on dietary pattern and intake relate to frequency of consumption of food items such as milk/curd, pulses/beans, green leafy vegetables, eggs, chicken, meat or fish. Prevalence of overweight and obesity among women is examined according to food habit and frequency of the intake of specific food items in Table 16.4. Vegetarian women were found to be more obese and overweight than non-vegetarian. There is a possibility that vegetarian people consume more fatty foods, particularly dairy products.

Further, looking at the consumption of milk or curd, it is again evident that higher the frequency of intake, higher the prevalence of overweight and obesity among women. More than 4 per cent of women are obese and about 13 per cent overweight among those who consume milk or curd daily as compared to less than 2 per cent obese and less than 10 per cent overweight who consumes these dairy items occasionally or never.

On the other hand, frequency of consumption of pulses or beans showed a mixed pattern of prevalence of obesity or overweight. Among women with more frequent intake of pulse or beans as well as among women who never consume pulse or beans, prevalence of obesity or overweight is found to be higher compared to women who consume pulses or beans weekly or occasionally. There is a possibility that women who never consume pulse or beans might be consuming non-vegetarian items more frequently. It is a common practice in India that vegetarian people consume dairy products and consume fatty diets as a substitute to non-vegetarian diets. Almost similar situation is apparent in case of frequency of consumption of eggs, meat or fish. Women consuming these items more frequently or never were found more obese and overweight than women who were found to consume these items occasionally. Women who consumed all such items like milk or curd, pulses or beans, green leafy as well as other vegetables and fruits on daily basis, were found to be more obese or overweight. Thus, higher amount of calories intake (more than the requirement) extensively aggravate the overweight or obesity among women.

Table 16.4

Food Consumption and Overweight or Obesity Body Mass Index (BMI) Levels among Women and Men Aged 15-49 according to Frequency of Consumption of Specific Food Items, India, NFHS-3, 2005-06

Type of Food	Body Mass Index (BMI) in Kg/m^2			
	Overweight or Obese Women[1] (≥ 25.0)	Number of Women	Overweight or Obese Men (≥ 25.0)	Number of Men
Milk or curd				
Daily or weekly	15.8	61,861	11.0	44,076
Occasionally or never	8.8	49,901	5.6	21,656
Pulses or beans				
Daily or weekly	12.8	99,894	9.5	59,566
Occasionally or never	11.2	11,868	6.8	6,168
Dark green, leafy vegetables				
Daily or weekly	12.7	103,873	9.5	61,471
Occasionally or never	12.6	7,871	6.4	4,260
Fruits				
Daily or weekly	19.2	44,360	13.5	30,955
Occasionally or never	8.3	67,320	5.5	34,760
Eggs				
Daily or weekly	15.1	36,431	10.6	27,095
Occasionally or never	11.5	75,297	8.3	38,633
Fish				
Daily or weekly	14.9	31,949	10.3	20,556
Occasionally or never	11.7	79,791	8.8	45,162
Chicken or meat				
Daily or weekly	17.1	25,398	12.4	18,436
Occasionally or never	11.3	86,335	8.0	47,286

Note: 1. Excludes pregnant women and women with a birth in the preceding.

2. months.

Consequences of Overweight and Obesity

The importance of obesity as a risk factor for a number of diseases including Type 2 diabetes, cardiovascular disease, hypertension, gallstones and certain cancers is well documented (WHO, 1998). Obesity or significant overweight can contribute to many problems in women's reproductive system like prolonged or heavy periods, menstrual pain, delayed ovulation, mid-cycle spotting, short luteal phase, premenstrual spotting, premenstrual syndrome, infertility, amenorrhea, fibroids, tumours of uterus, breast cancer, endometrial cancer, ovarian cancer, uterine prolapse etc. (Shannon, 1993). Several studies in India have related overweight conditions with diabetes, hypertension and heart disease (Venkatramana and Reddy, 2002; Misra *et al.*, 2001; Singh *et al.*, 2000; Gopinath *et al.*, 1994).

An attempt has also been made to look into some of the health problems of women and men by their BMI status (Table 16.5). Prevalence of asthma, diabetes and goitre was found to be significantly higher among obese and overweight women than normal or underweight women.

Table 16.5

Body Mass Index and Prevalence of Diabetes, Asthma and Goitre or Any Other Thyroid Disorders among Women and Men Aged 15-49, India, NFHS-3, 2005-06

Body Mass Index (BMI) in Kg/m^2	*Diabetes*	*Asthma*	*Goitre or Other Thyroid Disorders*	*Number*
		Women[1]		
Total thin (<18.5)	0.4	1.7	0.7	39,851
Normal (18.5-24.9)	0.8	1.6	0.8	57,890
Overweight or obese (≥ 25.0)	3.1	2.8	2.7	14,140
		Men		
Total thin (<18.5)	0.6	1.9	0.3	22,479
Normal (18.5-24.9)	1.1	1.5	0.4	37,176
Overweight or obese (≥ 25.0)	2.9	1.7	0.6	6,087

Note: 1 Excludes pregnant women and women with a birth in the preceding.
2. months.

In an earlier study using NFHS-2 data, it was found that prevalence of almost all maternal health problems like still birth, spontaneous abortion, induced abortion and caesarean births significantly to be higher among obese women. More than 25 per cent of overweight or obese women even had a terminated pregnancy compared to less than 20 per cent of normal and even underweight women. Also, at least one as well as two or more spontaneous abortions were found significantly higher among women with higher BMI. Induced abortion was also found significantly higher among women with higher BMI. About 10 per cent of obese or overweight women experienced induced abortion compared to five or less than five among normal and underweight women.

Caesarean births, which may be because of complications during pregnancy or child birth, were also found significantly higher among obese women followed by overweight and normal women. About 35 per cent of obese women have their last birth caesarean compared to 31 per cent among overweight women and 19 per cent among women with normal weight.

Conclusions

Overall in India, 3 per cent women are obese and 10 per cent overweight. There is not only significant differentials in the prevalence of overweight and obesity between rural and urban areas but overweight and obesity problem has assumed significant dimensions in urban areas particularly in metro cities. Even in the slum areas of Chennai and Hyderabad cities, more than 30 per cent of women are overweight or obese. The increasing overweight and obesity in urban population has serious implications, as still in India, the level of urbanisation is comparatively very low. Urbanisation and concentration of population in large cities will continue to increase bringing significant changes in the dietary habits and lifestyles of the people. Also, with changing socioeconomic scenario of the country more and more people may face overweight and obesity problems in near future. As seen, obese or overweight women and men are more at risk to health problems like diabetes and asthma. Among ever-married women, induced and spontaneous abortion and caesarean births were found to be negatively associated with overweight and obesity condition of women. It is high time that the traditional focus on undernutrition among women and men should be expanded to encompass all aspects of malnutrition including overnutrition.

References

Agrawal, P.K. (2002). "Emerging Obesity in Northern Indian States: A Serious Threat for Health", Paper presented at the IUSSP Regional Conference, Bangkok, June 10-13 (Unpublished).

Agrawal, P. and V. Mishra (2004). "Covariates of Overweight and Obesity Among Women in North India", *East West Center Working Papers, Population and Health Series*, No. 116, January.

Bellisle, F.R., McDebitt and A.M. Prentice (1997). "Meal Frequency and Energy Balance", *British Journal of Nutrition* 77: S57-S77.

Drewnowski, A. and B.M. Popkin (1997). "The Nutrition Transition: New Trends in the Global Diet", *Nutrition Reviews* 55(2): 31–43.

Gopalan, C. (1998). "Obesity in the Indian Urban 'Middle Class'", *Bulletin of the Nutrition Foundation of India* 19(1): 1-5.

Gopinath, N., S.L. Chadha, P. Jain, S. Shekhawat, and R. Tandon (1994). "An Epidemiological Study of Obesity in Adults in the Urban Population of Delhi", *Journal of Association of Physicians in India* 42: 212–215.

International Institute for Population Sciences (IIPS) & ORC Macro (2000). *National Family Health Survey (NFHS-2), 1998–99: India.* Mumbai: International Institute for Population Sciences.

Keys, A., K.F. Fidanza, M.J. Karvonen, N. Kimura and H.L. Taylor (1972). "Indices of Relative Weight and Obesity", *Journal of Chronic Diseases* 25: 329-343.

Lissner, L. and B.L. Heitmann (1995). "Dietary Fat and Obesity. Evidence from Epidemiology", *European Journal of Clinical Nutrition* 49: 79-90.

Maillard, G. *et al.* (1999). "Trends in the Prevalence of Obesity in the French Population between 1980 and 1991", *International Journal of Obesity and Related Metabolic Disorders* 23: 389-394

Misra, A., R.M. Pandey, J.R. Devi, R. Sharma, N.K. Vikram and N. Khanna (2001). "High Prevalence of Diabetes, Obesity and Dyslipidaemia in Urban Alum Population in Northern India", *International Journal of Obesity and Related Metabolic Disorders* 25(11): 1722–1729.

Pinstrup-Andersen, P., R. Pandya-Lorch (2001). "Emerging Food and Agriculture Concerns in the Developing World", International conference: *Sustainable Food Security for All by 2020. Entwicklung und Landlicher Raum* 4: 28-30.

Pishdad, G.R. (1996). "Overweight and Obesity in Adults Aged 20-74 in Southern Iran", *International Journal of Obesity and Related Metabolic Disorders* 20: 963-965.

Popkin, B.M. (2001). "Nutrition in Transition: The Changing Global Nutrition Challenge", *Asia Pacific Journal of Clinical Nutrition* 10 (Suppl): S13–S18.

————. (2002). "The Shift in Stages of the Nutritional Transition in the Developing World Differs from Past Experiences", *Public Health Nutrition* 5(1A): 205–214.

Popkin, B.M., S. Horton, S. Kim, A. Mahal, and J. Shuigao (2001). "Trends in Diet, Nutritional Status and Diet-related Non-communicable Diseases in China and India: The Economic Costs of the Nutrition Transition", *Nutrition Review* 59(12): 379–390.

Prescot-Clark, P. and P. Primatesta (eds) (1998). *Health Survey for England 1996*. The Stationery Office: London.

Schneider, D. (2000). "International Trends in Adolescent Nutrition", *Social Science and Medicine* 51: 955-967.

Shannon, M. (1993). "An Empathetic Look at Overweight", *CCI Family Foundation* 20(3): 3.

Shetty, P.S., and W.P.T. James (1994). "Body Mass Index—A Measure of Chronic Energy Deficiency in Adults", *Food and Nutrition Paper No. 56*. Rome: Food and Agricultural Organization.

Singh, R.B. *et al.* (2000). "Association of Dietary Factors and Other Coronary Risk Factors with Social Class in Women in Five Indian Cities", *Asia Pacific Journal of Clinical Nutrition* 9(4): 298-302.

Venkatramana, P. and P.C. Reddy (2002). "Association of Overall and Abdominal Obesity with Coronary Heart Disease Risk Factors: Comparison between Urban and Rural Indian Men", *Asia Pacific Journal of Clinical Nutrition* 11(1): 66-71.

Walker, A.R., F. Adam, B.F. Walker (2001). "World Pandemic of Obesity: The Situation in Southern African Populations", *Public Health* 115(6): 368-372, November.

Williamson, D.F. (1996). "Dietary Intake and Physical Activity as "Predictors" of Weight Gain in Observational, Prospective Studies of Adults", *Nutritional Review* 54: S101-109.

World Health Organization (WHO) (1998). *World Health Report: Life in 21st Century: A Vision for All.* Geneva: 132.

———. (WHO) (2000). International Association for the Study of Obesity (IASO) & International Obesity Task Force (IOTF). *The Asia-Pacific Perspective: Redefining Obesity and Its Treatment*. Geneva: World Health Organization.

———. (WHO) (2002). *The World Health Report 2002: Reducing Risks, Promoting Healthy Life*. Geneva: World Health Organization.

———. (WHO) (2003). Diet Nutrition and the Prevention of Chronic Diseases. *Report of a joint WHO/FAO expert consultation. Technical Report Series No. 916*. Geneva: World Health Organization.

Yoshike N., Y. Matsumura, M.M. Zaman, M. Yamahuchi (1998). "Descriptive Epidemiology of Body Mass Index in Japanese Adults in a Representative Sample from the National Nutrition Survey 1990-1994", *International Journal of Obesity and Related Metabolic Disorders* 22: 684-687.

Zargar, A.H., S.R. Masoodi, B.A. Laway, A.K. Khan, A.I. Wani, M.I. Bashir, and S. Akhtar (2000). "Prevalence of Obesity in Adults-An Epidemiological Study from Kashmir Valley of Indian Subcontinent", *Journal of the Association of Physicians of India* 48(12): 1170–1174.

17

Impact of Community Level Socioeconomic Inequality on Maternal Health

LAXMI KANT DWIVEDI AND ARIN KAR

Introduction

The Government of India identified the problem of poverty as one of the biggest challenges in development planning in India. Over the years, all levels of government in India have adopted a range of income, employment, health, education and social programmes to alleviate poverty and reduce socioeconomic inequality. The government's approach till late 1970s was that the growth process will take care of reducing poverty. However, the fruits of growth did not reach the poorer section of the country, especially in the rural areas. This lack of 'trickle down effect' of growth led the government to adopt special schemes for direct generation of income along with promotion of general growth. Persistence of the phenomenon suggests that national consensus on objectives did not and could not provide sufficient conditions for raising socioeconomic status or reduce socioeconomic inequality in rural India as around 80 per cent of the country's poor are to be found in the rural areas.

Poverty and health have been consistent in their negative association in both developed and developing countries. Poverty plays an important role in determining health status of the population as they interact to make it difficult for individuals with poor health to break out of a 'poverty-health trap' (Backlund *et al.*, 1996; Whitehead *et al.*, 2001). This lower socioeconomic status (SES) might have significant impact towards achieving the desired minimum nutritional status and access to and utilisation of health services especially for women. Women with poor SES comprise the most vulnerable section of the society with respect to their health status. Since women in general and particularly those residing in rural areas bear the burden of poverty, there is a gender divide in nutritional status. Women in the traditional Indian cultures have lower status and less social value than men. They tend to eat last and the least in their households. Therefore, if they live in poor families, they are the most likely members to be malnourished. However, they play a crucial role in shaping the nutritional status of the family. Malnourished women, who themselves are stunted, give birth to offspring with low birth weight. In rural India, these women have disadvantages during childhood and adolescence with numerous forms of neglect due to low SES. It is accepted that if special nutritional needs of women are not met, then physical and psychological insults to individuals become a drag on the development potential of entire households for multiple generations (Shetty, 2002).

This study uses Body Mass Index (BMI), an anthropometric measure as the indicator for nutritional status of women. Chronic energy deficiency in women is usually indicated by BMI of less than 18.5 where the unit is weight in kilograms per square of height in metres. Selection of BMI as the likely objective index for the assessment of nutritional status of women is based on the observation that BMI is consistently highly correlated with body weight and is relatively independent of the stature or height of the individual (Shetty, 2002).

The National Family and Health Survey (NFHS) data has not emphasised on the estimate of income and consumption expenditure inequality. So, this chapter uses average SES scores of the community as given in NFHS-2 (1998-1999) data. The scores are categorised into three socioeconomic categories of low, medium and high, and then the lower socioeconomic status is used as a proxy for poverty. However, the way of assigning weights to various asset holdings has been questioned in a study by Bhat and Zavier (1999). They mentioned that not only differences in income but differences in structure of economy and consumer preferences also affect asset ownership. Therefore, they constructed asset index specifically for rural areas. Land being a vital asset in rural areas, they assigned weight to each household asset ranging from 0 to 3 on the basis of inverse of possession ratios. They also suggested that an index score of 5 could be considered as the poverty line since 34 per cent of rural households at the all India level had asset scores lower than this.

Background and Literature Review

According to NFHS-2, more than 36 per cent women were reported to have BMI below 18.5 and among them 48 per cent have low standard of living, 36 per cent have medium and 17 per cent have high standard of living. During pregnancy, woman should gain about 10 kilograms on an average (WHO, 1995) but according to UNICEF, women in South Asia only gain about half of that (Shetty, 2002). On the linkages between poverty and malnutrition, Sukhatme (1987) opined that it is only when income generated from anti-poverty programmes like National Rural Employment Programme and Integrated Rural Development Programme enables the poor to modify their expenditure behaviour, it can be effective as an instrument in combating malnutrition. Significant changes in income and expenditure elasticities show that under sustained impact of anti-poverty programmes, the poor are being empowered. All these programmes are community level programmes, providing rationalisation for this study to understand the community level impact.

Community socioeconomic context affects health through two major pathways (Foster and McLanahan, 1996). First, it can reshape individuals' socioeconomic position by initiating opportunities and constraints persuaded in communities with different socioeconomic contexts affecting the educational attainment, job prospects and income level of individuals, which then more directly affect health. Secondly, by directly affecting the social service and physical environments of communities shared by residents. These affect the individual characteristics, conditions and experiences of individuals that more directly impact health (Robert, 1999). Studies have found that individual SES greatly mediates the relationship between community socio-economic level and individual health, with individual SES position explaining the association between community socioeconomic level and individual health. Even where independent effect was found, they were seen in socio-economically deprived communities. A 'double jeopardy' hypothesis might suggest that living in low SES communities may be particularly detrimental to the health of individuals who have lower SES themselves. Alternatively, a 'relative deprivation' hypothesis suggests that individuals with low SES may be worse off living in communities with higher SES than in communities with lower socioeconomic levels. This is because they might experience health effects of structural relative deprivation when competing with neighbours with higher socioeconomic position for scarce resources and/or psychosocial relative deprivation when comparing oneself to neighbours with higher socio-economic position. These theories provide contradictory but testable hypothesis (Robert, 1999). However, Diez-Roux *et al.*, 1997 have found no significant interaction between community socioeconomic context and individual socioeconomic position while predicting health. Contextual research simultaneously examines the effects of community level SES on individual level health, after controlling for individual and family level SES. This can conclude whether it is lower SES communities, individuals with lower SES, or both, that contribute to poor health (Robert, 1998).

Average education among women in communities has strong impact on use of maternity and other preventive health services. At individual level entire effect of education may not be seen. Community level contribution was seen in recent analysis of fertility from Africa (Kravdal, 2001) and India (McNay *et al.*, 2003), but possible importance of community status and education has been ignored in literature on maternal and child nutritional status in India. Three causal channels might explain the importance of community SES and education. These are 'social learning' (e.g. Bongaarts and Watkins, 1996) where knowledge and attitudes are transmitted directly from others by communication and observation. 'Social influence' refers to a more passive imitation of behaviour, driven by a desire to gain other people's approval or avoid sanctions (Kohler *et al.*, 2001). Indirect mechanism is where others' ideas, resources or behaviour can influence society and social institutions and thereby individual behaviour or events (Montogomery and Casterline, 1996).

Need for the Study

The major issues that have emerged from the review of earlier studies suggest that inequality in access to and utilisation of health services is a global phenomenon and SES is an important determinant. There is also evidence that inequality is less in preventive than curative health care, with higher dependence of poor households on publicly provided services. In market-oriented system, effective demand takes care of service availability and its quality. It is, however, not clear whether average SES of a region or community also affects distribution of primary health care services that can further affect nutritional status of mothers. Once the community with low SES has been identified, it was further examined whether increased concentration of low SES is associated with low health status by controlling for household economic status. Thus, it is to be seen whether the association between community socioeconomic context and aggregate and individual measures of health simply reflects: (a) relationship between individual socio-economic position and individual health of residents, or (b) affects characteristics of the community environment that can affect the health of all residents. If the association between community SES and health simply reflects the sum of relationships at the individual level, policy might target individuals with lower SES.

Though there is voluminous literature on association between poverty and health all over the world, there is dearth of literature exploring the community-level impact on health status of women in rural India.

Objective of the Study

The specific objective of this chapter is to examine the independent impact of socioeconomic status of community on maternal nutritional status by different regions of India.

The central hypothesis of this chapter is whether low socioeconomic status of community is associated with lower health status of women after controlling household socioeconomic status.

The other questions, which we want to address, are:

- Is there any systematic bias against relatively poor areas in terms of availability of sub-centre?
- Is the size of the village positively related with the socioeconomic status of community?

Data Source

The purpose of this chapter is to seek the effect of community level SES on nutritional status of women and it is sufficed by using NFHS-2 (1998-99) data. NFHS-2 provides the anthropometric measure by which nutritional status of women can be determined. NFHS is a national representative survey, which provides data at the household, village and individual level. The respondents are ever-married women in the age group 15-49. Data has been collected from 2,576 villages covering a total of 92,486 households and 90,303 sampled women. For the analysis, a sample of 52,540 has been considered after excluding pregnant women and missing cases with mean BMI of 19.58 kilograms per metre-square at the country level in rural areas. The number of missing cases has been found to be 4198 and is almost equally distributed among the household standard of living terciles. So this study has excluded the missing cases in further analysis.

Methodology

An asset index may be used as a measure of SES of households. Assigning weights to various asset holdings can create this index. The weights may be arbitrary or arrived at by factor analysis. But factor analysis does not directly take into account either the substitutability of assets or their market price (Bhatt and Zavier, 1999). In the present study, the rural households have been divided into low, medium and high terciles according to their standard of living score. The weights given to the housing characteristics such as type of house, type of cooking fuel, drinking water facility, sanitation facility etc., and household ownership of durable assets are the same as has been used in NFHS-2 (IIPS, 2000). The community standard of living, which has again been divided into low, medium and high terciles, is derived from the average of household standard of living scores in the concerned community. The standard of living has been used as a proxy for SES as mentioned in other studies (e.g., Bhat and Zavier, 1999; Khan *et al.*, 2005).

To look into the distribution of rural women according to household and community standard of living terciles having BMI of less than 18.5, simple cross-tabulation has been carried out. The same procedure has been used for determining the mean levels of BMI according to household standard of living terciles by village standard of living terciles. The difference of mean values of BMI among the community terciles for each household standard of living has been checked for statistical significance by using t-test.

For the regional analysis, all six regions have been considered—north, central, eastern, northeastern, western and southern. The states of Delhi, Haryana, Himachal Pradesh, Jammu and Kashmir and Punjab have been included in the northern region, while the central region consists of Madhya Pradesh, Uttar Pradesh, Rajasthan and Bihar. The states of Orissa and West Bengal comprise the eastern region and all the eight states of the northeast (Arunachal Pradesh, Assam, Manipur, Meghalaya, Mizoram, Nagaland, Sikkim and Tripura) have been clubbed to represent the northeastern region. Gujarat, Maharashtra and Goa have been categorised as the western region followed by Andhra Pradesh, Karnataka, Kerala and Tamil Nadu in the southern region. Logistic regression has been carried out after selecting each household's socioeconomic status. Interaction effect at 5 and 10 per cent level of significance between household and community socioeconomic status has been checked for each household standard of living category. BMI with less than 18.5 has been coded as one and zero for BMI value of greater than equal to 18.5.

Results

In the present study, BMI has been classified into two categories, i.e., BMI of less than 18.5 is considered as malnourished and BMI of greater than equal to 18.5 has been considered to be well nourished. It is to be mentioned here that there is no linear relationship between nutritional status and BMI and higher BMI value may also reflect poor nutritional status (Khan *et al.*, 2005). However, Gwatkin *et al.* (2003) showed the usefulness of the indicator. The study reveals that 41 per cent of ever-married women in rural areas of India are undernourished. Twenty-three per cent of rural women belong to both low household and community SES. Only 4.2 per cent of total women belonging to low SES households are living in high SES community whereas 3.6 per cent of women living in households with high SES actually reside in low SES community. About 14 per cent women are living in both high SES category of households and community.

Table 17.1 shows that about half of the women from the poorest household have low BMI. The percentage of people with BMI greater than equal to 18.5 and the mean BMI values increases with increase in household SES terciles. About 71 per cent of women from high SES category have BMI more than or equal to 18.5. The mean BMI value for women in the lowest and the highest terciles are 18.86 and 20.85 respectively. Distribution of women by two BMI categories among community standard of living terciles presents similar results as found in household level. About 47 per cent of women from the poorest community and 31 per cent from communities with high standard of living have low BMI. The percentage of people with BMI greater than equal to 18.5 increases with increase in community SES terciles. The mean BMI value for women in the lowest and the highest tercile are 19 and 20.61 respectively.

Table 17.1

Mean Levels of Body Mass Index (BMI) of Women according to Household and Community level Standard of Living (Terciles) in Rural India

Household Standard of Living (terciles)	*BMI<18.50 (in percentage)*	*Mean BMI*	*Standard Deviation*	*Sample*
Low	48.90	18.86	2.58	18851
Medium	41.80	19.40	2.87	16964
High	28.60	20.85	3.77	16725
Community Standard of Living (terciles)				
Low	46.60	19.00	2.65	17620
Medium	42.10	19.48	3.05	17185
High	31.20	20.61	3.70	17735

Note: Mean BMI in low/medium SES household/community is significantly lower than the mean BMI in high SES household/community.

Table 17.2 shows how community SES is associated with BMI after controlling for household SES. The proportion of women with BMI less than 18.5 in the community SES terciles decreases gradually as the community SES moves up from low to high after controlling the household SES. Fifty per cent in the low BMI category decrease to 43 per cent in the high community SES after controlling low SES households. When households with high SES are controlled, the number of women decreases sharply from 34 per cent in low BMI category to 25 per cent in high community SES. The difference of mean values of BMI between low and high community standard of living has been found to be statistically significant. The mean BMI for women in high socioeconomic status is 19.32 per cent with regard to low household SES whereas the mean BMI for women in high socioeconomic status is 21.30 per cent when households from high SES are selected. The differences of mean values of BMI are statistically significant in almost all the regions among low and high SES categories of communities except for the northern and central region when low household standard of living is selected.

Table 17.2

Mean Levels of Body Mass Index of Women according to Household Standard of Living (Terciles) and by Village Level Standard of Living (Terciles) in Rural India

Household Standard of Living (terciles)	*Community Standard of Living (terciles)*	*BMI <18.50 (in percentage)*	*Mean BMI*	*Standard Deviation*	*Sample*
Low	Low	49.60	18.78	2.49	10758
	Medium	49.50	18.85	2.61	5790
	High	43.40	19.32	2.96	2303
Medium	Low	44.50	19.11	2.62	5237
	Medium	42.40	19.37	2.85	6834
	High	36.50	19.94	3.22	4893
High	Low	34.00	20.12	3.31	1625
	Medium	31.90	20.46	3.58	4561
	High	25.00	21.30	3.94	10539

Note: Mean BMI in low/medium SES community is significantly lower than the mean BMI in high SES community for each household standard of living (terciles).

Table 17.3 shows the mean levels of BMI for ever-married women in the age-group 15-49 according to household standard of living and by village standard of living in six regions of rural India The differences of mean values of BMI are statistically significant in almost all the regions among low and high SES categories of communities except for the northern and central region when low household standard of living is selected.

Northern Region

When households with low standard of living are selected, greater percentage of women are found to be in the malnourished category at communities with high socioeconomic status than those with lower SES but it is statistically insignificant. Even in the medium SES communities, greater numbers of women are found to be in the malnourished category than those in the lower SES communities. Only in the medium community status more percentage of women have low BMI than those with BMI greater than or equal to 18.5 with regard to low household SES. When households having medium

SES are selected, the number of women having BMI less than 18.5 is almost equal in communities with low and high status but in the medium status there are more women in the malnourished category. However, the mean values are significantly lower in low SES communities as opposed to high SES communities. The results are similar when households with higher SES are considered.

Central Region

In the central region when low household SES is selected, almost equal percentage of women are found to be in the low BMI category of all the socioeconomic categories of the community. The difference in mean values of BMI at the community level is not found to be statistically significant. The differences in mean values of BMI between low and medium and between low and high are found to be significant among all the community categories. In case of households with high SES, about 30 per cent of women are found in low BMI category.

Eastern Region

In the eastern region, with regard to low SES households, lesser percentage of women is found in the low BMI category in communities with high SES. In the medium tercile communities, 60 per cent are found to have BMI less than 18.5. Mean values of BMI between low and high community terciles are found to be statistically significant. Similar results were obtained when medium and high household terciles have been selected separately. Around 22 per cent of women from both high community as well as high SES households are found to be in low BMI category. The mean BMI is highest (21.5) for women belonging to high SES communities on the basis of high household SES as compared to low and medium household SES.

Northeastern Region

The northeast shows that 29 per cent women have BMI less than 18.5 among communities with high SES when low household SES is considered. Around 19 and 17 per cent women belonging to high socioeconomic communities have BMI less than 18.5 when medium and high household categories are selected, respectively. The mean of BMI values between low and high socioeconomic categories of communities are found to be statistically significant in both the cases.

Western Region

In case of households with low SES, about 62 per cent of women at the lowest tercile community are found to have BMI less than 18.5, much higher as compared to corresponding percentage for medium and high household standard of living. Here, except for the difference of means between low and medium community terciles when low household status is selected, all other mean differences between low and medium and between low and high community socioeconomic statuses are statistically significant.

Southern Region

Communities in high socioeconomic categories are found to have lesser percentage of women having BMI lower than 18.5. With regard to households belonging to high SES, fewer percentage of women are found to have BMI less than 18.5 in the community socioeconomic tercile as compared to low or medium household SES. The differences of mean BMI values for women within the community tercile between communities of low and high SES are found to be statistically significant for each household SES.

Table 17.3

Mean Levels of Body Mass Index (BMI) of Women according to Household Standard of Living (Terciles) and by Village Standard of Living (Terciles) in Different Regions of Rural India

Region	Household Standard of Living (terciles)	Community Standard of Living (terciles)	BMI <18.50 (in percentage)	Mean BMI	Standard Deviation	Sample
North	Low	Low	31.40	19.80	2.64	116
		Medium	56.10	18.88	2.83	186
		High	41.70	19.52	3.07	421
	Medium	Low	31.00	19.89[a]	2.54	98
		Medium	38.60	19.62	2.80	429
		High	32.60	20.32[a]	3.49	1662
	High	Low	20.00	20.30[a]	2.27	15
		Medium	34.40	20.21	3.00	178
		High	20.90	21.80[a]	4.08	4286
Central	Low	Low	44.50	18.96	2.35	4261
		Medium	45.60	18.96	2.48	2293
		High	45.70	19.04	2.40	784
	Medium	Low	42.40	19.12[a,b]	2.46	2187
		Medium	40.60	19.30[a]	2.56	2932
		High	40.40	19.46[b]	2.70	1378
	High	Low	30.50	20.03[a]	3.01	532
		Medium	33.60	19.99	3.00	1894
		High	30.40	20.41[a]	3.32	2526
East	Low	Low	56.60	18.39[a]	2.30	2267
		Medium	60.40	18.33	2.35	639
		High	44.30	19.35[a]	2.82	125

contd...

...contd...

Region	*Household Standard of Living (terciles)*	*Community Standard of Living (terciles)*	*BMI <18.50 (in percentage)*	*Mean BMI*	*Standard Deviation*	*Sample*
	Medium	Low	53.50	18.64[a]	2.36	771
		Medium	49.70	18.95	2.63	453
		High	37.80	19.40[a]	2.82	147
	High	Low	40.40	19.62[a,b]	3.10	340
		Medium	31.30	20.42[a]	3.24	435
		High	22.30	21.48[b]	3.90	254
Northeast	Low	Low	32.00	19.65[a]	2.66	1681
		Medium	34.30	19.53	2.41	595
		High	29.10	19.85[a]	2.13	199
	Medium	Low	29.50	19.81[a]	2.70	906
		Medium	24.30	20.10	2.62	1039
		High	19.30	20.40[a]	2.61	600
	High	Low	26.10	20.48[a]	3.52	245
		Medium	21.60	20.47	2.60	552
		High	16.70	21.21[a]	3.31	1076
West	Low	Low	61.70	18.16[a]	2.28	718
		Medium	57.70	18.50[a]	2.64	548
		High	53.70	18.65	2.98	313
	Medium	Low	54.30	18.49[a,b]	2.33	321
		Medium	51.60	18.84[a]	2.81	610
		High	44.00	19.50[b]	3.07	399
	High	Low	47.70	19.50[a,b]	3.21	119
		Medium	37.40	20.07[a]	3.77	421
		High	29.10	21.00[b]	4.13	1094
South	Low	Low	50.00	18.95[a]	2.84	1715
		Medium	47.70	19.00	2.80	1529
		High	35.70	20.00[a]	3.48	461
	Medium	Low	41.50	19.53[a]	3.02	954
		Medium	40.70	19.79	3.30	1371
		High	31.80	20.64[a]	3.72	707
	High	Low	29.60	20.78[a,b]	3.67	374
		Medium	28.30	21.27[a]	4.23	1081
		High	20.80	22.20[b]	4.29	1303

Note: a and b denote mean BMI in low SES community is significantly lower than the mean BMI in medium/high SES community in each household standard of living (terciles) by different regions of India.

Logistic Regression

The interaction between household standard of living and community standard of living is found to be insignificant in case of households in low socioeconomic tercile in all the six regions considered.

Table 17.4(a) represents odds ratio of community level SES and other variables on BMI in comparison to their reference categories after selecting households belonging to low *SES*. It shows that in high SES communities of the northern region, the chances of women to be in low BMI category are more than that of women in low *SES* but is statistically insignificant. Expected odds of other religions to be in low BMI category are 0.596 times less likely than those of Hindu religion. For the southern region, women from the medium SES community are less likely to be in low BMI status than those in the community with low SES. Chances of women to have BMI less than 18.5 in high SES communities are significantly less than those in communities with low SES. Those belonging to other religions are 25 per cent less likely to have BMI less than 18.5. In the central region, odds of women in the medium SES community and those in the high SES are insignificantly more likely to have BMI values less than 18.5 than those in low SES community. Women belonging to other castes are less likely to be in low BMI category than those of Scheduled Castes and Tribes. Those women, who have reached menopause or infecundity, are more likely to have BMI below 18.5 than those who are fecund. For the western region, expected odds of those in high SES community are 0.752 times significantly less to be in low BMI category than those in communities with low SES. Those in other religions are 25 per cent less likely to have BMI less than 18.5. In the east, odds of being in low BMI category is 1.102 times more in communities of medium SES than women in communities with low SES. However, likelihood of being in low BMI category is halved in communities of high SES than women in communities with low SES. Those women, who have reached menopause, are more likely to have BMI less than 18.5 than those women who are fecund. In the northeast, women are less likely to have BMI less than 18.5 in communities of medium and high SES than women in communities with low SES.

Table 17.4(b) represents odds ratio of community level SES and other variables on BMI in comparison to their reference categories after selecting households belonging to medium *SES*. Interaction between community and household standard of living has been found significant in case of central and northeast regions. The impact of community level SES on maternal nutritional status is found to be insignificant in northern region. In the central, we failed to examine the independent impact of community level SES on BMI. However, the likelihood of having BMI less than 18.5 are more in case of contraceptive use, religion and women in the menopausal/infecund stage as compared to their reference categories. In the east, the interaction is not significant. Women in communities of medium and high SES category are less likely to have BMI below 18.5. In the northeast, the interaction is found to be significant. Those women in high SES community are found to be less likely to have BMI less than 18.5 than those in low SES community. In the west, odds of women having BMI less than 18.5, in medium and high SES communities are less than those women living in communities with low standard of living. The southern region also has insignificant interaction between the two levels of SES. Women belonging to high SES community, falling in the age-group 25-49, being literates, belonging to other castes, and using contraceptives are less likely to have BMI less than 18.5 as compared to their reference categories.

In this case of depicting odds ratio of community level SES and other variables on BMI in comparison to their reference categories after selecting households belonging to high *SES*, interaction has been found to be significant between community and household standard of living. Therefore, there is no independent role of community level SES on maternal nutritional status when household standard of living is high in all the six regions.

Table 17.4(a)

Odds Ratio of Community Level Socioeconomic Status and Other Variables on Maternal Nutritional Status among Low Socioeconomic Status of Household of Aged 15-49 Ever-married Women by Different Regions of India

Variables	*Category*	*North*	*South*	*Central*	*West*	*East*	*Northeast*
Socioeconomic status of community	Low®						
	Medium	2.275*	0.961	1.052	0.830	1.102	0.871
	High	1.480	0.712*	1.114	0.752*	0.560*	0.728*
Age	15-24®						
	25-34	0.433*	0.740*	0.970	0.947	0.861	0.959
	35-49	0.427*	0.592*	0.964	0.820	0.687*	0.844
Education	Illiterate®						
	Literate <middle school	1.091	0.751*	0.965	0.975	0.843	0.947
	Middle school complete	0.65	0.452*	1.043	1.001	1.004	0.976
	High school complete and above	0.007	0.669*	1.060	0.820	1.326	0.729
Religion	Hindu®						
	Others	0.596*	0.781*	1.228*	0.754*	0.948	0.830*
Caste	SC/ST®						
	Others	0.864	0.888	0.859	0.901	0.884	1.805*
Ever use of contraceptive	No®						
	Yes	1.176	0.988	1.184	1.095	1.264	1.091
Fecundity status	Fecund®						
	Infecund/ Menopause	1.269	1.202*	1.1690	0.947	1.403*	1.207
Parity (continuous)		1.125*	1.036	1.016*	0.995	1.020	1.024

Note: Interaction between household and community level socioeconomic is found to be insignificant. *p<0.05, ® Reference Category.

Table 17.4(b)

Odds Ratio of Community Level Socioeconomic Status and Other Variables on Maternal Nutritional Status among Medium Socioeconomic Status of Household of Aged 15-49 Ever-married Women by Different Regions of India

Variables	Category	North	South	Central	West	East	Northeast
Socioeconomic status of community	Low®						
	Medium	1.335	1.048	1.071	0.851	0.895	1.139
	High	1.169	0.905	1.233**	0.644*	0.577*	0.987
Age	15-24®						
	25-34	0.900	0.654*	1.092	0.957	0.861	0.999
	35-49	0.880	0.441	0.903	0.593*	0.687*	1.118
Education	Illiterate®						
	Literate <middle school	1.061	0.601*	0.967	1.125	0.843	1.135
	Middle school complete	0.999	0.651*	0.722*	0.740	1.004	1.001
	High school complete and above	1.266	0.460*	0.676*	0.866	1.326	1.100
Religion	Hindu®						
	Others	0.636*	0.635*	1.079	0.535*	0.948	0.972
Caste	SC/ST®						
	Others	0.853	1.126	0.785**	0.679	0.884	1.380*
Ever use of contraceptive	No®						
	Yes	0.816**	0.961	1.149*	1.164	1.264	1.256*
Fecundity status	Fecund®						
	Infecund/ Menopause	1.189	1.228**	1.170*	1.124	1.403*	1.100
Parity (continuous)		1.018	1.041	1.025**	0.960	1.020	0.978
Community SES* Household SES		NS	NS	0.999*	NS	NS	0.996*

Note: * p<0.05, ** p<0.10, NS= Not Significant, ® Reference Category.

Table 17.5 shows few characteristics for the best 10 per cent and worst 10 per cent villages according to their SES scores. There are 58 villages falling in the latter category. From the central region, there are 19 villages, 16 from the east, 20 villages from the northeast and 3 from the west. The mean BMI for women in these villages have been found to be 19.12. Around 38 per cent women have BMI less than 18.5. Only 14 per cent villages have a sub-centre. The mean distance from the sub-centre is 7.73 kilometres. About 69 per cent of women live in village size of 1500 or less (median size 1250). There are 254 villages falling in the best 10 scores. From the central region, there are 50 villages, 146 from the north, 21 from the northeast, 25 from the west and 12 villages from the south. The mean BMI for women in these villages have been found to be 21.45. Around 22 per cent women have BMI less than 18.5. About 48 per cent villages have a sub-centre. The mean distance from the sub-centre is 0.52 kilometres. About 32 per cent of women live in village size of 1500 or less (median size 3000).

Table 17.5

Mean Characteristics of Villages/Women according to Worst 10 per cent and Best 10 per cent Villages in Rural India

Characteristics of Villages/Women	*Worst Villages (10% of total villages) No. (percentage)*	*Best Villages (10% of total villages)No. (percentage)*
North	0 (0.00)	146 (57.48)
Central	19 (32.75)	50 (19.69)
East	16 (27.59)	0 (0.00)
Northeast	20 (34.48)	21 (8.27)
West	3 (5.17)	25 (9.84)
South	0 (0.00)	12 (4.72)
Total	58 (100.00)	254 (100.00)
Sub-centre	14.0	48.0
Mean distance from sub-centre (kms)	7.73	0.52
Median size of village	1025	3000
Mean BMI	19.12	21.45
BMI<18.5 (per cent)	37.80	22.20

Table 17.6 shows the means of village size and distance from sub-centres according to community socioeconomic terciles. In all the regions except the northeast, the mean village size increases with increase in SES. The mean distance from the sub-centre decreases as community SES increases. However, in the south, the mean distance is almost equal for low and high community SES.

Discussion and Conclusion

After categorising households into three socioeconomic categories by standard of living, it is found that at both the household and community level there is a consistent inverse relationship between SES and BMI status of women. This is consistent with findings in literature about relationship between SES and BMI status of women (Khan *et al.*, 2005). When low SES household tercile is controlled, the increase in mean BMI for women in lower to higher community terciles is found in every region. This implies that the community has an independent impact on health and its effect is manifested when household SES is lower. The result is more or less consistent when we control the medium SES households. When high SES households are controlled, we have failed to establish the relation found in lower SES households. This study is not compatible with the 'relative deprivation' hypothesis discussed earlier in review of literature. Women living in low household SES have been found to benefit from high community SES. So the community effect is found to be substantial on women's health status when household SES is low. Residing in communities with high SES may have an impact on women from low household SES through diffusion of knowledge about proper nutritional intakes and since high SES communities have better health facilities, the diffusion effect makes women in low household SES realise the need of proper nutrition and active life. A process of 'social learning' seems to interact between community SES and individual SES in case of low SES households residing in high SES communities.

Table 17.6

Mean Population Size of Village and Mean Distance of Sub-centre from Village according to Village Level Socioeconomic Status by Different Regions of India

Region	*Village Level Standard of Living (terciles)*	*Mean Distance from Sub-centre (kms)*	*Mean Population Size*
North	Low	11.9	1075
	Medium	5.7	2846
	High	3.5	3489
Central	Low	6.59	3391
	Medium	5.2	3420
	High	4.8	4245
East	Low	3.9	2625
	Medium	5.6	2975
	High	1.2	3217
Northeast	Low	11.0	5697
	Medium	4.9	2963
	High	3.8	4307
West	Low	7.3	2171
	Medium	2.8	3284
	High	1.5	9000
South	Low	3.7	3868
	Medium	3.0	7025
	High	3.8	17136

We have also examined the availability/distance of sub-centres from villages because primary health centres or sub-centres deliver most of the maternal health services in India (IIPS and ORC Macro, 2000). Unfortunately, there is no relevant information about the quality of these health centres. It is seen that availability/distance of/from sub-centres decreases with increase in SES of villages and higher the village size is, greater the SES of the villages and better the health facility.

References

Backlund, E., P.D. Sorlie and N.J. Johnson (1996). "The Shape of the Relationship between Income and Mortality in the United States: Evidence from the National Longitudinal Mortality Study", *Annals of Epidemiology* 6: 12-20.

Bhat, P.N.M. and F. Zavier (1999). "Findings of National Family Health Survey-Regional Analysis", *Economic and Political Weekly* XXXIV(42 and 43): 3008-3032.

Bongaarts, J. and S.C. Watkins (1996). "Social Interactions and Contemporary Fertility Transitions", *Population and Development Review* 22: 639-682.

Diez-Roux, A.V., Nieto, F.J. Muntaner, C. Tyroler, H.A. and Comstock, G.W. (1997). "Neighbourhood Environments and Coronary Heart Disease: A Multilevel Analysis", *American Journal of Epidemiology* 146(1): 48-63.

Foster, E.M. and S. McLanahan (1996). "An Illustration of the Use of Instrumental Variable: Do Neighborhood Conditions affect a Young Person's Chance of Finishing High School?", *Psychological Methods* 1(3): 249-260.

Gwatkin, D., S. Ruskin, K. Johnson, E. Suliman and A. Wagstaff (2003). *Socio-economic Differences in Health, Nutrition and Population*. 2[nd]edition Vol.1&2. Washington DC: World Bank.

International Institute for Population Sciences (IIPS) and ORC Macro. (2000). *National Family Health Survey (NFHS-2), 1998-99: India*. Mumbai: IIPS.

Khan, M.M., D.R. Hotchkiss, A. Berruti, A. Andres and P.L. Hutchinson (2005). *Geographic Aspects of Poverty and Health in Tanzania: Does Living in a Poor Area Matter?* Oxford University Press.

Kohler, H.P., J.R. Behrman and S.C. Watkins (2001). "The Density of Social Networks and Fertility Decisions: Evidence from South Nyanza District, Kenya", *Demography* 38: 43-58.

Kravdal, Ø (2001). "Importance of Education for Fertility in Sub-Saharan Africa is Substantially Underestimated When Community Effects are Ignored," *www.oekonomi.uio.no* [accessed on 22/03/07].

Kravdal, Ø (2003). "Child Mortality in India: Individual and Community Effects of Women's Education and Autonomy," *East West Center Working Papers, Population Series No.* 12.

Montogomery, M.R. and J.B. Casterline (1996). "Social Learning, Social Influence and New Models of Fertility", *Population and Development Review* 22: 151-175.

McNay, P. Arokiasamy and K.R. Cassen (2003). "Why are Uneducated Women in India using Contraception? A Multilevel Analysis", *Population Studies* 57(1): 21-40.

Robert, S.A. (1998). "Community Level Socio-economic Status Effects on Adult Health", *Journal of Health and Social Behaviour* 39: 18-37.

Robert, S.A. (1999). "Socioeconomic Position and Health: The Independent Contribution of Community Socio-economic Context", *Annual Review of Sociology* 25: 489-516.

Shetty, P.S. (2002). "Food and Nutrition", in *Oxford Text Book of Public Health (4th ed. 2004)*. London: Oxford University Press.

Sukhatme, P.V. (1987). "Poverty and Malnutrition", *Economic and Political Weekly* XXII(3): 83-84.

Whitehead, M. Dahlgren, G., and T. Evans (2001). "Equity and Health Sector Reforms: Can Low Income Countries Escape the Medical Poverty Trap?", *The Lancet* 358: 833-836.

WHO (1995). "Physical Status: The Use and Interpretation of Anthropometry". Geneva: World Health Organization.

18

HIV/AIDS in Bellary

*A Human Development Perspective**

INDRANI GUPTA, MAYUR TRIVEDI AND PRADEEP GUIN

Introduction

This chapter looks at the epidemic in the district of Bellary in Karnataka, using the human development approach. Bellary has remained central to much of the recent discussions on HIV and AIDS in Karnataka, because its HIV prevalence remains one of the highest in the state (Mahila Samakhya, 2002), despite a long history of interventions. The chapter focuses on three key factors that may alter the course of the epidemic: the quality of economic growth, the nature of governance, and the extent and adequacy of interventions and argues that all three are necessary for making an impact on the epidemic. Economic growth that is not consistent with human development can render a good set of interventions ineffective, even in well-governed areas. Similarly, quality economic growth and potentially effective interventions, when delivered in a poorly governed area may not achieve the desired results. The chapter uses this framework to analyse the HIV and AIDS situation in Bellary, and focuses on key factors that have played an important role in setting the course of the epidemic in the district.

Human Development and HIV/AIDS

The focus, worry and interest around AIDS epidemic have been unparalleled in its intensity in modern times. The rapidly increasing mortality experienced by countries in the Sub-Saharan Africa (SSA) region in the early days of the epidemic was reminiscent of the Black Death in Europe few centuries earlier, and viewed as a tool that had the potential of wiping out rapidly the meagre progress made in especially the poor countries. The essentially behavioural nature of the HIV epidemic meant that unlike the

---

*. This paper is based on a report entitled "Understanding HIV and Development: An Analysis from Bellary District in Karnataka, India", published by UNDP, June 2008. The funding for this research was provided by UNDP.

plague, there were fewer prevention tools available with the policy makers that could quickly bring the spreading virus under control.

An extensive literature review done on impact studies (Gupta *et al.*, 2007) point towards one common theme: the close link of the epidemic with low human development, especially poverty. It is now widely agreed that the most important cause of persistent poverty is too little economic growth, especially in the poorest countries. The other reason is persistent inequalities within countries that prevent the poor from participating in the growth that did occur (Chen and Ravallion, 2000).

The two charts below bring out very succinctly the relationship between human development indicators and HIV: the Human Development Index brought out by UNDP has been divided into four quartiles and plotted against the average HIV prevalence for: (a) all countries and (b) countries with non-zero prevalence. Both the figures indicate clearly that there is a very high negative correlation between HDI and HIV prevalence: HIV prevalence is lower on an average in countries with higher HDI and vice versa (Figure 18.1).

Figure 18.1

Human Development Index and HIV: A Comparison

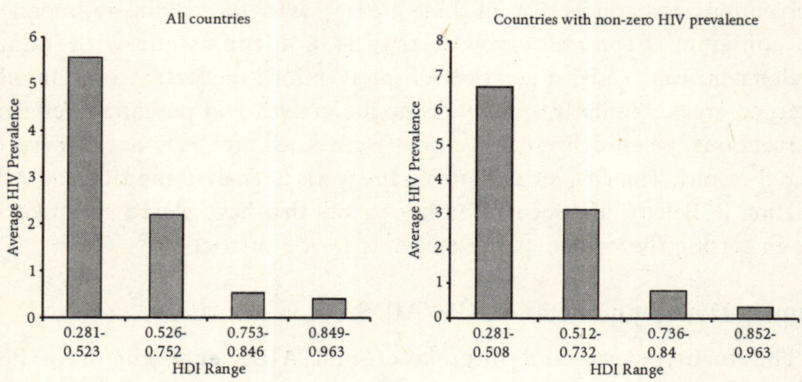

The presence of significant poverty and large groups of population with low human development make countries and populations within countries vulnerable to HIV (see for example Piot *et al.*, 2007, UNICEF, 2007, Kristensen, 2007). A study of 72 developing countries, done by Martha Ainsworth, Mead Over and others for the World Bank in 1997, showed that low incomes, high inequality, high ratio of urban males to females and significant male-female literacy gaps all contributed significantly to the spread of HIV levels (World Bank, 1999). Along with being vulnerable to the infection, the poor are most vulnerable to its greater impact as well. It is now confirmed and well documented that the epidemic worsens poverty and adds to the pool of poor. The problem of tackling poverty is therefore, bound to get worse in the worst affected countries of the region.

A very interesting and relevant paper in the present context that looked at the links between development and HIV prevalence, found that it is not sufficient for development to reduce high-risk behaviour. The authors argue that countries needed to reach a threshold level of development for sexual practices to become safer; else with lower levels of development, it was likely that even richer individuals will practice unsafe sex, given that most others are doing that as well (Clark and Vencatachellam, 2003). The authors contend that if the production technology evinces high human capital externalities, such that an individual's income depends on the aggregate level of income (or human capital) in the economy, and he expects a large proportion of the population to be engaged in unsafe sex, the person is more likely to engage in unsafe sex himself (income effect).

This finding is consistent with the hypothesis that a development pattern that generates a large pool of individuals with low income on the one hand and a small pool of individuals with very high income on the other may facilitate a faster spread of HIV, especially if there are other cultural and social practices (that promotes unsafe sex) already existing that act as catalysts in such situations. While more evidence on inequality and HIV will be presented later in this chapter, it is suffice to say here that the case of Bellary seems to fit well into this model. A key role in Bellary's development pattern is played by the rapid growth in the mining sector: there is now enough evidence from other parts of the world, especially Africa, that the mining sector with its typical workforce profile has been responsible for rapid spread of the infection. A report initiated by the Commission for Africa analyses several African countries and concludes that "the negative labour practices used in mining, construction and transport industries and domestic work, coupled with apartheid policies have contributed significantly to the spread of HIV." The situation in Bellary is no different and while Africa had apartheid policies, Bellary has a significant presence of backward classes (and women) with very low human development indicators.

Methodology and Data

The research was carried out for about one year, and included both quantitative and qualitative data/information collection and collation. A significant part of the methodology included workshops/meetings with key stakeholders, both within and outside the government structure. Various existing secondary sources of information were accessed and some key data was updated by engaging local researchers. Finally, primary data—both quantitative as well as qualitative—were collected, in the form of: (a) six hundred migrant households in three *taluks*, to analyse the magnitude, nature and characteristics of migration (one-month survey conducted in the month of June 2007), (b) survey among STD clinic attendees, women attending the Prevention of Parent to Child Transmission of HIV (PPTCT) centre and individuals attending the Revised National Tuberculosis Control Programme (RNTCP) at hospitals (data collected for 30 days in each of the three sites at Bellary and Hospet), and (c) nine Focus Group Discussions (FGD) and Key Informant Interviews (KI) among various groups.

Bellary: An Overview of Development

Bellary, a district in eastern Karnataka has a population of around 2.03 million, with two-third of its population residing in rural area. The district with seven *taluks* has around 36 per cent Scheduled Castes (SC) and Scheduled Tribes (ST), with the highest population of STs in the state (RGI, 2001). Below, we present some key economic and other social indicators of development and well-being in Bellary, to put the discussion of HIV and AIDS in the proper context. In addition, we discuss the mining sector in some detail, since it plays a pivotal role in the development of the district.

District Economy

In 2003-04, Bellary's share in state income was 4.8 per cent, ranking it as the 5th best district. While primary and secondary sectors contribute 21.4 and 35.4 per cent respectively, the share of tertiary sector (43.2 per cent) is below the state average of 54 per cent, indicating a relatively greater role of non-service industries in its economic development. Bellary tops among all districts in Karnataka in terms of the share of secondary sector in total income (GoK, 2005).

As can be seen from Figure 18.2, one-fourth of the total district income comes from the registered manufacturing industries, which includes textiles and steel industries. The share of mining and quarrying is at 8.1 per cent. However, if one takes into account the share of illegal mining in the district—discussed briefly below—these shares are likely to look different.

The rank of Bellary in terms of per capita net district domestic product (NDDP) increased from 9th to 3rd over 1990-91—2003-04, making it the third richest district of Karnataka, after Bangalore Urban and Dakshina Kannada. However, unlike these districts which saw rise in district income over a period, Bellary has seen a sharp increase in its income only recently; the district economy grew by 47 per cent between 1990-1991 and 1998-99 as compared to 63 per cent between 1998-99 and 2003-04.

Figure 18.2

Distribution of Income across Sectors in Bellary

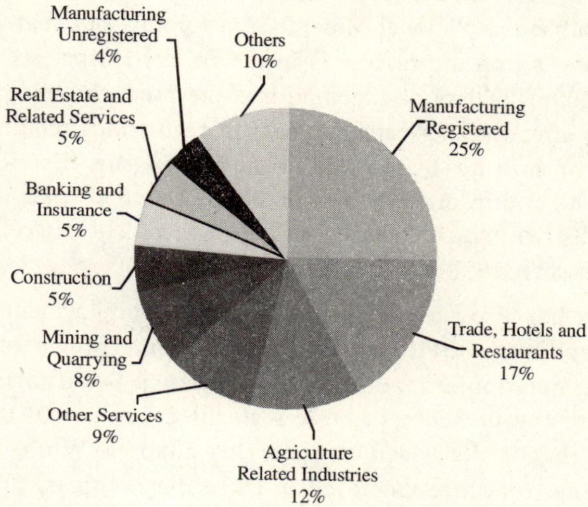

Further breakdown of growth by broad industries during 1999-2004, reveals that manufacturing (registered), mining and transport industries have seen spectacular rates of growth (248, 226 and 190 per cent, respectively). The share of registered manufacturing industry has doubled from 11 per cent to more than 25 per cent, whereas agriculture—which was topping the chart in 1998-99—has seen a sharp decline of 17 percentage points in its share in total income. In fact, it can be safely said that the mining sector has been containing the rapid decline in the share of primary sector in total income, which has experienced negative growth rates in areas like agriculture and fishing.

Bellary's primary sector presents an interesting picture with reference to two of its components—mining and quarrying, and agriculture. While the mining industry grew rapidly, the agricultural production nose-dived, mostly due to the continuous drought for almost four years, registering a negative growth between 1998-99 and 2003-04. While no studies exist to substantiate this, it is surmised that the growth of the many-layered agricultural sector is relatively more equalising than that of the almost bipolar mining industry, with its mine owners and operators on the one hand, and those who work for them on the other. This type of growth is more likely to lead to a concentration of wealth in a few hands, which is what Bellary has seen in the recent past.

Since the mining sector plays such a pivotal role in Bellary's development, a brief overview of this sector is given below.

Iron Ore Mining in Bellary

Karnataka, with 41 per cent of the total iron ore resource of India, is the richest among the 15 iron ore resource states (Indian Bureau of Mines, 2006). The recently published National Mineral Policy points out that about 16 per cent of the states's iron ore reserve is in the Bellary-Hospet sector (Planning Commission, 2006). Bellary has been an iron ore-producing district for a long time; however, after the 1999 amendments in regulations relating to mining, the number of mining leases for iron ore in the district increased dramatically. The reform of 1999 brought about a second spurt in the mining sector in the district, which experienced a growth of 214 per cent in iron ore production between 1998 and 2005.

The district has also seen a dynamic growth in employment in mines, as well as in ancillary activities like construction, trade, transport, etc. Employment generation around mining activities in Bellary has also got an impetus due to the presence of large-scale illegal mines in the district, a phenomenon that is discussed later in this chapter. While there are no estimates on the workforce employed in these illegal mines, the fact-finding report on child labour (Mines, Minerals and People, 2005 or MM&P from now onwards) gives some insight into the employment situation. The report mentions that an estimated 400,000 casual labourers are working in the iron ore mines in Bellary district, 50 per cent[1,2] being child labourers, mainly girls, and very young boys some of whom were as young as 5 years. Even the transportation sector employs at least 1.5 lakh casual workers in the three *taluks* of Bellary, Hospet and Sandur, most of whom are young boys.

Most of the workers, especially in the illegal mines, are migrant labourers working on a daily wage basis and are preferred to the local labourers by miners, mainly to avoid giving adequate perks and benefits. These casual labourers, including women and children, work under extremely hazardous situations and live in dismal condition.[3,4,5] The sudden emergence of STD

1. The fact-finding team observed that most of the children—who have no prescribed working hours or wages—were 'forced' into all forms of mining activities like digging, breaking stones, sieving, loading, dumping, transporting and processing activities of iron ore mining without adequate safety equipments, making them susceptible to injuries and accidents, apart from chronic mining-induced health problems.
2. *http://www.deccanherald.com/Content/Jun212007/metrothurs200706208478.asp*
3. *http://bellary.com/ironoreexport.htm* viewed on July 12, 2007.
4. *http://www.hinduonnet.com/fline/fl2311/stories/20060616002104300.htm*
5. *http://www.hindu.com/2007/05/21/stories/2007052107810300.htm*

clinics around Hospet and Bellary bears out the possibility of stepped up sexual activity, which in turn makes the mining sector a prime catalyst in the spread of HIV in this region (Anonymous, 2006; MM&P, 2005).

As can be seen from Table 18.1 which is based on different sources, it seems close to 55 per cent of the mining in Bellary is illegal, about 35-40 per cent alone by non-registered miners. Some put the estimate even higher, and contest that more than 80 per cent of mining is illegal.[6]

Table 18.1

Classification of Mining Activity in Bellary

Particulars	*Legal Mining*		*Illegal Mining*	
Classification of mining miner	Approved land Registered miner	Approved land Registered miner	Non-approved land Registered miner	Non-approved land Non-registered
activities	Declared quantity	Undeclared quantity	Undeclared quantity	Undeclared quantity
Estimated proportion of iron ore production	40-45	0-5	5-10	35-40

Source: Authors' estimation.

Mining and Development in Bellary

Most of the iron ores from Bellary is exported, due to a paucity of end users like large scale steel industries, which in turn have been constrained due to shortages in water and power (Planning Commission, 2006). The inability of the district to absorb a major part of the ore thus produced has made the development pattern of the district akin to countries that suffered from the phenomenon of "Dutch Disease", where exploitation of natural resources is accompanied by a development pattern which is detrimental to the economy of the area. While the Dutch Disease is associated with trading and effects of discovery of natural resources on exchange rate, the shift of "resources away from manufacturing sectors that generate 'learning by doing' might jeopardise a country's long-term growth potential by choking off an important source of human capital development." (Ebrahim-Zadeh, 2003).

The overall effect of the mining sector has been to generate a huge pool of temporary and migrant labour, many of whom do not enjoy basic human rights. It has also led to exploitation of children and women, and created a huge pool of individuals who are highly vulnerable to abuse, infections and diseases on the one hand, and behaviour patterns like visits to sex workers

6. *http://bellary.com/ironoreexport.htm*, accessed 23 July 2007.

and alcoholism on the other. These features, superimposed on cultural practices like the *Devadasi* system, play a key role in the context of the HIV and AIDS epidemic by creating a pool of individuals with significant vulnerabilities, while at the same time keeping Bellary in low human development equilibrium.

While there are other traditional industries in Bellary, like textiles, sugar and alcohol, the industry sector as a whole has not picked up despite such abundant mineral reserves, and Bellary remains one of the most backward districts of Karnataka, ranking 18th among 27 districts in 2001 (GoK, 2006).

Employment

Official employment statistics in Bellary does not indicate a significant rise in employment. Agriculture remains the major source of employment, though the category "other" seems to be increasing. The distribution of workers in medium and large scale industries (Figure 18.3) indicates the continued dependence on mining-related employment in the organised sector.

Figure 18.3

Distribution of Workers in Medium and Large Scale Establishments, 2005-06

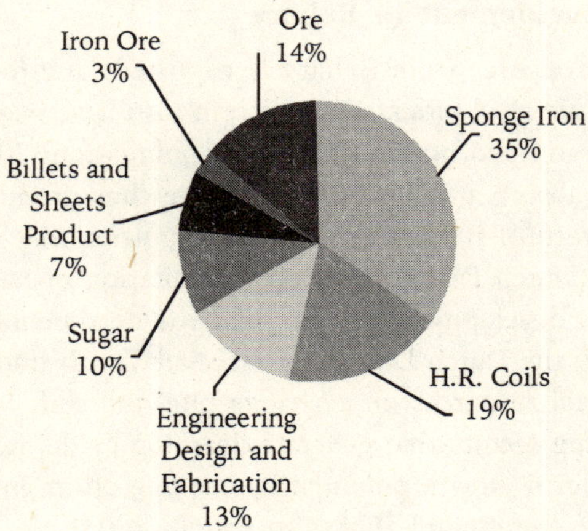

From various other sources, it is clear that Bellary has also seen an explosion in informal and unorganised sector employment, as also employment of women and children. The migrant workers are benefiting because they are finding work easily and probably getting better wages than their origin; however, this type of employment generation is not consistent with human development, since neither does it require high skills and education, nor does the work result in human capital formation.

Interestingly, the Child Workforce Participation Rate according to the 2001 Census was much higher (15 per cent) in Bellary than the state (7 per cent) and national average (5 per cent). It was one among the four districts (Koppal, Bellary, Raichur and Gulbarga) in the state, which had more than 10 per cent of their 5-14 years age group population in the workforce. Data indicates that while there are more male child workers in urban areas, female child workers are more prevalent in the rural settings.

Inequality and Poverty

The evidence on concentration of wealth in a few hands has been based on many discussions with stakeholders and experts, anecdotal evidence and newspaper reports. There is unanimity in the view that inequality has worsened in Bellary, with a few people becoming rapidly rich, and a large majority experiencing low rise in incomes. For example, there is evidence that the district has seen more and more private helicopters and imported cars in the recent past.[7] In fact, an estimate suggests that Bellary accounts for almost 10 per cent of the market for private flying machines in the country. It is noteworthy to mention here that no such private resources existed in the district during the last decade and evidence suggests that richer individuals—mostly miners—are buying helicopters to bypass the poor road network.[8]

Another important evidence of increasing inequality lies in the statistics on poverty. Despite being third in per capita income, and despite improving its head count ratio, as on 1999, Bellary still remained third in terms of incidence of poverty, with a head count ratio of 33.1 per cent. The improvement in poverty—in terms of decline of people living below poverty line—for the two richest districts i.e., Bangalore Urban and Rural has been phenomenal; the head count ratio of these two districts declined by 21 and 33 per cent respectively, while for Bellary this reduction was just 11 per cent. Rank-wise, while these two districts climbed from 12th and 13th to 7th and 3rd respectively, the rank of Bellary district has actually declined from 16th to 18th. Murgai *et al.*, 2003 estimated the poverty gap for 20 districts of Karnataka.[9] Bellary—with a poverty gap of 6 (which is way above the state average)—continued to be among the bottom five districts in the state.

Economic inequality also translates into social inequality: as the Karnataka HDR 2005 states: (a) "the greatest single issue that comes into focus is the wide gap between the Scheduled Castes and the general

7. *http://timesofindia.indiatimes.com/articleshow/1625531.cms*

8. *http://www.hinduonnet.com/fline/fl2311/stories/20060616002104300.htm*

9. Head count ratio and poverty gap data reproduced from Murgai *et al.*, 2003.

population along almost all human development indicators", and (b) "human development status of Scheduled Tribes is more than a decade behind the rest of the population of the state and they are the poorest and most deprived sub-populations in the state".

Similarly, the KHDR 2005 finds a trend in the state towards feminisation of poverty, with increasing trends of casualisation of female workforce, increasing dependence on agriculture and rising male-female wage differentials. As mentioned earlier, there is also a close correlation between class and gender in case of sex work, with many *Devadasis* and sex workers reportedly belonging to the lower castes.

The government failed to control for illegal mining and were also not able to control for the revenue, which could have gone to the state exchequer. This revenue would otherwise have been used to control for inequality. Neither of these has happened. Clearly, those who gained the most have also not invested on either of these areas in a visible manner. Thus, it stands to reason that the gains have remained in private hands, implying a significant worsening of inequality.

The link of inequality with HIV is increasingly being paid attention to: Sutherland (2007) analysed 57 countries including China, with HDI lower or equal than China's and found a statistically significant relationship between HIV prevalence and income inequality measured by Gini coefficient. The relationship understandably becomes weaker as higher HDI countries are included in the sample. The finding—reported earlier—that richer individuals are likely to practice unsafe sex in an environment that has unsafe sex as the dominant behaviour (Clark and Vencatachellam, 2003) fits very well and is very relevant for the case of Bellary: despite high incomes, it is probable that sexual behaviour continues to be risky among the rich, because the perception is that most others are indulging in multi-partner sex as well, given the socio-cultural norms of the district. Further, the increase in income, if unaccompanied by other improvements like improved education and knowledge, is likely to perpetuate or even accelerate high-risk behaviour due to higher disposable incomes, which in turn encourages commercial sex work.

The NFHS-3 report also shows that unsafe sexual practices increase with the rise in the wealth index; 5.5 per cent of men (in age group 15-54 years) in the second wealthiest quintile compared to 4.9 per cent in the lowest wealth index group reported having higher-risk sexual intercourse in the past 12 months of the survey. However, HIV prevalence was highest among the second wealthiest quintile (0.43 per cent) and lowest in the wealthiest quintile (0.18 per cent).

Human Development in Bellary

The overall development in Bellary in the recent past can be best gleaned from comparing the Human Development Index (HDI) values for 1991 and 2001. As is well known, HDI is based on three indices for health, education and income respectively. In Table 18.2 below, we present the HDI for Bellary and Karnataka, as well as the ranking among districts for Bellary.

Table 18.2

Human Development in Bellary, 1991 and 2001

Index	*Bellary*		*Karnataka*	
	1991	*2001*	*1991*	*2001*
Health	0.63 (10)	0.685 (7)	0.618	0.68
Education	0.506 (23)	0.618 (23)	0.602	0.712
Income	0.399 (9)	0.549 (9)	0.402	0.559
HDI	0.512 (18)	0.617 (18)	0.541	0.65

Source: GoK (2006).

While the overall HDI has improved for Bellary, as it has for Karnataka, its relative position has not changed among districts. Bellary has remained on 18th place (among 27) in these 10 years. Though in terms of the health index, Bellary has improved upon its previous status, this has not made a difference to its overall placement in Karnataka. As for education, Bellary continues to be in the bottom 5 districts in the state.

Development situation in Bellary was also substantiated by the updated Comprehensive Composite Development Index (CCDI) of the Nanjundappa report for assessing the development of *taluks*, which was based on 35 selected indicators. The relative ranking of the *taluks* have not changed much in these 5 years.

Education

While the literacy rate of Karnataka has been higher than the national average since the 1971 census (GoK, 2006), that of Bellary was much below the state and national average. The urban and rural literacy rates for Bellary were 70 per cent and 50 per cent, respectively. Though there has been a significant increase in the level of literacy among the SC/ST population in the district, it remains well below the state average. Female literacy and the gap between male and female literacy remain relatively adverse in the district. The continued low literacy levels of the district reaffirm its low human development oriented economic progress, which plays a key role in the HIV and AIDS epidemic.

Student dropout (standard I-VIII) statistics for two time points (1999-2000 and 2003-04) suggest that there has not been any significant improvement in the dropout situation in Bellary. While during 1999-2000, Bellary was ranked fourth among the bottom five districts in terms of dropouts (68.7 per cent), it slipped to bottom most position (67.1 per cent) during 2003-04. Even though the dropout rate among girls in the district showed some improvement during 2003-04, Bellary still topped among the districts in Karnataka in having highest number of girl students dropping out of school. High dropout rate in the district can be linked to three factors *viz.*, with poverty, parental attitude and status of girls/women playing major roles, both at work (in mines) and at home. Suffice to say that the education and literacy scenario in Bellary is not encouraging; though relative to its earlier performance, the situation has improved, the improvement has not been sufficient to make Bellary change its rank in the education index. In fact, as the HDI 2001 indicates, Bellary remains 23rd among 27 districts, as before in 1991.

Health

Official statistics indicate that Bellary has been able to keep pace with the average rates of change for Karnataka for many of the indicators, though the absolute values remain comparatively adverse in some cases, compared to the all-state averages. Infant mortality rate (IMR), crude death rate, life expectancy at birth are the three parameters that have better values than the state averages. However, couple protection rate and institutional deliveries—both relevant in the context of the AIDS epidemic—remain quite low. The extremely low value of institutional deliveries indicates that even if the deprivation indices mentioned from the Nanjundappa report were to be updated, Bellary would probably remain in the group of most deprived districts.

Status of Women, SC and ST

The results from the qualitative interviews among respondents coming to PPTCT and RNTCP sites in the government hospitals[10] indicate that Bellary continues to have a very traditional outlook about the status of women and upbringing of the girls, therefore, with lack of schooling, early marriage and lack of employment opportunities as factors are detrimental to their status in society. All these features indicate that women—poor as well as rich—may find it difficult to safeguard themselves against infections like HIV.

---

10. Details of this survey is discussed in Chapter 3.3 of this report.

Despite a sizeable population of SC and especially ST, Bellary has not been able to improve the status of these sub-populations significantly. The female and rural literacy remain dismally low, gross enrolment ratios are also lower and dropout rates are higher than the state averages, indicators of civic amenities are worse for this population compared to the general population.

Governance

The Karnataka Human Development Report 2005 presents some evidence on governance in the entire state, and indicates a picture of continued concern on several fronts: poor redressal of public grievances, a complex and non-transparent government structure, barriers to information making the Right to Information Act somewhat unusable, lack of proper indicators for evaluating quality of services, and lack of accountability evidenced by high teacher absenteeism etc. It can be assumed that a similar set of problems plague all the districts, including Bellary.

The boom of illegal mining is a clear evidence of non-compliance with government rules, which cannot happen without the cooperation of officials. The mining phenomenon has wide ranging implications: for example, deforestation due to hectic mining and quarrying activities in Bellary[11] seems to continue, and the mining sector is allowed to expand without regulations and control. Similarly, the roads in the district continue to be in very poor condition, without much action from the transport department to repair them. Poor provision of basic amenities, especially for the poor, the continued phenomenon of child labour and poor enforcement and implementation around the *Devadasi* system are some other indicators of poor governance.

HIV and AIDS in Bellary

Karnataka has been a high prevalence state, with a generalised epidemic among high-risk as well as low-risk segment of the population. Overall, infections remain high among all the sentinel groups, and the state presently has more than 500,000 HIV infected individuals (NACO, 2007).

Bellary is a high prevalence district in eastern Karnataka. It has 22,000 estimated HIV infections with 1.1 per cent HIV prevalence among general population (NACO, 2007). It is surrounded by three other high prevalence districts of the state and also shares its border with Anantpur and Kurnool districts of Andhra Pradesh, which have 2.25 and 0.75 per cent of HIV prevalence among ANC attendees, respectively; in fact, Kurnool has a HIV prevalence of 8.4 per cent among STD patients. Bellary has been showing

11. *parisara.kar.nic.in/PDF/Mining.pdf*

higher prevalence of HIV since the surveillance sites have been established there some eight years ago. In 1999, when HIV surveillance began in Bellary, the HIV prevalence in STD clinics was as high as 14 per cent, while the corresponding figure for ANC prevalence was 1.5 per cent. While the rate of infection at these sites has been fluctuating, it remained high enough to cause concern. Although not topping the list in terms of prevalence in surveillance sites, Bellary has the third highest estimated HIV infection in Karnataka followed by Bangalore Urban and Dharwad (UNDP, 2006). The following graphs compare HIV prevalence of Bellary sites with the average of Karnataka over the last few years (Figures 18.4 and 18.5).

Figure 18.4

HIV Prevalence in STD Clinics

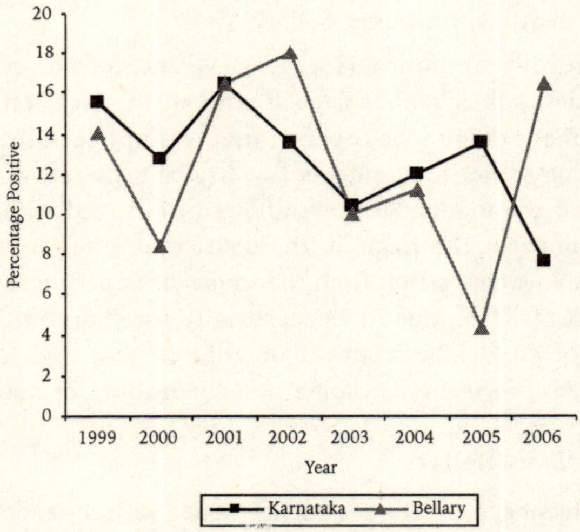

Source: Various HIV surveillance statistics from NACO.

As can be seen from the graphs, after increasing till 2002, the prevalence slowed down among STD patients, but the recent figures indicate a sharp rise again in the prevalence, making Bellary the district with the highest prevalence (16.4 per cent) among STD patients in the state. Similarly, prevalence among ANC went down significantly after 2002, but is showing a slight rise in 2006. Prevalence among ANC rural attendees has similarly gone up in 2006 and retained its earlier (2003) level of 1.75 per cent. Interestingly, the corresponding average figures for Karnataka do not show such a recent increase and in fact, the HIV prevalence among STD patients is the lowest in the recent years.

Figure 18.5

HIV Prevalence in ANC Clinics

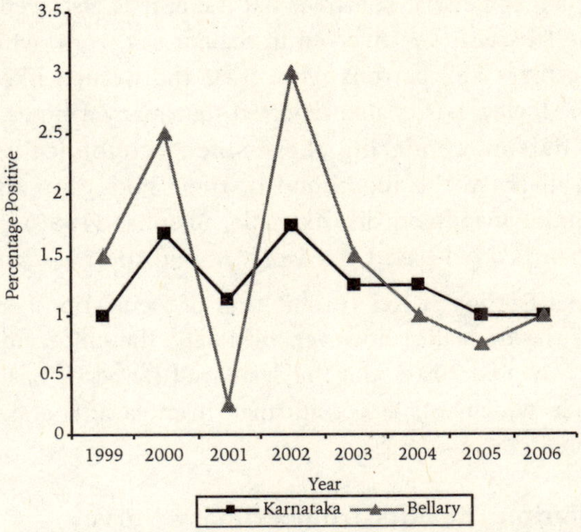

A mapping exercise carried out by the NGO SWASTI in 2004 gives interesting insights into the distribution of various high-risk groups (HRGs) across the towns of Bellary district. Firstly, it indicates that an estimated 4,300 persons—accounting for more than 0.42 per cent of the total adult population and 1.11 per cent urban adult population—are engaged in some kind of high-risk activities. The two major high-risk groups i.e., female sexual workers (FSWs)[12] and *Devadasis* comprised 87.5 percentage of total HRG population; the rest of about 12 per cent of the group included eunuch sex workers, *Jogappas* (male form of *Devadasis*), men who have sex with men (MSM) and a small number of injection drug users (IDUs).

It has been argued that the *Devadasi* (servant of God) system has degenerated into a culturally sanctioned system of initiating young girls into systemic—and so-called 'sacred'—prostitution (NHRC, 2004, Chawla, 2002; Tarachand, 1992). A report commissioned by the National Commission for Women (NCW) in India indicate that mostly lower caste women and girls are forced into the Devadasi system in several states of India. Devadasis generally belong to: a) poor families for whom marrying off their daughters would have been a financial burden, and b) families with only girl children, whose income would be essential for the household. There are an estimated 2.5 lakh *Devadasis* in the Maharashtra-Karnataka-Andhra Pradesh belt and the estimate suggests that around 23,000 of them are in Karnataka (Shankar,

12. The Karnataka Health Promotion Trust (KHPT), an agency, which is involved in HIV prevention activities in Bellary district, puts the estimates at 3852 FSWs.

1990); however, there are differing views about the total population of *Devadasis* in the country.

Although it is a somewhat controversial issue, it is also well accepted now that some of the *Devadasis* are involved in regular sex work, while others have fairly regular partners i.e., patrons who, treat the women like second wives (Chawla, 2002). However, it is also reported that many a times, these patrons terminate the liaison, rendering the women economically and socially vulnerable and increase the likelihood of their taking up commercial sex work as a means of livelihood; for example, Shankar (1990) reports around 40 per cent urban brothel-based sex work among the *Devadasis*.

The Karnataka Devadasis Act (Prohibition of Dedication) provides for the rehabilitation of the *Devadasis*; however, till lately, the enforcement of this act remained weak (Myrada, 2001) and the system of *Devadasis* has existed in one form or the other, which was also confirmed from various stakeholder/expert group discussions.

At-Risk Population: Results from Primary Survey

What are the characteristics of vulnerable population groups? In the absence of available data on the profile of at-risk population, it was decided to collect primary data on clients of three selected services: TB patients accessing treatment at RNTCP delivery points and pregnant mothers visiting PPTCT centres.

For RNTCP, roughly two-thirds (64.1 per cent) were male respondents.[13] Nearly half of the male (48.4 per cent) and three-fourths of the female (72.2 per cent) respondents of RNCTP were illiterate as compared to 41.2 per cent of PPTCT clients. For those who were literate, the average years of education for males and females were 6.6 years and 7.7 years respectively for RNTCP, and 8.3 years for PPTCT respondents. These results corroborate that individuals accessing these services are largely from lower socioeconomic strata and potentially vulnerable to various infections, including HIV. As for occupation, the proportion of working female was low for both the groups (RNTCP=43.2 per cent, PPTCT=35.9 per cent). Interestingly, a higher proportion of females were working than were literate, indicating the presence of unskilled and informal sector work in the area. This is corroborated by the result that among the working respondents, a majority were labourers that included daily wage labourers in agriculture, mining, construction and other industries. For RNTCP, 69.4 per cent of the males reported to be working.

13. All tables and graphs in this chapter are based on primary survey conducted for the purpose.

The evidence on education and occupation—including a high proportion of labourers in the two samples—reconfirm that there may be a high correlation between socioeconomic status and the likelihood of infections, including TB.

Information was collected on how often respondents needed to stay away from home for their work. Nearly 40 per cent of the male RNTCP respondents and half of the PPTCT respondents' husbands stay away from home for their work, with an average stay for around two months a year. More than 10 per cent were found to stay away for 2-6 months in a year. These figures indicate substantial mobility, which is now confirmed globally to be a key parameter in the HIV and AIDS epidemic.

The close link between alcohol and HIV has now found another dimension, with a recent research indicating that not only are people who abuse alcohol more likely to engage in risky behaviours such as unprotected sex (Fordham, 1995), alcohol consumption may increase susceptibility to infection upon exposure to HIV.[14] Data indicate that alcohol—especially country made liquor (*arrack*)—consumption is on the rise in Karnataka. Bellary ranks fifth, sixth and third highest in terms of consumption of beer, Indian-made liquor (IML) and *arrack* respectively during 2006-07. The data on RNTCP and PPTCT indicate that while on an average, more than half of the male RNTCP respondents and PPTCT respondents' husbands reported no consumption of alcohol, around 20 per cent of the male RNTCP respondents and 11 per cent husbands of PPTCT respondents were reported to be consuming alcohol daily. An additional 5-9 per cent consumed alcohol frequently (more than once a week). Given that self-admission of alcoholism may be lower than the actual incidence, it is probably safe to say that alcoholism cannot be ignored as a factor that may have implications about the vulnerability of women as well as high-risk behaviour.

More than two-third of the respondents were found to be aware of HIV/AIDS; the proportion of male RNTCP respondents who had heard of HIV was 74 per cent while corresponding proportion for female RNTCP respondents and PPTCT respondents were 69 per cent and 74 per cent respectively. An interesting result is that out of those who had never heard of HIV, more than three-fourths were married respondents, indicating, in turn, their and their spouses' potential vulnerability to infection due to lack of awareness.

While knowledge of 'unprotected sexual contact' as a route of transmission was found to be very high (almost 100 per cent in all categories), the knowledge of mother to child transmission was low in all the three

14. *http://news.bbc.co.uk/2/hi/health/2846471.stm*

categories. Again, nearly three-fourth of those who did not know about mother to child transmission were married. These responses are consistent with the findings from National Family Health Survey (NFHS) and Reproductive and Child Health (RCH) projects reported earlier.

As for the HIV testing, nearly 60 per cent of the women visiting PPTCT were tested for HIV as compared to 36 per cent of female and about half of the males of the RNTCP sample. Unless compared to other samples from other districts, it is not clear whether these numbers indicate high or low response to perception about risk behaviour. But the fact that these numbers are not insignificant, and higher than what one would expect from the general population, does seem to indirectly indicate the presence of high risk behaviour, which may be prompting respondents or their doctors to check the patients' HIV status.

The presence of any symptoms of sexually transmitted infections (STI) is another important indicator of vulnerability to HIV. The knowledge about the spread of STI was found to be abysmally low; only one-fourth of the total sample reported knowledge of how STI spreads. While nearly one fourth of the RNTCP respondents (23.7 per cent) and one-third of the PPTCT respondents (34.6 per cent) were reported to have shown some symptoms of STIs, only 10 per cent in RNTCP and 20 per cent in PPTCT could indicate sexual relationship as a source of their infection. The findings on STI, combined with the earlier results from the survey, make these groups seem very representative of populations that are highly vulnerable to HIV; the fact that there may be many more that do not seek treatment in these facilities, make the issue of targeted interventions very relevant.

Also, the STI issues drive home the point that messages of prevention and risks are not comprehensive; thus, while special programmes like PPTCT spread awareness about some components, these probably do not extend to topics that are not under their direct theme area. The lack of awareness about STI and the declining STI patients in public facilities are seemingly contrary findings, indicating a possibility of increasing recourse of patients to private providers, or lack of treatment-seeking due to stigma among the newer migrant populations (since earlier trends increased significant treatment seeking behaviour of STI, it stands to reason that the more recent additions to population may have less awareness or less familiarity with the provider set up in Bellary).

Overall, the results from the specially designed survey indicates a confluence of adverse parameters among the respondents, that all go to make such groups highly vulnerable to HIV, and indicate that mapping such populations may be one of the most important exercises for effective targeted interventions.

The results of the primary survey indicated low levels of knowledge about STI and HIV. Data from national databases including NFHS, RCH-RHS (rapid household survey) also corroborate these findings on knowledge and awareness, especially among women. The findings from the District Situation Assessment of Bellary—DSA, 2002 indicate that awareness of HIV among married women (39 per cent) in Bellary is much less compared to their unmarried counterparts (56 per cent). It also reveals that women above 25 years of age were either not aware or were partially aware of details of HIV. These findings are important when combined with other sets of findings like low education among women, low availability of information on sex and sexuality, low awareness of protection methods, high prevalence of multiple partners and bigamy among males, limited control of women over decision-making in personal issues, high prevalence of sexual abuse in the community, lack of adequate health services and poor treatment seeking behaviour (Mahila Samakhya, 2002).

Response to the Epidemic

Being one of the high prevalence districts, Bellary has always been a focus of HIV prevention and control interventions carried out by the Karnataka State AIDS Prevention Society (KSAPS). The sentinel surveillance site for ANC and STD clients has been operating in the district since 1999, followed by a number of other initiatives. A project named "Coordinated HIV and AIDS Response through Capacity building and Awareness (CHARCA)" that had a greater emphasis on District Situation Assessments (DSAs) leading to District Strategic Plans (DSPs) as planning tools, and focused on district ownership, participation and implementation was launched in 2001. Since then, a series of interventions aiming at awareness and capacity building is being carried out by a district level agency called Bellary District AIDS Prevention Society (BDAPS) with the help of the two NGOs *viz.*, MYRADA and Mahila Samkhya.

There is clear evidence that the interventions carried out by leading organisations/programmes in Bellary have made significant difference to the levels of knowledge and awareness in the population they have reached. However, the overall approach has been consistent with the targeted interventions approach widely prevalent in the country; while some attempt has been made to understand vulnerabilities, no significant efforts have been made to understand the underlying developmental factors that could have impact on the course of the epidemic. Thus, for instance, there was no evidence of sustained interventions with groups like *Devadasis*, workers in the illegal mines including child labourers, miners and middle-class men visiting sex workers, in a focused and sustained manner. Given the context of Bellary, these groups are key factors to the arrest of the epidemic in the district. While targeted interventions are important, these alone are not sufficient, and are unlikely to be effective in a sustainable way, if not nested within the larger socioeconomic context of the area.

Further, there has not been much evidence to demonstrate that such targeted interventions have been accompanied consistently by other policies that improve human development of the targeted groups. Such targeted interventions are unlikely to be sustainable in the long run, if one keeps in mind that the norms, cultural practices, socioeconomic vulnerabilities have not changed in the district, and the recent patterns of development have brought in a larger pool of vulnerable individuals with low human development levels.

Additionally, there is also no evidence of any efforts at mainstreaming the HIV and AIDS interventions with any existing socioeconomic policies of the district; the interventions have been carried out by NGOs or separate bodies, with little evidence of sustainability or incorporation in ongoing programmes of the district administration. Outside funding-dependent interventions are not only unsustainable, but extremely cost-ineffective, and cannot bring about long lasting changes in the fundamental determinants of vulnerability to HIV. Thus, Bellary is still grappling with high levels of infection, low awareness and high-risk behaviour, despite the presence of such interventions.

Finally though, the most important variable indicating the efficacy of these interventions is HIV prevalence, which, after decreasing for a while, has again shown an increase among groups like ANC attendees and STD patients. This is extremely worrisome and brings to the fore the need to evaluate such interventions for outcome—rather than process—indicators.

Conclusions and Recommendations

The two-way relationship between HIV and human development was examined in this chapter and the analysis centred on the status of human development and examined the progress made in the following areas: magnitude and type of economic development, literacy and education, health and risk factors, basic amenities including health infrastructure, status of backward classes, women and governance.

Each of these variables, in the light of the findings on the existing socio-cultural practices, were linked to the state of the epidemic in the district to bring out the extent of vulnerability to HIV and its consequent socioeconomic impact. The chapter also examined the response to the epidemic and the extent to which these were successful and brought out the possible constraints for a more rapid control of the epidemic in the district. The main findings and conclusions are listed below:

1. Bellary continues to be a high-prevalence district, and recently there has been an increase in HIV prevalence among key groups.
2. There has been a sudden and strong upsurge in economic growth in Bellary, fueled mainly by the mining industry.
3. The economic growth has not been consistent with progress in human development; it has been that of a typical natural resource-rich region, where the raw materials are mostly supplied out of the region, with the resultant effect of slow growth in manufacturing sectors.
4. Growth of employment has been much slower, and most of the employment generated has been in the informal/unorganised sector via the mining industry:
    a. The mining sector has attracted a large number of migrants, who have come in search of both any job/better wages. The textile industry, in contrast, continues to depend on local workers.
    b. Drought in agriculture and growth in other job opportunities has resulted in a slower growth in employment in agriculture and a greater tendency to migrate within and outside the district.
    c. Almost half of the mining industry in Bellary falls within different definitions of illegal mining, making the employment generated of a dubious quality from the perspective of welfare, with: a) low job security resulting in higher mobility and use of migrant workers, and b) large number of children and women employed, with serious implications about their welfare.
    d. Growth in other sectors related to the mining sector like transportation and construction workers.
5. The distributional aspects of the substantial economic growth have been adverse: employment growth has been low, poverty has remained high, inequality has increased and there has emerged a pool of often politically powerful rich class.
6. Status of SC/ST/OBC and women continue to be poor
7. Bellary has a history of the socio-cultural practice of *Devadasis*, which continues even today, in different forms.
8. Factors conducive to high risk behaviour: significant population of sex workers, presence of mobile populations, sudden increase in pool of rich men with high disposable incomes, significant alcohol consumption, low condom use, low knowledge of STI, high levels of STI, low status of women, low literacy and education, especially among women.

9. Indicators of child welfare continue to raise concerns.
10. Significant extent of prevention programmes, with evidence of partial success: limited interventions with *Devadasis*, migrants, transport workers, miners, high-income individuals and children; knowledge of HIV and AIDS high, but condom use and knowledge of STI still low; low education levels among target population constraining quick absorption of knowledge.
11. Many instances of inadequate governance.
12. No mainstreaming of HIV and AIDS policies with other social, economic and welfare policies of the district: short-term programmes funded from outside raising sustainability issue.

The analysis leads to some key conclusions. Firstly, the interventions would have been more effective had these not been constrained by the socio-economic environment, which has not been conducive to a more rapid absorption of prevention messages. The high prevalence among key groups, as well as the recent further rise, indicates that interventions may have had only short-term penetration; while knowledge and awareness have increased, this has not translated into significant behaviour change. In addition, the disconnect between governance and policies around HIV and AIDS in the district has severely limited the efficacy of the interventions. Thus, while such interventions are important for behaviour change, they are not sustainable unless mainstreamed and backed by social, economic and welfare policies accompanied by good governance that change the very environment in which these individuals live. Ultimately of course, the whole development paradigm needs to be altered in Bellary for lasting improvement in human development, which together with such key interventions, will definitely impact on the magnitude of the HIV and AIDS epidemic.

References

Anonymous (2006). "In the Mine field of Exploitation." (*http://naxalrevolution.blogspot.com/2006/06/in-mine-field-of-exploitation.html*, accessed 13 July 2007).

Chawla, Anil (2002). *Devadasis: Sinners or Sinned Against*. (*http://www.samarthbharat.com/files/devadasihistory.pdf*, accessed 8 May 2007).

Chen, Shaohua, and Martin Ravallion (2000). "How Did the World's Poorest Fare in the 1990's?", Policy Research *Working Paper* 2409. Washington D.C.: World Bank.

Clark, C. Robert and Désiré Vencatachellum (2003). "Economic Development and HIV/AIDS Prevalence." CIRANO Scientific Series 2003s-25. Montreal: CIRANO. (*http://cirano.qc.ca/pdf/publication/2003s-25.pdf*, accessed 10 August 2007).

Dzenovska, Dace, Nadia Rasheed and Bjørg Sandkjær (2005). "HIV/AIDS and Human Development Thematic Guidance Note", National Human Development Report Series, NHDR *Occasional Paper* 4. New York: UNDP.

Ebrahim-Zadeh, Christine (2003). "Back to Basics: Dutch Disease: Too much Wealth Managed Unwisely", International Monetary Fund, *Finance and Development* 40(1), March.

Fordham, G. (1995). "Whisky, Women and Song: Men, Alcohol and AIDS in Northern Thailand", *Australian Journal of Anthropology* 6: 154–177.

Government of Karnataka (2002). *High Power Committee for the Redressal of Regional Imbalances: Final Report*. Bangalore: Government of Karnataka.

———. (2005). *Economic Survey 2004-05*. Bangalore: Department of Planning and Statistics. (*http://planning.kar.nic.in/esurvey200405.htm*, accessed 12 July 2007).

———. (2006). *Karnataka Human Development Report 2005*. Bangalore: Planning and Statistics Department, Government of Karnataka.

Gupta, Indrani, Mayur Trivedi and Pradeep Guin (2007). "Socio-Economic Impact of HIV and AIDS: Mainstreaming Policies of Impact Mitigation." Report submitted to Futures Group International India Pvt. Ltd. February.

Indian Bureau of Mines (2006). *Indian Minerals Yearbook 2005*. Nagpur: Controller General, Indian Bureau of Mines.

International Institute for Population Sciences (IIPS) and ORC Macro (2000). *National Family Health Survey (NFHS-2), 1998-99: India*. Mumbai: IIPS.

International Institute for Population Sciences (IIPS) and Macro International (2007). *National Family Health Survey (NFHS-3), 2005-06: India: Volume I*. Mumbai: IIPS.

Kristensen, Kirsten Marie (2007). "AIDS Hits Poor People Harder", Copenhagen: DanChurchAid. (*http://www.danchurchaid.org/sider_paa_hjemmesiden/what_we_do/issues_we_work_on/hiv_aids/read_more/aids_hits_poor_people_harder*, accessed 3 November 2007).

Mahila Samakhya-Karnataka (2002). *Vulnerabilities of Young Women to STIs / HIV in Bellary District, Karnataka: A District Situation Assessment*. Draft (2) for discussion. Bangalore: MSK.

Mehu, Sowmya Aji (2006). "CM steels Reddy's Thunder!". Bangalore: *The Times of India*. (*http://timesofindia.indiatimes.com/articleshow/2003888.cms*, accessed 18 July 2007).

Mines, Minerals and People (2005). *Our Mining Children: Fact Finding*. (*http://www.mmpindia.org/childlabourfactfindingreport.PDF*, accessed 23 July 2007).

Murgai, Rinku, M.H. Suryanarayana and Salman Zaidi (2003). "Measuring Poverty in Karnataka: The Regional Dimension", *Economic and Political Weekly*. January 25.

Myrda (2001). *Empowerment of Devadasis: An Evaluation Study for NOVIB*. Belgaum.

National AIDS Control Organization (2007). *Karnataka Fact Sheet on HIV Surveillance*. Unpublished. New Delhi: NACO.

National Human Rights Commission (2004). *A Report on Trafficking in Women and Children in India 2002-03, Volume I*. NHRC-UNIFEM-ISS Project. New Delhi: NHRC. (*http://nhrc.nic.in/Documents/ReportonTrafficking.pdf*, accessed 12 August 2007).

Piot, Peter, Robert Greener and Sarah Russell (2007). "Squaring the Circle: AIDS, Poverty and Human Development." *PLoS Med* 4(10): *e314. doi:10.1371/journal.pmed.0040314*

Planning Commission (2006). *National Mineral Policy: Report of the High Level Committee.* (*http://mines.nic.in/* accessed 18 July 2007).

Registrar General of India (2001). Census of India 2001, Primary Census Abstract. New Delhi: RGI.

Shankar, Jogan (1990). *Devadasi Cult—A Sociological Analysis*. New Delhi: Ashish Publishing House.

Shesana, O. and L. Letlape (2004). "The Impact of HIV/AIDS on the Sub-Saharan African Economy", *Background paper* commissioned for *Our Common Interest: Report of the Commission for Africa.* March 2005. (*http://www.commissionforafrica.org/english/report/background/shisana_and_letlape_background.pdf*, accessed 4 November 2007).

Sutherland, Dylan (2007). "Exploring the Economic and Social Terrain of Epidemic Disease in China: Income Inequality and HIV/AIDS—Is There a Relationship?", Conference paper of 2007 Conferences on 'Governance of HIV/AIDS Response: Making Participation and Accountability Count', 5-6 November, Radcliffe House, University of Warwick. (*http://www2.warwick.ac.uk/fac/soc/csgr/activitiesnews/conferences/2007/hivaids/papers/sutherland.doc*, accessed 28 February 2008).

Tarachand K.C. (1992). *Devadasi Custom – Rural Social Structure and Flesh Markets*. New Delhi: Reliance Publishing House.

United Nations Children's Fund (2007). "UNICEF Situation Report Lesotho—External." 21 June 2007. (*http://www.unicef.org/infobycountry/files/Lesotho_EXTERNAL_SitRep_21Jun07.pdf*, accessed 3 November 2007).

United Nations Development Programme (2006). *CHARACA Annual Report 2006*. New Delhi: UNDP.

World Bank (1999). *Confronting AIDS: Public Priorities in a Global Epidemic*. World Bank Policy Research Report. Washington D.C.: World Bank.

Section VI

Ageing and Health Insurance in India

19

The Economics of Ageing

The Pangs of Female Elderly in India

K. SHANTHI

Introduction

Ageing has implications for the physical, mental and psychological well-being of the individuals. As age advances, the physical and mental stamina comes down forcing the individuals to depend on others. This in turn shatters their self-image and dignity causing behavioural changes in them. Often they are not supported to lead a positive and fruitful life. Poverty and consequent economic insecurity further aggravates the situation. Not only the aged are agitated because of their dependency but also the young who support them are restless and would like to shift the burden of caring the elders on somebody else's shoulders. The root cause for this new phenomenon is longevity of life. The drastic reduction in death rate, rise in the nutrition standards of people, tremendous advancements in the field of medical care have contributed to the longevity of life. Since life expectancy at birth for females is higher than for males, women live longer than men. Women by and large in the Indian society are non-earners or intermittent earners. They have no pension or independent source of income. This forces them to be at the mercy of somebody during their old age. They are vulnerable to violence, ill-treatment and neglect. The custom of marrying a girl to a man who is elder to her by few years increases the likelihood of widowhood at a comparatively young age. Women being caregivers for the sick and the old, encounter lot of strain, work out a trade-off between career and home, forgo their leisure, neglect their own health and spend materially also, on the elderly, invariably parents-in-law and sometimes parents, if happen to be widows. When these women who support their elders are themselves getting aged, the problem gets compounded. This means women suffer on both counts—as women in their old age and as caregivers during their young age. In developing countries where social security system is almost absent or its coverage is limited, the problem of ageing should be addressed in its proper perspective.

The Ageing Society: International Scenario

The median age of the US population is steadily rising. In 1900, out of 25 Americans one was 65 or over. By 2050, that figure will rise to one in five. The US Census Bureau has projected that over 65 population will more than double between 2000 and 2050. The proportion of the 'oldest old' i.e., 85 and over is likely to increase by four times. By the year 2020, the ratio of over 65 individuals to the working age adult population will be about one to four. But one advantage in the case of America is, the new legislation allows re-entry to labour force upto 69 after retirement at 65 and hence of the 9.2 million people in the age bracket 65-69, 23 per cent are working. This is over two million senior workers (Sam, 2000).

Table 19.1

Percentage of Population Aged 60 Years or Over in Selected Countries

Country	*2000 (Per cent)*	*2050 (Per cent)*
Italy	24	41
Germany	23	35
Japan	23	38
Spain	22	43
Czech Republic	18	41
USA	16	28
China	10	30
Thailand	9	30
Brazil	8	23
India	8	21
Indonesia	7	22
Mexico	7	24

Source: United Nations, 1998.

The situation with regard to certain other countries is clear from Table 19.1. India though has only 8 per cent, in absolute numbers it is a huge population in view of the large population base. China has 10 per cent indicating India's comparative better position. For India, the percentage of the aged will increase to 21 in 2050 and for China to 30. What this means in terms of absolute numbers even by 2025 is clear from Table 19.2.

The UN Projection for 2050 for India is 326 million which is a staggering figure. This should be compared to the 20 million elderly in 1951. The male-female break up projections by the UN reveals that the proportion of the male elderly in total male population will be 20.2 per cent and for females, it will be 22.4 per cent in 2050 (UN Population Division, 1999). India and China being the major countries in Asia, no doubt make Asia occupy the first rank among the continents in the world.

Table 19.2

Absolute Numbers (Million) of Persons above 60 Years of Age in Countries with About or More than 100 Million Inhabitants (in 2002)

Country	*2002*	*2025*
China	134.2	287.5
India	81.0	168.5
Brazil	14.1	33.4
Nigeria	5.7	11.4

Source: Hoskins, Irene (n.d.) *"A Global Perspective on Active and Healthy Ageing: Current and Future Trends"*, Geneva Ageing and Life Course Programme, WHO.

Table 19.3

Distribution of World Population Over Age 60 by Region

Region	*2002 (Per cent)*	*2025 (Per cent)*
Asia	53	59
Africa	7	7
Oceania	1	1
North America	8	8
Latin America & Caribbean	7	8
Europe	24	17

Source: United Nations, 2001.

While the percentage of 60+ population will remain the same for Africa, Oceania and North America even in 2025, for Latin America and Caribbean it is going to increase only by one percentage point. But for Asia it will go up from 53 per cent to 59 per cent. For Europe, there will be a fall in the elderly population percentage.

The differences between developed and developing countries are worth exploring here. In developed countries, the rate of the population ageing was slower when compared to that of developing countries. France took 115 years to double the number of older population from 7 per cent to 14 per cent whereas it doubled in China, Thailand and Colombia in about 25 years (Nampudakam, 1999a). Thus, three-quarters of all deaths in developing countries would be age related. This should be compared to the situation in 1950 when the average life expectancy was 46.5 years. Till the 1980s, the developing and the developed countries shared the aged in equal proportion but as things stand today, Asia alone is expected to share 50 per cent of the world's elderly. India and China being the two most populous countries in Asia will thus, have a significant share in the world's elderly (Rajan *et al.*, 1999). The World Bank estimates also conform this. By 2030, population aged 60 years and above is expected to reach 1.4 billion, most of the growth taking place in developing countries (World Bank, 1994). This has lot of implications to developing countries in terms of resource management and health care costs. Developing countries are yet to be free from infectious diseases, malnutrition and complications from childbirth. In addition to it, now they have to address the chronic illnesses such as heart disease, cancer and depression, which mean the 'double burden of disease'. No doubt the medical care of the elderly takes a back seat.

The Indian Scenario

By the year 2020, it is estimated that the population of the elderly will increase to 142 million or about 11 per cent of the country's population. One more factor which is of serious concern is: the grey population is getting more mature i.e., population in the age bracket of 80 years is only 10 per cent in the population over 60 years of age as of now which is expected to rise to 25 per cent by the year 2050. According to the 1991 census, out of 100 elderly persons in India, four-fifths are found in rural areas and the remaining in urban areas. Coming to inter-state comparisons, as of 1991 the highest proportion of the elderly among the states and union territories was found in Kerala with 8.77 per cent and the lowest proportion was observed in Andaman and Nicobar Islands.[1] About 17 states are expected to have more than 10 per cent elderly by 2021. Since different states are in different stages of demographic transition in terms of fertility and mortality, generalisations are difficult. But since India is expected to have a faster decline in fertility compared to mortality (because the latter is already at a low level), the ageing process will be faster than in certain other developing countries.

As per 1991 census, four-fifth of the elderly persons live in rural areas and the female elderly outnumber the male elderly. They are mostly illiterate, work beyond 60 years of age and are widowed. In the informal sector where our majority Indian labour force is employed, there arises no question of formal retirement. They neither have social security nor pension benefits on their past work. As Dr. Gro Harlem Brundtland, the then Director General of

1. The percentage of children below 14 years in Kerala was 43 in 1961 which declined to 30 in 1991 and is projected to reach 19 by 2021, whereas the percentage of people above 60 years was just 6 in 1961, 9 in 1991 and is expected to reach 16 by 2021. (Nampudakam Mathew, *op.cit*).

World Health Organization rightly observed, "While developed countries became rich before they became old, developing countries may become old before they become rich. Therefore, we must be determined to eliminate the greatest enemy of good health i.e., poverty particularly in its most extreme forms" (Nampudakam, 1999). NSS 52nd Round (July 1995-June 1996) throws light on the socioeconomic profile of the aged in India (*Sarvekshana* XXIII(3) January-March, 2000). Information relating to number of living children, living arrangement, state of economic independence, number of dependent persons supporting the aged, disability, chronic ailments, state of health and their familial roles in the household are available for the sample population of the aged. This information helps us to discern the male-female gap in dependency, health status, etc.

Pangs of the Female Elderly

Table 19.4 is indicative of females living longer than males. The 52nd Round indicates that for every 1000 aged males (above 60), there are 1017 females in the rural areas and 1043 females in the urban areas. The urban sex ratio is higher than the rural sex ratio. Quoting other studies the NSS report says, "elderly population would become more feminine in the future owing to the expected larger increment in the longevity of females."

The dependency factor is obvious in Table 19.5. Among females for every 1000, while 706 are fully dependent on others among males, only 313 are fully dependent as far as rural areas are concerned. In urban areas, the situation is worse. While only 297 males out of 1000 males are fully dependent, for females the figure is 757. Elderly urban women's status seems to be much more vulnerable when compared to rural elderly women. The figures in bracket indicate the situation in 1986-87 based on 42nd NSS Round. It is very clear that both for rural and urban women as well as for men, the number of 'fully dependent on others' has come down, may be due to the fact that people are aware of the changing reality and try to be self dependent. The figure for 'not dependent on others' for rural females has gone up from 88 per 1000 in 1986-87 to 121 per 1000 in 1995-96. For rural males, it has gone down from 511 to 485. But for urban males, it has gone up from 457 per 1000 to 515 per 1000. The increase is much higher in the case of urban females shooting up from 48 to 115. To quote the report, "as many as 70 per cent of the aged had to depend on others for their day-to-day maintenance. The situation is worse for elderly females. Among them about 85-87 per cent were economically dependent either partially or fully. In this respect males were much better off—among them 49 to 52 per cent did not depend on others for their livelihood."

Table 19.4

Sex Ratio (Number of Females for 1000 Males) among Aged Persons Obtained from Census and NSS Surveys (India)

Source	*Rural*	*Urban*	*Combined*
1	2	3	4
Census 1981	954	986	960
NSS 43rd Round (1987-88)	971	1032	983
Census 1991	922	960	930
NSS 50th Round (1993-94)	963	1060	984
NSS 52nd Round (1995-96)	1017	1043	1023

Source: NSS 52nd Round; *Sarvekshana* XXIII(3): 91.

Table 19.5

Per 1000 Distribution of Aged Persons by State of Economic Independence for Each Sex (India)

Sex	*Not Dependant on Others*	*State of Economic Independence*		
		Partially Dependant on Others	*Fully Dependant on Others*	*Total (including No Reported Cases)*
		Rural		
Male	485 (511)	180 (162)	313 (327)	1000
Female	121 (88)	146 (137)	706 (775)	1000
Person	301 (340)	163 (152)	511 (508)	1000
		Urban		
Male	515 (457)	169 (169)	297 (374)	1000
Female	115 (48)	110 (91)	757 (861	1000
Person	311 (289	139(157)	532 (574)	1000

Note: Figures in parentheses give the corresponding estimates obtained from NSS 42nd Round (1986-87).

Source: NSS 52nd Round, *Sarvekshana* XXIII(3): 93.

About 74 per cent of the elderly depend on their children, about 14-16 per cent on their spouses, 5-6 per cent on their grandchildren and the rest i.e., 6-7 per cent on 'others' including non-relations. The work participation rate details reveal that the work participation rate among the aged in the rural area is 39 per cent, which is double that of in the urban areas (21 per cent). The male-female differences are also pronounced. In the rural areas, the work participation rate of aged females was 17 per cent while that of males was 60 per cent. But in urban areas, for males it was 35 per cent and for females 8 per cent. This difference should be attributed to the category of job. Most of the men and women in the urban areas work in regular wage employment which are protected by retirement benefits and there is a fixed age of superannuation. But in rural areas, work is irregular and people who work in their own farm and non-farm enterprises continue to work even after the age of 60.

The prevalence of disability, which is found in Table 19.6, reveals that for all kinds of disability both for rural and urban, the incidence is higher among females when compared to its incidence among males.

Table 19.6

Prevalence Rate (per 1000 Persons) of Physical Disability among Aged Persons by Type for Each Sex (India)

Sex	*Visual*	*Hearing*	*Speech*	*Locomotor*	*Amenesia/ Senility*	*Any Disability*
Rural						
Male	249	139	32	107	96	380
Female	291	156	38	115	113	425
Person	270	148	35	111	105	402
Urban						
Male	225	111	29	80	61	333
Female	260	132	34	94	80	367
Person	243	122	32	87	70	350

Source: NSS 52nd Round, *Sarvekshana* XXIII(3): 100.

Dependency details for rural and urban females are available in Table 19.7 for the major states of India. While 40-55 per cent of males (both for rural and urban India in almost all the states) are not dependent on others, for females the figures are very discouraging. Not even 20 per cent of the females are independent. Though the elderly urban females are slightly better, the situation is almost the same for all the states. Inspite of the fact that majority of the women in the poverty-stricken households are economically active during their productive age since they work in the unorganised sector, they have no protection in the form of pension benefits to sustain themselves during old age. Thus, the overall conclusion of the above analysis is that the share of the aged female in general is higher than that of the aged male and is also higher in the rural areas than in the urban areas.

The Fate of Widows

The total number of widows in India as per 1991 census was 33 million or 8 per cent of the total female population. Sixty plus women constitute 60 per cent of the widows. Widows are a particularly disadvantaged social group.

Research studies indicate that the children of widows are prone to ill-health because of the economic deprivation of their mothers and are forced to go for work for survival. The life and status of widows vary greatly between regions and social groups and the cultural practices followed by different communities. Parents/brothers are often quite unwilling to re-absorb the widows due to the economic hardship and changing lifestyle which stresses on nuclear family system. With the kith and kin of the husband, the widows find it difficult to unite and a sense of alienation haunts them. The system of patrilocal residence and patrilineal inheritance has the effect of isolating the women. Patriarchal norms coupled with hierarchical social order impose many restrictions on their mobility, effectively preventing them from being gainfully employed. Dependence on others for material support makes them still more vulnerable. If they live alone with their children, they are more vulnerable to sexual violence and often feel threatened. Research studies indicate that after the death of the head of the household, a drastic reduction in the per capita income of the household is witnessed and the wealth holding also comes down either due to sale or mortgage of property. Old-age is a period of helpless dependency and often dreaded by many elderly women since without support they cannot look after themselves. Sons with unequal earnings often quarrel among themselves as to who should keep the widowed mother with them. Or they may decide to keep them in rotation. The widows have to keep moving from one son to another adjusting to each one's way of life. This is a very great mental strain especially during old age. Often the widows feel humiliated, forsaken and insecure which in turn has repercussions on their physical health. In the case of young widows, there is social stigma for their remarriage. Widow remarriage rates are higher in north India than in south India due to the practice of levirate marriages in north and north-west India. This again indicates the deep-rooted backwardness in gender development than to be rejoiced as revolutionary and forward-looking.

Issues

Factors, which are of grave concern for the aged, are their health and economic status. In many poor countries, old people do not receive any pension. In India where 85-90 per cent of the workforce is employed in the unorganised sector, dependence on children during old age is inevitable. Unfortunately the traditional social fabric i.e., joint family and extended family system are fast vanishing. The youth have migrated to the urban areas in search of better opportunities leaving the elderly to fend for themselves. Old age health problems such as cardio-vascular disorders, respiratory disorders, tuberculosis, gastro-intestinal disorders warrant continuous health expenditures which many families can ill afford. When providing food and shelter itself is considered as drain on resources in this age of consumerism and materialism, expenditures on health care of the old is not generally relished.

Table 19.7

Per 1000 Distribution of Aged Persons by State of Economic Independence of Each Sex

State	Not Dependent on Others			
	Rural Male	*Urban Male*	*Rural Female*	*Urban Female*
Andhra Predesh	441	615	169	163
Assam	349	384	29	12
Bihar	576	498	167	80
Gujarat	431	443	104	59
Haryana	493	477	87	165
Himachal Pradesh	569	610	236	389
Jammu & Kashmir	553	512	106	52
Karnataka	438	496	107	65
Kerala	497	449	92	112
Madhya Pradesh	514	566	181	135
Maharashtra	509	506	148	135
Orissa	446	400	116	104
Punjab	445	514	15	72
Rajasthan	546	535	117	110
Tamil Nadu	446	488	189	173
Uttar Pradesh	478	487	98	71
West Bengal	499	530	22	75
All India	485	515	121	115

Source: NSS 52nd Round, *Sarvekshana* XX111(3): S396–S398.

The dimensions of deprivation experienced by the elderly especially the female elderly can be listed as follows:

- Poverty: This refers to lack of physical necessities, assets and income.
- Social exclusion and a feeling of neglect: As children and other members in the family spend less and less time with them due to their own pre-occupations, the aged feel neglected and left-out.
- Isolation: This refers to the sufferings of elders in the villages who had been left behind while the younger generation migrated to the city in search of better prospects. They are isolated in terms of communication, contacts, information, access to social services and markets. They invariably lack social and economic support.

- Physical and mental illness: The physical weakness which automatically sets in with ageing coupled with the mental trauma due to isolation and neglect lead to low morale.
- Vulnerability: This refers to increased exposure to risk, shocks, stress and humiliation.
- Powerlessness: The old especially the women being powerless are unable to bargain. They lack the courage to demand their eligible share.

In the Indian context between male and female elderly, the female elderly are much more vulnerable due to their subordinate status and socioeconomic dependence. Repeated pregnancies and self-denial of food when young make them very weak and fragile during their old age. Moreover, women till their death are not relieved from the household chores and bringing up of children and grandchildren. The two major concerns, which need attention, are financial support and physical care needs of older people.

In the traditional family ideologies, the family was identified as the appropriate arena for the care of the elderly. It was firmly believed that the family members have a moral responsibility, and the supportive and enduring security provided by the family cannot be substituted with impersonal and bureaucratic care of the old age homes and government centres for the aged. But the current trend of thinking is—the fast changing family values and lifestyles are incompatible with elder care. The state being a 'welfare state' should take up this responsibility. Dr. Sharatchandra Gokhale, an eminent social scientist based in Pune when honoured with a special award by the International Federation on Ageing at Montreal for his service to the aged said, "My belief is that longevity is a basic human right and hence it becomes the business of the state to provide for healthy aging. I feel aging has to be recognised as a development issue and has to be addressed at social political and economic levels. The notion that the aged are a social and economic burden needs to be discarded fast. To me, starting old age homes is an altogether misleading concept. On the contrary, it is important to strengthen the family, provide day-care services and provide income security to people" (Nampudakam, 1999b). Another researcher observes, "For an aging woman, maintaining functional capacity within the support system of family may still be construed as autonomy. Being dependent on children may not threaten sense of self worth. It is not independence and autonomy that are important rather being interdependent, being integrated that seem important to women" (Jaiprakash, 1997). So the view that family should continue to play a vital role in the care of the elderly is very much emphasised in the Indian context. Such being the case, what impact it has on women's domestic work burden and their labour force participation and attachment are crucial issues. Unfortunately, research studies are few and far apart in this area. However, the research findings pertaining to USA are worth analysing here.

A study conducted by the National Alliance for Care Giving and the American Association of Retired Persons brings out the adverse impact of elder care on career advancement of women. This sample study on 1200 people who provided care giving assistance to some one above 50, reveals that 11 per cent of caregivers took leave of absence, 7 per cent opted to work fewer hours, 4 per cent lost job benefits, 3 per cent turned down a promotion and 10 per cent took early retirement or quit their jobs. Collectively for the country as a whole, family caregivers spend $2 billion of their own assets each month to assist relatives. It is feared that women's progress toward shattering the glass ceiling will be slowed down because of the increasing burden of elder care (Sam, 2000). If this is the case in a country where plenty of part-time and flexi-jobs are available, one can imagine the impact of elderly care on career women in India where a compromise between the two is unimaginable.

There is another group, which believes in state-family partnership wherein the burden of family caring will be lessened but at the same time limiting the power of professionals and state bureaucrats over people's lives. The expansion of state care is being emphasised by the feminist gerontological researchers. They consider caring of older people as another aspect of women's unpaid domestic labour. This restricts their mobility, paid work and reinforces women's dependence and subordination. Taking into consideration the increasing material and emotional cost care of the elderly, the feminists point out the need for expansion of state care.

Caring refers to comfort and psychological support and provision of services like personal and nursing care, taking them to health care centres, and managing their finances. Private initiatives are coming up in a big way though the big corporates are yet to be involved as they are the 'monied people' who can do on a mass scale. In India, 234 old age homes, 398 day care centres and 40 mobile medical units are supported by the Government of India. About 4 million destitute elderly women are provided old age pension as a part of the National Social Assistance Programme (NSAP). In 1999 by way of response to the 'International Year of the Older Persons', the Ministry of Social Justice and Empowerment, Government of India announced a national policy for older persons. The objective of the policy is to help the older persons to spend the last phase of their life with purpose, dignity and peace. The main features of the policy are: (a) expanding old age pension scheme to the private sector, (b) subsidising health care with private sector involvement, (c) legalising parents' right to be supported by their children, (d) easy access to housing loans (e) increased standard tax deductions for senior citizens, and (f) special provisions in the Indian Penal Code for protection of older persons. As usual like any other policy, this policy is gender neutral. The vulnerability of female elders when compared to male elders is not being appreciated.

Another issue, which is of prime importance, is the nexus between gender and poverty. Among the poor, women constitute a sizeable proportion. Since women live longer than men, 'feminisation of ageing' and 'feminisation of poverty' go hand in hand. Patriarchal hierarchies within the family and outside force women to bear a disproportionate part of the burden in poverty. Recently understanding has grown that poverty affects men and women differently and hence, one single poverty alleviation policy is of no avail. But still gender issues are rarely openly acknowledged in national anti-poverty strategies. A disproportionate share of the burden of poverty is suffered by women though little data and information are available about the health status of the bottom 20 per cent of the world's poorest of which women constitute a high proportion.

Table 19.8

Percentage of Population Below International Poverty Lines in Countries with a Population Close to or Above 100 million in the year 2000

Country	Population (Million)*	Percentage with <1$ Per day**	Percentage with <2$ per day**
China	1.275	18.5	53.7
India	1.008	44.2	86.2
Brazil	170	9.0	25.4
Nigeria	113	70.2	90.8

Note: * UN World Population Prospects the 2000 revision.

** Adjusted for purchasing power parity.

Source: World Development Indicator Database 2001, World Bank.

Active and Healthy Ageing

WHO response to population ageing is one of active and healthy ageing (Hoskins). Active ageing is the process of optimising opportunities for health, participation and security in order to enhance quality of life as people age. Health refers to physical, social and mental well-being. Quality of life refers to physical health, psychological health, level of independence, social relationships and physical environment. Active ageing is more inclusive than healthy ageing as it recognises the multiple factors that affect how individuals and people age. WHO policy framework complements the international plan of action on ageing. The approaches include life course approach. Maintenance of maximum functional capacity at older ages, risk factor approach, development approach, continuum of care, and universal and equal access to health care services. The broader framework includes training of workers of public health centres in geriatrics and gerontology. Active ageing policies and programmes include working towards fewer premature deaths in the highly productive stage of life, fewer disabilities associated with chronic diseases of older people, more people enjoying a positive quality of life as they grow older, more people participating actively as they age in the social cultural economic and political aspects of security in paid and unpaid roles and in domestic, family and community life and lower cost related to medical treatment and care services. The developing countries are prepared to face the challenge of population ageing lest they may face an 'agequake' with concomitant adverse outcomes (Wallace, 1999).

Plan of Action: Points for Pondering

The Government of India is still complacent that the joint family system and traditional values would provide the social security in old age. But the weakening support mechanisms and the increasing number of the elderly make the care and support of the aged an urgent social issue. The following measures are worth considering:

a. Construction of disaggregated data by age-group and gender. And understanding the role of internal migration on the structure of family and on the care of the elderly.

b. Promotion of research studies on different economic groups on the nature of elderly care and details on caregivers' time allocation.

c. Research in geriatrics and treating chronic ailments and health care provision.

d. Equal opportunity to women in inheritance and other economic means of living.

e. Productive capacity of older women identified, mainstreamed and strengthened to give them identity and involvement.

f. Prevent or postpone disability through 'age friendly' policies and enable those with disability to fully participate in community life.

g. Encourage voluntary work of the elderly and make use of their services.

h. Promote an inter-generational approach that recognises the importance of relationships among and between family members.

i. Last but not the least is devising a pension system which will take care of the older women whether they worked or not during their working age.

Conclusion

In this age of 'youth oriented society', older men and women struggle with ageism. Because of double standards, women are labelled 'old' at an earlier age. Because of the heavy burden of domestic chores and frequent child birth they also start looking aged even when young. The custom of marrying men older to them by many years pushes them to dependency and widowhood at a comparatively young age. The mental trauma suffered by them is simply taken for granted. Feminisation of poverty and feminisation of ageing are vital issues for immediate policy attention. Unless measures are worked out to tackle the problem, the situation may go out of control causing untold misery to humankind. It is just not a "woman's issue" but it is very much a "social issue". The need for intervention is very urgent in the case of developing countries than in developed countries in view of the absolute number of women to be attended to.

References

Hoskins, Irene (n.d.) *A Global Perspective on Active and Healthy Ageing: Current and Future Trends.* WHO Ageing and Life Course Programme, Geneva.

Jaiprakash, Indira (1997). "Hindu World View and Well-Being of Aging Women", *Research and Development Journal* (A Journal of Help Age, India) 3(2): 43-49.

Nampudakam, Mathew (1999a). "Greying Blues", *Health for the Millions* 25(5): 3, Sep.-Oct.

———. (1999b). "The National Policy for Older Persons", *Health for the Millions* 29, Sep.-Oct.

Rajan, Irudaya. S., U.S. Mishra and P. Sankara Sarma (1999). *India's Elderly: Burden or Challenge?.* Sage. p.16.

Sam, Ervin L. (2000). "Fourteen Forecasts for an Aging Society", *Futurist* 34(6): 24-29, Nov-Dec.

UN Population Division (1999). "World Population Prospects 1998 Revision", *New York Vol I: Comprehensive Survey Tables, Vol II: Sex and Age and UN World Population Projections to 2150 New York.*

Wallace, Paul (1999). *Agequake: Riding the Demographic Rollercoaster, Shaking Business, Finance and Our World.* London: Nicholas Bready Publications.

World Bank (1994). *Averting the Old Age Crisis: Policies to Protect the Old and Promote Growth.* Oxford University Press.

20

Health Insurance and Health Care Financing in India

An Empirical Study with Special Reference to Social Health Insurance

AVISHEK HAZRA AND SUBRATA LAHIRI

Introduction

In recent times, there has been a growing concern with the increasing cost of health services and the existing mechanisms for financing health care costs. Like other developing countries, in India, the Ministry of Finance seems to undervalue health development particularly for the rural and tribal population because all modern health facilities are getting concentrated in the urban areas. As a result, for health service development, tax collection increasing beyond the limits seems to be critical option for the government (Green, 1992). In such a situation, a significant viewpoint has emerged to manage the problem. Taxing the poor most heavily to pay for the health for all may be better than making the sick more sicker, but it is hardly in the line with health for all policies, which identify poverty as major cause of ill health. It would be shocking to advocate making the poor still poorer by taxation (Abel-Smith, 1986). The triumph over such complexity of taxation in relation to improve health status and quality of life of the people, health insurance emerges as a potentially better option. For the reason that health insurance offers a means of obtaining a substantial part of the funds for urban health services from employers and employees, so that the government can release tax based revenue for preventive and promotive actions for primary health care where coverage is very inadequate and totally absent especially in remote rural and tribal areas.

In influencing the choices that make for better health and lowered financial burden of ill health, the society is typically faced with three key challenges. The first has to do with controlling the cost incurred in the provision of health interventions that it supports—be it care, health care regulation or provision of insurance—given that resources are limited and face competing demands for their use. The second is to achieve an equitable distribution of the financial burden of ill health and morbidity. This is a direct consequence of the fact that societies are concerned not just about improvements in "average health" but also, especially, about the health and economic welfare of the socially and economically marginal groups in society. A third issue is to ensure the quality of medical care that is provided, because of its central importance to people who need care, and also because of its direct link to the cost-effectiveness of care provision.

Risk pooling initiative for sharing costs among the healthy and the sick leading to insurance schemes act as a substitute for or as supplementary to state provision for minimum uniform services. The well-to-do segment of the population, both in rural and urban areas have acceptability and affordability towards medical care, at the same time cannot be said about the people who belong to poor segment of the society. More than 75 per cent of the population utilises private sector for medical care. Unfortunately, medical care is becoming costlier day by day and it has become almost out of reach of the poor people. Today, there is need for injection of substantial resources in the health sectors to ensure affordability of medical care to all. Health insurance seems as an important option, which needs to be considered by the policy makers and planners.

The present chapter tries to address the importance of health insurance for equitable health care utilisation, and whether health insurance can be a healthy option for health care financing in India. Before entering into the analytical part of the study, the existing methods for financing health care services in general and the scenario of existing health insurance schemes as a risk-pooling mechanism in particular have been portrayed. With the help of secondary data, it is investigated how the health insurance coverage varies across different income quintiles, and whether health insurance status makes any difference in health care utilisation. In the last section, the chapter intends to focus on Employees State Insurance Scheme (ESIS), a social health insurance meant for social security and which is one of the major flagships of the health insurance scheme directly run by the government. The chapter investigates the quality of care provided in the health facilities under the aforementioned social security scheme and whether it affects health care utilisation among the insured or not.

Health Financing in India

The share of public financing in total health care is just about one per cent of GDP compared to 2.8 per cent in other developing countries.

Beneficiaries are both poor as well as well-fed section of society. Over 80 per cent of the total health financing is private financing, much of which is out-of-pocket payments (i.e., user charges) and not any prepayment schemes. Public spending in health care is very low at 17 per cent and the National Health Policy has recognised this. More than 86 per cent of health care financing is through unplanned for, non-contributory spending.

A number of methods exist for financing health care services: (i) Personal payment (out-of-pocket) (ii) Voluntary insurance (iii) Social insurance (iv) General revenues (v) Charity (vi) Industry and (vii) External financing. In most of the developing countries including India, the first four sources finance the health care service and the last four sources contribute negligible amount. Out of the first four, the former two are private and the later two are public (Sandhya, 2005).

Quality of Care and Health Insurance

Internationally, few studies have examined the relationship between health insurance, health costs and health care utilisation (Dafny and Gruber, 2000, French and Kamboj, 2002). Most have been observational studies, which analyse outcome differences between insured and non-insured populations. And most of these studies focus mainly on the utilisation and do not capture the aspect of quality of care.

It is needless to say, that the quality of health services provided is an important matter of concern when people seek medical care. Studies conducted in Ghana (1989), Peru (1987), Switzerland (1990) and Zaire region (1989) revealed that quality of health care is a significant factor in influencing 'demand for health care' (Creese, 1990) and consequently health care utilisation. It may also influence the choice of health facilities. The decision to choose between different health care providers involves evaluating the cost and quality of care in each of the options available. Studies in India show that people spend large amounts out-of-pocket for curative care, by preferring to visit private, rather than public health facilities (Sundar, 1995, Visaria and Gumber, 1994). It has been observed that higher-priced options, such as treatment in the private sector, are usually associated with higher quality of health care. There has been substantial analysis on the quality of the public health care services and the consensus is that, "...this is not as inexpensive as it seems, is often not of the best quality and is also inaccessible" (Gupta and Dasgupta, 2000). The private sector on the other hand is much more expensive, but easily accessible (Dreze and Sen, 1995, World Bank, 1995). The choice of facility reveals that the vulnerable sections still have a higher probability of visiting the government facilities, mainly because of price differentials. If they end up visiting private facilities, it imposes a severe economic burden on them, and on the other hand if they go to the government facilities, coupled with the issue of availability and accessibility, quality of medical care becomes important (Gupta and Datta, 2003). It is not surprising that with enrolment in health insurance schemes, 'consumers hope to get better quality of health care'. This has implications about what kind of system the health insurance companies would want to bring with them, which would ensure high quality (Gupta, 2000). According to Ahuja (2004), health insurance, which strengthens the demand, makes sense only when the supply of health care is reasonably well-developed and where this is not so, health insurance loses its importance. When there exists any facility-based insurance mechanism, the issue whether quality of care receives priority or the risk-reduction/cost minimisation, remains unexplored. The present study focuses on Employees State Insurance Scheme (ESIS), which is one of the major flagships of the health insurance scheme directly run by the Government. ESI scheme has a wide reach and the highest coverage among all the existing health insurance schemes in India. In order to understand the effect of risk-sharing towards better utilisation of public health services, a careful study of the functioning of such scheme is called for. Unlike most other public and private sector health insurance schemes, there are service facilities designed for the ESI scheme members and their families. This in turn may make difference in ESI beneficiaries' health seeking behaviour with that of general population or of those having some form of insurance scheme other than the ESI scheme. Feasibility of such publicly provided health insurance schemes in India, catering to the specific requirements of the disadvantaged sections of the population needs to be studied as a health financing option for a healthy nation of tomorrow.

Data and Methods

The chapter utilises secondary as well as primary data. The secondary data source is the dataset of National Family Health Survey-3 (2005-06). For the first time in NFHS, information on health care prepayments or health insurance of household members have been collected from the head of the household and is given in the household data file. And that provide a chance to link the insurance status with the utilisation of health care services. To capture the domain of client satisfaction and quality of care provided by such public health facilities, 150 patients availing the facility of the selected ESI hospital and dispensaries have been interviewed following an exit interview technique in two districts of the state of West Bengal. Simple frequency distribution and bivariate analysis is used for the study. A composite index of quality of care has been constructed to depict the quality of care provided in the ESI facilities.

Results and Discussion

Health insurance coverage in India is far from satisfactory, despite the existence of a large population living below the poverty line and/or illiterate, which lives under great health risks. Existing insurance is largely limited to a small proportion of people in the organised sector (IIPS and WHO, 2006). NFHS-3 asked the respondent in the household questionnaire whether any member of the household is covered by a health scheme or health insurance. Health insurance schemes can be categorised as follows: (1) mandatory or government run schemes such as the Employees State Insurance Scheme (ESIS) or Central Government Health Scheme (CGHS), (2) schemes offered by non-governmental organisations or community based health insurance, (3) employer-based schemes, and (4) voluntary health insurance schemes or private-for-profit schemes.

Findings from NFHS-3 show that only a small proportion of households (5 per cent) have at least one usual member covered by a health scheme or health insurance. The state-wise percentages shows that in Bihar, Uttar Pradesh and Orissa, less than 2 per cent of households are having a member covered by any health scheme or health insurance plan, whereas in Gujarat and Karnataka, more than 10 per cent of households are having a member covered by any health scheme or health insurance (Figure 20.1).

Figure 20.1

Percentage of Households Covered by any Health Scheme or Health Insurance Coverage in India and Major States, NFHS-3, 2005-06

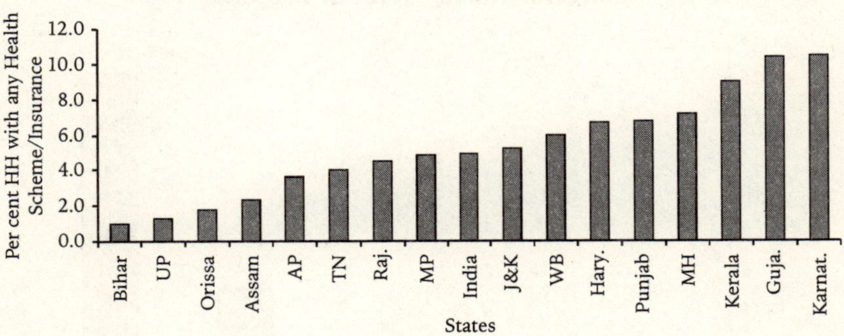

The proportion of urban households covered under a health scheme or insurance is 10 per cent, compared with only 2 per cent of rural households.

Higher coverage is reported in households falling in the highest wealth quintile (16 per cent). Among households in the lowest three wealth quintiles, the proportion having a household member with health insurance does not exceed 2 per cent (Figure 20.2). Survey data clearly highlights the poor health insurance coverage in the country, a situation urgently requiring remedial steps.

Figure 20.2

Health Insurance Coverage by Types of Health Schemes/ Health Insurances, India, NFHS-3, 2005-06

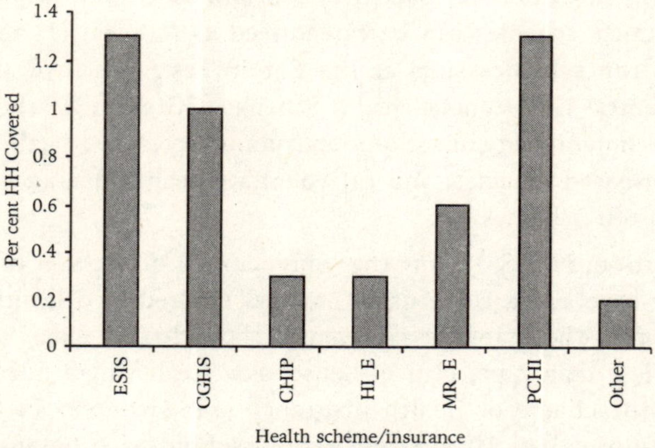

Note: ESIS: Employees State Insurance Scheme; CGHS: Central Government Health Scheme; CHIP: Commercial Health Insurance Programme; HI_E: Health Insurance provided by Employer; MR_E: Medical Reimbursement through Employer; PCHI: Privately purchased Commercial Health Insurance.

Figure 20.3

Health Insurance Coverage by Wealth Index Categories, India, NFHS-3, 2005-06

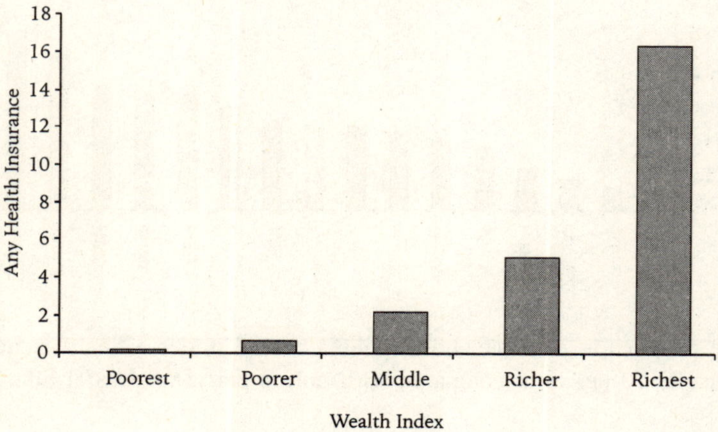

Respondents who reported someone in the household to be covered by a health insurance scheme were asked to identify the type of scheme or insurance. While it was possible to report more than one health insurance scheme, 98 per cent of households with coverage reported only one type. Those with insurance are most likely to have privately purchased the insurance (28 per cent) or to be covered under an ESIS (26 per cent). The third most common form of coverage is under a CGHS (20 per cent). The remaining households with insurance are reimbursed by their employer (12 per cent), covered under some other insurance with their employer (6 per cent), or included in a community health insurance programme (5 per cent). The type of health scheme or insurance coverage clearly indicates the predominance of mandatory schemes and employer-based schemes such as the ESIS, CGHS, insurance through employers and medical reimbursement from employers rather than voluntary health insurances/schemes. Private providers of health insurance have only recently emerged as big players in the Indian health insurance market, after liberalisation of the economy.

Table 20.1 shows the per cent distribution of respondents who availed treatment facility in the ESI service dispensaries and hospitals in the selected two districts of West Bengal. Majority of them are Hindu, belong to general category, in the working age-group and male. Two-third of the patients came from a distance of more than 5 kilometres for treatment. The patients who came for treatment to the ESI service dispensaries were asked, "Are you satisfied with the ESI scheme?". Surprisingly only about 35 per cent responded positively which is really a serious matter of concern (Table 20.2). In response to the question, "In presence of other facility, would you have still chosen the ESI facility?", only 15 per cent of the respondent said affirmative. Those who responded that they are not satisfied with the ESI facility were asked about the prime reasons for choosing ESI facility for treatment. Among the responses, 'treatment is free of cost' (68 per cent) becomes the most important reason followed by 'customary' (35 per cent), 'others' (30 per cent) and 'medical leave benefit' (26 per cent). Therefore, it may be said that quality of care outweighs the risk-reduction, or in other words, to the ESI beneficiaries, mostly living in rural areas and with lower economic condition, 'treatment free of cost' is much more important than the quality of services. They do not have the ability or capability to bear the expenses of getting treatment from the private facilities.

There were 14 questions on several aspects of quality of care of services rendered in the ESI service dispensaries. The questions were asked on a three point scale of good, average and poor. As per the ratings of the respondents, most of the parameters got the average rating. Ninety per cent of the patients rated 'long' for the waiting time for getting treatment. Around 82 per cent and 68 per cent of the respondents gave 'poor' ratings to confidentiality/ privacy and time spent by doctor for examination/diagnosis. There was a direct question on overall satisfaction. Based on the score values, it comes out that only about six per cent of the respondents rated 'good'. On the other hand, when we computed a composite index of quality of care considering all these 14 parameters, the quality of care in the ESI dispensaries is rated 'good' by one-third of the respondents (Table 20.3).

Table 20.1

Background Characteristics of the Respondents who have Received Treatment Facility in the ESI Service Dispensaries and Hospital, West Bengal

Background Characteristics	*Per cent*
Religion	
Hindu	72.3
Non-Hindu	27.7
Caste	
SC/ST/OBC	30.5
General	69.5
Age	
< 35	40.4
35-59	48.2
60+	11.3
Sex	
Male	70.9
Female	29.1
Distance from Home (Km.)	
<=5	33.3
5-10	36.9
10+	29.8
N	150

Note: N refers to total number of respondents.

Table 20.2

Percentage Distribution of Respondents who Availed Treatment from ESI Service Dispensaries by Various Treatment Related Characteristics, West Bengal

Characteristics	*Per cent*
Consulted anywhere before coming to ESI facility	40.4
Place of last consultancy	
ESI panel doctor	15.0
Govt. facilities	25.0
Private facilities	52.5
Chemist/medical shop	7.5
Reason for choosing ESI for treatment	
Customary	34.3
Treatment free of cost	81.8
Facility is nearby	5.1
Facility is of good quality	2.0
To get benefit of leave	10.1
Others	3.0
Waiting time for doctor	
<=1 hr	65.7
1-2 hrs	23.2
>2 hrs	11.1
Time spent by doctor with you	
<=2 minutes	41.4
2-5 minutes	50.5
>5 minutes	8.1
Frequency of using ESI facility more than other facility	32.3
Satisfied with the scheme	
No	61.6
Yes	35.4
DK/CS	3.0
In presence of other facility still chosen this facility	
No	50.5
Yes	15.2
DK/CS	34.3
If not satisfied in ESI services, reason for choosing ESI for trt.	
Customary	34.8
Treatment is free of cost	68.2
Facility is nearby	4.5
To get medical leave benefit	25.8
Others	30.3
If were not ESI beneficiary, preferred place for treatment	
Only govt. facilities	32.3
Only private facilities	38.5
Both facilities	29.2
Future preferred place for similar health problem	
Only ESI facility	21.2
Only non-ESI facility	48.5
Both ESI & non-ESI facility	12.1
Cannot say	18.2
N	99

Note: N refers to total number of respondents.

Table 20.3

Percentage Distribution of Respondents who Availed Treatment from ESI Hospital by Various Treatment Related Characteristics, West Bengal

Characteristics	*Per cent*
Consulted before coming to ESI hospital	54.8
Place of last consultation	
ESI panel doctor	48.0
Private facilities	48.0
Chemist/medical shop	28.0
Visit of doctor regular	76.2
Examined in separate room	9.5
Doctors spent enough time	45.2
Doctors listen carefully about health problem	66.7
Prescribed medicine easily available	66.7
Doctor explained properly	32.5
Satisfied with the ESI scheme	57.1
In presence of other facility still would have chosen this facility	29.3
Reason for choosing ESI for treatment although not satisfied in ESI services	
Customary	50.0
Treatment free of cost	88.9
Medical leave benefit	33.3
Others	22.2
If were not ESI beneficiary, preferred place for treatment	
Only govt. facilities	52.4
Only private facilities	11.9
Both facilities	35.7

Table 20.4

Quality of Care in the ESI Service Dispensaries, West Bengal

Parameters	*Good*	*Average*	*Poor*
Convenient location of the facility	44.0	46.2	9.9
Availability of doctor/physician	14.3	68.1	17.6
Behaviour of doctors	33.0	51.6	15.4
Behaviour of paramedical staffs	14.3	39.6	41.8
Time of examination/diagnosis	1.1	27.5	68.1
Confidentiality/privacy	1.1	11.0	82.4
Technical competence of doctor	7.7	36.3	2.2
Availability of medicines	9.9	63.7	26.4
Quality of medicine	3.3	48.4	34.1
Cleanliness of surroundings	47.3	50.5	2.2
Special treatment	6.6	64.8	28.6
General comfort	1.1	38.9	50.0
Waiting time for getting treatment	0.0	9.9	90.1
Waiting time for getting medicine	5.5	75.8	18.7
Overall satisfaction	5.5	48.4	46.2
Quality of care index	**33.3**	**42.2**	**24.4**

Table 20.5

Quality of Care in the ESI Hospital, West Bengal

Parameters	*Good*	*Average*	*Poor*
Convenient location of the facility	54.8	38.1	—
Availability of doctor/physician/nurse	17.9	74.4	5.1
Behaviour of doctors	30.8	59.0	10.3
Behaviour of paramedical staffs	—	59.0	28.2
Time spent by doctor for examination/diagnosis	—	53.8	41.0
Confidentiality/privacy	—	23.1	64.1
Technical competence of doctor	25.6	17.9	56.4
Availability of medicines	7.7	82.1	7.7
Availability of beds	28.2	53.8	15.4
Availability of diagnostic/surgical equipments	2.6	23.1	25.6
Quality of medicine	2.6	66.7	7.7
Quality of food	2.6	30.8	66.7
Cleanliness of surroundings	—	48.7	51.3
Special treatment	—	20.5	10.3
General comfort		64.1	23.1
Waiting time for getting treatment	2.6	64.1	33.3
Waiting time for getting medicine	2.6	79.5	17.9
Waiting time for getting bed	20.5	66.7	12.8
Overall satisfaction	7.7	66.7	25.6
Quality of care index	**25.6**	**38.5**	**35.9**

References

Abel-Smith, B. (1986). "Funding Health for All-Is Insurance the Answer?", *World Health Forum 7.*

Ahuja, Rajeev (2004). "Health Insurance for the poor in India", *ICRIER Working Paper No. 123.* New Delhi: Indian Council for Research on International Economic Relations.

Card, David, Carlos Dobkin and Nicole Maestas (2004). "The Impact of Nearly Universal Insurance Coverage on Health Care Utilization and Health: Evidence from Medicare", *NBER Working Paper No. 10365.*

Creese, A. L. (1990). "User Charges for Health Care: A Review of Recent Experiences, Current Contents", *SHS Paper, Number 1,* Division of Health Services Strengthening, WHO.

Dafny, Leemore and Jonathan Gruber (2000). "Does Public Insurance improve the Efficiency of Medical Care: Medicaid Expansions and Child Hospitalizations", *National Bureau of Economic Research (NBER) Working Paper No. 7555.*

Dreze, J. and A. Sen (1995). *India: Economic Development and Social Opportunity.* Oxford. Ellis: Clarendon Press.

ESIS (2004). *Report on the activity of the ESI Corporation.* Employees' State Insurance Corporation, Kolkata, West Bengal.

Finkelstein, Amy and Robin McKnight (2005). "What did Medicare do (and was it worth it)?", *NBER Working Paper No. 11609.*

French, Eric and Kirti Kamboj (2002). "Analyzing the Relationship between Health Insurance, Health Costs and Health Care Utilization", *Economic Perspective.* 3Q/2002.

Green, A. (1992). *An Introduction of Health Planning in Developing Countries.* Oxford: Oxford University Press.

Gupta, Indrani and Arindam Datta (2003). "Inequities in Health and Health Care in India: Can the Poor hope for a Respite?". New Delhi: Institute of Economic Growth.

Gupta, Indrani and Purnamita Dasgupta (2000). "Demand for Curative Healthcare in Rural India: Choosing between Private, Public and No Care", *Discussion Paper No 14.* New Delhi: Institute of Economic Growth.

Gupta, Indrani (2000). "Willingness to Avoid Health Costs: Results from a Delhi Study", *Discussion Paper No 15.* New Delhi: Institute of Economic Growth.

International Institute for Population Sciences (IIPS), World Health Organization (WHO), and World Health Organization (WHO) - India – WR Office (2006). *Health System Performance Assessment: World Health Survey 2003 India.* Mumbai: IIPS.

Sandhya, S. (2005). "Health Financing Reforms in India: Lessons from Other Countries", *Journal of Social and Economic Development* 7(1): 53-90.

Sundar, R. (1995). "Household Survey of Health Care Utilization and Expenditure", *NCAER Working Paper No. 53.* New Delhi: National Council of Applied Economic Research.

Visaria, P. and A. Gumber (1994). *Utilization of Primary Health Care in India, 1986-87.* Ahmedabad: Gujarat Institute of Development Research.

World Bank (1995). *India Policy and Finance Strategies for Strengthening Primary Health Care Services.* Report No. 13042-IN.

21

Perspective on Age Structural Transition and Economic Growth in India

Consequences on Demographic Dividend

NEELANJANA PANDEY AND FAUJDAR RAM

Introduction

India is emerging as a major demographic bonus state due to changing demographics. It will remain both young and old for most of this century. Young, owing to the past fertility and its momentum; and old because of their changing demography and added life span. These demographic trends contribute to change the economic scenario of the country. India's population is projected to grow from 1029 million to 1400 million in 2026 according to office of Registrar General of India. As per the census figure for 2001, 54 per cent of the population is below 24 years of age. This forms the basis of the demographic dividend notion, implying that there are natural advantages of having a younger population.

Population growth rates are subjected to change in fertility, mortality and migration, all of which play a vital role in the multi-dimensional process of demographic transition. The crux of India's population problem lies in the states of Bihar, Madhya Pradesh, Rajasthan and Uttar Pradesh. According to latest expert group projections, out of projected increase in population of 371 million in India during 2001-2026, 187 million is likely to occur in seven states of Bihar, Chhattisgarh, Jharkhand, Madhya Pradesh, Rajasthan, Uttar Pradesh and Uttarakhand (termed as BIMARU states, since it was so before division) (R.G.I., 2006).

In international literature, the Kerala model of demographic transition has received considerable attention. The same is not true of Tamil Nadu which is a much larger state than Kerala, in both area and population. The factors which have contributed to the significant reduction in the birth rate in Tamil Nadu are different from those operated in Kerala. Leaving aside the tiny state of Goa, which has the lowest birth rate in India, Kerala and Tamil Nadu are success stories in the field of population control. As a matter of fact, all the southern states, Kerala, Tamil Nadu, Andhra Pradesh and Karnataka are doing well in family planning, whereas the four large states in the north, Uttar Pradesh, Bihar, Madhya Pradesh and Rajasthan, are lagging far behind. As a result, a peculiar situation has arisen in India in terms of what we call 'north-south demographic divide' (Bose, 1996).

In the 1990s, different scholars have pointed out that population growth will not be evenly distributed across the different age-groups during the demographic transition (Chesnais, 1990; 1992). On the contrary, as the demographic transition unfolds, the growth rate of different age-groups will follow an uneven pattern (Malmberg and Sommestad, 2000). Age structure transition is a consequence of speed and timing of fertility and mortality decline, so it is important to understand priori the fertility and mortality trends in India and its states. Generally, the gap in life expectancy at birth has been narrowing down among all the states but onset and speed of fertility decline differ significantly.

Apart from demographic diversity, there were little evidence of comparable convergence among Indian states, this raises an important question as to why some regions demonstrate inter-regional convergence while others do not. In India, it appears that geographical variation across regions may block or slow the convergence of incomes (Sachs *et al.*, 2002). In the Indian context with wide regional variations in terms of socioeconomic development, economic reforms have been initiated at different levels across states. Most of the economic reforms have been pursued in the industrial sector, the spread and growth of which show considerable regional variations. Availability of infrastructure, which is a strong determinant of industrial productivity and competitiveness on the one hand and occupation, mobility and earnings of the population on the other, also varies significantly across states (Mitra, 1997).

Asia's record of economic growth has been associated with changes in three key factors: (1) the share of population in the prime working ages, (2) the productivity of labour in all sectors of the economy, and (3) the allocation of labour to the low productivity agriculture sector and the high-productivity industry and service sectors. It is insisted that all three factors have potentially strong linkages to various aspects of demographic change, especially changes in the age structure. So, it has become essential to examine these factors and their suitability in country like India which is as diverse as Asian countries.

Despite the fact that India is a fast developing economy, difficulties have led the government to conclude that far more needs to be done to create more employment opportunities for the majority of Indians, to enable them to participate in the benefits of growth and to contribute to that growth. The growing numbers have always been perceived as the cause and consequence of underdevelopment and poverty. This growth is consequence of the demographic transition that has taken place over time. Most often, planners and policy makers in the country have not taken cognisance of the demographic transition and this result in wastage on the economic front. The present stage of India's demographic transition poses typical problems of increasing numbers in the working ages as well as old ages as a consequence of high fertility in past and higher survival rate in recent times. On economic front, the agenda should be to generate more employment in order to accommodate the increased supply of labour force (Rajan *et al.*, 1993).

The chapter addresses two main issues, first, the age structural transition and population ageing process and its linkages with economic growth among the different states of India and second, to study the nature and factors of employment and economic growth.

Data and Methods

Methodology

To show the diversity of degree of demographic transition completed an index of transition for five zones as well as for selected 14 major states has been computed, using formula proposed by Cho and Togashi (1984) which has been modified for Indian condition. Although the index may not be the perfect indicator but still it provides useful and concise information.

The index of the percentage of demographic transition completed has been constructed using the following formula:

$$Index = 0.40\left[\frac{TFRmax - TFR}{TFRmax - TFRmin}\right] + 0.40[1 - (\frac{e_{0max} - e_0}{e_{0max} - e_{0min}})] + 0.20[u]$$

Where,

TFR = total fertility rate per woman

e_o = life expectancy at birth, and

u = proportion of population urban

To obtain minimum and maximum value of TFR and life expectancy at birth, we have revisited the estimates made by Ram *et al.* (1995), Rele (1987) and Mukherjee (1976). Following values are observed during the transition:

$TFRmax = 7.4 \quad TFRmin = 2.1$ (replacement level fertility)

$e_{omax} = 75 \quad e_{omin} = 31.5$

To study the age structural change, conventional dependency ratios and index of ageing have been calculated. Difference between the growth rate of working age population and total population has been used to indicate demographic opportunity phase. For this purpose, age-wise population estimates of states provided by Sample Registration System have been used. Beyond the year 2005, we have used population projections made by an expert group.

An attempt has been made to modify the index of ageing, as the traditional measure of ageing gives only head-count ratio which reflects only the numbers that are old, but does not take into account the extent of oldness (Basu and Basu, 1987). As shown by them, a family of poverty measure in economics offers idea for developing an index which captures the underlying notion of ageing.

$$I(P) = \frac{1}{n}\sum_{j=1}^{k} m(P_i) * \frac{(P_i - 60)^2}{60^2}$$

Where,

j = 1, 2...k i.e., classes of old age above age 60

n = number of people in the population

m (pj) = number of people aged in the age-group j and

Pi = age of ith oldest person.

Based on this index, the trend of population ageing in India and different regions has been illustrated.

Industrial Classification of Workforce

The description of industry was relevant to the type of economic activity. Using NIC-1998[1] classification, we have made the comparability of National Sample Survey data (tables in appendix) by classifying into broad sectors as:

(I) Primary sector (agriculture and mining)

(II) Secondary sector (manufacturing and construction) and

(III) Tertiary or service sector (transport, commerce, administration, IT, etc.)

1. National Industrial Classification-1998 is a standardised classification of economic activities undertaken by the economic units.

The analysis is carried out in Stata using weighted sample. The unemployment rate is defined on the basis of usual activity status. The variables used in the analysis are state, age, sex, industry, education etc. The economic performance at all India as well as state level has been examined by broad sectors namely primary, secondary and tertiary sector. The net state domestic product (NSDP) has been used as the proxy of economic growth of state. Various rates and ratios have been calculated to understand the coping mechanism of economic growth.

Annual compound rate of growth has been worked out applying the simple log linear model for NSDP with respect to time (t), defined as

$$NSDP2 = NSDP1\ (1 + r)^t$$

Taking natural logarithm of above, we can calculate the compound growth rate as

$$r = \left\{ \exp\left(\frac{\dfrac{\ln NSDP2}{\ln NSDP1}}{t} \right) \right\} - 1$$

Aggregate as well sectoral employment elasticity has been calculated to capture labour force absorption. Employment elasticity has been defined as

$$E = \frac{\Delta emp}{\Delta out}$$

Where, Δemp = Annual growth rate of employment, Δout =Annual growth rate of output.

To study the sources of economic growth, a decomposition analysis has been carried out.

We begin by considering the possible role that changes in the number of workers per capita and in sectoral composition play in explaining economic growth in India.

We start with an accounting identity that links income per capita (Y/N) to income per worker (Y/L)

$$\frac{Y}{N} = \frac{Y}{L} * \frac{L}{WA} * \frac{WA}{N}$$

In this identity, WA represents the population of working age. The identity merely states that the level of income per capita equals the level of income per worker times the labour participation rate (L/WA) times the ratio of working age to total population (WA/N). Defining

$y = \log(Y/N)$, $z = \log(Y/L)$, $\rho = \log(L/WA)$, $\omega = \log(WA/N)$

and totally differentiating the identity, we have that the growth rate of income per capita equals the growth of income per worker plus the growth of labour participation plus the growth of the ratio of working age to total population, i.e.,

$$y = z + \rho + \omega$$

Growth in income per worker can result from increases in worker productivity in each sector, or from the reallocation of workers from low-productivity to high-productivity sectors. We can decompose the effect of changing sectoral shares on economic growth more formally by writing

$$y = z_a b_a + z_i b_i + z_s b_s,$$

according to which NSDP per worker is a weighted average of the output per worker in the agriculture, industry and service sectors, given by Z_a, Z_i and Z_s, with the weights being the respective shares of each sector in total employment, given b_a, b_i and b_s.

Totally differentiating and dividing by z, we can again decompose output per worker in

1) The growth of worker productivity in each sector and
2) The growth of each sector's share in total employment.

$$\left(\frac{dz}{z}\right) productivity = \left(\frac{Y_a}{Y}\right)\left(\frac{dz_a}{z_a}\right) + \left(\frac{Y_i}{Y}\right)\left(\frac{dz_i}{z_i}\right) + \left(\frac{Y_s}{Y}\right)\left(\frac{dz_s}{z_s}\right)$$

Where each sector's productivity growth rate is weighted by share of that sector in total NSDP (Ya/Y is the share of agricultural output in total output). The increase in output per worker due to change in sectoral composition is given by

$$\left(\frac{dz}{z}\right) \text{sectoral} = \left(\frac{z_i}{z} - \frac{z_a}{z}\right) db_i + \left(\frac{z_s}{z} - \frac{z_a}{z}\right) dbs$$

Where we have used the fact that $d_{ba} = -db_i - db_s$ due to adding up constraint that the share of the three sectors must sum to one.

To examine the linkages between population change and economic growth within the framework that permits bi-directional causality, we begin by examining the effect of demographic variables on the pace of economic growth, taking into account other influences on growth that are standard in the economics literature. The multivariate regression techniques permit us, in principle, to decompose the correlation between demographic change and income growth into two parts, one that reflects the effect of demographic change on income growth and another that reflects the reverse effect of income growth on demographic change.

Sources of Data

The following data sets have been used for the study:

i. Annual Statistical Report of Sample Registration System (SRS) for 1971-2005 and population projection made by Expert Committee/ Technical Group, Registrar General of India for 2006-2026.

ii. National Sample Survey (NSS) conducted by the Central Statistical Organisation–The 50th, 55th and 60st rounds of NSS have been used for the study.

iii. To study the economic performance of the states, database built by Economic and Political Weekly Research Foundation (EPWRF): *Domestic Product of States of India: 1960-61 to 2000-01* and *Handbook of Statistics on Indian Economy, 2005-06*, published by R.B.I. have been used.

Sample Registration System (SRS) provides reliable estimates of fertility and mortality data from 1971. It also provides vast information on age structure of the population at national as well as state level. Beyond year 2005, Expert Committee/Technical Group projections have been used. Though there are various other projections available but the present study uses the expert committee projections because they are based on trends of fertility and mortality data available from SRS and thus confirms the comparability and direction.

The present study uses the 50th round (July 1993-June 1994), 55th round (July 1999-June 2000) and 60th round (January-June 2004) of National Sample Survey. All the rounds are based on conceptual framework given by Dantwala Committee, which confirms the consistency in comparability of concepts, definitions and procedures used in the survey.

As a proxy of economic growth at state level, net state domestic products have been used from EPWRF's publication which provides data on state domestic product available on a comparable basis for different periods in the post-Independence period. For the year 2004, incomes of states have been taken from *Handbook of Indian Economy*, Reserve Bank of India.

Selection of Study Population

To address the question of regional performance, we narrow our focus to the 14 major states, which excludes the Himalayan states, the northeastern states and the six union territories. Fourteen major states are selected for the study, i.e., Andhra Pradesh, Bihar, Gujarat, Haryana, Karnataka, Kerala, Madhya Pradesh, Maharashtra, Orissa, Punjab, Rajasthan, Tamil Nadu, Uttar Pradesh and West Bengal. These states account for 93 per cent of population and 91.5 per cent of net domestic product (NDP) in the country and may, therefore, be taken as representative for the purpose of analysis. To study the regional variations, 14 states have been divided into five zones (Mukherjee, 1976), i.e.,

South: Andhra Pradesh, Karnataka, Kerala, Tamil Nadu

North: Punjab, Haryana, Rajasthan

Eastern: Bihar, Orissa, West Bengal

Western: Gujarat, Maharashtra

Central: Madhya Pradesh, Uttar Pradesh

Findings

Diversities in Demographic Transition in India and States

Population growth rates are subject to change in fertility, mortality and migration, all of which play a vital role in the multi-dimensional process of demographic transition in India. There is a wide diversity between the states which means pace of change has varied strikingly from one region to another. Figure 21.1 displays the change in the index for the zones in India from 1961-1966 to 1996-2001 and Table 21.1 presents corresponding values for the selected states. Several points of interest emerge from this table. First, a brief comparison of the five zones, illustrated in Figure 21.2 reveals that although each sub-region recorded a continuous rise in the degree of demographic transition completed during last four decades, there are substantial disparities in the tempo of transition among them. In 1961-1966, the value of this index was highest for southern zone (0.36) by small margin from central zone (0.24). The difference between southern and central becomes wide over time, particularly after the 1970s. In the remaining three zones, western zone is quite close to south while eastern zone is following the similar path of central zone with a small margin.

Secondly, as shown in Table 21.1 on state specific basis, Kerala completed its demographic transition by 1990s with highest value of index (0.7) among the states, followed by Tamil Nadu and Karnataka in mid-90s. The most urbanised state Tamil Nadu is very close to complete its demographic transition. Thirdly, states which achieved intermediate level of completion (0.4 to 0.6) are Bihar, Madhya Pradesh, Uttar Pradesh and Rajasthan still maintaining their acronym of BIMARU states. Insofar as the outlook of demographic transition in the five sub-regions is concerned, the value of the index of demographic transition is expected to rise continuously up to year 2026, as illustrated in Figure 21.2.

Figure 21.1

Index of Demographic Transition for Five Zones, 1961-1966 to 1996-2001

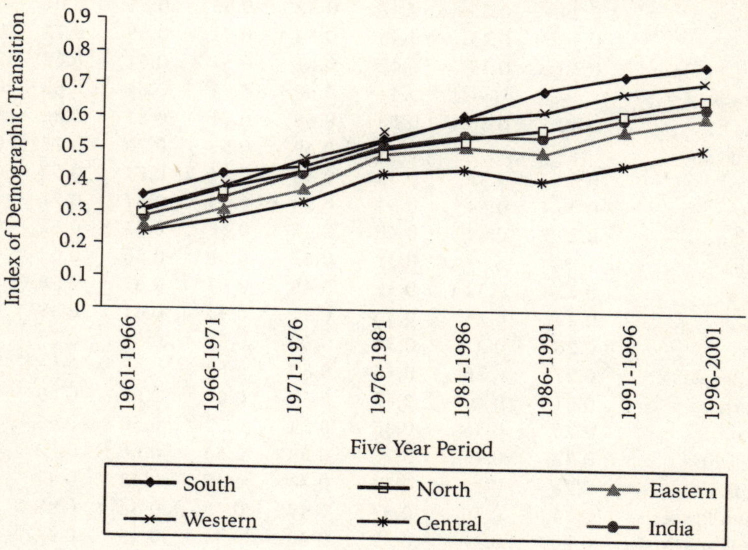

Figure 21.2

Index of Demographic Transition for Five Zones, 2001-2006 to 2021-2026

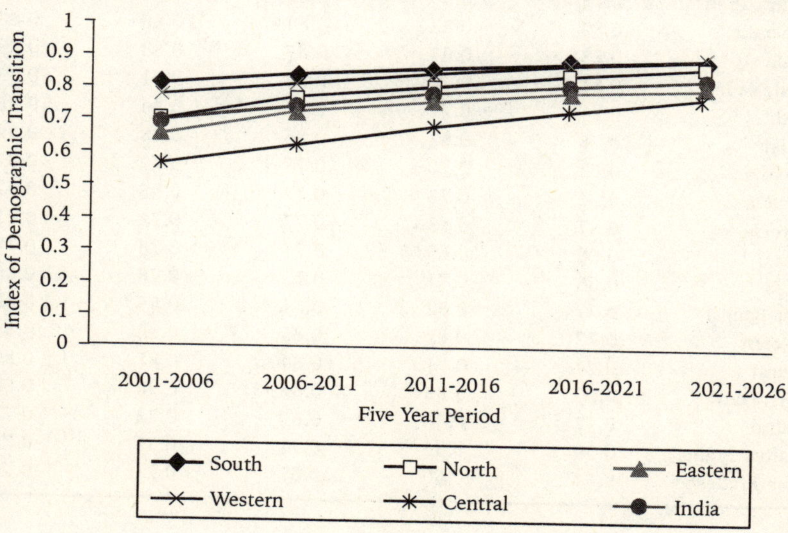

Table 21.1

Index of Demographic Transition for India and Selected States, 1961-1966 to 2021-2026

Period	1961-1966	1966-1971	1971-1976	1976-1981	1981-1986	1986-1991	1991-1996	1996-2001
India	0.29	0.35	0.42	0.52	0.55	0.55	0.61	0.65
South	0.36	0.43	0.46	0.54	0.61	0.69	0.74	0.78
Andhra Pradesh	0.30	0.35	0.42	0.51	0.57	0.61	0.68	0.72
Karnataka	-	-	0.44	0.50	0.61	0.64	0.69	0.74
Kerala	0.42	0.50	0.58	0.66	0.71	0.81	0.86	0.86
Tamil Nadu	-	-	0.41	0.49	0.55	0.70	0.76	0.79
North	0.30	0.37	0.43	0.49	0.54	0.57	0.62	0.66
Punjab	0.35	0.44	0.53	0.59	0.63	0.67	0.72	0.76
Rajasthan	0.29	0.34	0.40	0.47	0.48	0.47	0.52	0.56
Haryana	-	-	0.38	0.42	0.50	0.56	0.62	0.67
Eastern	0.25	0.32	0.39	0.49	0.52	0.51	0.58	0.61
Bihar	0.22	0.28	0.33	0.41	0.43	0.41	0.49	0.51
Orissa	0.26	0.31	0.38	0.50	0.53	0.51	0.57	0.61
West Bengal	0.27	0.36	0.45	0.57	0.59	0.62	0.67	0.72
Western	0.31	0.40	0.48	0.57	0.60	0.63	0.69	0.73
Gujarat	0.26	0.36	0.45	0.54	0.57	0.60	0.66	0.70
Maharashtra	0.37	0.43	0.50	0.59	0.64	0.66	0.72	0.76
Central	0.24	0.29	0.34	0.44	0.45	0.42	0.47	0.51
Madhya Pradesh	0.24	0.30	0.37	0.47	0.48	0.44	0.49	0.54
Uttar Pradesh	0.24	0.27	0.32	0.40	0.41	0.39	0.44	0.49

Period	2001-2006	2006-2011	2011-2016	2016-2021	2021-2026
India	0.71	0.74	0.78	0.81	0.83
South	0.81	0.84	0.86	0.88	0.89
Andhra Pradesh	0.75	0.80	0.82	0.83	0.84
Karnataka	0.82	0.82	0.84	0.86	0.88
Kerala	0.85	0.87	0.87	0.88	0.89
Tamil Nadu	0.81	0.87	0.89	0.91	0.93
North	0.71	0.77	0.81	0.84	0.86
Punjab	0.78	0.83	0.86	0.88	0.89
Rajasthan	0.63	0.70	0.75	0.79	0.82
Haryana	0.72	0.78	0.82	0.85	0.87
Eastern	0.67	0.73	0.77	0.79	0.81
Bihar	0.56	0.65	0.71	0.76	0.79
Orissa	0.66	0.71	0.75	0.78	0.80
West Bengal	0.77	0.82	0.84	0.85	0.86
Western	0.77	0.82	0.85	0.88	0.89
Gujarat	0.74	0.81	0.84	0.87	0.89
Maharashtra	0.80	0.83	0.86	0.88	0.90
Central	0.57	0.63	0.69	0.73	0.77
Madhya Pradesh	0.59	0.66	0.71	0.75	0.79
Uttar Pradesh	0.54	0.60	0.67	0.71	0.76

Age Structural Change, Population Ageing and its Linkages with Window of Opportunity

In this section, an attempt has been made to answer the questions: How does age structure change during demographic transition and what will be the future speed of ageing in India? Due to both pronounced fertility declines and remarkable improvement in life expectancy among the states, the age composition of each of these states has been changing swiftly since 1980s. As shown in Table 21.2, from 1980 to 2005, the total dependency ratio has fallen substantially in all states except for two high fertility states (UP and Bihar). The extent to which the dependency ratio for each state has decreased over this period is closely related to magnitude with which its fertility has been lowered, as reflected in young dependency ratio. Among the states, which show a decline in dependency ratio between 1980 and 2005, Haryana has the largest reduction by 21.07 points from 87.41 to 66.33. Haryana is followed by Karnataka (20.40 points), Kerala (17.85 points) and Tamil Nadu (17.0 points). All of these states have already attained status of economically forward states or are approaching it promptly. This may indicate that such faster declines of dependency ratio have facilitated their rapid economic growth performance.

On the basis of population projection given by the Registrar General of India, as shown in Table 21.3, indicate that states with high dependency ratios will face considerable reduction of the burden placed on working age population in 2016 and beyond. In these states, the declining dependency ratios are likely to facilitate their developmental process. In contrast, states with low dependency ratios are expected to go under substantial increase, mainly due to rapid rise in proportion elderly.

Tables 21.2 and 21.3 also document the change in old age dependency ratio for all the states and for regions. In the states whose onset of fertility reduction was early, the change in this ratio are most pronounced. Southern states have the largest gain. Kerala showed considerable increase, i.e., from 11 per cent in 1980 to 17 per cent in 2005, whereas northern and central zone states are still considered to be young.

A brief comparison of index of ageing, however, yields a substantial different picture. Because the effect of fertility reduction is immediately reflected in this index, a marked increase in the value of this index is observed. Presently, only Kerala has the most aged population but the index indicates that the population ageing has been under way in all the states of south India. Although value of index is quite low for north zone (22) and central zone (16), there is no sign of ageing at least till 2026. More importantly, primarily because of fertility decline in southern states has been

Table 21.2

Age Structural Changes for India and Selected States, 1980-2005

States	1980 Dependency Ratio			1980 Index of Ageing	1990 Dependency Ratio			1990 Index of Ageing	2005 Dependency Ratio			2005 Index of Ageing
	Total	Young	Aged		Total	Young	Aged		Total	Young	Aged	
India	77.71	67.48	10.24	15.17	73.34	62.59	10.75	17.18	68.67	56.66	12.01	21.19
South	73.44	62.96	10.48	16.65	66.83	55.46	11.38	20.51	55.43	41.73	13.69	32.81
Andhra Pradesh	74.55	64.11	10.44	16.28	71.58	60.27	11.30	18.75	57.66	45.66	12.01	26.30
Karnataka	78.06	68.04	10.02	14.73	72.24	61.90	10.34	16.71	57.66	45.97	11.69	25.43
Kerala	72.41	61.34	11.07	18.04	62.07	49.27	12.80	25.99	54.56	37.71	16.85	44.67
Tamil Nadu	68.98	58.60	10.38	17.70	62.04	51.05	10.99	21.52	51.98	37.84	14.13	37.35
North	80.61	69.33	11.28	16.27	76.76	66.02	10.74	16.26	68.69	56.27	12.42	22.08
Punjab	72.29	59.17	13.13	22.19	70.07	57.82	12.24	21.18	60.67	46.39	14.29	30.80
Rajasthan	82.82	72.96	9.85	13.51	82.94	73.03	9.91	13.57	80.22	68.88	11.33	16.45
Haryana	87.41	76.67	10.74	14.01	77.76	67.79	9.96	14.70	66.33	54.83	11.50	20.97
Eastern	80.32	70.42	9.91	14.07	76.04	65.85	10.19	15.48	71.33	58.99	12.34	20.91
Bihar	91.94	80.42	11.52	14.32	90.67	79.05	11.62	14.70	89.94	77.99	11.95	15.33
Orissa	77.40	67.50	9.90	14.66	70.99	60.58	10.41	17.18	67.11	53.09	14.02	26.42
West Bengal	72.71	64.25	8.46	13.17	68.12	59.40	8.72	14.69	59.68	48.64	11.04	22.70
Western	75.73	66.02	9.71	14.71	69.49	59.32	10.17	17.14	62.18	49.59	12.58	25.37
Gujarat	77.21	67.85	9.36	13.79	68.24	58.49	9.75	16.67	61.81	50.32	11.49	22.83
Maharashtra	74.28	64.22	10.06	15.66	70.77	60.17	10.60	17.61	62.54	48.86	13.68	28.00
Central	83.25	72.95	10.30	14.12	82.24	71.31	10.93	15.33	79.84	68.32	11.52	16.86
Madhya Pradesh	84.16	74.36	9.80	13.17	80.18	69.37	10.81	15.58	75.53	64.44	11.09	17.21
Uttar Pradesh	82.35	71.55	10.80	15.09	84.35	73.30	11.05	15.08	84.35	72.38	11.97	16.54

Table 21.3

Age Structural Changes for India and Selected States, 2016-2026

States	2016 Dependency Ratio			Index of	2026 Dependency Ratio			Index of
	Total	*Young*	*Aged*	*Ageing*	*Total*	*Young*	*Aged*	*Ageing*
India	56.34	41.94	14.40	34.33	55.83	36.39	19.44	53.42
South	52.11	33.90	18.21	53.70	55.10	30.32	24.78	81.71
Andhra Pradesh	50.30	34.53	15.77	45.65	52.59	30.95	21.65	69.95
Karnataka	51.82	35.61	16.21	45.53	53.76	31.49	22.27	70.73
Kerala	54.40	32.92	21.48	65.26	58.57	29.68	28.89	97.33
Tamil Nadu	51.98	32.52	19.45	59.81	55.61	29.13	26.48	90.91
North	54.75	40.56	14.19	34.99	51.77	33.16	18.60	56.10
Punjab	51.75	35.36	16.39	46.35	51.67	29.55	22.12	74.87
Rajasthan	60.51	47.19	13.32	28.23	54.71	38.02	16.69	43.90
Haryana	52.29	39.48	12.80	32.43	49.03	32.04	16.99	53.02
Eastern	53.43	39.00	14.43	37.01	54.06	34.03	20.02	58.82
Bihar	61.13	47.90	13.23	27.61	55.92	38.79	17.13	44.18
Orissa	51.98	36.63	15.35	41.91	53.37	32.21	21.17	65.71
West Bengal	47.78	33.14	14.64	44.20	52.91	31.19	21.71	69.61
Western	52.98	37.92	15.06	39.72	52.52	32.26	20.26	62.80
Gujarat	52.83	37.98	14.85	39.11	52.91	32.06	20.86	65.07
Maharashtra	53.13	37.86	15.27	40.32	52.13	32.47	19.66	60.56
Central	65.23	52.48	12.75	24.29	60.08	43.76	16.32	37.29
Madhya Pradesh	61.75	49.27	12.48	25.33	56.99	40.50	16.48	40.70
Uttar Pradesh	68.87	55.84	13.03	23.33	63.30	47.15	16.15	34.26

substantially quicker than the rest of the region, the speed of population ageing in the former has been and will be much faster than that observed in latter. Thus, southern states need to shift the emphasis from 'how many dependants' to 'what kind of dependants' the working population has to support.

Figure 21.3

Refined Ageing Index

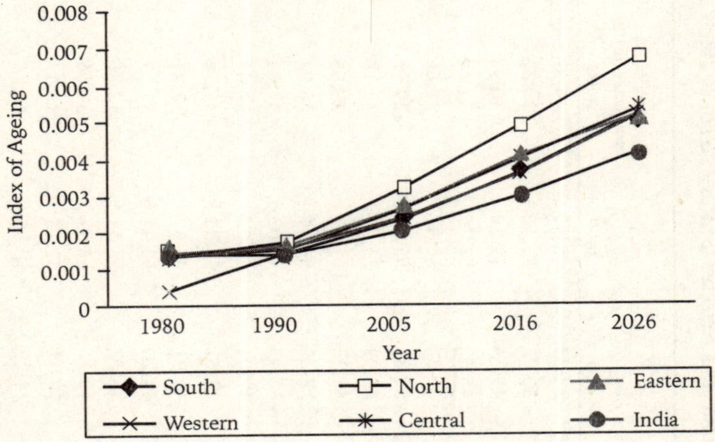

Figure 21.4

Conventional Ageing Index

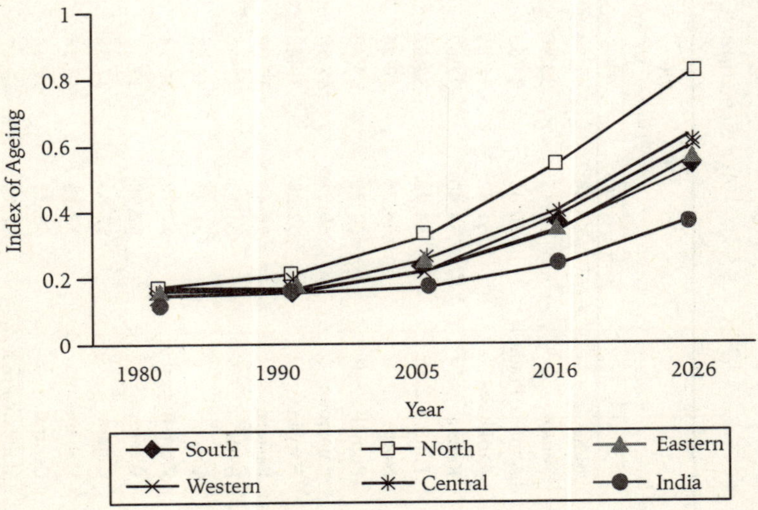

To discuss this issue, a modified ageing index *I (p)* has been calculated in Table 21.4, this index reveals a clear trend towards further ageing in India. It is more sensitive and registers a steeper and larger increase in comparison to conventional index of ageing. Though the value of this index goes beyond unity, for which Kulkarni (1988) has proposed an improvement but that does not affect the extent of oldness and proportion change in aged population.

Table 21.4

Expected Trend in Ageing of Population according to Modified Ageing Index (I (p) per 1000): 1980-2026

Period	*1980*	*1990*	*2005*	*2016*	*2026*
India	1.42	1.59	2.37	3.69	5.04
South	1.49	1.73	3.20	4.89	6.73
Andhra Pradesh	1.43	1.56	2.39	4.11	5.72
Karnataka	1.44	1.61	2.63	4.29	6.03
Kerala	1.68	2.20	4.61	6.04	7.99
Tamil Nadu	1.42	1.57	3.18	5.12	7.16
North	1.59	1.61	2.79	4.11	5.17
Punjab	1.96	2.00	3.55	5.00	6.30
Rajasthan	1.30	1.33	2.18	3.52	4.51
Haryana	1.51	1.52	2.63	3.82	4.71
Eastern	0.43	1.45	2.32	3.66	5.20
Bihar	0.00	1.55	2.02	3.18	4.52
Orissa	1.29	1.52	2.71	4.05	5.59
West Bengal	0.00	1.29	2.22	3.76	5.49
Western	1.32	1.51	2.64	4.04	5.32
Gujarat	1.27	1.50	2.50	3.74	5.42
Maharashtra	1.37	1.52	2.78	4.34	5.23
Central	1.40	1.53	2.13	3.04	4.16
Madhya Pradesh	1.29	1.53	2.01	3.04	4.17
Uttar Pradesh	1.51	1.53	2.26	3.04	4.14

The combination of differential rate of mortality and fertility over demographic transition among the states would contribute to varying disordered flows of age cohorts between these states. Over period of time, these cohorts turn into working age population and economically dependent population. Thus, growth rate of working age population over growth rate of total population give us idea about the phase of demographic opportunity. Population projection along with SRS based growth rate of population and working age population growth helps to pinpoint when such a demographic bonus period would occur during the transition. In the light of available data (see Table 21.5), demographic bonus phase for each region in India has been determined:

India: 1995-2000 to 2011-2016, **South:** 1985-1990 to 2005-2016, **North:** 1995-2000 to 2016-2021, **Eastern:** 1995-2000 to 2016-2021, **Western:** 1995-2000 to 2016-2021 and **Central:** 2005-2011 to 2021-2026.

Table 21.5

Difference Between Growth Rate of Working Age Population and Total Population 1980-1985 to 2021-2026

Period	*1980-1985*	*1985-1990*	*1990-1995*	*1995-2000*	*2000-2005*	*2005-2011*	*2011-2016*	*2016-2021*	*2021-2026*
India	-0.17	0.62	-0.24	**0.57**	**0.27**	**0.97**	**0.48**	0.18	0.24
South	0.16	**0.59**	**0.44**	**0.63**	**0.47**	**0.4**	**0.22**	-0.01	-0.07
Andhra Pradesh	-0.18	0.5	0.03	0.83	0.83	0.67	0.34	0.03	0
Karnataka	-0.18	0.68	0.85	0.82	0.27	0.6	0.35	0.03	0
Kerala	0.66	0.6	0.49	0.3	0.3	0.19	0.12	-0.09	-0.12
Tamil Nadu	0.34	0.57	0.37	0.57	0.47	0.14	0.06	0	-0.17
North	-0.26	0.51	-0.17	**0.78**	**0.44**	**1.01**	**0.62**	**0.37**	0.3
Punjab	-0.13	0.23	-0.26	0.91	0.56	0.8	0.35	0.23	0.11
Rajasthan	-0.78	0.58	0.25	0.31	-0.03	1.22	0.85	0.52	0.44
Haryana	0.14	0.74	-0.49	1.13	0.79	1.01	0.65	0.38	0.34
Eastern	-0.35	0.45	-0.07	**0.53**	**0.18**	**1.31**	**0.75**	**0.23**	0.04
Bihar	-	-0.04	0.07	0.15	-0.07	1.81	1.11	0.52	0.39
Orissa	-0.14	0.87	-0.3	0.56	0.39	1.1	0.59	0.14	0.03
West Bengal	-	0.53	0	0.89	0.22	1.02	0.54	0.03	-0.28
Western	0.12	0.58	0.08	**0.67**	**0.25**	**0.75**	**0.41**	**0.25**	0.06
Gujarat	0.13	0.86	0.19	0.63	0.06	0.76	0.38	0.29	0
Maharashtra	0.11	0.3	-0.03	0.71	0.44	0.73	0.44	0.2	0.11
Central	-0.44	0.52	-0.32	0.35	0.3	**0.91**	**0.58**	**0.48**	**0.42**
Madhya Pradesh	-0.08	0.49	-0.21	0.49	0.27	0.88	0.6	0.58	0.33
Uttar Pradesh	-0.81	0.54	-0.43	0.22	0.32	0.94	0.56	0.39	0.5

Figure 21.5 shows the difference between working age and total population. It has been observed that except central region, there is around 0.5 per cent point increase in growth of 15-59 population to the total population which provide opportunity for raising productive capacity and human capital formation. From the graphs, it is clear that during 2000-2020, growth rate of working age population would exceed the growth rate of total population for India. The demographic bonus would be larger in the states where pace of demographic change is slower. The figure also shows the similar plot for all the regions in India, it is evident that southern region had

already entered the demographic bonus phase by the 1990s. Perhaps the economic optimism being currently seen in south is a reflection of its favourable demographic conditions. But it is expected to slip out of this phase in 20-years time. On the other hand, central region will enter this phase in the period 2005-2011, and remain in this phase until 2026.

Figure 21.5

Window of Demographic Opportunity in India and Five Zones

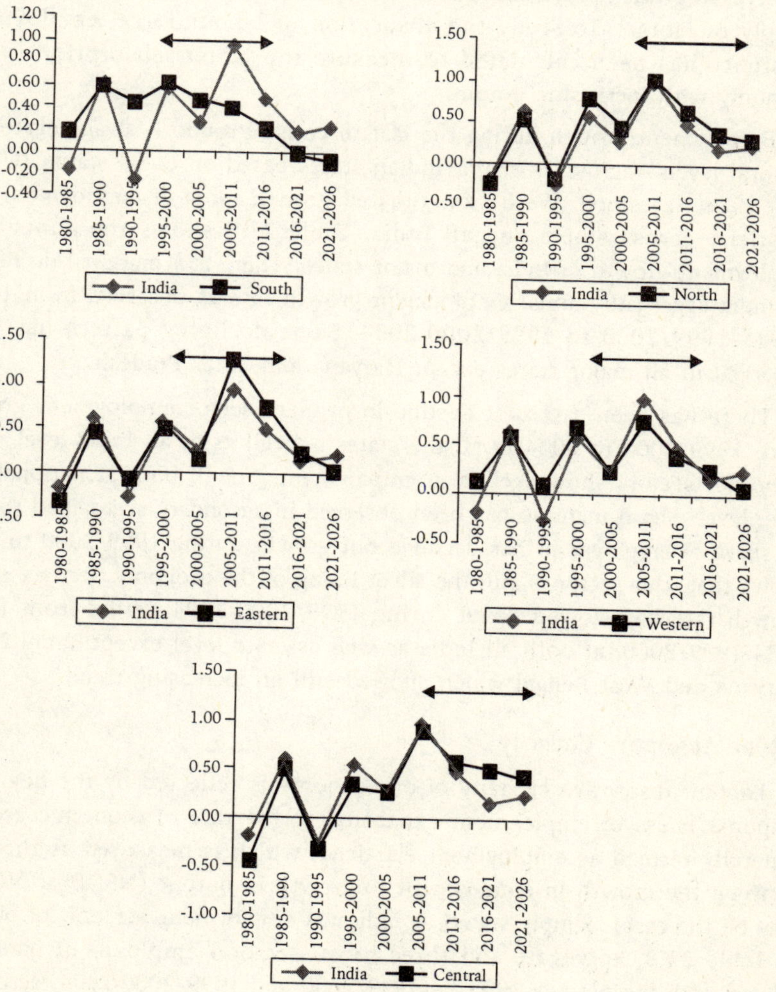

Employment Growth and Elasticity in India and Major States

Aggregate and Sector-wise Employment Growth

Expansion and creation of employment opportunities is necessary for economic development and for productive utilisation of increased working age population and labour forces. After the introduction of New Economic Reforms in India, it is expected that economy will be a booming one. Though the output in terms of NSDP has spectacular growth but along with that there is increasing unemployment among youths which indicates the wastage of supply of labour. To study the absorption of labour force, employment elasticity has been calculated to measure the labour absorption in the economy with increasing output.

Employment growth during the last three NSS rounds—at aggregate and sectoral levels—across 14 major Indian states based on usual status (UPSS) have been examined. We have estimated growth rates of employment and elasticity across states and all India. Table 21.6 shows the annualised employment growth of India and major states. There is a marginal decline in all India aggregate annual employment growth rate as observed from 1993/1994—1999/2000 to 1999/2000-2004. Same declining pattern has been observed in all major states except Haryana and Uttar Pradesh.

There has been a secular decline in primary sector employment growth since 1999/2000 to 2004 in all the states as well as at all India level while the other sectors show decline in employment growth both at national and state level. Sharp increase has been observed in secondary sector and though its share of employment has declined but growth during 1999/2000 to 2004 shows that, this sector is still the silver lining of the economy. Tertiary sector growth rate has slowed down during 1999/2000-2004 period from 1993/1994-1999/2000, at both all India as well as state level except Tamil Nadu, Haryana and West Bengal which showed still an increasing trend.

Labour Absorptive Capacity

Labour absorptive capacity of an economy is reflected by the degree of responsiveness of employment expansion to the rate of economic growth, generally termed as employment elasticity, which is measured as the ratio between the growth in employment to growth in output (NSDP or NDP, as may be the case). Simply stated, it indicates employment per unit of output. In Table 21.8, aggregate and three broad sectoral employment elasticity related with the periods 1993/94-1999/2000 and 1999/2000-2004, across 14 major states and India has been calculated. Aggregate employment elasticity at the all India level for the period between 50th and 55th round suggests

Table 21.6

Annualised Growth Rate of Employment for India and States, 1993-94 to 2004

	Aggregate		*Primary*		*Secondary*		*Tertiary*	
	1993-94 to 1999-2000	*1999-2000 to 2004*	*1993-94 to 1999-2000*	*1999-2000 to 2004*	*1993-94 to 1999-2000*	*1999-2000 to 2004*	*1993-94 to 1999-2000*	*1999-2000 to 2004*
India	1.87	1.26	1.31	0.42	-5.62	11.03	3.66	2.34
South								
Andhra Pradesh	1.43	-0.01	0.64	-0.75	-2.31	5.79	4.10	1.35
Karnataka	1.93	-0.22	2.98	-1.71	-6.37	7.41	3.75	0.98
Kerala	2.58	2.27	-2.97	1.69	-1.02	8.53	7.24	4.90
Tamil Nadu	-0.22	0.97	-0.68	-0.04	-2.42	3.82	1.07	2.41
North								
Punjab	0.31	2.85	-0.17	1.53	-11.31	18.88	0.69	1.94
Rajasthan	3.03	0.52	-0.46	-2.85	-7.53	16.99	3.35	3.19
Haryana	0.78	1.98	0.91	0.80	-11.22	16.20	1.34	5.62
Eastern								
Bihar	3.91	-0.03	3.05	-0.63	-1.56	11.85	5.73	1.14
Orissa	0.32	0.66	-0.45	-0.93	-11.73	21.12	1.53	3.14
West Bengal	1.01	1.11	1.72	0.03	-5.17	4.71	0.90	4.95
Western								
Gujarat	2.61	1.45	3.54	-0.11	-8.39	12.91	4.04	2.85
Maharashtra	2.60	1.87	1.86	1.14	-2.22	8.43	4.82	2.29
Central								
Madhya Pradesh	2.11	1.61	2.64	1.61	-10.69	12.14	3.90	1.06
Uttar Pradesh	1.90	2.13	0.40	1.33	-6.34	17.66	3.83	1.27

that it was around 0.32 which declined to 0.25 during 55th to 60th NSS rounds. Primary sector labour absorption has declined from 0.56 to 0.25 for all India but for few demographically as well as economically backward states like Madhya Pradesh and Uttar Pradesh, this sector is still the largest pool of labour absorption on aggregate level. Secondary sector employment elasticity has increased at all India level.

Apart from other states and regions, Tamil Nadu, Maharashtra and Bihar has shown decline in employment elasticity of secondary sector. Tertiary sector too displayed decline in employment elasticity from 0.45 to 0.33 during NSS rounds for all India. At regional level, Tamil Nadu from southern zone, Haryana, Rajasthan and Punjab belonging to northern region and Orissa and West Bengal from eastern region has shown increase in elasticity of this sector. Although tertiary sector output growth had seen mild decrease (see Table 21.7), much of the decline in tertiary sector employment elasticity is accounted for by a significant reduction in employment growth from 3.7 to 2.3 per cent for the period under consideration. Interestingly, it is the service sector, which appears to have improved employment elasticity in the post-reform years.

Results of Decomposition Analysis

A decomposition analysis has been carried out to capture demographic as well as structural shift (sectoral composition). Table 21.9 performs the decomposition of NSDP/SDP growth in India and all five regions for period 1993/94-2004. Perusal of Table 21.9 reveals that faster the growth in output per worker accounts for most of the speed up growth in India as well as regions, with modest contribution from rising participation and increase in working age share of the total population. Growth in income per worker can result from increase in worker productivity in each sector, or from the reallocation of workers from low—productivity to high-productivity sectors. Table 21.10 reports the share of employment in primary, secondary and tertiary sector for each region, which shows that there is a noticeable movement of worker from agriculture and allied activities to industry and services except eastern and central zone. We can decompose the effect of changing sectoral shares on economic growth so that the growth in output per worker depends on: (1) the growth of worker productivity in each sector and (2) the growth of each sector's share of the total employment. These two effect can be separated and is shown in Table 21.11. The effect of growth in sectoral productivity is calculated by weighing each sector according to its share in NSDP at the beginning of period. The effect of changing employment shares is weighted using productivity levels at the beginning of the period. Calculations in Table 21.11 suggest that most of the growth of NSDP per

Table 21.7

Annualised Growth Rate of NSDP/SDP for India and States, 1993-94 to 2004

	Aggregate		Primary		Secondary		Tertiary	
	1993-94 to 1999-2000	1999-2000 to 2004	1993-94 to 1999-2000	1999-2000 to 2004	1993-94 to 1999-2000	1999-2000 to 2004	1993-94 to 1999-2000	1999-2000 to 2004
India	5.87	4.94	2.33	1.69	6.34	2.62	8.22	7.03
South								
Andhra Pradesh	5.42	6.68	1.86	3.91	6.60	6.16	7.36	8.25
Karnataka	7.33	6.11	3.98	-4.80	4.40	10.04	10.92	10.08
Kerala	5.45	5.31	1.68	-4.48	6.42	1.51	7.13	9.40
Tamil Nadu	6.34	2.59	1.25	-6.31	4.11	-1.45	9.74	6.57
North								
Punjab	5.69	6.54	1.86	2.49	6.73	6.36	8.75	9.30
Rajasthan	4.54	3.62	2.31	1.56	5.10	1.43	6.96	6.35
Haryana	8.23	5.52	4.86	6.94	12.44	2.14	8.99	5.93
Eastern								
Bihar	3.90	4.36	0.87	3.84	3.72	-6.08	7.00	5.65
Orissa	4.18	4.43	-0.69	2.94	8.79	2.11	6.87	6.20
West Bengal	7.22	7.04	3.97	3.13	7.13	3.59	9.35	10.01
Western								
Gujarat	7.36	8.00	2.17	14.11	7.36	7.71	9.71	5.77
Maharashtra	5.95	3.62	2.67	-2.07	5.25	-1.77	7.42	7.20
Central								
Madhya Pradesh	6.10	2.17	2.37	0.83	7.86	1.82	8.78	3.25
Uttar Pradesh	4.52	3.16	3.39	1.52	2.86	3.08	6.05	4.46

Table 21.8

Employment Elasticity across India and Major States, 1993-94 to 2004

	Aggregate		*Primary*		*Secondary*		*Tertiary*	
	1993-94 to 1999-2000	*1999-2000 to 2004*	*1993-94 to 1999-2000*	*1999-2000 to 2004*	*1993-94 to 1999-2000*	*1999-2000 to 2004*	*1993-94 to 1999-2000*	*1999-2000 to 2004*
India	0.32	0.25	0.56	0.25	-0.89	4.21	0.45	0.33
South								
Andhra Pradesh	0.26	0.00	0.34	-0.19	-0.35	0.94	0.56	0.16
Karnataka	0.26	-0.04	0.75	0.36	-1.45	0.74	0.34	0.10
Kerala	0.47	0.43	-1.77	-0.38	-0.16	5.65	1.01	0.52
Tamil Nadu	-0.03	0.38	-0.55	0.01	-0.59	-2.64	0.11	0.37
North								
Punjab	0.05	0.44	-0.09	0.61	-1.68	2.97	0.08	0.21
Rajasthan	0.67	0.14	-0.20	-1.82	-1.48	11.85	0.48	0.50
Haryana	0.10	0.36	0.19	0.11	-0.90	7.58	0.15	0.95
Eastern								
Bihar	1.00	-0.01	3.50	-0.16	-0.42	-1.95	0.82	0.20
Orissa	0.08	0.15	0.65	-0.32	-1.33	9.99	0.22	0.51
West Bengal	0.14	0.16	0.43	0.01	-0.73	1.31	0.10	0.49
Western								
Gujarat	0.36	0.18	1.63	-0.01	-1.14	1.67	0.42	0.49
Maharashtra	0.44	0.52	0.70	-0.55	-0.42	-4.76	0.65	0.32
Central								
Madhya Pradesh	0.35	0.74	1.11	1.95	-1.36	6.66	0.44	0.33
Uttar Pradesh	0.42	0.67	0.12	0.88	-2.21	5.74	0.63	0.28

Table 21.9

Sources of Growth in India and Region, 1993/94-2004 (Annual Average Growth Per cent)

	India		South		North		Eastern		Western		Central	
	1993/94-1999/2000	1999/2000-2004	1993/94-1999/2000	1999/2000-2004	1993/94-1999/2000	1999/2000-2004	1993/94-1999/2000	1999/2000-2004	1994/94-1999/2000	1999/2000-2004	1994/94-1999/2000	1999/2000-2004
Growth rate of NSDP per capita	3.69	6.3	4.16	4.03	3.91	3.35	2.01	5.93	3.05	5.07	3.63	4.06
Decomposition of Growth Rate of NSDP Per Capita:												
Growth rate of NSDP per worker	4.53	5.45	4.71	3.89	4.5	2.52	2.72	5.26	3.29	4.2	4.58	3.1
Growth of labour force participation rate	-0.78	0.14	-0.83	-0.51	-0.82	0.01	-0.52	-0.06	-0.31	0.28	-0.82	-0.07
Growth rate of ratio of population 15-59 to total population	-0.03	0.66	0.31	0.63	0.27	0.77	-0.17	0.69	0.08	0.55	-0.09	1

Table 21.10

Share of Employment by Sector, 1993/94-2004

	1993/94			1999/2000			2004		
Region	Primary	Secondary	Tertiary	Primary	Secondary	Tertiary	Primary	Secondary	Tertiary
South	58.3	22.1	19.6	51.4	23.1	25.5	51.3	23.3	25.4
North	48.2	30.3	21.5	41.3	35.1	23.6	40.7	35.2	24.1
Eastern	66.4	17.9	15.7	58.9	20.6	20.5	60.5	20.4	19.2
Western	57.7	22.6	19.8	55.1	21.6	23.3	54.1	22.8	23.1
Central	69.0	17.5	13.6	62.4	19.6	18.0	65.8	19.8	14.4

Table 21.11

Productivity Growth: Shift Share Analysis

	South		North		Eastern		Western		Central	
	1993/94 to 1999/2000	*1999/2000 to 2004*	*1993/94 to 1999/2000*	*1999/2000 to 2004*	*1993/94 to 1999/2000*	*1999/2000 to 2004*	*1993/94 to 1999/2000*	*1999/2000 to 2004*	*1993/94 to 1999/2000*	*1999/2000 to 2004*
Growth rate of NSDP per worker(% annual average)	4.71	3.89	4.5	2.52	2.72	5.26	3.29	4.2	4.58	3.1
Decomposition:										
Due to growth of productivity within sector(with base year sector share)	3.17	4.35	4.98	2.33	1.92	6.27	2.57	2.15	1.55	3.46
Due to change in sector shares (with base year productivity)	1.91	-0.03	0.1	0.21	1.92	-0.62	1.15	-0.36	2	-0.97

capita in both the period 1993/94-1999/2000 and 1999/2000-2004 was due to increased productivity within sector except northern and western region, all other region show more than two percentage point growth due to growth in productivity. The result from Tables 21.9 and 21.11 together suggest that increase in labour force participation, a rising share of working age population to the total population and a movement out of primary into secondary and tertiary sector accounts for 1.4 percentage points of growth in south (one-third of the observed growth rate) during 1993/94-1999/2000 while in next period, it has declined sharply. North region has just started taking advantage of rising participation and increased working age population. Eastern region in which basically Bihar, Orissa and West Bengal falls, shows an increased growth of NSDP per worker but contribution from participation change, share of working age and sectoral change is very low in 1999/2000-2004 in comparison to previous period. The same situation can be observed for central region. The analysis is mechanical and the interpretation, which attributes the results to separate productivity and labour force effects, assumes that sectoral employment shares do not change productivity per worker, which is unlikely to be true.

The Contribution of Demographic Factors to Economic Growth

Table 21.12 reports the results of ordinary least square. In Model 1, all the variables are acknowledged to play a role in growth process. It has been found that level of fertility has significant effect on level of income per capita and with the unit increase in level of TFR, the NSDP per capita may decline by eight per cent. Proportion of population with secondary and above education is positively related with level of income. Share of primary sector employment also comes out to be significant as it affects the level of income per capita in negative direction i.e., if share of primary sector employment increase by 10 per cent, level of income may decline by two per cent.

To capture the change due to region and time, we adopt a panel study approach, including regional dummy and time period indicators (Model 2 in Table 21.12). Explanatory variable included here, have already been discussed in methodology. Due to high collinearity between TFR and difference between working age to total population growth rate, we have dropped TFR.

The models suggest that with increasing level of life expectancy, level of income per capita will increase significantly. Log share of 15-29 age population is also significantly related to the positive growth in income per capita. Female labour force participation rate does not show consistent results, the probable reason behind this may be the fact that there has been no significant change in female labour force participation in the last decade.

Difference between growth rate of working age and total population is also an important predictor in explaining economic growth. Its coefficient suggest that with the increase of one per cent point in this difference, level of income per capita may increase by five per cent. Population density has also come out to be significant in explaining level of income per capita as high population density may put pressure on agricultural production and level of income may decline. The above results show that demographic factors are playing a large role in India's economic growth, but the analysis presented here assumes that effect of demography on economic growth is automatic.

Table 21.12

Regression Results Explaining Economic Growth in India (Dependent Variable = Log of NSDP Per Capita)

Independent Variables	Unadjusted Regression Coefficient	
	Model 1	Model 2
Constant	3.50***	-3.117
Log of TFR	-0.081*	
Log of proportion of pop. with secondary education	0.086*	-0.066
Log of percentage of urban population	0.350***	0.357***
Log share of pop. in primary sector	-0.202***	-0.0372
Log of life expectancy		1.93**
Log share of 15-29 age pop.		0.897*
Log share of 60+ aged pop.		0.007
Female labour force participation rate		-0.0026
Difference in growth rate of working age and total pop.		0.054*
Log of pop. density		-0.0588**
Log ratio of working age to total population		0.029
Reg_dummy=2		0.0439
Time= 1999/2000		0.0667*
Time= 2004		0.111***
R square	0.826	0.941
Durbin-Watson statistics		2.5
Mean VIF (variance inflation factor)	1.4	5.42

Note: ***p<0.01, **p<0.05, *p<0.1.

The Effect of Income on Life Expectancy and Fertility

This section has approached the issue of feedback effects income on vital rates. Table 21.13 shows us the effect of change in income on life expectancy, this effect is supposed to be felt only in long term, because health status is related to many events. The short run effect may mislead about the long run effect. To capture the long run effect, we focus on estimating the relationship between life expectancy and income level, rather than the changes in each. We adopt panel study approach, including two time dummies and an indicator variable for two regions to capture the effect on life expectancy of regional conditions. As we know, that NSDP per capita depends directly on the age structure of the population, so it cannot be taken as independent variable when explaining life expectancy and fertility. We therefore use NSDP per worker as our independent variable. Estimates suggest that a 10 per cent rise in income per worker increases life expectancy by 0.4 per cent, adding regional indicator variable in model, suggest that life expectancy is some 2 per cent lower in region 2 (which includes northern, eastern and central region) than we would expect, given their income levels.

To study the effect of income on fertility (as measured by total fertility rate), we follow exactly the same approach as for life expectancy; estimates are reported in second panel of Table 21.13. The coefficient of NSDP per worker suggests that 10 per cent higher income is associated with 2.5 per cent lower fertility. At regional level, fertility of region 2 (northern, eastern and central) is 33 per cent higher than we would expect given its income. Technically, this regression analysis may not capture decline in TFR over time (may be because of short time duration).

Table 21.13

Regression Results, Indicating the Effect of Income on Life Expectancy at Birth and Total Fertility Rate in India, 1993/94-2004

Dependent Variable: Life Expectancy	*Basic OLS*	*Dependent Variable: Total Fertility Rate*	*Basic OLS*
Constant	1.4305***	Constant	3.376***
Log NSDP per worker	0.0376***	Log NSDP per worker	-0.245***
Reg_dummy=2	-0.0191***	Reg_dummy = 2	0.328***
Time=2000	0.0018	Time = 2000	-0.0455
Time=2004	0.0181**	Time = 2004	-0.0927839
R square	0.6667	R square	0.6053

Note: *** $p<0.01$, ** $p<0.05$.

Summary and Conclusion

The study shows India's wide diversified experience in demographic transition along with economic growth. It is evident that faster demographic transition facilitated the economic growth in some of the states, e.g., Haryana, Karnataka, Kerala and Tamil Nadu. Decline in labour force absorption capacity among all the sectors suggest that age structural change along with structural transformation in the economy may be responsible for increasing unemployment. Apart from this, it may be noted that growth in productive capacity plays an important role in raising income level of tertiary sector as its growth is less labour-intensive. Findings indicate that the interaction between demography and economic growth gives rise to the possibility of cumulative causation, increases in life expectancy and growth of working age population along with reductions in fertility, can provide a strong boost to economic growth. This growth in turn leads to further reductions in fertility rates, and to an increase in life expectancy. These demographic changes then set up another round of economic growth, this virtuous cycle. However, there are enough reasons to believe that beneficial effects of demographic transition may be lost, if we do not take remedial measures to meet the demand of labour in terms of education and technical requirement.

The interaction between demographic change and economic growth means that we must view the growth process as a system of causality running both ways. This interaction also supports an endogenous growth process. Our findings indicate that the interaction between demography and economic growth gives rise to the possibility of cumulative causation, but only for a limited period of time. Initial increases in life expectancy and reductions in fertility and in the youth dependency ratio can provide a strong boost to economic growth in developing states. This growth in turn leads to further reductions in fertility rates, and perhaps to an increase in life expectancy. These demographic changes then set up another round of economic growth; this virtuous cycle, however, has a natural limit.

Policy Implications

The implication is clear. Just as the "excess population" argument failed to recognise the benefits that can be gained if these excess workers could be put to work, the "demographic dividend" argument ignores the fact that available workers are not automatically absorbed to deliver high growth. Though government has made many strategies and policies for increasing employment and vocational training, which may be useful to exploit the demographic window of opportunity that India is experiencing today. India's experience during the liberalisation years suggest that markets do not necessarily ensure that utilisation of the potential human resources that the country's demographic transition temporarily offers. To realise the effect, it is necessary to support it with appropriate economic, social and political institutions and policies. Otherwise, it would only lead to higher levels of unemployment and social unrest.

India's recent growth has been impressive, with real GDP rising by over eight per cent a year since 2004—accompanied by a jump in innovative activities. Growth has been driven by rapid expansion in export-oriented, skill-intensive manufacturing sector and services. India needs to transform its immense young labour pool into a skilled workforce, which will be able to take advantage of the new and existing knowledge. The larger, healthier and better educated workforce will only bear economic fruit if extra workers can find suitable jobs. Several key policy variables have been identified in this study which can influence the nations' ability to realise and exploit its "demographic dividend". To fully unleash India's potential as an innovation economy, the government needs to improve the delivery of basic skills to both the formal and informal sectors, improve the flexibility of labour force, encourage participation of females into labour force, employment for semi-skilled and unskilled man power, vocational training institutes for providing technically sound labour force as to meet the current demand for skilled labour. If the appropriate employment avenues are created to absorb the skilled manpower, India can surely take advantage of this 'demographic dividend' to boost its economic growth and social development.

References

Adabar, K. (2007). *Economic Growth and Convergence in India*. Bangalore: Institute for Social and Economic Change. Accessed on August 1.

Ahluwalia, M.S. (2001). "State Level Performance under Economic Reforms in India", *Working Paper* No. 96. Stanford University: Center for Research on Economic Development and Policy Reform.

Basu, A. and K. Basu (1987). "The Graying of Population: Concepts and Measurment", *Demography India* XVI: 80-89.

Barro, R. and X. Sala-I-Martin (1995). *Economic Growth*. New York: McGraw-Hill Inc.

Bhat, P.N. Mari, (2004). *Demographic Scenario*, 2025. New Delhi: Institute of Economic Growth.

Bhattacharya, B.B. and S. Sakthivel (2002). "Economic Reforms and Jobless Growth in India in the 1990s", *Working paper*. New Delhi: Institute of Economic Growth.

Bloom, D.E., D. Canning and P. Malaney (2000). "Demographic Change and Economic Growth in Asia", *Population and Development Review 26*(supp.): 257-290.

Bloom, D.E. and D. Canning (2001). "Cumulative Causality, Economic Growth, and the Demographic Transition", in *Population Matters: Demographic Change, Economic Growth, and Poverty in the Developing World*, edited by N. Birdsall, A.C. Kelley, and S.W. Sinding. Oxford: Oxford University Press. pp.165-200.

Bloom, D.E., D. Canning and J. Sevilla (2003). "The Demographic Dividend: A New Perspective on the Economic Consequences of Population Change", *Population Matters Monograph MR-1274*. Santa Monica: RAND.

Bloom, D.E., D. Canning, Linlin Hu, Yuanli Liu, A. Mahal and W. Yip (2006). "Why has China's Economy Taken off Faster than India's?" *PGDA Working Paper* No. *20 http://www.hsph.harvard.edu/pgda/working.htm*, June.

Bose, A. (1996). "Demographic Transition and Demographic Imbalance in India", *Health Transition Review, Supplement to Volume* 6: 89-99.

Business Line (2007). "India must leverage the Demographic Dividend", The Hindu Group. March 28.

Chandershekhar, C.P., J. Ghosh, A. Roychowdhury (2006). "The 'Demographic Dividend' and Young India's Economic Future", *Economic and Political Weekly* 41(49): 5055-64.

Chesnais, J.C. (1990). "Demographic-Transition Patterns and Their Impact on the Age Structure", *Population and Development Review* 16(2): 327-336.

————. (1992). *The Demographic Transition. Stages, Patterns and Economic Implications: A Longitudinal Study of Sixty-Seven Countries Covering the Period 1720-1984*. Oxford: Clarendon Press.

Cho, L.J. and J.Y. Togashi (1984). "Industrial Transition and Demographic Dynamics of Asian-Pacific Region", pp-41-59 in proceedings of the *International Symposium on the Role of the Asia-Pacific Region in World Economic Development*. Tokyo: College of Economics, Nihon University.

Coale, A.J. (1986). "The Decline in Fertility in Europe since the Eighteenth Century", *Demographic History*. Princeton: Princeton University Press.

Dahlman, C., A. Utz (2005). *India and the Knowledge Economy Leveraging Strengths and Opportunities*. World Bank.

EPWRF (2003). *Domestic Product of States of India: 1960-61 to 2000-01*. Mumbai: EPW Research Foundation.

India Times (2007). "India to have Zero Unemployment by 2010", *India Times*, July.

Kulkarni, P. M. (1988). "Measures of Ageing: A Proposed Amendment", *Demography India* 17(2): 273-277.

Malmberg, B. and L. Sommestad (2000). "The Hidden Pulse of History: Population and Economic Change in Sweden, 1820-2000", *Scandianvian Journal of History*.

Mason, A. and R. Lee (2006). *Reform and Support Systems for the Elderly in Developing Countries: Capturing the Second Demographic Dividend*. GENUS.

Mitra, Arup (1997). "Infrastructure and Human Development", *Productivity* 38(2): 200-206.

Mukherji, J. (2006). "*Economic Growth and India's Future*" Available online via *www.sas.upenn.edu/casi*, Accessed on 7th October 2007.

Mukherjee, S.B. (1976). "The Age Distribution of the Indian Population: A Reconstruction for the States and Territories, 1881-1961".

Navneetham, K. (2002). "Age Structural Transition and Economic Growth: Evidences from South and Southeast Asia", *Asian Meta Center Research Paper Series No. – 7*, National University of Singapore.

National Accounts Statistics of India (2003). *EPW Research Foundation*, Mumbai, June.

NSSO (1996). "Key Results on Employment and Unemployment: NSS 50th round, July 1993-June 1994", Report No: 406, Ministry of Health and Programme Implementation, Government of India, New Delhi.

———. (2001). "Employment and Unemployment Situation in India: NSS 55th round, July 1999-June 2000", Report No: 458(55/10/2), Ministry of Health and Programme Implementation, Government of India, New Delhi.

———. (2005). "Employment and Unemployment Situation in India: NSS 60th round, January-June 2004", Report No: 506(60/10/1), Ministry of health and Programme Implementation, Government of India: New Delhi.

Ogawa, N and N.O. Tsuya, (1994). "*Demographic Change and Human Resource Development in the Asia-Pacific Region: Trends of the 1960s to 1980s and Future Prospects*". Japan: Nihon University.

Population and Human & Social Development FACTS-I accessed at *http://populationcommission.nic.in/facts1.htm*

Prskawetz, A., T. Kogel and S. Scherbov (2004). "The Effects of Age Structure on Economic Growth: An Application of Probabilistic Forecasting to India", *Working Paper*, March 2004. Vienna Institute of Demography.

Ram, F., U. Ram and K. Namboodiri (1995). "Fertility Transition in India". India: IIPS.

Rajan S.I., U.S. Mishra and P.S. Sarma (1993). "Demographic Transition and labour Supply in India", *Productivity* 34(1): 11-20.

Registrar General, India (2006). *Population Projections for India and States 2001-2026*. New Delhi: Government of India.

———. (1999). "Compendium of India's Fertility and Mortality Indicators 1971-97", Sample Registration System. New Delhi: Government of India.

Rele, J.R. (1987). "Fertility Levels and Trends in India: 1951-81", *Population and Development Review* 13(2): 513-531.

Sachs, J.D, N. Bajpai and A. Ramiah (2002). "Understanding Regional Economic Growth in India", *CID Working Paper No.88*. Harvard University: Center for International Development.

Shetty, S.L. (2003). "Growth of SDP and Structural Changes in State Economies: Interstate Comparisons", *Economic and Political Weekly* 38(49): 5189-200.

The Economic Times (2006). "Demographic Dividend: How to Make it Pay?", *The Economic Times* December.

Appendix A-21.1

Estimated and Projected TFR for India and States, 1961-2026

Period	*1961-1966*	*1966-1971*	*1971-1976*	*1976-1981*	*1981-1986*	*1986-1991*	*1991-1996*	*1996-2001*	*2001-2006*	*2006-2011*	*2011-2016*	*2016-2021*	*2021-2026*
India	6.05	5.78	5.37	4.65	4.46	4.00	3.54	3.26	2.98	2.60	2.30	2.20	2.00
South	5.24	4.83	4.35	3.73	3.17	2.65	2.26	2.11	1.99	1.88	1.83	1.80	1.80
Andhra Pradesh	5.51	5.41	5.15	4.45	3.90	3.38	2.78	2.42	2.16	1.90	1.80	1.80	1.80
Karnataka	5.88	5.58	5.15	4.49	3.66	3.36	2.88	2.48	2.32	2.00	1.90	1.80	1.80
Kerala	5.04	4.43	3.79	3.14	2.62	2.08	1.74	1.82	1.76	1.80	1.80	1.80	1.80
Tamil Nadu	4.80	4.49	4.12	3.55	3.22	2.52	2.16	2.04	1.88	1.80	1.80	1.80	1.80
North	6.60	6.11	5.59	5.02	4.75	4.09	3.76	3.36	3.03	2.53	2.20	2.00	1.87
Punjab	6.01	5.27	4.63	4.28	3.86	3.34	3.00	2.60	2.26	2.10	1.90	1.80	1.80
Rajasthan	6.58	6.44	6.15	5.62	5.52	4.70	4.50	4.16	3.82	3.10	2.60	2.30	2.00
Haryana	7.20	6.62	5.99	5.17	4.86	4.22	3.78	3.32	3.00	2.40	2.10	1.90	1.80
Eastern	6.37	6.09	5.65	4.78	4.62	4.15	3.58	3.27	3.06	2.47	2.17	2.00	1.87
Bihar	6.31	6.25	6.09	5.62	5.62	5.16	4.54	4.44	4.30	3.30	2.70	2.30	2.00
Orissa	6.07	5.94	5.58	4.55	4.24	3.76	3.22	2.90	2.62	2.20	2.00	1.90	1.80
West Bengal	6.72	6.07	5.27	4.18	4.00	3.52	2.98	2.48	2.26	1.90	1.80	1.80	1.80
Western	6.08	5.53	4.95	4.27	3.90	3.50	3.04	2.81	2.55	2.25	2.05	1.90	1.85
Gujarat	6.50	5.74	5.04	4.39	4.12	3.56	3.16	2.98	2.82	2.30	2.10	1.90	1.90
Maharashtra	5.66	5.31	4.86	4.14	3.68	3.44	2.92	2.64	2.28	2.20	2.00	1.90	1.80
Central	6.45	6.38	6.14	5.40	5.42	5.05	4.72	4.36	4.07	3.60	3.10	2.75	2.40
Madhya Pradesh	6.56	6.33	5.94	5.10	5.08	4.76	4.32	3.98	3.76	3.20	2.80	2.50	2.20
Uttar Pradesh	6.33	6.42	6.33	5.70	5.76	5.34	5.12	4.74	4.38	4.00	3.40	3.00	2.60

Note: Estimates for 1961-1971 have been taken from Rele, estimates from 1971 to 2005 have been borrowed by Sample Registration System. Beyond year 2006, projections of TFR are given by Technical group/Expert committee, R.G.I.

Appendix A-21.2

Expectation of Life at Birth for India and States, 1961-2026

Period	*1961-1966*	*1966-1971*	*1971-1976*	*1976-1981*	*1981-1986*	*1986-1991*	*1991-1996*	*1996-2001*	*2001-2006*	*2006-2011*	*2011-2016*	*2016-2021*	*2021-2026*
India	48.05	52.55	56.65	60.45	62.45	57.90	60.30	62.20	66.45	66.95	68.45	69.95	71.05
South	49.35	53.85	53.37	55.90	58.80	64.43	66.23	67.63	68.41	69.93	71.16	72.24	73.20
Andhra Pradesh	44.40	49.40	54.00	58.30	60.30	59.80	61.80	63.40	65.60	67.40	68.90	70.25	71.35
Karnataka	0.00	0.00	55.20	56.30	60.70	62.00	62.50	64.30	67.05	68.80	70.15	71.25	72.25
Kerala	54.30	58.30	61.90	65.20	65.70	70.50	72.90	73.60	73.40	74.40	75.40	76.15	76.90
Tamil Nadu	0.00	0.00	43.00	46.20	50.00	60.80	63.30	65.00	67.60	69.10	70.20	71.30	72.30
North	53.10	57.10	59.63	60.93	63.10	60.73	63.33	64.73	66.62	68.88	70.17	71.23	72.27
Punjab	53.45	57.45	61.05	64.35	64.85	64.60	67.50	68.30	66.85	70.15	71.25	72.25	73.15
Rajasthan	52.75	56.75	60.35	63.65	64.15	55.90	59.10	60.90	65.65	67.65	69.15	70.25	71.35
Haryana	0.00	0.00	57.50	54.80	60.30	61.70	63.40	65.00	67.35	68.85	70.10	71.20	72.30
Eastern	47.70	52.20	56.30	60.10	61.27	56.77	59.30	60.80	64.83	66.53	68.15	69.60	70.77
Bihar	45.10	50.10	54.70	59.00	61.00	55.10	59.30	60.60	65.15	66.90	68.65	69.90	71.00
Orissa	47.70	52.20	56.30	60.10	61.10	54.20	56.50	58.10	61.30	63.15	65.15	67.15	68.65
West Bengal	50.30	54.30	57.90	61.20	61.70	61.00	62.10	63.70	68.05	69.55	70.65	71.75	72.65
Western	49.00	53.25	57.10	60.65	61.40	60.75	62.90	64.70	67.48	69.35	70.78	72.00	73.10
Gujarat	46.80	51.30	55.40	59.20	60.20	58.20	61.00	63.30	66.95	69.10	70.85	72.20	73.40
Maharashtra	51.20	55.20	58.80	62.10	62.60	63.30	64.80	66.10	68.00	69.60	70.70	71.80	72.80
Central	46.53	51.03	55.13	58.93	59.93	53.40	55.75	57.70	61.43	63.55	65.68	67.63	69.30
Madhya Pradesh	47.40	51.90	56.00	59.80	60.80	53.50	54.70	56.60	60.90	62.90	64.90	66.90	68.65
Uttar Pradesh	45.65	50.15	54.25	58.05	59.05	53.30	56.80	58.80	61.95	64.20	66.45	68.35	69.95

Appendix A-21.3

Estimated Proportion of Urban Population in India and States, 1961-2026

States	*1961-1966*	*1966-1971*	*1971-1976*	*1976-1981*	*1981-1986*	*1986-1991*	*1991-1996*	*1996-2001*	*2001-2006*	*2006-2011*	*2011-2016*	*2016-2021*	*2021-2026*
India	18.63	19.62	20.91	22.65	24.10	25.10	26.12	27.16	28.30	29.40	30.50	31.70	32.80
South	21.82	22.94	24.25	25.88	27.59	29.42	31.33	33.38	35.70	38.00	39.90	42.23	44.30
Andhra Pradesh	17.81	18.75	20.11	22.12	24.02	25.78	26.89	27.01	27.40	27.60	27.80	28.00	28.20
Karnataka	22.73	23.72	25.23	27.52	29.29	30.30	31.52	33.06	34.70	36.30	38.00	39.60	41.30
Kerala	15.34	15.90	16.74	17.99	20.28	24.13	26.35	26.11	25.90	26.00	25.40	25.20	25.00
Tamil Nadu	27.40	29.19	30.80	32.14	33.20	33.83	36.13	40.96	46.50	51.70	56.30	61.90	66.60
North	19.02	19.43	20.45	22.38	23.99	25.12	26.39	27.88	29.50	31.13	32.83	34.60	36.37
Punjab	23.19	23.53	24.52	26.50	28.09	29.11	30.57	32.68	35.00	37.30	39.70	42.20	44.60
Rajasthan	16.55	17.23	18.31	20.02	21.42	22.33	22.98	23.23	23.50	23.80	24.00	24.30	24.60
Haryana	17.32	17.53	18.50	20.61	22.46	23.92	25.63	27.74	30.00	32.30	34.80	37.30	39.90
Eastern	13.33	13.99	14.89	16.15	17.13	17.67	17.96	17.87	18.00	18.50	18.87	19.27	19.63
Bihar	8.74	9.53	10.49	11.73	12.61	12.96	12.63	11.28	10.50	10.50	10.50	10.60	10.60
Orissa	6.74	7.78	9.09	10.78	12.12	12.94	13.74	14.51	15.40	16.30	17.20	18.20	19.20
West Bengal	24.51	24.66	25.09	25.95	26.65	27.10	27.50	27.83	28.10	28.70	28.90	29.00	29.10
Western	27.52	28.84	30.31	32.03	33.77	35.52	37.23	38.88	40.65	42.35	44.05	45.85	47.55
Gujarat	26.23	27.39	28.68	30.19	31.76	33.41	34.99	36.47	38.00	39.50	41.00	42.60	44.10
Maharashtra	28.81	30.29	31.94	33.87	35.77	37.62	39.46	41.30	43.30	45.20	47.10	49.10	51.00
Central	13.89	14.68	15.95	17.93	19.61	20.82	21.99	23.07	23.85	24.50	25.10	25.70	26.30
Madhya Pradesh	14.69	15.69	17.09	19.09	20.87	22.33	23.90	25.63	26.70	27.40	28.00	28.60	29.20
Uttar Pradesh	13.08	13.67	14.81	16.77	18.34	19.31	20.07	20.51	21.00	21.60	22.20	22.80	23.40

Appendix A-21.4

Distribution of Indian System of Industrial Classification

Primary	Section "0"	A. Agriculture, hunting & forestry
		B. Fishing
Secondary	Section "1"	C. Mining & quarrying
	Section "2"	D. Manufacturing
	Section "3"	
	Section "4"	E. Electricity, gas & water supply
	Section "5"	F. Construction
Tertiary	Section "6"	G. Wholesale & retail trade; Repair of motor vehicle, motor cycle and personal & household goods
		H. Hotels & restaurants
	Section "7"	I. Transport, storage & communication
	Section "8"	J. Financial intermediation
		K. Real estate, renting & business activities
	Section "9"	L. Public admn. & defence, compulsory social security
		M. Education
		N. Health & social work
		O. Other community social & personal services
		P. Private household with employed persons
		Q. Extra territorial organisations and bodies

22

Health Status of Elderly in Rural Maharashtra

Do Socioeconomic Differentials Matter?

DHANANJAY W. BANSOD AND BALRAM PASWAN

Introduction

One of the most important demographic events of the 20th century is population ageing and it is going to remain till 21st century. This global phenomenon of ageing has also affected India. There were around 20 million aged population in India in 1951, which increased to 76.6 million (7.4 per cent to total population of India) in 2001. India is passing through a technological, social, cultural and demographic transition. Consequently, increase in quality of life, awareness of health care and improvement in the quality of health care, and ultimately increase in the life expectancy, which laid to increase of elderly population. Along with the growing number of the aged, the traditional family support system is seen to be disappearing from the Indian society. The aged persons are one of the most vulnerable and high-risk groups in terms of health, development and socioeconomic status in society. Today, the health of elderly is the major concern in India.

The WHO defines "Health as a state of complete physical, mental and social well-being and not merely the absence of disease or infirmity". To the psychologist, health is principally the normal functioning of the mind. To the physician, health is principally the normal functioning of the body. As age increases, the health of the elderly deteriorates. The old aged people suffer from multiple kinds of diseases. The effects of ageing are quite visible on their motivations, emotional life, adjustment etc. Old age comes with different psychological pressure on the mind of the people. Old people may also face the problem of adjustment due to the loss of spouse.

Several studies (Banerjee, 1998; Chakraborty, 2004; Madhu and Darshan, 2003; Mohanty, 1997; Radha Devi *et al.*, 1999) reveal that loss of respect, authority, status, interaction, effective roles and social relation of elders are the root cause of other psychological and health problems. As a result, majority of elders had multiple health problems and were also found depressive. The analysis of National Sample Survey data for 1986-87 reveals that about 45 per cent of the rural elderly are chronically ill among whom 45 per cent are men and 45.8 per cent are women. Cough, joint pain, high blood pressure, heart disease and urinary problems are more common among the elderly. In rural areas, 5.4 per cent of elderly (6.8 per cent females and 4.4 per cent males) are physically disabled. The proportion of female physically disabled is more than the male (Kohli, 1996). Literacy and income play a crucial role in determining health conditions of the aged (Yadav *et al.*, 1996).

For this study Amravati district of Maharashtra state is purposely selected. Maharashtra is one of the industrial states of India. Maharashtra has 8.7 per cent (2001) elderly population to total population, which is the highest among all Indian states. The same figure for Amravati district is 10 per cent, which is a matter of major concern.

It has been found from various studies that many factors are responsible for the health of the elderly population. However, for this study it has been conceptualised that all the socioeconomic and demographic variables may have influences on health of elderly through the intervening variables like living arrangement, relation with family members, his/her decision-making role and lifestyle. The lifestyle like food, habits (drinking, smoking), prayer and exercise influence the health of the elderly in a big way. The conceptual model has been graphically represented in Figure 22.1.

Objectives

The main objective of the chapter is to investigate the socioeconomic and demographic influences on health of the elderly. However, the specific objectives are:

(i) to know the health problems and disability of elderly;

(ii) to know the determinants of perceived health status of elderly; and

(iii) to know the functional health status and determinants of mental health of elderly.

Figure 22.1

Conceptual Framework of the Study

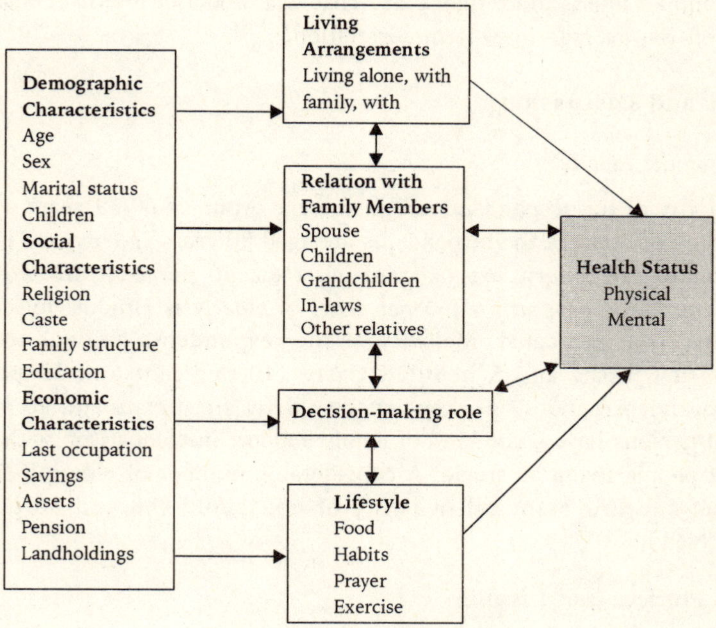

Methods and Materials

This study is based on primary data collected from Amravati district of Maharashtra state of India. Three stage sampling design has been adopted with the selection of blocks in the first stage, villages in the second stage and households in the third stage to collect information from 600 respondents in 15 villages of the Amravati district. After random selection of a block, villages were stratified into three strata on the basis of population size. A sampling frame of aged 60 and above was then prepared for the selected villages by house listing. This was followed by selection of aged respondents using systematic random sampling. A mix of qualitative as well as quantitative research techniques has been applied to gather the necessary information, such as in-depth interviews, focus group discussions and structured interview schedule. Univariate, bivariate, chi-square test and multivariate analysis has been applied to analyse the data. To capture the health status of elderly, activity of daily living (ADL), mental health scale and mood assessment scale has been computed. Adjustment inventory scale has also been used to assess the social adjustment of elderly. Reliability analysis has been done to check the association of the variables before constructing the above scales. Alpha value has been checked for all the items before constructing the scale. Only those items have been included in the scale for which alpha value is more than 0.56. That is a model of internal consistency, based on the average inter-item correlation.

Result and Discussion

Profile of the Elderly

Majority of the respondents are in the age group of 60-69 years whereas, only seven per cent of the respondents are aged 80 years and above. Fifty-nine per cent of the elderly are married whereas, 40 per cent are widowed/ widowers. Large proportion (60 per cent) of elderly is Hindus, followed by Buddhists (36 per cent). Majority of the respondents belongs to Other Backward Classes and Scheduled Caste (40 per cent and 39 per cent respectively). Around 37 per cent of the elderly are literate and 90 per cent of aged persons have some kind of family support in comparison with 10 per cent of people living as single. A considerable number of elderly belong to medium and low standard of living of household (38 and 36 per cent respectively).

Health Problems and Disability

It can be noticed from Table 22.1 that 13 per cent of elderly were suffering from asthma/breathing problem; around 8 per cent and 5 per cent of elderly were suffering from blood pressure and diabetes respectively and 2 per cent of them were suffering from heart, kidney lung problems. Whereas 7 per cent of elderly were suffering from arthritis, back pain, liver damage, piles, paralysis and tuberculosis. The asthma, blood pressure and arthritis are the main health problems among the elderly in rural part of Amravati district.

Table 22.1

Per cent Distribution of Elderly Suffering from Various Health Problems in Amravati District of Maharashtra

Problems	*Percentage*	*Frequency*	*Total No.*
Blood pressure	8.2	49	600
Heart, kidney or lungs	2.0	12	600
Asthma or breathing problem	12.8	77	600
Diabetes/sugar problem	4.5	27	600
Others*	7.0	42	600

Note: * Arthritis, back pain, liver damage, piles, paralysis and T.B.

The analysis reveals that 50 per cent, 48 per cent and 45 per cent of the elderly have visual disability, walking disability and hearing disability respectively (Table 22.2). It is also found that more females are having all three kinds of disabilities such as hearing, visual and walking than their male counterparts.

Table 22.2

Per cent Distribution of Elderly by Sex and Various Type of Disability in Rural Area of Amravati District of Maharashtra

*Type of Disability**	*Male*	*Female*	*Total*	*No.*
Hearing	42.5	49.1	45.7	274
Visual	46.0	55.1	50.3	302
Walking	46.3	49.8	48.0	288

Note: * Multiple responses.

Perceived Health Status of Elderly

The elderly were asked "At present how do you feel about your health?" and the responses were coded as good, average and not good. Thirty per cent (Figure 22.2) of the elderly said that their health is good and 37 per cent elderly reported average health. Whereas 33 per cent of the elderly cited that their health is not good. Sex-wise distribution shows that more males (39 per cent) as compared to 20 per cent female perceived their health status is good. Whereas 43 per cent of females perceived their health status is not good as compared to 23 per cent male. The perceived health status of elderly by socioeconomic characteristics has been presented in Table 22.3. It seems that age is playing a more important role in explaining elderly perceived health status. As expected it is found that as age increases the problems among the elderly also increases. It is seen that 25 per cent of the elderly in the age of 80 years and above said that their health is good compared to 33 per cent elderly in the age group of 60-69 years. However, 65 per cent of the elderly of 80 years and above feel that their health is not good as compared to 27 per cent in the age group 60-69 years of elderly. A larger proportion of females (43 per cent) perceive that their health is not good than their male counterparts (23 per cent). Similarly, 46 per cent of the widowed/widower felt that their health is not good as compared to 24 per cent married elderly. A higher proportion of elderly having high standard of living index (SLI), joint family and economically independent said their health status to be good compared to their counterparts. The elderly having comfortable living conditions perceived their health status as good compared to the elderly living with uncomfortable living conditions.

Figure 22.2

Distribution of Perceived Health Status of Elderly

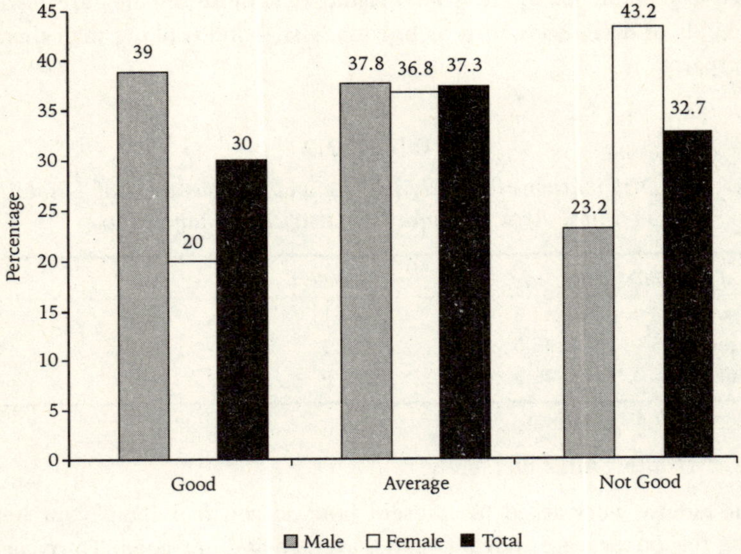

Logistic Regression Analysis of Perceived Health Status of Elderly

Table 22.4 gives the result of logistic regression. The dependent variable is perceived health problems (i.e., 1 = having problem, 0 = not having problem). It was observed that elderly in the age of 80 years and above is more likely to perceive poor health than those elderly in the age group of 60-69 years, they are two times more likely to perceive poor health compared to elderly belonging to age group 60-69 years, which is also coming out statistically significant. The widowed/widowers are more likely to perceive poor health status than married elderly. It was observed that elderly living with family are less likely to have poor health than those who are living single and this association is found to be significant. The economic status of the elderly is playing an important role in explaining health status of the elderly. Economically dependent elderly are three times more likely to perceive poor health than economically independent elderly. Elderly having any disability are more likely to perceive poor health status than elderly having no disability but the same is not statistically significant.

Table 22.3

Perceived Health Status of Elderly by Background Characteristics

Background Characteristics	*Feeling About Health* *Good*	*Average*	*Not Good*	*No.*
Age group				
60-69	32.9	40.0	27.1	365
70-79	25.6	37.9	36.4	192
80+	25.0	10.0	65.0	40
Sex				
Male	39.0	37.8	23.2	315
Female	20.0	36.8	43.2	285
Marital status				
Married	38.1	38.4	23.6	352
Widowed/widower	17.8	36.4	45.9	242
SLI				
Low	28.8	37.1	34.2	445
Medium	29.1	41.8	29.1	141
High	78.6	0.0	21.4	14
Type of family				
Single	17.7	33.9	48.4	62
Nuclear	23.2	43.7	33.1	263
Joint	39.3	32.0	28.7	275
Economic status				
Independent	37.4	41.2	21.3	342
Dependent on others	20.2	32.2	47.7	258
Disability				
No disability	31.3	42.9	25.9	112
Any disability	29.7	36.1	34.2	488
Living conditions				
Comfortable	38.2	23.6	38.2	157
Satisfactory	26.5	46.7	26.8	362
Uncomfortable	29.6	22.2	48.1	81
Total no.	180 (30.0)	224 (37.3)	196 (32.7)	600

Functional Health

Functional health is defined in terms of functioning ability based on ADLs (Activity of Daily Living) and IADLs (Instrumental Activity of Daily Living). Activities of daily living (ADLs), is a way to describe the functional status of a person. There are six basic ADLs: eating, bathing, dressing, toileting, transferring (walking) and continence. An individual's ability to perform ADLs is important for determining what type of long-term care (e.g., nursing-home care or home care) and coverage the individual needs (i.e., medicare, medicaid or long-term care insurance).

Table 22.4

Logistic Estimates of the Effect of Selected Characteristics of Elderly on Perceived Health Status

Variables	*Exp (B)*
Age group	
60-69[(R)]	
70-79	1.291
80+	2.317**
Marital status	
Married[(R)]	
Widowed/widower	2.161***
Caste	
General[(R)]	
SC/ST	1.247
OBC	0.550
Type of family	
Single[(R)]	0.789
Nuclear	0.512*
Joint	
SLI	
Low	
Medium	0.972
High	0.904
Economic status	
Independent[(R)]	
Dependent on others	3.007***
Disability	
No disabled[(R)]	
Any disabled	1.691**
Constant	0.185

Note: *** P < 0.001, ** P < 0.005, * P < 1.01; [(R)] Reference category.

Prevalence rate of activity of daily living (ADL) is showing in Figure 22.3. In case of personal care like getting out of bed, go to toilet and taking bath, more than 90 per cent of the elderly are independent and they can do their work by their own. In case of indoor household work, some elderly need assistance and it was seen that more than one-fifth of the elderly are dependent on others. Similarly, for outdoor work like travelling and shopping personal items, most of the elderly are independent. Fifty per cent and more elderly are independent for outdoor work, they can do their work independently without taking anybody's help. Table 22.5 shows the functional capacity index of elderly by sex. From the table it can be noticed that travelling, going to toilet, bathing and in shopping personal items, males are found to be more independent than females. As expected, in case of house work and meal preparation, females are more independent than males. Females are more independent for indoor work but are dependent on others for outdoor work.

Figure 22.3

Share of Functionally Impaired With and Without Assistance

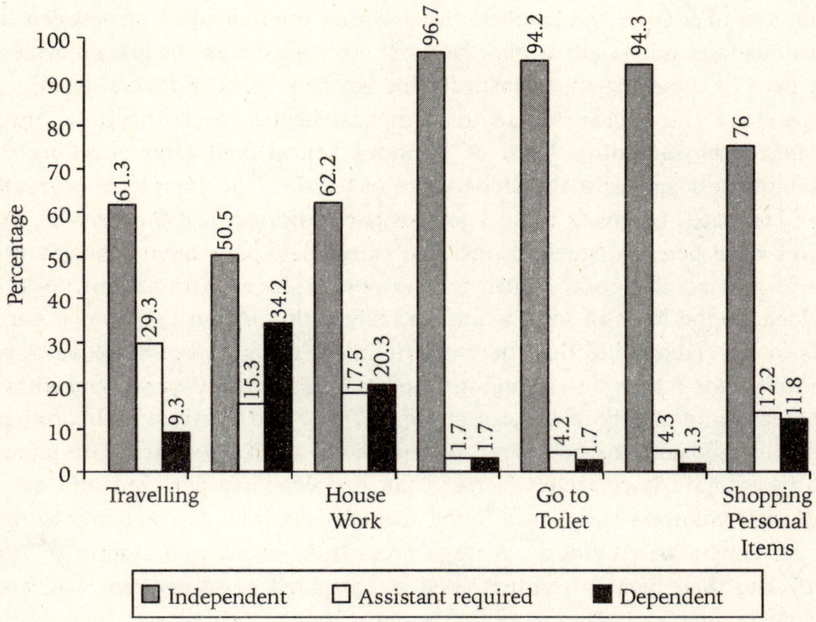

Table 22.5

Functional Capacity Index of Elderly 60 Years and Above by Sex

Daily Activities (ADL)	*Independent*		*Assistant Required*		*Dependent*	
	Male	*Female*	*Male*	*Female*	*Male*	*Female*
Travelling	77.8	43.2	17.1	42.8	5.1	14.0
Preparing meals	35.2	67.4	16.5	14.0	48.3	18.6
House work	56.8	68.1	19.4	15.4	23.8	16.5
Get out of the bed	96.8	96.5	1.3	2.1	1.9	1.4
Go to toilet	97.1	90.9	1.6	7.0	1.3	2.1
Bathing	96.5	91.9	2.2	6.7	1.3	1.4
Shopping personal items	89.5	61.1	6.7	18.2	3.8	20.7

Mental Health Status of Elderly

Mental health is more than the mere lack of mental disorders. Concept of mental health includes subjective well-being, perceived self-efficacy, autonomy, competence, intergenerational dependence and recognition of the ability to realise one's intellectual and emotional potential. Concisely stated, mental health is that quality of mental and emotional well-being which provides one with effective and enjoyable living. It is living a purposeful life of accepted accomplishment that gives consuming satisfaction and enjoyment with a minimum of friction and conflict, either within the individual or between the individual and others about him. Not just accomplishment or just enjoyment, but both of these together constitute the cofactor index of mental health. To understand the overall situation of mental health, a composite score is computed by including 9 out of 12 items (questions) after checking the reliability test and with the alpha value of 0.6429. The composite score has been computed by giving value 1 for positive indicators and 0 otherwise. The scores have been categorised into two categories: poor mental health (0-5 score) and good mental health (6 and above score). The cut-off point is decided on the basis of total scores and bifurcating it into two similar parts. It is found (Table 22.6) that more elderly in the age group of 60-69 years are mentally good than in the age group of 70-79 and 80 years and above. Whereas more elderly in the age group of 70-79 and 80 years and above are mentally not good as compared to age group of 60-69 years. The mental health of male is relatively better than female. Fifty per cent and above widowed/widowers elderly are found mentally not well as compared to only 32 per cent married elderly. A large proportion of married elderly (67 per cent) said their mental health is good as compared to 44 per cent widowed/ widowers. It clearly indicates that elderly living with spouse have better mental health. Married elderly have moral support of their spouse so that they can live better life as they both can share the problems together, on the other hand in most of the cases the widowed/widowers elderly depend primarily on their children or other family members, who in many case tend to ignore the needs of elderly, that results into various physical and mental disorders. A large number of elderly with Buddhist religion said their mental health is not good than Hindu and Muslim elderly. Education also plays an important role among the elderly and their mental health. Half of the illiterate elderly said their mental health is not good as compared to literate elderly, however more than 70 per cent literate elderly found to be mentally good. The elderly living with family are found to be mentally good than living alone. Living with family makes more difference for anyone's mental health, which shows its effect at later ages. Elderly with low standard of living index were mentally weak than medium and high SLI. More than 70 per cent economically independent elderly were found to have good mental health condition as compared to dependent elderly. The main cause of weak mental health status is financial and health seeking dependency on their children or other family members.

Table 22.6

Per cent Distribution of Elderly by Mental Health Status and Background Characteristics in Amravati District of Maharashtra

Background Characteristics	*Mental Health*		
	Not Good	*Good*	*Total*
Age group			
60-69	39.5	60.5	365
70-79	46.2	53.8	195
80+	45.0	55.0	40
Sex			
Male	28.9	71.1	315
Female	56.5	43.5	285
Marital status*			
Married	32.4	67.6	352
Widowed/widower	56.2	43.8	242
Religion			
Hindu	37.0	63.0	359
Muslim	36.4	63.6	22
Buddhist	50.7	49.3	219
Caste			
General	30.0	70.0	50
SC	45.9	54.1	233
ST	51.3	48.8	80
OBC	37.6	62.4	237
Education			
Illiterate	50.0	50.0	382
Primary	29.9	70.1	144
Middle school & above	24.3	75.7	74
Type of family			
Single	54.8	45.2	62
Nuclear	44.5	55.5	263
Joint	36.7	63.3	275
SLI			
Low	49.5	50.5	216
Medium	40.6	59.4	229
High	33.5	66.5	155
Economic status			
Independent	29.2	70.8	342
Dependent	58.9	41.1	258
Total	42.0 (252)	58.0 (348)	100.0 (600)

Note: * Never married and separated has not been considered in the analysis because of very less number i.e., only 6 respondents.

Mood Assessment Scale

Mood assessment scale is mainly used to assess the depression level among the older people. Originally it was 15 items (questions) scale and the scoring for the scale was one point for each of these answers. Before using these items into scale, reliability analysis was done to check the relationship within these items. After reliability test, three items included in the questionnaire were dropped from the analysis. So, 12 items were included in the analysis out of 15 items. The cut-off range for normal depression: 0-4, mild depression: 5-8 and severe depression: 9-12, have been adopted. This scale was used to measure the depression level among the elderly. The mood assessment scale shows that 42 per cent of the elderly are normal, while one-third of elderly found to be mild depressed and one-fourth (25 per cent) of elderly found to be in severe depression (Figure 22.4). Among the age group of 60-69, it is found (Table 22.7) that depression level is normal, whereas in the age group of 70-79 years, the elderly are severely depressed than other age groups. However, in the age group of 80 years and above the elderly are found to be mildly depressed than age group of 60-69 and 70-79 years. More females are found depressed than males. The elderly widowed/widowers were found more depressed than their married elderly counterparts. More Hindu elderly are found to be normal while elderly belonging to Muslim and Buddhist religion are found to be in mild depression. Elderly belonging to Scheduled Tribe are found to be more depressed than other ethnic groups. The illiterate elderly is found to be more depressed than literate. Higher proportions of elderly living in joint family are found to be normal as compared to elderly living single and in nuclear family. Elderly in nuclear families were found to be mildly depressed than those living in joint families and living single. The higher percentage of elderly living single found to be severely depressed as compared to elderly living with families. Standard of living and level of depression are also associated with each other. Elderly with high SLI were found to be normal compared to low and medium SLI. Elderly having low and medium SLI are found more depressed than the elderly with

Figure 22.4

Distribution of Elderly by Mood Assessment Scale

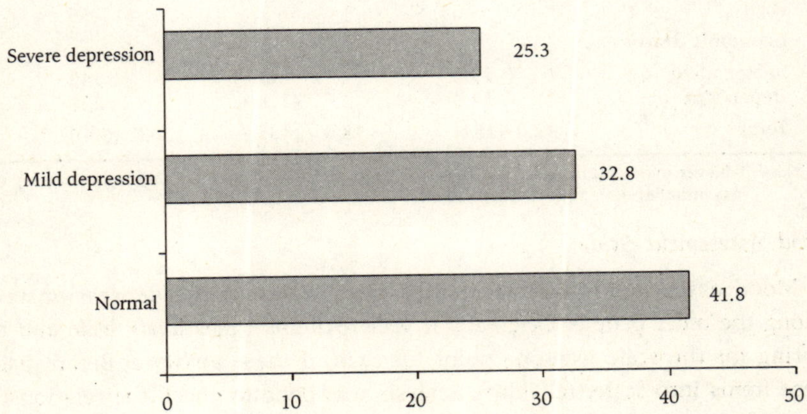

high SLI. Those elderly who are economically dependent on others are found to be depressed than economically independent elderly. The economically independent are found to be normal, they are enjoying life without any tension as they are self-dependent and they don't have to ask for money or any kind of help from others.

Table 22.7

Per cent Distribution of Elderly by Mood Assessment Scale and Background Characteristics in Amravati District of Maharashtra

Background Characteristics	*Mood Assessment Scale*			
	Normal	*Mild Depression*	*Severe Depression*	*Total No.*
Age group				
60-69	44.1	31.5	24.4	365
70-79	37.9	33.3	28.7	195
80+	40.0	42.5	17.5	40
Sex				
Male	52.7	27.6	19.7	315
Female	29.8	38.6	31.6	285
Marital status*				
Married	49.4	30.7	19.9	352
Widowed/widower	31.0	36.4	32.6	242
Religion				
Hindu	45.1	31.2	23.7	359
Muslim	36.4	36.4	27.3	22
Buddhist	37.0	35.2	27.9	219
Caste				
General	40.0	36.0	24.0	50
SC	39.5	33.9	26.6	233
ST	32.5	37.5	30.0	80
OBC	47.7	29.5	22.8	237
Education				
Illiterate	35.9	35.6	28.5	382
Primary	47.9	29.9	22.2	144
Middle school & above	60.8	24.3	14.9	74
Type of family				
Single	25.8	29.0	45.2	62
Nuclear	39.9	34.2	25.9	263
Joint	47.3	32.4	20.4	275
SLI				
Low	33.3	34.3	32.4	216
Medium	42.8	33.6	23.6	229
High	52.3	29.7	18.1	155
Economic status				
Independent	54.7	26.9	18.4	342
Dependent	24.8	40.7	34.5	258
Total	41.8 (251)	32.8 (197)	25.3 (152)	600

Note: * Never married and separated has not been considered in the analysis because of very less percentage i.e., only one per cent.

Summary and Conclusion

The analysis reveals that socioeconomic condition of the elderly has an impact on their health status. It is observed that there is a significant relation between age and health status of the elderly. As age increases, health deteriorates, and the elderly perceived poor health. A large proportion of widowed/widower elderly perceived their health as not good. It is obvious that in every society, after the death of a spouse a person feels lonely and also there may not be any one to look after. Elderly with low standard of living, elderly living alone and economically dependent elderly are more likely to perceive the status of their health to be poor. Elderly persons having some disability are prone to perceive and report poor health status. The functional capacity index of elderly reveals that in getting out of the bed, going to toilet and bathing, more than 90 per cent of elderly are found to be independent. While in case of preparing meal and home work, more than 15 per cent of elderly required some sort of assistance. Male are more independent in outdoor work and females are more independent in indoor work. A close look at the functional capacity by age suggests that elderly aged 80 and above are found to be dependent. Fifty per cent and above widowed/widower elderly are found mentally not well as compared to 32 per cent married elderly. Similarly, those elderly living with family are found to be mentally better off than those living alone. Elderly with low standard of living and economically dependent on others were found to be mentally weak. The main cause of weak mental health status is financial and health seeking dependency on their children or other family members. The mood assessment of the elderly also shows similar results. Female elderly, widowed/widower elderly, SC/ST elderly are found to be more depressed. Higher proportions of elderly living in joint families are found to be normal as compared to elderly living single and in nuclear families. The higher percentage of elderly living single, having low standard of living and being dependent on others are found to be severely depressed. The hypothesis that elderly females tend to have more health problems as compared to their male counterparts are ascertained in this study.

References

Alam, M. and M. Mukherjee (2005). "Ageing Activity of Daily Living Disabilities and the Need for Public Health Initiatives: Some Evidence from a Household Survey in Delhi", *Asia-Pacific Population Journal* 20(2): 47-76.

Banerjee, S.K. (1998). "Life Beyond Sixty Living Arrangements, Economic and Health Transition among Male Elderly: A Case Study of West Bengal", *Unpublished Ph.D. Thesis*. Mumbai: International Institute for Population Sciences.

Bansod, D.W. and B. Paswan (2006). "From Home to Old Age Home: A Situational Appraisal of Elderly in Old Age Homes in Maharashtra", *HelpAge India Research & Development Journal* XII(3), New Delhi.

Chakraborti, R.D. (2004). *The Graying of India: Population Ageing in the Context of Asia*. New Delhi: Sage Publication.

Dandekar, K. (1996). *The Elderly in India*. New Delhi: Sage Publications.

Devi, Radha D., S. Santosh, A. Ashraf, and T.K. Roy (1999). "Aged in A Changing Society: A Case Study of Kerala". Mumbai: International Institute for Population Sciences.

Field, M. (1968). "Ageing with Honour and Dignity", in H.S. Bhatia, *Ageing and Society: A Sociological Study of Retired Public Servants*. Udaipur: Arya's Book Publishers. p.87.

Gaur, Rajan and Amarjot Kaur (2004). "Health Status and General Attitudes of Institutionalized and Non-institutionalized Aged Persons living in and around Chandigah", *Man in India* 84(3-4): 153-166.

Gold, D.T. (1989). "Sibling Relationships in Old Age: A Typology", *International Journal of Ageing and Human Development* 28(1): 53-66.

Kohli, A.S. (1996). *Social Situation of the Aged in India*. New Delhi: Anmol Publications Pvt. Ltd.

Kothari, C.R. (1990). *Research Methodology: Methods and Techniques*, Second edition. New Delhi: Wishwa Prakashan.

Lakshinarayanan, T.R. (1993). "A Comparison of Male and Female Rural Aged in Adjustment", *Ageing and Society: The Indian Journal of Gerontology* 3(3): 13-25.

Madhu, S. Varmani and S. Darshan (2003). "Changing Social Status of Elders in Rural Haryana," *Ageing and Society: The Indian Journal of Gerontology* 13(1): 1-16.

McGhee, J.L. (1984). "The Influence of Qualitative Assessment of the Social and Physical Environment on the Morale of the Rural Elderly", *American Journal of Community Psychology of Ageing* 12(16): 709-723.

Mohanty, M. (1997). "Socio-Economic Problems of Aged Santals of Mayurbhanj Orissa", in Chakravarty's (eds.), *Life in Twilight Years*. Calcutta: Kwality Book Co. pp-115-127.

Shanas, E. (1968). "The Psychology of Health", in B.L. Neugarten (eds.), *Middle Age and Ageing*. Chicago: University of Chicago Press. pp. 212-219.

Yadav, N.C., S. Surendar, R.E. Robert (1996). "Ageing and Health Hazards in Rural Northern India", *Health and Population Perspectives and Issues* 19(1): 1-18.

Section VII

Population Growth Prospects and its Developmental Implications in India

23

Population Projections for India and States, 2001-2051

K.S. NATARAJAN

Introduction

India has witnessed unprecedented growth in population during the 20th century. From a population of 238 million in 1901, the population has increased to 1028 million in 2001 or more than four times. This rapid increase in population growth is mainly due to the rapid decline in mortality after 1921, particularly after Independence. Though many parts of India have shown fertility decline in recent periods, the decline in fertility started much later only after 1971. The decline in fertility accelerated during 1981-1991 and gained momentum during 1991-2001.

A number of attempts have been made by individual researchers and organisations to project the population of India. Almost all the projections made earlier to 2001, proved to be under estimates. With the announcement of the results of 2001 census, there have been renewed attempts to project the population of India. Important among them are the following:

1. *Population Projections for India and States 2001-2026: Report of the Technical Group on Population Projections* constituted by the National commission on population, May 2006.
2. *World Population Prospects 2006*, by the United Nations Population Division, New York.
3. *Population Projections for Countries of the World* by US Bureau of Census.
4. *The Future Population of India—A Long-range Demographic View* by Population Reference Bureau and Population Foundation of India, August 2007.
5. *Indian Demographic Scenario, 2025* by P.N. Mari Bhat, Institute of Economic Growth, Delhi.

6. "India's population—the future" by Tim Dyson in *Twenty-first century India: Population, economy, human development and the environment*, published by Oxford University Press.

This chapter attempts to review the assumptions regarding fertility, mortality and migration made in these projections and project the population of India till the middle of 21st century using the latest information. Of the above projections, projections by the technical group (TG) at Population Foundation of India (PFI) and that by Tim Dyson, are more elaborate and include projections for states of India. The other three projections are only at national level. Mari Bhat's projections, present separate estimates for two broad categories, north and south India. Projections by TG, UN and PFI use smoothed age-sex distribution of the 2001 census. Other projections use 1991 census age distribution, suitably modified.

Implications of the projection for various regions, urbanisation, dependency ratio, young and old, labour force and old age populations are discussed. This chapter may be divided in to three sections. Section 1 discusses the fertility, mortality and migration assumptions used in these projections. Section 2 develops the assumptions for a new set of projections. Section 3 discusses the results.

Review of Previous Projections

UN Projections 2006

The 2006 revision of the *World Population Prospects* released by the United Nations Population Division includes eight projection variants and three AIDS scenarios. The eight variants are: low; medium; high; constant fertility; instant replacement fertility; constant mortality; no change (constant fertility and constant mortality); and zero migration. The *World Population Highlights* focuses on the medium variant of the 2006 revision.

The first five variants, namely, the low, medium, high, constant fertility and instant replacement fertility, differ among themselves exclusively in the assumptions made regarding the future path of fertility. The sixth variant, named "constant mortality", differs from the medium variant only with regard to the path followed by future mortality. The seventh variant, denominated "no change", has constant mortality and constant fertility and thus differs from the medium variant with respect to both fertility and mortality. The eight variant, denominated "zero migration", differs from the medium variant only with regard to the path followed by future international migration. Generally, variants differ from each other only over the period 2005-2050.

In addition, the 2006 revision includes three AIDS scenarios named no-AIDS, high-AIDS and AIDS-vaccine. These scenarios are variations of the medium variant and differ from each other and from the medium variant in terms of the path mortality follows, because they each incorporate different assumptions regarding the course of the HIV/AIDS epidemic.

Medium-Fertility Assumption

Total fertility in all countries is assumed to converge eventually toward a level of 1.85 children per woman. However, not all countries reach this level during the projection period, that is, by 2045-2050. Projection procedures differ slightly depending on whether a country had a total fertility above or below 1.85 children per woman in 2000-2005. The medium projection for India assumes that TFR will decline from 3.11 in 2000-2005 to 2.32 in 2015-2020, to 2.13 in 2020-2025 and reach 1.85 in 2045-2050. In the same period, the expectation of life at birth for both the sexes will improve from 62.9 years.

Mortality Assumption

Mortality is projected on the basis of models of change of life expectancy produced by the United Nations Population Division. These models produce smaller gains the higher the life expectancy already reached. The selection of a model for each country is based on recent trends in life expectancy by sex. For countries highly affected by the HIV/AIDS epidemic, the model incorporating a slow pace of mortality decline has generally been used so as to reflect a slowdown in the reduction of mortality risks not related to HIV/AIDS.

In particular, medium fertility assumptions and mortality assumptions for India are presented in Table 23.1. The population of India is expected to increase to 1448 and 1658 million respectively in 2025 and 2050. TFR of 2.1 is expected to be reached in 2025.

Table 23.1

Population Projections for India-UN 2006

	2000-2005	*2005-2010*	*2010-2015*	*2015-2020*	*2020-2025*	*2045-2050*
TFR	3.11	2.81	2.54	2.32	2.13	1.85
$E^{\circ}_{\circ}$	62.9	64.7	66.6	68.4	70	75.6
IMR	62.5	55	48.8	43.4	38.9	23
Under 5 mortality	89.9	78.6	68.6	60.1	53	29.7

Mari Bhat's Projection

Based on the provisional population totals, the population of India as on March 1, 2001 was estimated at 1010 million. The smoothed age-sex distribution of the 1991 census was brought forward. This is the starting point of the projection. Two projections were made. They differed in fertility assumptions. These consider two alternate scenarios of achieving population stabilisation. The first one was termed optimistic and the second one realistic. In the first projection, it was assumed that India would be able to achieve the demographic goals set in the National Population Policy 2000 (NPP, 2000). The NPP had set a target of achieving TFR of 2001 and Infant mortality rate of 30 by 2010. The IMR goal would implicitly lead to an expectation of life of 68 years for males and 71 years for females. After 2010, it has been assumed that the TFR would remain constant at 2.1 and life expectancy would increase further to 72 years for males and 76 years for females by 2025. In a more realistic scenario, it has been assumed that TFR would fall from 3.4 in 2000 to 2.8 in 2010 and reach very close to replacement level by 2025. Life expectancy would increase by only 4 years during the next 15 years. By 2025, it would reach 67 years for males and 71 years for females i.e., five years less than the optimistic assumption. The projected population would be 1380 million under the first assumption and 1403 million under the second.

Tim Dyson's Projection

Projections were made for each state of India and India as a whole. Sample Registration System (SRS) based on the smoothed age distribution of 1991 census were brought forward to 2001 census for provisional population totals. Linear regressions were fitted to the state-level SRS TFRs for 1986-1998 and these were used to extrapolate the future trend in total fertility until it reached the floor level of 1.8. With a few minor amendments, this approach produced reasonable TFRs, which declines for most states. However, for UP it produced an unusually slow pace of decline, implying that total fertility would be around 3.2 births during 2021-2026, while in all other states it would be about or below replacement. Yet if linear extrapolation produces a TFR for Bihar in 2021-2026 of 2.1, it seems improbable that the TFR in UP will be over one birth higher. Therefore, it was assumed here that the TFR in UP during 2021-2026 will be 10 per cent higher than that in Bihar (as applied during 1996-2001). This admittedly arbitrary adjustment implies that UP's total fertility rate will fall linearly to about 2.3 births in 2021-2026 which means that this key state is not left as the sole. The mortality assumptions are based on UN's medium model patterns of decline. After estimating the likely level of expectation of life at birth for the year 2011-2016, the expectations were reduced by an amount to account for deaths due to HIV/AIDS. This varied from state to state. To help gauge what impact these levels of infection may have on future levels of state-level mortality, UN data for all countries for which 'with' and 'without AIDS' estimates of life expectation have been made, and estimated levels of adult HIV prevalence in 1997 below 2 per cent, were examined. Specifically, the estimated levels of HIV prevalence in 1997 were compared with the estimated future reductions in national life expectations for the period 2011-2016.

This exercise suggested that, on an average, for every 1 per cent increase in adult HIV prevalence in 1997, the level of life expectation during 2010-2015 would be reduced by 2.15 years. The implied reductions in future state-level life expectation which arise when this indication is applied to the estimates of HIV prevalence in the major states in 1998 were that, in most cases the implied decreases were small, but in the southern states they were quite significant. It has been assumed here that in the period 2011-2016 and 2021-2026, state-level life expectations will rise at half the quinquennial rates assumed for the period between 1996-2001 and 2011-2016. At the national level, the expectation of life at birth projected for 2021-2026 was 67.6 and 70.7 years for males and females, respectively. No adjustment was done for migration. The projected population in 2026 was 1419 million. Two points need to be mentioned. Recent estimates have indicated that HIV prevalence in India is much lower that estimated earlier. Secondly, comparison of expectation of life at birth for the period released by SRS indicate that in most of the states and India, the slow path of the UN model mortality improvement would prevail than "medium" path.

Report of the Technical Group on Population Projections

A Technical Group was constituted by the National Commission on Population (NCP) in 2001 under the Chairmanship of the Registrar General, Government of India to prepare population projections for the period 2001-2025. The mandate given to the Group was, among other points, to review the methodology of population projections adopted in the past and prepare fresh projections up to the year 2025 with age, sex, urban-rural and states/UT break-ups for the five-year intervals. After the release of the age-sex distribution data of the population for India/states and migration data based on Census 2001, with the latter released only in November 2005, the projection was released in May 2006. Component method of projections were adopted for 21 states and India. For all other states and union territories, mathematical method of projection was adopted. The smoothed age data of

2001 census was the starting point of the projection. A Gompertz's curve was fitted to SRS TFR from 1981 to 2001.

$$\ln(-(\ln(TFR-L)/(U-L))) = \ln(-\ln a) + t.\ln b,$$

The fitted curve was used to extrapolate the TFR for years beyond 2001. In the above equation, U and L are the upper and lower limit of the curve and a and b are constants. In fitting the Gompertz's model, three types of upper asymptotes have been taken for the states depending upon whether the particular state is a higher or medium or low TFR state. The upper asymptote (U) has been taken as 6 for southern states and 7 for the northern states. For western and eastern states, U has been taken as 6.5. The lower limit was taken as 1.8. The weighted average of the projected state TFRs has been used for India as a whole. This implied that at national level, fertility would reach replacement level in the year 2021. Sex ratio at birth for the period 1998-2000 presented in the report of the Sample Registration System, 2000 published by the Office of the Registrar General, India, for the country and the major states have been used for the projection exercise. This varied from 103 in northern states and Chhattisgarh to 125-26 in Haryana and Punjab. Expectation of life at birth based on SRS life tables for the period 1999-2001 centred at year 2000 as base level estimates. For projecting the likely levels of expectation of life at birth (e0), working models developed by the UN have been adopted. To decide whether high, medium or low improvement should be assumed for each state, the e0s for the periods 1990-1994 and 1995-1999 obtained from SRS life table have been examined and pattern obtained through this for e0 has been assumed to continue in future for India and all the states. Based on the migration data of Census of India 2001, inter-state net migrants during decade 1991-2001 has been assumed to remain constant throughout the projection periods for all the states. The population of India is expected to increase from 1029 million to 1400 million during the period 2001-2026—an increase of 36 per cent in 25 years.

The Future Population of India—A Long Range Demographic View by Population Reference Bureau and Population Foundation of India, August 2007

This is the latest in the series of population projections for India. The projections have been made up to the year 2101. This makes use of the smoothed age-sex population of the 2001 census. Component method of projection was used for all the states and union territories. The state and union territory populations were projected under two scenarios labeled A and B. Scenario A assumed that states with a current TFR above "two children" would decrease to 2.1 and then remain constant. The other assumed that the TFR decline would continue until it reached 1.85 children per woman. A logistic curve was used to project the TFR. For states with very low TFRs such as Kerala, Tamil Nadu, Goa and Puducherry, TFR was assumed to remain constant throughout the projection period.

TFRs based on SRS were used for bigger states. For smaller states and union territories, TFRs were estimated by reverse projection of smoothed 2001 census populations and by matching SRS crude birth rates. Based on SRS age specific mortality rates, life tables were constructed for the period 1999-2003, centred at 2001. For smaller states and union territories, the life tables were selected from those of bigger states. It was assumed that expectation of life at birth would be 85 years for males and 90 years for females. Life expectancy was projected using logistic curve. Coale and Demeny's west model life tables were used to calculate the survival ratios. Net migration rates from 2001 census were made use of. It was assumed that net migration rates would increase slowly from the level assumed in 2001.Under the two scenarios prepared for this study, India's population would near the 1.8 billion mark by mid-century and may even exceed 2 billion by 2100 unless fertility rates decline more rapidly in India's largest and poorest states. A summary of the results is presented below.

Table 23.2

Projected Population of India: Two Scenarios

(in million)

	2001	*2026*	*2051*	*2101*
Scenario A	1029	1464	1825	2181
Scenario B	1029	1449	1751	1853

Population Projections 2001-2051—Assumptions

This section attempts to project the population of India till the middle of 21st century. Such a projection is important to throw light on the likely implications for food production, infrastructure development, environment and ecology. The projection has been undertaken using component method of projection. In this method, separate assumptions have been made regarding the three components of growth of population *viz.*, fertility, mortality and migration. The populations of India and 15 major states i.e., Andhra Pradesh, Assam, Bihar, Gujarat, Haryana, Karnataka, Kerala, Madhya Pradesh, Maharashtra, Orissa, Punjab, Rajasthan, Tamil Nadu, Uttar Pradesh and West Bengal, each with a population of over 10 million in 2001, have been projected separately. These 15 major states contribute about 96 per cent of India's population. The states of Jharkhand, Uttarakhand and Chhattisgarh have been carved out of Bihar, Uttar Pradesh and Madhya Pradesh respectively.

According to the 2001 census, Jharkhand, Chhattisgarh and Uttarakhand comprised respectively 24.5, 25.6 and 4.9 per cent of the former populations of Bihar, MP and UP respectively. Compared to the states to which they formerly belonged, the new states each experienced appreciably lower population growth rates during 1991-2001. In the absence of relevant time series and demographic data for these states, no projection has been attempted for these and other states and union territories.

Base Year Population

The projections are based on smoothed age-sex distribution of 2001 population. Table 23.3 shows the estimated population in 2001 of India and major states. This population together with the age data has been used as a base level for projection. Cohort component method of projection has been used to project the population. Under this method, separate assumptions have been made regarding the trends in fertility, mortality and interstate migration. While fertility and mortality assumptions are based on analysis of Sample Registration System data, interstate-inter-decadal migration rates have been derived from 2001 census.

Table 23.3

Base Population, Age Distribution and Interstate Migration

State	*Population 2001*	*% of All India*	*Population Age Distribution (%)*			*Interstate Net Migration 0-9 Years*	*Net Migration Rate (per 100)*
			0-14	*15-59*	*60+*		
Andhra Pradesh	76210007	7.4	32.1	60.8	7.2	-209,079	-0.274346
Assam	26655528	2.6	37.4	57.4	5.2	-154,654	-0.580195
Bihar+Jharkhand	109944338	10.7	41.5	53.1	5.4	1,844,138	1.6773
Gujarat	50671017	4.9	32.8	60.5	6.7	689,160	1.360067
Haryana	21144564	2.1	36.0	57.1	7	670,118	3.169221
Himachal Pradesh	6077900		31.1	60.2	8.8	50,723	0.834548
Karnataka	52850562	5.1	31.9	60.8	7.3	130,528	0.246976
Kerala	31841374	3.1	26.1	63.4	7.3	-164,657	-0.517117
Madhya Pradesh +Chhattisgarh	81181826	7.9	38.2	55.5	6.3	459,276	-0.5657375
Maharashtra	96878627	9.4	32.1	59.6	8.3	2,383,018	2.459797
Orissa	36804660	3.6	33.2	59.0	7.8	207,275	0.563176
Punjab	24358999	2.4	31.4	59.9	8.7	336,636	1.381978
Rajasthan	56507188	5.5	37.4	57.4	5.2	-261,684	-0.463099
Tamil Nadu	62405679	6.0	27	64	9	-378,160	-0.605970
Uttar Pradesh +Uttarakhand	174687270	17.0	40.8	53.1	6.1	2,665,761	1.5260
West Bengal	80176197	7.8	33.3	60.1	6.6	253,502	0.316181
All India	1,027,015	100.0	35.4	57.7	6.9	1.072	-

Projection of Fertility Trends

Projecting fertility and mortality trends can be subject to errors, particularly when the projections are long term. In India, most of states have shown consistent decline in fertility during the last 30 years. The quantum of decline varies from state to state. The fertility assumption for each state has been operationalised by assuming future changes in total fertility rate (TFR) and calculating age specific fertility rates that are consistent with the assumed TFR. For most of the states of India, the age pattern of fertility has been assumed to follow the customised pattern. The age specific fertility rates (ASFR) and the total fertility rates (TFR) for the years 2001-2005 have been made use of. TFRs have been projected using Gompertz's model. In the year 2021 when TFR for India attains a value of 2.1 (replacement level fertility), the ASFR pattern of Tamil Nadu for the year 2000 can be assumed to be operative for India. At the end point, two patterns have been assumed. For states like Punjab and Himachal Pradesh, it has been assumed that this pattern is consistent with early nuptiality and peak fertility in the age groups 20-24 and 25-29.

Annual estimates of TFR are available for most of the major states and India on a regular basis from SRS for over quarter century 1971-1996. For the states of Bihar and West Bengal, SRS based rates are available from 1981 onwards on a regular and uninterrupted basis. This data set was utilised to predict the future trends in fertility. A Gompertz's curve of the form

$$\frac{TFR-L}{U-L} = ((a)^{b})\ \hat{}\ t$$

Or alternatively,

$$Ln\ (-\ (Ln\ (TFR-L)/(U-L))) = Ln\ (-Ln.a) + t.Ln.b$$

Where U and L are the upper and lower limits of TFR respectively and a and b are constants and t is the year. The above curve was fitted using least square method. It was further assumed that once TFR reaches a level of 1.7, it would not decline further and would remain at the same level. The TFR value of 1.7 is the level achieved by Kerala and Tamil Nadu.

For all the states except Himachal Pradesh, Bihar and West Bengal, the observed values of TFRs from 1971-2005 were considered for projecting the future levels of TFR. As reliable estimates from SRS are available for Bihar and West Bengal from 1981 onwards, these were made use of. For Himachal Pradesh, similar data were available for the period 1991-2005. Separate estimates of fertility have been released for the states of Jharkhand, Chhattisgarh and Uttarakhand only recently and that too for the period 2000-2005. No separate projection of fertility has been undertaken for these states.

Table 23.4 shows the projected TFRs. When the projected TFR is less than 1.7, it has been assumed to remain at the same level, thereafter. It is seen from Table 23.4 that TFR of 2.1, corresponding to replacement level of fertility is likely to be achieved by 2006 in AP, Himachal Pradesh, Punjab and West Bengal. TFR in Kerala and Tamil Nadu had already reached that level by 1996. Haryana, Gujarat, Karnataka and Maharashtra are likely to achieve it before 2011. While Orissa and Assam is likely to attain the replacement level fertility during 2011-2016, 2016-2021 respectively. The remaining four states, MP, Rajasthan, Bihar and UP will continue to have fertility above replacement level even after 2025. While UP may according to present trends, attain net reproduction rate (NRR) of one by 2025 and MP by 2026, Rajasthan around 2030, Bihar is expected to achieve it even by 2033. Efforts to control fertility are, therefore, needed to be concentrated on these states.

Table 23.4

Projected TFR 2006-2051 using Gompertz Curve

Year	*India*	*AP*	*AS*	*BH*	*GJ*	*HR*	*HP*	*KA*	*KE*	*MP*	*MH*	*OR*	*PJ*	*RJ*	*TN*	*UP*	*WB*
1	*2*	*3*	*4*	*5*	*6*	*7*	*8*	*9*	*10*	*11*	*12*	*13*	*14*	*15*	*16*	*17*	*18*
2001	3.1	2.3	3.0	4.4	2.9	3.1	2.2	2.4	1.8	3.9	2.4	2.6	2.4	4.0	2.0	4.5	2.4
2006	2.8	2.0	2.7	3.9	2.3	2.3	2.0	2.2	1.7	3.4	2.2	2.4	2.1	3.6	1.8	3.8	2.0
2011	2.5	1.9	2.4	3.5	2.1	1.9	1.8	2.0	1.7	3.0	2.0	2.2	1.9	3.2	1.7	3.3	1.9
2016	2.3	1.8	2.2	3.1	1.9	1.8	1.8	1.9	1.7	2.7	1.9	2.0	1.8	2.9	1.7	2.7	1.8
2021	2.1	1.7	2.0	2.7	1.8	1.7	1.7	1.8	1.7	2.4	1.8	1.9	1.7	2.5	1.7	2.3	1.7
2026	1.9	1.7	1.9	2.4	1.7	1.7	1.7	1.8	1.7	2.1	1.8	1.8	1.7	2.3	1.7	2.0	1.7
2031	1.8	1.7	1.8	2.1	1.7	1.7	1.7	1.7	1.7	1.9	1.7	1.7	1.7	2.0	1.7	1.8	1.7
2036	1.8	1.7	1.8	1.9	1.7	1.7	1.7	1.7	1.7	1.8	1.7	1.7	1.7	1.9	1.7	1.7	1.7
2041	1.7	1.7	1.7	1.8	1.7	1.7	1.7	1.7	1.7	1.7	1.7	1.7	1.7	1.8	1.7	1.7	1.7
2046	1.7	1.7	1.7	1.7	1.7	1.7	1.7	1.7	1.7	1.7	1.7	1.7	1.7	1.7	1.7	1.7	1.7
2051	1.7	1.7	1.7	1.7	1.7	1.7	1.7	1.7	1.7	1.7	1.7	1.7	1.7	1.7	1.7	1.7	1.7

The second column of Table 23.4 shows the projected value of TFR for India used in the projection. The 15 states of India discussed above contribute 96 per cent of India's population. There are regional variations in fertility levels and pace of decline. It was, therefore, decided to estimate the fertility using the weighted average of the TFR of 15 states, the weights being female population in the reproductive age group 15-49.

Assumptions Regarding Mortality

For projecting mortality, three working models, fast life expectancy rise model, medium life expectancy rise model and slow life expectancy rise model have been developed by UN population division. Based on historical patterns, all these models assume that improvement becomes slower as life expectancy rises. It was further assumed that life expectancy may rise to a maximum of 80 years. In case the model indicated a life expectancy of more than 80 years, for subsequent period the e^o of 80 was assumed.

To decide whether high, medium or low improvement should be assumed for each state, the expectation of life at birth for the periods 1970-1975, 1976-1980, 1991-1995, 1996-2000 and 2001-2005, based on Sample Registration System based life tables were examined. The improvement pattern indicated by 1996-2001 and 2001-2005 SRS life tables were assumed to continue in future. In most of the states, except Himachal Pradesh, Rajasthan and West Bengal males, in all other states and India as a whole, the improvements followed a slow pattern indicating that the improvement in life expectancy has slowed down in the last 10 years for which data are available. In these states, the improvement for males was fast.

Table 23.5

United Nations Mortality Model Working Model for Mortality Improvement

Initial Mortality Level(e_0^0 in Years)	*Quinquennial Improvement in Expectation of Life at Birth According to Initial Levels of Mortality*					
	Fast		*Medium*		*Slow*	
	Males	*Females*	*Males*	*Females*	*Males*	*Females*
52.5-55.0	2.5	2.5	2.5	2.5	2	2
55.0-57.5	2.5	2.5	2.5	2.5	2	2
57.5-60.0	2.5	2.5	2.5	2.5	2	2
60.0-62.5	2.5	2.5	2.3	2.5	2	2
62.5-65.0	2.3	2.5	2	2.5	2	2
65.0-67.5	2	2.5	1.5	2.3	1.5	2
67.5-70.0	1.5	2.3	1.2	2	1	1.5
70.0-72.5	1.2	2	1	1.5	0.8	1.2
72.5-75.0	1	1.5	0.8	1.2	0.5	1
75.0-77.5	0.8	1.2	0.5	1	0.3	0.8
77.5-80.0	0.5	1	0.4	0.8	0.3	0.5
80.0-82.5	0.5	0.8	0.4	0.5	0.3	0.3
82.5-85.0		0.5		0.4		0.3
85.0-87.5		0.5		0.4		0.3

Assumptions Regarding Migration

Apart from fertility and mortality, migration is a component of population growth. Data from 2001 census reveals that the decadal net migration rate based on place of residence with duration of residence 0-9 years in place of enumeration was less than one per cent per decade for most of the states. Only in the states of Haryana, Gujarat, Punjab, Maharashtra, Uttar Pradesh and Bihar, the interstate inter-decadal migration contributed by more than one per cent. In the first four states, net in-migration contributed for more than one per cent of the 2001 population of the state. In the other two states, net out-migration resulted in lowering the population growth rate. It has been assumed that at least this quantum of migrants would continue during the entire projection period. The age distribution of the net migrants was assumed to be same as reported in 2001 census.

For other states, the migration rates were found to be very low. Accordingly, no separate assumption regarding migration was made for these states.

The projections were made using DemProj software developed by Futures Group. The above projections by component method has been attempted for India and 15 major states. In the absence of fertility, mortality and migration data, no projections has been attempted for the remaining states and union territories.

Projection of Urban Population

For projecting the urban population, the Urban-Rural Growth Differential (URGD) method as given in Manual–VIII of UN has been adopted. This method is based on the fact that the urban-rural growth differentials follow a logistic pattern. The URGD for the period 1991-2001 has been assumed to be same in future as well up to 2051. In case of Tamil Nadu, the urban proportion has risen sharply from 34.2 per cent in 1991 to 44 per cent in 2001. If the same URGD is assumed, the projected urban proportion is likely to be over 68 per cent by 2051 which appears unlikely. In view of this, the URGD for the period 1971-2001 has been adopted for this state.

The simulation exercise based on the assumptions leads to following broad conclusions:

1) India's population is poised to increase by 47 per cent during the period 2001-2051 from 1.028 billion in 2001 to 1.51 billion, an increase of 480 million in 2051 and stabilise thereafter. Population growth rate will be zero. Demographic transition started around 1921,

with falling mortality and increasing life expectancy. While mortality is still falling, fertility started falling around 1975. This process of falling fertility is likely to be complete in all the states of India by 2030.

2) Due to falling fertility, the crude birth rate is likely to fall from 25 per thousand at the beginning to about 11 in 2051. Crude death rate which was around 9 in 2001 is likely to decline to 7.9 till 2021 and then increase to about 10.8 in 2051. This increase is due to changing age structure of the population, particularly the increasing number of old age population in later years.

3) The infant mortality rate (IMR) is likely to decline to 23 in 2051. In Himachal Pradesh, Kerala, Maharashtra and Tamil Nadu, the IMR levels are likely to be below 20. In Uttar Pradesh and Rajasthan, it is like to be above 30. In all other states, it is likely to range between 20 and 30.

4) Of the projected increase, around 350 million or (73 per cent of the increase) is likely during the first quarter of the century, 2001-2026. During 2026-2051, the increase is likely to be only 130 million. Four states of Bihar, Madhya Pradesh, Rajasthan and Uttar Pradesh together contribute 290 million or 62 per cent of the projected increase.

5) The lowest per cent increase is likely to be in Tamil Nadu (10.7 per cent) and highest in Rajasthan (84 per cent). Population of Uttar Pradesh is also likely to increase by 73.0 per cent. Most of the growth is likely during 2001-2026. There would be very little population growth during 2026-2051 (around 5 per cent) in the states of Andhra Pradesh, Karnataka, Kerala, Orissa, Tamil Nadu and West Bengal. In Gujarat, Haryana, Maharashtra and Punjab, the natural increase is likely to reach zero. Only migration will propel the population growth. In Kerala, the population is likely to decrease after 2036. In states like Andhra Pradesh, Karnataka and Tamil Nadu, the population is likely to decline during 2041-2046. In Himachal Pradesh, Orissa, Punjab and West Bengal, it is likely to decline during 2046-2051. Only in five states, Assam, Bihar, Madhya Pradesh, Rajasthan and UP, the population is likely to increase even during 2046-2051. The states of Maharashtra, Punjab and Haryana would continue to show slight positive growth rate because of in-migration.

6) One consequence of the decline in fertility is that the child population of India, i.e., population in the age group 0-14, will decline from 365 million in 2001 to 258 million in 2051. The decline start from 2001

and continue throughout the period. The population of children aged 0-4, will decline steadily from 121 million in 2001 to 82 million in 2051.

7) Another important consequence will be that the population in school going age group 5-14, will increase to 243 million in 2001 and will decline steadily thereafter to 120 million in 2051. As a consequence of this, young age dependency ratio, defined as the percentage of population aged 0-14 to population in the working age group 15-64, will decline from 69 per cent in 2001 to 35 per cent in 2051.

8) The most significant increase will be noticed in the working age group 15-64. The population will double from 620 million in 2001 to 1046.5 million in 2051. Most of them will be in labour market. Providing employment to such a huge population will be the biggest challenge India will face in the first half of the 21st century. Very significant increase will also take place in the old age population i.e., population in age group 65 and over. Their number will increase 4.6 times from 45 million (or 4.37 per cent of the population) to 205 million (or 1.59 per cent of the population). Providing for old age security through various legal measures and providing medical and health facilities for old people will be another significant area of action.

24

India's Population Growth, Issues and the 'Demographic Dividend'

K. NARAYANAN UNNI

Introduction

The population of India has been continuously growing throughout the 20th century except for a slight decline during the decade 1911-1921. The growth spurred by decline in mortality has resulted in the country having a young population as it entered the 21st century. Though fertility has also been declining, the country is still decades away from reaching 'zero' population growth. The demographic changes have not been uniform across the country. States like Kerala and Goa achieved reduction in fertility and mortality comparatively early and were followed by Punjab, Tamil Nadu, etc. On the other hand, larger states like Uttar Pradesh, Bihar, Rajasthan and Madhya Pradesh are way behind in demographic transition. This diversity has resulted in significant changes in the geographic distribution of population that is expected to grow in the near future. These changes have significant socio-cultural and economic implications.

The age structure of the population has been changing over the years and is poised for much faster changes. The population would become 'older' and the number of 'aged' will be increasing fast. The population in the working age group would be seeing a period of rapid growth in the immediate future. On the other hand, the number of births is likely to remain at the same level for some more time due to the demographic momentum of the past. So the country need to invest substantially in human resource development, health systems, old age care and generate employment at a much larger scale than in the past. This chapter focuses attention on some of these important issues. The population projections for the country that indicates the likely magnitude of these problems has been used as the main source of information for the analysis.

The views directly or indirectly expressed in the article are those of the author and not necessarily that of National Sample Survey Organisation or Government of India.

There has been several references in the popular media and elsewhere of the 'young' population of India being an 'asset' as the population in advanced countries are ageing. However, there are other countries too with population as young or even younger. They would also be in a position to provide the same services that we are able to provide. While our younger population may be an 'asset' in the short term, how far it would hold into the future is a difficult question to answer. However, considering it an 'asset' in the short term is also not as simple as it looks and is fraught with issues relating to converting it into a productive asset. The later part of this chapter would look at this issue, keeping the international scenario in view.

Population Projections for India

Population of India has grown from about 238 million at the start of the 20th century to 1027 million in 2001 when the last census was taken. The 'Technical Group on Population Projections' appointed by the National Population Commission, has projected that it will reach about 1400 million by 2026. According to the long-term population projections made by United Nations, India's population is expected to grow to about 1658 million in 2050. It is expected to overtake China as the most populated country in the world by about 2025 as per the assessment made by United Nations in *World Population Prospects 2006*. The first half of the 21st century will see the population increasing by almost 50 per cent in the country. The net addition of 514 million to the population during 2000-2050 is as much as the total population of 548 million at 1971 census.

It is anticipated that the population may reach a maximum of about 1557 million by about 2065 and may eventually stabilise in the range of 1300-1400 million. In the following discussions, the projections made by United Nations have been used wherever the figures beyond 2026 are required or where the projections by the Technical group are not available. Otherwise the projections made by the Technical group have been used as it also provides the state-wise break-up.

Table 24.1 indicates the growth prospects of the population of India, China, Africa and the rest of the world over the 21st century.

From about 16.75 per cent in 2000, the share of India's population in the world is expected to be about 17.2 per cent by 2050 and decline thereafter to about 16 per cent by the end of the century. The decline in the share is more due to the higher growth of population in Africa in the second half of 21st century, resulting in the proportion of population of Africa going up from 13.1 per cent in 2000 to 20.2 per cent in 2050 and reaching almost a quarter of the world's population by 2100. Figure 24.1 shows the changing share of India's population in the world during 1900-2100.

Table 24.1

Population Projections 2000-2100: India, China and Selected Regions of the World (millions)

Year	*India*	*China*	*Rest of Asia*	*Africa*	*Europe*	*Rest of the World*	*World Total*
2000	1,046	1,270	1,389	821	729	870	6,124
2025	1,447	1,446	1,886	1,394	715	1,122	8,011
2050	1,658	1,409	2,199	1,998	664	1,263	9,191
2100	1,458	1,182	2,379	2,254	538	1,253	9,064

Note: Totals may not tally due to rounding.

Sources: United Nations - *World Population Prospects, 2006* assessment for the data for 2000-2050. United Nations - *World Population to 2300,* for the data for 2100.

Figure 24.1

Changing Proportion of India's Population in the World, 1900-2100

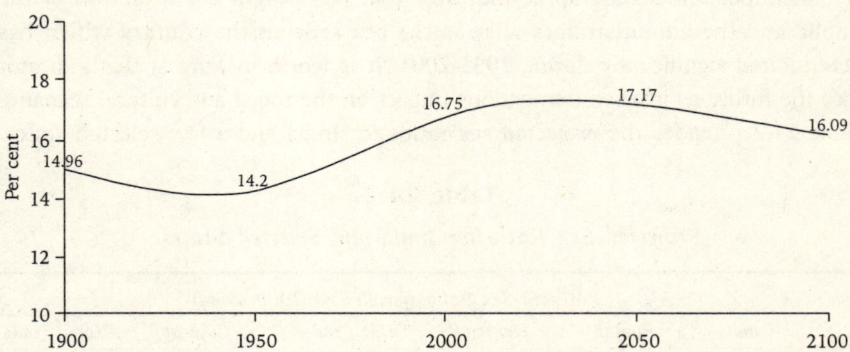

It is expected that the birth and death rates in India would continue to fall in the first quarter of the 21st century. Death rate may start rising in the second half of the 21st century to result in a negative growth rate for some time. As with any projections, while one can expect these events to happen, the precise time point of the occurrence of these events would depend on a variety of factors. The projections indicate that population density in India would go above 500 per sq. km which would be significantly higher than that of most of the populous countries of the world. Among the larger countries, Bangladesh

(1997), Uganda (837), Pakistan (530) and Republic of Korea (508) are the only ones expecting to have population density of over 500 by 2100.

Fertility rates are likely to fall below replacement level by 2021-2025. Birth rate is expected to be under 20 by 2011-2015 and to about 16 by 2021-2025, still significantly above that of advanced countries. However, this high birth rate is the consequence of the demographic momentum resulting from the large population in the reproductive age group. The anticipated fall in infant mortality rate (IMR) is much slower than targeted. Though the National Population Policy 2000 aims at reducing IMR to 30 per 1000 live births by 2010, the Technical group on population projections does not expect it happening even by 2021. According to the committee's report, the IMR is likely to be about 40 even in 2021-2025. As per the latest data from Sample Registration System, the IMR was 57 in 2006. If the health programmes are able to bring down the IMR to levels lower than those anticipated in the projections, then the death rates will be lower and population may be slightly higher than that projected by the Technical group. However, this is not going to significantly alter the conclusions of the present analysis.

Sex Ratio

An important demographic indicator that has caught the attention of the public and the administrators alike is the sex ratio in the country which has deteriorated significantly during 1991-2001. It is worth looking at this indicator into the future as it has a tremendous impact on the social and cultural scenario. Table 24.2 provides the projected sex ratios for India and a few selected states.

Table 24.2

Projected Sex Ratio for India and Selected States

Year	*Projected Sex Ratio (females per 1000 males)*					
	India	*Punjab*	*Haryana*	*Uttar Pradesh*	*Gujarat*	*Tamil Nadu*
2001	933	876	861	898	920	987
2006	932	867	855	898	912	990
2011	932	859	850	898	904	992
2016	931	852	845	898	896	995
2021	930	845	842	899	889	997
2026	930	840	839	901	882	1000

Source: Report of the Technical Group on Population Projections.

The table shows that though there may be only a slight fall in the sex ratio at national level, there is considerable divergence in the behaviour of states. While in some states, like Punjab, Haryana and Gujarat, the sex ratio is likely to become more adverse to females; in states like Tamil Nadu, the situation may improve. It is heartening to note that in Uttar Pradesh, the largest state in the country, it is likely to be stable in terms of the sex ratio. Deterioration of the sex ratio of children had caused much debate and sparked action in the recent past. However, the prospects of this indicator is not being discussed here in as its estimates are heavily dependent on the assumption used in making the projections—that of the sex ratio at birth observed in 1998-2000 continuing unchanged in the next 25 years.

Projections for the States of India

Since the states in the country are at various levels of demographic change and many of them are large enough to be considered as independent units in any analysis, it is useful to analyse the sub-national projections. Table 24.3 provides the projected population of the country and that of the major states as projected by the Technical group on population projections. The average annual growth rates for the periods 2001-2006 and 2021-2026 and the contribution of the states to the total population of the country in 2001 and 2026 are also presented.

All states, except Delhi, are expected to experience significant decline in growth rates over the next two decades. Even then, the population would be growing at about 1 per cent or more per annum even during 2021-2026 in the states of Delhi (2.7%), Uttar Pradesh (1.2%), Haryana (1.1%), Madhya Pradesh (1.1%), Rajasthan (1%) and Maharashtra (1.0%). While the higher growth rate in Delhi and Maharashtra can be attributed to migration to these states, those in other states resulting from the demographic momentum will take more time to slow down. Of the anticipated increase of 371.2 million in the population of India during the next 25 years, about 82 million (22%) would be contributed by Uttar Pradesh alone, followed by Maharashtra (36.4 million, 9.8%) and Bihar (30.8 million, 8.3%).

The share of various states in the population of the country would also change significantly in the future. In 2026, Uttar Pradesh would have 17.8 per cent of India's population as against 16.2 per cent in 2001. The share of Delhi (2% in 2026), Rajasthan (5.8%) and Madhya Pradesh (6.3%) would also be higher by more than 0.25 percentage points compared to 2001. On the other hand, Tamil Nadu (0.9 per cent lower in 2026), Andhra Pradesh (0.7%), West Bengal (0.6%), Kerala (0.4%), Karnataka (0.4%) and Orissa (0.3%) would be having significantly lower share of population of the country. It is worth noting that the four out of the first six states in terms of the quantum of decline in their share of population are in the southern region.

Table 24.3

Population of Major States of India 2001, Projections for 2011 and 2026, Growth Rates for 2001-06 and 2021-2026 and Share of the States in India's Population in 2001, 2026

State	Population (million)			Average Annual Growth Rate		Per cent Contribution to Population of India	
	2001 (census)	Projected					
		2011	2026	2001-06	2021-26	2001	2026
INDIA	1,028.6	1,192.5	1399.8	1.6	0.9	100.0	100.0
1. Andhra Pradesh	76.2	84.7	94.1	1.2	0.5	7.4	6.7
2. Assam	26.7	30.6	35.6	1.5	0.8	2.6	2.5
3. Bihar	83.0	97.7	113.8	1.8	0.8	8.1	8.1
4. Chhattisgarh	20.8	24.3	28.6	1.6	0.9	2.0	2.0
5. Delhi	13.9	18.5	28.0	2.9	2.7	1.3	2.0
6. Gujarat	50.7	59.0	69.3	1.6	0.9	4.9	4.9
7. Haryana	21.1	25.4	31.1	2.0	1.1	2.1	2.2
8. Jammu & Kashmir	10.1	11.7	13.4	1.5	0.7	1.0	1.0
9. Jharkhand	26.9	31.5	37.4	1.7	0.9	2.6	2.7
10. Karnataka	52.9	59.4	66.9	1.3	0.6	5.1	4.8
11. Kerala	31.8	34.6	37.3	0.9	0.4	3.1	2.7
12. Madhya Pradesh	60.3	72.2	87.7	1.9	1.1	5.9	6.3
13. Maharashtra	96.9	112.7	133.3	1.6	1.0	9.4	9.5
14. Orissa	36.8	40.8	45.3	1.1	0.6	3.6	3.2
15. Punjab	24.4	27.7	31.3	1.4	0.7	2.4	2.2
16. Rajasthan	56.5	67.8	81.5	1.9	1.0	5.5	5.8
17. Tamil Nadu	62.4	67.4	71.9	0.9	0.3	6.1	5.1
18. Uttar Pradesh	166.2	200.8	248.8	2.0	1.2	16.2	17.8
19. Uttarakhand	8.5	9.9	11.7	1.6	0.9	0.8	0.8
20. West Bengal	80.2	89.5	100.5	1.2	0.6	7.8	7.2

Source: *Report of the Technical Group on Population Projections*, Government of India for population figures and the growth rates. The remaining are author's calculations.

Age Distribution

Age structure of India's population would be undergoing significant changes in the future. The age distribution varies across the states significantly and this diversity would continue for some more time. The changes in the population size in various age groups over the years will have significant impact on education, employment, etc. Table 24.4 presents the population in the broad age groups in 2001 and 2026 for selected states along with the per cent change during 2021-2026.

The child population (ages 0-14 years) that constituted more than a third of the total population in 2001 would decline to about 29 per cent in 2011 and to about 25 per cent in 2021. According to these projections, even in absolute terms the child population would start declining by 2010. The UN has called the age structure having less than a third of the population below 15 years with the proportion of those above 65 years being below 15 per cent as the demographic window and both the UN projections as well as the official projections for India agree that by about 2010, India would be entering this phase of demographic change.

During 2001-2026, the population in the age group 0-14 years would be declining in all larger states barring Uttar Pradesh and at national level. While Andhra Pradesh (22.1%), Orissa (22.1%) and West Bengal (23.1%) expect declines above 20 per cent, Madhya Pradesh and Maharashtra are the only large states where the decline will be below 10 per cent. A look at the data by age groups shows that in all states other than Uttar Pradesh and Delhi, the population in the age groups 0-4 and 5-9 years would decline during 2001-2026. Even in Uttar Pradesh, the population in these age groups would peak by about 2016 and and start declining thereafter. In Delhi, where the population growth would continue to be on account of migration, the population in the age group 0-4 years is likely to continue increasing till 2026. These changes would mean that the infrastructure requirement for infant and child care as well as primary education in quantitative terms has almost reached the peak in most states. However, considering the regional disparities that exist in larger states, there may be areas within many states where capacity increase may still be necessary. Investments may also be necessary in some cases to cater to population in far-flung areas. However, it is definite that the focus has to shift to quality improvement and in reaching the educational and health services for children to inaccessible areas in a sustained manner.

The most important aspect of the age structure is the growing numbers in the age group 15-59 years. From about 593 million in 2001, it is projected to increase to 747 million in 2011 and 859 million in 2021 with annual growth rates of 2.3 per cent and 1.4 per cent per annum in the two decades. It may touch 900 million by 2026. In proportionate terms, the population in this age group is expected to rise from 57.7 per cent in 2001 to 62.6 per cent in 2011 and to 64.2 per cent in 2021 and may remain at the same level in 2026. This growth will have tremendous impact on the higher education and employment scenarios. Both educational facilities and employment generation has to grow much faster than the population growth rate. The break-up of this age group into 15-29 and 30-59 brings out several interesting features of the expected changes at state level.

Table 24.4

Population in Broad Age-Groups in 2001 and 2026 and per cent Change during 2001-2026, India and Selected States

State	0-14			15-29			30-59			60+		
	2001	2026	change*	2001	2026	Change*	2001	2026	Change*	2001	2026	Change*
INDIA	364.6	327.0	-10.3	278.0	340.0	22.3	315.3	559.7	77.5	70.7	173.2	145.0
1. Andhra Pd.	24.4	19.0	-22.1	21.3	20.7	-3.0	25.0	41.0	63.8	5.5	13.4	145.7
2. Bihar	34.9	28.3	-18.9	20.3	30.6	50.6	23.2	42.4	82.8	4.5	12.5	175.5
3. Gujarat	16.6	14.5	-12.7	14.3	16.3	14.0	16.3	28.9	77.4	3.4	9.5	179.2
4. Haryana	7.6	6.7	-11.8	6.0	7.8	29.6	6.0	13.0	115.4	1.5	3.6	141.6
5. Karnataka	16.9	13.7	-18.8	14.9	14.9	0.2	17.3	28.7	65.9	3.8	9.7	152.3
6. Kerala	8.3	7.0	-15.8	8.7	7.6	-12.5	11.5	15.9	38.1	3.4	6.8	102.4
7. Madhya Pd.	23.3	22.6	-2.9	16.0	23.0	43.6	17.3	33.0	91.0	3.8	9.1	142.3
8. Maharashtra	31.1	28.4	-8.7	26.9	31.8	18.1	30.8	55.9	81.3	8.0	17.3	115.6
9. Orissa	12.2	9.5	-22.1	9.9	10.4	4.3	11.8	19.2	62.7	2.9	6.3	119.5
10. Punjab	7.6	6.1	-20.1	6.9	7.1	2.4	7.7	13.6	76.8	2.1	4.6	115.3
11. Rajasthan	22.7	20.0	-11.8	14.9	21.5	44.7	15.6	31.2	99.8	3.4	8.8	160.8
12. Tamil Nadu	16.8	13.4	-20.1	17.5	14.7	-16.3	22.4	31.5	40.4	5.6	12.3	117.9
13. Uttar Pradesh	68.2	71.8	5.2	42.7	65.7	53.9	45.2	86.9	92.1	10.1	24.5	142.7
14. West Bengal	26.7	20.5	-23.1	22.1	22.0	-0.2	26.1	43.8	67.5	5.3	14.2	168.0

Note: * change is expressed as per cent change from 2001 figure.

Kerala (12.5%) and Tamil Nadu (16.3%) are the only major states where population in the age group 15-29 years is expected to decline by more than 10 per cent during 2001-2026. In Andhra Pradesh (3.0%), Karnataka (0.2%), Orissa (4.3%), Punjab (2.4%) and West Bengal (-0.2%), the change is below 5 per cent. In all other states, the population in this age group is expected to increase significantly with Uttar Pradesh (53.9%) at the top of the list followed by Bihar (50.6%), Rajasthan (44.7%) and Madhya Pradesh (43.6%). As the children complete their education and start looking for employment, while in this age group, the changes noted above are very important. The larger states will have a significantly large number of people seeking avenues for secondary and post-secondary education as well as employment.

School enrolment ratios have been improving over the years while dropout rates are falling. Thus, there would be more children aspiring to have secondary and higher education even without the increasing population. The increasing population would add to the demand for higher education. Thus, significant capacity increase of the order of 25 per cent or more for secondary and higher levels of education would be required in the immediate future in several large states. Though interstate mobility for higher education is growing, the states showing a decline in population in this age group would not be in a position to fill in the gap as there is an increase of about 22 per cent in the population in this age group at the national level.

Employment generation would be another important issue in the coming years. As larger number of educated persons would start searching for jobs, there would be need for creating employment opportunities commensurate with the educational levels. At the national level, the population in the age group 25-29 would be almost 40 per cent higher in 2026. In the age group 30-59, the population would go up from 315 million to about 560 million, i.e., by about 77 per cent during 2001-2026. As per the latest estimates, the labour force participation rate (LFPR) for the population aged 30-59 is about 74 per cent.[1] About 175 million persons have to be additionally provided employment by 2026 to retain the current level of LFPR. This excludes the requirement for those aged 25-29 years. This estimate also does not take into account the fact that more women are likely to take up employment in the future instead of remaining homemakers. It is also worth noting here that the population in this age group would be increasing in all states. Even in Kerala and Tamil Nadu where the increase is lowest, it is expected to be higher by about 40 per cent in 2026. This means that interstate migration may not be of help in reducing unemployment in any state.

---

1. An approximate estimate arrived at using the projected population and age specific work labour force participation rates from NSSO 61st round.

Elderly population is set to increase rapidly in the years to come. From about 71 million in 2001, the population aged 60 years and above is likely to increase to 173 million in 2026, an increase of 145 per cent in 25 years. Kerala, with a high proportion of population in this age group, has the lowest increase and even there, the population of aged is likely to double during this period. Since more people in this age group are likely to continue to be economically active, it will further add to the demand for employment. The population above 80 years, the age group that would need specialised care, was about 3.2 million in 2001 and is expected to be in the range of 20 million by 2025.

The effect of changes in these age structure on the dependency ratios shows interesting patterns. Table 24.5 provides the dependency ratio defined as the number of persons of age below 15 or above 59 per 1000 persons in the age group 15-59 years. Considering the fact that more people would continue to be economically active beyond the age of 60 years, it may be appropriate to take the age of 65 years for defining 'elderly'. However, the definition used in the official projections has been retained to avoid confusion and comparison over time.

In 2001, Tamil Nadu had the lowest dependency ratio followed by Kerala. Among these two states, Kerala had more of elderly dependants (28.9%) compared to Tamil Nadu (25.1%). By 2026, the dependency ratio may fall slightly in case of Tamil Nadu, while it will significantly increase in Kerala. In 2001, Bihar (907) and Uttar Pradesh (891) had the highest dependency ratios. In 2026, though at a much lower level, Uttar Pradesh would continue to occupy the top position while on its downward movement. On the other hand, Kerala, on its upward movement due to increasing elderly population, occupy the second position.

The contribution of elderly population to the dependency ratio would change significantly over the years. At national level their contribution would increase from about 16.2 per cent to 34.5 per cent. While Kerala (28.9%), Tamil Nadu (25.1%) and Punjab (21.7%) were the only states in 2001 where elderly people formed more than 20 per cent of the dependants, by 2026 every state would cross this level and Uttar Pradesh at the lowest end will have 25 per cent of the dependants being elderly. Kerala, Tamil Nadu and Punjab would continue to be at the top levels. Almost half of the dependants in Kerala would be 'elderly', closely followed by Tamil Nadu (47.7%). More than 40 per cent of the dependants would be 'elderly' in Andhra Pradesh, Karnataka and West Bengal also.

Table 24.5

Dependency Ratios and Percentage of Elderly among Dependants, 2001-2026

State	2001			2026			% of Elderly (60+)	
	Young	Old	Total	Young	Old	Total	2001	2026
INDIA	614	119	734	363	192	556	16.2	34.5
1. Andhra Pradesh	528	118	645	309	217	526	18.3	41.3
2. Assam	653	91	744	370	170	540	12.2	31.5
3. Bihar	803	104	907	388	171	559	11.5	30.6
4. Chhattisgarh	654	114	768	393	182	575	14.8	31.7
5. Gujarat	543	111	654	321	209	530	17.0	39.4
6. Haryana	631	122	752	322	171	493	16.2	34.7
7. Jammu & Kashmir	618	107	724	331	188	519	14.8	36.2
8. Jharkhand	721	90	811	382	175	558	11.1	31.4
9. Karnataka	524	119	644	314	222	536	18.5	41.4
10. Kerala	412	167	578	298	290	588	28.9	49.3
11. Madhya Pradesh	701	113	813	404	163	567	13.9	28.7
12. Maharashtra	539	139	678	324	197	521	20.5	37.8
13. Orissa	563	131	694	323	212	535	18.9	39.6
14. Punjab	524	145	669	295	221	516	21.7	42.8
15. Rajasthan	744	111	855	379	168	547	13.0	30.7
16. Tamil Nadu	421	141	562	291	266	558	25.1	47.7
17. Uttar Pradesh	776	115	891	470	160	630	12.9	25.4
18. Uttarakhand	647	129	776	380	183	563	16.6	32.5
19. West Bengal	554	110	664	312	216	528	16.6	40.9

The above discussion indicates that the elderly population would be increasing across the country and points to the need for developing a dependable old age care system in the near future. The task of providing for old age care in across of the country, including even the remote rural areas, appears ominous.

Urban Population

According to the official projections, by 2026, a third of India's population will be living in urban areas, up from 27.9 per cent in 2001. This means that about 472 million people would be living in urban areas by 2026 compared to 291 million in 2001, showing an increase of 63 per cent over 25 years at an annual growth rate of 1.95 per cent. If the present climate for industrialisation continues and more industries are set up, it is likely that the level of urbanisation may be higher. United Nations has projected that by 2025, about 520 million people in India would be living in urban areas.

Long-term projections for individual cities are hazardous to attempt and are not available. UN projections indicate that by 2015, Mumbai (21.9 million), Delhi (18.6 million) and Kolkata (17.0 million) would be among the world's eight largest urban agglomerations. It is not possible to guess as to how many new towns would emerge in the country. However, going by the past experience, it can be easily said that the growth of existing towns and cities, including natural growth, migration and expansion of these by merger of areas in the periphery, is going to fuel the urban growth. By 2015, cities with population above 500,000 would account for more than half of the urban population (about 16 per cent of the total population) of the country. Thus, the available urban infrastructure would be undergoing tremendous pressure in the near future. Due to high rentals and transportation problems in the central areas, many cities are expanding outwards. Providing for water, sanitation, waste disposal/recycling, transportation, etc., would require tremendous investment in almost all towns and cities.

Almost a quarter of the urban population is living in slum areas according to the 2001 census results. Their proportion is as high as 54 per cent in Mumbai and 32 per cent in Kolkata. There are towns in the country where more than 90 per cent of the population were living in slum areas in 2001. Population living in slum areas contribute substantially to the services sector. However, it is inhuman to allow the conditions in the slums to continue as such. The number of slum dwellers is likely to increase in absolute terms as more migration takes place from rural areas in search of work.

Food Supply

One of the first issues that come to mind when looking at the growing population is that of food supply. Ramesh Chand (2007) has estimated that by 2020-21, the country would require about 261.5 million tonnes of cereals, 19.1 million tonnes of pulses for domestic consumption. As against this, the country produced 192.8 million tonnes of cereals and 14.2 million tonnes of pulses in 2004-05. It is important to note that an annual growth rate of about 1.86 per cent during the Eleventh Plan and 2 per cent beyond would be required to ensure self-sufficiency. This growth rate appears high when compared with the actual growth rate of only 0.48 per cent during 1997-98 to 2006-07. In case we are unable to increase the growth rate to the desired level, we may end up being dependent on imports of food grains.

The Young Population—An Asset or a Liability?

As the population in the developing countries are ageing and their population in the working age group declines, there would be demand for labour. Countries like India having a relatively younger population would be in a position to fill up the void by providing workers, which would be beneficial to both countries (the so called 'demographic dividend'). However, how far India can benefit from this would depend on several factors. The first question would be whether the market for such labour is sufficiently large so as to have a significant impact on the employment situation in the country. India is not the only 'young' country and neither is the population of India the only one being considered an asset. For example, Kamuzora (2005), has argued that African population would be a critical global asset for development. The quality of workers that we can provide to the developed countries is another important factor to be considered.

The population of India appears young when compared to that of the developed countries. The median age of the population is estimated to be 22.5 years in 2000 and it is expected to increase to about 31.4 years by 2026 according to the Technical group's projections. However, the UN projections estimate the median age to be 23.4 years in 2000 and expects it to become 37.9 by 2025. The difference in the median age at the initial years between the two sources may be due to the differences in the age distributions considered for making projections. Population of the 15 most populous countries (as per the population in 2000), their median age and dependency ratios (number of persons aged below 15 or above 65 per 100 persons in the age group 15-64) in 2000 and 2025 are given in Table 24.6.

It may be seen that the median age of the population is in the range of 20-24 years in India (23.4), Indonesia (24.6), Bangladesh (20.0), Mexico (22.9), Vietnam (23.1), the Philippines (20.9) and Turkey (24.2), while Pakistan (18.8) and Nigeria (17.3) have still lower median age. Thus, out of the 15 most populous countries of the world, 9 have median age below 25. The countries with median age above 35 years are Japan (41.3), Germany (39.9), Russian Federation (36.8) and USA (35.2). Only countries like Japan, Germany and to some extent Russian Federation may be having difficulty of finding enough workers now. At present, it does not appear that there would be sufficient demand for younger workers from India as a result of ageing in developed countries. By 2025, Nigeria would be the only one among the larger countries with mean age below 25 years. Bangladesh, India and Pakistan would have mean ages in the range 27-30 years. Declining dependency ratio would imply that there would be more people in the employable ages in the

Table 24.6

Population and Median Age—Selected Countries, 2000 and 2025

Country	Population (millions)		Median Age		Dependency Ratio	
	2000	2025	2000	2025	2000	2025
1. China	1,297.0	1,445.8	30.0	39.4	47	46
2. India	1,046.2	1,447.5	23.4	29.9	65	48
3. United States of America	284.8	354.9	35.2	38.3	51	58
4. Indonesia	211.7	271.2	24.6	33.8	54	43
5. Brazil	174.1	228.8	25.4	33.5	54	49
6. Russian Federation	147.4	128.2	36.8	41.9	44	48
7. Pakistan	144.3	224.9	18.8	26.8	83	55
8. Japan	127.0	121.6	41.3	50.7	47	68
9. Bangladesh	139.4	206.0	20.0	27.8	68	50
10. Nigeria	124.7	210.1	17.3	21.1	93	68
11. Mexico	99.7	124.7	22.9	33.5	62	47
12. Germany	82.3	80.3	39.9	47.8	47	60
13. Vietnam	79.1	106.4	23.1	33.5	64	44
14. Philippines	76.2	115.9	20.9	27.2	70	52
15. Turkey	68.2	89.6	24.2	33.7	55	44

Source: United Nations: *World Population Prospects 2006* database (website).

future. It is seen that apart from India, the dependency ratio will significantly decline in Indonesia, Pakistan, Bangladesh, Nigeria, Mexico, Vietnam and the Philippines. This means that by 2025, there would be enough competing countries in the employment market. Considering the size of India's population in the employable age group (which will be largest in the world by 2025), it does not appear feasible that the overseas employment opportunities would absorb sufficiently large numbers so as to have a significant impact on the unemployment situation in the next 10-15 years. Beyond that period, the competition may become more intense as other developing countries from Asia and Africa would also be trying to get a share of the employment opportunities.

The educational level of the persons in the younger age groups who are already seeking employment or would soon start seeking jobs would be an important factor in determining the ability of the country in taking advantage of the labour scarcity in the world. Table 24.7 presents the distribution of population in selected age groups by educational level as per the 2001 census.

Table 24.7

Distribution of Population by Educational Level in Selected Age-Groups, 2001

Educational Level	Population (million)			Per cent Distribution		
	15-19	20-24	25-29	15-19	20-24	25-29
Total	100.2	89.8	83.4	100.0	100.0	100.0
Illiterate	20.8	24.0	27.5	20.7	26.8	33.0
Literate but below middle school	27.7	21.6	20.7	27.7	24.0	24.9
Middle but below matriculation	44.6	25.5	20.6	44.5	28.4	24.7
Matriculate but below graduation	7.1	11.9	6.7	7.1	13.3	8.1
Graduation and above	0.0	6.8	7.9	0.0	7.5	9.5

Source: Office of the Registrar General, India - Census of India 2001, Table C-8.

In the 15-19 age group, by which time children should have completed middle school, 20.8 million accounting for a fifth of the population in that age group are illiterate. Another 27.7 million (27.7%) are educated below middle school only. In the last five years, this population would have reached the age group 20-24. The picture in the age group 20-24 is also not very different. About 45.6 million (50.8%) are below middle school level and only 6.8 million (7.5 per cent) being graduates. In 2001, in the age group 25-29, the age group in which most of the people start working, a third were illiterate. Graduates constituted less than 10 per cent only. It is likely that the employment opportunities available in the countries with shortage of employable people are for specific occupational categories. Persons having such skills may not be available in sufficient numbers to cater to the domestic requirement and for the external demand unless the educational system can reorient to the needs.

The school enrolment and dropout rates to have an idea of the enormity of the task involved in transforming the population into an asset. Table 24.8 presents the enrolment and gross enrolment ratio in primary and upper primary levels and the dropout rates.

Both enrolment of children in schools and the enrolment ratios have been steadily improving over the years. Still, the enrolment in upper primary stages is below 70 per cent. The children who will be available for employment by 2025 are already in schools. The dropout rates are as high as 30 per cent in primary classes (I-IV), 50 per cent in the elementary classes (I-VIII) and 62 per cent by the time children complete their the secondary schooling. Unless these come down drastically over the next few years and more children go to the higher secondary schools, we may not have enough educated persons who can effectively compete in the international job market. Normally, improvements in these indicators is a gradual process that takes time.

Table 24.8

Enrolment, Gross Enrolment Ratio (GER) and Dropout Rates by Stages, Selected Years

Year	Primary (IV)		Middle/Upper Primary (VIVIII)		Dropout Rate (%)		
	Enrolment	GER (%)	Enrolment	GER	I-V	I-VIII	I-X
1990-91	97.4	100.1	34.0	62.1	42.6	60.9	71.3
2000-01*	113.8	95.7	42.8	58.6	40.7	53.7	68.6
2001-02*	113.9	96.3	44.8	60.2	39.0	54.6	66.0
2002-03*	122.4	95.3	46.9	61.0	34.9	52.8	62.6
2003-04*	128.3	98.2	48.7	62.4	31.5	52.3	62.7
2004-05*	130.8	107.8	51.2	69.9	29.0	50.8	61.9

Notes: 1. Enrolment figures are in millions.
2. GER- Gross Enrolment Ratio.
*Provisional.

Source: Government of India, Ministry of Human Resource Development - Selected Educational Statistics, 2004-05.

It is necessary that educational standards—both in terms of levels and skills—of the population in the employable age groups are improved dramatically over the next few years for the country to take advantage of the opportunities for skilled jobs. It is doubtful whether it will be possible to continue exploiting the market for unskilled labour in the face of competition from other developing countries in Asia and Africa. More importantly, even if India is able to exploit the overseas employment opportunities effectively, the job markets in the countries with older populations are not large enough to make a substantial dent in the unemployment situation in the country.

Conclusions

The population projections for the country indicate that the number of children in most of the states have reached the peak. This would mean that the demand for infant and child care facilities as well as primary education may not increase in quantitative terms, though geographical variations exist. However, there is a need for qualitative improvements and ensuring accessibility in a sustained manner.

Population in the age group 15-29 years is poised for a substantial increase over the next 20-25 years in many large states. This would, along with increasing enrolment rates and falling dropout rates, result in huge demand for secondary and post-secondary education as well as employment generation.

The population in the age group 30-59 would increase from 315 million in 2001 to about 560 million during 2001-2026. Even to retain the current level of work participation, employment has to be provided to an additional 175 million people by 2026, excluding the likely demand due to increasing labour force participation of women and the additional requirements in the age groups 15-29 and 60+ years.

The elderly population (aged 60+) is set to more than double over the next 25 years. The proportion of elderly among dependants would increase from 16.2 per cent to 34.5 per cent. It may be above 40 per cent in several states with Kerala (49.3%) followed by Tamil Nadu (47.7%) at the top end. Providing for the care of the elderly across the country would be a daunting task.

Though the population of India is young, considering its huge size, providing workers to advanced countries may not significantly affect the employment scenario in the country. The distribution of population by education, enrolment ratios and dropout rates indicate that a lot needs to be done if India's 'young' population has to take advantage of the shortage of young people in advanced countries.

References

Census of India (2001). Tables C8 – *Educational Level by Age and Sex for Population aged 7 years and above.*

Chand, Ramesh (2007). "Demand for Food Grains", *Economic and Political Weekly*, December 29, 2007-January 4, 2008.

Government of India (2007). *Selected Educational Statistics, 2004-2005*. Ministry of Human Resource Development.

———. (2006). *Employment and Unemployment Situation in India 2004-05*– Report No. 515, NSS 61st Round.

———. (2006). *Population Projections for India and States—Report of the Technical Group on Population Projections*. National Commission on Population.

Kamuzora, C L (2005). "Africa's Population: A Critical Global Asset for Development", An invited paper to the CODESRIA 11th General Assembly, Maputo, Mozambique, 6-10 December 2005.

United Nations Department of Economic and Social Affairs Population Division (2006). *World Population Prospects* – 2006 Revision (online database).

———. (2006). *World Urbanization Prospects* – 2005 Revision (online database).

———. (2004). *World Population to 2300.*

25

Current and Future Health Scenario *vis-a-vis* Development in Major States of India

N.P. DAS and URVI SHAH

Introduction

The present study has examined recent national and state level data to understand the existing pattern of population growth *vis-à-vis* the economic growth and its likely health consequences in the future in the context of economic development and the national population policy and programmes in the country.

National Population Policy and Programmes

India has a long history of population and developmental planning as reflected by the formulation of the country's five year plans. It was also the first country to launch a national programme of family planning as early as 1951. Over time, the focus of this national programme has evolved from population control to include aspects of family welfare and maternal and child health. The programme, as it stands today, aims to address the health needs of both men and women across the life cycle and includes components of sexual and reproductive health, which had remained unacknowledged. There is also a strategic shift in service delivery and the programme is need-based, client centred and demand-driven rather than provider-driven. The recent period has also witnessed the formulation of new initiatives and policies aimed at achieving the goals of replacement level fertility, population stabilisation and health for all. For instance the National Population Policy (NPP) 2000 provides a policy framework for advancing goals and prioritisation of strategies during the next decade to meet the reproductive and health needs of the people. The immediate objective of the NPP 2000 is to address the unmet needs of contraception, health infrastructure, health personnel and to provide integrated service delivery for basic reproductive and child health care; the medium-term objective is to bring TFR to replacement level by 2010 through vigorous implementation of inter-sectional operational strategies while the long-term objective is to achieve population stabilisation by 2045, at a level consistent with the requirements of sustainable economic growth, social development and environmental protection.

In the health sector, the National Health Policy (NHP) 2002 was formulated with the main objective to achieve an acceptable standard of good health amongst the general population of the country. The approach of the policy is to increase access to decentralised public health system by establishing new infrastructure in deficient areas and upgrading the infrastructure in the existing institutions. The overriding aim of the NHP 2002 is to ensure a more equitable access to health services across the social and geographical divide of the country.

To meet the targets laid down in both the National Population Policy 2000 and National Health Policy 2002, the National Rural Health Mission (NRHM) was launched throughout the country from 11 May 2005. The primary objective of the Mission is to improve access of the rural population, especially women and children, to equitable, affordable and effective primary health care. In order to achieve this objective, the NRHM aims to carry out necessary architectural correction in the basic health care delivery system in the rural areas. It envisages the provision of a female health activist in each village and the development of a village health plan by a local team headed by the health and sanitation committee of the *panchayat*. In order to improve health infrastructure, it seeks to strengthen the existing PHCs and CHCs and ensure the provision of a 30-50 bedded CHC per 1 lakh population, which is in accordance with the Indian Public Health Standards (IPHS), defining personnel, equipment and management. In effect, the Mission adopts a synergistic approach by relating health to its various determinants *viz.*, nutrition, sanitation, hygiene and safe drinking water which are translated into programmatic action through a district plan for health.

In view of the goals of achieving population stabilisation in the country and bringing about improvements in the quality of life of its citizens through an acceptable standard of health, it becomes necessary to understand the pattern of social and economic development in the various states of the country as well as the health conditions of the people, particularly the women and children, to be able to ascertain how near (or far) the various states are towards the achievement of these goals by the target date.

The present paper therefore has first examined the socioeconomic and demographic status and pattern of future population growth in the major states of the country. This is followed by an assessment of the morbidity and nutritional data to understand the disease and the health status of various population groups, particularly children, women and the elderly.

Finally, the relatively well developed states are also compared with other less developed states on various health indicators, as certain states have already progressed well towards achieving replacement level fertility despite having almost similar health programme initiated by the Central government. In this regard, the poor performing states are also identified for special focus under the programme to facilitate their movement towards the long-term goal of population stabilisation.

Data

The study has essentially analysed recent data from the census, the National Family Health Survey (NFHS 1-3), Sample Registration System (SRS) and other relevant studies.

Results and Discussion

This section begins with a brief description of the socioeconomic and demographic condition prevailing in the major states in the country, which is followed by an examination of the present and future population growth and the morbidity and mortality pattern in the country.

Social and Economic Development

Table 25.1 presents data on various parameters of socioeconomic status in the major states as well as at the all-India level. The level of female literacy is moderate to high (58–88 per cent) in the southern states, except Andhra Pradesh where it is 51 per cent, as well as in Maharashtra and Gujarat in the west, West Bengal in the east and Punjab and Uttarakhand in the north. On the other hand, level of female literacy is very poor (45 per cent) in states like Bihar, Uttar Pradesh, Jharkhand, Jammu & Kashmir and Rajasthan. Although the progress in the rate of literacy during the 1990s is quite impressive (Appendix Table A-25.1), it will be difficult to achieve universal elementary education in the country because of a number of constraints such as physical access to schools, outlay on expenditure etc., availability of qualified teachers (Kingdon *et al.*, 2004). The per cent of urban population shows a similar pattern as states like Bihar, Uttar Pradesh, Jharkhand, Jammu & Kashmir and Rajasthan including Assam and Orissa are found to be the least urbanised. This indicates that except for Rajasthan and Andhra Pradesh, the western and southern states respectively are well placed on social development *vis-a-vis* other states in the country. The projections of urban proportions by Registrar General of India (1996) indicate that India's current 30 per cent urban population (in 2006) is expected to rise to almost 34 per cent by 2016. These urban proportions are expected to vary widely across the states from a low of 14 per cent in Assam to a high of 48 per cent in Maharashtra during 2016 (data not shown). The projection of urban population based on the 2001 Census by Dyson and Visaria (2004) also indicate a similar pattern of urbanisation. They estimate that the country's urban population will be about 36 per cent by 2026, with wide variation across the states, from as high as 68 per cent in Tamil Nadu, 52 per cent in Maharashtra and 45 per cent in Gujarat to as low as 17 per cent each in Bihar and Assam. In fact, the western and southern states like Maharashtra, Gujarat, Tamil Nadu, Karnataka, Kerala, Andhra Pradesh are likely to be more urbanised than the northern and eastern states like Uttar Pradesh, Bihar, Orissa and Assam; but the size of the urban population even in the less developed states in the northern and eastern regions will be quite large in the next 10 years. It is therefore important that the quality of life of this large group be improved, in view of the inadequate infrastructure, limited resources and increasing urban slum settlements housing the urban poor. The level of social development including urbanisation is closely associated with its economic development as evident from Table 25.1.

Here again, except Rajasthan, the other states in the western region and most of the states in the northern and southern region are well placed on the economic indicators such as per capita state domestic product (SDP), household wealth index and level of poverty. On the other hand, states like Bihar, Jharkhand, Orissa, Uttar Pradesh, Madhya Pradesh and Rajasthan once again merit special attention as they fare poorly on all the three economic indicators.

In fact, most of the states experienced economic growth during the last decade (1993-94 to 2005-06), as evident from data on per capita net state domestic product by state in India (Appendix Table A-25.2). There are however concerns about progress in the slowest growing states, typically the poorest states like UP, MP, Bihar, Assam and Orissa, while states such as Maharashtra, Tamil Nadu, Gujarat, Punjab and Haryana which were initially relatively wealthy, were the fastest growing states during 1990s. The other states like Karnataka, Kerala, Andhra Pradesh, West Bengal, Himachal Pradesh and surprisingly Rajasthan, also did relatively well after the economic reforms that began in the 1990s. Unfortunately, such economic reforms may have increased the divergence between the rich and poor states for varied reasons (Acharya *et al.*, 2004). Nevertheless, the country's economy which is growing annually at a rate of 5 per cent, on an average, will depend on the progress made by the poor states. As will be noted in the next section on the impact of changing population age structure, the economically active population in the age group 15-59 will increase rapidly in most of the states except states

Table 25.1

Socioeconomic Condition of the People in the Major States of India, 2001

Region/States	*Characteristics*				
	% of Females (7+) Literate (2001)	*% of Urban Population (2001)*	*Wealth Index (% of Population in the Highest Wealth Quintile, 2005-06)*	*SDP Per Capita, 2003-04 (Rs. Per Year)*	*Poverty Ratio in % (1999-2000)*
India	54	28	20.0	11799	26
North					
Haryana	56	29	31.0	15752	9
Himachal Pradesh	68	10	35.1	12765	-
Jammu & Kashmir	42	25	35.1	-	3
Punjab	64	34	48.1	16119	6
Uttarakhand	60	26	32.8	9471	-
Central					
Chhattisgarh	52	20	10.2	8383	37
Madhya Pradesh	50	27	13.1	8284	37
Uttar Pradesh	43	21	13.6	5975	31
East					
Assam	56	13	11.8	6466	36
Bihar	34	11	9.4	3557	43
Jharkhand	39	22	11.9	7732	43
Orissa	51	15	9.9	6487	47
West Bengal	60	28	13.9	11612	27
West					
Gujarat	59	37	31.9	16780	14
Maharashtra	68	42	32.5	16478	25
Rajasthan	44	23	19.1	9685	15
South					
Andhra Pradesh	51	27	17.1	11756	16
Karnataka	58	34	19.8	13141	20
Kerala	88	26	44.8	12328	13
Tamil Nadu	65	44	19.5	12976	21

Source: (1) Census of India, 2001.

(2) Cassen, R. and K. McNay (2004). "The condition of the people", in Tim Dyson, Robert Cassen & Leela Visaria (eds.), *Twenty-first Century India-Population, Economy, Human Development and the Environment*. New Delhi: Oxford University Press.

(3) Central Statistical Organisation (CSO) website as on 23-2-2006.

(4) NFHS-3 (IIPS & Macro International, 2007).

like Kerala and Tamil Nadu during the next 25 years. This addition to the workforce and an associated decline in the dependency ratio offers an opportunity for faster growth in the country's economy, although this potential will transform into reality depending on the effectiveness of the policies and programmes to ensure skill acquisition and an acceptable level of health among this workforce. Increased allocation of funds from the Centre particularly to less developed states in the social sectors as well as creation of job opportunities will help such states come out of the nexus between high population growth and low socioeconomic and health development.

The Pattern of Population Growth in the Recent Period

According to the 2001 Census, the population of India is about 1027 million, which is growing at an annual rate of 1.93 per cent. The country seems to have entered the third stage of demographic transition since 1981 (with decline in growth rate), as birth rate also started declining and continued to do so during the last decade. However, the speed with which the country can move to the next phase of transition to bring about a new balance of fertility and mortality at lower levels depends on the further transformation of the society and the process of modernisation including improvements in women's status and standard of living in the major states as well as in the country as a whole.

Data supports that rate of population growth is on the decline in the country as a whole although there is much variation across the states. In fact, there is a clear north-south divide with the northern and central states stagnating or lagging much behind the southern states in their advancement towards population stabilisation. Table 25.2 presents the changes in percentage decadal growth rate of population and in different states of India during the last two decades. The percentage decadal growth rate of the country as a whole declined from 23.9 during 1981-1991 to 21.3 during 1991-2001—a fall in India's decadal growth rate by 2.6 percentage points, which is the sharpest decline since Independence. However, it is a matter of serious concern that population growth rate has not come down to the desired level, particularly in the northern and central states, including Rajasthan in the west and Bihar and Jharkhand in the east (Table 25.2). In fact, none of the backward states like Uttar Pradesh, Jharkhand, Bihar and Rajasthan made a significant contribution to the decline in growth rate at the all-India level during the last decade.

As against this, all the southern states (Andhra Pradesh, Karnataka, Tamil Nadu, Kerala) and certain eastern states like West Bengal, Assam and Orissa recorded a decline in growth rate of varying degrees. The biggest southern state, Andhra Pradesh, recorded the highest decline of 10.3 percentage points during the decade 1991-2001.

Table 25.2

Changes in Growth Rate of Population in the Major States of India during the Last Two Decades

Region/States	Percentage Decadal Growth Rate		Percentage Point Change
	1981-1991	1991-2001	
India	23.9	21.3	-2.6
North			
Haryana	27.4	28.1	0.7
Himachal Pradesh	20.8	17.5	-3.3
Jammu & Kashmir	30.3	29.0	-1.3
Punjab	20.8	19.8	-1.0
Uttarakhand	24.2	19.2	-5.0
Central			
Chhattisgarh	25.7	18.1	-7.6
Madhya Pradesh	27.2	24.3	-2.9
Uttar Pradesh	25.6	25.8	0.2
East			
Assam	24.2	18.9	-5.3
Bihar	23.4	28.4	5.0
Jharkhand	24.0	23.2	-0.8
Orissa	20.1	15.9	-4.2
West Bengal	24.7	17.8	-6.9
West			
Gujarat	21.2	22.5	1.3
Maharashtra	25.7	22.6	-3.1
Rajasthan	28.4	28.3	-0.1
South			
Andhra Pradesh	24.2	13.9	-10.3
Karnataka	21.1	17.3	-3.8
Kerala	14.3	9.4	-4.9
Tamil Nadu	15.4	11.2	-4.2

Source: Computed from Census data of 1981-2001, Office of The Registrar General, India, New Delhi.

Among the western states, Maharashtra, despite having a positive net migration (mainly due to the migration towards the city of Mumbai) recorded a decline in its decadal growth rate by 3 percentage points. Yet another big state in the western part of the country, Gujarat, has shown an increase in decadal growth rate of 1.3 per cent, which is mainly due to moderate positive net migration. In the remaining states, although declines of varying order are indicated, a special mention is needed of the developed states, *viz.*, Punjab and Himachal Pradesh which have already shown only a decline which remained almost stable in their growth rates during 1981-1991.

Thus, on the whole, the four southern states, West Bengal from eastern India, Maharashtra from western India and Himachal Pradesh and Punjab from northern India are nearing replacement level fertility (hence much advanced towards population stabilisation) and their future contribution to the country's population growth rate reduction will be limited (discussed later in the sections to follow). In this context, for further reduction in the country's growth rate, the fertility rates of the remaining states have to substantially decline in future. However, the states like Gujarat, Orissa, Jammu & Kashmir and Assam whose level of fertility is moderate and is lower than the all-India level, have the potential to follow the southern and other low fertility states and therefore also deserve focused attention under the National Rural Health Mission and RCH programme.

Marriage Pattern and Level of Fertility, 1999-2006

Increase in age at marriage plays a significant role in the reduction of fertility. In several Asian countries like Sri Lanka and West Malaysia, and Kerala in India, it is seen that change in age at marriage has played an important role in fertility decline. Teenage marriage, closely followed by childbearing is evident from data presented in Table 25.3 for the major states in the country.

Despite reduction in teenage marriage in majority of the states, proportion of women aged 20-24 married by age 18 is still very high (more than 50 per cent) in the states of Bihar, Jharkhand, Rajasthan, Uttar Pradesh, Madhya Pradesh, Chhattisgarh, Andhra Pradesh and West Bengal, while it is relatively low (less than 2 per cent) in Kerala, Tamil Nadu, Himachal Pradesh, Jammu and Kashmir and Punjab. Similarly, 50 per cent of women aged 25-49 years in majority of the states had their first birth by the age of 19-20 years, although the relatively more developed states like Kerala, Tamil Nadu, Punjab, Haryana, Himachal Pradesh and Gujarat were found to have a higher median age at first birth (above 20 years). In fact the median age at first birth is almost 23 years in Kerala and has shown a tendency to increase in majority of the states as well as at the national level over the last 7 years (Table 25.3). Similarly, sex preference appears to have slightly reduced and the use of contraception has also increased during the recent period as per cent of women with 2 living daughters wanting no more children and per cent of women using any family planning method increased substantially during the last seven years in majority of the states, although large differentials in the above two indications do exist by state (Table 25.3). For example, proportion of women with 2 living daughters wanting no more children varies from as low as 20 per cent in Bihar to as high as 90 per cent in Tamil

Nadu, while the proportion of women using any family planning method is again very low (34 per cent) in Bihar as against 73 per cent in Himachal Pradesh and it is 56 per cent at the all-India level. The level of fertility in a state is more or less consistent with the above fertility behaviour indicators including use of contraception. The level of total fertility rate (TFR) has declined considerably in most of the states during the last seven years, although it still varies widely across the states. For example, the level of TFR is 3-4 births per woman in states like Bihar, Uttar Pradesh, Rajasthan, Jharkhand and Madhya Pradesh, while the developed states like Kerala, Tamil Nadu, Karnataka, Maharashtra, Punjab and Himachal Pradesh and even a relatively less developed state like Andhra Pradesh have largely attained TFR of 2.1 or less by 2005-06. The other states occupy intermediate position (TFR ranges between 2.2 and 2.9), although some of them are close to achieving replacement level fertility.

The Pattern of Future Population Growth

An examination of various projections for India (done by the United Nations, 2001; US Census Bureau, 1999; World Bank, 2004 and Dyson, 2004) suggest that the population of India will be between 1.34 and 1.41 billion by the year 2026 and between 1.57 and 1.65 billion by the year 2051. In other words, another at least half a billion population would be added to India's population by 2051 because of its large base. For example, Table 25.4 presents results of the standard run (medium fertility assumption) population projection for India (projections made separately for states and adjusted for all-India) by developing simple yet plausible rules for generating assumptions about the future course of fertility and mortality (Dyson, 2004).

This projection is based on 2001 census data and SRS vital rates. The population weighted TFRs and life expectancies which emerge from the assumptions and projection results for all-India suggest that the total fertility rate will be close to replacement level by the period 2016-2021 and below replacement level by 2021-2026. The expectation of life for both sexes combined is projected to reach about 69 years by 2021-2026. As per standard projection, the country's population is expected to reach to about 1.42 billion by 2026 and to about 1.58 billion by 2051 (Table 25.4).

A state-wise analysis of this projection, presented in Table 25.4, reveals that the four southern states and surprisingly Orissa are expected to grow at a much slower pace and their population would increase by 15-24 per cent by 2026, while as expected, the northern states like Uttar Pradesh, Bihar, Madhya Pradesh (as per their earlier geographical boundaries) and Rajasthan will grow at a much faster pace (45-55 per cent). The developed states like

Table 25.3

Marriage Pattern, Childbearing Practices and Level of Fertility by Major States in India, 1998-2006

State	Indicators														
	Per cent of Women Aged 20-24 Married by Age 18 (1)			Median Age at 1st Birth for Women Aged 25-49 (2)			Married Women with 2 Living Daughters Wanting No More Children (3)			Per cent of Women using any Family Planning Method (4)			Total Fertility Rate (5)		
	1999	2006	% Change	1999	2006	% Change	1999	2006	% Change	1999	2006	% Change	1999	2006	% Change
India	50.0	44.5	-11.0	19.3	19.8	2.6	47.0	62.1	32.1	48.2	56.3	16.8	2.9	2.7	-6.0
North															
Haryana	41.5	39.8	-4.1	20.1	20.3	1.0	17.6	25.8	46.6	62.4	63.4	1.6	2.9	2.7	-6.6
Himachal Pradesh	10.7	12.3	15.0	20.5	21.2	3.4	50.2	63.7	26.9	67.7	72.6	7.2	2.1	1.9	-9.3
Jammu and Kashmir	22.1	14.0	-36.7	20.3	21.4	5.4	26.6	38.6	45.1	49.1	52.6	7.1	2.7	2.4	-12.2
Punjab	11.6	19.4	67.2	21.5	21.4	-0.5	24.4	43.4	77.9	66.7	63.3	-5.1	2.2	2.0	-10.0
Uttarakhand	25.9	22.6	-12.7	20.1	20.5	2.0	35.4	49.4	39.5	43.1	59.3	37.6	2.6	2.6	-2.3
Central															
Chhattisgarh	61.3	51.8	-15.5	17.8	18.8	5.6	22.1	46.8	111.8	45.0	53.2	18.2	2.8	2.6	-6.1
Madhya Pradesh	64.7	53.0	-18.1	18.7	19.4	3.7	19.5	37.6	92.8	44.1	55.9	26.8	3.4	3.1	-9.0
Uttar Pradesh	64.3	53.0	-17.6	18.8	19.4	3.2	16.5	30.8	86.7	27.1	43.6	60.9	4.1	3.8	-5.9
East															
Assam	40.7	38.0	-6.6	19.9	20.7	4.0	44.3	67.1	51.5	43.3	56.5	30.5	2.3	2.4	4.8
Bihar	71.9	60.3	-16.1	18.9	18.7	-1.1	10.8	20.0	85.2	23.5	34.1	45.1	3.7	4.0	8.1
Jharkhand	64.1	61.2	-4.5	18.7	18.9	1.1	28.2	32.1	13.8	27.6	35.7	29.3	2.8	3.3	19.9
Orissa	37.6	36.3	-3.5	19.6	20.0	2.0	35.0	53.2	52.0	46.8	50.7	8.3	2.5	2.4	-3.7
West Bengal	45.9	53.3	16.1	19.2	19.0	-1.0	63.3	74.3	17.4	66.6	71.2	6.9	2.3	2.3	-0.9

contd...

...contd...

	1999	*2006*	*% Change*	*1999*	*2006*	*% Change*	*1999*	*2006*	*% Change*	*1999*	*2006*	*% Change*	*1999*	*2006*	*% Change*
West															
Gujarat	40.7	33.5	-17.7	20.1	20.6	2.5	32.0	48.8	52.5	59.0	66.6	12.9	2.7	2.4	-11.0
Maharashtra	47.7	38.8	-18.7	19.0	19.9	4.7	41.4	55.1	33.1	60.9	66.9	9.9	2.5	2.1	-16.3
Rajasthan	68.3	57.1	-16.4	19.4	19.6	1.0	12.5	33.1	164.8	40.3	47.2	17.1	3.8	3.2	-15.1
South															
Andhra Pradesh	64.3	54.7	-14.9	18.0	18.8	4.4	70.3	85.0	20.9	59.6	67.7	13.6	2.3	1.8	-20.4
Karnataka	46.3	41.2	-11.0	18.9	19.9	5.3	67.2	76.9	14.4	58.3	63.6	9.1	2.1	2.1	-2.3
Kerala	17.0	15.4	-9.4	21.9	22.7	3.7	85.8	86.4	0.7	63.7	68.6	7.7	2.0	1.9	-1.5
Tamil Nadu	24.9	21.5	-13.7	20.6	21.0	1.9	73.6	90.0	22.3	52.1	61.4	17.9	2.2	1.8	-17.8

Source: Computed from NFHS-2 (1998-99) and NFHS-3 (2005-06) reports (IIPS and ORC Macro, 2001; IIPS and Macro International, 2007).

Maharashtra, Punjab and West Bengal will grow at a moderate rate and would increase by 28-30 per cent by 2026. The population of the remaining states like Assam, Gujarat and Haryana would increase by 35-39 per cent by 2026 (Table 25.4).

Table 25.4

Projected Population (in millions) in Major States of India Based on Standard Run Population Projection (Medium Fertility Assumption), 2001-2026

Region/States	Population		
	2001 (Base)	2026 (Projected)	Expected Percentage Increase in Population during 2001-26
India	1027.0	1419.2	38.2
North			
Haryana	21.1	29.4	39.4
Punjab	24.3	31.0	27.6
Central			
Madhya Pradesh+	81.2	118.0	45.3
Uttar Pradesh+	174.5	271.0	55.3
East			
Assam	26.6	36.0	35.2
Bihar+	109.8	166.1	51.4
Orissa	36.7	45.5	23.8
West Bengal	80.2	104.3	30.0
West			
Gujarat	50.6	68.1	34.6
Maharashtra	96.8	123.9	28.0
Rajasthan	56.5	83.3	47.5
South			
Andhra Pradesh	75.7	91.7	21.1
Karnataka	52.7	65.5	24.2
Kerala	31.8	38.5	20.8
Tamil Nadu	62.1	71.7	15.5

Note: + Based on their earlier geographic boundaries.

Source: Dyson, Tim (2004). "India's population- The future", in Tim Dyson, Robert Cassen and Leela Visaria (eds.), *Twenty-first Century India, Population, Economy, Human Development and the Environment*. New Delhi: Oxford University Press.

The Impact of Changing Population Age Structure

One way by which demographic trends affect the socioeconomic conditions is through changes in the age composition of the population. Trends in fertility rate, mortality rate and migration have some repercussions on the age structure of the population. Table 25.5 presents the selected output from the standard run population projections for India's 15 states (Dyson, 2004). The change in the proportion of children, the proportion of working age population and that of the elderly for the next quarter of a century can be studied from this table. In all the states, the proportion of the population aged 0-14 will decrease in the next 25 years. These numbers are directly relevant for the educational planning in the states. Even in the four high fertility states (Uttar Pradesh, Rajasthan, Bihar and Madhya Pradesh), the decrease in the proportion of child population is of the order of more than 10 percentage points. However, this does not imply a decrease in absolute number of children. At the all-India level, the proportion of child population will decrease by 11 per cent points. However, in the present low fertility states, the reduction in the proportion of child population is less.

An equally important aspect will be changes in the structure of the working age population. According to Table 25.5, all the states, except for Kerala and Tamil Nadu will experience an increase in population aged 15-59 in the next quarter of the century. The proportion of population in this age group (workforce) in the states of Kerala and Tamil Nadu will remain almost the same during this period. One of the inevitable consequences of the demographic transition is population ageing or the increase in the proportion of the elderly population. The ageing population is defined as those above 60 years of age. According to Table 25.5, the percentage of the elderly population for the country as a whole will increase from the present 7 per cent in 2001 to about 12 per cent in the next quarter of the century. Among the states in India the two southern states, *viz.*, Kerala and Tamil Nadu, which had undergone substantial fertility reduction in the last two decades have the highest proportion (Kerala 9.6 per cent and Tamil Nadu 8.5 per cent) of elderly population in 2001. However, this proportion will increase to around 16 per cent for both Kerala and Tamil Nadu by 2026. Among other states, all except the present high fertility states (Uttar Pradesh, Rajasthan, Bihar, Madhya Pradesh) will have a proportion of elderly population of about 10-15 per cent by 2026. The proportion of elderly in the present high fertility states will increase from 6-7 per cent in 2001 to around 9-10 per cent by 2026. This increase of 3-4 per cent seems to be small, but by virtue of their large population size, the absolute numbers of the elderly in these high fertility states will be very high in 2026. In the years beyond 2026, the elderly population will again rise as these states progress towards demographic transition (when fertility reduces substantially).

Table 25.5

Likely Age Structure of the Population in Major States of India, based on Standard Run Population Projection, 2001-2026

Region/States	Population							
	0-14 Years		*15-59 Years*		*60+ Years*		*Median Age in Years*	
	2001	*2026*	*2001*	*2026*	*2001*	*2026*	*2001*	*2026*
India	34.4	23.2	58.6	65.2	7.0	11.6	22.7	31.6
North								
Haryana	35.8	20.8	57.2	68.4	7.0	10.8	21.5	32.4
Punjab	31.6	19.2	60.5	67.0	7.9	13.8	24.0	35.0
Central								
Madhya Pradesh (including Chhattisgarh)	37.2	24.8	56.3	65.4	6.5	9.6	21.4	29.0
Uttar Pradesh (including Uttarakhand)	38.7	28.5	54.6	62.4	6.7	9.1	20.2	26.2
East								
Assam	36.4	21.3	58.3	68.2	5.3	10.5	21.3	32.5
Bihar (including Jharkhand)	38.6	27.0	55.0	62.9	6.3	10.1	20.2	27.7
Orissa	32.7	20.0	59.9	67.4	7.4	12.6	23.7	34.4
West Bengal	33.0	20.3	60.5	66.5	6.5	13.2	23.4	34.9
West								
Gujarat	31.9	20.1	61.4	67.2	6.7	12.7	23.8	33.7
Maharashtra	32.0	19.9	60.5	66.5	7.5	13.6	24.3	34.7
Rajasthan	38.3	24.6	55.4	65.6	6.3	9.8	20.3	29.9
South								
Andhra Pradesh	31.7	19.7	61.0	66.5	7.3	13.8	24.1	35.9
Karnataka	31.7	19.7	61.1	67.0	7.2	13.3	23.8	35.3
Kerala	25.8	18.8	64.6	64.9	9.6	16.3	27.1	37.6
Tamil Nadu	26.5	18.9	65.0	65.6	8.5	15.5	27.0	37.1

Source: Dyson, Tim (2004). "India's population—The future", in Tim Dyson, Robert Cassen and Leela Visaria (eds.), *Twenty first Century India, Population, Economy, Human Development and the Environment*. New Delhi: Oxford University Press.

Health of Women and Children

In the context of population growth and socioeconomic development, we discuss here the health status of women and children in the recent past. The nutritional status of women, as measured by BMI, anaemia and obesity, indicates that 56 per cent of women have anaemia, one-third of them have a

BMI which is below normal (<18.5, indicating mild to severe thinness) while 15 per cent are found to be obese (Table 25.6). These proportions increase sharply in the less developed and more populous states, with little improvement overtime. Apart from nutritional deficiency reflected in these data, another cause of concern is the rise in proportion of women who are obese as noted in most of the states. Data on anaemia among men indicate that about one-fourth were found to have any anaemia which varies from 8 per cent in Kerala to as high as 40 per cent in Assam (data not shown). The health of women is further likely to deteriorate during pregnancy as about half of them had not availed the necessary antenatal services (including nutritional supplementation), and 60 per cent had not delivered at a health or medical facility (Table 25.6). The situation, as expected, is worse in the less developed states, although marginal improvements on these two aspects have been noted over time. With regard to the nutritional status and other health care of children, it is noted that as high as four-fifth of children aged 6-35 months are found to be anaemic in India with little variation across the states, which is a cause of concern due to its association with child mortality (Table 25.6). Child health care is equally poor, particularly in the less developed states as slightly more than two-fifth of children aged 12-23 months were fully immunised.

Morbidity among the General Population

This section discusses the diseases and ailments among the general population followed by that among the elderly population in the states and in the country. The 60th round of the National Sample Survey (NSS) on morbidity, health care and condition of the aged carried out during 2004 provides insight into the health condition of men, women and children as well as that of the elderly (NSSO, 2006).

An examination of these data indicates that the incidence of morbidity for a reference period of 15 days preceding the survey was about 4444 per 100,000 population at the all-India level, with the incidence being slightly higher for women (4647) than men (4251). Furthermore, the incidence is much higher at younger ages, particularly at 0-4 years (9463). Interestingly, the incidence rate among this age group is found to be more for boys (9888) than girls (9013). There is a marked decrease in the incidence of ailments after age 10 years which, however, peaks at age 60 years and above. The incidence of morbidity moreover is relatively much higher for women after age 30 years compared to men at similar ages (NSSO, 2006: Appendix Table 38). Needless to say these data once again suggest the need to improve the reach of the much-needed health care services, particularly curative services under the national programme among young children, women and the elderly.

Table 25.6

Health Status of Women and Children by Major States in India, 1998-2006

State	Indicators											
	Per cent of Mothers who had at least 3 Antenatal Care Visits for their Last Birth			Institutional Delivery (for Births that Occurred during 3-5 years Preceding the Survey)			Per cent of Children Aged 12-23 Months Fully Immunised			Per cent of Women Whose Body Mass Index is Below Normal		
	1			2			3			4		
	1999	2006	% Change	1999	2006	% Change	1999	2006	% Change	1999	2006	% Change
India	44.2	50.7	14.7	33.6	40.7	21.1	42.0	43.5	3.6	36.2	33.0	8.8
North												
Haryana	38.2	58.8	53.9	22.4	39.4	75.9	62.7	65.3	4.1	25.9	27.8	-7.3
Himachal Pradesh	61.6	62.6	1.6	28.9	45.3	56.7	83.4	74.2	-11.0	29.7	24.3	18.2
Jammu & Kashmir	67.2	74.2	10.4	35.7	54.3	52.1	56.7	66.7	17.6	26.4	21.3	19.3
Punjab	58.4	72.5	24.1	37.5	52.5	40.0	72.1	60.1	-16.6	16.9	13.5	20.1
Uttarakhand	19.7	44.8	127.4	20.6	36.0	74.8	40.9	60.0	46.7	32.4	25.7	20.7
Central												
Chhattisgarh	33.2	54.7	64.8	13.8	15.7	13.8	21.8	48.7	123.4	48.1	41.0	14.8
Madhya Pradesh	27.1	40.2	48.3	22.0	29.7	35.0	22.6	40.3	78.3	35.2	40.1	-13.9
Uttar Pradesh	14.6	26.3	80.1	15.2	22.0	44.7	20.2	22.9	13.4	36.5	34.1	6.6
East												
Assam	30.9	36.3	17.5	17.6	22.7	29.0	17.0	31.6	85.9	27.1	36.5	-34.7
Bihar	15.9	16.9	6.3	14.8	22.0	48.6	11.6	32.8	182.8	39.1	43.0	-10.0
Jharkhand	24.5	36.1	47.3	13.9	19.2	38.1	8.8	34.5	292.0	41.1	42.6	-3.6
Orissa	48.0	60.9	26.9	22.6	38.7	71.2	43.7	51.8	18.5	48.0	40.5	15.6
West Bengal	57.4	62.4	8.7	40.1	43.1	7.5	43.8	64.3	46.8	43.7	37.7	13.7

contd...

...contd...

	1			2			3			4		
	1999	2006	% Change	1999	2006	% Change	1999	2006	% Change	1999	2006	% Change
West												
Gujarat	61.2	64.9	6.0	46.3	54.6	17.9	53.0	45.2	-14.7	37.0	32.3	12.7
Maharashtra	66.2	75.3	13.7	52.6	66.1	25.7	78.4	58.8	-25.0	39.7	32.6	17.9
Rajasthan	23.6	41.2	74.6	21.5	32.2	49.8	17.3	26.5	53.2	36.1	33.6	6.9
South												
Andhra Pradesh	80.2	86.0	7.2	49.8	68.6	37.8	58.7	46.0	-21.6	37.4	30.8	17.6
Karnataka	72.4	79.3	9.5	51.1	66.9	30.9	60.0	55.0	-8.3	38.8	31.4	19.1
Kerala	98.6	93.9	-4.8	92.9	99.5	7.1	79.7	75.3	-5.5	18.7	12.5	33.2
Tamil Nadu	90.9	96.5	6.2	79.3	90.4	14.0	88.8	80.8	-9.0	29.0	23.5	19.0

State	Indicators								
	Per cent of Women Who are Overweight or Obese 5			Per cent of Ever Married Women aged 15-49 who are Anaemic 6			Per cent of Children Aged 6-35 Months who are Anaemic 7		
	1999	2006	% Change	1999	2006	% Change	1999	2006	% Change
India	10.6	14.8	39.6	51.8	56.2	-8.5	74.2	79.2	-6.7
North									
Haryana	16.6	21.0	26.5	47.0	56.5	-20.2	83.9	82.5	1.7
Himachal Pradesh	13.1	17.3	32.1	40.5	40.9	-1.0	69.9	58.8	15.9
Jammu & Kashmir	13.8	22.7	64.5	58.7	53.1	9.5	71.1	68.1	4.2
Punjab	30.2	37.5	24.2	41.4	38.4	7.2	80.0	80.2	-0.3
Uttarakhand	9.2	16.0	73.9	45.6	47.6	-4.4	77.4	61.5	20.5

contd...

...contd...

	5			6			7		
	1999	*2006*	*% Change*	*1999*	*2006*	*% Change*	*1999*	*2006*	*% Change*
Central									
Chhattisgarh	4.1	6.7	63.4	68.7	57.6	16.2	87.7	81.0	7.6
Madhya Pradesh	6.8	8.6	26.5	49.3	57.6	-16.8	71.3	82.6	-15.8
Uttar Pradesh	7.3	11.1	52.1	49.0	50.8	-3.7	73.8	85.1	-15.3
East									
Assam	4.2	9.0	114.3	69.7	69.0	1.0	63.2	76.7	-21.4
Bihar	3.9	5.3	35.9	60.4	68.3	-13.1	81.1	87.6	-8.0
Jharkhand	3.2	5.9	84.4	72.9	70.4	3.4	82.4	77.7	5.7
Orissa	4.4	7.6	72.7	63.0	62.8	0.3	72.3	74.2	-2.6
West Bengal	8.6	12.5	45.3	62.7	63.8	-1.8	78.3	69.4	11.4
West									
Gujarat	15.8	20.3	28.5	46.3	55.5	-19.9	74.5	80.1	-7.5
Maharashtra	11.7	17.1	46.2	48.5	49.0	-1.0	76.0	71.9	5.4
Rajasthan	7.1	10.2	43.7	48.5	53.1	-9.5	82.3	79.6	3.3
South									
Andhra Pradesh	12.0	17.7	47.5	49.8	62.0	-24.5	72.3	79.0	-9.3
Karnataka	13.6	18.1	33.1	42.4	50.3	-18.6	70.6	82.7	-17.1
Kerala	20.6	34.0	65.0	22.7	32.3	-42.3	43.9	55.7	-26.9
Tamil Nadu	14.7	24.4	66.0	56.5	53.3	5.7	69.0	72.5	-5.1

Source: Computed from NFHS-1 (1992-93), NFHS-2 (1998-99) and NFHS-3 (2005-06) reports (IIPS, 1995; IIPS & ORC Macro, 2000; 2007.

Yet another aspect to understand the health of the people is to assess the prevalence of chronic diseases such as diabetes, asthma and tuberculosis. Data from the NFHS provide a glimpse of the prevalence of these diseases as reported during the survey. The data on these aspects are summarised in Tables 25.7 and 25.8.

Table 25.7

Number of Persons per 100,000 Usual Household Residents Suffering from Tuberculosis by State, India, 1992-2006

State	Number of Persons per 100,000 suffering from Tuberculosis			
	1992-93	*1998-99*	*2005-06*	*% Change (1992-2005)*
India	467	544	445	-4.7
North				
Haryana	327	358	340	4.0
Himachal Pradesh	242	259	182	-24.8
Jammu and Kashmir	245	428	104	-57.6
Punjab	238	207	201	-15.5
Uttarakhand			345	
Central				
Chhattisgarh			310	
Madhya Pradesh	435	602	353	-18.9
Uttar Pradesh	560	551	450	-19.6
East				
Assam	638	710	654	2.5
Bihar	595	989	797	33.9
Jharkhand			659	
Orissa	555	833	418	-24.7
West Bengal	357	492	605	69.5
West				
Gujarat	308	438	538	74.7
Maharashtra	293	282	321	9.6
Rajasthan	724	397	371	-48.8
South				
Andhra Pradesh	407	592	449	10.3
Karnataka	136	269	141	3.7
Kerala	586	526	275	-53.1
Tamil Nadu	703	479	508	-27.7

Source: Computed from NFHS-1 (1992-93), NFHS-2 (1998-99) and NFHS-3 (2005-06) reports (IIPS, 1995; IIPS & ORC Macro, 2000; 2007).

It is evident from Table 25.7 that the prevalence of tuberculosis was found to be 445 per 100,000 usual household members, and that the incidence has reduced slightly or remained more or less same overtime in majority of the states except for certain states like West Bengal, Gujarat, Bihar and Maharashtra, which have in fact shown a substantial rise in prevalance rate.

It is further important to note that the reported incidence of tuberculosis is relatively much higher in the states of Bihar, Assam, West Bengal, Jharkhand, Tamil Nadu and Gujarat compared to other states during the recent period (Table 25.7). With regard to asthma, about 1627 men and 1696 women per 100,000 reported to be suffering form asthma at the all-India level (Table 25.8). The prevalence rate varies from 407 among men in Jharkhand to 4365 men in West Bengal, while the incidence of asthma among females is lowest in Himachal Pradesh (384) which increases to 4037 in Kerala. Another chronic disease which is a cause of concern is diabetes among men and women. The incidence rate of diabetes is found to be 1051 per 100,000 among men as against 881 among women. Here again there is a large variation across the states.

The incidence among men is much higher in Kerala (3078), West Bengal (2323), Andhra Pradesh (2116), Tamil Nadu (1351) and Orissa (1179). A similar state-wise pattern of prevalence among women is noted with the addition of states like Haryana and Himachal Pradesh also having higher incidence of diabetes (Table 25.8). This pattern of morbidity therefore suggests that the public health system be equipped to identify and manage the condition of ill-health arising out of these diseases. In fact, diabetes, which is a lifestyle disease, is also linked to obesity which has increased as already been noted in this examination. Similarly, pollution linked to asthma, both of which are on the rise has also been noted.

Morbidity among the Elderly

Understanding the health status of the elderly is important in view of their growing numbers in the Indian population. Data from 60th round of the NSS (conducted during 2004) reveal that about 6454 elderly persons (60+ years) per 100,000 reported some ailment during the 15 days prior to the survey, at the all-India level, with average duration of the ailment being 54 days (NSSO, 2006). The incidence of the ailment was noted to be higher among women (6803) than men (6108). Furthermore, the incidence rate varies widely across the states. It is surprising to note that the incidence of ailments is much higher in the states of Kerala, West Bengal, Punjab and Assam (data not shown). The ailments commonly reported were gastrointestinal infections, cardiovascular diseases, eye ailment and disability (data not shown). In fact, analysis of data from an earlier round of NSS reveals that the elderly were found to suffer from chronic diseases/ailment such as cough, piles, joint problems, heart disease, urinary problems, diabetes and cancer. The incidence rate was reported to be 52034 per 100,000 aged persons while the incidence of physical disabilities was reported to be 20955 (Das and Shah, 2001). In

Table 25.8

Number of Women and Men Aged 15-49 Per 1000,000 who Reported they have Diabetes, Asthma by State, India, 2005-06

	Health Problems			
	No. of Women Per 100,000		*No. of Men Per 100,000*	
State	*Diabetes*	*Asthma*	*Diabetes*	*Asthma*
India	881	1696	1051	1627
North				
Haryana	1169	1552	608	1266
Himachal Pradesh	1048	384	344	527
Jammu and Kashmir	540	897	278	816
Punjab	849	945	802	802
Uttarakhand	825	537	965	972
Central				
Chhattisgarh	659	746	932	858
Madhya Pradesh	558	1283	555	1102
Uttar Pradesh	383	1089	456	1225
East				
Assam	402	1411	601	1105
Bihar	1024	1696	940	981
Jharkhand	652	1291	629	407
Orissa	556	2533	1179	1592
West Bengal	1641	3304	2323	4365
West				
Gujarat	968	1530	524	1844
Maharashtra	479	1714	906	1855
Rajasthan	282	1565	362	1739
South				
Andhra Pradesh	838	2151	2116	2189
Karnataka	681	1259	973	691
Kerala	2549	4037	3078	2984
Tamil Nadu	2188	1126	1351	687

Source: Computed from NFHS-3 (2005-06) report (IIPS & Macro International, 2007).

addition to incidence of illness, the 60th round of NSS also provides important data on hospitalisation required for illness during the 365 days prior to the survey. It is noted from these data that about 2.7 per cent of the elderly at the all-India level were hospitalised during the one year reference period. This proportion is highest in Kerala (12.3 per cent), followed by Tamil Nadu (4.0 per cent), Haryana (3.7 per cent) and Maharashtra (3.6 per cent), while it is much lower in Bihar, Jharkhand and Assam (about 1 per cent each). The other major diseases/ailments for which the elderly required hospitalisation were cardiovascular diseases, gastro-intestinal problems, eye ailments (especially cataract), psychiatric disorders, fractures/poisoning/accident/injuries and cancer and other tumours.

Mortality Pattern and its Future Scenario

The health condition of the people can ultimately be judged by analysing the data on mortality by age and sex to understand its emerging pattern across the life cycle and its likely trend in the future at the national and state level. This section therefore primarily aims to examine the pattern of mortality, particularly among infants, children, women of reproductive ages and the elderly, using a number of indicators, based on recent SRS and NFHS data. Understanding the emerging mortality pattern among these groups during the recent period can provide valuable information for policymakers and health professionals who are concerned with improving the survival of men and women across the life cycle, particularly among the vulnerable population groups.

Trends in the Average Expectation of Life at Different Ages

A life table is a convenient summary tool to analyse mortality pattern as well as to understand the implication of age-specific mortality rates in terms of average life expectancy. An attempt has therefore been made to establish the trend in the expectation of life at different ages during the last three decades. This analysis is basically done using the SRS time series data and has been summarised in Appendix Table A-25.3. It is evident from this table that life expectancy at different ages has improved substantially for both males and females during the last three decades. Such an increase is however, relatively more in case of females than males. For example, a life expectation at birth of 50.5 years for males and 49.0 years for females during 1970-1975, increased to 61.8 years for males and 63.5 years for female during 1999-2003. The sex differentials in e_0^0 which were almost non-existent or rather in favour of males during the early seventies or before, increased overtime in favour of females. Similarly, the life expectation at ages 1, 5, 50 and 70+ is higher among females than males, particularly at age 5 during the recent period. Furthermore, life expectancy at age 1 is higher than at birth by 3-4 years for both males and females, even during the recent period, indicating that the level of infant mortality is still high in the country. Thereafter, the average expectation of life (that is, after age 1) for males and females reduces with age. However, life expectancy at all ages is relatively higher for females than for males. Furthermore, it is important to note that the survival chances are relatively much higher for females than males after age 50, the increase in life expectancy being 21 per cent at age 50 and 29 per cent at age 70+ for females as against 16 per cent and 23 per cent respectively, for males during the last three decades (between 1970-1975 and 1997-2001).

The average expectation of life at selected ages by region based on analysis of NFHS data reveals that there is a wide variation in the level of mortality across the country (Das and Patel, 2007). It appears that the level of mortality is still very high in the northeastern regions, while it is relatively less in the northern as well as in the southern and western regions. For example, the e_0^0 is found to be highest in the northern region (68.3 years), followed by western (67.1) and southern (65.8) regions, while it is lowest in the eastern (60.7 years), followed by the central (61.1) and northeastern regions (62.4). The level of infant mortality is still very high in the country and varies considerably across the regions, which is reflected from the fact that the average expectation of life at age 1 for both males and females increase by almost 5 years in the northeastern and central regions after crossing the crucial period of infancy, while the corresponding increased is about 2-3 years for other regions. We will come back to the issue of infant mortality a little later. With regard to the likely future trend in e_0^0, it is evident from Figure 25.1 that e_0^0 for males and females is likely to increase further to about 67.8 and 71.3 years respectively by 2015, if the present rate of decline in mortality continues in the future.

With the rise in e_0^0, the differential between the sexes is likely to increase further (in the country to about 3 years by 2015 in favour of women, which matches well with the pattern currently prevailing in the more developed countries).

Infant Mortality

Time series data on IMR from the SRS indicate that there is a consistent decline in the level of infant mortality in the major states as well as at the all-India level during the last decade (Appendix Table A-25.4). At the all-India level, the IMR declined by more than one-fourth between 1992 and 2004, although such a decline is relatively lower in the some of the underdeveloped states. If this pace of decline continues, IMR at the all-India level would reduce to about 47 per 1000 live births by 2012 and to about 43 by 2015 (Figure 25.2). This clearly indicates that India will fail to meet its national target of reducing IMR to 30 per 1000 live births by the target date.

Figure 25.1

Observed and Expected Trend of Expectation of Life at Birth (e_0^0) at the All-India Level, 1970-2015

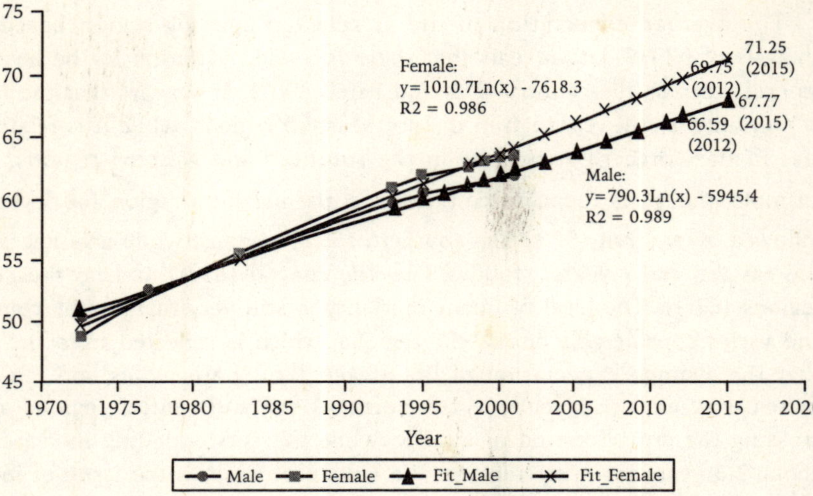

Figure 25.2

Observed and Expected Trend of Infant Mortality Rate (IMR) at the All-India Level, 1992-2015

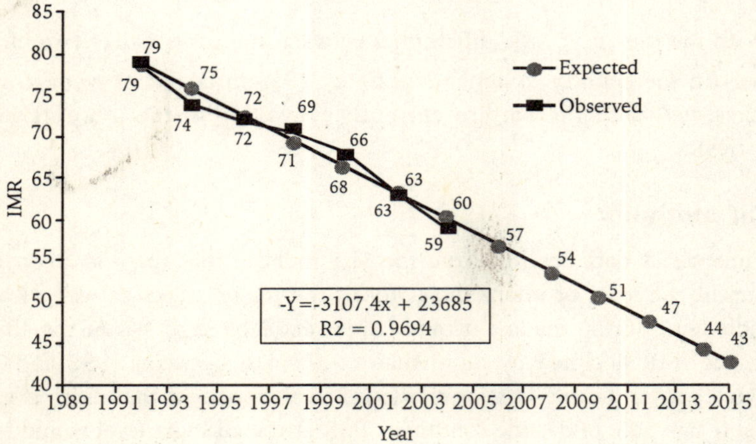

Under-Five Mortality

Analysis of data from the three rounds of NFHS once again reveals that there is a decline in the under-5 mortality in most of the states as well as at the country level. For example, the level of under-5 mortality reduced by almost one-third from 109 deaths per 1000 live births during 1992-93 to 74 deaths during 2005-06 at the all- India level (Appendix Table A-25.5). As expected, such a decline varies widely across the states from as low as 13 in Jammu and Kashmir to as high as 59 in Tamil Nadu. With the present pace of decline in under-5 mortality, it appears that its level would reach about 48 deaths per 1000 live births by 2015 in the country as a whole (Figure 25.3). The further decline in the under-5 mortality will depend on the speed of its decline in the underdeveloped states like Uttar Pradesh, Rajasthan, Madhya Pradesh, Assam and Orissa where the level is still very high (85 or more child deaths per 1000 live births). Unless concerted efforts are made to improve the reach of nutrition, immunisation and other health and medical services for mothers and children, the country will not only fail to meet its national goal but also its international commitment to reduce under-five mortality by two-third by 2015.

Figure 25.3

Observed and Expected Trend of Under-Five Mortality Rate at the All-India Level, 1992-2015

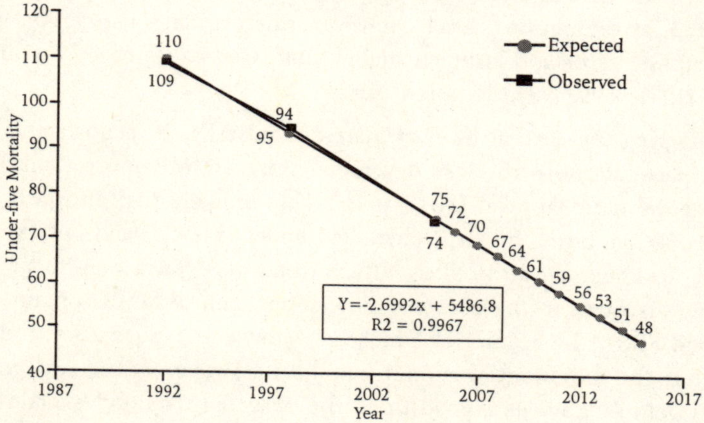

Maternal Mortality

Maternal health can best be judged by the level of maternal mortality ratio prevailing in a country or region. Maternal mortality ratio is defined as the number of maternal deaths per 100,000 live births and which provides an indication of the obstetric risk of death. This measure is based on annual number of female deaths to usual residents of the sample households that occurred during pregnancy, childbirth or within two months after termination of pregnancy or childbirth.

Table A-25.6 presents the direct estimate of MMR based on SRS for the period 1997-98 to 2001-2003, which reveals that maternal mortality has shown a decline over time in a number of states as well as in the country as a whole. However, estimates of MMR for certain states for the period 1997-2003 appear to be inconsistent, suffer from large sampling errors, and unexpectedly indicate a rise in its level during the period. As a result in case of some states, the apparent decline in MMR is not statistically significant during this period, although the decline at the national level is significant because of a relatively much lower margin of error in the estimate. It is further evident from Appendix Table A-25.6 that despite a large margin of error in the estimates, there are wide differentials in the level of maternal mortality across the states even during the recent period. The maternal mortality ratio is relatively lower (< 200) in some of the southern states like Kerala and Tamil Nadu as well as in certain northern states like Punjab and Haryana, while it is much higher (> 350) in the central and eastern region (except West Bengal). At the all-India level, the SRS estimates MMR at 301 (with 285-317 at 95 per cent CI) during 2001-2003, which declined from 398 (378-417) prevailing during 1997-98. The SRS national level estimate of 1997-98 appears to be grossly underestimated in view of the NFHS–2 (1998-1999) estimate of 540 with a 95 per cent confidence interval ranging from 428 to 653, at the national level. However, this estimate also suffers from a large sampling error and is much higher compared to its earlier estimate of 437 (NFHS–1, 1992-93), as noted earlier.

Considering the current level of maternal mortality in major states in the country, particularly in the less developed states (MMR more than 400) as well as at the national level (301), it is highly unlikely that an MMR of 100 per 1,00,000 live births by 2012 envisaged under the NPP and NRHM can be achieved. To understand the likely future trend of MMR a non-linear model, $y = e^{a+bt}$, was fitted to the observed time series data of MMR (obtained from NFHS and SRS), the results of which are shown in Figure 25.4. It may be noted that the exponential model which is however based on only four observed points, provides a good fit to the observed data and explains about 92 per cent of the variance in MMR. As can be seen from Figure 25.4, the pace of decline is slow during the recent period and the level of MMR will not decline beyond 200 by the stipulated date, that is, 2012. India's commitment to the Millennium Development Goal of reduction in MMR is also likely to remain unrealised as MMR will not reduce beyond 183 by 2015 unless there is political will to accelerate the pace of decline in MMR through rigorous implementation of programmes that address all aspects of maternal health including improvement in nutritional status.

Figure 25.4

Observed and Expected Trend of MMR, India, 1992-2015

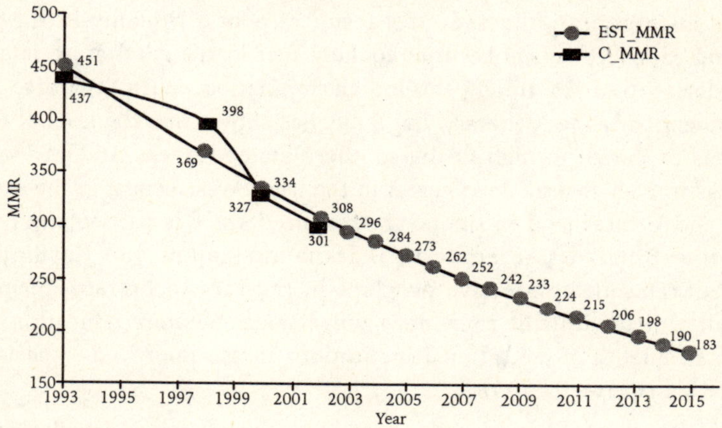

Conclusions

The widening divergence of population growth rates and economic development between the main northern and southern states has been clearly revealed by our study. Population projections suggest that demographic growth rates in the central states including Bihar in the east, Rajasthan in the west and Jammu and Kashmir in the north will continue to be significantly higher than those in the south during the years to come. The most populous states are already experiencing difficulties because of their sheer demographic size. While Uttar Pradesh will become still more of a population giant, other northern states which are also fast growing will increase their weight in total. The stage is set for uneven future demographic growth and increasing economic divergent which have grave implications on the health and development of the people. A serious fallout of demographic growth is on the health of women and children. While mortality levels have fallen throughout India, partly due to decline in fertility, in the absence of good quality of obstetric services, lack of control of diarrhoeal diseases, absence of universal immunisation etc., mortality among women and children continues to remain high. Simultaneously, the country is now also facing the threat of HIV/AIDS, the spread of which will slow down the overall rate of decline in mortality. The increasing presence of the HIV/AIDS virus has seen a resurgence of old diseases, especially TB. Other communicable diseases, such as malaria also continue to pose a risk to the health of the people. In fact, development projects and urban expansion and growth of urban slums very often create breeding grounds for vector-borne and communicable diseases. Nutritional deficiency disorders and resultant mortality is yet another scourge we are fighting, while recent data also show an increase in obesity and other nutritional and metabolic diseases like diabetes and hypertension. The increase in respiratory illnesses as a result of poor air quality in the urban areas and exposure to smoke from cooking fuel in the rural areas is adding to the disease burden among the Indian population. With regard to social development particularly literacy, our study has shown that the level of female literacy is moderate to high in the southern states (except Andhra Pradesh) as well as in Maharashtra and Gujarat in the west, West Bengal in the east and Punjab and Uttarakhand in the north. Female literacy is particularly poor in states like Bihar, Uttar Pradesh, Jharkhand, Jammu and Kashmir and Rajasthan. Despite impressive progress in the rate of literacy during the 1990s, it will be difficult to achieve universal elementary education if the access and quality of educational institutions is not improved, especially in the rural and peri-urban areas.

On the economic front, while most of the states experienced economic growth during the last decade, there is a concern about the progress in the slowest growing states, typically the poorest states like UP, MP, Bihar, Assam and Orissa compared to states like Gujarat, Maharashtra, Tamil Nadu, Punjab and Haryana.

The economy in the various states can be strengthened if the growing workforce in the age group 15-59 can be brought within the fold of formal education and technical/skill acquisition training. Needless to say, this workforce can bring the much-needed economic dividends if they are assured a disease-free life. In this regard, increased allocation of resources from the Centre, particularly to the less developed states in social sectors of health and education as well as creation of job opportunities in these states will enable them to come out of the nexus between high population growth and low socioeconomic and health development.

The desirable progress in the health of women and children has not been achieved despite improvements overtime and special focus being given under the RCH programme. The nutritional status of women and children is poor as is the utilisation of the major needed and child health maternal services to partially offset the nutritional deficiency and minimise risks during pregnancy and infancy. The situation is particularly worse in the more populous and less developed states. Yet another group of population which will need more focused attention under the health programme is that of the elderly, whose numbers will continue to increase in the decades to come even in the high fertility states.

Similarly, the disease profile of the general population which includes women, children and the elderly suggests that the incidence of tuberculosis is on the rise. Moreover, diabetes and asthma will also take a toll on the quality of life of individuals especially on the working force. The rise in levels of obesity as a result of modernisation is the other health concern in recent times. These are the current and future health needs which the programme will have to address.

Finally, the present study has examined the available date on the pattern of mortality especially among infants, children and women of reproductive ages, since this is the ultimate indicator of health. Life expectancy at different ages has increased substantially for both men and women during the last three decades. Moreover, the edge in survival which men had over women prior to and during the early seventies has reversed in favour of women thereafter. The average expectation of life at different ages in the various states indicates a wide variation in the level of mortality across the states. The level of mortality is still very high in the northeastern region and relatively low in the northern, southern and western regions. However, if the present rate of decline in mortality continues in the future, the sex differentials in mortality will increase further (in favour of women) and by 2015 the country will witness a pattern of e_0^0 currently prevailing in the developed countries of the world. There is still no place for complacency since the level of infant mortality, despite consistent decline in the major states of India, continues to remain high. The current pace of decline in infant mortality suggests that at the all-India level, IMR would be about 47 per 1000 live births in 2012 which is much higher than our national target of 30 per 1000 live births by that date. Similarly, the country's commitment to the MDG of reducing under-five mortality by two-third by 2015 is also likely to remain unrealised unless concerted efforts are made to accelerate the decline in child mortality in the underdeveloped states like Uttar Pradesh, Rajasthan, Madhya Pradesh, Assam and Orissa where its level is still very high. Needless to say, substantial achievements to curb infant and child mortality can only be made by vigorous efforts to improve the reach of nutrition, immunisation and other health and medical services among mothers and children, which are already part of the national programme. These efforts will simultaneously also yield the much-needed improvements in maternal health, since the prevailing level of maternal mortality is still very high in the country, with wide state-wise variations even during the recent period. Despite the limitation of data and consistency of estimates, maternal mortality is relatively lower in the some of the southern (Kerala and Tamil Nadu) and northern (Punjab and Haryana) states while it is much higher in the central and eastern regions. The pace of decline in MMR is slow during the recent period and its level will not decline beyond 200 by 2012 and 183 by 2015. India's commitment to the Millennium Development Goal of reduction in MMR by three-fourth (i.e., about 100), will also remain unattained in the absence of necessary political will to improve maternal health ensure institutional delivery and emergency obstetric care as emphasised under the NRHM. Addressing these concerns, therefore, as well as planning for the growing numbers of elderly working age population is the most pressing challenge before the country today.

References

Acharya, S., R. Cassen and K. Mc Nay (2004). "The economy-past and future", in Tim Dyson, Robert Cassen & Leela Visaria (eds.) *Twenty-first Century India – Population, Economy, Human Development and the Environment*. New Delhi: Oxford University Press. pp. 202-227.

Bose, A. (2001). *India's Billion Plus People 2001 Census Highlights, Methodology and Media Coverage*. Delhi: B.R. Publishing Corporation.

Cassen, R. and K. McNay (2004). "The condition of the people", in Tim Dyson, Robert Cassen & Leela Visaria (eds.) *Twenty-first Century India – Population, Economy, Human Development and the Environment*. New Delhi: Oxford University Press. pp. 178-201.

Das N.P. and R.M. Patel (2007). "Region and community specific life tables for India, 1991-98: Use of repeat surveys of the same population to maximise precision of the estimates", *Demography India* 37(1): 111-145.

Das N.P., R.M. Patel and Urvi Shah (2007). "Revisiting maternal mortality in India", *A paper prepared for the Ministry of Health and Family Welfare*, Government of India, New Delhi: Population Research Centre, Baroda.

Das N.P. and Urvi Shah (2001). "The socio-demographic and health status of the elderly in India: Evidence from recent national level data", *A project report prepared for the Ministry of Health and Family Welfare*. New Delhi: Government of India, Population Research Centre, Baroda.

Dyson, Tim (2004). "India's population—The future", in Tim Dyson, Robert Cassen and Leela Vasaria (eds.), *Twenty-First Century India: Population, Economy, Human Development, and The Environment*. New Delhi: Oxford University Press. pp. 74-107.

Dyson, T. and P. Visaria (2004). "Migration and urbanisation retrospect and prospects", in Tim Dyson, Robert Cassen & Leela Visaria (eds.) *Twenty-first Century India—Population, Economy, Human Development and the Environment*. New Delhi: Oxford University Press. pp. 108-129.

Kingdom, G., R. Cassen and K.Mc Nay (2004). "Education and literacy", in Tim Dyson, Robert Cassen & Leela Visaria (eds.) *Twenty-first Century India – Population, Economy, Human Development and the Environment*. New Delhi: Oxford University Press. pp. 130-157.

International Institute of Population Sciences (IIPS) (1995). "National family health survey (MCH and Family Planning)", India 1992-93. Mumbai: IIPS.

International Institute for Population Sciences (IIPS) and ORC Macro (2000). National Family Health Survey (NFHS–2), India, 1998–99: Country report and state level reports of Gujarat, Maharashtra, Rajasthan, Goa and Tamil Nadu.

________ and Macro International (2007). National Family Health Survey (NFHS-3), 2005-06: *India, Volume I:* Mumbai: IIPS.

Ministry of Health and Family Welfare (n.d.). *National Rural Health Mission 2005-2016*. Mission Document. New Delhi: Government of India.

Office of the Registrar General, India (1996). *Population Projections For India and States 1996-2016*. New Delhi.

Registrar General, India (1996). *Census of India 1991*. Ministry of Home Affairs, Government of India, New Delhi.

United Nations (2001). *World Population Prospects: The 2000 Revision*. New York: United Nations.

U.S. Bureau of the Census (1999). *World Population Profile, 1998*. Report WP/98. Washington DC: U.S. Government Printing Office.

World Bank (2004). "World Development Indicators - 2005", *CD Rom*, Washington DC.

Appendix Table A-25.1

Female Literacy Rate in States, 1991-2001

State	Female Literacy Rate		
	1991	*2001*	*% Change*
India	39.3	54.2	14.90
North			
Haryana	40.5	56.3	15.80
Himachal Pradesh	52.3	68.1	15.80
Jammu and Kashmir	Na	41.8	Na
Punjab	50.4	63.6	13.10
Uttarakhand	41.6	60.3	18.60
Central			
Chhattisgarh	27.5	52.4	24.90
Madhya Pradesh	29.4	50.3	20.90
Uttar Pradesh	24.4	43.0	18.60
East			
Assam	43.0	56.0	13.00
Bihar	22.0	33.6	11.60
Jharkhand	25.5	39.4	13.90
Orissa	34.7	51.0	16.30
West Bengal	46.6	60.2	13.70
West			
Gujarat	48.9	58.6	9.70
Maharashtra	52.3	67.5	15.20
Rajasthan	20.4	44.3	23.90
South			
Andhra Pradesh	32.7	51.2	18.50
Karnataka	44.3	57.5	13.10
Tamil Nadu	51.3	64.6	13.20
Kerala	86.2	87.9	1.70

Source: Bose, A. (2001). *India's Billion Plus People.*

Appendix Table A-25.2

Per Capita Net State Domestic Product at Factor Cost State-wise (at Constant Price)

State	Per Capita Net State Domestic Product		
	1993-94	*2005-06*	*% Annual Growth*
India	7690	12416	5.12
North			
Haryana	11097	16872	4.34
Himachal Pradesh	7870	14320	6.83
Jammu and Kashmir	6543	8040	1.91
Punjab	12710	16756	2.65
Uttarakhand	6896	9471	3.11
Central			
Chhattisgarh	6539	8383	2.35
Madhya Pradesh	6584	8199	2.04
Uttar Pradesh	5066	6138	1.76
East			
Assam	5715	7020	1.90
Bihar	3037	4034	2.74
Jharkhand	5897	8025	3.01
Orissa	4896	6555	2.82
West Bengal	6756	11612	5.99
West			
Gujarat	9796	16780	5.94
Maharashtra	12183	16479	2.94
Rajasthan	6182	9603	4.61
South			
Andhra Pradesh	7416	13135	6.43
Karnataka	7838	13141	5.64
Tamil Nadu	8955	13999	4.69
Kerala	7983	13321	5.57

Source: Central Statistical Organisation (CSO) website as on 23-2-2006; *http://rbidocs.rbi.org.in/rdoc/publications/pdfs/72639.pdf*

Appendix Table A-25.3

Life Expectancy at Selected Ages by Sex, India, 1970-1975 to 1999-2003

Age	Period	Average Expectation of Life of a Person e_x^0		
		Total	*Male*	*Female*
0	1970-1975[a]	49.7	50.5	49.0
	1981-1985[a]	55.5	55.4	55.7
	1991-1995[a]	60.3	59.7	60.9
	1993-1997[c]	61.1	60.4	61.8
	1996-2000[b]	61.9	61.0	62.7
	1997-2001[b]	62.2	61.3	63.0
	1998-2002	62.4	61.6	63.3
	1999-2003	62.7	61.8	63.5
1	1970-1975[a]	56.2	57.0	55.6
	1981-1985[a]	60.9	60.8	61.1
	1991-1995[a]	64.5	63.9	65.1
	1993-1997[c]	65.3	64.5	66.0
	1996-2000	65.7	64.7	66.6
	1997-2001	65.9	64.9	66.8
5	1970-1975[a]	57.5	57.5	57.5
	1981-1985[a]	60.8	60.1	61.8
	1991-1995[a]	62.9	61.8	63.9
	1993-1997[c]	-	-	-
	1996-2000	63.8	62.3	65.2
	1997-2001	64.0	62.5	65.6
20	1970-1975[a]	45.1	44.8	45.6
	1981-1985[a]	-	-	-
	1991-1995[a]	-	-	-
	1993-1997[c]	-	-	-
	1996-2000	50.2	48.6	51.9
	1997-2001	50.4	48.7	52.2
50	1970-1975[a]	20.4	19.8	21.3
	1981-1985[a]	22.4	21.4	23.8
	1991-1995[a]	23.5	22.3	24.8
	1993-1997[c]	-	-	-
	1996-2000	24.2	22.8	25.5
	1997-2001	24.4	23.0	25.7
70+	1970-1975[a]	8.9	8.6	9.2
	1981-1985[a]	10.2	9.7	11.0
	1991-1995[a]	10.6	10.0	11.0
	1993-1997[c]	-	-	-
	1996-2000	11.1	10.4	11.7
	1997-2001	11.3	10.6	11.9

Note: a SRS data based abridged life tables constructed by Registrar General (1999), India: New Delhi.

b SRS data based abridged life tables constructed by Registrar General (2004), India: New Delhi.

c Abridged life tables constructed based on two rounds of NFHS data under the present study.

Appendix Table A-25.4

Estimates of Infant Mortality Rate (IMR) based on Three-Year Moving Average for Major States of India, 1992-2004

Region/State	1992	1994	1996	1998	2000	2002	2004	% Change (1992-2004)
India	79	74	72	70.6	67.8	63	58.7	-25.7
North								
Haryana	75	70	68	67.2	65.4	62.8	60	-20.0
Himachal Pradesh	68.8	59	62	62.2	58.4	53.2	49.7	-27.8
Jammu & Kashmir	-	-	-	47	47.2	47.7		
Punjab	56	53	51	52.2	52.2	49.6	46	-17.9
Uttarakhand	-	-	-	47.8	44.4	41.7		
Central								
Chhattisgarh	-	-	-		76.5	71.6	64.3	
Madhya Pradesh	104	98	97	93.2	89.2	83.8	79	-24.0
Uttar Pradesh	98	88	85	84.4	82.8	78.6	73.7	-24.8
East								
Assam	76	78	74	75.4	74	70.2	67	-11.8
Bihar	73	67	71	66.8	63	61.2	60.7	-16.8
Jharkhand	-	-	-		63.5	56.6	50	
Orissa	115	103	96	96.4	93.4	86.4	78.3	-31.9
West Bengal	65	62	55	53.2	51.2	47.4	41.3	-36.5
West								
Gujarat	67	64	61	62.4	61.8	58.4	54.7	-18.4
Maharashtra	59	55	48	48	47	43.2	38	-35.6
Rajasthan	90	84	85	82.6	80	75.6	70	-22.2
South								
Andhra Pradesh	71	65	65	65	65	62.2	58.3	-17.9
Karnataka	73	67	53	55.8	57.2	54.2	50.3	-31.1
Kerala	17	16	14	16	16	16	15	-11.8
Tamil Nadu	58	59	53	52.4	49.8	45.6	40.3	-30.5

Source: Computed from various *SRS Bulletins*, Sample Registration System, Office of the Registrar General, India, New Delhi, 1997-2006.

Appendix Table A-25.5

Under-Five Mortality Rates for the Five-Year Period Preceding the Respective Survey

State	Under-Five Mortality 1992-93	1998-99	2005-06	% Change (1992-2006)
India	109.3	94.9	74.3	-32.0
North				
Haryana	98.7	76.8	52.3	-47.0
Himachal Pradesh	69.1	42.4	41.5	-39.9
Jammu and Kashmir	59.1	80.1	51.2	-13.4
Punjab	68.0	72.1	52.0	-23.5
Uttarakhand	-	-	56.8	-
Central				
Chhattisgarh			90.3	
Madhya Pradesh	130.3	137.6	94.2	-27.7
Uttar Pradesh	141.3	122.5	96.4	-31.8
East				
Assam	142.2	89.5	85.0	-40.2
Bihar	127.5	105.1	84.8	-33.5
Jharkhand			93.0	
Orissa	131.0	104.4	90.6	-30.8
West Bengal	99.3	67.6	59.6	-40.0
West				
Gujarat	104.0	85.1	60.9	-41.4
Maharashtra	70.3	58.1	46.7	-33.6
Rajasthan	102.6	114.9	85.4	-16.8
South				
Andhra Pradesh	91.2	85.5	63.2	-30.7
Karnataka	87.3	69.8	54.7	-37.3
Kerala	32.0	18.8	16.3	-49.1
Tamil Nadu	86.5	63.3	35.5	-59.0

Source: Computed from NFHS-1 (1992-93), NFHS-2 (1998-99) and NFHS-3 (2005-06) reports (IIPS, 1995; IIPS & Macro International, 2000; 2007).

Appendix Table A-25.6

Estimates of Maternal Mortality Ratio (MMR) and its Trend for Major States of India, 1997-2003

Region/State	Maternal Mortality Ratio (maternal deaths per 100,000 live births)			
	SRS Estimate+			
	1997-98	1999-2001	2001-2003	% Change (1992-2004)
India*	398(378-417)@	327(311-343)	301(285-317)	-24.4
North				
Haryana	136(82-191)	176(113-239)	162(102-223)	19.1
Himachal Pradesh	-	296(261-331)**	257(223-290)**	
Jammu & Kashmir	-	214(183-246)**	215(184-247)**	
Punjab	280(185-376)	177(99-254)	178(100-257)	-36.4
Uttarakhand	-	-	-	
Central				
Chhattisgarh	-	-	-	
Madhya Pradesh	441(370-512)[1]	407(332-482)[1]	379(306-452)[1]	-14.1
Uttar Pradesh*	606(544-668)[2]	539(481-596)[2]	517(461-573)[2]	-14.7
East				
Assam	568(460-677)	398(309-486)	490(393-588)	-13.7
Bihar*	531(464-597)[3]	400(340-461)[3]	371(313-430)[3]	-30.1
Jharkhand	-	-	-	
Orissa	346(264-427)	424(336-512)	358(277-439)	3.5
West Bengal*	303(240-366)	218(165-271)	194(111-243)	-36.0
West				
Gujarat	46(19-74)	202(141-262)	172(116-228)	273.9
Maharashtra	166(117-216)	169(114-224)	149(97-201)	-10.2
Rajasthan	508(425-590)	501(423-580)	445(371-519)	-12.4
South				
Andhra Pradesh	197(132-261)	220(155-286)	195(132-257)	-1.0
Karnataka	245(185-305)	266(202-311)	228(169-287)	-6.9
Kerala	150(90-210)	149(91-207)	110(59-161)	-26.7
Tamil Nadu	131(81-182)	167(111-224)	134(83-185)	2.3

Note: 1 Includes Chhattisgarh 2 Includes Uttarakhand 3 Includes Jharkhand

\+ Based on SRS Special Retrospective Surveys on Maternal Mortality in India: 1997-2003 (Registrar General India, 2006).

@ Figures within parenthesis indicate 95 per cent confidence interval.

* The decline in MMR during 1997-98 and 2001-2003 is significant ateast at .01 level.

** Based on estimates derived indirectly by Das *et al.*, 2008.

26

Implications of India's Future Population Growth for Education and Employment Scenario with Focus on Large States

SUMATI KULKARNI

Introduction

The Vision 2020 Document of the Planning Commission (2004) envisages that "by 2020 the people of India will be more numerous, better educated, healthier and more prosperous than at any time in our long history." While achievement of 8 per cent GNP growth rate, IT boom and prospects of demographic dividend have generated optimism about the feasibility of achieving the 2020 targets, skepticism also prevails due to the dismal performance on the agricultural front, farmers' suicides and India's low rank among countries in terms of human development index. It is, therefore, essential to have objective assessment of the task ahead, as reflected in the available data. Poverty reduction is a formidable challenge and success in this respect is inevitably linked with employment generation on a large scale. Lack of adequate quality education, however, poses a big constraint for employability of large masses in the non-agricultural sector. Substantial qualitative improvement in these sectors again is constrained by the huge numbers involved. Apart from the magnitude of the problem, locating the problem and identifying the areas where it is going to be acute is also crucial in view of the regional imbalance in India. As per the projected levels of TFR (Registrar General, Government of India), Uttar Pradesh and Madhya Pradesh are likely to reach replacement level in 2027 and 2025 respectively while Bihar and Rajasthan are likely to reach it by 2021. These are the states which have lagged behind both in terms of demographic transition as well as socio-economic indicators. Population of four large north Indian states constituted 36 per cent of India's population in 2001 and they together are estimated to contribute 45 per cent of population growth in India during 2001-2021. Maharashtra, though one of the leading states in terms of development indicators, is also next to UP in terms of population size and is estimated to contribute about 10 per cent to India's population growth during 2001-2021.

So far India's success on economic front is largely due to the performance of certain sectors and a few states but translating the Vision 2020 into reality in totality, especially its human development component, largely depends on how far the success can be achieved in these five states which together are going to contribute substantially (55 per cent) to India's population growth during 2001-2021.

Keeping Vision 2020 in view, this chapter proposes to assess the magnitude of the task ahead in these states, with focus on education and employment scenario. Discussion about development implications in this chapter is based on the projections for these sectors as well as for per capita net state domestic product for the above five states, made by making suitable assumptions, as explained in the following sections. Comparison with magnitude of the task ahead for India is mostly made on the basis of available projections for India. *Population Projections for India and States 2001-26* published by the Office of the Registrar General (2006), *Labour Force Projections for All India* made by Mari Bhat (2007), Economic tables from 2001 Census, Economic Survey, 2006-07 (Govt. of India) and All India School Education Survey (NCERT, NIC, 2007) are the data sources used for analysis.

Per Capita State Income

It is envisaged that, compounded effect of the GDP growth rate of 8.5-9 per cent over 20 years, would result in quadrupling the per capita income and almost eliminating the poverty by 2020. On the basis of data available in the Economic Survey, it is estimated that to reach the per capita income level four times the level in 2001, India's net national product (NNP) will be about Rs. 90,80,500 crores at 2001-02 prices in 2020. Assuming that percentage share of each state in total NNP will remain the same as in 2001, state incomes (NSDP) are estimated and using the projected state population figure for 2020, per capita NSDP at 2001-02 prices for five states was estimated (Table 26.1). It shows that if by 2020 India's per capita income is to be quadrupled but the relative difference between states remains the same, the NSDP of five states will have to increase at slightly higher rate during 2001-2020 i.e., Bihar 4.34 times, MP 4.15 times, Rajasthan 4.17 times, UP 4.06 times and Maharashtra 4.34 times. Even after such increase, Bihar's per capita income in 2020 at 2001-02 prices (Rs. 21,696) will be only marginally higher than the per capita income of Kerala and Tamil Nadu in 2001 (20287, 20326). In 2001-02, as compared to NSDP of Maharashtra, Bihar's was one fifth, MP's was half, UP's was 39 per cent and Rajasthan's was 56 per cent. The estimated figures indicate that in 2020 the disparity will slightly widen. This is obviously the result of difference in their population growth rates as other things are kept constant.

Table 26.1

Per Capita Net State Domestic Product 2001-02, 2020-21 at 2001-02 Prices and Index No. Indicating Comparison with Maharashtra

State	*Per Capita NSDP Rs.*	
	2001-02 (Index No.)	*2020-21 (Index No.)*
Maharashtra	24044 (100.0)	104458 (100.0)
Bihar	5004 (20.8)	21696 (20.8)
M.P.	12209 (50.8)	50656 (48.5)
Rajasthan	13621 (56.6)	56827 (54.4)
U.P.	9320 (38.8)	37868 (36.2)

Source: For 2001-02 figures: *Economic Survey*, Government of India, 2006-07.

Education

Due to the effect of expected fertility decline, India's population of boys and girls in the primary school age group (6-11) is likely to decline during 2001-2020, by 5.5 and 6.8 million respectively (Table 26.2). Among the states under study, U.P. which is the least advanced in demographic transition, will experience increase in 6-11 population of both boys and girls and M.P. will have moderate increase only for boys. The other three states are likely to have decline for both boys and girls in the range 0.25 to 1.11 million for boys and 0.35 to 0.91 million for girls.

Table 26.2

Primary School Age Pop., Enrolment in Classes I-V and Expected Increase Upto 2020 by Sex

Boys	*6-11 Million*			
State	*Pop.6-11 (2001-02)*	*Pop.6-11 (2020-21)*	*Enrolment* 2006*	*Expected Increase 2006-2020 if 100% Enrolment*
Col.1	*Col.2*	*Col.3*	*Col.4*	*Col.5 (Col.3-Col. 4)*
Maharashtra	6.57	6.29	5.71	0.58
Bihar	7.37	6.26	5.50	0.76
M.P.	4.87	5.01	4.15	0.86
Rajasthan	4.78	4.53	4.31	0.22
U.P.	14.64	15.72	12.23	3.49
India	77.20	71.74	65.36	6.38
Maharashtra	5.99	5.55	5.18	0.37
Bihar	6.58	5.67	4.06	1.61
M.P.	4.44	4.42	3.60	0.82
Rajasthan	4.26	3.91	3.54	0.37
U.P.	12.91	13.57	10.50	3.07
India	70.47	63.63	57.55	6.08

Note: * Source for Enrolment in Classes I-V: NCERT & NIC Seventh All India School Education Survey (AISES) Enrolment in Schools, 2007, Table 18.

In spite of this decline, the number of students enrolled in primary school will increase as shown in Table 26.2, if the goal of universal primary education is to be achieved by 2020. UP accounts for half the expected increase in primary school enrolment of boys and girls in India during 2006-2020 and the four large north Indian states account for more than 80 per cent increase in boys' enrolment and even higher share in case of girls. This pinpoints the need to concentrate the investment in primary education in these four states for coverage, reduction in dropout as well as for quality education.

As for the population in the age group for middle school level education (12-14), for India as a whole, it is expected to decline from 37.4 to 35.8 million for boys and from 33.5 to 31.8 million for girls during 2001-2020. Among the four states, UP, MP and Rajasthan are likely to experience increase in population aged 12-14. But the prospects of achieving 100 per cent enrolment are bleak for both boys and girls in Bihar and UP and for girls in Rajasthan as shown below:

Gross Enrolment Ratios for Classes VI-VIII

State	*Boys*	*Girls*
Bihar	39.66	24.29
M.P.	98.04	86.51
Rajasthan	84.82	54.80
U.P.	57.82	46.29

Source: Government of India, Economic Survey 2006-07.

Employment

Mari Bhat's (2007) projections of labour force (working + seeking work) are available for all India for the period 2002-2022. He has projected the labour force participation rates (LFPR) taking into account the changes in the educational composition and the education–specific participation rates. Age-specific participation rates used by him to project the total labour force, thus are the result of expected changes in the educational composition and propensity to participate in labour force at different educational levels. For the states, 2001 age-specific participation rates are available. Age-specific participation rates for 2020 were calculated for males and females by applying the all India ratio of 2020 LFPR/2001 LFPR of the corresponding age groups to the 2001 state LFPR of that age group. Thus, it was assumed that though the levels of state rates are different from all India rates, they will have the same proportionate change during 2001-2020 but the changes in the educational composition of each state were not taken into account. To obtain the size of labour force in 2020 in different age sex groups, LFPRs thus projected were applied to the projected population in the corresponding age sex group. Assuming that child labour will be eliminated by 2020, (consistent with 100 per cent enrolment), labour force projections were made only for 15+ populations. Results for five states and India are presented in Table 26.3.

Table 26.3

Workers (2001), Projected Size of Labour Force (2020) by Sex and Additional Jobs Required during 2001-2020

Age Group		Maharashtra	Bihar	M.P.	Rajasthan	U.P.	India
			Males (Million)				
15-59	2001	22.26	15.26	12.61	11.70	29.73	216.11
	2020	40.08	30.34	24.75	23.79	60.08	390.80
60+	2001	1.91	1.82	1.18	0.89	3.88	19.95
	2020	3.58	3.40	2.08	1.75	6.44	39.21
15+	2001	24.17	17.08	13.79	12.58	33.61	236.05
	2020	43.66	33.74	26.83	25.54	66.52	430.01
			Females (Million)				
15-59	2001	9.32	3.15	4.55	4.15	4.32	65.85
	2020	23.66	9.02	12.68	11.90	12.30	168.76
60+	2001	0.83	0.24	0.33	0.22	0.46	4.66
	2020	2.15	0.78	0.88	0.67	1.32	14.28
15+	2001	10.15	3.40	4.88	4.37	4.78	70.51
	2020	25.81	9.80	13.56	12.57	13.62	183.04
			M+F (Million)				
15+	2001	34.32	20.48	18.67	16.95	38.39	306.56
	2020	69.47	43.54	40.39	38.11	80.14	613.05
Addi. Reqd.		35.15	23.06	21.79	21.16	41.75	306.49

It reveals that male labour force of 15+ is likely to double itself during 20 years in the four large north Indian states while in Maharashtra, it is expected to increase by 80 per cent. About one-third (33 per cent) of the all

India male labour force is accounted by these four states in 2001. In 2020, it is expected to be slightly more (35 per cent). Maharashtra is likely to continue having 10 per cent of all India male labour force in 2020.

In India and Maharashtra, female labour force in 2020 is likely to be two and half times the size in 2001 but in the four large north Indian states, it is expected to be three times. Female labour force 15+ in the four large north Indian states was 25 per cent of all India female labour force 15+. Even after 20 years, its share is likely to increase marginally (to 27 per cent). Maharashtra's share is likely to be 14 per cent, the same as 2001.

In 20 years, about 300 million more jobs are likely to be required to absorb those who are available for work. Out of these, more than 100 million are expected to be required in the four large north Indian states i.e., about 35 per cent, of which U.P. alone is likely to require 14 per cent. About 12 per cent of the total additional jobs (35 million) are likely to be required by Maharashtra. If the state economies are not able to meet these requirements, it has implications in terms of migration, poverty and social unrest. Employability of those available for work is also a critical issue. In today's competitive set-up, especially after liberalisation, vocational training is a crucial requirement. Only 5 per cent of country's labour force in the age-group 20-24 has undergone such training as compared to 28 per cent in Mexico and 96 per cent in Korea. (Vision 2020, p.36) Enrolment rates at middle level education, discussed earlier indicate that prospects of 100 per cent enrolment even in classes VI-VIII are not very bright. It is well recognised in the Vision that "development of human resources is the most important determinant of development and more than doubling of investment in education from the current level of 3 per cent to 4 per cent of GNP is the soundest policy for quadrupling the GNP per capita" (Vision 2020, p.35). One wonders whether increase in expenditure on education alone will do the magic. Appropriate changes in the educational system to suit the changing times and changing demographic scenario also need to be given high priority.

References

Bhat, P.N. Mari (2007). *A Note on Labour Force Projections for the 11th Five Year Plan.*

Government of India (2007). *Economic Survey 2006-07.*

NCERT & NIC (2007). *Seventh All India School Education Survey—Enrolment in Schools.*

Office of the Registrar General & Census Commissioner, India (2006). *Population Projections for India & States 2001-2026.* New Delhi: Office of the Registrar General & Census Commissioner, India.

Office of the Registrar General & Census Commissioner, India). *Census of India 2001, Economic Tables.*

Planning Commission, Government of India (2004). *India Vision 2020.* New Delhi: Academic Foundation.